Desmond Bowen

History and the Shaping of Irish Protestantism

PETER LANG
New York • Washington, D.C./Baltimore • San Francisco
Bern • Frankfurt am Main • Berlin • Vienna • Paris

BX
4839
.B67
1995

Library of Congress Cataloging-in-Publication Data

Bowen, Desmond.
History and the shaping of Irish Protestantism/ Desmond Bowen.
p.   cm. — (Irish studies; vol. 4)
Includes bibliographical references and index.
1. Protestants—Ireland—History. 2. Ireland—Church history.
3. Catholic Church—Ireland—Relations—Protestant churches. 4. Protestant
churches—Ireland—Relations—Catholic Church. I. Title. II. Series: Irish
studies (New York, N.Y.); vol. 4.
BX4839.B67   941.5'008'82—dc20   94-47553
ISBN 0-8204-2750-0
ISSN 1043-5743

Die Deutsche Bibliothek-CIP-Einheitsaufnahme

Bowen, Desmond:
History and the shaping of Irish protestantism / Desmond Bowen. - New York;
Washington, D.C./Baltimore; San Francisco; Bern; Frankfurt am Main; Berlin;
Vienna; Paris: Lang.
(Irish studies ; Vol. 4)
ISBN 0-8204-2750-0
NE: GT

Photo on the cover: Copyright © Belfast Telegraph Newspapers Ltd.

The paper in this book meets the guidelines for permanence and durability
of the Committee on Production Guidelines for Book Longevity
of the Council of Library Resources.

© 1995 Peter Lang Publishing, Inc., New York

Printed in the United States of America.

History and the Shaping
of Irish Protestantism

Irish Studies

Robert Mahoney
General Editor

Vol. 4

PETER LANG
New York • Washington, D.C./Baltimore • San Francisco
Bern • Frankfurt am Main • Berlin • Vienna • Paris

Dedication

To the Protestant peacemakers of
Ireland, from William Bedell to
Eric Elliott and John Morrow.

CONTENTS

Foreword

The origins of this work lie first of all in a discussion I had a few years ago with one of the Anglican bishops serving on the Anglican-Roman Catholic International Conversations body, following publication of the ARCIC-I report. We were talking about how the report was received by the Protestants in Ulster, and he confessed that the members of ARCIC II were finding it difficult to understand the Irish Protestant mind, particularly in Northern Ireland, as they pursued their exercise in ecumenical dialogue. It was at that time that I began to ponder the value of presenting an account of how the sensibilities of the Irish Protestants have developed during Ireland's turbulent history.

My resolve to press on with such a study strengthened after professor Brendan Bradshaw presented his controversial interpretation of 'Nationalism and Historial Scholarship in Modern Ireland' in volume XXVI of *Irish Historical Studies* in 1989. In his article professor Bradshaw pleaded for sound critical scholarship which would respond: 'sensitively to the totality of the Irish historical experience'. He concluded his argument by suggesting that such historical exercise should include not only an 'imaginative and empathetic approach' to the Irish nationalist tradition, but also to that of the Irish Protestants. This study contends that at the heart of the Irish Protestant tradition is an abiding conviction, which has indeed become an integral part of its 'faith' — 'the right of individual freedom in matters of religion is among the dictates of the law of nature'.[1] The first section deals with the pre-Reformation period because of the Protestant claim, from the time of archbishop James Ussher in the seventeenth century, that their community can trace its history back to the time of St. Patrick. The study concludes with the assessment of contemporaries who consider those relations between the Roman Catholic and Protestant communities, which so bewilder the ARCIC divines and many other observers of Irish religious affairs.

Preface

Partition does not depend upon a physical boundary which can be
removed by political action; it depends upon very important differences
in outlook between two groups of people: and though these differences
may be accentuated by political division they will not necessarily
disappear as a result of enforced political union. The most fundamental
difference is probably that of religion... the real partition of Ireland is
not on the map but in the minds of men.[1]

Professor James Beckett produced this insight prior to the beginning of the
modern 'troubles' in Northern Ireland in 1969, a struggle which a great many
Ulster Protestants choose to view as a 'war of independence' to keep themselves
from being assimilated into what they view as the Roman Catholic 'confessional
state' of the Republic of Ireland. Cardinal Conway discussed the religious
element during the political upheavals of the time when he addressed the fourth
international Synod of Bishops in Rome in October, 1970, and concluded that:

By an accident of history those who favour union with Britain are
Protestant and most of those who wish for a united Ireland are
Catholics. But that accidental fact does not make the conflict a war of
religion.[2]

Earlier the cardinal had joined the province's other ecclesiastical leaders when
they issued a joint statement to assure the world that the conflict was not
essentially a 'religious struggle', in spite of so many 'sectarian' murders.[3]

Twelve long years later, however, the Roman Catholic archbishop of
Armagh, Tomas Cardinal O'Fiaich told the readers of the Roman Catholic
weekly, *The Universe*, that the Ulster war was in large measure a religious one,
reflecting wide-spread bigotry among the people of Ulster. He also suggested
that ninety percent of the bigotry was to be found among the Protestant people.[4]
Two years later, in an address in Hamborn, West Germany, cardinal O'Fiaich
identified the most important and troubling element at the heart of the Ulster

We Catholics find this hard to understand, yet we must take it seriously and seek to dispel it by reaching out to Protestants in brotherhood and love.[5]

Cardinal O'Fiaich was a historian, and his experience as an 'ethnarch' representing his people's political as well as their religious aspirations, had convinced him of the reality of this Protestant apprehension. He understood that, however latent it appeared to be at times, there existed within the Protestant mind a conviction that the spirit of the Counter–Reformation still had to be reckoned with in Ireland: an anachronistic determination to bring 'recalcitrant heretics' back into the fold. This fear was particularly to be found among the Ulster Protestants. They treasured both the religious freedom and the political settlement which they had, and when they looked at the partly successful assimilation of the southern Protestants into the conservative Roman Catholic society of the Republic they were determined to resist every encouragement or pressure to force them into a united Ireland. So far as they were concerned neither the blandishments of southern political leaders, nor Republican terrorism was going to persuade them to 'surrender'. However simplistic or historically misplaced may be such suspicions and anxieties, the marching banners of the Protestants, with their reaffirmation of ancient causes, reveal an abiding distrust of Roman authority. As recently as 1988 the General Assembly of the Irish Presbyterian Church solemnly debated whether it was still necessary to subscribe to that part of the Westminster Confession of Faith which referred to the pope as the Antichrist, the man of sin.[6]

One southern political leader who recognized these northern sensibilities was the one time taoiseach Garret Fitzgerald. In his 1972 work, *Towards a New Ireland*, he expressed his sympathy for those northern Protestants who resisted the pressures put upon them to accept incorporation into the religiously conservative society of the Republic. He noted the drastic reduction in numbers of the Protestant population in the south since 1922, much of which was the result of the implementation of the rules of the Roman Catholic Church governing inter-faith marriages. This policy had resulted in a 'leakage of perhaps 25% from the Protestant community in the Republic'.[7] Nine years later, in a pamphlet with the same title, Fitzgerald confessed that: 'If I were a Northern Protestant today, I cannot see how I could be attracted to getting involved in a state which is itself sectarian':

> ... and we expected the Northern Unionists to join a state which in 1979 was bringing in laws based on the theology of one church? ... that has to change, and what I want to do is to lead public opinion towards that.[8]

For many reasons Ulster Protestants have never been successful in winning the world's approval for their 'primal sense of siege'[9]: their continuing resistance to perennial attack by forces which threaten to destroy their identity as a separate people. Part of the reason is that in our secular western world the media, in particular, have refused to take seriously the claim of the Protestants that theirs is a defensive struggle, one of liberation, to deny Rome an exercise in ecclesiastical 'triumphalism', and Dublin its 'imperial ambitions'. Nevertheless most Ulster Protestants remain convinced they must fight to survive as a people religiously and culturally. This is difficult for many Protestants in the Republic to comprehend, let alone the Catholic majority in the island, but it is a widely held conviction. As professor John Barkley of Belfast's Presbyterian College once wryly remarked: 'just because we are paranoiac does not mean that we are not being attacked'.[10] Many of the Ulster Protestants, if not most, view themselves as a suffering people under constant threat of extinction. Like their forefathers they still reject both 'home rule' and 'Rome rule'.

It is the latter entity that the Ulster Protestants particularly fear; the juridical power of the Roman Catholic Church, the authority of the Vatican, exercised throughout the world through the agency of the episcopal hierarchy. From the time of the Reformation Ireland's Protestants have resisted the 'special powers of teaching, ruling and sanctifying' claimed by what has traditionally been referred to as 'the court of Rome'. Like the 'Reformed Church' German princes, and some of the representatives of the free cities, who protested the 1529 attempt at the Diet of Speyer to bring them back under Roman ecclesiastical jurisdiction, the latter-day 'protestors' of Ireland reject every pressure which they believe would bring them under papal authority. At the heart of historic Protestantism has always been the demand for recognition of the primacy of the individual's conscience that Paul Tillich has called 'the Protestant principle': 'the protest against any human attempt to limit or circumscribe, or even define for another the will of God'.[11]

Unlike their strident co-religionists in Ulster, the minority Protestant community in the Republic has been a timorous one since 1922, but recently even it has begun to demand recognition of the sanctity of the individual's conscience over and against Rome's hierarchical and juridical authority. This boldness is partly explained by a new spirit of 'protest' against the 'court of Rome' which has appeared among many Roman Catholics who are also opposed to the 'juridicism' and 'exclusivism' of traditional Tridentine ecclesiastical government:[12]

> Catholicism insisted on the role of the church as a visible community, but the community is hierarchically structured with special powers of teaching, ruling, and sanctifying given to the offices of pope and bishop. In reaction to Protestantism, post-Tridentine Catholicism tended to define itself not primarily as the people of God, but as a hierarchically structured society.[13]

Protestant leaders in the Republic have also been emboldened by encouragement given by English liberal churchmen and by European groups like the Dutch based International Humanist and Ethical Union who decry the cultural and political pressures against non-Roman Catholics in the Republic of Ireland:

> People who do not adhere to the dominant religion cannot escape an integrated system of religious ethics that permeates every aspect of Irish public life.[14]

Such reinforcement has persuaded some southern Protestants strongly to express their opinions in recent referenda on moral issues, and even to demand change in the ecclesiastical laws governing mixed marriages which have greatly affected the minority community.

In the Protestant mind is the belief that from the time of the Counter-Reformation the freedom of the individual has been greatly diminished in any area where the state recognized the ecclesiastical and religious authority of the papacy. As many emigré Irish priests were to discover, a continental university under the eye of the Inquisition, or run by the Jesuits, did not allow much latitude in thought. To accept the authority of the 'court of Rome' was to surrender to a collective consciousness of mind which, to Protestants, was anathema. When this collective mind was in a political position to impose its ways of thought and its values upon a community, over a long period of time, it was able to nurture a distinctive way of life, a culture. In Ireland, as we will see, the struggle by the 'court of Rome' to impose its values upon the majority of the Irish people was a long one, and it was not until the post-famine period of the nineteenth century that the Irish ultramontane victory allowed Rome to make 'its claims a reality'.[15] A new order was now to be imposed upon Ireland:

> The triumph of the post-famine church was also the victory of one culture over another, and when modern Irish Catholicism came into its inheritance it did so only by means of the destruction of the rival world.[16]

Within this new triumphalist culture there inevitably appeared a refinement in historical thought, 'the Irish canon of history',[17] which interpreted the ultramontane victory as a blessing of divine providence. An example of this kind of thinking is presented in monsignor Patrick Corish's *Irish Catholic Experience* where, from the time that Tridentine reformers established their 'new plantation in religion', their new 'civility', down to the ultramontane victory of the nineteenth century, Irish history is seen as a reflection of the people becoming self-conscious of their destiny: 'as the Irish lost one identity they found another, and the new identity was Catholicism'. This religious-cultural triumph was made manifest in Dublin in the International Eucharistic Congress of 1932: 'the greatest fusion of Catholic and national pride', when a million people 'knelt at the papal legate's mass'. The blessing of heaven was further revealed in the 1937 Constitution, the preamble of which refers to the guiding hand of the deity guarding Ireland's majority faith: 'given the facts of Irish history, clearly the sustainer of the Catholics rather than of the Protestants'.[18]

In the writing of Irish history many scholars have chosen to discuss how the destiny of the Irish people, and the shape of their culture has been formed by British imperialism.[19] Few writers, however, have considered how much Irish historical development has been influenced by the other great external authority 'the court of Rome', which has imposed religious discipline, cultural values, and political authority upon the lives of Irish Catholics. It is the presence of Roman imperial power in Irish society which Irish Protestants, even in our own age of ecumenism, find threatening. As cardinal O'Fiaich noted, they fear that Rome still shares the spirit of Counter-Reformation triumphalism, and that the papacy is as intent as ever upon bringing all the inhabitants of the island back into the one true church. This is partly why Ulster's Protestants consider their defensive struggle, fought at great cost since 1969 as one of 'liberation'. They will never accept Dublin rule, the quasi-confessional culture represented by the Constitution of 1937, nor the society which would threaten their identity—as it did many of their grandparents who fled to the north in 1922.[20]

Few Irish Protestants see any evidence to dispel their belief that the Irish hierarchy is one of the most conservative and Tridentine-minded bodies in the entire Catholic communion. The liberal Catholicism which has struggled for life since Vatican Council II has not had much influence in the Republic of Ireland, as recent referenda on moral issues have revealed. The outspoken Irish political figure, Noel Browne, believes that the Irish hierarchy makes an 'implicit claim' to the real government in the Republic; its political and ecclesiastical power is not seriously questioned; and, in the words of Sean O'Faolain: 'the slightest word from this quarter is tantamount to the raising of the sword'.[21] Recent church surveys have indicated that the Roman Catholic church in the Republic is losing the support of the young, and it may be that, in the future, ultramontane authority in the society in the south may go the way of that in Quebec, but the Ulster Protestants refuse to risk their future upon that hope.[22]

It was not only cardinal O'Fiaich who was aware of Protestant sensibilities about freedom in the last decade, and this was revealed when the Roman Catholic bishops made their submission to the New Ireland Forum in January, 1984. In their presentation they admitted that they were bound by the authority of Rome, and that in any future united Ireland matters of private morality would be determined by the doctrinal view of the majority church. Cardinal O'Fiaich made it clear that: 'the Catholic code of morality should be followed by all the citizens of the State and that code be given the sanction and protection of the civil law'.[23] The Irish hierarchy did not see this demand to be an unjust one: 'it is not unreasonable to require sacrifice of minorities in the interests of the common good'.[24] Ulster Protestants, however, who have resisted for so long the I.R.A. 'dragonnade', British pressures for conciliation or union with the Republic, and the blandishments of the southern government, have no intention of accepting Roman imperial diktat in concerns of morality or ethics. They may no longer be able to consider their northern territory as 'a Protestant land for a Protestant people', but they have no intention of allowing themselves to be united with a church-state system which could impose upon them a 'code of morality' which was not of their own choosing.

There is nothing new in such northern Protestant intransigence, which is not unlike that of their forefathers in any generation. They remain unyielding in their opposition to the 'court of Rome' which they believe would bring them under its rule. However unrealistic this stance based on a traditional anxiety may be, it is an abiding reality in the Irish Protestant psyche and any consideration of Irish history is distorted if it is ignored. Deep in their folk memory is 'the experience of catastrophe and heroic endurance'.[25] The Irish Protestants have no fear of Irish Catholicism as a religion of the people, and seldom has the Protestant struggle for survival been characterized by direct attack on the symbols of faith. Yet they do believe that the 'court of Rome' is not to be trusted. Every 'religious' indignation or outrage visited upon them in any age is interpreted, only too often, as directed by the central authority of the Roman Catholic Church which in our twentieth century, as in every period since the Reformation, is intent upon extending its *imperium* at the expense of Protestant freedom.

The historian Marc Bloch has argued that: 'in the last analysis it is human consciousness which is the subject matter of history'.[26] It is hoped that this study of one part of the human consciousness of the Protestants of Ireland will help to explain what seems to be an atavism to many people: the haunting presence of the mentality of the seventeenth century in so many Irish affairs, particularly in Ulster. In that age the post-Tridentine Roman church was passionately dedicated to a reorganization of religious and ecclesiastical affairs in the western world, to bring them under a centralized authority: 'complete liturgical and disciplinary as well as dogmatic uniformity in the western churches under its rule'.[27] The seventeenth century papacy which directed the Roman campaign to enforce 'conformity' had no sympathy for ideas of religious or ecclesiastical pluralism, and it was intent upon promoting its Counter-Reformation policies, even at the point of the sword. Many Irish Protestants of our day, especially those in Ulster, see little evidence to suggest that the Tridentine zeal of earlier times has disappeared from either the thinking of the Roman curia, or the members of the Roman hierarchy in Ireland. They simply do not believe that ideas of cultural or religious pluralism will ever be positively appreciated in the Irish Roman Catholic church as it is presently constituted. However desirable peace between the warring ecclesiastical bodies in Ireland might be, the Protestants believe they will retain their freedom only through constant vigilance and by resisting an authority that will never grant them full toleration as a people. Fear always distorts human reasoning, and it is hoped that what this study reveals of the evolution of the Irish Protestant mind will bring some compassion for the understanding and reaction of a people who have long been convinced they are perennially under siege: 'highest justice is found in the deepest sympathy with erring and straying men'.[28]

To some readers, particularly those southern Protestants who have found an albeit uneasy accommodation with the Republic of Ireland, the emphasis on the Irish Protestant's fear of assimilation in an overwhelmingly Roman Catholic united Ireland may seen exaggerated and simplistic. This study argues, however, that historical experience has persuaded the Protestants of Ireland that religiously and culturally they remain a people under siege; many in Northern Ireland consider themselves also to be under political threat. It is the 'besieged minority' complex of Ireland's Protestants which has produced in their succeeding generations the spirit of suspicious intransigence in ecclesiastical affairs which has puzzled ecumenically-minded people like the Roman Catholic and Protestant prelates engaged in the ARCIC meetings. As we have noted, however, insightful observers such as Garret Fitzgerald or Tomas Cardinal O'Fiaich have reckoned with the sensibilities that historical experience and recollection have nurtured among Ireland's Protestant people. When times of crisis have brought soul searching among them, as at the times of the universally-condemned outrages at Darkley or Enniskillen, it has been very difficult for them not to react in an atavistic way redolent of the seventeenth century rather than the present day.

This attempt to 'put the thought and actions of contentious men in their historical setting'[29] is produced at a time when more and more people, in Britain and in the European community are concerned to find historical explanation for Ireland's bitter and seemingly irrational civil and religious conflict. Too often studies of the Irish 'troubles' have been confined to developments in Ireland alone, but in this historical critique constant reference is made to affairs in Britain and on the continent which, it is hoped, may help to explain the influence of external events upon the formation of the Irish Protestant mind and its contribution to sectarian strife. At the 1987 Irish inter-church conference at Ballymascanlon the Church of Ireland primate, archbishop Eames, suggested with the concurrence of cardinal O'Fiaich, that the churches should encourage investigation of the historical causes which have contributed to Ulster's endemic sectarian warfare:

It is a big subject, and it may be discovered that some of the major contributions to sectarianism are to be found in church doctrine—which could be embarrassing to both sides. The attitude of the Irish Catholic church to mixed marriages is one example of how divisions can be created... similarly adherence to traditional doctrines like the Presbyterians' Westminster Confession of Faith is open to misinterpretation.[30]

As long ago as 1981 cardinal Daly, then bishop of Down and Connor, in conciliatory fashion commented on a printed sermon of mine by saying: 'A primary ecumenical duty is the duty to trust our separated fellow-Christians. We should try to see other Christian communities as they see themselves'.[31] It is hoped that this study may in part explain how historically Irish Protestants have interpreted and responded to the authority of the 'court of Rome', and the majority Irish population when, led by ultramontane bishops and clergy, it has sought, many Protestants believe, to impose religious and cultural uniformity upon all inhabitants of the island.

Ireland's Protestants have traditionally claimed they reject 'politics from Britain and religion from Rome'.[32] This study deliberately narrows its concern to that of the religious authority coming from the Holy See. Whether the Norman invasion of Ireland with papal blessing is considered, or the attitude of pope Innocent XI to the campaign of William of Orange is discussed, or the political machinations of Counter-Reformation popes of any age are noted, the focus of the study will be the historical pressure of the Roman authority in Irish affairs and, it is hoped, from the perspective of 'liberal Catholicism'. History is written usually by the victors in any conflict, and until the latter years of the present century there has been little criticism of the ultramontane version of Catholic-Protestant relations in Ireland. There has always existed a minority tradition in Irish Catholicism, however, representative of the 'Gallican' outlook of prelates such as James Doyle and Daniel Murray in the nineteenth century. It is presumed that the appreciation of Roman political authority in the study will be welcomed by those Irish Catholics who belong to this tradition, and will help to put the long history of religious struggle in Ireland in a new perspective.

The intention of this work is eirenical. When a 'black and white' or simplistic interpretation is presented through reference to some militant Protestant source the assessment is not that of the writer. I have spent some thirty years wrestling with the problem of religious and ecclesiastical antagonism in Ireland, and have been greatly helped in my understanding by clergy and laity of all denominations. Lecturing and writing in both parts of Ireland has convinced me that there are no simple solutions to the perennial 'troubles' particularly in the realm of religion. At the same time I have been convinced that a comprehensive study of what lies at the heart of Protestantism, even in its most intransigent form, needs to be considered and reflected upon by intelligent members of both of Ireland's contending communities.

I am greatly indebted to both the Humanities and Social Science Research Council of Canada, and Carleton University, Ottawa, for the research and publishing assistance they have provided for me during the years. I owe a special debt of gratitude to Mrs. Joan Collett of the Queen's University, Belfast, library for the great help she had provided for so long. Mrs. Margaret Jones of Ottawa, who has acted as production assistant in bringing this study into print, has been of immense help to me, and her patience has been much appreciated. My thanks are particularly extended to my wife, Jean Bowen, for her on-going support and encouragement during the creation of this work, as well as for her valuable insights into Catholic-Protestant tensions among the Irish in the British army. Last of all I am grateful to the mature ordinands of the Church of Ireland, from all parts of the island, to whom I have tried to lecture and who have revealed to me something of the complex 'mind' of Irish Protestantism.

Desmond Bowen,
Ottawa, Canada, 1994.

Chapter I

Introduction

Ireland's Dual Protectorate

'It was in Rome that Christianity found its favourable environment'
Benito Mussolini, 14 May, 1929,
Scritti e Discorsi, Milan, 1934, VII,
pp. 34–35.

I   **Rome, Reform and Ireland**

Apart from the apostles themselves, the most venerated churchmen in Roman Catholic hagiography have been the series of powerful popes who proclaimed papal supremacy in the early centuries. Leo the Great (440–461) attributed the authority of the Roman see to the mystical gift of Peter and Paul:

> It is they who have raised thee to thy present pinnacle of glory, in order that—as a holy family, a chosen people, a priestly as well as a royal city that has become the capital of the world in virtue of being Blessed Peter's Holy See—thou mightest reign over a wider realm in the strength of our divine religion than in the exercise of an earthly dominion.[1]

By the time that Gregory VII, (1073–1085) was leading the great eleventh century reform movement he reiterated what he believed to have been the conviction about papal supremacy held by his predecessors like Gelasius I (492–496):

> Although it is fitting that the faithful should submit themselves to all priests who perform their sacred functions properly, how much the more they should accept the judgment of that prelate who has been appointed by the supreme divine ruler to be superior to all priests.[2]

Concern for *imperium* has haunted holders of the papal office, and this passion for authority has persuaded thinkers as diverse as Thomas Hobbes, Edward

Gibbon and J.B. Bossuet to regard the papal church as the 'ghost' of the Roman empire.

Geography and history denied the Roman version of Christianity from establishing itself in Ireland before the legions were withdrawn from Britain in the fifth century, but the evangelist Ninian who had been consecrated bishop in Rome in 394 before he set out to convert Scotland, may have crossed over into Ireland. About the same time pope Celestine I probably sent a bishop named Palladius to a Christian community which had been established in Leinster for some time. The Irish had long traded with both Britain and the continent, and as Roman rule waned they had engaged in large-scale raiding of settlements along the western coast of the larger island. It was on one of these raids that Patrick, a Romanized Briton of extraordinary personality and spiritual stature, was first brought to Ireland. After a conversion experience, and a period of study on the continent, Patrick returned to Ireland to evangelize its peoples.

Patrick's mission probably took place during the pontificate of pope Leo the Great who with the aid of a rescript from the emperor Valentinian III had asserted his authority over all the western provinces of the empire, but there is no evidence that Patrick's work among the savage Irish during their 'generations of chaos'[3] was Roman directed. Patrick's work in Ireland was charismatic in origin, neither blessed nor hindered by papal direction. In his *Confessio* he stressed how unlearned he was, yet he proclaimed himself to be a bishop: 'most assuredly I believe that what I am I have received from God'.[4]

By the last years of the fifth century, with Italy under the rule of the Ostrogoths who were officially recognized by Constantinople, pope Gelasius I took advantage of the situation to assert papal independence from imperial control. He argued that of the two powers ruling in the world the *sacerdotium* of the church, governed by the papacy, was superior to the *imperium* of the state, because it was the instrument of human salvation. When in the sixth century Constantinople attempted a reconquest of the west, however, and incessant warfare reduced Rome to the status of a provincial town, the Roman pontiffs had little authority in church or state. Bishops made use of the prevailing anarchy to act as local temporal sovereigns, and where there was a transmission of the faith by them, and what was left of Greco-Roman culture, it occurred through accommodation with the half-Romanized Ostrogoths.

When religious revival began it was as charismatic in origin as the Irish mission of Patrick in the previous century. Benedict of Nursia rejected contemporary licentiousness to withdraw from the world to live as a hermit at Subiaco, and by 525 he had moved to Monte Cassino to establish what became the Benedictine monastic order. Benedict himself was not ordained, nor does it appear that he contemplated founding an order for clerics. One of the great churchmen of Rome, however, Gregory, when he was prefect of the city from 573, became a patron of the new monastic development, founded six monasteries, and entered the one in Rome himself to lead a very austere life. He became pope in 590, and it is from the time of Gregory I that there was a close identification between Benedictine monasticism and the papacy.

Gregory was a powerful personality who used his office to establish the temporal power of the papacy in Italy, as well as the claim that the Roman pontiff was the supreme authority in spiritual affairs. He took advantage of imperial weakness to conclude peace with the savage Lombards who had invaded Italy, and ignored the exarch in Ravenna who represented the ecclesiastical power of the eastern emperor. He granted the Benedictines privileges which set them partly free from episcopal jurisdiction, and he encouraged them to engage in a major missionary campaign. One of the most successful of the Roman directed missionaries was Augustine of Canterbury, who had been prior of St. Andrew's monastery in Rome before Gregory sent him to Britain, as archbishop of Canterbury, to bring the Anglo-Saxons within the Roman sphere of ecclesiastical influence. Pope Gregory also directed work in Gaul, Spain and Northern Italy, but he lacked the resources to contemplate work in Ireland.

Scholars disagree to what extent there was in the post-Patrick age 'a Celtic church as such' and whether there was in any real sense an 'emotional link of the Irish church with Rome'[5] for the faith seemed to have been easily assimilated by the Irish who gave it an expression that was uniquely their own. No martyrs appeared during the spread of what passed as Christianity in Ireland, and it is probable that neither pope Gregory nor the Benedictine missionaries of the time would have appreciated Ireland's curiously tribal and monastic expression of religious and ecclesiastical life. Though monastic schools such as that of Clonard, founded under Welsh inspiration, produced pious saints like Colum Cille and Columbanus, who became *peregrini,* voluntary exiles from their tribes, and extended their Irish version of the faith in Britain, Gaul and Italy, such inspired ascetics were not typical representatives of the Irish church: 'they were outsiders... tolerated on the fringe of society'.[6] Christianity enriched tribal life, but the values of pre-Christian poets and seers were as important as those of the Irish monks. By the eighth century Irish monasteries were almost totally a part of tribal life, powerful institutions, often wealthy, and subject to no hierarchical direction. Monks took part in the incessant warfare of the age, and on occasion whole communities fought each other to the death:

> The Christian church had embraced all that was congenial in heroic society, its honour and generosity, its splendour and display, its enthusiasm, its respect for learning; in so doing she had shed some of her classical trappings and become a Celtic church. Her strength and weakness lay in her full adjustment to her environment.[7]

In the seventh century Ireland and Northumbria formed part of the same cultural area, and Irish missionaries were at work in the north of Britain from about the year 635. Augustine's Roman mission was well established in Kent and elsewhere in the south, however, by the early years of the seventh century and, at the Synod of Whitby in 664 it was agreed that the Roman ecclesiastical system would be the dominant one in Britain. When, under Theodore of Tarsus as archbishop of Canterbury, a reformed episcopal government was established the Irish resented it and began a cultural and religious withdrawal across the Irish sea. It may be true to say that: 'no scholar nowadays, on the basis of these disputes, holds that the Irish church rejected Rome',[8] but it is clear that the kind of Roman influence that Theodore as archbishop of Canterbury brought to Britain did not extend to Ireland.

Rome in the period following the Synod of Whitby was concerned with survival issues as it tried to reassert the equality of the patriarchates of Constantinople and Rome, and contend with Lombard power. It allied itself with the upstart Carolingian dynasty, and the Donation of Pepin (756) established what were to become the estates of the church in central Italy. From this time the papacy had a powerful military ally outside Italy which tacitly recognized the claim of the popes to be the heirs of the Roman empire, at least in the central Italian lands that legally belonged to the eastern empire. This alliance with the Franks allowed the reappearance of the exalted view of the papacy previously held by Leo I, Gelasius I and Gregory I. They were strongly presented by Nicholas I (858–867), one of the few great popes between Gregory I and Gregory VII. For him the pope was God's representative on earth, with authority over the whole church, synods serving merely as organs for carrying out his decisions. No prince was to interfere in church affairs, except when the pope requested protection and support, but the church had the right to watch over and influence the state. Nicholas's successors were not strong men, however, and papal prestige fell in the tenth century as feudal authorities dominated the papacy effectively, denying it either spiritual or temporal power. Even Nicholas I had neither the means nor the opportunity to promote a papal mission in Ireland. There is evidence of Irish scholars communicating with both Italy and Spain, and the historian Einhard refers to Irish scholars corresponding with Charlemagne, but the period before the Viking invasions was a particularly insular and depressing one for the Irish church.

No church synod was held in Ireland for almost a hundred years after a synod at Birr in 697, and no ecclesiastical authority existed to control abuses such as open warfare between monastic communities. Some hope appeared in the reform movement of the Céli Dé (servants of God), but this minority movement of pious ascetics was not representative of the state of the Irish church and even it was in decline by the middle of the ninth century. More representative was the career of the infamous Feidlimid, king of Munster. He identified himself with the reformers in the church, but he was in fact a brutal ecclesiastical war-lord who used the excuse of enforcing reform to attack wealthy monasteries such as those of Durrow, Kildare and Clonmacnois.

In spite of the savagery of the time the two centuries before the Viking invasions gave Ireland culturally a Golden Age represented by the art and erudition found in some monasteries. This brought Englishmen to study in Ireland, and Irish intellectual genius had influence not only in Britain but on the continent. By the time that Feidlimid died as abbot of Clonfert, however, Viking invaders were wintering in Ireland forcing scholars to flee with their manuscripts to the continent, while the newcomers pillaged the countryside paying particular attention to those secularized and often wealthy monastic settlements where tribal valuables were stored. It was not until the period when Alfred the Great in England was checking Danish depredations that the Irish were strong enough to destroy the chief Viking town of Dublin in 902. By this time conversion of the Vikings, to Christianity had begun and, when Ireland was spared the second wave of attack that devastated England, a slow process of accommodation with or assimilation to Irish society increased among the Vikings. Trade prospered, English coinage was used by the Vikings in Ireland and, although the Norse defeat at Clontarf in 1014 limited their influence to the areas around their coastal cities, Ireland was opened up to external influences from the Viking world. By 1017 Cnut was ruling a northern empire which consisted of Denmark, Norway and England.

During this period, when the Irish and the English were trying to cope with the shock of the Viking invasions, no one paid much attention to the papacy which had degenerated into a local and secular institution following the pontificate of Nicholas I. Only strong feudal lords kept Italy from domination by invading Saracens and Magyars, and the papacy endured its nadir, the age often referred to as 'the Pornocracy'. The Roman aristocracy dominated the papal curia, and the infamous Marozia, a member of the Crescentii family, was the mistress of pope Sergius III, and mother of pope John XI. She later imprisoned John XI, and her family maintained an intermittent supremacy in Rome for most of the tenth century. During this time the papacy was without political power as the western church became a loose organism, its parts controlled by 'national' bishops who afforded Rome neither spiritual prestige nor ecclesiastical authority.

The myth of imperial Rome was strong among the barbarian people who were settling in western Europe, however, and in 961 the Saxon emperor, Otto the Great, responded to a call for help from the eighteen year old profligate grandson of Marozia, pope John XII, and made a significant expedition to Italy. Otto agreed to protect the pope and the patrimony of Peter, and in return pope John anointed Otto and his queen in St. Peter's to inaugurate the concept of the Holy Roman Empire. Otto also solemnly confirmed the earlier donations of land to the papacy made by Pepin and Charlemagne which extended the papal state to include about two thirds of Italy. Pope and emperor soon fell out, however, John was deposed, and for another hundred years the papacy was dominated by the German emperors and their vassals the counts of Tusculum. During this period the bishops of the church everywhere became increasingly dependent on kings and feudal nobility, and more and more secular in outlook.

Britain was another area where the myth of Roman grandeur had immense influence among the newly converted and pilgrimages to the tombs of the apostles, Peter and Paul (*ad limina apostolorum*) began to have particular appeal to the Norse rulers. The English already had a permanent colony in Rome, the *Schola Saxonum,* which had been established and set free from taxation from the time of Alfred the Great, and it was visited by king Cnut in a splendid pilgrimage he made in 1027. Earls, thegns and lesser people followed his example, all of them eager to venerate the holy places in the Eternal City, to be impressed by the basilicas and other ancient buildings, and to reverence Rome's many relics of apostolic times. When spiritual authority was once more granted to the papacy in the late eleventh century the reforming cardinals considered the English among the most loyal of all those who reverenced Rome as the mother church of the faith:

> No other daughter could show a greater tradition of love and untroubled obedience than the Anglo-Saxon community, and there were even elements in England's willing subjection to Rome which could lead the more ambitious and legally-minded popes of the later eleventh century to believe that the kingdom of England itself was subordinate to the papacy.[9]

Because of the close Norse connections between the two islands Cnut's pilgrimage inspired the Irish Viking people to emulate his example. One of those who made a similar visitation to the Roman shrines was Sitric, the recently converted king of Dublin. On his return to Ireland he founded a bishopric in Dublin, that of Christchurch, and installed Donatus as the first bishop, although there is a tradition that the consecration took place at Canterbury. Other Irish royal pilgrims also made their way to Rome, including the king of Munster who died there in 1065. By the end of the eleventh century the Irish were well enough established in Rome to have their own monastery, but there was at the time a much closer link between Rome and England where it was by then accepted that the English church paid tribute to the pope, and that archbishops were to visit Rome to receive the pallium, symbolizing acceptance of 'the plenitude of the papal office'. From the standpoint of the papacy in the period prior to the Norman invasion of England, however, the Irish church was in such a quasi-barbaric state that any formal identification with Rome would have to be preceded by a major reform both religious and ecclesiastical.

When a spirit of reform appeared in the universal church it was not in Rome. At the time when pope Sergius III came to the papal throne by murdering two of his rival contenders, William the Pious, Duke of Aquitaine was busy founding the monastery of Cluny, near Macon in Burgundy. Its first abbot, Berno of Baume set a very high standard of monastic observance, and his successor Odo persuaded not only neighbouring monasteries but others such as

Monte Cassino to return to the original zealous spirit of Benedictine monasticism. This Cluniac revival exercised decisive influence in the life of the whole church in the eleventh and twelfth century. It was the spirit of this movement which finally brought an end to a century and a half of papal decadence when the emperor Henry III forced upon the papal throne his kinsman and a strong supporter of the Cluniac reform movement, Bruno the bishop of Toul, who took the title Leo IX. Leo surrounded himself with able advisers, including the powerful Hildebrand, a Tuscan monk who became the virtual guide of the papacy until he became pope Gregory VII in 1073.

Gregory VII, like his predecessors, Leo the Great, Gelasius I, Gregory the Great and Nicholas I, held grandiose ideas of papal supremacy in both spiritual and temporal affairs. He was convinced that only the papacy could carry out a reform of the church, and that the needed reform would only be possible when the church was freed from its domination by the feudal rulers of the age. This resolve led him into a protracted struggle with lay rulers, and gave him his exalted mystique of papal authority. In his *Dictatus Papae,* produced only two years after he became pope, Gregory in twenty-seven remarkable propositions presented his view of papal authority. To him the pontiff, as the judge and legislator appointed by God, was to root out abuses in both the church and secular society. His authority included the right to depose any prince, temporal as well as spiritual, who opposed what became the Gregorian revolution in the universal church:

> the Cluniac aim of freeing the churches, particularly monastic churches, from direct lay control—an aim expressed in the programme of 'free election'—was soon merged in a policy of raising the standards of lay society itself, because it was evident that the freedom of religious houses from aristocratic exploitation and control could never be assured unless lay society itself were purified and the worst excesses of feudalism eradicated.[10]

It was inevitable that sooner or later the unreformed state of the Irish church would concern the Gregorian reformers. Nowhere was there a more urgent need to free the monasteries from lay control, or to raise the standards of a lay society which was only nominally Christian. The historical record of the eleventh century are filled with accounts of Ireland's unending warfare when monasteries and churches were regularly raided and burned. Sometimes the aggressors were the recently converted Norsemen, but in a society where sons succeeded fathers as abbots of monasteries which were secularized institutions filled with men who often took neither religious orders nor monastic vows, the attackers were only too often rival 'monks':

> The successful monastery was now in fact an ecclesiastical territorial

state, its centre the monastic city or *ruam*. Around this lay its wide
possessions, held by lay tenants who made up the community (*muintir*)
of the monastery equally with its monks and ecclesiastics; every citizen
of the monastic jurisdiction was legally a 'monk' (*manach*). It had its
relations with other states, and these were sometimes put to the test of
war, for the monastic state had its army. Monastic forces might be
involved in secular wars, and monastery might even fight monastery...
The Annals record in 807 'a battle between the community of Cork and
the community of Clonfert, among whom there was a slaughter of
countless ecclesiastics and of the noblest of the community of Cork.'[11]

The decadence within the Irish church was too well established by the eleventh
century to be easily eradicated, but when the citizens of Dublin asked Lanfranc,
the new Norman archbishop of Canterbury to consecrate their bishop elect,
Patrick, in 1074, a long correspondence began between England, Ireland and
Rome on the state of the barbaric Irish church.

It seems clear that communication between Ireland and Rome was then rare,
for Gregory VII in a letter of uncertain date to Turlogh O'Brien, king of
Munster, indicated that it broke a long: 'silence towards Ireland which had lasted,
apparently, since the year 640'.[12] Gregory was very much in contact with the
church in England, however, for he had allied the papacy with the Normans
during the struggle over lay investiture with the German emperor Henry IV, and
it was Gregory who had interceded and obtained blessing from his predecessor,
pope Alexander II , for the invasion of England by William the Conqueror. The
Norman alliance did not help him in England, however, for William made it
clear that he had no intention of becoming a papal vassal. He kept a tight
control on all episcopal appointments, and he let it be known that no papal bull,
brief or legate was to be allowed in the country without royal approval. Gregory
accepted this situation for he was a political realist, and he had no wish to fall
out with the Normans. He was consoled, furthermore, when he knew that
William's choice as archbishop of Canterbury was Lanfranc, a strong supporter
of the Gregorian reform programme.

Lanfranc soon showed that he intended to bring reform to the Irish church as
well as that in England. He believed that from the time of Augustine and the
Venerable Bede Canterbury had: 'exercised primacy... over the whole of the
island called Britain, as well as over Ireland'.[13] Many of the Irish bishops were
one-time monks of the Canterbury province who at the time of their consecration had sworn to give canonical obedience to the archbishop of Canterbury, and
the new primate believed that if William would only help him a reform of the
decadent Irish church was possible. When a dispute arose between the Gaelic
Irish and the 'foreigners of Dublin' an appeal was made to Lanfranc on the
grounds that Irish churchmen had always accepted the jurisdiction of his
predecessors: 'from whom we are mindful we received ecclesiastical rule'.[14]

Lanfranc's response was to suggest to the king that now was the time for him to reform the unruly Irish:

> ... to order the bishops and all religious men to come together, and preside over their assembly in your own person, with your nobles, and strive to banish these evil customs and all others which are forbidden by the church's law from your kingdom.[15]

William, however, had his hands full consolidating his rule in England, and apart from his concern that Ireland might be used by the sons of Harold as an invasion base, he had no interest in the smaller island. He was also suspicious of serving a papal influenced reforming crusade which would be expensive, and might put him in the position of promising fealty to the pope. He had experienced the political machinations of Gregorian reformers in Normandy, and he was concerned about and closely supervised all ecclesiastical affairs. The chief prelates were obliged to attend the Great Council, and William extended his power of veto even to local councils. He knew that he could never have this sort of control in Ireland also, without help from the papacy, and though he could not ignore its strategic importance he chose not to get bogged down in an Anglo-Papal reforming crusade.

William's successor, William Rufus was draconian in his control of the English church, taking over the revenues of the see of Canterbury when Lanfranc died. The choice of the clergy for primate was another reformer, Anselm of Bec, but Rufus refused to accept him or to allow papal legates to enter the country, for he distrusted greatly the new spirit of reform which was sweeping the church. The pope from 1088 was Urban II, one time prior of Cluny and a strong supporter of the Gregorian reform programme. At the Council of Clermont in 1095 he proclaimed the 'Truce of God' as a law of the church and, as a further way of controlling the endemic violence in society, he initiated the First Crusade. The latter action brought the papacy great prestige, and enthusiastic support, but Urban's influence in England was limited by the running quarrel between Rufus and Anselm.

It was not until 1093, when William Rufus thinking he was dying made up his quarrel with the church, that Anselm was allowed to occupy his see. Urban had tried to avoid involvement in the struggle, for the king supported an imperial-appointed anti-pope but, once Rufus recognized Urban, Anselm began to press for reform in the church. When he refused to receive the pallium from the king, however, he had to leave the country. He went to Rome where he remained until the death of Rufus. The new monarch, Henry I, continued the struggle over control of the English church almost immediately he was crowned, and by 1103 Anselm was again in exile for refusing to consecrate bishops whom Henry had invested. It was not to be until 1109, two years before he died, that Anselm, with the help of Urban II, was able to return to England and to occupy his see.

Because of these ecclesiastical and political tensions Anselm had little time or opportunity to oversee affairs in the Irish church. He did reply to an appeal from the clergy and citizens of Waterford for him to consecrate a bishop for the small Norse-Irish city, however, and he admonished both Irish bishops and local kings to rid the church of notorious abuses which were contrary to the canon law. One of the kings responded to Anselm's appeal, Murtagh of Munster, and he called an assembly of clergy and laity to Cashel in 1101. This was not a national synod for no northern representatives were present, and it is likely that Murtagh had a political motive when he responded to Anselm's appeal: 'deliberately choosing Cashel as a southern counterpart to Patrick's church in Armagh'.[16] On the other hand Murtagh was sincere enough that he made over to the church, free of any lay encumbrance, the Rock of Cashel which had been a royal seat and fortress since prehistoric times.

The Cashel synod was limited in terms of the clergy and laity who attended it, but it was important because it heralded the kind of reform movement that had to be brought into Ireland if the Irish were to become part of the mainstream development which was changing church and society in Britain and on the continent. The Cashel decrees showed that during its long years of isolation Ireland had evolved a native culture and religious expressions which the reformers in Rome or Britain were never going to tolerate. There were laymen who ruled in the Irish church; more than one bishop existed in some churches; clerical concubinage was tolerated; kinship marriages were arranged; wives were casually abandoned; and poets as well as clergy were granted freedom from the jurisdiction of civil courts. What was obviously called for was a cultural and religious revolution, which would only be carried out when help was received from Rome or Britain, and chieftains, bishops, clergy and laity could be persuaded that they must accept the civilizing discipline of the universal church.

The next step towards realizing this ideal was in 1111 when a larger synod was held at Rath Bresail, between Thurles and Templemore. This synod, modelled on the old Frankish type, had the king, Murtagh, preside with his principal nobles. An advance on Cashel, however, was the presence of representatives from Ulster, and the recognition of a chief ecclesiastic. This was Gilbert, the first bishop of Limerick, a friend of Anselm of Bec whom he had visited and corresponded with about reform affairs. Gilbert was also recognized as papal legate, and he made clear once again that from the standpoint of the British reformers, or the authorities in Rome, no progress could be made in the Irish church until the customs which had shocked Anselm were eliminated. There had to be an end to the loosely structured church which tolerated numerous bishops for single towns or cities, and still maintained in most parts of the country, in Roman eyes, a reprehensible monastery-based and tribal-dominated organization. Gilbert succeeded, with the help of king Murtagh and the fifty or so bishops at the synod, in persuading the host of clergy and laity who attended that a new territorial diocesan system, like that found in Britain and elsewhere in the universal church, had to be accepted in Ireland. It was certain, however, that this would not be an easy task; the council, for example, revealed the depth of jealousy and suspicion between Ulster and the rest of Ireland.

Little was done after Rath Bresail because of tensions between Britain and Rome. When Anselm died Henry I did not make an appointment for five years and, when he did, the new primate showed little interest in church reform in England let alone Ireland. Rome was unsuccessful in sending emissaries to the English church who might encourage reform, and Henry showed no interest in working with the papacy in such a cause. After his death England was in a state of anarchy during the reign of Stephen; a reforming archbishop of Canterbury, Theobald, was in exile after receiving the pallium in Rome; and pope Eugenius III finally laid England under interdict. When the English crown was in such a state of tension with the papacy there was little desire shown by either authority to continue the reform movement in Ireland which had begun with the synods at Cashel and Rath Bresail.

By this time the Cluniac reform movement had lost much of its early zeal, and when a new spirit appeared to carry on reform it began with an Englishman, Stephen Harding, who initiated an austere expression of the Benedictine rule at the monastery of Citeaux in Burgundy where he was abbot. At first his ascetic house had little appeal, but from 1112 it became an influential spiritual centre because of the support it was given by one of the giants of monastic history Bernard of Clairvaux. Out of his work evolved a new reforming spirit, associated with the Cistercian order, which founded over 500 abbeys by the end of the twelfth century. The new movement was welcomed in the English church during the latter years of the reign of Henry I with the founding of great abbeys at Rievaulx in 1131 and Fountains the following year. Within twenty years the latter foundation had eight daughter houses. It was this reforming movement which carried on the work begun by the Gregorian reformers, and enabled the church in Britain to transcend the political tensions between Henry I, Stephen and Rome.

The Cistercian revival spirit appeared in Ireland when the archbishop of Canterbury consecrated as bishop of Waterford a monk of Winchester called Malchus.[17] He in turn influenced a monk from Armagh, Malachy, who visited Malchus when he was prior of the monastery at Lismore. From there, Malachy went north to be bishop of Down and Connor, ministering to people who, according to Malachy's biographer, Bernard of Clairvaux, lived lives of primitive pagan savagery:

> When he began to administer his office, the man of God understood that he had been sent not to men, but to beasts. Never before had he known the like, in whatever depth of barbarism: never before had he found men so shameless in their morals, so wild in their rites, so impious in their

faith, so barbarous in their laws, so stubborn in discipline, so unclean in their life. They were Christians in name, in fact they were pagans.[18]

Malachy, nevertheless, devoted himself to trying to reform the church and its people, but by 1127 incessant warfare drove him out of the north and he retired once more to the monastery at Lismore. From there, with the help of lay patrons, he was made archbishop of Armagh, but only after a struggle to end the power of a family that had controlled the see for some two hundred years. Once he was established he set out for Rome in 1139 to receive the pallia for the sees of Cashel and Armagh from the pope. According to strict canon law the papacy had to grant these symbols of archiepiscopal office before an archbishop could function, and Malachy wanted as much authority as he could obtain for his reforming mission.

His greatest support, however, proved to be spiritual rather than ecclesiastical. On his way to Rome he visited the reformed monastery of Clairvaux, and it was there that his devotion to the Cistercian reform movement was confirmed, and his close personal friendship with Bernard began. So great was his attachment to the Cistercians he sought permission from pope Alexander II to join the order and resign his see when he got to Rome, but the pontiff insisted Malachy return to Ireland to carry on with his mission activities. He granted Malachy the title of papal legate, to assist him in his work, but he refused to give him the pallia until a reforming council was held, and the church and people of Ireland showed signs of spiritual regeneration. On his way back to Ireland Malachy revisited Clairvaux, leaving there four of his companions for training as Cistercians. One of these men was later to become a papal legate in Ireland.

Malachy had an eight year apostolate in Ireland that was not an easy one, and little would have been heard of it but for his friendship with his biographer, Bernard of Clairvaux who was then at the height of his fame. When Malachy did finally hold a reforming council, on the island of Inis Padraig off the coast of County Dublin it met without the needed support of an Irish king. After holding the council Malachy set off for Rome to request the pallia once more, but he became ill on the journey and died in the arms of Bernard at Clairvaux in 1148. Bernard made sure that the heroic labours of the saintly Malachy were not forgotten, and Eugenius III, the first Cistercian pope, sent the legate, John Paparo, to Ireland with four pallia for the archbishops in Armagh, Dublin, Cashel and Tuam. These were presented at a reforming synod held at Kells in 1152, to give the Roman Catholic Church in Ireland the form of hierarchy which it has held to the present day. The annalists tell us that among the many reform issues discussed was the problem of imposing a new morality among the clergy: from that time they were to eschew clerical concubinage, rape, robbery, and the imposing of extortionate dues for baptism and anointing.[19]

Tribal life remained turbulent in Ireland, however, and reform minded churchmen in Britain and Rome knew that even the labours of a Malachy, or the pious intentions of synods, would not bring about reformation in a church and society long used to the savagery that accompanies endemic warfare. Monarchs of the tribes like Turlough O'Connor, or Murtagh MacLochlainn were constantly ravaging the countryside, including churches and monasteries, in their never-ending 'hostings'. The king of Leinster, Diarmuid MacMurrough, might appear civilized when he attended a synod, founded a monastery, or acted as patron to Laurence O'Toole, who introduced the reforming Arrouaisian order into his cathedral when he became archbishop of Dublin. Diarmuid could also contrive the public rape of the abbess of Kildare by one of his warriors, and was as barbaric and ruthless as the other Irish kings and chieftains of the time. It would not be easy for British or continental reformers to persuade such men, or their subjects, to accept moral reform and a new civility. Offences against the canon law of the universal church in affairs of sex and marriage remained common in Ireland, and there was little ecclesiastical censure of them when most church offices were in the gift of tribal leaders.

Both Bernard of Clairvaux, and pope Eugenius III, who had done so much to promote reform, died in 1153 but by that time a resolve to raise clerical and monastic standards, and to improve moral behaviour was common in the universal church. The Cistercian order was becoming increasingly wealthy and influential, numbering twenty-six abbeys in England alone by the end of the twelfth century.[20] Bernard of Clairvaux had been convinced that the work of salvation called for man's activity to cooperate with the love and grace of God, and he had little difficulty in convincing church reformers, and secular rulers of the crusading era that the spreading of Christian culture by force of arms was worthy of consideration. When the Cistercian pope Eugenius III invited churchmen to a synod at Rheims he developed the doctrine that through St. Peter Christ had granted the pope supreme authority in temporal as well as spiritual affairs. In 1146 he proclaimed the Second Crusade, and commissioned Bernard of Clairvaux to preach it. The successor of Eugenius, pope Anastasius IV, sought conciliation with the English crown by sending the pallium to the archbishop of York who had been deposed through Cistercian influence, and it was clear that by mid-twelfth century a rapprochement with Britain was desired by the papacy. This would be the time, in the minds of many reformers when the English crown should with papal blessing launch another 'crusade'—this time in Ireland to put an end to abuses in the church, and barbarism in society.

New tensions arose in England, however, with the coming to the throne of Henry II. The new king was intelligent, well-educated, strong minded, and determined to maintain his royal prerogatives in his hybrid 'empire' which included much of France as well as Wales, Scotland and Ireland. This soon brought him into conflict with the church for, during the chaotic reign of Stephen, clerical courts with their well-developed system of canon law had begun seriously to encroach on those of the monarch. 'Benefit of clergy', which granted tonsured clerks and nuns exemption from trial by a secular court, was particularly resented when it was extended to include even homicides. The king was emotionally involved in this issue after his personal friend, Thomas Becket, whom he had made archbishop of Canterbury, led the resistance to the crown over such concerns. When the crown extended its jurisdiction at the expense of the church's law in the Constitutions of Clarendon in 1164, Becket was forced to flee into exile. He later returned, excommunicated bishops who supported the king, and was murdered in his own cathedral in 1170. The scandal shocked Europe, and Henry was obliged to swear that he had never intended Becket's death, that he would be faithful to the pope in the future, that he would allow appeals to Rome, and if necessary he would go on a crusade. Becket's tomb at Canterbury became one of the most popular pilgrim shrines in Europe, and when Becket was canonized in 1173 Henry was also obliged to attend. Most importantly, he had to tolerate the exercise of 'benefit of clergy' which became almost scandalous, and to accept a great increase in appeals made to Roman courts.[21]

Henry was not the only European monarch to experience the new spirit of papal aggressiveness. Though Eugenius III may be regarded as the last representative of the reforming zeal which accompanied the rise to influence of the Cistercians, the papacy as an institution was asserting itself effectively in political affairs. It survived the establishment in Rome of a commune government set up by the anti-hierarchical renegade monk, Arnold of Brescia, while the successor of Eugenius III, Anastasius IV, a tough-minded Roman native used his diplomatic skills in the service of the Holy See, as we have seen, during this time of testing. He astutely extended the influence of the Roman court in many parts of the church, and during his reign a very able legate, cardinal Nicholas Breakspear successfully organized the payment of Peter's Pence by Norway and Sweden. When Anastasius died, Breakspear, a strong-willed and clear-sighted Englishman, was unanimously elected pope Hadrian IV.

Determined to assert the full monarchical claims of the papacy, Hadrian continued to use diplomacy and political alliances to protect Rome from its enemies. When he crowned Frederick Barbarossa in St. Peter's in 1155 he significantly altered the service so as to bring out the emperor's subordination to the pope. When friction increased between pope and emperor over imperial rights Hadrian made an alliance with William I of Sicily, recognizing his Norman rule over southern Italy, with special rights over the church in Sicily. In return William acknowledged the pope's feudal suzerainty and agreed to pay Rome an annual tribute. Before he died Hadrian threatened the emperor Frederick Barbarossa with excommunication because he had infringed on papal prerogative, and had been ungrateful as a vassal for the benefits the papacy had bestowed upon him. It was during the pontificate of Hadrian IV that the use of the title 'Vicar of Christ' for the pope became current, although it had existed since the eighth century.

Hadrian's closest counsellor, cardinal Roland, a celebrated professor of law at

Bologna, carried on the temporal policies of his predecessor when he succeeded him as pope Alexander III in 1159. He assiduously sought to assert the authority of the holy see over other rulers within the limits of the politically possible. It was Alexander who supported Thomas Becket in his quarrel with Henry II over control of the English church, and laid fullest sanctions upon the king after the murder of the archbishop. In 1179 Alexander held the Third Lateran Council which was impressively attended, and marked an important stage in the development of papal legislative authority. Alexander was the first great lawyer pope, resolutely in the reforming tradition, and not a pontiff who would tolerate the abuses in the unreformed Irish church. Neither was he a pontiff who having urged force to be used against the Cathar heretics in the south of France would be one who would hesitate to use the power of his Norman ally in England to bring about order in Ireland.

In the Irish nationalist canon of history there has been considerable questioning of the authenticity of the bull of Hadrian IV, *Laudabiliter,* which authorized Henry II to carry out on behalf of the papacy a religious reformation in Ireland:

Whereas then, well-beloved in Christ, you have expressed to us your desire to enter the island of Ireland in order to subject its people to law and to root out from them the weeds of vice, and your willingness to pay an annual tribute to the blessed Peter... we...do thereby declare our will and pleasure that, with a view to enlarging the boundaries of the church, restraining the downward course of vice, correcting evil customs and planting virtue, and for the increase of Christian religion, you shall enter that island and execute whatsoever may tend to the honour of God and welfare of the land.[22]

A pontiff such as Hadrian IV, however, thought in just these terms as the vicar of Christ upon earth, combining royal with sacerdotal powers in his supervision of the nations and their rulers. So far as he and Alexander III were concerned there was no doubting of: 'the papal principle that St. Peter was the feudal overlord who through his successor, the pope, enfeoffed kings and princes'. [23] Rome was aware of the state of Irish church and society in this period, after the legatine report on the synod of Kells of 1152, and it was almost inevitable that Rome would authorize the English crown to carry out a papal directed religious reformation. Henry II was in a suppliant mood after the Becket scandal, and was willing to undertake such a crusade, as Alexander III reminded the kings and princes in Ireland in 1172. The Normans were coming as defenders of the faith, to deliver the people of Ireland from barbarism to guarantee that:

... there shall reign in your land greater peace and tranquility and that the Irish people, in proportion as through the enormity and filthiness of their vices, they have fallen so far from the divine law, so they shall be all the more surely moulded in it and receive all the more fully the discipline of the Christian faith.[24]

II   The Anglo-Roman Settlement

The Anglo-Norman invasion of Ireland began in 1169, with the king arriving in 1171. Henry II's land-hungry Anglo-Norman forces had comparatively little difficulty in penetrating to every corner of the island, establishing their sword-land, erecting their castles, and overcoming Irish counter-attacks. Rome gave its full approval to the Anglo-Norman exercise. A cardinal-legate, Vivian, was sent in 1177 to hold a council of bishops in Dublin and to threaten excommunication for any who opposed the rights of the English crown. The papacy also ensured that lay-rulers understood that the oaths of fealty they were forced to make to the invaders were to be honoured. In 1182 pope Lucius III accepted the nomination of the archbishop of Dublin by the crown, and four years later a legate placed a crown on the head of prince John to proclaim him king of Ireland. The Anglo-Roman dual protectorate which was to operate in Ireland throughout the medieval period was well established by the end of the twelfth century. Though Rome was to admonish the crown from time to time for wrongs committed in Ireland: 'the papacy was never before the Reformation seriously to reconsider its authorization of the English claim to sovereignty over Ireland'.[25]

Wherever the invaders could govern with any degree of peace they introduced their comparatively sophisticated feudal way of life built around castles, churches and reformed monasteries. The religious dimension of this imposed social order was greatly strengthened when members of the new mendicant orders came to Ireland in the thirteenth century, to have influence in the Gaelic as well as the Anglo-Norman territories. On the whole, however, the way of life of the Anglo-Normans was rejected by the majority of the Gaelic population who chose to cling stubbornly to cultural expressions that were anathema to both Canterbury and Rome. By the thirteenth century the newcomers, who were seldom reinforced by new Norman arrivals, were on the defensive, struggling to resist assimilation into the Gaelic culture which showed amazing resilience. Rome was regularly informed when religious reform languished, even among the Cistercians: abbots were murdered, monks were blinded in tribal warfare, and visitations carried out by reformers from continental houses had little influence. In 1231 the general chapter of the Cistercian order appealed to pope Gregory IX for help, but the most that the great patron of the Franciscans could do was to condemn dissident Irish monks as 'beasts who have rotted in their own dung'.[26] He also called on his docile vassal, Henry III of England, to do something about the continuing barbarism that threatened church and society in Ireland, but neither the papacy nor the English crown in the thirteenth century were in a position to promote the needed crusade.

At the beginning of the century papal authority was at its zenith during the pontificate of Innocent III (1198–1216). Yet his mystical dream of the papacy ruling Christendom as a single entity in which moral unity would prevail was unfortunately negated by exercises in political opportunism. The sack of Constantinople during the Fourth Crusade, the extermination of the rich culture of part of southern France during the Albigensian Crusade, and Innocent's ruthless attempts to root out the political power of the house of Hohenstaufen revealed a secularizing spirit in Rome which many Christians deplored.

Resentments over papal power exploded in England when Innocent appointed Stephen Langton as archbishop of Canterbury in 1205. A protracted quarrel with the crown resulted in Innocent putting England under interdict, with king John by 1213 forced to surrender his crown and kingdom to Roman authority, to receive them back only when he agreed to pay an annual tribute and to acknowledge himself vassal of the pontiff. This was no mere symbolic gesture for during a period of years when the nation was threatened by civil war a series of able and determined papal legates not only kept order in government but systematically extended Roman authority in the English church. Prior to his recall in 1222 one of these curial officials, Pandulf, was the virtual ruler of England during the minority of king Henry III. By the time Henry was able to rule on his own he was well conditioned to accept Roman authority in the kingdom, including a sophisticated system of taxation, and appeal procedures for 'Rome runners' who sought redress of grievance in the papal courts.

To pay for its expanding administration in England Rome increasingly provided curial appointees to English benefices, such as Pandulf who finally retired to Rome as titular bishop of Norwich. As more and more foreigners were appointed to English livings, often without even visiting them, and the outflow of English money to Rome continued, popular resentment increased against these:

> ...wretched men without manners, full of cunning, proctors and 'farmers' of the Romans, seizing whatever in the country is precious and serviceable and sending it away to their lords living delicately out of the patrimony of the Crucified.[27]

The same process took place in other parts of western Christendom for Aragon, Bulgaria, Denmark, Hungary, Poland, Portugal and Serbia were, like England, obliged to recognize the pope as feudal suzerain as well as the spiritual arbiter of a universal Christian commonwealth. Even in distant Ireland, lying, in Roman eyes, 'on the very edge of the world', papal emissaries strove to improve ecclesiastical administration, which would extend curial authority, through legates like Cardinal John of Salerno (1193–1203) or the papal collector, John of Frosinone who spent most of his life in Ireland prior to his death in 1274. The extortionate activities of these functionaries were as resented in Ireland as they were elsewhere.

The climax of Innocent III's claims for spiritual and temporal authority had been the Fourth Lateran Council of 1215 attended by 400 bishops, 800 abbots and representatives of the monarchs of Christendom. His successors, however, became increasingly worldly as they sought the outright destruction of the imperial house of Hohenstaufen and became more and more involved in Italian political affairs. By the end of the thirteenth century Boniface VIII, lawyer, diplomat and man of affairs, as well as a sceptic in religion, substituted on occasion imperial dress for papal vestments and indignation against papal authority and taxation intensified throughout the universal church. Edward I of England, and Philip IV of France, particularly rejected the ideological pretensions of the secularized papacy, choosing to oppose and humiliate Boniface whom they dismissed as a petty Italian prince as much concerned with the aggrandisement of his family as he was with the welfare of the church universal.

The secularization of the papacy developed further in the period 1305–1378 when the popes, dominated by the French, had their court at Avignon. There the administration procedures and taxation policies of the papal curia became the most sophisticated in Europe, with most of its income spent on war and entertainment.[28] John XXII, was one of the most secular of the Avignon popes, incurring the wrath of the Spiritual Franciscans who regularly denounced the worldliness of the papal court. In the late fourteenth century the scandal of the secularized papacy continued with the Great Schism, and the spectacle of rival popes excommunicating each other. The first half of the fifteenth century was the period when lay rulers and church reformers forced upon the papacy reforming councils, but by the time a strong pope, Martin V, 'a Roman of the Romans' emerged out of the council of Constance in 1417 the papacy's principal concern was political ascendancy and survival not religious or ecclesiastical reform. What spiritual fervour there was in the church was to be found among the underground movements like the Lollards in England, or the Hussites in Bohemia. The Renaissance popes of the fifteenth century were not the men to provide leadership for a new reform movement as in the days of Gregory VII or Eugenius III.

English resentment of papal exactions had increased during the reign of Henry III as legates and nuncios extended the power of the Roman courts in the kingdom, and collectors became ever more rapacious in their financial demands. In 1253 even the pious Robert Grosseteste, bishop of Lincoln, in the last year of his life burst out in exasperation against the papal encroachments: 'with all filial respect and obedience I will not obey, I resist, I rebel'.[29] Under Edward I the statute of *Mortmain* established crown control of benefactions made to religious houses, and by the time of Edward III the series of statutes called *Provisors* and *Praemunire* sought to control papal appointments to English benefices, and appeals to the papal court at Avignon. The English parliament had supported the resistance of the crown by stating that king John had had no authority to make the nation a papal fief without its consent, and this expression of popular sentiment put an end to the payment of tribute which John had promised to Innocent III. Most importantly in the 1370's, John Wyclif, who had helped the government in negotiations with the papacy over ecclesiastical appointments revealed the depth of anti-papal feeling in England when he began his radical criticisms of the theocratic concepts which were so important to the papal system. Though repressed in England, the ideas of this 'morning star of the Reformation' spread as far as Bohemia where they greatly reinforced the anti-papal resistance of the Hussites. Nor did the followers of Wyclif bow to the pressures put upon them by the ecclesiastical establishment. Lollardy as an underground movement maintained its resistance to the worldliness of the papacy, and the corruption within the church, until the time of the Reformation.

The tensions between the English crown and the papacy ensured that Ireland's two 'protectors' had little interest in promoting reform in either church or society in distant Ireland. There the people were divided between their identification with the way of life of either the Anglo-Normans or the Gaelic chieftains, and were constantly at war. The prevailing anarchy was at its height when Edward Bruce led a Scots army to Ireland in 1315 to savage the land for three terrible years: 'to the common ruin of the Galls and Gaels of Ireland'.[30] The result of this time of chaos was a waning of the rule of any law, with the central government ignored, and finances strained to the breaking point. When the Black Death reached Ireland in the summer of 1348, devastating the whole of the eastern seaboard and destroying almost totally the relatively sophisticated society of Dublin and Drogheda, there were few barriers left to a reversion to traditional tribal life anywhere in the island. The English 'nation' in Ireland was particularly the victim of the plague, and Richard FitzRalph archbishop of Armagh believed it lost two thirds of its population.[31]

The papacy was appealed to during the Bruce invasion when many of the Irish supported him. In the midst of the turmoil the Gaelic Irish sent to pope John XXII at Avignon a *Remonstrance* which revealed the depth of hatred which existed between the two 'nations'. The Gaelic chieftains castigated the Anglo-Normans for their 'arrogance and excessive lust to lord it over us... there cannot be in the present or in the future any sincere good will between them and us':

> We have a natural hostility to each other arising from the mutual, malignant, and incessant slaying of fathers, brothers, nephews and other near relatives and friends so that we have no inclination to reciprocal friendship in our time or in that of our sons.[32]

John's response to the *Remonstrance,* like that of his predecessor Gregory IX a century earlier, was to castigate the friars, 'agents of the devil' who were fomenting dissension in Ireland, but apart from excommunicating all supporters of Edward Bruce he sought to avoid papal involvement in the troubles. He naturally exhorted Edward II, as a Christian prince, to bring a just settlement to the war-torn land, and he avoided replying to those who complained about crown injustice. The Avignon papacy did not intend to lose support of the English crown, and to show his good will the pope promoted members of the Dublin administration to the archbishoprics of Dublin and Cashel for John XXII: 'was not a whit less committed to supporting the English lordship of Ireland than had been his predecessors'.[33]

At the same time the Avignon curia was not about to lose its financial interest in Ireland which had become an integral part of the papal fiscal system, the Florentine banking firm of Sapiti handling its affairs. Irish churchmen who wished to revert to the traditional system where ecclesiastical offices became hereditary, and church lands were controlled by tribal chieftains, found that the papal curia was only too willing to bargain with them in return for a financial consideration. All the issues that the reformers of Malachy's era had struggled over became a problem once more as dispensations were granted readily for clerical bastards, and hard bargaining obtained papal provision to bishoprics, abbeys, rectories and other benefices. The only area where there was resistance to this surrender to the earlier unreformed state of ecclesiastical order was around Dublin where common law procedures inhibited the work of the papal agents. By the end of the fourteenth century, however, a cynical bargain had been made between Rome and the unreformed churchmen of Ireland: 'by 1399 virtually the whole episcopate held office in right of papal provision'.[34]

Moral decline was greatest in the Gaelic areas, especially in those areas farthest from the English lordship where even the reform movement of the twelfth century had made little impact upon church or tribal custom. There churches were regularly burned during savage clan struggles, warrior bishops died in combat, and the chieftains appropriated more and more church land. Old abuses such as clerical concubinage were condoned, with offenders openly defending their way of life by declaring that: 'old statutes had ceased to bind and that they were guilty at most of a mere technical or legal offence':

> Councils, synods, visitations and various forms of disciplinary action were all invoked from time to time by conscientious prelates and superiors to recall delinquent clergy to a sense of duty, but the rot had gone deep and the spirit of the time was opposed to moral reform.[35]

One of the few reforming prelates in the middle years of the fourteenth century was Richard FitzRalph, archbishop of Armagh, who sought help from the courts in both London and Avignon as he tried to check the moral decline in church and society. He was identified with English authority, however, and regardless of his fame as a theologian, his piety, and his reforming zeal, he found that churchmen refused to recognize his authority, especially in the Gaelic areas.

There the resistance to reform was led by the friars who regularly objected to the censures the archbishop tried to levy when he opposed their ecclesiastical irregularities:

> In my diocese of Armagh, so far as I can reckon, I have two thousand subjects who are involved every year in sentences of excommunication by reason of sentences that I have decreed against deliberate murderers, public robbers, incendiaries and such like; and of all these scarce forty a year come to me or my penitentiaries. Yet all these receive the sacraments like other men and are absolved; and it is believed beyond doubt that they are absolved by the friars, for there are no others to absolve them.[36]

The tragedy of the Irish church in the fourteenth century was that even when it produced a superior prelate like Richard FitzRalph, there was no reforming movement such as that of the Cistercians, nor a charismatic figure such as Bernard of Clairvaux to reinforce his activities. Instead there was the worldly politicizing religious ethic of the age, which in Ireland took the form of dividing the people between its two 'nations'. Though the archbishop was dismissed by the Gaelic church militants as an agent of English authority, he had spent seven years at Avignon, and had communication with the centre of continental ecclesiastical power, but there was no reformer in the curia to support him. Cynical churchmen in Ireland, of course, knew this and were willing to promote political and ethnic divisions as a means to avoid change in church and society.[37] The secularized papacy that was to withstand the challenge of reform presented by Jan Hus and others during the conciliar struggle cared not to apply itself seriously to the problems of the barbarous Irish.

Neither was the English crown concerned about redressing the wrongs in Ireland which would call for a major military operation and massive expenditure. By the middle of the fourteenth century the need of the Irish administration was to protect the Anglo-Norman settlers from assimilation into the culture of the 'mere Irish' who lived under the 'servile condition' of the Brehon law. In 1366 the government tried to curb this process by legislating comprehensive statutes in a parliament held at Kilkenny. They were intended to protect the culture of the English nation by separating radically its people from their Gaelic neighbours, and prelates were called upon to pronounce solemn anathema against those who would ignore the statutes by: 'forsaking the English language, fashion, mode of riding, laws and usages, live and govern themselves according to the manners, fashion and language of the Irish enemies'. The Anglo-Irish were also urged to avoid the 'divers marriages and alliances' between members of the two nations which made certain that: 'English laws are put in subjection and decayed'.[38] The Statutes of Kilkenny achieved little, however, for both the Anglo-Irish and the Gaelic Irish knew they would not be reinforced by any

coercive power. Though the Peace of Bretigny in 1360 gave England a breathing
space in the Hundred Years War in France, both church and state were so weak
that there was little likelihood of anyone showing interest in redressing the Irish
situation.

When England did show interest in Ireland again was during the reign of
Richard II at the end of the fourteenth century. The papacy was then enduring
the scandal of the Great Schism, with rival popes in Avignon and Rome, and its
struggle to survive ensured that the king would have freedom to impose his own
settlement in Ireland. The king was on good terms with parliament which
reenacted the anti-papal statutes of *Provisors* in 1390, *Mortmain* in 1391 and
Praemunire in 1393, and agreed to give him financial backing in an attempt in
1394 to settle finally the Irish problem. The island's people were radically
divided by this time, however, between the 'wild Irish', the Gaelicized Normans,
and the 'obedient' English, and though Richard demanded homage from a great
many chieftains and other leaders little was accomplished when a resurgence of
Lollardy and other problems brought him back to England. He returned in 1399
after his heir, Roger Mortimer, whom he had left in Ireland as his representative,
was killed in a tribal battle but his absence from England lost him his throne to
Henry IV.

William the Conqueror had been too occupied establishing Norman rule in
England to do anything about Ireland, but he had recognized that its nearness was
a potential threat should he get overly involved there, or any enemy decide to
make use of it as a base for future invasion. Richard II, to his cost in 1399,
realized the same truth, which was to haunt Anglo-Irish relations from then to
the present day. In terms of international and domestic politics Ireland was too
close to England, and its people too involved within a common way of life, for
English rulers to leave it alone. The strategic importance of the smaller island
of the archipelago could not be ignored. This was made clear again during the
fifteenth century Wars of the Roses when the pretenders Lambert Simnel and
Perkin Warbeck both attempted to make use of Ireland and its dissident people
before moving on to England to contest the throne.

Civilization did not advance in fifteenth century Ireland. The breakdown of
law and order and the prevailing anarchy was so great that perhaps half the
English population returned home during the reign of Henry V. England was in
no position to do anything about affairs in Ireland as it endured the dreary civil
war between the houses of Lancaster and York though Richard of York, as
viceroy in mid century, tried to ingratiate himself with colonists and natives
alike at the expense of virtually abandoning English rule in Ireland. As for the
papacy, it was fighting to maintain its authority during the great councils of
Pisa, Constance and Basel. 'Pragmatic Sanctions' recognized the loss of taxing
authority by the papacy in both France and Germany; local ecclesiastical
assemblies asserted themselves at the expense of Roman prerogatives; and even
the strong minded Martin V who emerged out of the council of Constance could

do little to advance the prestige of the secularized papacy. The fall of Constantinople in 1453 persuaded pope Callistus III to organize a crusade for the recapture of the eastern Christian capitol but his zeal had little influence on western monarchs. Callistus sold papal treasures to pay for galleys built in the Tiber, and his successor Pius II died at Ancona while he waited for a crusading force to appear and follow him east.

None of the successors of Pius II showed interest in crusading or directing the universal church in a way that would once more allow the papacy to assert its authority. The 'Renaissance popes' of the last half of the fifteenth century were generally effete, worldly, and more interested in the aggrandisement of their families through Italian political intrigues than in giving leadership to western Christendom.[39] From the standpoint of earlier reformers their personal lives were scandalous: Innocent VIII dined publicly with ladies, and openly recognized his children; Alexander VI's life was shocking even by the standards of the age; and Julius II (1503–1513) was more a statesman than a priest, not averse to wearing armour when going into battle. There was little concern for promoting reform in Ireland, or anywhere else, in Renaissance Rome. Julius II opened a council held at the Lateran between 1512 and 1517 but it showed small enthusiasm for promoting serious reform in the church, and Julius tried to use the council to condemn curbs on papal financial policies like the Pragmatic Sanction of Bourges, for at the time he was fighting the French with his Venetian, Spanish, English and Swiss allies in the Holy League formed in 1511. European leaders generally agreed with the Florentine historian Guicciardini who said there was nothing of the priest about this pope except his dress and his name.

The fifteenth century papacy left the government of the church and state in Ireland to the English in the years immediately prior to the Reformation. Martin V in 1417, for example, provided to the archbishopric of Dublin a powerful individual, Richard Talbot who was as much a politician as he was a churchman, serving at times as justiciar and even as king's lieutenant as well as prelate. His brother John ruled as viceroy several times and used military might often in his attempt to build up an administration that would give strong and impartial government. Yet even dedicated officials like the Talbots appeared helpless as the numbers of rebels increased, warfare was endemic, and anarchy prevailed. The Irish parliament described for the king the state of Ireland in 1435:

His land of Ireland is well-nigh destroyed and inhabited with his enemies and rebels, in so much that there is not left in the nether counties of Dublin, Meath, Louth and Kildare, that join together, out of the subjection of the said enemies and rebels, scarcely thirty miles in length and twenty miles in breadth there, as man may surely ride and go, in the said counties, to answer the king's writs and to his commandments.[40]

In this situation neither censures by churchmen nor punitive actions by the government were of much avail. The borders of the Pale continued to contract, and Irish officials in Dublin knew that little could be done to curb the arrogance of the Gaelic chieftains and their allies the rebel Anglo-Irish lords. John Talbot was so repressive in his counter-insurgency measures that the annalists of the time compared him to Herod,[41] but the Irish were so intransigent, and disaffection from the crown so widespread, that nothing could be accomplished unless a major reinforcement of government forces was made. This the Irish knew would not happen so long as civil war, or the threat of it, existed in England: 'England's difficulty was Ireland's opportunity'.

What hope there was for moral reform lay in the church, but without help from outside Ireland it lacked the spiritual resources to do much more than struggle for survival as an institution. Within the Irish church there had remained always unreformed areas such as Kerry where even the reformers of the twelfth century had had little influence. There the great abiding threat to the Irish church, its assimilation into the traditional Gaelic society, never disappeared. The custom of certain families having hereditary rights in certain parishes, including that of presentment, still was common.[42] Privileges of sanctuary and immunity were regularly disregarded, and during the endemic warfare the clergy served more as servants of the tribe than of the church. The rot was most clearly seen in the Gaelic and Gaelicized areas where in the monasteries observance of celibacy was widely abandoned and abbots and monks openly married. Inevitably monastic property became quasi-hereditary, visitations for reform by Pale or English superiors could only be carried out with the help of an armed force, and often in distant dangerous areas even these exercises had to be abandoned. Even the Cistercians, the great reformers of the twelfth century, fell into decadence, and the great monastery of Mellifont, which lay within the Pale and was purely English, shared in the decline. It contained monks who never took orders and lived as laymen, and the abbot said that outside the Pale the rule of the order was seldom observed, or the Cistercian habit worn. The only sign of reform was among some of the friars in the Gaelic areas who served the Observant movement but: 'it did not survive the Reformation, and little is known about it in detail'.[43] Clerical life was if anything even more deplorable among the secular clergy:

> Mismanagement and civil strife begot a numerous and evil progeny—pluralism, non-residence, neglect of divine service, dilapidation, a lowering of standards for candidates to the priesthood, and clerical engagement in the trades and professions.[44]

For political as well as religious reasons the prelates of the English nation would have liked to remedy the state of the Gaelic church, if they had received help from Canterbury or Rome. They knew well that the church in Gaelic

Ireland was becoming so secularized, so much a part of the traditional tribal way of life, that reform was by now almost an impossibility. Within the territory which recognized English authority, although the situation was bad, some attempt was made to control the worst abuses. The other ecclesiastical authority, that of Rome, also operated in Ireland, however, and the numerous papal collectors, showed little interest in pressing for reform. Rather they were willing to overlook glaring offences against good ecclesiastical government for the sake of the financial return that was theirs for papal dispensation:

> During the second half of the fifteenth century it became the practice to grant provisions to members of the great and influential families who were barely in minor orders or were even still laymen but had declared intention to take orders. In the sixteenth century this practice became more and more widespread... when a great man had secured possession of an abbey or benefice no power existed which could effectively secure his removal.[45]

Evidence provided by the papal registers of the late fifteenth century indicate clearly that Rome's interest in Gaelic Ireland, in particular, was limited to obtaining money from its church. Whatever the disreputable arrangement wanted by the Irish chieftain who coveted position or property in the church an accommodation was made possible for him by a papal agent in return for a financial consideration. Few historians would disagree with the judgment: 'the papacy was not interested in remedying these grave abuses, indeed its toleration of them, unthinkable by thirteenth century papal standards, undoubtedly fostered them':

> The papacy made of its right to provide to benefices a major industry... the whole complex system of ecclesiastical office was exploited often as a purely fiscal operation of which the aim, at least in practice, was more financially than religiously motivated... As far as Gaelic Ireland was concerned, this papal centralization led to a considerable increase in 'Rome-running'.[46]

Rome's toleration of Irish abuses reflected her loss of spiritual leadership. The truth was that from the time of the Council of Constance there was little authority granted to the papacy generally by either the secular leaders of Europe, or by an increasing number of churchmen. The German monk, Dietrick Vrie, a historian of the council, expressed the anti-papal sentiment which even the repressive measures of the conservative hierarchies of the time could not contain:

> The pope, once the wonder of the world has fallen... Now is the reign of Simon Magus, and the riches of this world prevent just judgment.

The papal court nourishes every kind of scandal, and turns God's houses into a market... Golden was the first age of the papal court; then came the baser age of silver; next the iron age set its yoke on the stubborn neck. Then came the age of clay. Could aught be worse? Aye, dung; and in dung sits the papal court. All things are degenerate; the papal court is rotten; the pope himself the head of all wickedness, plots every kind of disgraceful scheme, and, while absolving others, hurries himself to death.[47]

After the fall of Constantinople the one-time humanist pope Pius II published at Mantua in 1460 a remarkable document, *Execrabilis,* which sought to assert, in the strongest of terms, the traditional authority of the papacy. The call of Pius for a crusade against the Turks was virtually ignored, however, as we have noted, and the papal statement's phrasing was noticeably defensive:

A horrible and in earlier times unheard of abuse has sprung up in our period. Some men, imbued with a spirit of rebellion... suppose they can appeal from the pope, vicar of Jesus Christ; from the pope to whom it was said in the person of the blessed Peter 'feed my sheep' and 'whatever you bind on earth will be bound in heaven'... but... no one is allowed to violate or daringly oppose this, our expression of what is to be desired, condemned, reproved, voided, annulled, decreed, asserted and commanded. If, however, anyone should be presumptuous enough to attempt this he should know that he will incur the indignation of almighty God and of his blessed Apostles, Peter and Paul.[48]

When the worldly and ineffectual pope Leo X, published reform decrees from the Lateran council initiated by Julius II they were also largely ignored. Few secular rulers, or the churchmen they appointed, recognized the court of Rome on the eve of the Reformation as an agency of moral or ecclesiastical regeneration.

Certainly those rulers and churchmen who dominated society in Gaelic or Gaelicized areas of Ireland did not look to Rome as an agency to reprove or to change their way of life which by the beginning of the sixteenth century was as wicked and dissolute as that which had been decried by Malachy and the early Cistercian reformers. Rather they looked upon the court of Rome, and its agents who drew wealth from Ireland, as singularly accommodating, only too willing to tolerate their control of church temporalities, and their idiosyncratic culture: 'Christianity fitted this society with the comfort of an old shoe'.[49] There was never in late medieval Ireland the radical disillusionment with the worldly secularized papacy of the age that appeared elsewhere, for the Irish church readily adapted itself to the Roman curia and its compliant administration. Unlike the capricious, meddling English, whose ecclesiastical authorities tried to harass the Irish church, the curia made it clear that so long as imperial tribute was paid the insular way of life of the Irish would be left undisturbed.

It might have been expected that the Roman contact would have brought at least some Renaissance refinement of manners to Ireland but, with a few notable exceptions, this was not the case. The 'Rome-runners' who sought papal dispensations met with sophisticated curial officials, but they gained little from them except an increase in their native business acumen. Both clergy and laity became remarkably astute as they bargained with the avaricious and omnipresent papal collectors. On the eve of the Reformation there were few parts of the Irish church where a dispute over property, or the need for dispensation from some irregularity had not brought contact with the court of Rome.[50] Slowly there was being formed an administrative organization of Irish ecclesiastical affairs which linked the Gaelic and Gaelicized Irish especially with the curia.[51] In the long run this kind of communication was to be important when there was a falling out, at the time of the Reformation, between Ireland's traditional protective authorities. Irish churchmen never were at ease in their dealings with either Canterbury or London, but they were very much at ease with the cynical yet accommodating world of the curia in Renaissance Rome.

The English authorities in church and state were too close to the Irish, and too involved ecclesiastically and politically to accommodate themselves to a people they believed were continually intriguing politically, annexing land, and pursuing a policy of never ending warfare which denied the growth of civility in the land. The crown's intent, if it was possible, was to act in the manner of the Anglo-Normans of the twelfth century, forcing upon the Irish 'enemies', when it had the time and the means, reforms in both church and society. This alone, it was believed, would bring these semi-barbaric people into the main-stream of European development. What the English intended for them was unforgetably revealed to Gaelic and Gaelicized Ireland during the parliament of 1494–1495, summoned by the viceroy, Edward Poynings. His resolve, he made clear, was to reduce the Irish to perfect obedience, to put an end to the endemic murders, burnings and warfare throughout the Lordship. The parliament reenacted the Statutes of Kilkenny, condemned the Brehon Law, as well as the culture which sustained it, and planned for an expansion of the social order found within the Pale. Nothing came from Poynings' initiative in the long run, apart from the bridling of the power of the Dublin government, but the Irish were reminded how powerful was the authority across the Irish sea—and the likelihood of another Poynings coming with greater might to impose upon them a way of life that was not of their choosing. Fear and resentment of English authority in both church and society had become an abiding element in Irish sensibilities on the eve of the Reformation. The Irish stubbornly defended their 'anachronistic hibernocentric perspective',[52] and looked for reinforcement of their traditional way of life from the other great *imperium* of the age, the distant and accommodating court of Rome. There, they knew from experience, their cause would be listened to in a way it would never be in Canterbury or London. The Irish were ready to make use of either of the traditional authorities which had long governed them, so long as it was to the advantage of their cherished insular way of life. There is some truth in the observation that if England had remained Catholic at the Reformation Ireland, in some sense, would have become Protestant. Rome could be reverenced, but the immediate threat to the Irish and their passionately insular way of life was always the threatening power of the English people across the Irish sea.

Chapter II

Ireland and the English Reformation

'The clash of two civilizations exacerbated by the clash of two religions'

> C.V. Wedgwood, *Thomas Wentworth*,
> 1961, p. 128.

I   **The Tudor Reformation Inheritance**

When Henry VII of the house of Tudor came to the English throne in 1485 he was bent upon developing a royal absolutism that would put to an end the anarchy created by the Wars of the Roses. The parliament at Drogheda in 1494–1495 which gave Ireland statutes like Poynings' Law was a reflection of this policy, but the new king was so intent upon maintaining the stability in England that he left Irish affairs in the hands of Garret More, the earl of Kildare, who from 1496 until his death in 1513 managed the Irish parliament in a kind of 'home rule'. Though the Pale was much reduced this 'uncrowned king of Ireland' as deputy and earl marched over more of Ireland than any viceroy had for generations, battling chieftains like Ulick Burke, his son-in-law who had usurped the royal town of Galway. When Henry VIII became king in 1509 his early years were spent seeking glory in futile expeditions on the continent and in fighting the Scots while, like his father, he was willing to leave affairs in Ireland in the hands of the house of Kildare. Garret Oge carried on his father's policies when he succeeded him as early and chief governor in 1513.

Ireland may not have been a threat to nominal crown authority during this period, but the endemic warfare continued to erode what civilization there was, particularly on the borders of the Gaelic areas where: 'at the beginning of the reign of Henry VIII, if the Irish mind was dwelling in the ninth century the Anglo-Irish mind was still in the thirteenth or fourteenth'.[1] The concern of Kildare and the Irish parliament to bring the chieftains into feudal submission did nothing to end the social chaos in all parts of the island. The published *State Papers (Ireland) Henry VIII* abound with reports on the need for 'reformation' in society, and even within the church:

> ... no land in this world of so long continual war within himself, nor of so great shedding of Christian blood, nor of so great robbing, spoiling,

preying and burning, nor of so great wrongful extortion continually as Ireland.[2]

Hugh Inge, who had been provided by the pope to the bishopric of Meath in the early sixteenth century described to Cardinal Wolsey 'the sorrowful decay in good Christianitie' in his diocese where, he said, religious life was about what you would expect to find in Turkey.[3] He was then echoing the same sentiments of Bernard of Clairvaux who, nearly four hundred years earlier, had found the Irish 'Christians in name, in fact pagans' when he wrote the story of Malachy's mission.[4] There may have been some hope of Malachian reform continuing in Ireland as late as the thirteenth century but, as we have seen, little remained that was hopeful as the fifteenth century came to an end. Alienation and dilapidation of church property was common, and the clergy were guilty of pluralism, absenteeism, and the neglect of divine services. The moral life of the clergy was scandalous. Celibacy was often ignored, the clergy were often partakers in tribal warfare, and rivalry between the Gaelic and English parts of the church was intense. Violent excesses led pope Alexander VI in 1497 to shut down the popular devotional centre in Lough Derg because of quarrelling over the abbacy, misappropriation of revenues, and failure to celebrate divine service.[5] Though allowance must always be made for invention and exaggeration, innumerable entries in papal registers at this time show an Irish church in a state of degeneracy:

> The general impression... is that the late medieval Irish church was in a state of lamentable disorder, and that metropolitan and episcopal government no longer sufficed to remedy these grave abuses.[6]

If there is any truth in the opinion that, when Henry VIII came to the English throne in 1509, Gaelic Ireland lived in a pre-feudal culture, and the Anglo-Irish still thought in feudal terms, then tension with the government and society across the Irish sea was inevitable. Like the rest of Europe in the age of the Renaissance England was changing rapidly, producing a new civility which reflected advances in literature, in philosophy, in science, in law and in politics. A university had been considered in Ireland in the reign of Edward II when Anglo-Norman power was still ascendant, but it never came into being, and two further attempts to found one in the fourteenth century had also failed. The cultural gap between the peoples on the two islands of the archipelago was great, and it was difficult for the English authorities to try to ignore Irish conditions, as they did during the time of the Fitzgerald era of 'home rule'. Thomas Wolsey began his rise to power in the year of Garret More's death, and it was this powerful ecclesiastic who dealt with Irish affairs while the king was engaged in his continental excursions. As a cardinal, papal legate, and chancellor he was a power to be reckoned with. The reports he received about Irish affairs spoke of a continuing resurgence of the Gaelic way of life, with Gaelic chieftains and Old English lords allied, with intermarriage common among them, and all of them displaying the arrogance of 'over-mighty subjects'. In a state paper of 1515 sixty principal chieftains are listed who 'live by the sword', demanding tribute from the inhabitants of English areas while they savage the land and despoil the church.[7] Report after report was made of the same nature, insisting that a reformation of Irish society had to be undertaken to bring civility and true religion to these unruly people.

All the portents were there to suggest that, as in the twelfth century, pressure was going to be exerted by the traditional 'protectors' of Ireland, the papacy and the English crown to end Ireland's long period of isolation from the mainstream of European development. The pope was Leo X, the polished Renaissance prince of the house of Medici, whose chief interest was to keep Italy and his native Florence free from foreign domination. He was quite prepared to lend his support to whatever policy cardinal Wolsey and Henry VIII might initiate in Ireland, so long as it did not involve for him economic expenditure or political trouble. Leo favoured Henry for the English king had strongly opposed the revolt against the papacy initiated by the Augustinian monk, Martin Luther, and by 1521 the pope was to reward Henry with the title 'Defender of the Faith' for his polemical writing against the reformers in Germany. In 1519 Henry finally decided that the time had come to do something about Ireland; he summoned Garret Oge to London, and sent the earl of Surrey with a small force to see what he could do to establish good order in the country. Surrey's report was that only an expensive major reconquest promised a solution to the situation of near anarchy in the country. As for the church, its 'barbarity' was reported to Wolsey by his servant John Kite, whom he had made archbishop of Armagh and, in the words of another respondent on the state of religion, the cause of the scandal lay in the spiritual ignorance of the people:

> For there is no archbishop, no bishop, abbot nor prior, parson,nor vicar, nor any other person of the Church, high or low, great or small, English or Irish, that is accustomed to preach the word of God, saving the poor friars beggars.[8]

The 'poor friars beggars' were the 'observant' or reformed members of the Franciscans, Dominicans and Augustinians, who had some influence in these years just before the Reformation began, as we have noted.

Full scale conquest might have been the answer to the Irish problem, as Surrey recommended, but he also had reported that such an exercise would be not only expensive but a continuing drain on royal resources. Henry was much more concerned with continental affairs, and so the decision finally made was to try using 'sober ways, political drifts, and amiable persuasions' which would encourage the Irish lords and chiefs to surrender their tribal lands to the crown and receive them back as estates granted to them by the king.[9]   The English assumed the hard pressed popes of the period, would have no objection to this Tudor policy, if it was workable, and so Irish church reform was left to the direction of cardinal Wolsey who was a serious contender for the papal throne upon the death of Leo X in 1521. The conclave, however, chose Hadrian VI, one time tutor in the Hapsburg household and a favourite of the emperor Charles V. This ascetic and devout pontiff had to face problems such as the invasion of Europe by the Turks under Suleyman the Magnificent, the Lutheran revolt in Germany , and the hostility of Francis I of France who stopped the transfer of money to Rome and was preparing to invade Lombardy. By the time he died in 1523, worn out by his exertions, Hadrian was in political and friendly alliance with England, and quite willing to leave affairs in Ireland to the care of Wolsey.

Wolsey having once more missed election as pope fell from grace over his failure to obtain a royal divorce for Henry VIII from the new pontiff, Clement VII, an ecclesiastical careerist whose political ineptitude contributed to the schism between England and the papacy. Clement's bowing to Hapsburg pressure brought about the excommunication of Henry VIII; and this led to the indictment of Wolsey on a charge of *Praemunire* for having exercised Roman legatine authority in England. Henry made sure that he carried the country with him when he made his break with Rome, and he cannily held his Reformation Parliament from 1529 until 1536 when the crown's religious affairs were directed by Wolsey's successor, Thomas Cromwell, a strong advocate of royal supremacy in church and state. It was Cromwell who arranged for the dissolution of the English monasteries between 1536 and 1539, and before his fall from favour in 1540 he pressed for an alliance between England and the Protestant princes of Germany.

Henry VIII still maintained his reservations about what was emerging theologically in Germany, however, and his tentative overtures to Lutheranism reflected political concerns of the moment. What he wanted was a royal control of the church like that exercised by the Spanish crown where the Inquisition, for example, was very much a royal instrument of power. Politically he wanted to put pressure on the papacy, and to ensure that the court of Rome was denied both spiritual and temporal authority in England. Much has been written about the implications of the Royal Supremacy, but what is clear is that:

> On statutory evidence it could be argued either that it was a personal
> attribute of the king derived directly from God, or that it was sprung of
> the whole body politic, and exercised by the king in Parliament...
> Henry's Supremacy was far more stringent than anything the Lutheran
> princes had won and was looked at askance by the Reformers...
> Authentic Protestantism looked for a prince who would serve true
> religion, not one who would take upon himself the role of autocratic
> *summus episcopus*... it could never easily live with hierarchy sprung

from above and a 'descending theory of Royal Supremacy'.10

On 15 May, 1532 in the submission of the clergy the English convocations surrendered to the demands made by the king. They recognized the monarch as supreme in all ecclesiastical causes, and less than two years later their acceptance of his authority was incorporated into an act of parliament which coupled it with legislation for the restraint of appeals to Rome. Henry, in England, had now inherited both the power and the problems of the papacy. The king was to be acknowledged as 'Protector and Supreme Head of the English Church and Clergy'. There was to be no dual allegiance for the clergy tolerated, as the king ominously warned a deputation of the Commons when they were summoned before him:

> Well-beloved subjects, we thought that the clergy of our realm had been
> our subjects wholly, but now we have well perceived that they be but
> half our subjects, yea and scarce our subjects: for all the prelates at their
> consecration make an oath to the pope clean contrary to the oath they
> make to us, so that they seem to be his subjects and not ours.11

Henry left the direction of Irish affairs in the hands of Cromwell until 1540, and it was during the period when he was in authority that serious trouble began. Silken Thomas, son of Garret Oge, began a rebellion which was of little political or military significance but for his appealing to both the emperor Charles V and the pope against the excommunicated English king who, he declared, had forfeited his lordship in Ireland because of heresy. Thomas was duly captured and executed in London, and from this time English direct rule began in earnest. The rebels had murdered the archbishop of Dublin during the rising, and his replacement George Browne worked with Cromwell to establish a new ecclesiastical settlement in Ireland. An Irish Reformation Parliament met under the Deputy, Lord Grey; the properties of the abbeys were put in the hands of the crown after they were dissolved; and the crown annexed to the king annates and other incomes which had traditionally gone to Rome. An act of supremacy was passed, and it was acknowledged that from that time Ireland was united with England under the Crown. Sufficient bishops were found to take the supremacy oath, and it seems that what emerged in Ireland under Henry was a traditional church in liturgical matters, the only real sign of the imposition of English custom being the requirement to preach in English in Leinster and areas where there was an English population.

Care was taken to ensure that the king was not seen as merely the viceroy of the pope in Ireland. An act of June, 1541 passed in the Irish parliament declared the king to be ruler of Ireland by right of inheritance and conquest, to disabuse the Irish of: 'a foolish opinion among them, that the bishop of Rome should be king of their land'.12 Some historians have argued that at this time: 'the majority of the Irish regarded their country as a papal fief held by the crown of England in virtue of Adrian's donation',[13] and though this opinion would undoubtedly have been expressed by the papal collectors, it is doubtful that tales of ancient papal prerogatives would have mattered much to the Irish. Of more consequence to them was possible indictment for *Praemunire*, and the reality of the large and purposeful royal army which could be deployed by the Deputy, Sir William Skeffington. This was the immediate concern they had to contend with, not the ideological claims of the effete papacy of the time, nor the political machinations of Henry's European enemies. It was to take a while, however, for the Irish to realize that the traditional dual protectorate provided by London and Rome had come to an end. In the reign of Henry VIII Irish attitudes were still unformed, and they did not want to face the challenge of choosing between the *dominium regale* or the *dominium papale*.[14]

As for the English authority it was not anxious to involve itself any more than was necessary in the quagmire of Ireland's political and ecclesiastical problems. The Hapsburg emperor, however, was clearly prepared to use the Silken Thomas rebellion as a means of putting pressure on Henry, and the king was left with no option but: 'to pursue the policy he had always rejected—the establishment of a permanent English administration, controlled from Westminster and backed by a standing army'.[15] The Catholic authorities had no intention of ignoring the 'Turk on the Thames', and the Irish government was soon aware of papal agents negotiating with the earl of Desmond in Ireland. This alerted both the English and Irish administrations to an alarming new spirit which was appearing in Rome. It was first associated with the new pontiff, Paul III who came to power in the same year that Henry proclaimed himself the Supreme Head of the English church.

Paul III in his early years was as secular in his manner of life as any Renaissance prince. His sister was a mistress of Alexander VI who made him a cardinal. He was not ordained priest until later, and his own noble Roman mistress bore him three sons and a daughter. He was also a confirmed nepotist, intent upon making his house of Farnese one of the great ones in Italy. After his ordination he displayed a new seriousness about ecclesiastical affairs, however, and this continued after he succeeded Clement VII as pope. He may not have been the initiator of the reform movement in the Roman church, the Counter-Reformation, but he took seriously the two tasks of halting the Protestant advance, and protecting the papacy from domination by the Hapsburgs. He made a series of brilliant nominations to the sacred college, including Reginald Pole, who was sent to negotiate with Charles V and Francis I about a deposition of Henry VIII. Paul also excommunicated Henry again (Clement VII's earlier sentence had been suspended), placed England under interdict, and urged sanctions by the continental Catholic powers against the heretics. To put the universal church on an ideological war-footing he encouraged reforms in the religious orders, established the Roman Inquisition, approved the Society of Jesus, and opened the general council of Trent. Pope Paul also supported the emperor in his attempt to crush the Protestant Schmalkaldic League in Germany, encouraged Francis to persecute the Huguenots in France, and showed interest in taking advantage of the Irish situation as a means of hitting at the English heretics.

At the time that Henry was proclaimed king of Ireland there were seditious clerics there under Roman direction to be reckoned with, but this is a confusing era as the state papers show. The anarchy continued in all its 'barbarous wildness, crueltie and ferocity'[16] to such an extent that many settlers began to return to England. Within the church the archbishop of Dublin, George Browne worked with the civil administration to persuade the clergy and laity to accept the new ecclesiastical settlement and, as the chieftains and lords submitted to the royal authority so did the representatives of the church.[17] Browne, a one-time Augustinian friar, showed considerable political skill in dealing with resentment over the dissolution of the monasteries when great lords like the Butlers, O'Briens and O'Neills augmented their wealth at the expense of churchmen, for he recognized the Reformation in Ireland to be: 'a social rather than a religious problem'[18] There were churchmen who listened to Franciscan and other dissidents and refused to accept that the king was now head of the church rather than the pope[19] but on the whole it seems clear that the bishops at least reckoned with the power of the crown which was much more immediate than the distant one on the Tiber:

> The feeble hold which, in Henry's time at least, the Pope had on the inhabitants of Ireland is manifested by the fact that the nominees whom he tried to intrude into the sees of Ireland were unable to maintain their positions. Henry's nominees held them, and their rivals were left to look elsewhere for emoluments and scope for their ministrations.[20]

Most of them were able to find positions, but only after they had repudiated any connection with the Roman authority.

It would seem that most senior Irish churchmen were in a state of confusion over which of the traditional authorities they should serve in matters ecclesiastical. At the beginning of the Reformation the archbishop of Armagh was George Cromer who, apparently, opposed the royal supremacy and the policies of George Browne. On the other hand by 1539 he was under papal ban, accused of heresy, and the administration of his see given over to a Scot, Robert Wauchop, by the papacy. Wauchop, who was to attend the Council of Trent in 1546–1547 was a devotee of the papal supremacy, and a skilled diplomat. He was favoured in Armagh by Con O'Neill, but when he managed to have two Spanish Jesuits brought over from Scotland in 1541 to help organize papal jurisdiction in the Irish church, neither he nor the Jesuits found support for their mission among the Ulster chieftains. The Jesuits were appalled by the prevailing state of anarchy: 'disorder, turmoil and danger on all sides'. Their report castigated the uncivilized behaviour of the barbarous natives whose chieftains had sworn obedience to the crown and the royal supremacy, and had promised to burn any papal briefs that fell into their hands.[21] It may well be that many churchmen simply avoided responding to the demands of such diplomatic manoeuvering yet still served their traditional expression of religion; but in the struggle for allegiance of the nobles and chieftains the papal authority was clearly on the defensive. A year before the death of Henry VIII a memorial sent to the king praised the governance of church and state carried out by prelates like George Browne, and the Deputy, Sir Anthony St Leger:

> Oh, if only our ancestors had had governors of this sort! They would have lived more holily in the eyes of God, more obedient to the laws of man. We, too, their descendents, easily schooled thereto from infancy, would have walked in their footsteps and have obeyed your Majesty's behests with an ever-growing readiness and a more perfect acquiescence in the divine will.[22]

As early as 1542 the Irish council had been able to make the remarkable announcement that Ireland was at peace, and when the king died five years later it claimed that: 'Henry VIII held his title in opposition to the pope and acquiescence in Ireland seemed general'.[23] The traditional dual protectorate in Ireland had come to an end; succeeded, in theory, by the authority of the new Church of Ireland.

At the time of Henry's death, however, Europe was moving towards its fearful time of religious warfare, and, to the Catholic powers, Ireland as a possible bastion on the extreme flank of the line between the Protestant forces of northern Europe and the allies of the papacy in the Mediterranean area, was never forgotten. For political as well as religious reasons: 'the idea was already born that Ireland must be kept true to the old faith, whatever the cost might be'.[24] Martin Luther died a year before Henry VIII and Germany was torn asunder by contending Catholic and Protestant princes in the Schmalkaldic War. The religious peace of Augsburg brought a pause in the contest, but the tensions between Catholics and Protestants increased after the abdication of emperor Charles V in 1556. His territories were divided between those ruled by his fanatically Catholic son Philip II of Spain, and his brother, Ferdinand of Bohemia and Hungary whose equally fanatical descendants were to begin the terrible Thirty Years War. The first round of hostilities, however, was to take place in France. There a Protestant minority, the Huguenots, influenced by the militant Protestantism John Calvin had evolved in Geneva, were organizing themselves to withstand pressure from the strongly Catholic house of Guise.

The ferocity so often displayed by Catholic armies during the sixteenth and seventeenth century wars of religion was not only a counterpart of that of the

Protestant zealots whom they fought, but it was a reflection of the passion of the zealous and powerful popes who directed the Counter-Reformation crusade against heresy. The first of these was that most intransigent of popes, Paul IV (1555–1559). Not only the Protestant heretics were to bow to his authority, for no pontiff lusted more for power:

> His lofty notions of the dignity attaching to the Holy See, together with his personal pride, led him to a theocratic concept whose anachronism he does not appear to have understood: kings, emperors and peoples must kneel before the pope; there must be no nations, only large groups absolutely subject to the Vicar of Christ.[25]

Dreaded by many, this militant old pontiff reorganized the papal Inquisition, and did not hesitate to send to the galleys two hundred recalcitrant Roman monks whom he excommunicated. He seemed to be always at war, using every religious sanction and every temporal means possible to extend the imperial authority of Rome. When Reginald Pole, the papal legate in England under Mary Tudor, questioned the papal use of violence he was deprived of his authority and summoned back to Rome. But for the queen refusing to allow him to go Pole would probably have ended up in the dungeons of the castle of Sant' Angelo. There cardinal Morone, bishop of Modena was imprisoned on a charge of theological laxity, as well as archbishop Carranza of Toledo who had criticized the new catechism. Such was the local hatred of this pontiff that on his death rioting crowds stormed the Inquisition headquarters to free its wretched prisoners, and they tore down a statue of the pope on the Capitol.

Roman power was curbed during the pontificate of Paul IV, however, for the pope had developed a great hatred of the Hapsburgs, when tensions arose because of his inhuman severity in his role as head of the Inquisition. Without temporal aid from Spain, or some other Catholic power, he could do little to bring papal authority to England or Ireland; though he did demand unsuccessfully that Elizabeth I submit her claim to hold lands of the church to his jurisdiction. His successor, Pius IV (1559–1565) was less despotic. He put to death two of Paul IV's powerful nephews, but he sought to bring an end to the alienation of the Roman population which his predecessor had generated. He also discarded Paul's anti-Hapsburg policies, entering into friendly alliance with both Philip II of Spain and the emperor Ferdinand. At the same time he kept them from dominating the Council of Trent which he reconvened, and by the time it ended in 1563 it was agreed that the pope as universal pastor had full power to rule the universal church. Authentic interpretation of the decrees of the council were reserved to the pope. In 1564 Pius ordered all bishops, superiors and doctors to subscribe to the new 'Profession of the Tridentine Faith'—the famous 'Creed of Pius IV' which was to be so fiercely attacked by the Irish Protestants of the nineteenth century.

The rigorist spirit of Paul IV reappeared in the next pope, Pius V, who had been made Inquisitor General in 1558. A member of the Dominican order he was an intense ascetic, devoted to implementing the decrees of Trent, ruthlessly stamping out immorality, and accused by his contemporaries of trying to turn Rome into a vast monastery. No pope was more universal in his vision as he sought to extend the authority of the decrees of Trent as far away as Mexico, Goa and the Congo. He was also determined that Protestantism would not gain a foothold in Italy. In spite of the protests of the imperial ambassador he had a Protestant minister burned at the stake by the Inquisition in Mantua, and though he resented royal control of the church in Spain he approved of the smoke of many an auto-da-fé of Philip II as it rose to the sky. He blessed the pillaging of the Low countries of the duke of Alva, and sent military and financial aid to Catherine de Medici in her persecution of the Huguenots. Single minded, devout to the point of bigotry, and utterly relentless in his fight against heresy this saint of the Roman church (he was canonized in 1712) represented the Counter-Reformation at its most militant. No mercy was to be shown to any people who rejected the authority of the court of Rome. Pius built a new palace for the Inquisition, tightened up its rules and practices, and personally attended many of its sessions. He left a Tridentine impress on the church that was to shape the Roman mission for decades.

The temporal authority of the papacy was at its height in this age when Pius succeeded in forming with Venice and Spain a 'holy league' against the Turks which at the battle of Lepanto shattered Turkish superiority in the Mediterranean. His fellow zealot, Philip II of Spain, said in all sincerity: 'I would give a hundred lives and my kingdom rather than have heretics as subjects', and Pius shared the same spirit, when he considered what had once been Western Christendom.[26] While Pius greatly irritated Catholic monarchs by his uncompromising stand against secular domination of the church in his bull *In coena Domini* of 1568, with its exalted claims for the papacy, Spain especially was willing to work with Rome in any future holy league against the heretics in England where, under Elizabeth, the state was firmly in control of the church. Madrid immediately offered to give Pius temporal assistance should he ask for it when he excommunicated Elizabeth in 1570, and purportedly deposed her—the last such sentence on a reigning monarch by a pope. To Philip II Protestantism was not only an international conspiracy directed against the true faith, but it was an affront to Catholic pride in Spain where crusaders had driven the Moors from Christian lands. In the Netherlands Philip's forces were to be resolute in their determination to exterminate the Protestant heretics, and this would be the spirit in which the Armada was sent against England. In the words of the Jesuit Ribadeneyra in his exhortation to the Spanish forces:

I consider this enterprise the most important undertaken by God's church for many hundreds of years. Every conceivable pretext for a just and holy war is to be found in this campaign... This is a defensive, not an offensive war: one in which we are defending our sacred religion and our most holy Roman Catholic faith; one in which we are defending... our peace, tranquillity and repose.[27]

The crusading alliance of Rome and Spain was continued by the successor of St. Pius V, Gregory XIII (1572–1585). His patron had been Paul IV who had compared diseases of the body, which could only be checked by the burning of infected clothing and houses, with diseases of the soul which called for similar drastic measures to contain contagion.[28] Gregory agreed with this attitude. He attended the Council of Trent as an expert in canon law, had helped to draft its decrees, and then went to Spain as papal legate. During his time in Spain he won the confidence of Philip II, and it was the latter's influence which ensured he became pope. As supreme pontiff he was resolute in his support of the Counter-Reformation; when news of the St. Bartholomew's massacre reached the Holy See he celebrated it with a *Te Deum* in thanksgiving for the victory. He urged Philip II to attack both the Netherlands and Ireland, as a means of getting at England, and when his dreams of an Irish invasion of England collapsed in 1578 and 1579, as we shall see, Gregory gave his personal support to plots to have Elizabeth assassinated. This very political pontiff who strongly supported the Jesuits as shock troops of the Counter-Reformation was as hated in the Papal States as had been Paul IV. By the time he died they were filled with lawless bandits and disgruntled nobles who resented the papal pillaging and extortions of the land for the sake of the crusade against the heretics.

Such was the bigotry of these fierce popes that few English were inclined to disagree with the judgment of Hugh Latimer, bishop of Worcester, who described the Roman pontiff as: 'that Italian bishop yonder, the devil's chaplain'.[29] There was not much opposition when during the reign of Edward VI the church in England became more Protestant liturgically, and continental reformers like Peter Martyr, Martin Bucer and John à Lasco used their time as refugees in England to shift the climate of English religious opinion. Though the full militancy of the Counter-Reformation had not yet begun to assert itself in Edward's reign the first sessions of the Council of Trent were taking place and Jesuit authority was increasing. When the half-Spanish and fanatically Roman Catholic Mary was cautiously welcomed to the throne on Edward's death in 1553 the church was divided and anxious as it waited to see what restoration of the Church of England to the Roman jurisdiction might mean.

In Ireland a 'wait and see' policy prevailed during the brief reign of Edward VI. John Bale, a one-time Carmelite friar tried to promote the new radicalism coming out of Geneva when he became bishop of Ossory, but he received little encouragement from archbishop Browne or anyone else. The first prayer book of 1549 was printed in Ireland, and read in Christchurch, Dublin, before the lord deputy, Sir Anthony St. Leger, but the more radical prayer book of 1552 was never officially used. On its part Rome made no attempt to provide for vacant sees in Cashel, Derry, Ossory and Ross, and the time was one of unusual quiet and relative prosperity. Unease over what was taking place on the mainland may have prevailed, but most of the chieftains did not hesitate to renounce the papacy and take an oath of allegiance to the young king. Within the church the majority of the bishops and the inferior clergy maintained the beliefs and practices of former times, as in England where many managed to hold their places in the church right through from the reign of Henry VIII to Mary. On the question of the royal supremacy, however, they were content to recognize the prevailing authority.

When the Princess Mary was proclaimed queen she was declared to be 'supreme head of the churches of England and Ireland', and it was clear that in England and Ireland it was going to be difficult for the papacy to extend once more its full authority over the church and the people. In 1555 the religious peace of Augsburg recognized that the Reformation was a reality that had to be reckoned with, and Paul IV who became pope the same year immediately and fiercely showed that the time for compromise between Catholic and Protestant authorities was past. Mary realized this also when she made the error of signing a marriage treaty with her kinsman, Philip of Spain. No one wanted England to be drawn into the world of Spanish influence, and from the time that Mary began to try to undo the religious reforms carried out by Henry VIII and Edward VI the English were concerned politically as well as religiously over any changes she carried out. Unease was general when Reginald Pole arrived as papal legate in 1554 and old laws against heresy were revived. Parliament agreed it would annul all ecclesiastical legislation since 1528, but it refused to return the monastic lands to the church. When the heresy laws were implemented, and the number of martyrs increased, popular opinion turned against Mary and cardinal Pole. Then England was drawn into a disastrous war with France, political unrest spread, and when Mary and Pole both died in 1558 it seemed to most English a providential deliverance. In the words of a contemporary, when news of the queen's demise was received: 'the same day all London sang and sayd Te Deum laudamus in evere chyrche in London.'[30]

Mary's programme in Ireland was as disastrous as it had been in England, for she offended many people both religiously and politically. The earl of Sussex was sent over as lord lieutenant in 1556, and it seems that in the Dublin parliament there was no great enthusiasm for Mary's demand that the religious legislation of the last two reigns should be repudiated. Conservative Catholic historians have argued that: 'the return of "whole papism" under the Catholic queen was almost universally welcome'.[31] There is little evidence for this assumption, however, as the 'wait and see' mentality of the previous reign continued, without any significant interruption:

The changes in liturgical form that had been required by the state in

Ireland during the period 1540–1553 were so modest in character that on the accession of Queen Mary the community could revert to the original form of catholic worship without noticing that a change had taken place.[32]

It is doubtful that in any real way the short reign of the Catholic queen 'provided the opportunity for the Counter-Reformation to establish itself'[33] for the people were now religiously noncommittal—at least among those who had had opportunity for travel or education. In the Pale, in particular, following Mary's reign:

> ... those few who did have contact with London or the universities would have become firmly attached to the state religion, and despite having suffered a consequential isolation from their localities, they would never have contemplated forsaking their newly discovered true religion for the redefined heresies of Trent.[34]

There simply does not exist evidence to sustain the belief that after mid-sixteenth century there was a dramatic turning once more to the papal authority or the Tridentine expression of the faith. In Galway the response to the Reformation was such that the president of Connacht, Richard Bingham, 1584–1596, believed that the continued identification with the new version of the faith promised that the town had: 'the prospect of it becoming a second Geneva from which all Ireland would be reformed'.[35]

Mary's reign may not have had great religious impact upon Ireland, but politically her policies were of great importance. When she sent the earl of Sussex to Ireland to restore the whole Catholic system, he was also commanded to confiscate land and to dispossess a whole body of native lords in Leix and Offaly. The affected lands were to be 'planted' with new settlers, English subjects born in either England or Ireland. The O'Mores, the O'Connors, and other Gaelic kings who found themselves reduced to small landlords became rebels, opposed to what Mary was imposing upon Ireland and, if she had lived longer, it is likely there would have been in Ireland a general reaction to what she was trying to force upon the Irish in both politics and religion. The Irish might have become: 'the most violent Calvinists in Europe'.[36]

II   The Elizabethan Settlement

Elizabeth had been brought up as a Protestant, and as soon as she came to the throne she repealed the religious legislation of Mary and re-enacted the laws of her father relating to the church, including an act of supremacy which recognized her as 'supreme governor' of both church and state. During her reign there was also an act of uniformity, a *via media* revision of the Prayer Book, and in 1563 the adoption of the Thirty-Nine Articles. This established in England a compromise church, largely Protestant in doctrine though many of the religious articles were deliberately ambiguous. Elizabeth was the most politically astute of all the Tudors; she knew how much the extreme religious policies of her Catholic half-sister had been loathed, and throughout her reign, so long as the Catholics did not pose a political threat, she tried to accommodate 'tender consciences' in ,matters of religion. By nature she was not passionate about religious matters. She deliberately did not work through convocation where religious opposition might be encountered, but through parliament which accepted her wisdom in seeking compromise.

What opposition in parliament there was to her policies came from representatives of the extreme Protestants who had fled the country during the reign of Mary, and were now returned filled with resolve to establish in England the kind of theocratic régime they had experienced in Geneva and elsewhere. Many of these zealots were only nominally within the Church of England, where they formed a subversive organization intent upon making the religious settlement and ecclesiastical organization more radically Protestant. Whatever Elizabeth did in church affairs, in either England or Ireland, she had to reckon with the power of these so called Puritans. Particularly she had to recognize their popular support in many areas in the country, and their abiding hatred of Roman Catholicism. It was always to be difficult for Elizabeth to find a middle way in religious affairs, to try to spare England and Ireland the terror of sectarian conflict, like that which raged in France and the Low Countries.

Pope Pius IV refrained from excommunicating Elizabeth in the hope that England might once more return to the Roman obedience, but the queen knew how friendly the pope was to her enemies, Philip II of Spain and the emperor Ferdinand. She also knew of his reconvening of the Council of Trent, and the resolve of himself, and his successor Pius V, to promote a universal acceptance of the decrees of Trent. Elizabeth was convinced that no possible accommodation could be made with either the papacy or the Catholic continental powers, and her belief was strengthened from the time that Mary, queen of Scots, fled to England to become the centre of Roman Catholic intrigue in the nation. It was Mary's presence in England, and a series of plots against Elizabeth which finally persuaded Pius V in 1570 to excommunicate the English queen, to declare her deposed, and her subjects dispensed from their oaths of allegiance to her.[37] The Spanish Jesuit, Juan de Mariana, had published his infamous book, *De Rege et Regis Institutione* a year after Elizabeth became queen, and the English government took note of the tyrannicide doctrine it promoted. This was a time when England was flooded with young Counter-Reformation zealots coming out of Douai and other continental seminaries, and a papal-directed threat to the monarch was taken seriously. No one was surprised when it was discovered that a papal secretary had sent to the nuncio in Madrid a letter which justified assassination of Elizabeth: 'whosoever sends her out of the world with the pious intention of doing God's service not only does not sin but gains merit'.[38] By the 1580's Catholic plots against the Protestant queen were becoming frequent, until in 1587 they lessened with the execution of Mary Stuart, after a fourteen year imprisonment. From this time the Catholic dissidents looked for external help from Spain to support their cause, and it was clear that there was not to be any English rapprochement with Rome. The government passed legislation which excluded from the country all Jesuits, seminary priests, or anyone who might be considered a Spanish agent capable of assassination.

The government's fear of what the Roman-Spanish alliance might visit upon England was shared by most of the population, and the anti-recusant policies of the time were given general support. Approval was also given to the harrying of those Irish who refused to accept the royal supremacy, and considered alliance with the Roman-Spanish power. Religious passion dictated that there was to be no compromising on either side in an age when religion was used to excuse appalling atrocities. When Gregory XIII was told of the massacre of St. Bartholomew he is reported to have said that the news was more gratifying than fifty battles of Lepanto.[39] The work of the duke of Alva in the Low Countries was viewed as a crusade by Catholic authorities, and the Huguenots of France had no difficulty in finding rationale for their excesses. A fanatic in Protestant eyes was Sixtus V, who became pope in 1585, the year that Elizabeth sent aid to the Protestant insurgents in the Low Countries following the assassination of William of Orange. The Protestants had some justification for their assessment of this energetic, violent and inflexible pontiff. He had been so severe as an inquisitor in Venice that Rome had had to recall him. His immediate intention after he became pope was to bring law and order in the papal states where he carried out thousands of public executions and mercilessly punished any who opposed the papal authority. This zealous 'Iron Pope' was so execrated by his subjects that when his death was announced a mob tore down his statue on the Capital—as it had that of Paul IV thirty years earlier. Sixtus confined his opposition to heresy in England to the promise of aid for Philip II and his planned invasion—though he refused to pay after the failure of the Armada.

The Elizabethan English generally reacted to the threat of invasion by the forces of Philip II and Sixtus V in the way of united resistance that their descendants were to show when Bonaparte and Hitler promised similar action in later centuries. In the hysteria of the time some 250 Catholics who defied the laws were put to death, and the defeat of the Armada was looked upon not only as a national victory but an escape from religious oppression.[40] The English had not forgotten what they had endured under Mary Tudor, and they feared the fanaticism of their Counter-Reformation opponents. A year after the Armada the last member of the House of Valois, Henry III, was murdered by a friar, Jacques Clement. The deed was praised by the Spanish Jesuit, Juan de Mariana. It was not to be until the very last days of Elizabeth's reign that England could breathe a little easier when, under Clement VIII, the papacy sought to free itself from Spanish domination, and there were some hopeful signs that the early Tridentine fervour might be passing.

If Elizabeth and her government resented and feared Roman intrigue and Spanish might, the Protestant minority in Ireland, surrounded by a hostile and warlike population was almost paranoiac about a league against them by Counter-Reformation agents with Spanish help. More and more English were coming into Ireland, as part of the European expansion westwards, and usually their presence was bitterly resented. When the earl of Sussex in Mary's reign had tried to expel the Scots from Antrim he discovered how greatly the English were loathed. The Ulster chieftains showed no great concern about their traditional rivals, the Scots, but they: 'said plainly that Englishmen had no right to Ireland'.[41] Also in Munster, in some areas there were 'close working relationships that developed between natives and newcomers', but as numbers of settlers increased from 4,000 in 1598, to 5,000 in 1611, to 14,000 in 1622, and 22,000 by 1641,[42] there was inevitably a negative response by the local power élite, both Old English and Gaelic. Although religion did not, at first, play an important part in the growing migration from the larger island, it soon became an issue. This was especially so in Dublin where an English-born junta appeared, led by Hugh Curwen. He had been appointed archbishop of Dublin by Mary, yet he survived under Elizabeth, and was generally held in little respect for being: 'a complier in all reigns'.[43] Together with the other prelates who tried to force acceptance of the Supremacy Act, and the Act of Uniformity, and demanded use of the Book of Common Prayer, Curwen and his supporters were widely resented for being both English and Protestant. As resentment grew, more attention was paid to the solicitations of the 'Rome-runners' of old, or the new agents of the Counter-Reformation, who were ready to remind the native Irish that the pope had traditionally been their feudal suzerain, that he had declared Elizabeth a heretic, and deposed her for her iniquities. The resentful Irish who listened to the Roman advocates were often persuaded that opposition to the crown had religious merit.

Most of the dignitaries of the church, like their English counterparts, were primarily concerned with their own survival and convictions. In distant parts of the island where neither Rome, London, nor Dublin had much influence, the bishops had to reckon first with the ruthless rule of chieftains like Shane O'Neill in Ulster. These warlords tried to control church appointments and, at the time of Elizabeth's first parliament the sees of Armagh, Clogher, Kilmore and probably Achonry were vacant. Endemic warfare was such that the government focused only on the primatial appointment, and left appointment to the tribes in the other cases. The bishops chosen sometimes followed custom, notwithstanding the threat of *Praemunire*, and then sought confirmation of their appointment in Rome where, in 1563, no less than fourteen priests hastened to claim appointment to the see of Raphoe.[44] On the other hand Eugene O'Harte, relative of a local chieftain, ignored Rome and renounced papal authority when he was appointed to the see of Achonry on the recommendation of Sir John Perrot, the Lord Deputy. He later promulgated the decrees of the Council of Trent, and when he died in 1603 at the age of 100 he was recognized as bishop of Achonry by both the crown and the papacy.

Ecclesiastical affairs were very confused in Ireland at the time that Elizabeth's first parliament authorized reform of the church, but it does seem clear that the majority of bishops, however reluctantly, accepted the authority of the crown:

> A striking feature of the writings of the counter-reformation apologists is that none of them made reference to the disposition of the body of Irish bishops to the Elizabethan ecclesiastical revolution. Evidently there was no tradition of significant episcopal opposition to the religious changes.[45]

This was understandable for there was always the possibility that Elizabeth might follow the example of continental princes and attempt to impose total conformity: 'a draconian intervention of the state supported by the missionary endeavours of the clergy'.[46] In an area like Munster, where communication with Britain was regular, and resentment of new settlers qualified, it is possible that this might have worked. This was certainly the conviction of later Protestants who were critical of the crown for not intervening in religious affairs more directly:

> Planters in Ireland, throughout the seventeenth century were fully satisfied that if compulsion had been used consistently 'all or the most part of the inferior sort of people... would have long since been reclaimed to our religion'.[47]

The experience of Ulster was to show, however, that the further away from the Pale and the centre of crown control the more difficult it would be to enforce religious conformity.[48]

What Elizabeth, like any other monarch of her age, ideally wanted was: 'uniform parochial observance'.[49] Her resources were limited, however, she was at war for most of her reign, she had urgent tactical requirements, like the support of the Protestant rebels in the Low Countries, which took precedence, and she knew how expensive it would be to carry out a campaign to impress Protestantism upon all the Irish people. She also preferred persuasion to coercion in religious matters, as her English policies showed. This mentality reflected her seeking a *via media* in religious matters. It was also an expression of 'the Protestant principle'—the respect for the conscience of the individual. It is interesting to note that as the British expanded overseas there was seldom in their territories the kind of church-state exercise in coercion that was so characteristic of what occurred in the Spanish colonies.[50] The Elizabethan respect for 'tender consciences' has sometimes been interpreted as a secular expression of the Calvinist doctrine of exclusivity of salvation. This, however, is not what the Elizabethans were about. They did not deliberately seek:

> ... an élitist anglicized church, serving only a small section of the population, willing to abandon whole parishes to the catholic priests... content to let the people 'go to hell' in their own way.[51]

Such an exercise in religious magnanimity was one that could not be risked. The government felt, with some reluctance, that it had to offer the Irish the traditional 'protection' of the crown in religion and other affairs, with the hope that the Irish would accept it. To allow them full freedom in religious expression realistically was not a possibility. In the circumstances of the late sixteenth century, any decision to allow the Irish to go 'to hell in their own way' would have begged the entry of the rival religious *imperia* of Rome and Spain into the country.

The government was intent upon keeping out of the country any Roman emissaries who would offer such an alternative but, in spite of the failure of the abortive Jesuit mission in 1541, Roman agents began to enter the country again. One of the ablest was David Wolfe, a native of Limerick who arrived in 1560. He had been sent by the Jesuit general, James Laynez, a passionate supporter of papal absolutism who was notorious for his ruthless extermination of would-be Protestants in Piacenza and other northern Italian cities. Presumably Wolfe shared his superior's convictions when he was entrusted with the wide commission to establish: 'the spiritual superintendence of the religious life of the country'.[52] Wolfe, of course, knew that even those Irish who had reservations about the royal supremacy might not consider accepting Rome's authority as an alternative. He knew this was especially true of the Anglo-Irish, and Wolfe avoided working in the Pale. Rather he focused his attentions on the Gaelic Irish who had maintained some communication with the papacy through the 'Rome-runners', as well as those friars who tolerated the traditional expression of the faith, and supported the Counter-Reformation papacy. The place where Wolfe found the most ready acceptance of his promise of external aid to those who resisted the government's policies was in Ulster. There he persuaded Shane O'Neill to pronounce himself a papal champion. Soon O'Neill was offering to attach himself to the king of France if he was sent military aid, begging the fiercely anti-Huguenot cardinal of Lorraine: 'Help us we implore you to chastise the heretics and schismatics and to bring our country to the Holy See'.[53] Wolfe had trouble with O'Neill, however, when the latter wanted his unlearned younger brother to be appointed archbishop of Armagh. When the papacy appointed Wolfe's friend, Richard Creagh, as primate, Shane showed his displeasure by burning the cathedral and town of Armagh. This savage act brought on Shane not only Roman displeasure, but excommunication by the Protestant primate, Adam Loftus. Shortly afterwards western chieftains joined the royal standard and Shane was killed by the MacDonnells of Antrim in a tribal dispute.

In most areas of Ireland the lords, chieftains and bishops were not unlike Shane O'Neill: only too willing to take advantage of either of the external authorities of London and Rome, so long as it enabled them to live in their traditional, and to the outsiders, barbaric way of life. On the ecclesiastical level Wolfe raged against 'hireling' bishops who moved easily from papal to royal jurisdiction, and religiously he would have agreed with Edmund Tanner, the papal bishop of Cork and Cloyne, who told cardinal Moroni in 1571 that all, clergy and laity, were so demoralized that a pious Catholic could not be found.[54] There is considerable insight in the nineteenth century opinion of the historian J.A. Froude about the loyalties of the Irish leaders in Elizabethan times:

> The Irish chiefs were ready to swear any number of oaths, upon their knees, when in the Deputy's preserve, and broke them without scruple when safe amongst their own people again. The spiritual lords need not have been more scrupulous as they may have qualified their submission and taken the oath of allegiance with a saving clause.[55]

Elizabeth and her advisers, if they could have had their way, wanted no war at all in Ireland. They were certainly not about to impoverish the treasury in an expedition to subdue the lords and chieftains politically, nor to enforce recognition of the royal supremacy in religious affairs. Their war-budget barely allowed them means to support the campaign in the Low Countries, even with the Dutch paying for the English regiments sent there. The government feared that it might have to increase substantially its support of the French Huguenots, and thinking as it did in continental strategic terms it dreaded getting bogged down in an Irish 'second front'. It watched the duke of Alva trying to cope with guerilla warfare in the Netherlands, and the English government knew how expensive a similar kind of campaign would be in Ireland. In the later words of Matthew Hutton, archbishop of York, in May 1600, when the rising of Hugh O'Neill was dragging on, and threatening to inflame the whole of Ireland:

> I take it to be against good policy for a great prince to keep a long and lingering war with a subject nation, though the people be never so base, for it teacheth them to be skillful, stout and resolute, as appeareth by the Low Countries.[56]

Yet a struggle between the English crown and the Irish people, led by their nobles and chieftains seemed increasingly likely. More and more 'adventurers' were moving into Ireland, and dispossession of the lands of the people was carried out through a searching of titles and other questionable procedures. An Irish Court of High Commission established in 1564 had limited influence as it sought to enforce religious conformity, but it added greatly to the general resentment of the external authority from across the water which was trying to change the traditional Irish way of life. As in the past it was probable that the Irish, threatened as they were by the immediate authority of the traditional enemy, the English crown, would turn for help to the distant power of Rome, with which they had always kept contact.

For its part Rome still considered Ireland important as a mission field and politically. It had no intention of surrendering its long time influence, especially in the Gaelic areas, to its one time ally and now bitter enemy, the English crown. Pius V who had excommunicated Elizabeth in 1570 was sure that he had in Philip II a Catholic champion: 'whose fanaticism amounted to moral insanity'.[57] His successor, Gregory XIII, was deep in the confidence of the Spanish king, and he realized how much Philip wanted to strike back at Elizabeth, whose troops were opposing the crusade in the Netherlands. So it was inevitable that Rome showed great interest in the 1570's in the invasion of Ireland scheme of a dissident Munster chieftain, James Fitzmaurice Fitzgerald, as well as that of an English Catholic freebooter, Sir Thomas Stukeley. A ready hearing was given to Fitzmaurice who argued that a Roman-Spanish landing would persuade the Irish not: 'to forsake the catholic faith by God unto his church given and by the see of Rome hitherto prescribed to all Christian men'.[58] Fitzmaurice finally received full backing from Gregory XIII in 1579, when Philip was convinced that something had to be done to advance the Roman Catholic cause in both the Netherlands and in Ireland, but Stukeley was then no longer available to help the expedition for he had died in the service of the king of Portugal the previous year.

There was no doubting the religious nature of the Fitzmaurice expedition. Two of his advisers were Nicholas Sanders, an English Jesuit who represented English Catholics at the Spanish court, and the papal bishop of Mayo, Patrick (O'Helius) O'Healy. When his force landed at Dingle in County Kerry on 18 July 1579 it was reported that:

> Two friars in their habits were his standard bearers, and they went before him with two standards. A bishop with a crozier and his mitre was next the friars. After came the traitor himself, and he had in his company about a hundred. He makes fires on the high hills and looks for more ships.[59]

The looked for reinforcements arrived in four ships which had sailed from Corunna with another 600 men, mostly Italian, but including Jesuits and friars. When they had built a fort at Smerwick they raised the papal flag, and sought support from the local tribesmen. Few of them responded to Fitzmaurice's invitation to join the papal army, however, and within a month of his arrival Fitzmaurice was shot during a skirmish with members of the Burke clan.

The government finally responded to this invasion when news came through that some dissident lords like Sir John of Desmond, and viscount Baltinglass had begun to pillage in Munster and even within the Pale. By then the authorities feared that the Desmonds were about to join with Fitzmaurice in what might become a general rising of the Geraldines. A squadron of ships was sent to patrol the western coast and cut off further Spanish aid, but because of cost Elizabeth was at first reluctant to furnish extra troops. After Youghal was savagely sacked, however, and the Desmond forces flaunted the papal ensign and shouted 'Papa Aboo',[60] the queen reacted decisively. Sanders by this time was spreading in England and the continent tales of the papal success, and though the queen still urged pardon for lesser rebels she indicated that this was not to be extended to the papal envoy. As soon as it was known that the crown had taken military control of the situation support for the rebels fell away, and finally the fort at Smerwick fell, with a butchery of all foreign troops (except officers held to ransom). It was a brutal age, when the Elizabethan 'adventurers' whether settlers or in the military were as ruthless with the native Irish as their descendants were to be with the Indians in North America. It was felt at the time that no apology had to be made for the slaughter at Smerwick when: 'after the fall of Haarlem Alva butchered three or four times as many as perished at Smerwick'.[61] For the first time in Ireland, in the age of religious wars, the papal flag had been raised challenging directly the royal authority, and in the sixteenth century it was accepted that the punishment was fitting. Certainly no official complaint was made by the Roman Catholic authorities. As the campaign went on the crown policy was lenient for the age inasmuch as captured priests were offered their lives if they would acknowledge the royal supremacy. Whether the same treatment would have been offered Nicholas Saunders who was with the Desmond forces is doubtful, but he died of disease. By 1583 the earl of Desmond, who had joined the rising, was killed by the Moriartys and the rising was at an end.

Three years later with the ending of Desmond power Elizabeth approved final plans for a plantation on the lands of the defeated lords, The new settlers included hard men, like Sir Walter Raleigh, who ended up with some 40,000 acres and much local enmity. Other settlers like Sir Nicholas Browne, ancestor of the earls of Kenmare, were often easily assimilated, some of them becoming Roman Catholic in the process. From the standpoint of the government such families were a worrying reinforcement of the local indigenous society. Their loyalties were confused, however, and as the treatment of the Armada survivors showed the Romano-Spanish power could not take for granted any substantial Irish support—at least in the southern part of the island. On the other hand the English realized that they could not relax their military presence. Sixtus V had promised Philip of Spain huge subsidies for the Armada enterprise, and Elizabeth was not surprised when another attempt was made by the continental powers to reinforce Irish dissidents, this time in Ulster where acceptance of the royal writ was strongly opposed.

In Ulster the restive Gaelic tribesmen were strongly reinforced by Scots mercenaries who controlled most of North Antrim. The Irish leader was Hugh O'Neill who had lived in London, was well acquainted with English military tactics, was recognized by the crown as earl of Tyrone, yet was passionately opposed to the government's intention of extending English culture in Ulster. Rather than accept a forced assimilation of the Irish to English ways he wanted them to become part of the mainstream of European development but on their own terms; 'voluntary conformity as inhabitants of the periphery to common European standards'.[62] It has been argued that in religious affairs O'Neill and his fellow Ulster chieftains did show interest in ending abuses like clerical concubinage during their long (1595–1603) and bloody rebellion,[63] but the main concern of O'Neill was how to make use of the Roman-Spanish power in his struggle for freedom for the Ulster tribes. As early as 1593 he was appealing for Spanish help, assuring Philip II that what he sought was: 're-establishing the Catholic religion... to restore the faith of the church, and to secure you a kingdom.'[64] When he fought his protracted war he wanted the gentry of the Pale to join him in a religious-political confederacy: 'to assist Christ's Catholic religion... to aid God's just cause'.[65] At the climax of the struggle Clement VIII issued on 18 April, 1600, a 'Bull of Plenary Indulgence to the Irish in arms against Queen Elizabeth'.[66] It was Hugh O'Neill who chiefly brought Ireland out of its long period of isolation from the European wars of religion: 'the fateful decision... to enter into an alliance with Spain... committed the fortunes of Ulster to a whirlpool of international politics over which he had no control'.[67]

During his prolonged war O'Neill received considerable ideological help from clerics like Matthew da Oviedo, who had first come to Ireland with the Smerwick expedition, and did his best to encourage the Irish to support the rebellion on religious grounds. The Irish, he said, should give no allegiance to a monarch who had been declared deposed by three popes; those who did support the queen were sharing in her heresy. Yet there were then only five Jesuits in the country, and it seemed likely that, however diligently they laboured, the state of the clergy and laity was such that few of them would be persuaded to become converts to the cause of the Counter-Reformation. The lords, chieftains and their followers cared little about papal authority, or Tridentine reforms, however much they greatly resented the alien government of the crown which ignored them, while it did much to support the rapacious New English who were flooding into the country:

> The behaviour of those captains who sought more after private gain...
> than the reformation of the country was such, according to one writer,

that their Irish critics could plausibly argue that the queen did not wish the regeneration of the Irish.[68]

The Irish people also bitterly resented the levying of a cess to support the forces of the crown; they had contempt for unlearned and rascally clergymen who came from England to exploit the people and the land in any way they could; and they loathed those Irish who chose to serve in the Protestant establishment, the 'common clergymen' so castigated by Edmund Spencer.[69] Even in the Pale there was little enthusiasm for the religion established by the English crown, for it was but part of the culture which the New English wished to impose upon the country.

The evidence of a diligent and hard working reformed church bishop such as William Lyon of the diocese of Ross, and then of Cork and Ross, reveal the shift in opinion that was taking place in Munster. When he was appointed to Ross the Desmond rebellion was then in its final stage, and he told the Lord Justices how the oppression by the army and the levying of cess was driving even loyal subjects into opposition to the government. Yet when the Armada was defeated the people joined in the thanksgiving services for deliverance from a possible Spanish Catholic invasion; in Cork the bishop preached to over two thousand worshippers. By the time that the O'Neill rebellion was at its height, however, Lyon was writing in despair of the control of the minds of the people by papal agents who were urging the cause of sedition. The service of his church was called 'the Devil's service' and its ministers 'devils'. All this he said reflected the work of 'seditious priests' and the papal legate who were identified with Hugh O'Neill 'in his rebellious career'. Writing to Burghley in 1596 Lyon said:

... the Jesuits will not allow the physicians and surgeons of Cork to visit in their sickness such as hold ecclesiastical preferment; many people would willingly come to the service of the church but that they are sworn to the contrary; they are charged not to reason with the ministers of the church; a customary prayer after meals was for the safe return of Desmond's son.[70]

The Jesuits and friars who served the Counter-Reformation cause in west Cork were led by Owen MacEgan, the bishop designate of Ross, and Dermot Creagh, papal bishop of Cork and Cloyne. The former during the rebellion was in charge of the money and munitions which Hugh Roe O'Donnell raised in Spain and also acted as a papal nuncio. He died during the fighting in Ulster, after the defeat at Kinsale.[71] Creagh was a cousin of Miler Magrath, the protestant archbishop of Cashel, who warned Creagh when danger threatened him. In his underground capacity he was recognized as a papal legate who 'useth all manner of spiritual jurisdictions in the whole province'. He had also served the earl of Desmond in his rising: 'being in accion of rebellion with him'.[72] Had the Spanish army which landed at Kinsale prevailed with the help of O'Neill and O'Donnell these two papal agents would have been instrumental in establishing a Counter-Reformation political and religious settlement.

Shortly after the death of Elizabeth the militant Paul V, whose reign saw the beginning of the terrible Thirty Years War, urged in a brief to the Irish Catholics that they 'be faithful to their ancestral religion',[73] and it is probable that papal toleration of traditional expressions of Irish Catholicism contributed much to the winning of popular support for the counter-Reformation cause. A zealot like Paul V had every intention of bringing Tridentine authority, and then reform, to the Irish people, but the establishment of ecclesiastical power was the first step in the process. In the last years of Elizabeth's reign this meant an all-out political struggle to ensure with the help of Spain and the Irish tribal insurgents, that the jurisdiction of the Roman court be extended throughout Ireland. Wherever possible there was encouragement for Irish priests to give up obvious abuses such as clerical concubinage but, as in the twelfth century, the papacy recognized that force would have to be used to impress reforms like those of Trent upon the Irish. The work of the Inquisition was successful in areas like Bohemia, as well as parts of Germany and France once Catholic power was established, and the militant continental mission provided a model for the Irish situation where reform was so badly needed. Accommodation should be used to establish Roman authority—the Counter-Reformation religious mission would follow. So the papal envoys remained tolerant of tribal warfare and other abuses in Irish folk religion at this period, and tried to avoid confrontations which would deny them popular support for their causes. This was recognized by the authorities, of course, and one of the Lord Justices, Sir Henry Wallop explained the lack of popular support for the state religion on these grounds:

> The great affection they generally bear to the popish religion, which agreeth with their humour, that having committed murder, incest, theft, with other execrable offences, by hearing a mass, confessing themselves to a priest, or obtaining the pope's pardon, they persuade themselves they are forgiven. And hearing mass on Sunday or holyday, they think all the week after they may do what heinous offences soever it is dispensed withall.[74]

The toleration of ancestral practices by the papal emissaries, whose immediate task was to win the support of lords, chieftains and people to the Roman-Spanish-O'Neill cause, helps partly to explain the allegiance slowly granted by many Irish to the Counter-Reformation mission. The alien English version of the faith usually had less appeal, especially in the Gaelic areas, but there were contemporaries who argued that if the Protestant power had used force consistently to impose a reformed religious settlement it would have been successful. Experience had taught political and religious authorities in Europe that if imposed conformity was followed by intensive evangelization it was often enough to enforce compliance upon people who would not otherwise accept an ecclesiastical settlement. This was certainly argued by many of the New English reformers who believed that, as in the twelfth century in Ireland, there had to be a forceful overthrow of the native ruling order before evangelization would be possible.[75] The enforcement of conformity by the government was never consistent, however, nor was there an evangelization campaign launched to bring about a new spiritual consciousness among the Irish. Few of the English churchmen even showed much interest in taking the first step in successful evangelizing—learning the Irish language.

The toleration of traditional religion by the papal emissaries, and the reluctance to impose even a uniformity of religious observance by the Protestant authorities, however, did not mean that in the last years of Elizabeth's reign there was any mass movement to accept Roman direction of Irish society. It was, of course, difficult not to accept the Roman order in any area where the Ulster rebels established themselves, but the general picture seems to be that most of the population carried on traditional religious practices without showing enthusiasm for either of the ecclesiastical authorities which sought their allegiance. As for hazard of the crown imposing its will in matters religious the Elizabethan viceroys had much to say about abuses in the church in Ireland, but even Mountjoy after the defeat of O'Neill showed no interest in doing anything about the condition of religion.

> Like other viceroys before and after him, Mountjoy, when political expediency demanded it, would not have hesitated to condone ecclesiastical abuses, and would have enforced a compliance with the legal semblance of conformity, when administrative necessity required it. He was no real help to the Church of Ireland in its spiritual mission; he probably was a hindrance.[76]

By the end of the sixteenth century the Reformation had only shallow roots in some parts of the island. The Counter-Reformation, similarly lacked the power to establish papal authority with the collapse of the O'Neill rebellion and the defeat of the Spanish forces at Kinsale. The most the Roman militants could do was to fulminate like the Jesuits at Salamanca who, in 1602, announced that the war of O'Neill and his followers was just and good, and that Catholics who supported the queen risked eternal damnation. The majority of the native population remained outside the authority of either of the rival ecclesiastical bodies, and continued to practice their traditional pre-Reformation and pre-Tridentine version of the Christian faith.[77]

It may be that one of the reasons why Mountjoy and others did not try to take advantage of their victory by using compulsion to bring about religious uniformity was a positive religious one—a reflection of the 'Protestant principle', with its *via media* respect for the sanctity of the individual conscience. He told government figures in Dublin who wanted to pressure the recusants to conform, (and as he later told Cecil), persecution was wrong tactically, and in itself was not a means of spreading the reformed faith: 'I am of opinion that all religions do grow under persecution. It is truly good doctrine and example that must prevail'.[78] What Mountjoy wanted was to maintain the traditional Tudor policy, which had worked in England, of demanding no more than nominal conformity. 'Seditious instruments' of foreign power were to be punished, but there was to be no religious or state pressure used against those: 'as doe professe to bee faithful subjects to her Majestie and against whom the contrarie cannot be proved'.[79]

There were churchmen who hoped that Trinity College, Dublin, would be as zealous in promoting a reformed church mission as were its papal counterparts on the continent. Trinity received its crown charter in 1592, a year before Philip II established the college of St. Patrick in Salamanca. In fact the charter of the college indicates that one of the reasons for its foundation was to counter the appeal of colleges like that of Salamanca:

> whereby knowledge and civilitie might be increased by the instruction
> of our people there, whereof many have usually heretofore used to travel
> into France, Italy, and Spain, to get learning in such foreign
> universities, whereby they have been infected with Popery and other ill
> qualities, and so become evil subjects.[80]

Yet the college never received enough crown funds to be as effective as it might have been in this cause, and perhaps this reflected not only Elizabeth's parsimonious nature, but also her concern for the Puritan ethos of the new Irish foundation. From the time that Thomas Cartwright, a militant Puritan divine, had been in Ireland from 1565 to 1567, churchmen there had been influenced by his party which the queen loathed. Adam Loftus, the first provost of Trinity, was a graduate of Puritan Cambridge, and when he was translated from Armagh to Dublin he had earnestly recommended as primate Thomas Cartwright. Loftus was thought to be an advanced Calvinist, and the provosts who succeeded him were also Puritans, while the immediate successor of Loftus, Walter Travers was considered by John Whitgift, the archbishop of Canterbury, to be: 'one of the chief and principle authors of dissension in the Church'.[81] Elizabeth was not likely to support a major mission from Trinity College Dublin when it might be dominated by Puritan divines who would seek confrontation with Irish papists rather than their conversion.

For a complex of reasons the crown policy was to try in Ireland what had worked in England: to insist upon no more than public conformity to the royal supremacy and what was demanded by the Act of Uniformity. But Ireland was not England and, even after the defeat of Hugh O'Neill and the Spanish, church and society suffered from the many years of prolonged warfare. At the end of the century matters were no better in most parts of Ireland than those described for the queen by Henry Sydney, the Lord Deputy, in 1576. He described the diocese of Meath, then outside the war zone, as blessed with a bishop, Hugh Brady, who was considered to be honest, zealous and learned. The church, however, was in extreme disrepair, much of its land impropriated, with absentee clergy, and a people who lived 'without little or no reformation, either of religion or manners'. Among the curates only eighteen could speak English: 'the rest Irish priests, or rather Irish rogues, having very little Latin, less learning or civility'. The laity in this, 'the best inhabited county of all this realm' were so profane and heathenish that even the sacrament of baptism was ignored among them. [82] It would seem that from the religious point of view, indeed, there was little improvement in conditions in most parts of the church as a whole during the sixteenth century. [83] As for the clergy who did not conform, and lived according to their traditional style, the papal agents from David Wolfe to Rinuccini in the next century had little to praise in their way of life. When the dean of Raphoe went to Rome to seek a bishopric in 1561 Wolfe referred to him as: 'a rude, coarse man, fitter to be a soldier than a churchman'. [84] The Catholic laity, apart from the minority who were directly touched by the Tridentine reform movement, were in Roman eyes still living lives of singular barbarity.

Elizabeth's English policy of tolerating the minority of recusants, so long as they kept out of politics, failed in Ireland primarily because the majority of the people chose to serve and protect their traditional expression of the faith. The reason why they did so lay in their reaction to, and resentment of, what was brought upon them by their powerful neighbour from across the Irish sea. A new vibrant mercantilist and expansionist culture was developing in England, and its values were brought to Ireland by an increasing number of settlers whose wealth and industry were changing life in both the towns and the countryside. So far as most of the native Irish were concerned, whether Old English or Gaelic Irish, this folk migration and extension of an alien culture had to be resisted— and part of the culture was the religious settlement which Elizabeth offered to them. They watched uneasily as reformers like Adam Loftus, or William Lyon rebuilt churches, began systematic visitations, weeded out incompetents, and brought bibles and prayer books into the country. The queen even sent over a printing press with Irish type, and by 1602 parts of the new Testament were appearing in Irish, much of the translation being the work of a Kilkenny native, William Daniel, who became archbishop of Tuam in 1609. 'Civilitie' including 'true religion' was being foisted upon the Irish, and when they rejected the common law, shires, sheriffs, justices on assizes, juries, and English land-tenure and local administration, so did they reject the new ecclesiastical settlement. More of them might have accepted the new church, if the crown had indicated that it was intent upon enforcing acceptance of the Act of Supremacy and the Act of Uniformity but this did not happen. Like the English recusants those of Ireland were allowed to maintain their traditional form of religion, so long as they kept out of politics. The great difference was that in Ireland the recusants formed the majority of the population and, from the time of the O'Neill alliance with the papacy and Spain, Ireland was now part of the maelstrom of Europe's era of religious warfare.

The crown was aware of what was taking place in Ireland. In Galway, which had once been considered a Protestant stronghold, a report on the religious condition of Connaught in 1591 said:

> For the town of Galway as the same hath bene once the paradisse of Ireland in nomber and zeal of professers of the Gospell, so now what through the negligence of the magistrates for not preserving the heate and furtheringe the fruitfullness as by reason of certayne Romish flatterers secrettly seducinge them are exceedingly fallen away so farre... now very few of their men, and not of the cheefest wilbe seene to frequent the same (the Church).[85]

Loftus warned London that the number of recusants was increasing rapidly among 'gentlemen of account' who were openly refusing to attend sermons or receive communion in the reformed church: 'they have grown to such obstinacy and boldness that it is to be feared—if some speedy remedy be not provided—upon pretext of religion they will shake off all duty and obedience'.[86]

English policy in Ireland during the last years of Elizabeth's reign was based on the assumption, or hope, that even the restless recusants that Loftus referred to could be tolerated in a 'new civilitie'; one that would reflect the new economy and increasingly sophisticated social organization that was being established. Religion was then recognized as an essential element in the promotion of the new 'civilitie', but the government did not give support of the Protestant mission high priority, for it promised to be expensive to maintain. Neither did it protect the church from exploitation by the greedy newcomers flocking in from the mainland,[87] nor did it give aid which might have helped to win disaffected Old English and the Gaelic chieftains from their traditional ways of religious expression.[88] It was almost inevitable that the rebuffed Irish leaders would pay increasing attention to the missionaries among the people who served the cause of the Counter-Reformation papacy, and to the offer of help from distant Spain which was still made after the disaster at Kinsale. The alternative to the indifferent offer of nominal conformity to the decayed Protestant church, which was brought to the Irish with zeal and effectiveness was the universal power of Rome supported by Spanish might. Acceptance of the Counter-Reformation cause was a slow process, however, for: 'if the mission of the Established Church was feeble, it would be a mistake to regard the success of the Catholic mission as in any way inevitable'.[89]

The strength of the Roman Catholic mission in Ireland reflected the Counter-Reformation spirit of the Holy See which was at its apogée during the pontificate of the authoritarian, inflexible and violent Sixtus V. Imposing his own Franciscan standards of morality upon the church he accumulated great wealth, becoming one of the richest princes in Europe, determined to use his economic power in extending effectively the decrees of the Council of Trent. His greatest accomplishment, however, was his lasting reorganization of the church's central administration to put it on a war-footing. Sixtus showed the power of his new government first by a ruthless repression of banditry in the papal states when thousands of brigands were publicly executed. For years after his death in 1590 the people of Rome remembered the zeal of this single-minded pontiff, devout to the point of bigotry, who terrorized so many. It was said that for years Roman mothers quieted their crying children by admonishing: 'Here comes Sixtus'.[90] The pope who harried the people of the papal states to enforce conformity was even more fanatical when the opportunity arose to persecute heresy. Sixtus V represented everything that was threatening in the imagination of the Protestants who were determined to keep his authority out of both England and Ireland.

After Sixtus died Spanish pressure ensured the election of three short-lived pontiffs, then another model of Tridentine piety became pope as Clement VIII. A passionate supporter of militant reform he was too busy elsewhere to cause Elizabeth much trouble in her last days, though he intervened in English Catholic disputes. Elsewhere he exercised his ascetic idealism by sharpening the severity of the inquisition which in his reign sent more than thirty heretics, including the ex-Dominican philosopher, Giordano Bruno, to the stake. There were signs during Clement's pontificate that some of the zeal of the Tridentine reformers was passing, and Clement himself was concerned to free the papacy from Spanish domination. Yet it was unlikely that any of the young Irish emigrés, coming out of continental colleges and seminaries, would be likely to return to Ireland without sharing in the Counter-Reformation idealism of the time. On occasion they could protest that they would, 'conduct religious propaganda and remain unconnected with the temporal operations of the papacy and its high ecclesiastics', but they knew well their mission in Ireland was part of the greater project: 'an introduction to... the papal conquest of England'.[91]

The greater chieftains and wealthier citizens could send their sons to Oxford or Cambridge, but the rest of the gentry and other citizens followed the advice of papal ecclesiastics and were likely to send their boys to get a good and cheap education in the Roman colleges and universities in France and Spain. Many of the young men who came back from these colleges were passionate supporters of the Tridentine papacy, and what they wanted for the Catholic church in Ireland was more than the mere 'accommodation' of their faith offered by the policies of the crown. Whether they were priests, friars, or laymen, their intention was to bring Ireland into what they considered Providence, through the Vicar of Christ upon earth was ordering. They came as servants of a great imperial power whose ideas and practices were not unlike those of the new monarchies of Spain, France and England:

> The sixteenth century counterpart in Catholicism of what used to be called the new monarchy is the counter-reformation papacy, not only in general spirit but also in precise method: the taking into papal hands of all the new tasks that the Counter-Reformation in all its aspects required; enforcement of the Tridentine decrees; establishment of new relations with secular powers; extension of mission work in heathen lands; reorganization of pastoral and controversial equipment in Europe, and the counter-attacks on Protestantism.[92]

The imperial authority of the papacy was determined by the time that Elizabeth died in 1603 to take over Irish Catholicism, and to direct the Irish people in crusade against the English heretics, and the apostates who had joined the Church of Ireland. Hugh O'Neill's agent in Rome, Peter Lombard, a Waterford native who had studied at Louvain in the Spanish Netherlands, was made papal archbishop of Armagh at O'Neill's request in 1601 and, with others, he was intent upon building in Ireland a rival ecclesiastical establishment to that of the Church of Ireland. Ireland was not to be spared the great political-religious power struggle which tore Europe apart, and brought about such terrible suffering for so many people:

> On one side was a Church contaminated by State Control, unable to move an inch without an Order in Council, forbidden to exercise its natural functions by political exigencies, poor, needy, and weak, regarded as legitimate prey by every agrarian adventurer, staffed with a Clergy who were the heirs of Pre-Reformation traditions, and reft of parishes by the fact that more than half its advowsons were in the control of its enemies. On the other hand was a Mission, financed by a great European Power, and supported by the dominant political interests of the moment. What was more, it was controlled autocratically by an outside Power, the Vatican at Rome.[93]

Chapter III

William Bedell's Ireland

'The union of Catholics in Ireland was, from first to last, a protestant achievement, not a catholic one'.

Aidan Clarke, *Old English in Ireland*, Preface

I   The Crown, the Papacy and Jacobite Ireland

It is very difficult to know with any certainty where the Irish people stood with regard to the traditional two religious *imperia* at the time of Elizabeth's death.   During the war years of the O'Neill rebellion protestant leaders complained of the growth of recusancy, and when news of Elizabeth's death reached Cork and Waterford protestant ministers were expelled and there was a demand that private catholic worship should be tolerated in the communities. There is no doubt that there had been a change in Old English religious sensibilities during the 1590's. They were 'consciously Catholic', in the sense that they rejected the religious establishment served by the New English who were now settling among them, but they were: 'ill-instructed by the standards of the Counter-Reformation'.[1] Their shift in allegiance from loyalty to the crown to service of the papal mission was to be a slow one, partly a reaction to the New English who were increasing rapidly in numbers in Ireland and, more importantly, a response to external circumstances produced by the relationship between the house of Stuart and the papacy.

At the time of Elizabeth's death religious affairs in England were in a chaotic state, with a great struggle shaping up between supporters of the extreme Protestant party, the Puritans, who had been cowed but not defeated by the policies of the archbishop of Canterbury, John Whitgift. He had forced them to conform, however nominally, to Elizabeth's *via media* settlement, with its attempt to comprehend 'tender consciences'. This did not satisfy the extreme Calvinists of the Puritan party, but they settled for the 'wait and see' attitude of so many churchmen who had been forced to respond to the religious changes imposed upon them in the time of Henry VIII, Edward VI, Mary and Elizabeth. The 'wait and see' attitude was also characteristic of the Old English in Ireland, in particular. There were at the most about a hundred Counter-Reformation agents in the country, and their influence was decidedly limited. They were known to the New English in Dublin and elsewhere, who reported to the crown how the country did 'swarm with Jesuits, seminary and massing priests, yea and friars' all trying to seduce 'the natural people of the country' for service in the cause of the Antichrist of Rome.[2]

These exaggerated reports made by the New English settlers are not sustained by what is known about the state of religious allegiance in the country, however. There is general truth in Canon G.V. Jourdan's judgment:

> At the close of Elizabeth's reign, and for some years after, the cleavage in religion was not so distinctly marked as we are prone to imagine. Except for Ulster, the whole country had conformed. That does not mean that the people of Ireland were what we today would call Protestants. Up to this time no proper presentation of Protestant doctrine had been laid before them.[3]

Neither did the people know much about the Tridentine form of Roman Catholicism. Their religious affirmation was unreformed by the standards of either Canterbury or Rome, and most were willing to accept the nominal conformity demanded by the crown, so long as they were left alone to pursue their traditional way of religious life. Their clergy were 'impoverished, illiterate men who knew little or no theology'.[4] Like their flocks they chose to conform as an exercise in 'conservative survivalism',[5] while as crypto-catholics they practiced traditional forms of their faith, hoping this would not bring upon them social or political censure. There seems to be enough evidence to indicate that when James I came to the English throne many of the native clergy and their flocks were at least nominal members of the established church—even in Gaelic Ireland as a visitation of 1615 reveals.[6]

At the time of James' accession the pope was Clement VIII, who was devoted to Catholic reform and pressed hard to encourage the spirit of the Council of Trent: he enlarged the Index, harried the Jews, and involved himself in the last stages of the French religious wars. His acceptance of the Edict of Nantes, granting the Huguenots qualified religious and political liberty, was grudging: 'this crucifies me... liberty of conscience for each and every one is the worst thing in the world'.[7] Though he gave his blessing to the O'Neill forces in 1600, when it looked like they might prevail with Spanish help, his continental involvement left him little time to interfere in England or Ireland. In fact, Elizabeth said of Clement's general attitude towards her affairs that: 'she had nothing to complain'.[8] The queen and her advisers knew that Catholic influence had practically vanished from her court by the end of her reign, the secession of individual Catholics was increasing, and Rome was put on the defensive as the royal policy of qualified repression had results. The hope for Rome at the time of the queen's death was a reversal of policy by James Stuart, king of both England and Scotland, as well as Ireland.

James had considerable trouble with extreme Calvinists in Scotland, and his first concern when he became king of England was to curb the pretensions of the arrogant Puritan party. Both James and his wife, Anne of Denmark, a Catholic convert, had written to Clement VIII in 1599, when the soon to be king sought a rapprochement with the Catholic church that would enable him to consider how he might deal with religion in the future. He told the earl of Northumberland, a leading Catholic nobleman that his intention was to demand no more than nominal conformity from the recusants:

> As for catholics I will neither persecute any that will be quiet and give
> but an outward obedience to the law, neither will I spare to advance any
> of them that will by good service worthily deserve it.9

In his first parliament James had said that he acknowledged the Roman church as the mother church in Christendom, 'although defiled with some infirmities and corruptions', and he acknowledged the pope's position as 'Patriarch of the west'.10 It is little wonder that Clement had hopes that under the Stuart king Britain would again return to the Roman obedience.

Unfortunately for Clement James heartily resented not only the authority claimed by the Scottish Kirk, but any assertion of ecclesiastical authority from any quarter. He strongly held belief in the doctrine of Apostolic Succession in the church, and the Divine Right of Kings when it came to government generally. He may have had a Catholic mother, but this pedantic monarch and would-be theologian had such a high opinion of his own abilities that he was unlikely to accept papal authority which would interfere with his assertion of what he believed to be his ecclesiastical and political prerogatives. To James kings were 'breathing images of God upon earth':

> The state of monarchy is the supremest thing upon earth; for kings are
> not only God's lieutenants upon earth, and sit upon God's throne, but
> even by God himself they are called Gods.11

James was bound to have difficulties with the papacy for in 1605 there came to the papal throne a pontiff, Paul V, who held ideas of the papal prerogatives that would have pleased Gregory VII or Boniface VIII. Paul had no doubt that the pope was the vicegerent of Christ who had granted him the power of the Keys and, as such, he should be reverenced in all humility by all nations and princes. This one-time inquisitor of Rome was elected with both Spanish and French backing when he was only 52, and he was convinced that his unexpected elevation was the result of divine intervention. His exalted concept of papal power, and how it should be exercised, was shown soon after his election when he had a pamphleteer beheaded on the bridge of Sant Angelo for comparing Clement VIII to Tiberius.12

The relationship between James I and Paul V got off to a bad start because of the outcry associated with the   This was the work of Catholic extremists, led by Robert Catesby and Guy Fawkes, who attempted in 1605 to blow up the king, lords and commons in parliament in one enormous explosion. The pope immediately wrote to James telling him to ensure that the unsuccessful assassination attempt did not bring suffering upon the Catholics of England. The plot inevitably led to a tightening up of laws against recusants, however, as well as the demand by parliament that all Catholics take an oath denying the pope's right to depose monarchs. Paul immediately denounced this action, and forbade Catholics to take the oath. When the Catholic archpriest, George Blackwell, urged the people to comply with what the government demanded he was replaced by Rome. The Gunpowder Plot became part of British folk memory, and put an end to any real hope of reconciliation with the papacy for the next two hundred years. James, 'the wisest fool in Christendom', chose this time to show his theological prowess by engaging in a dispute with cardinal Bellarmine defending the oath imposed on the recusants. His 1607 publication entitled *Apologie for the Oath of Allegiance* was addressed 'to all quietly minded papists', and it promised them that he was intent upon carrying on the qualified toleration of the recusants exercised by earlier rulers. The oath, said James, was: 'good proofe that I intended no persecution against them for conscience sake, but onely desired to be secured of them for civill obedience'.[13] His *apologia* failed to please Paul V because it dismissed the deposing power of the papacy as imperious and heretical.[14] Nor did it please the Puritans who were furious over such a controlled reaction to the Gunpowder Plot.

Popular suspicion of James' relationship with Rome was increased by a confusing foreign policy which bewildered not only the English people but many European governments with whom he negotiated during the years leading up to the beginning of the Thirty Years War. There was general Protestant satisfaction when his daughter Elizabeth was married to the strongly Protestant Elector of the Palatinate in 1613. In five years time this 'Winter King' was to ally himself with the Bohemian rebels against the might of the Hapsburgs at the start of the great religious-political conflict which was to visit so much suffering on so many people between 1618 and 1648. James promptly undid his popularity by beginning prolonged negotiations with Spain for the marriage of his son Charles to a Spanish princess. Charles visited Spain, letters were exchanged with the pope, and by 1621 parliament was submitting a petition to the king against popery and the Spanish marriage. Two years later negotiations began again to negotiate a marriage treaty with terms so favourable to the Catholics that parliament was furious. When the marriage attempt fell through Charles was married to the Catholic Henrietta Maria, sister of Louis XIII of France, in 1625. The house of Stuart was now set upon its way to direct confrontation with the strongly Protestant parliament.

The Irish knew little about what was going on in Europe; they cared little for the pretensions of either James I or Paul V; nor were they interested in the theological disputes between Reformation and Counter-Reformation churches or powers. What concerned them was the folk migration of the New English among them, even before the Ulster Plantation began. In Munster the influx was most evident, increasing to about 18,000 with their dependants by 1630.[15] The newcomers were generally rapacious, able men, adventurers to be reckoned with, ruthless in their handling of the natives, and hated by the Old English and the Gaelic Irish alike. One of the most remarkable of these men was Richard Boyle, who arrived in Munster the year before Elizabeth died. By a series of shrewd initiatives he purchased the lands of Sir Walter Raleigh, and before he died in 1634 Boyle had been created the first earl of Cork.[16] The native Irish were convinced that they had friends neither in court nor in Dublin, and that whenever a legal or political decision was to be made the appointment or whatever was at issue would go to one of the new English settlers. It was the bitterness associated with this wide-spread experience which convinced many of the Old English in particular, that they needed external support to withstand the powerful new settlers. They naturally turned to the other traditional protective power which had been important in Irish life prior to the Reformation—the papacy. Its agents, the Jesuits and others, were now not hard to find in the country.

A good example of an Old English family changing slowly its political-religious allegiance is provided by the Stanihursts, a wealthy Pale family, one of whose members had been lord mayor of Dublin in 1489. Very much part of the Anglo-Irish ascendancy the family did well out of the dissolution of the monasteries, their young were traditionally educated in London, and by 1570 James Stanihurst was speaker of the Irish House of Commons. All of them had been nurtured on tales of the savagery of their 'prowling mountain neighbours', the Gaelic Irish. In religious matters the family chose to continue their traditional observances, and found that they had no trouble with the benign Irish administration. When James' son Richard Stanihurst attended Oxford, however, he had as his tutor the strong minded and gifted Edmund Campion. Richard fell under the spell of this remarkable man who visited Dublin in 1569 before leaving the Church of England to become a Roman Catholic and a Jesuit. Richard followed him, and became in turn a devotée of the Counter-Reformation movement which was intent upon changing the religious and political settlement in England and Ireland: 'to integrate these countries into the political system being devised and reflected upon in Madrid'.[17] During his time in Spanish territory Richard had published in Antwerp in 1584 his remarkable history, *De rebus in Hibernia gestis*, an account of the traditions of his ancestors and the state of the society in which he grew to manhood. In the work Stanihurst expressed his wish that the once feared Gaelic Irish could join with the Anglo-Irish in accepting the blessings of Counter-Reformation religion and Roman-Spanish 'civilitie'. In actual fact, like many others his own father, James was a 'trimmer' who had survived under both Mary and Elizabeth, and was not only a pliant instrument of government policy, but a strong advocate for: 'the ideal of English civilization thrusting out from Old English areas'.[18] This was a task that James Stanihurst did not want to see abandoned to direction by the New English who talked much about conquest and plantation.

Much has been made by historians of the 'identity crisis' of the Anglo-Irish, and there is no doubt that it was increased by James I's conciliatory attitude after the Gunpowder Plot, his continuing toleration of the recusants, and his lack of interest in talk of Protestant mission to the Irish Catholics. If the Church of Ireland had been given massive and sustained support by the crown and the Dublin administration, under the leadership of men like William Daniel, the scholarly archbishop of Tuam, and other graduates of Trinity College, a serious mission to promote 'true religion and civilitie' might have been attempted. On its own, however, the Church of Ireland was without the spirit or the means to do other than struggle for survival. Much of its land was alienated by powerful lords and chieftains, many of them openly Catholic, and its leadership so corrupt that even its own bishops enriched their families by taking over church lands. Among the bishops of the period was Miler Magrath: 'more fit to sacrifice to a calf than to intermeddle with the religion of God'.[19] The ultimate allegiance of these bishops to either king or pope was always in doubt; the parish clergy were so impoverished, uneducated and lacking in zeal that little in terms of mission could be hoped for from them. They held in theory two or three benefices, usually, but this barely provided them with income for survival:

> For all their pluralities they are most of them beggars, for their patron
> or ordinary, or some of their friends, take the greater part of their profits
> by a plain contract before their institution; so that many gentlemen, and
> some women and some priests and Jesuits, have the greatest benefit of
> our benefices, though these poor unlettered clerks bear the name of
> incumbents.[20]

A report made by the Lord Deputy, Sir Arthur Chichester, on a visitation he made to Monaghan, Fermanagh and Cavan, in 1607 revealed how desperate was the situation of the Church of Ireland in areas far from the oversight of Dublin:

> It appeared that the churches (of the diocese of Clogher) for the most
> part are utterly waste: that the king is patron of all; and that their
> incumbents are popish priests, instituted by bishops authorized by
> Rome; yet many of them, like other old priests of Queen Mary's time
> in England, ready to yield to conformity.[21]

Whether clergy of this sort were 'popish priests' or not is arguable. Certainly they were 'poor, ragged, ignorant creatures' in official report language 'illiterati, infecti papismo',[22] very much part of the problem of religious identity in Ireland.

What helped to define the position of many Irish was the political crisis which accompanied the famous 'flight' to Rome of the earls of Tyrone and Tyrconnell in the same year that Chichester made his northern visitation. Theirs was a premeditated action, with Hugh O'Neill hoping to use Spanish diplomatic leverage, or Spanish military power to assist him to return to his one time position of great power.[23] It failed for the ship carrying himself and other chieftains did not reach Spain. It landed in France, and via the Spanish Netherlands, O'Neill reached Rome, which became the centre for his intrigues. Welcoming O'Neill were Peter Lombard, titular archbishop of Armagh, Florence Conry, titular archbishop of Tuam, and other exiles who were dedicated to overthrowing the authority of the crown in Ireland with Roman and Spanish help. The response of the government to the departure of the earls was to accuse them of treason, and to begin a new Pale through the confiscation of their tribal lands. This plantation, 'the best vehicle for promoting civility in Ireland' filled many of the hitherto loyal Anglo-Irish and Gaelic Irish with alarm. By 1630 a total of 14,500 newcomers, most of them redoubtable Lowland Scots, were settled in Ulster. Including their women and children this folk migration brought close to 34,000 new settlers into Ireland.[24] Like the Puritans in England, the Calvinists in Scotland, or indeed the Huguenots in France the Catholics of Ireland developed a deep distrust of the crown which ultimately brought them into armed conflict with its authority.

The Scots from the very beginning of Irish history had interfered in affairs in Ulster, and Tudor policy had been to keep them out. James, however, long before he ascended the English throne had sought to extend his authority to the north-west of Scotland and, as part of that policy, he had encouraged Scots to establish themselves in counties Antrim and Down. This meant that when the Lowlanders poured into Ulster from 1609 onward they found Scots colonies already established there, and this bridgehead helped them in their massive take-over of land. They had to be a sturdy people to survive for the land was wasted by years of war and famine, and the people were hostile to their presence. Some of the Scots, like the Hamiltons, were not only Catholics but strong supporters of their religion. Most of the newcomers wanted a replica of the reformed Church of Scotland, organized on Presbyterian lines in their settlements, however, and they shared in the loathing that John Knox had had for the pope, the Antichrist. In their church and community there was to be retained nothing: 'that ever flowed from that Man of Sin'.[25] From the moment they arrived in Ulster their religion, and the way of life it nurtured, radically separated them from their Catholic neighbours. Sir Humphrey Gilbert's charter for land in Munster had commissioned him to bring the blessings of 'Christian civility' to the Irish barbarians, but the Scots in Ulster needed no royal commission to exercise their own form of religious and cultural imperialism. They were never sufficient in number, even with English reinforcement to take over Ulster completely, in the way their contemporaries established themselves in Virginia, but they were determined to impress 'civility' upon those whom they dispossessed from being proprietors to being 'tenants-at-will'.[26] In the western part of Ulster, especially, the planters found themselves sparsely numbered amidst a hostile and Catholic population who opposed them whenever possible culturally, religiously and politically. This in no way dismayed the Ulster Scot who was willing to live with 'the sword in one hand the axe in the other'.[27] They did have anxieties, however, about what their situation would be if the Ulster Catholics were reinforced from outside. In the words of one observer in 1612:

> If the king of Spain were to land 10,000 men in Ireland, all the settlers would be at once massacred, which is not difficult to execute in a moment, by reason they are dispersed, and the native swords will be in their throats in every part of the realm, like the Sicilian Vespers.[28]

The Scots who came to Ulster were tough, self-reliant men and so were their clergy. Robert Blair was one of the religious reformers in their number and his opinion of the ungodly clerical adventurers who came with the first Scots settlers was scathing:

> Although amongst those whom Divine Providence did send to Ireland there were several persons eminent for birth, education and parts; yet the most part were such as either poverty, scandalous lives, or, at the best, adventurous seeking of better accomodation had forced thither, so that the security and thriving of religion was little seen to be among those adventurers, and the preachers were generally of the same complexion with the people.[29]

Although the Scots clergy were mostly Presbyterian in sympathy if not conviction they did not hesitate to intrude themselves into Church of Ireland livings, with the help of compliant Scots bishops, like Andrew Knox of Raphoe, or Robert Echlin of Down. Once they were secure within the establishment they acted like their Puritan counterparts in the Church of England, reviling the Church of Ireland and its bishops. At the same time they were far from exemplary in their own spiritual lives and Blair, who had been episcopally ordained, and a professor at Glasgow before going to Ireland, further castigated them as: 'indolent or remiss, if not lewd and scandalous, while even the most regular appeared to have contented themselves with the more routine duties of their profession'.[30] Blair, at the same time, had much to say about the 'northern Irishes': 'remaining not only obdured in Popish superstition and idolatry, but also in their idleness and incivility'.[31] It was the rapacious and brutal lives of the first Scots settlers who convinced the Ulster Catholics that to survive they had to fight the intruders, with the aid of any external help that was available to them. Blair was soon to build up a reform party among the Irish Presbyterians, convinced that Providence had brought the Scots to Ulster to establish there a truly Christian community.[32] They shared the opinion that they were to have as little communion as possible with the degraded papists among whom they were obliged to live, and their insolence was to have far-reaching consequences:

> The sweeping denunciations made by this new cult of every existing tradition and custom did more to assist the reaction of the counter-reformation than all the preaching of the friars.[33]

The development of plantation in Ulster was very different from what was attempted in Munster. There, sectarian tension was at first not a problem and many English recusants came to the south convinced that in Ireland they would find less anti-catholic prejudice that in England. There was very little reaction to the Gunpowder Plot in Ireland, and reaction was mild when a papal emissary, David Rothe, produced a work in 1616 comparing James I with Julian the Apostate, and described the English as dogs or beasts.[34] Even the clergy who came to the south of Ireland with the Protestant planters encouraged social and religious conciliation wherever it was possible: 'it was not the case that the clergy was full of contempt for the Irish population, or that they believed them consigned to damnation'.[35] The crown avoided giving direct support to the Protestant church, and even countenanced native objections to the legality of titles to land held by the new settlers. The general attitude of the government seemed to be that the rival ecclesiastical organizations could contend as they wished for the allegiance of natives and settlers alike. In return for such a concessionary outlook the papal primate Peter Lombard refined a theory that allowed Irish Catholics to accept James as their 'lawful king' in spite of his being a heretic.

No such spirit of accommodation appeared in Ulster, however, where the land-grabbing Lowland Scots were resented by not only the Roman Catholic but by many members of the Church of Ireland. Many of the Scots planters were crypto-Presbyterians, they were constantly reinforced by their co-religionists from the Scottish mainland, and as their numbers grew so did their arrogance. The Church of Ireland Protestants resented them, but the dispossessed Catholics began to nurture a loathing of the Scots that took the form of clan hatred. Inevitably, some of them began to look for political and religious reinforcement and began to pay serious attention to the Roman-Spanish agents who wished to organize them and to put them on a war-footing in support of the Counter-Reformation. News of what was taking place in the north inevitably influenced developments in the rest of the island. Among the Old English especially in the other areas of planter penetration, Munster and Dublin, resentments increased as did the withdrawal of loyalty to the crown, ostensibly on the 'grounds of religion'. The mercantilist culture of the southern planters and officials, was now seen to be reinforced by this massive northern migration, and it was inevitable that the Irish would turn for help to the 'protective' authority of old that was so eager to help them oppose the heretical English. At the same time that the Protestants in England were becoming restive and resentful over the Catholic alliance promised by the Spanish marriage of Prince Charles, the Catholic primate, Peter Lombard, began to take hope that the Roman and Spanish power might yet win over to the Counter-Reformation cause the Irish Catholics.[36]

> The mishandling of the Plantation accomplished what not all the labour of the papal emissaries had been able to bring about—a drawing of the rural Irish into a close union with the Anglo-Irish of the towns, and that too on the grounds of religion... the last hope of the Church of Ireland retaining in her fold that large body of Irish countrymen which up to this date and for a few years more oscillated indeterminately between parish church and 'massing house' now began to fade.[37]

The real division of the Irish people into warring religious bodies began during the reign of James I, and much of the blame for it can be attributed to his confusing political and religious policies. One of his tutors, as a boy, had been George Buchanan, an extreme Protestant who had produced a work, *De iure regni apud Scotos* justifying tyrannicide, and James learned from him how easily religious convictions could be a threat to any ruler. He knew that in a crisis there was apt to be a meeting of minds between Scots Presbyterians and English Puritans, who shared the same Calvinist theology. However much he proclaimed his royal prerogatives the very presence of such a body of critical Protestant opinion greatly influenced his decisions. At times the Protestants displayed outright rancour over the king's vacillating foreign policy, and they strongly condemned his indecisiveness when the one-time Huguenot leader, Henry of Navarre, who had become a Roman Catholic and king of France, was murdered by a religious fanatic, Francois Ravaillac. In England the king responded to Protestant pressure by enforcing with considerable severity the penal laws against Catholics, and negotiations for the Spanish marriage were quietly dropped. In Ireland there remained, however, increasing disquiet among the Protestants for Henry of Navarre had been considered to be the chief opponent of the fanatical Catholicism and overgrown power of Philip III of Spain. Continental affairs mattered to them because they were aware of the politico-ecclesiastical agitation of clerics like Florence Conry, the Catholic archbishop of Tuam, a supporter of Hugh O'Neill. They were close to their co-religionists in England and when James began again negotiations for the Spanish marriage, they shared the alarm which led the Commons in 1621, three years after the beginning of the Thirty Years war, to draw up a petition against popery and the Spanish marriage. Once more the recusants were granted more and more privileges in both England and Ireland. The Venetian ambassador wondered in 1622 if the king was not sowing the seed of civil war with his flaunting of both parliament and public opinion when: 'the catholic religion has never been practiced in this realm so freely as at present.' His successor, as ambassador feared that the Puritans would react and seek a king, 'after their own heart', and 'then one might fear the extirpation of the catholic plant'.38

There was a close ideological connection between the leaders of the Protestant churches in both England and Ireland at this time, and the continental Calvinists. The latter had always held the prevailing expression of Calvinism in England to be too moderate or 'Arminian' in its expression, but it was the prevailing theology in the Church of England, and even John Whitgift, archbishop of Canterbury who so harried the Puritans, was a Calvinist as his Lambeth Articles of 1596 reveal. George Abbott, who became English primate in 1611 was not only a Calvinist who ensured that England was represented at the Calvinist Synod of Dort in 1618, but he was accused by many of having Puritan sympathies. In Ireland the Convocation of the Church of Ireland in 1615 drew up 104 articles of faith that were decidedly Calvinist. In them the necessity of episcopal ordination was ignored, absolute predestination was taught and the pope was affirmed as the Antichrist. These Irish articles which were to influence greatly the later Westminster Confession of Faith were strongly defended by James Ussher who became archbishop of Armagh just before James I died. One of the great scholars of the age, Ussher was a professor of divinity at Trinity College, Dublin, when the Irish Articles were drawn up. He was famous as an international controversialist, and though he had many reservations about the Ulster Scots and their religious opinions, he was part of the Protestant world which closed ranks in the years of European religious conflict when the Counter-Reformation papacy was committed to establishing its authority by force. The Scots were closely identified with the fortunes of the continental Calvinists and were to play a prominent military role in the Thirty Years War. By the time that Charles Stuart married his French princess, Henrietta Maria, England was also being drawn into the world of European religious conflict—and so was Ireland. It was impossible for Ireland's contending Catholics and Protestants to withstand the reinforcement offered by the external Counter-Reformation or Reformation forces. The Irish people were to endure in their own theatre of conflict the same stupid waste of human resources which characterized the Thirty Years War on the continent:

> Morally subversive, economically destructive, socially degrading, confused in its causes, devious in its course, futile in its result, it is the outstanding example in European history of meaningless conflict.39

II   Ireland and the European Wars of Religion

When the Thirty Years War began in 1618 with a revolt of Bohemian Protestants against the emperor Ferdinand of Hapsburg, who had been educated by the Jesuits as a strict Roman Catholic, the third parliament of James I voted a supply in support of the Protestant forces led by James' son-in-law Frederick V of the Palatinate. As James was again negotiating the Spanish marriage for his son Charles he showed little enthusiasm for the idea of becoming a leader in the Protestant alliance. His lack of sympathy for the Protestant cause was not a surprise for English churchmen who knew how seriously the 'English Socrates' took his 'Divine Right' role as head of the Church of England. James was not ready to take advice in ecclesiastical affairs from the leaders of any continental Protestant Union anymore than he was willing to consult with the archbishop of Canterbury, George Abbott. On one occasion he informed the English primate:

> I hope no honest man doubts the uprightness of my conscience: and the best thankfullness that you, that are so far my creature, can use towards me, is to reverence and follow my judgment, except where you may demonstrate to me that I am mistaken or wrongly informed.[40]

It was this kind of folly that estranged James from the English Protestants and set the Stuarts on their way to religious confrontation. In the early years of his reign James had had the opportunity to play an important diplomatic role in the manoeuvrings of the great powers of the day, and if he had allied himself with the continental Protestant cause at that time the whole course of European history might have been different. Instead he quarrelled with the Puritans in parliament over the imposing of episcopacy upon the church in Scotland, and the Spanish marriage negotiations. His obsession with his insular concerns meant that he missed the opportunity to identify himself with the Protestants on the continent at the time of the Venetian interdict crisis of 1606–1607. It also meant that there was little likelihood of James sustaining any Protestant mission in Ireland. He was not pleased when the Provost of Trinity College, the learned Puritan William Temple defied the archbishop of Canterbury, then Chancellor of the university and with his colleagues refused to wear surplices in the college chapel.[41]

The Venetian crisis was important insomuch as the convoluted diplomacy of James convinced both the Protestant powers on the continent and the Venetians, that the English king was not to be trusted when it came to religious affairs.[42] Venice had always had trouble with the papacy, suffering from interdicts in 1284, 1309 and 1483. On the other hand she was friendly towards England, because Henry VIII had shown sympathy for the Venetian cause when Julius II had joined together with the Empire, Spain and France for a despoiling of the Republic in the League of Cambrai in 1508. From that time Venice was very wary of the court of Rome, particularly when Counter-Reformation policies led to the papal alliance with Spain which occupied nearby Milan.

Venice was strongly Catholic at the beginning of the seventeenth century, inasmuch as its people made much of traditional religious expressions of the faith, but she had no intention of allowing the Counter-Reformation court of Rome to interfere in her internal affairs. Venice played no active part in the proceedings of the Council of Trent, and though the Inquisition was permitted to operate in her territories its proceedings were kept under scrutiny and control. In opposition to Rome's wishes, Venice welcomed German Protestants into the university of Padua, allowed a small Protestant community to develop in Vicenza, printed books that were on the papal Index, and refused to send suspected heretics to Rome for trial. During the reign of James I the English ambassador was allowed to import Protestant books, and to hold private Anglican services in his chapel, in spite of the protests of the Inquisition. At the same time Venice's use of diplomacy in her dealings with the Protestant powers was so sophisticated that both Rome and Spain hesitated to interfere directly in the affairs of the Republic.

This accommodation was disturbed when Paul V, with his extreme ideas about papal prerogatives, caused an international furore by using once more the papal weapon of interdict against the Republic. The papal action threatened to give an excuse for a Spanish take-over of Venetian territories, which was of special concern to Henry IV of France, the one-time leader of the French Huguenots. Other European powers, on the eve of the Thirty Years War were also intensely concerned about how events in Venice might disturb the balance of power between Catholic and Protestant nations, and though the Roman-Venetian confrontation was to last for only a year it was a crisis of international concern and importance.

The trouble began when Venice refused 'benefit of clergy' to two criminal clerks, and Paul V took affront at their being punished by the secular arm of the Republic. When he pronounced the interdict Venice responded by banishing from her territories the Counter-Reformation orders, the Jesuits, the Capuchins and the Theatines. Most importantly, she put herself on a war-footing by appointing as state theologian a brilliant man of letters, an eminent scientist, and shrewd diplomat, Fra Paolo Sarpi of the Servite order. He sought aid from England and Holland, as well as from Henry IV of France, yet such was his skill in his negotiations that Spain never found sufficient reason to invade Venetian territory as champion of the papacy. Rome was very disturbed by the Venetian crisis, fearing as it did that the outright apostasy of Venice, as well as a European war, were distinctly possible. Finally French mediation was accepted, and the papacy found itself forced to compromise its position, or continue to lose prestige:

For Pope Paul and his Curia, there was a terrible truth to be faced. The interdict had failed. The most dreaded weapon in the papal armoury—that same weapon the very threat of which, in the Middle Ages, had been enough to bring kings and emperors to their knees—had lost its power. Worse, its failure had been revealed to the world. The effect on papal prestige, already incalculable, was growing with every day that this farcical sentence continued to operate.[43]

This use of the interdict was the last one in the history of the Catholic church. No pope ever dared risk another and, coming as it did just before the beginning of Europe's war of religion, the Venetian revolt revealed the weakness at the heart of Rome's secular policies. Only eleven years later the son-in-law of James I, the Calvinist Elector Palatine, Frederick, was also to stand up to the Roman-Hapsburg alliance.

Sarpi did not give up his civic duty as state theologian immediately, and he drove a hard bargain with the papacy. Venice was to continue to deny 'benefit of clergy'; the Jesuits and other Counter-Reformation orders were to be kept out of her territories; and no statement was to be made that the Republic was in the wrong, or regretted its actions. The result was almost physically fatal for Sarpi. Assassins tried to murder him outside his Venetian convent, and when they were later seen fully-armed on Roman streets contemporaries took for granted that their attack had been directed by papal authorities. Papal resentment of Sarpi never abated when he had published in England in 1619 his much acclaimed *History of the Council of Trent*, in which conciliar decrees were dismissed as the work of 'power-hungry curialists', a 'deformation' of the church universal.[44]

It is unlikely that Sarpi, knowing the caution of the Venetian government, and the near-by presence of the Spanish army in Milan, ever seriously considered a formal alliance with the Protestant powers in Europe. Yet he corresponded voluminously with 'the Huguenot pope', Phillipe du Plessis-Mornay, who had been Henry IV's trusted adviser before Henry became king of France; he persuaded Dutch troops to come to fight for the Venetians, and he would have made use of English forces if James I had made them available. Sarpi believed during the crisis that England was 'the best friend we have', and Rome certainly feared English aid might be forthcoming both military and religious. Sarpi appreciated the traditional Venetian expression of Catholicism, 'religion should be kept inviolate in all its parts, avoiding every change and novelty of any kind whatsoever'. Yet he recognized that each 'community of believers' would have their own expression of the faith, like the 'folk Catholicism' of the Venetians, with a whole range of local variation: 'what is useful to one state is not useful to another'. For Sarpi the church universal: 'so far as it existed at all in this world was... simply a federation of local churches which properly varied considerably from each other'.[45] It was this respect for 'religious pluralism' which contributed to his deep abiding antipathy to the court of Rome which sought to impose Tridentine uniformity on Venice at the point of the sword.[46]

He never forgot the fate of his colleague, Fra Manfredi, who went to Rome to plead the Venetian case, only to be charged with heresy and burnt at the stake.[47]

An interesting historical anomaly is that this late Renaissance polymath, whom Galileo described as his master, had influence in the development of Irish Protestantism. Through historical accident, Paolo Sarpi's intellectual distinction between the concept of Catholicism as a religious expression of a community, rather than an obedience to the religious-legal authority of the court of Rome, was brought to Ireland to have consequence in Catholic-Protestant relations. The medium through which Sarpi's ecclesiological convictions appeared in Ireland was the system of thought of an English cleric who became provost of Trinity College, Dublin, and then bishop of Kilmore—William Bedell.

William Bedell was a graduate of Emmanuel College, Cambridge, a Puritan stronghold, and was a skilled patristic scholar who spent seventeen years at Cambridge until his appointment as chaplain to Sir Henry Wotton, English ambassador to Venice in 1607. He arrived just after the end of the interdict crisis, when Wotton had hopes of persuading Paolo Sarpi to ally himself with the Protestant cause in Europe. To press his case Wotton arranged soon after the arrival of Bedell that he should meet with Sarpi, ostensibly to study Hebrew. The two men found quickly that they had much in common intellectually, and in religious matters they agreed 'on essentials of the faith'. For nearly three years the two men were closeted together on almost a daily basis, free from interference by the papal nuncio, while they gained greatly in their appreciation of each other's intelligence. During this time Bedell had the work of John Jewel, the bishop of Salisbury in Elizabeth's reign, the *Apologia Ecclesiae Anglicanae*, smuggled into Venice, and Bedell translated several of Sarpi's anti-papal works into English. As the two scholars worked together Bedell appreciated increasingly the distinction the state theologian made between Catholicism as a religion and the organization and direction of the faith by the court of Rome. Bedell, in return, shared with Sarpi his own biblically based faith:

> This is the man whom Padre Paolo took, I may say, into his very soul, with whom he did communicate the inwardest thoughts of his heart, from whom he professed to have received more knowledge in all divinity, both scholastic and positive than from any that he had ever practiced in his days.[48]

Bedell also greatly influenced Sarpi's secretary and constant companion, Fulgenzio Micanzio. By 1609 the latter was preaching biblically based Lenten sermons to a select group of young Venetians. Among them was Nicolo Contarini who later became Doge. It seems possible that if James I of England had given consistent and real support to the Venetians during their struggle with Paul V that some form of Gallican Catholic church would have emerged in

Venice.[49] At least the support that Bedell gave to Sarpi helped him in his communication with both the French Gallicans, and eirenical Huguenots, who sympathized with the Venetian struggle for Republican liberty, and the seeking for an alternative to the war against evangelical religion desired by Paul V and Philip III of Spain.

Bedell returned to England in 1610 and for the next sixteen years lived the life of a quiet country clergyman, though he continued to translate Sarpi's anti-papal works. He showed how much he was indebted to the latter's thought in correspondence with a contemporary James Wadsworth, an old college friend, who had gone to Spain to be tutor and chaplain to the Infanta, then promised to be married to Prince Charles. His religious development was significantly different from Bedell's, however, for having arrived in Spain about the same time Bedell went to Venice he became a Roman Catholic, in Bedell's words: 'he was cheated out of his religion by the Jesuites, and turn'd apostate; and there lived and died, and return'd no more to his native country'.[50] Wadsworth soon began to regret his decision to serve the Counter-Reformation, but when he tried to open communication with his onetime Cambridge colleagues Bedell was the only one who paid any attention to him. Their correspondence was published in 1624,[51] and in it Bedell displayed not only an ecumenical spirit that was remarkable for the age, but he expounded on Sarpi's distinction between the spiritual worth of Catholicism, and the regrettable Roman love of ecclesiastical coercion.

> One thing I would again desire that... you would forbear to be lords over our faith, nor straightaway condemn of heresy our ignorance or lack of persuasion concerning things we cannot perceive to be found in Holy Scripture. Enjoy your own opinions, but make them not articles of our faith.[52]

Bedell was to become of great importance in Irish religious history because he was that rarest of seventeenth century ecclesiastical figures, an ecumenist. He developed his eirenical ideas during his years in his English country living after he returned from Venice. There he corresponded with theologians at Cambridge whose intellectual descendants in the next generation were to be known as Cambridge Platonists. They were individuals who were beginning to move beyond the sterile polemics of the time, and to explore reconciliation among churchmen. Bedell agreed with the thought of Benjamin Whichcote, fellow of Emmanuel College from 1633, who argued that: 'truth is truth, whoever speaks it, and I will readily agree with Papist, Socinian or any, so far as he asserts it; because it is not his but God's.[53] He also corresponded with like-minded churchmen on the continent such as Samuel Hartlib and John Durie.[54] At the same time Bedell's Venetian experience, and the mind-sharing he had had with Paolo Sarpi persuaded him that it would be difficult to deal with the court of

Rome through: 'the honest use of reason and conscience'.[55] Bedell knew that the intransigent popes of the Thirty Years War era would make no concessions lest the authority of the council of Trent might be questioned, and he knew the struggle that the Reformation power represented by the: 'spiritual leadership of the papacy, Spanish might, Jesuit élan, and Tridentine doctrine'.[56]

While Bedell spent his years of rustication in study, Paul V suffered a stroke during a procession to celebrate the 1620 defeat of Frederick V, Calvinist king of Bohemia, and son-in-law of James I of England. His successor was Gregory XV, the first Jesuit-trained pontiff, and the choice of Paul V's Borghese family. Gregory XV had only a short pontificate but during it he was very active politically in support of the Counter-Reformation cause, and showed himself to be as militant as his predecessor, the kind of pope that Bedell deplored. In 1622 the new pontiff founded the Sacred Congregation for the Propagation of the Faith, to supervise missionary activity not only in heathen lands but in countries which had become Protestant and lost their hierarchies. In fact, Propaganda, as it was known, became headquarters of the Counter-Reformation, uniting the Catholic princes in a great offensive to rid Christendom of the Protestant heretics. The English were bought off by promise of the Spanish marriage, in return for James softening the penal laws against Catholics. Philip III was persuaded to break the truce in the Netherlands, and papal troops showed their Counter-Reformation zeal in a brutal slaughter of Protestants in the Valtelline pass between Spanish and French territories. Gregory had only been pope for two years when he died in 1623, but his rule committed the papacy to an all-out identification with the Hapsburg cause. His pontificate saw the canonization of Ignatius Loyola, founder of the Jesuit order.

III   Catholics and Protestants in Caroline Ireland

When Gregory XV died in 1623, two years before James I, Rome had expectations, as did the Irish, that the English king was not going to be a supporter of continental Protestantism, and that Counter-Reformation influence was to spread in both islands. Ireland, in particular, was of concern to the Roman-Spanish authority for, if it could be brought into subjection, England might reconsider its tactic of supporting the rebel Dutch or the Huguenots as it had in the past. Peter Lombard, the titular archbishop of Armagh was particularly hopeful that the tolerance by the crown of Irish recusants would have important strategic results.[57] Urban VIII (1623–1644) was Gregory's successor, an able and authoritarian pope who had been made a cardinal by Paul V and shared his militant spirit. He was the pope who directed ecclesiastical affairs during the Thirty Years War, and carried out the shifting of the papal alliance from Spain to France, a development of significance in England where the presence of queen Henrietta Maria gave an important French entrée into the royal court. For all his assurance in diplomatic affairs Urban was not a great pope, however, and his pontificate showed how much the early zeal of the Counter-Reformation, as a reform movement, had waned. A flagrant nepotist, he was in his personal life a throw back to the popes of the Renaissance. In his closing years he allowed his greedy family to persuade him to engage in a petty Italian war over a papal fief which rejected his authority and allied itself with Venice and other anti-papal states. The war led to devastation in the papal states, crippled papal finances, and brought about a dreadful oppression of the people. The Roman populace broke into riotous jubilation when his death was announced—a joy not shared by the pro-French lobby in England and Ireland.

Through the influence of the Duke of Buckingham there was some English support given to the Huguenots during the early years of Charles I's reign, but after his murder in 1628 the king became greatly influenced by his French Catholic queen, Henrietta Maria. She had her private chapel in St. James' palace and to the English Protestants she was the centre of a continuing intrigue. Charles was a 'high church' Anglican devoted to sacramental religion, but when he used the archbishop of Canterbury, William Laud, to force the Puritans out of the established church if they did not conform to its regulations, he convinced his critics that his policies were pro-papal and too much encouraged by the queen. In the words of Francis Routh in the House of Commons, Charles and Laud were: 'ready to open the gates to Romish tyranny'.[58] Unfortunately for both the monarch and the archbishop neither really appreciated how their policies alienated the English people who were strongly anti-papal as the terrible struggle developed on the continent. The year before Laud was made primate Urban VIII had ordered thanksgiving masses to be celebrated in Rome when news came through of the death of the Protestant champion, Gustavus Adolphus, the king of Sweden. This action was not well received in England.

Three successive papal agents came to England during Charles' reign, hoping for the conversion of the king, and Laud's acceptance of a cardinal's hat. One of these men, a Scot named George Con, won the confidence of the king enough that they engaged in theological discussion about events such as Paolo Sarpi's attempt to find a *via media* religious expression in Venice.[59] Yet none of these emissaries had lasting influence with the king, although they reinforced the presence of the French Capuchins in the queen's chapel, and greatly increased Protestant suspicions. Such royal indiscretion took place at a time when the power of the Puritans was steadily increasing, there were no prominent English Catholic figures to organize a Counter-Reformation movement, and even the emigration of young Englishmen to the Catholic seminaries on the continent was decreasing. The Venetian ambassador, Marc Antonio Correr, expressed his amazement as conversions to Roman Catholicism took place in the court, and it seemed that Con was about to persuade the king to rule by his own authority, even at the cost of a civil war.

It was from the England of Charles I, filled with its deep resentment of

Roman Catholicism that William Bedell was to go to Ireland as Provost of Trinity College, Dublin in 1627. There the recusants were in a different position than they were in England where they were so much a minority. Urban VIII had given Propaganda its own missionary training seminary, and by 1630 the early emissaries in Ireland like David Rothe and Peter Lombard had been reinforced by zealous graduates of it and other continental seminaries, intent upon introducing Roman discipline into ecclesiastical affairs, as well as a Tridentine religious culture. There was soon a bishop in every see in Ireland, about forty Jesuits and forty Dominicans in the country, and probably a thousand diocesan priests and Franciscans who had some degree of Tridentine training. Mass houses were tolerated and, though there was an occasional move to enforce conformity on the part of the officials in Dublin, the recusants were generally given total freedom of religious expression. The weakness of the Roman mission was that not all Irish Catholics welcomed those missioners who spoke of bringing to the country a 'new plantation in religion', a 'new civility' like that found on the continent. Although the first permanent Jesuit mission was Old English in character, and the Old English wanted a transition to 'civility', what most wished for was to be identified with the diffusion of English, culture, manners and government.[60] The demoralized Gaelic Irish, on the other hand, wanted a restoration of their traditional religion and culture and talked once more of armed resistance backed by help from Spain. Churchmen in both communities, however, were united in their wish for a spiritual revival especially among the clergy whose continual quarrelling was deplored by the laity, both Old English and Gaelic Irish. Patrick Comerford, papal bishop of Waterford, described his clergy as 'undisciplined', many of them apostates, whose moral life with reprehensible. They seldom catechized, had sons who sought ordination, and drinking and gambling was common among them.[61] Some of their failings he attributed to the Irish climate:

> The weather is so rainy and drowsy continually, that it doth imprint and indent in a man's heart a certain Saturn quality of heaviness, sluggishness, lazyness and perpetual sloth.[62]

As might be expected the situation was not greatly different in the Church of Ireland, as William Bedell found out when in 1629 he became bishop of Kilmore. The primate was James Ussher who came from an Old English Pale family. A scholarly retiring man he wanted true religion and civility to be brought by the established church to all the Irish, if that was possible, but he had all the ingrained suspicions of the Gaelic Irish which were common in the society in which he had been nurtured. He had been the first professor of divinity at Trinity College, but he lacked any great commitment to mission among the people. In Irish religious matters he was far from being a bigot, although he loved theological controversy. He argued, for example, in his

Answer to a Jesuit of 1624 that the Protestant episcopal succession could be traced back to the twelfth century Synod of Kells. As for Roman Catholicism it shared a 'foreign succession' and was theologically wanting because it: 'disalloweth of many chief articles which saints and fathers of the primitive church of Rome did generally hold to be true'.[63] He consulted with Luke Wadding, head of the Irish Franciscan and Ludovisian colleges in Rome, on scholarly matters, and even obtained a royal license in 1631: 'to confer with popish priests, bishops and Jesuits, if it be for the good of the church'.[64]

Ussher recognized that when James was negotiating the Spanish marriage there was little likelihood of the crown encouraging a Protestant mission, and he lacked any personal desire to encourage activities that might upset the recusants and thus the government. Yet he was uneasy when the people were abandoned to the authority of 'popish titulars... exercising a foreign jurisdiction'.[65] Ussher was a strong Calvinist, and he believed: 'toleration involved becoming an accessory to the papal abomination':

> The religion of the papists is superstitious and idolatrous, their faith and doctrine erroneous and heretical; the church in respect of both apostatical. To give them therefore a toleration, or to consent that they freely exercise their religion and profess their faith and doctrine is a grievous sin.[66]

He was appalled when Urban VIII issued a bull calling on the Irish not to take an oath of allegiance to Charles I when he ascended the throne, and he went so far as to call a meeting of Protestant bishops in his Dublin home, and there they brought out a protest against the government's toleration of disloyal recusants.

Ussher had been 'reared in an atmosphere of minimal conformity and of Calvinist doctrine'[67] and, however much he appreciated English support for the maintenance of the Church of Ireland, he wanted religious independence for the establishment of which he was primate. In the Convocation of 1615 he persuaded the Irish prelates not to adopt the Thirty-Nine Articles of the Church of England: 'the majority conceived it more consistent with the character and independence of their national church to frame a new confession of their own'.[68] This reflected the thinking of many churchmen of the Pale who had no difficulty in affirming the pope as the Antichrist, at the same time they taught absolute predestination and ignored episcopal ordination in their Irish Articles. When archbishop Laud and Thomas Wentworth as Lord Deputy later forced the Irish Convocation of 1635 to accept the Thirty-Nine Articles Ussher insisted that there should also be retained subscription to the Irish. Like his ancestors of the Pale, Ussher's instinct was to practice a kind of 'apartheid', when it came to relations with the Gaelic and other Irish who practised their traditional version of the faith. At the same time he had no intention of allowing the Church of Ireland to become a colonial ecclesiastical establishment governed by and for the sake of the English.

When William Bedell first came to Ireland, his appointment as provost of Trinity College, Dublin, was at the urging of Sir Henry Wotton, but it also met with the approval of Ussher who greatly respected his scholarship. What the primate had not counted on was an English churchman coming to Ireland who was intent upon peacemaking, in Bedell's words: 'the worthiest and principallest thing... what the Apostle calls the Ministry of Reconciliation'.[69] Bedell espoused still the viewpoint of Paolo Sarpi, so that while he strongly opposed the authority of the court of Rome he had the utmost charity for the spiritually neglected people of Ireland: 'like sheep without a shepherd, the prey of the sanguinary wolves of Rome'.[70] Almost inevitably Bedell's convictions were to lead him into contention with Ussher who had no desire to engage in direct controversy with the Irish Catholics whatever provocation arose. Ussher was primarily a scholar, rather than an ecclesiastical leader, and so long as the papal agents, or the Irish Catholics left the Church of Ireland in peace he was satisfied. Unfortunately for Ussher Bedell caused tension in Ireland almost from the day he arrived.

Bedell from his Cambridge contacts knew something of the Irish situation before he arrived, and he became convinced that in Ireland he would be of 'better use to my country and to God's church'[71] than he was in his English country parish. His way in Ireland was not to be an easy one, however. When he got to Trinity College he found the Fellows quarrelling among themselves, financial mismanagement of the college treasury, and such a neglect of religion that the eucharist had not been celebrated in the chapel for eleven years. Bedell immediately began to put the college's finances in order, to reorganize and implement the college statutes, and to impress upon both the faculty and the students that the primary task of the college was the promotion of Protestant mission to all the Irish people:

> Nothing being aimed at either for the addition of maintenance or outward splendour to himself or the fellows, but that every fellow should study divinity, and after seven years stay should goe out into some employment in the church.[72]

Bedell knew that if a serious attempt were to be made to bring the reformed faith to the people the Fellows, and anyone who worked among them, would need to learn Irish. He had been told of the translation of the New Testament into Irish by William Daniel in 1602, before he became archbishop of Tuam. Daniel had also translated the Book of Common Prayer into Irish, and Bedell was intent upon making the study of Irish part of the college curriculum so that Fellows and graduates would be: 'the fitter to convert their countreymen, the Irish'.[73] To set example Bedell himself began to learn the language, wrote an Irish primer and he also began the translation of the Old Testament into Irish.[74] He also planned a history of the college, but the statutes were in such great confusion that the bringing of good order among the seventy scholars and sixteen Fellows left him little time for 'leisure as to set up my books, much less to use them'.[75]

Bedell was never to find time for scholarly leisure again for at the age of 59 he was appointed as bishop of Kilmore and Ardagh. There he found the people in a state of physical and spiritual destitution in their thirty-two parishes served by some sixty-six Catholic priests and thirty-two Protestant clergymen. The Church of Ireland was particularly impoverished for previous bishops had alienated church property, giving long leases to wives, sons or relatives, and had looked upon the ecclesiastical lands as 'spoils of a conquering race'. The lesser clergy had their ministrations weakened by the need to hold several livings to give them an income, with accompanying scandal. To set an example to the clergy Bedell divested himself of the diocese of Ardagh, and addressed himself to finding remedies for the evils of non-residence and pluralism. In a long letter to his friend Samuel Ward in Cambridge he described the:

> ... detestable practice of many of our nation who have gotten four, five, or six to eight benefices apiece... which is yet worse maintain no curates unless it be sometimes for two or three livings, by means whereof the popish clergy is double to us in numbers and having the advantage of the toung, of the love of the people, of our extortions upon them, of the very inborne hatred of subdued peoples to their conquerors, they hold them still in blindness and superstition, ourselves being the chieftest impediments of the works that we pretend to set forward.[76]

Bedell's concern for the poor almost immediately led him into conflict with the local Protestant authorities, especially the chancellor of the Kilmore diocese whose courts handled matters of probate, divorce, relief works and education. The Irish Catholics, for whom Bedell also felt responsible, suffered greatly from the rapacious exactions of these officials who imposed civil penalties on those who offended the church courts. His answer to this problem was to take over direction of the courts himself so that their administration would be honest and their sentences just. The result of his reforming efforts was that: 'the rage of Satan and men's malice flew against him, at his very first stirring, though gently, for some reformation'.[77] Bedell also drew upon himself the wrath of the chief justices for opposing an army levy and, more dangerously, he caught the critical eye of Thomas Wentworth who from 1633 to 1640 sought to bring about a 'thorough' reorganization of Irish society, including the Church of Ireland. Such opposition did not deter Bedell, however, who had no intention of tolerating abuses in the Protestant establishment:

> ... its diversion of ecclesiastical resources to rapacious landlords, the

veniality of officials, the weakness of the clergy in number and quality, the failure to provide for services or instruction in the Irish language, and the growth of Presbyterian elements in the north.[78]

Bedell knew that if any kind of evangelism was to be carried out there had to be a new spirit among the clergy, like that shown by the Jesuit Matteo Ricci who was so successful in China.[79] To inspire them he began the habit of regular visitations, including dining with the poorest of them rather than with the local lay magnates, and this caused considerable local resentment. When he held a synod in 1638 to promote diocesan reform his enemies immediately charged him with *Praemunire*. Bedell, however, successfully defended himself with archbishop Laud, and explained what had gone on in the 'Presbyteriall Conventicle of Kilmore',[80] although he never attempted another such gathering. This did not mean that he ceased his reform campaign, and he never let up on his opposition to the exploitation of the people in the Protestant 'consistory courts, vile and mercenary places'.[81]

Whereas Bedell stood up to Laud courageously, he was very disappointed when he became aware of the trouble his reform programme was causing archbishop Ussher. He found that Ussher had no desire to carry out a national mission, for this would have meant a reorganization of the whole church, and for that task he was temperamentally unsuited:

> The truth is, he so gave himself wholly over to the search of the fathers and all antiquity, and to that apostolick work of praying and preaching the word, that he had no time scarse once to think of the discipline of the church, or to regulate anything that was amiss, tho', according to his place and station in the church... God had required it of him, and put it in his power to doe it.[82]

Bedell told Samuel Ward that he had always presumed from the time he came to Ireland that he and the primate were 'of accord', but as time went on he found that there was a difference between himself and Ussher when it came to dealing with the Irish Catholics:

> I kept telling him that I had ever professed here and in England and in Italy that the difference betweene us and the church (or court rather) of Rome were not in fayth (which we had in common) but in certain additions forreine to it, which by corrupt custome were crept in, which he acknowledged.[83]

Ussher's instinctive response as a Palesman to the Gaelic Irish, in particular, was to share the opinion of John Bramhall who became bishop of Derry in 1634: 'the native Irish were a barbarous and degraded people, unworthy and incapable of civilization'.[84] He qualified this opinion when he talked to Bedell, however, and he never showed sympathy for Bedell's critics who dismissed the bishop of Kilmore as: 'a papist, an Arminian, an equivocator, a politician and a traveller into Italy'.[85]

If the learned, judicious, and kindly Ussher had a difficult time to accept Bedell's distinction between the traditional Catholic faith of the Irish people, and the external authority of the 'idolatrous' Roman court which governed 'unchristian Babylon',[86] other Protestant leaders were openly critical of what Bedell was attempting. They noted his toleration of 'popish customs', such as making the sign of the cross, his indifference over where the communion table should be placed in church, and his mystical view of the eucharistic sacrifice. Like Ussher they worried lest religious accommodation for the sake of mission might be spiritually dangerous: 'toleration involved becoming an accessor to the papal abomination and would set religion and the souls of the people to sale'.[87] Equally disquieting had they but known was that when Bedell wrote to his Catholic counterpart in Kilmore he addressed him as 'his reverend and loving brother' who was with the Protestant bishop a member of 'one common Christian religion'.[88]

The Protestant leaders felt uneasy about what Bedell was attempting in terms of ecumenism and evangelicalism, but the Catholics also had their reservations. In the seventeenth century as in eighteenth and nineteenth centuries, there was intense suspicion on the part of Catholic leaders when the Protestant church showed interest in preaching in Irish. It was a clear signal that the kind of 'apartheid' long practiced by the Anglo-Irish, and encouraged by Ussher and other churchmen was about to be abandoned for the sake of a Protestant religious and cultural mission. The Catholic hierarchy wanted no religious controversy if it could be avoided, nor did it want to contend culturally for the allegiance of the people. Bedell, in his quiet way soon showed in Kilmore that he was intent upon bringing the reformed biblically-based faith of the Church of Ireland to the Irish people, and that he wished to promote the mission through the medium of the Irish language.

When he was at Trinity College Bedell had provided for Irish speaking scholars to be instructed in their own language, had arranged for a lecture in Irish, and had Irish prayers said in the chapel on holy days. His successor as Provost, Robert Ussher had carried on this tradition with a directive that a chapter of the Irish testament should be read by a native scholar each day during dinner. As we have noted, Bedell had also begun to supervise a translation of the Old Testament into Irish, at the same time he studied the language intensively.[89] When he was settled in Kilmore he planned that two Catholic scholars, Murtagh King and James Nangle would collaborate with him to complete his translation of the Old Testament into Irish. At the same time he urged each of his clergymen to keep an English school which should be open to all children regardless of their ecclesiastical allegiance. So far as Bedell was concerned 'the sabbath was made for man', and the ecclesiastical divisions tolerated by Canterbury and Rome should not be an excuse to deny the people the opportunity to rid themselves of their ignorance through education. Bedell had no hesitation in using Catholic schoolmasters when no Protestants were available.

In the collective mind of the Protestants of Ireland Bedell became a legend, the model, the paradigm of a bishop whose concern was to bring the Gospel and the blessings of civilization to all his people regardless of their ecclesiastical allegiance. An Englishman, a Puritan, a scholar who kept abreast of the rapidly changing theological world of Cambridge, he was remarkably open-minded for his age, thanks to his time in Venice and his closeness to Paolo Sarpi. He was able to establish an empathy with the Irish Catholics that has been the wonder and the envy of many Irish Protestants ever since his death during the Irish rising of 1641. Generation after generation of Irish Protestant scholars have produced studies of him, and his worth continues to be appreciated, not least among those who would promote biblical studies in Irish. What he sought was the ecumenical ideal which has yet to be realized in Ireland, an 'accommodation' between the rival ecclesiastical systems which would allow the contending churches to serve the Irish peoples and their needs. He had little sympathy for the exactions put upon the people by the secular Protestant administration, as we have seen. Neither had he toleration for what the Roman Catholics of the Counter-Reformation wished to impose upon the people. An abiding conviction in his thought was the difference between traditional Catholicism, and the power-seeking designs of the Court of Rome, which he had first appreciated in his Venetian days in the company of Sarpi:

> He considered the corruptions of that church as effectual cause for enervating the true design of Christianity; and this he gathered not only from speculation but from what he saw and knew during his long abode in Italy.[90]

There is no doubt that the Catholics of Kilmore appreciated greatly the efforts of this reforming prelate. They respected him for his understanding of their culture, language, and all that was good in their traditional expression of the faith. They also had affection for him as the story of his last days as a prisoner of the insurgents of 1641 reveals. When he died his body was borne by a great company of the Sheridans and other local people to the cemetery to be buried. On the way they met a party of the O'Reillys, led by the local sheriff, accompanied by musketeers, the entire gathering intent upon showing their respect to the Protestant bishop who had stayed in Kilmore throughout the rising:

> O'Reilly and those with him applied themselves in most courteous and

condoling language to the bishop's sons, speaking respectfully and comfortably to the living... the sheriff told the bishop's sons that they might use what prayers, or what form of burial they pleased; none would interrupt them. And when all was done, he commanded the musqueteers to give a volley of shot, and so the company departed.[91]

IV   Thomas Wentworth and the Pacification of Ireland

William Bedell's death in 1641 marked not only the end of the earthly life of a saintly man, but also the hope for the development of religious accommodation if not toleration in Ireland. The European wars of religion had finally extended their horror to Ireland, and the relations between Catholics and Protestants in the years after 1641 were to be bloody ones as the Irish found themselves caught up by ruthless external forces which they could neither counsel nor control. The year after Bedell was appointed to Kilmore the Thirty Years War which cost Germany up to half its population was moving to its climax with the entry of Gustavus II Adolphus of Sweden as Protestant champion, astutely supported by cardinal Richelieu of France who feared the growing power of the house of Hapsburg. 1631 witnessed the sack of Magdeburg by the Catholic generals Tilly and Papenheim when most of the population was put to the sword and, except for the cathedral the city was burned. The countryside throughout Germany was ravaged by savage mercenary leaders, Catholic and Protestant alike, the most notorious of them Albrecht von Wallenstein becoming a name to invoke terror in all, until his assassination at the instigation of an Irish colonel named Butler. The pope of the time, Urban VIII, had little authority among the Catholic contestants when he sought to maintain an uneasy neutrality as the division between Spain and France deepened.

By 1630 England was at peace with both France and Spain, but involvement in the political-religious passions of the age was almost inevitable. Charles I took seriously the profound belief in the Divine Right of Kings which he had inherited from his father, and in matters dealing with religion and ecclesiastical affairs he found himself at odds with parliament, whose Calvinist members were sure that their opposition to royal policies also reflected the will of Providence. Because of the king's continuing toleration of Roman Catholic envoys in the queen's entourage the Protestants were convinced that whatever the monarch attempted in church affairs was a portent of a papal inspired or directed plot: 'whosoever shall bring in innovation of religion, or by favour or countenance seek to extend or introduce popery or Arminianism or other opinion disagreeing from the true and orthodox Church, shall be reputed a capital enemy to this kingdom and commonwealth'.[92] Faced with this kind of Calvinist intransigence Charles tried to govern by royal prerogative after dissolving parliament.

Assisting him in government were two powerful individuals, Thomas Wentworth, who in 1640 was made earl of Strafford, and William Laud who became archbishop of Canterbury in 1633. Both men were extremists in their use of force in a policy of 'thorough' to bring the country to heel.

Resistance to the royal rule first appeared in the form of armed opposition in Scotland, where the Protestant spirit had become increasingly uncompromising. Bishops had been resented in the Kirk in both Elizabeth's and James' reigns, and Charles decided that he would force the full episcopal system of England upon the Kirk. This included a Prayer book for Scotland, which the Scots believed to be even more Catholic than the English Book of Common Prayer. It was publicly rejected in a riot in St. Giles cathedral in Edinburgh in 1637 amidst cries that 'the mass is entered amongst us'. In a great public demonstration of loyalty to Scotland and to Presbyterianism the majority of the population signed the Covenant, a pledge to defend the Protestantism of the Kirk. In 1639 Scotland was at war with England. This forced Charles to summon parliament and convocation and when the Scots were not defeated the king had to negotiate with parliament. Strafford was impeached and put to death; Laud was imprisoned to suffer the same fate four years later; and in the Root and Branch Petition, which split the Puritans, the episcopal government of the church was denounced for increasing Romish superstition and ceremonial. A year later parliament's Grand Remonstrance demanded the holding of a synod to which foreign Protestants should be admitted, and for the removal from the church of 'idolatrous and Popish ceremonies introduced into the Church by the command of the bishops'.[93] The next year the bloody Civil War began.

William Laud had usually advised Thomas Wentworth in ecclesiastical affairs but he had less influence over him, apart from issues like the rebuking of Bedell, after Wentworth was sent to Ireland as Lord Deputy in 1633, While the king was having his difficulties with the Puritans in parliament he did not want obstinate opposition to the crown to appear in Ireland, as it did in Scotland, and Wentworth's pro-consular brief was for him to be 'thorough' in establishing order in Ireland in both church and state. He was strongly to persuade the Old English, the Gaelic Irish and the New English to accept a new order which would serve the cause of the king in England. He began by curbing the Irish Puritans whom he forced in convocation to accept the legal formulary of the Church of England, the Thirty–Nine Articles but, as we have noted, James Ussher insisted that the Calvinistic articles of 1615 should also be retained as authoritative in the Church of Ireland. Wentworth also intimidated those 'overmighty subjects' like Richard Boyle, the earl of Cork who had alienated much church property, and in St. Patrick's in Dublin had erected a glorious family tomb: 'in the proper place of the altar... as if it were contrived on purpose to gain the worship and reverence which the chapter and the whole church are bound by special statute to give towards the east.'[94] What Wentworth sought to establish in the Church of Ireland was the same expression of the traditional Catholic faith which Laud was trying to impose in England. In the words of his chaplain, and later bishop of Derry, John Bramhall:

> The Church of England before the reformation and the Church of England after the Reformation are as much the same church as a garden before it is weeded and after it is weeded is the same garden; or a vine, before it is pruned and after it is pruned and freed from the luxuriant branches is one and the same vine.[95]

To the job of tidying up the Church of Ireland administratively and religiously he dedicated his characteristic ruthless contempt of opposition giving: 'strict mandates to my lords the bishops to see the churches repaired, adorned and preserved free from profanation throughout the whole kingdom'.[96]

The result of Wentworth's rule in Ireland between 1633 and 1639 was the establishing of a tyrannical authority which alienated the Catholics and Protestants alike. He bullied landowners and prelates as his courts reviewed their titles to their land, and he sought to increase the royal rent, and to recover tithes and advowsons. He was resolute in maintaining pressure against magnates like the earl of Cork, and he meddled with the finances of the London companies among the northern planters, making many enemies in the process. He offended the Gaelic Irish with plans for plantation in Connaught and Clare, and added to the royal exchequer by heavily fining those who resisted this project. Most importantly of all he built up an Irish army, and by the time the Scots revolt against the crown reached the crisis point this largely Catholic force was assembled, 9000 strong, at Carrickgus ready to be used to defend the monarchy against rebellious Scots, and dissident Puritans in parliament.

Not all that Wentworth attempted was resented by the Irish Protestants, who rejoiced when Christchurch, Dublin, was reformed by having a 'popish tavern' in its vaults removed. They were also pleased when, after the queen suggested a restoration of St. Patrick's Purgatory shrine on Lough Derg, Protestant outrage persuaded Wentworth to tell the queen: 'this devotion was allowed to rest awhile'.[97] Still the Protestants remained deeply suspicious of the policy of 'reducing this kingdom to a conformity with the Church of England', an intention 'deeply set in his majesty's pious and prudent heart',[98] and few of them were other than reluctant to support Wentworth's ecclesiastical policies.

Laud directly intervened in Irish affairs when he looked for a provost at Trinity College who would carry out his High Church reforms, and he found his man in an acquiescent divine from Cambridge, William Chappell. He succeeded the Puritan, Robert Ussher, and immediately on Laud's orders drew up new statutes to attack the Puritans: 'to use the university as an instrument through which the Irish Church might be attached more closely to the High Church party in England'.[99] Senior Fellows from Cambridge who also shared Laud's vision were imposed upon the college to support the new Provost.[100] Chappell so pleased Laud that he was made bishop of Cork, while he was still provost, but in Protestant eyes he was a thorough-going 'papist' who insisted on daily chapels, and the wearing of the surplice on Sundays.[101] The Protestants knew that what could be forced upon Trinity College would sooner or later become the rule for the whole church, and most of them resented greatly the Laudian program to curb Irish Protestant freedom of religious expression.

The part of Ireland where there was the greatest opposition to the Laud and Wentworth reforms was in Ulster, for there the Scots settlers had no intention of accepting Wentworth's reform policies: 'for the better ordering of this poor church which hath thus long laid in the silent dark'.[102] When the Scots swarmed into counties Antrim and Down, in particular, they were often accompanied by their Presbyterian ministers who occupied pulpits within the Church of Ireland:

> On entering upon the ministerial office in Ireland, while they objected to matters of government, and were particularly careful not to be ensnared into an approbation of prelacy, they cheerfully acquiesced in the confession of the Irish Church, which was strictly Calvinistic, and unobjectionable either to Scottish Presbyterians or English Puritans.[103]

Wentworth's chief aide in his harrying of the northern Presbyterians because of their nominal conformity was his chaplain, John Bramhall, bishop of Derry from 1634. An able man with Laud-like zeal, Oliver Cromwell referred to him as 'that Irish Canterbury', and his treatment of the Presbyterians won him great hatred.

Bramhall did not have an easy time for by the age of Wentworth and his Laudian reform programme Presbyterianism was as strongly rooted in Ulster as the Counter-Reformation version of Catholicism was in other parts of Ireland. In the dioceses of Down and Connor Bramhall reported that the Clergy were so resolutely Presbyterian in their sympathies that: 'it would trouble a man to find twelve Prayer Books in all their churches'.[104] In their liturgical practices they did not hesitate to sit on the holy table: 'and receive the sacrament together like good fellows'.[105] Bramhall was determined to put an end to this 'Prescopalian' period of churchmanship, however, and with the aid of Henry Leslie, bishop of Down and Connor, he was able in 1637 to report to Laud that the ringleaders of the nonconformists had been driven out of the church and back to Scotland. There they played a prominent part in the Scots' resistance to Laud's ecclesiastical policies which began that same summer.[106] Little had been accomplished with the departure of the ministers, for Henry Leslie told Wentworth the following year:

> All the puritans in my diocese are confident that the arms raised against the King in Scotland will procure them a liberty to set up their own

discipline here amongst themselves.[107]

Everywhere in the province was to be found: 'the spirit of ecclesiastical antipathy, the most virulent and malevolent expressed, with the utmost acerbity of invective'.[108]

The Protestants of Ireland generally were uneasy and suspicious over Wentworth's religious programmes, which included providing hospitality for Catholic leaders, such as the titular archbishop of Dublin. When at the same time the lord deputy was imposing upon Scottish settlers in Ulster the 'Black Oath', which called for loyalty to king Charles, and an abjuration of any other oath or covenant they might have taken, the Protestants were convinced that Wentworth cared not for 'true religion' but only for exploiting Ireland for the sake of the crown. They no longer saw him as an ecclesiastical reformer, but as a tyrant intent, like cardinal Richelieu in France, in establishing royal autocracy. He was charged by some with joining forces with the Hapsburgs of Austria and Spain, with the intention of suppressing Protestant liberty, to bring upon them a:

> Romish hierarchy of bishops, commissaries, vicars-general, and other
> officials... and to the establishing of a foreign state, and jurisdiction in
> all things ecclesiastical.[109]

The Protestants resented appointment of justices of the peace and high sheriffs who were Catholics; they suspected that Wentworth's policies did not welcome as settlers either English Puritans or Scottish Presbyterians; and they feared the largely Catholic army with its Old English and Gaelic commanders that had been moved into Ulster. When news of the execution of their one-time lord deputy reached Ireland in May, 1641 there was general rejoicing in the Protestant community that the revolution he had attempted, and they had found so threatening, had now come to an end. One of Wentworth's great enemies, whom he had driven out of Ulster, was Sir John Clotworthy. He supported the Covenanters in Scotland, became a member of the Long Parliament, and never let the English Puritans forget what was the most abiding result of Wentworth's policies, the armed and trained body of Catholics in Ireland who were ready to support the king. In one petition to the Long Parliament which Clotworthy presented on behalf of the Ulster Protestants a major grievance was said to be the crown's toleration of popery: 'titular bishops are by them winked at in the exercise of jurisdiction from foreign power'.[110] The Protestants of Ulster feared the kind of military and religious action,which was soon to be visited upon them, long before it happened.

If the Protestants were fearful about a coming holocaust, so were many of the Irish Catholics. They were grateful that Wentworth had never used penal laws against them: a fact that was grimly noted by his Puritan detractors when he was impeached and brought to trial. The Catholics recognized that

Wentworth's Irish policy was based on the hope that a toleration of their culture and their religious practices might one day persuade them to conform. At the same time they knew that friars and other Counter-Reformation agents were spreading rumours about incipient rebellion in Connaught, and were talking of an anti-Protestant crusade where the heretics would be treated as the Moors and Jews had been in Spain.[111] Such talk made most Irish Catholics uneasy for if there was continental interference of any sort their whole situation would change, because neither Wentworth nor Bramhall would have any sympathy for those who supported the: 'papal court that hath ruined the church'.[112] The intelligent, at least, among the Catholic leaders feared the general suffering that would be visited upon Ireland if the conflict that was then devastating Germany was brought into Ireland.

Laud in an appeal for relief of ministers in the Palatinate had tried to ease the ideological tension of the time by removing the phrase 'antichristian yoke' when he referred to the papal supremacy, but for most Protestants in both Ireland and England there was no doubt that the pope was the biblical Antichrist. Neither James Ussher nor William Bedell had any problem with this identification, and when George Abbott, archbishop of Canterbury, died in 1633 he expressed his conviction that the pope was Antichrist even in his will.[113] Ussher attacked a writer who had argued that the Antichrist had not yet come by calling his work 'rotten stuff':

> ... a book neither pious nor learned, written by one wholly savouring of the spirit of Antichrist, and ignorant of the main scope of the Gospel.[114]

Confronted with such passionate anti-papal prejudice on the part of the Protestants in both England and Ireland, and knowing it was shared by the Scots Calvinists, the Catholic Old English and Gaelic Irish shared a growing apprehension over what lay ahead if the papacy managed by any means to drag Ireland into Europe's war of religion.

Bedell's distinction between Catholicism and the court of Rome allowed him to identify the pope with the Antichrist, but it did not lessen his commitment to the bringing of peace and reconciliation between Catholics and Protestants in Ireland. Unfortunately for Christianity as a whole, he was one of the few churchmen in either the Catholic or Protestant churches who sought conciliation while the Thirty Years war on the continent moved into its final phase of bloodshed and irrationality, and religious bigotry became commonplace in both Ireland and Britain. Griffith Williams, who became bishop of Ossory immediately before the rising of 1641, and longed for religious peace, infuriated the Puritans by his writing about the need for spiritual 'meeknesse' in his eirenical *Right Way to the Best Religion* of 1636.[115] Thomas Ram of Ferns and Leighlin endeavoured to win over the recusants to conformity by using only the methods of friendly discussion and argument, but earlier he had signed the Protestation of 1626 opposing the toleration of popery.[116] When he tried to provide education for all the community in his diocese through a school-building programme, he quickly discovered how little his efforts were appreciated. The Roman Catholic clergy threatened excommunication for any parent who allowed their children to attend a Protestant school, and Ram despaired when he was told about the re-baptism of converts from Protestantism carried out by the Catholic clergy. He ended up by nailing up the doors of newly-built Catholic chapels. The experience of well-meaning bishops such as Williams and Ram show how remarkable was the peace-seeking administration of Bedell in his diocese which was never abandoned by him. It made a great impression upon his contemporaries, as we have noted, and thanks to the scholarly work of his son,William Bedell, his chaplain Alexander Clogie, and later writers such as the historian, Gilbert Burnet, his life and work have been remembered by many in Ireland's Protestant community. Even on the level of popular writing reference has been made to Bedell since the time of his death unto the present day; a 'singular fascination' with his life and work maintained.[117]

Chapter IV

Ireland's Wars of Religion

'The Calvinist-Catholic struggle was in one sense the last medieval crusade, in another the first modern war between nation-states.'

Richard Dunn, *Age of Religious Wars*, New York, 1970, p. 4.

I   The Rising of 1641

To watch the banners carried by members of the Orange Order during its marching season in any generation, is to realize how important the Catholic rising of 1641 has been in Protestant folk memory. In any large parade there is almost always some representation of one of the massacres of the time, such as the drowning of Protestants in the river Bann by Catholic soldiers driving women and children into the water. It is religious iconography reflecting the Protestant belief that given the chance the Irish papists would force the whole reformed church community into submission to the authority of the court of Rome. Not every Protestant is an Orangeman, of course, but the banners do demonstrate at the very least an atavistic fear among many Ulstermen that they still need to be on guard against the designs of the Roman Catholic church militant.

The pope at the time of the rising, as we have noted, was Paul V's protegé Urban VIII who intrigued so much in political affairs that the Catholic general Wallenstein spoke seriously of leading an expedition against Rome.[1] By the time of his death the Counter-Reformation papacy was exhausted, ecclesiastically, economically and politically: 'by the death of Urban VIII in 1644 the moment would seem to have passed when Catholicism could have established itself in any depth in the heart of the rising civilization of northern Europe'.[2] The long and bitter ideological crusade against the heretics in Europe had begun to falter as the Peace of Westphalia was to show in 1648 when pope Innocent X could do nothing about the concessions the Hapsburgs were willing to grant to the Protestant powers. From that time the Roman see was to be restricted from interfering in religious matters in Germany, and a papal brief denouncing the terms of Westphalia was universally ignored.

No one in Ireland was aware of the slow demise of Roman authority, and nothing contributed more to the bitterness of warfare in the 1640's than the Protestant reaction to the political meddling of the Counter-Reformation agents who tried to take over the Irish rebellion and use it in the service of the continental struggle against the Protestant heretics. It has been argued that the Catholic continental powers never took seriously the strategic importance of Ireland, the Protestant held bastion on the edge of Europe's religious battlelines, or considered making use of the dissident Catholic population:

> So far as Ireland's strategic importance was concerned, the ambiguities and flexibility of political relationships there rendered it a very slippery stone towards England. The continental powers knew this. And the government in England knew this.[3]

It is true that the crossing of the Irish Sea would be a formidable challenge for Counter-Reformation forces if they did manage to establish themselves in Ireland. Yet they would be reinforced by well-trained Irish Catholics in the north especially, after the disbandment of Wentworth's army, the Scots were unpredictable, civil war was expected by many of the English Puritans, and they worried about royalist forces being reinforced from across the North Channel. The Puritans also knew that in Rome and Madrid were pensioned the descendants of the chieftains who had fled in 1607, and that they would use their influence to ensure that a Catholic rising in Ireland would be strongly supported by Spanish forces. Many Irish Catholic graduates of the continental seminaries were important in continental military circles, some even holding high rank in the Catholic armies, and they would certainly urge support for any Irish rising. They would also make sure that agents kept alive the hatred the Ulster natives felt towards the Protestant planters, their religion and their culture. The Catholic emigrés were dedicated to bringing the Irish into the continental religious wars.

Ultimately what the Roman Catholic zealots could count upon to draw the Irish into the religious wars were the passions of the age, the *zeitgeist* of the seventeenth century, so incomprehensible to most liberal historians. These passions were seldom strictly religious, but sectarian certainties made them ferocious. Count Peter Ernst Mansfeld, a Protestant condottiere led English, French and German troops into the Lower Palatinate in 1621 slaughtering Catholics, and ravaging the land and the people indiscriminately: 'it was difficult to distinguish this "protection" of the Lower Palatinate from its devastation.'[4] The Flemish count Johan Tilly who directed the extirpation of the Protestants in Bohemia, and the sack of Magdeburg, had his army carry images of the Virgin on their standards, and their battle cry was 'Santa Maria'.[5] During Laud's harrying of the Puritans a fanatical Scot, Alexander Leighton, offended the archbishop by calling for a holy war against Spain. His sentence in the Court of High Commission was to have his ears cut off, his nose slit and his cheeks branded, among other punishments.[6] Europe's age of religious warfare was savage:

> Committed church historians avoid the conclusion that the most far reaching, because secularizing outcome of the Reformation and Counter-Reformation... was outburst after outburst of iconoclasm, civil and national war, and the torture and execution of religious opponents on the ground that their opinion was dangerous to society. This was the uncomfortable face of Christianity and historians have therefore tried hard to disconnect the violence from Christianity.[7]

Nowhere was the 'uncomfortable face of Christianity' to be presented more vividly or for so long as in Ireland during, and since, the seventeenth century time of religious struggle.

The Ulster Irish were always concerned with affairs in Scotland and they did not overlook the concessions the Scots won from Charles I from the time they raised their army in 1639. Sir Phelim O'Neill and the other leaders of the Ulster rising which began in the autumn of 1641 had no intention of beginning a religious-political crusade against a heretical Protestant government. At most they wanted to capture the administration under the crown and to: 'slip into the authority previously exercised by the English.'[8] This they believed was possible in Ulster, where Wentworth had effectively disarmed the Scots planters who might otherwise have supported their people across the water: 'so they shall not stir to their own prejudice'.[9] O'Neill, and the other leaders intended to reassure parliament by promising not to 'meddle' with Scots possessions, then—with help from the southern Irish who were to take Dublin—they would eliminate Lisburn and other Protestant strongholds, and negotiate their moderate demands. They wanted an Irish parliament set free from the shackles of Poynings' law—the 'controlling' legislation enacted in the fifteenth century—with full civil and religious rights given to the Catholic population.

In the climate of 1641, however, any such limited revolution was impossible. With the civil war about to break out in Britain, and the Thirty Years War at its bloody climax, it was going to be impossible for the Catholic-Protestant contest in Ireland not to become part of the general European struggle. Rumours soon abounded that: 'a covenanted army under General Lesly would soon come over to extirpate Catholicism in Ulster'.[10] In reaction to such a probability, for the rumour was taken seriously, the conspirators opened negotiations with their kinsmen in the Catholic armies on the continent. Owen Roe O'Neill, a colonel in the Spanish army in the Low Countries, when approached for help in 1641 immediately replied that he would come to Ulster to lead a Catholic army. Within six weeks Ulster was in chaos as Protestants were driven from their land, forfeited estates were reclaimed, and the war was extended to the south. Dublin could not be taken, but savage treatment was visited upon the Protestants everywhere.

The rising of 1641 has been interpreted in many ways by many historians, some dismissing the importance of 'the myth of the Bloody Massacre' as being of limited consequence although acknowledged as: ' a major force in perpetuating flaws in the Anglo-Irish relationship'.[11] Others have viewed it as: 'the gravest event in Irish history, the turning-point on which all later controversies between England and Ireland hinge'.[12] From the standpoint of Irish Protestantism there is no doubt that it was viewed then, as it is now, as much more than a myth. It was indeed a 'turning point' at least in Catholic-Protestant relations in Ireland, a confirmation of the worst fears of the supporters of the reformed churches. Historians still debate the number of victims of the rising but considering the temper of the times, and the deep religious and social division between natives and planters it would be surprising if they were not substantial. There seems little doubt that a very large number of helpless people were savagely treated or put to death. There is enough evidence in the Trinity College 'depositions', evidence taken from survivors after the event, to support the belief that a massacre as shocking as that of St. Bartholomew in France had taken place:

> For all the exaggeration and repetition of rumour in the depositions, there are enough eye-witness accounts of robbery and murders, some times by several deponents describing the same event, to satisfy the most sceptical critic of the depositions.[13]

Regardless of the numbers who died, what was important about the stories of massacre was that they were believed in England. Parliament was shaken when it assembled and heard the news of the atrocities. It was now believed that the 'popish faction' in Ireland was confederate with Spain and France, and that what was sought was not only the take over of Ireland, but an extension of the rebellion to England and Wales, which would put an end to British support for the Dutch and other European Protestant peoples.[14] It was also believed that the king had long intended to make use of the papists: 'wild and savage heathens who were capable of greater barbarities than the fearsome Turk'.[15] Pamphlets warned the populace that the Irish catholics were about to join with their English and Welsh co-religionists in an organized slaughter of Protestants:

> Ireland is not unfitly termed, a back doore into England: and of what dismall portendence it must needs be to you and your nation, to have the pope keeper of the keyes of your back dore, I shall not represent unto you... If you let Ireland goe, the peace and safety of your own land and nation (it is much to be feared) will soone follow after it.[16]

The mood in the Long Parliament following the rising was such that the Puritans were inclined to agree that: 'the conversion of the papists in Ireland was only to be effected by the Bible in one hand, and the sword in the other'.[17]

The planters in Derry had long been expecting some kind of rising,[18] and London knew as early as 1639 from its agents in Madrid that the Irish exiles were plotting an insurrection with hope of support from Spain.[19] Nobody was surprised when Owen Roe O'Neill arrived in July 1642 to take over command of the Catholic forces from Sir Phelim O'Neill. He was very much a Counter-Reformation champion, used to the merciless sectarian fighting of the continent. When he exhorted his troops just before his victory of 5 June, 1646 at Benburb, county Tyrone, he borrowed the war-cry of Count Tilly's hosts:

So let your manhood be seen by your push of pike; and I will engage, if you do so, by God's assistance and the intercession of His blessed mother and all the holy saints in heaven, that the day will be your own. Your word is *Sancta Maria*; and so in the name of the Father, Son and Holy Ghost, advance, and give not fire till you are within picket-length.[20]

O'Neill had been encouraged to come to Ireland by Rome through the recommendation of the Franciscan, Luke Wadding, one time president of the Irish College in Salamanca, then theologian to the Spanish mission in Rome. O'Neill was followed by another condottiere from the Spanish army in Flanders, Thomas Preston. Richelieu promised to discharge all Irish troops in the French army that they might return home, and also assured the rebels of financial assistance. From 1641 there had been no turning back as Ireland was swept into the vortex of Europe's age of religious war:

Important as the acquisition of experienced officers and military supplies was to the rebels, the decisive continental contribution to the war in Ireland was perhaps one of attitude: there was introduced to Ireland an extremist element, at least in religious outlook, which was unfamiliar and unconcerned with the circumstances in which the rebellion had originated, and which was determined to impose upon the war a purpose related to religious preconceptions rather than to Irish realities.[21]

The ferocity that was brought into the conflict made an indelible impression upon Protestant folk memory, like the reported drowning at Portadown of the host of children and poor Protestants who could not be ransomed.[22] Such savagery they believed represented: 'the direful passions of hatred and revenge which the Roman priesthood had for years been fostering in the breast of their people against their Protestant neighbours.'[23] Few Protestants who survived the holocaust would have disagreed with the royalist commander, Sir Henry Tichborne, when he surveyed the fury which the war brought upon the area around Ardee and Dundalk: 'there was little mercy shown in those times'.[24] The Protestants in their turn were merciless in their treatment of the Catholic insurgents who, they were convinced, were fanatically inspired by popish bishops such as Heber MacMahon (Emer Mattheus) who later led the rebel army on the death of Owen Roe O'Neill.[25]

By the time that the Catholic Confederation of Kilkenny came into being in May, 1642, there was no doubt that the recusant bishops and clergy were interpreting the rising in a militantly religious sense. They wanted ambassadors sent to the Catholic kings of France and Spain, as well as the pope, the army was to take the sacrament once a month, and always before a battle. Excommunication was to be the punishment for crimes such as arson, robbery and murder.[26] They also demanded a break with the Protestant monarchy. It seems that the Counter-Reformation zealots had some success with those followers of O'Neill and Preston who had served the Spanish Catholic cause on the continent, and were not 'excommunication proof' as were many of the native Irish. It was said that Preston lost the battle of Dungan Hill in 1647 because he followed the advice of Nicholas French, papal bishop of Ferns.[27] Most of the Catholic laity, however, were primarily concerned with secular matters such as where they stood with regard to the king, and wanted to negotiate with the marquis of Ormond who urged them to serve the royal cause and be content with whatever terms the monarch granted to them.[28] The Old English, in particular, were reluctant rebels, much more concerned with their lands and their social position under the crown than they were with the crusading spirit of the Counter-Reformation.

What held the Confederation of Kilkenny together was the fear of the Puritans of the Long Parliament, but when the long dreaded Protestant reaction took place it began in 1642 with the coming of a Scots army under Robert Monro, who led 2,500 troops, many of them veterans of the savage continental wars. From Carrickfergus they moved south, carrying out a massacre of Catholics on Islandmagee, killing some 700 country people in their plundering of Newry, and raiding as far south as Westmeath and Longford.[29] Catholic fears magnified when parliament's Adventurers' Act declared forfeit the estates of leading rebels, and the king was denied the right to grant pardon to them. It was abundantly clear to the Old English and Gaelic lords what faced them if the king lost his struggle with parliament. It was not easy for the Old English to identify themselves with their traditional enemies, however, and they looked askance at the actions of the O'Neill, Magennis, MacMahon and Maguire septs who had little appreciation of civility. They were appalled when the O'Neills followed the example of their tribal leader Shane of Elizabeth's time and burned Armagh again, defending their barbarity by saying it was in retaliation for excesses committed by the Scots:

> The cathedral with its steeple and with its bells, organ and glass
> windows, and the whole city with the fine library, with all the learned

books of the English on divinity, logic and philosophy. Many lives were also taken by the Irish in revenge for Monro's severities.[30]

The 'reprisal' morality of the European wars of religion had arrived in Ireland with a vengeance.

The Irish recusants' point of no return came when Charles I, having arranged a Cessation of Arms in Ireland, began to bring Irish troops into England. The Puritans had long believed that Henrietta Maria and her Catholic entourage had somehow been responsible for the 1641 rising, as part of a papal directed conspiracy, and that the weak-willed king had been won over to support of the venture. There was actually some evidence to suggest that the king was privy to plans for a *coup d'état* in Dublin in the spring of 1641,[31] and if this was suspected by the Catholics it was easily believed by the Puritans in parliament. Some of the army that were brought over from Ireland were English, but it was believed that: 'fully half the men aboard the crown's fleet were Irish'.[32] The Kilkenny rebels for their part did not hesitate to refer to themselves as 'queen's men', and even moderate Protestants began to believe that the king was somehow involved in a Catholic plot.[33] The Irish lords by 1643 knew that if parliament won its battle with the crown they would pay a heavy price for being Catholic, regardless of what part they had taken in the rising.

Shortly before Urban VIII died in 1644 he sent an Oratorian, Piero Francesco Scarampi, to Ireland who urged the Catholics at Kilkenny to ignore the Cessation of Arms and to drive the Scots out of Ulster. He also persuaded them to allow recruiting agents for the Spanish army to operate in Ireland, and when this was agreed to France made a similar demand. Scarampi's attempt to take over the Irish rebellion and to make it part of the Counter-Reformation crusade was tolerated for it was authorized by a papal brief, and he brought with him both financial aid and arms and ammunition. The Catholics gave him a hearing also because shortly after the 1643 Cessation of Arms, to which they had agreed, the English parliamentarians had signed the Solemn League and Covenant, promising to make the religions of England, Scotland and Ireland as nearly uniform as possible, and to stamp out popery and prelacy. The following year, when Scarampi arrived, the Covenant was also brought to Ulster where the Protestants still had power in places like Londonderry and Coleraine. By this time Oliver Cromwell was emerging as the leading military figure in the parliamentary army, and the Catholics of Ireland knew that to survive at all they would need, however reluctantly, to negotiate for further support from the continental Catholic powers.

The Irish soldiers sent to help Charles were defeated at the battle of Nantwich, and early in 1645 the Irish found themselves negotiating with the crown as well as the papacy, with Charles willing to make great concessions in return for military support.[34] It was at this time that Scarampi's mission was reinforced by the arrival of a papal nuncio, Giovanni Rinuccini, bishop of

Fermo, who was intent upon persuading the confederates to serve the papal rather than the royal cause. Rinuccini's commission gave him almost unlimited ecclesiastical authority, and his first move was to ensure that the clergy generally were willing to help him instill among the confederates the kind of religious fervour so often found in the continental Catholic armies. Ireland was once more to become a protectorate of the papacy, through a submission to the cause that Rinuccini was commanding them to serve:

> ... to restore and re-establish the public exercise of the catholic religion in the island of Ireland, and further to lead her people, if not as tributaries to the Holy See such as they were five centuries ago, to subject themselves to the mild yoke of the pontiff, at least in all spiritual affairs.[35]

Rinuccini was not a successful ambassador because, however determined and zealous he was, the Irish had no desire to give unqualified support to the cause served by 'the Italian bishop', Ireland's 'unbidden guest'. Like Scarampi he brought with him a large quantity of arms, as well as money from Rome and France, but few of the confederates were interested in a continental style crusade against the Protestants. The supreme council of the confederates generally supported the thinking of one Catholic leader who said:

> He would neither contest with his prince, or lose himself a foot of his estate for all the mitres in Ireland: that it was indifferent for him to have mass with solemnity in Christ or St. Patrick's church, as privately by his bedside.[36]

Even the Catholic bishops were divided over the church surrendering itself to Roman authority (Rinuccini appointed ten new bishops in 1647 alone)[37] and most of them appeared content to settle for the religious toleration they had known under Henry VIII and Elizabeth. In doing so they shared the attitude of most of the Old English whom Rinuccini and the Gaelic Irish described: 'as Henrican or Elizabethan Protestants rather than real Irish Catholics'.[38]

It is interesting to contrast the opinion of Rinuccini and the Gaelic Irish about the Old English among the Kilkenny Confederates with the hind-sight view of some latter-day Catholic historians:

> The Old English in general developed a new sense of identity with Catholic Europe, especially with France. They spoke of a 'new plantation in religion', a 'new civility', much as their forefathers had had their hopes of a 'new civility' in the very different circumstances of the 1540's. Tridentine Catholicism had been implanted in Ireland, even if it did have to adapt somewhat to circumstances there.[39]

From the standpoint of Rinuccini the 'circumstances' indicated an almost total rejection of his policies by the Old English, and a decided reluctance on the part of the confederates to shift their focus from British affairs to the large European scene of sectarian conflict. Usually the tactic of historians who think in terms of ultramontane inevitability is to glide over the results of the Rinuccini mission, for the evidence suggests that only the Gaelic Irish fully welcomed the papal nuncio with his wide-ranging powers to bring the Irish back to the Roman obedience.

Hostility against the nuncio came into the open when he held a synod at Waterford to denounce those who sought to negotiate with Ormond, the royalist commander. He announced he would excommunicate any who sought conciliation, and this brought him into head-on confrontation with the Old English:

> A few days after my arrival in Kilkenny some lawyers inquired from Father Scarampi if I were going to erect a tribunal. When he said yes, they replied that they would not put up with it by any means... In the public assembly Viscount Muskerry said that the day of my arrival was a fatal one for the country; in short they have shown in every action that they cannot endure the authority of the pope; they are even not ashamed to say in private and in print that his succours were empty hopes, vanity and vexation.[40]

Where Rinuccini had support was among those who followed Owen Roe O'Neill, whose standing was high after his victory over Robert Monro at Benburb, and those who served in the forces of Thomas Preston. Both these military leaders had long served in the Spanish army on the continent and it was their troops who thought in terms of religious-political crusade.

The Old English and many of the Gaelic Irish leaders were hesitant about identifying with the Counter-Reformation powers for practical as well as ideological reasons. The aged Innocent X celebrated a *Te Deum* in S. Maria Maggiore when news reached Rome about the victory at Benburb. He was not a pope of resolution, however, and was dominated by his sister-in-law Donna Olimpia Maidalchini, a venial woman of insatiable ambition and rapacity. Innocent's authority as we have noted, was ignored at the Treaty of Westphalia, which brought the terrible Thirty Years War to an end, and he had little influence in Spain which was preoccupied with revolts in Portugal, Naples and Catalonia. His influence was even less in France where cardinal Mazarin carried on Richelieu's policy of building up royal absolutism. There was little likelihood of Innocent X maintaining his authority among the continental Catholic powers whose appetite for religious crusade had ended with the Treaty of Westphalia, and many of the Catholic people in Ireland knew this. Certainly most of the confederate leaders in Ireland realized that they were on their own when they dealt with the Puritans in the English parliament and anticipated the fury that was to be unleashed upon them, sooner or later, after the events of 1641.

Yet Rinuccini, O'Neill and Preston still thought in terms of an age that was passing, and in September 1646 they deposed and imprisoned the Irish leaders at Kilkenny, to set up the nuncio as president of a new supreme council. When he carried out his excommunication threat, and laid towns under interdict, the alliance of confederates began to disintegrate. Their military commanders would not campaign together, they suffered defeats in the field, and shortly before Rinuccini finally left Ireland in February, 1649 he expressed his despair over the Anglo-Irish who clearly wanted to accept the Anglican Reformation settlement:

> I have now only to lament that at this moment the Catholic Confederation is under the power of a heretic (Ormonde); that Munster is in the possession of a Calvinist (Inchiquin) and that the Protestant bishops and parish priests are already preparing to take possession of the ecclesiastical income.[41]

As for the Irish Catholic people, Rinuccini had no high opinion of them, and considered that they lacked the moral fibre which was necessary for them to serve the Counter-Reformation crusade he wanted to initiate:

> This nation, perhaps more than any other in Europe are negligent by nature of all that might with industry and activity might improve them... whence we find neither in ecclesiastical nor in secular affairs any solicitude or extraordinary diligence.[42]

The only place that Rinuccini could discover the latent zeal that he was looking for was among the recusants in Ulster who were inflamed by the excesses of the Scots. Of them he said, grudgingly, they were: 'barbarous enough by nature, although good catholics'.[43]

It was in Ulster that the sectarian divisions of the seventeenth century were never laid to rest. The 'good catholics' in Ulster that Rinuccini referred to were reacting in many cases to atrocities carried out by Scots who served with the Catholic MacDonnells—but there was no confusion in the folk memory of the Ulster Protestants over which people had visited the horrors of 1641 upon them. To the Protestants that protracted sectarian slaughter was on the level of the worst atrocities carried out by the Catholic forces in France and Germany. When direction of the Catholic forces was taken over by the Spanish general Owen Roe O'Neill, and the papal nuncio Rinuccini, the sinister hand of Rome behind the slaughter was clearly revealed to them. Just as Ulster Catholics nurse their mythology of the penal laws of the eighteenth century so in Ulster the Protestants have never forgotten the rising of 1641:

> Here if anywhere the mentality of siege was born, as the warning

bonfires blazed from hilltop to hilltop, and beating drums summoned men to the defence of castles and wall towns crowded with refugees.[44]

It was indeed out of this experience of 'siege' following the rising of 1641 that the characteristic Protestantism of Ulster came into being. When the Scots army of Robert Monro appeared to deliver the Protestants many of them saw the arrival of his troops as an act of Providence. Among them were Presbyterian chaplains and officer-elders, and it was from the worship organized by these seventeenth century religious commissars that there came into being the presbytery at Carrickfergus in 1642: 'a little appearance of a formed church in the country'.[45] This small beginning of organized Ulster Presbyterianism was soon reinforced by Presbyterian clergy who earlier had been driven out of Ireland by Wentworth. Most of these men were supporters of the Solemn League and Covenant which the Scottish Assembly had approved, as had the English Puritans in their parliament. Their theology was embodied in the Westminster Confession of Faith of 1643. It identified the pope as the Antichrist,[46] and the convictions of the covenanters reflected well the prevailing thought of the Ulster Protestants and their Scots brethren across the water:

> The Covenanters stood for the Reformation (against Rome), Calvinism (against Arminianism), Presbyterianism (against prelacy), Constitutionalism (against tyranny), Scottish independence (against English interference), and Puritanism in morals, art and everything (against the Devil).[47]

The Ulster Scots were an assertive people who seemed at times to dislike English churchmen almost as much as they did the papists. John Milton expressed the Puritan view of them when he dismissed them as: 'the blockish presbyters of Clandeboye... unhallowed priestlings... ingrateful and treacherous guests'.[48] They had little use for the Puritans in parliament who departed from the Solemn League and Covenant, nor did they like the royalists who 'combined themselves with papists and other notorious malignants'. The political results of the Ulster Scots intransigence was very confusing when they refused to help General George Monck who had taken over the Protestant forces after Monro was defeated at Benburb. This drove the parliamentarians to seek aid from the native Irish:

> The complexities and paradoxes of this period of Ulster history reach their climax when the city of Derry is besieged by Presbyterian forces and defended by Coote, the parliamentary commander, assisted by Owen Roe O'Neill.[49]

Yet the Ulster Scots had to be reckoned with for during this time of chaos an increasing number of new settlers came over from Scotland; then as now, the Scottish people seemed to be the only ones who had sympathy for the Protestants of Ulster.

The Ulster Protestant community arose out of the ashes of 1641 and at the heart of its self-awareness was and is an abiding suspicion of the designs of Rome; the fear that papal religious and cultural imperialism would be extended at their expense. At the mid-point of the seventeenth century Ulster Protestants found themselves at war with the native Irish, and at odds with the Anglo-Irish, and with the English parliamentarians. Though the community was shocked by the regicide of Charles I it had been estranged from the crown for a long time. The Ulster Protestants had few friends:

> It is to that period of peril, suffering, and isolation that we may look for an explanation of much of the neighbourliness, the communal self-sufficiency, the pride, the carelessness of outside opinion and the stubborn self-will that have distinguished Ulster people ever since.[50]

II   Cromwell's Irish Protectorate

The folk memory of the massacres of 1641 and Catholic sectarian savagery was mostly an Ulster phenomenon:

> Many attempts were made during the insurrection to persuade the Protestants to forsake their religion, the principal argument used being that no one but a Roman Catholic should ever possess a foot of land in Ireland again... It was reported that a Fermanagh priest had reconciled to the Church of Rome between forty and fifty Protestants, and that therefore, finding them 'in a good faith' he and others cut all their throats lest they should return to their heresy again.[51]

The evidence suggests that the atrocities varied greatly from district to district and, in the walled towns of the south many Protestant clergy carried on their duties without serious interruption: 'Robert Browne officiated at Fermoy from 1641 to 1663, and there must have been others who were able to do the same'.[52] Only a minority of the recusants wanted to respond to the Rinuccini and Owen Roe O'Neill call for crusade: 'for the extirpation of heresy'. The Protestant bishops seemed to have no difficulty escaping. Ussher was in England buying books when the rising took place, and he never returned. John Bramhall of Derry left Ulster when the Scots army arrived, yet he returned briefly in 1648 before going into exile on the continent until the Restoration. One of the last to depart was John Leslie of Raphoe, who carried out a spirited defence of his episcopal palace until he was forced to flee. William Bedell, as we have noted, escaped maltreatment when he remained at his post. His apostolate was recognized by his captors at the time of his burial:

> They gave him a volley of shot and said: *Requiescat in pace ultimus Anglorum*! For they had told him at their first rising, that he should be the last English man that should be put out of Ireland; because he was styled *ultimus et optimus episcorum* by men of understanding.[53]

The absence of open and wide-spread religious tension at this time probably reflect the influence of the crown policies as they had been implemented under Wentworth. There was certainly to be a forceful administration of political affairs in Ireland, but there also was to be a widespread toleration of the religious life of the people. Even during the time Rinuccini was in the country religious accommodation was sought, and by the time the fanatical nuncio had left his views and those of the confederates 'had reached the stage of mutual incomprehension'.[54] Yet the Old English, as well as the Gaelic Irish knew that this time of relative religious peace would pass when the victorious parliamentarians would come from England with their armed might. They would come as 'the army of the Lord', seeking vengeance for the atrocities of 1641, and they would be draconian in their treatment of any who in any way supported the Catholic cause: 'the day of battle would show God's wishes, and God's will would be done by the soldiers'.[55] The time of religious concession was about to pass:

> The 20,000 strong parliamentary army which assembled in Dublin under the command of Oliver Cromwell on 15 August, 1649, was possibly the best fighting unit in all of Europe at this time; it was fully equipped with the most advanced weaponry and... more to the point the morale of the army was extra-ordinarily high because of its recent victory in England, and the officers and men were of one mind with their commander on what their purpose in Ireland should be.[56]

Before this army sailed for Ireland the ringleaders of those who objected to the expedition, by arguing that the 1641 rising was a justified response of a subdued people to their oppressors, had been put to death.[57] When Cromwell first landed he told the Dublin populace in a speech near College Green that he was called to them by Divine Providence, to restore the 'bleeding heart of Ireland to its former happiness and tranquillity'.[58] How he went about this task has never been forgotten by Ireland's Catholics. In their memory it is remembered with the same bitterness with which the Protestants recall the events of 1641.

As judicious a historian as W.E.H. Lecky has pointed out that Cromwell forbade the plundering by the army that was common in the age, and that his troops were well disciplined. Others have indicated that as late as the time of Wellington's campaign in the Peninsular War military custom dictated the sacking of a besieged town that refused surrender. Yet it is not easy to justify the savagery of the sieges of Drogheda and Wexford: 'the massacres that accompanied them deserve to be ranked with the most atrocious exploits of Tilly or Wallenstein'.[59] At least half the garrison in Drogheda were English Catholics, who could not possibly have taken part in the 1641 rising, but most of the inhabitants perished at the hands of the Puritan soldiers delivering the chastisement of the Almighty. Cromwell's excuse for this terror tactic was the one to be used in the modern day for the bombings of Hamburg, Dresden or Hiroshima:

> I am persuaded that this is a righteous judgment of God upon these barbarous wretches who have imbrued their hands in so much innocent blood, and that it will tend to prevent the effusion of blood for the future, which are satisfactory grounds to such actions, which otherwise could not but work remorse and regret.[60]

Following the sacking of Drogheda and Wexford other royalist strongholds were subdued in the south, crops were destroyed to encourage submission, and bubonic plague ravaged the countryside. When the war ended at last in 1652 there was little sign of 'happiness and tranquillity' in the 'bleeding nation of Ireland'. Sir William Petty, physician to the English forces, estimated that a third of the population perished at this time, over an eleven year period, from the sword, famine and plague. All the horror of Europe's age of religious warfare, with its specious special pleading for justification, was now visited upon poor Ireland:

> The name of Cromwell even now acts as a spell upon the Irish mind, and has a powerful and living influence in sustaining the hatred of England and Protestantism. The massacre of Drogheda acquired a deeper horror and a special significance from the saintly professions and the religious phraseology of its perpetrators.[61]

From the Protestant standpoint the most that can be said on behalf of the Cromwellian subjugation of Ireland is that it was no more savage than other exercises of a similar nature at that time. Cromwell viewed himself as one of the Protestant champions of Europe, the ally of those who opposed the papal authority, and he held up a commercial treaty with the French when he heard that French troops, including some Irish, had taken part in a massacre of Waldensian Protestants in Piedmont in 1655. He was so enraged by the sufferings of the Waldenses (Vaudois), which were probably more prolonged and genocidal than the suffering imposed on Ireland, that he threatened to use the navy against the French. This persuaded cardinal Mazarin to intervene with the duke of Savoy who was exterminating the Piedmont Protestants, but the program of genocide went on for thirty years.[62]

Cromwell left Ireland in 1650, never to return again, leaving the administration of the conquered island to the rapacity of the army and various adventurers who flocked there. He was never happy with the handling of the Irish situation, and he did pay attention to critics such as Vincent Gookin of Kinsale, a friend of William Petty who deplored the treatment of the people:

> Five parts of six of the whole nation are destroyed, and after so sharp an execution is it not time a length to find a retreat?... Justice? wherefore is justice invoked against them, was it not for cruelty? God has avenged it, let others take heed now they become guilty, especially they that avenge it.[63]

Protests such as this persuaded Cromwell to modify transplantation and even to have second thoughts about a massive new plantation, or a radical policy of forcing an anglicized Protestant civility or religious settlement upon the people. What the Lord Protector finally settled for in Ireland was not much different from the traditional Tudor policy of an earlier time: so long as the Catholics kept out of politics they were for the most part ignored. The erosion of power of the Catholic landlords who had been patrons of the church hurt the Catholic ecclesiastical structure, as did the execution of about a hundred priests, and the exiling of another thousand. Some of the exiles soon returned, however, and the harrying of the priests was not consistent:

> If a comparison with contemporary Bohemia can be sustained... Ireland experienced no evangelisation drive similar to that promoted by the Habsburg state and the Catholic church in downtrodden Bohemia, and the opportunity was lost in Ireland to bring the mass of the native people to conform with the requirements of the state in matters religious.[64]

Cromwell had no use for popery in any form, but as an Independent he shared with his son Henry, who governed Ireland for him, a reluctance to impose a religious settlement upon individuals who conscientiously objected to what was offered to them by the government. The Lord Protector refused to countenance an episcopal church in Ireland, and the Church of Ireland was denied use of the Book of Common Prayer. On the other hand each congregation could choose its pastor and form of Protestant worship, and there was no close inquiry when traditional churchmanship was followed. Similarly with the Presbyterians of Ulster, of whom Cromwell was always suspicious, ideas of transplanting some of them to Tipperary were dropped;[65] meetings of Presbyterians as well as Independents in the army were tolerated; and there was even allowed a new migration of ministers into Ulster:

Though there were not above twenty-four ministers planted belonging
to the presbytery in the year 1653, yet they had multiplied to near
eighty within a few years thereafter; even in the sight and to the
angering of their adversaries on all hands.[66]

Some five thousand foot and nearly half as many horse were stationed in Ulster
when England was at war with Catholic Spain from 1656 until 1659, and
because there was a common enemy to guard against, tensions soon eased
between the Independents and the Presbyterians in the army.

These were the years when the Catholics were often obliged to worship at
mass rocks, when there was a sporadic hunting of priests, and some forced
deportation of people to the Barbados and other New World colonies, but Henry
Cromwell found that a total domination of the population was impossible. He
continued hunting the Tories, or bandits, who hid in the hills and were supplied
with arms by French and Spanish ships which also brought in priests, but he
thought little of petty persecutions such as an oath of abjuration of catholic
doctrines which was demanded of the recusants: 'the great engine by which the
popish clergy stir up the people, and whereby they move foreign states to their
assistance':

I wish this extreme course had not been so suddenly taken, coming like
a thunderclap upon them. I wish the oath for the present had provided
(though in severest manner) for their renouncing all foreign jurisdiction;
and as for other doctrinal matters, that some means had been first used
to have informed their judgments with ordinary smaller penalties as
former experience has found effectual.[67]

Even for Henry Cromwell, with so much power at his disposal, when it came to
finding a workable religious policy for Ireland his answer was not much different
from that of previous English governors: the religion of the people was to be
tolerated, but not the political and ecclesiastical machinations of the Roman
court.

The Presbyterians of Ulster were not pleased about Henry's solution to the
recusant problem. In 1649 the Presbytery in Belfast had published a manifesto
attacking the Independents for their ambiguous support of the Solemn League
and Covenant, and their ideal of 'a universal toleration of all religions'. This
was too much for John Milton, then Secretary of the Lord Protector, and the
great champion of civil and religious freedom. Answering the charge that the
government had not tried to extirpate prelacy and popery, as the Covenant
demanded, Milton, as we have noted, poured his scorn on these religious
rigorists who wanted a persecution of the recusants:

... nor doth the Covenant in any way engage us to extirpate or prosecute the men, but the heresies and errors in them, which we tell these divines and the rest that understand not, belongs chiefly to their own functions in the diligent preaching and insisting on sound doctrine, in the confuting—not railing down —encountering errors, both in public and private conference, and by the power of truth—not a persecution.[68]

It is difficult, in spite of John Milton, to argue that any true freedom of conscience was tolerated during the Commonwealth: 'but only a limited freedom for those whose religion did not inconvenience the objectives of the government'.[69] This was shown by the government's treatment of the Quakers, for George Fox and his followers presented it with a dilemma over how it might satisfy the conscience of those difficult people. The Quakers were also a problem in Ireland where they sought converts in the army, especially in the Limerick area. Henry Cromwell banished some back to England, but others came over later to plead the Quaker cause. Because he thought them a threat to civil order their sufferings did not come to an end, but there is no doubt that the sanctity of the individual conscience was of concern to the Cromwells and the other Independents. Fear of the external threat of Roman, Spanish and French power in most cases denied toleration to the Catholics, especially in the 1652–1656 period, when persecution of continental Protestants infuriated the Puritans, and it is little to be wondered that in Irish Catholic memory the oppression by the Cromwellians has never been forgotten. Yet the French ambassador could comment with amazement that English Catholics were allowed freedom to celebrate mass in private,[70] while in Ireland the vicar-general of Dublin was sentenced to death for murder, then released to go into exile, and finally was allowed to return as archbishop of Armagh.[71] Anomalies like this, however, never mitigated the Irish Catholic remembrance of Cromwell and his Puritans as the cruellest of all the English invaders.

III   Restoration and Catholic Resurgence

Most English and Irish Protestants joined in the loathing which the Irish recusants had for the Puritan protectorate. The English Protestants had detested the period of religious totalitarianism which they had experienced under Mary Tudor, and to a similar degree they never forgot the bleak life imposed upon them during the Commonwealth. Few mourned in either England or Ireland when Oliver Cromwell died in 1659, Henry Cromwell returned to England, and it was clear that the rule of the 'saints' had come to an end. Richard Cromwell succeeded his father briefly, but nobody wanted a continuation of the rule of the: 'anabaptists and persons of like fanatic spirits'.[72] When Charles II came to the throne in 1660 almost every faction gave a sigh of relief in both England and

Ireland.

Before he left his place of exile in Holland, Charles promised in the Declaration of Breda as much religious liberty as would be possible: 'a liberty to tender consciences'.[73] The new monarch had many faults, but: 'his own inclination was to forgive and forget all the treasons and betrayals and rebellions'.[74] The duke of Ormond was appointed viceroy in Ireland to begin his first term in this position from 1662–1669 (he returned again in 1677–1685). He was considered to be hostile to the Catholics during the 1660's, but his bias did not represent government policy. One of his successors, John Robartes was thought to be pro-Presbyterian, while another John Berkeley raised Protestant suspicions when he clearly favoured the Roman Catholic clergy. Ireland was radically divided on religious lines by 1660, and the majority of the population took no pleasure in the re-establishment of the Church of Ireland while: 'papists, presbyterians, independents, anabaptists and quakers were not to be allowed "unlawful assemblies"'.[75]

The new established church was fortunate to have as its first primate John Bramhall, who was one of the eight bishops who survived the Commonwealth period. He worked closely with the state to fill up the episcopal bench with mostly English bishops, and he strove to recover church lands which had been impropriated by the laity during the long years of warfare. Very much a high churchman Bramhall affirmed the catholicity of both the Church of England and the Church of Ireland. In his *Just Vindication of the Church of England from the Unjust Aspersion of Criminal Schism*, he argued that what separated the ecclesiastical bodies was the papal system of government:

> It was not we but the Court of Rome itself that first separated England
> from the Church of Rome, by their unjust censures, excommunications
> and interdictions.[76]

The Church of Ireland, like her sister church in England, as we have noted, was the same church as it was before the Reformation but in a reformed state: 'a vine, before it is pruned and after it is pruned and freed from luxurious branches, is one and the same vine'.[77] But the Roman church since the Council of Trent, in particular, was not a pure Christian church: 'it is your new Roman creed that hath ruined the faith; it is your papal court that hath ruined the church.'[78] Bramhall never at this time identified the pope with 'that great Antichrist',[79] but he granted no authority religious or ecclesiastical to the Church of Rome.

It was not only Bramhall who engaged in the religious ideological debate of the age. James Ussher in his 1641 work, *Reduction of Episcopacy unto the Form of Synodical Government* had presented an ecclesiological viewpoint that had won even the respect of the forbearing Puritan divine, Richard Baxter.[80] Such a blurring of differences between church systems did not suit the Restoration period, however. When Bramhall died in 1663, worn out by his labours, his funeral sermon was preached by Jeremy Taylor the immensely learned bishop of Down. Taylor is best known for his devotional works, such as his *Holy Living and Holy Dying*, but he was also a considerable polemicist. Early in his life he had pleaded the cause of religious toleration in his 1647 treatise, *Liberty of Prophesying*, but that was before he had to deal with the Ulster Presbyterians. When he first encountered them they told him bluntly that theirs was a divinely appointed system of church government, and they needed no other. They wanted an end to episcopacy, wished for universal subscription to the Solemn League and Covenant, and a radical reordering of the traditional forms and rituals of the Church of Ireland. His answer to their intransigence was to expel thirty-six Presbyterians who had occupied church parishes in his diocese. He also dealt severely with the Quakers. As for the recusants, his 1664 work, *Dissuasive from Popery* was a powerful defence of the Church of Ireland as a reformed episcopal body. He had no use for the Romanists and their court which by 'defining the church to be an infallible judge... usurped an empire over consciences'.[81]

Unfortunately for the Church of Ireland at this time, when the various religious bodies were seeking for more than mere toleration, most of the bishops were not of the calibre of the strong willed Bramhall, or the intellectual Taylor. The primate from 1663 until 1678 was James Margetson a gentle and conciliatory Yorkshireman whose chief interest was in rebuilding Armagh cathedral which Phelim O'Neill's troops had burned in 1641. He sought conciliation with both the recusants and with the Presbyterians, though he demanded of the latter that they must abandon the Solemn League and Covenant. His attempt to pacify the Catholics was not ill-timed for in 1666 a synod was held in Dublin in which the recusant nobility and gentry indicated they were willing to sign a loyal 'remonstrance'. The overwhelming mass of priests and friars refused to sign it, however, for although the penal laws against the Catholics were in practical abeyance and the viceroy, Lord Berkeley, openly favoured the titular archbishop of Dublin, Peter Talbot, the Roman hierarchy wanted more than mere toleration. The brother of the archbishop, who dominated the Irish government, was Richard Talbot earl of Tyrconnell, and everywhere recusant influence was increasing in the administration. By the letter of the law it was a criminal offence for a priest to say mass, or for a layman to hear it. All recusants, in theory, were subject to a fine for not attending the services of the Church of Ireland. In reality, however, William Petty and others noted that during the reign of Charles II the exercise of Catholic functions was very seldom interfered with: 'the papists lived happily. There was a liberty of conscience by connivance, though not by law'.[82]

As might have been expected the gentle Margetson had his trouble with the northern Presbyterians who took advantage of his lack of resolve. The year he became primate there was a Presbyterian plot involving Colonel Thomas Blood, who later attempted to steal the crown jewels, and his brother-in-law, William

Lecky, a Presbyterian minister. The conspirators wanted to seize Dublin Castle and the Lord Lieutenant, and to reassert a truly Protestant government. Their coup sought to bring about:

> ... an overturning of the state of bishops and rectifying the civil government, and restraining the papists from that great liberty and countenance they had enjoyed, and furthermore securing a liberty of conscience to themselves as they had enjoyed in Cromwell's time.[83]

The plot failed, Lecky was caught and executed, the rest fled to Scotland, but Margetson was shaken by the event. Radical Scots Covenanters, driven out of their homeland, were settling in Ulster to: 'strangely pervert the people',[84] and before he died Margetson was as wary as Jeremy Taylor had been about the Ulster Presbyterians:

> As long as those ministers are permitted amongst us there shall be a perpetual seminary of schism and discontent... they are looked on as earnest and zealous parties against the government.[85]

There was during the reign of Charles II little threat from the Independents, however, for most of their ministers had fled, and there were left only one or two congregations in Dublin and Munster.[86]

The Ulster Presbyterians were an anxious people as events in England and Scotland indicated to them that the king was not a strong supporter of Protestantism. The Presbyterians had been driven out of the established church by the series of enactments known as the Clarendon Code, the Covenanters had been crushed when they attempted to revolt in Scotland, and there were many indications that Charles II was, like his father, falling under the influence of papists. His mother had been a Roman Catholic, he himself married Catherine of Braganza, daughter of the king of Portugal, and by 1670 Charles had signed with parliamentary approval the Treaty of Dover, promising to support Louis XIV of France in his wars. A secret provision of the treaty was the promise that both Charles and his brother, James, Duke of York, would openly join the Church of Rome when it was expedient. James at once professed his change of religious allegiance. When, in 1672, Charles issued a Declaration of Indulgence, freeing both nonconformist Protestants and Roman Catholics from restrictions, the Presbyterians knew that the recusants gained far more from this than they did. At the same time they gladly accepted the royal bounty, the *regium donum*, as a bribe to buy their peace. It also gave them establishment status of a sort: in the presbytery of Antrim there was reference to their body being 'ye church off Ireland'.[87]

In many ways the Presbyterians were stronger at this time than was the established church. Margetson's weak primacy was followed by that of Michael

Boyle who also acted as lord chancellor and devoted himself to secular affairs and self-aggrandisement rather than building up the fabric of the church which had deteriorated greatly during the war years. When the Restoration service had been held in St. Patrick's cathedral in Dublin in 1661 there was a real danger of the roof falling upon the heads of the newly consecrated bishops. Nearby Christchurch cathedral was in even worse condition.[88] This state of affairs in Dublin was typical of the church as a whole, with only one church in seven fit for worship, and with a deplorable deficiency of clergy to serve the people. In Derry city and county the people were too poor to consider restoring their ruined churches and: 'the holy offices of God's publick worship were, for the most part, administered either in a dirty cabin or in a common alehouse'.[89] What the Church of Ireland lacked was a strong leadership at this time, one that could obtain the kind of commitment to sustain it that seemingly was offered to both the Presbyterians and the recusants.

By the time that James, duke of York, married the Catholic, Mary of Modena, he emerged as the leader of a strong recusant party. Those who opposed the duke of York in the English parliament had passed the Test Act of 1673, which compelled holders of public office to take oaths of allegiance, to recognize the royal supremacy, to adjure the Roman doctrine of transubstantiation, and to take the sacrament of the Church of England. Anxiety about Roman Catholicism expressed itself on the popular level by the Popish Plot hysteria of 1678. Titus Oates, son of an Anabaptist preacher, inflamed public opinion with a tale of Don Juan of Austria, and Père Lachaise, the Jesuit confessor of Louis XIV, plotting to kill Charles to put his brother James on the throne. Substance seemed to be given to the story when the correspondence of the confidential secretary of James, duke of York, was seized and published. It contained letters to the French king's confessor which discussed plans for the forcible conversion of the English, Scots and Irish:

> We have a mighty work upon our hands, no less than the conversion of three kingdoms, and by that the subduing of a pestilent heresy, which has dominated over a great part of this northern world for a long time. There was never such hope of success since the death of Queen Mary as now in our days when God has given us a Prince who is become zealous of being the author and instrument of so glorious a work.[90]

By this time it was not only in Ireland that among Protestants there was fear that '1641 was come again'.

The political results of the hysteria were alarming. Innocent Catholics were pursued to their death, James left the kingdom, and the Papists' Disabling Act was passed to exclude Roman Catholics from parliament—not to be repealed until 1829. In Ireland Peter Talbot the Catholic archbishop of Dublin was arrested, to die in prison. Oliver Plunket, the Catholic primate, was accused by dissident priests of planning for a French landing in Ireland, and he was executed in London in a trial that was a travesty of justice. Soon, however, there was a reaction in parliament to the excesses of the Whigs during the anti-Catholic panic, and many of the Tory squires and High Church clergy became ultra-royalists, so obsessed with their zeal to defend the Anglican church against the Dissenters that they almost abandoned their traditional fear of Rome. Some talked of unconditional submission to the royal will, and within the court debated to what extent the crown should ally itself with the French Catholic king who was attacking Protestants in the Palatinate and in the Netherlands.

Louis XIV's ambition was to rule some day a Catholic Europe, and thirty of his long fifty-four year reign was spent in a series of wars to that end. Spain was in decline after its long war with France, following the end of the Thirty Years War, and the papacy found it had little influence with Louis when it suggested a crusade against the Turks. When the French-Spanish conflict came to an end in 1659, in the Treaty of the Pyrenees, the pope of the time Alexander VII was excluded from its deliberations. Louis humiliated him further by threatening to invade papal enclaves at Avignon and Venaissin, and even the papal states, should he have trouble with the Roman authority. He continued his bullying of the next pope, Clement IX, (1667–1669) and obtained from him a free hand in church appointments. Clement X (1670–1676) also found he could not persuade Louis to support a defensive alliance against the Turks. Rather Louis persuaded this aged pontiff that the French attempt to conquer Holland was a holy war for the restoration of Catholicism. At the same time Louis claimed an unrestricted right to *regalia*, the appointment to ecclesiastical offices, and used intimidation to have pro-French nominees made cardinals. By the time that Clement X died it was clear that the Catholicism the Protestants of Europe had then to fear was French rather than Roman.

The authority of the papacy was reasserted at this juncture by Innocent XI (1676–1689) whom even Voltaire praised for being 'a courageous, resolute and magnificent prince'[91] who stood up to Louis XIV. Morally earnest, he was no friend of the Jesuits, and he dedicated himself to sweeping away abuses in the papal court. Almost immediately he found himself in conflict with Louis XIV who wished to extend even further his control of the *regalia*. This led to the adoption by the French clergy of the Gallican Articles of 1682, which affirmed ancient liberties of the French church, asserted the superior authority of general councils over that of the pope, and denied the pope authority over either temporal affairs, or the rule of the king. The Gallican Articles put Innocent very much on the defensive, but he continued to stand up to Louis and his policies. He approved in principle the Revocation of the Edict of Nantes, which took away the religious privileges of the Huguenots, but he deplored Louis' use of the *dragonnades*, using the brutality of dragoons quartered in Protestant homes as a persuasive to force them either to convert to Catholicism, or to flee from France. His action led Lord Acton, in later years, to refer to Innocent as 'the Protestant pope',[92] and the historian Ranke also praised him for opposing such tyranny: 'it was not of such method that Christ availed himself: men must be led to the temple, not dragged into it'.[93]

This prolonged religious-political struggle between France and Rome greatly influenced events in Britain and in Ireland. The British saw Louis' experiment in caesaropapism as part of his expansionist policy of enslaving other nations who refused to accept his 'divine right of kings' form of authority, which included religious conformity: 'I do not doubt that it is God's will that I endeavour to lead back to his ways all subjects'.[94] Few of the Catholic leaders in Ireland knew much about affairs of church and state on the continent, however, and their interest in other than insular matters was usually confined to what was happening in England. There they knew, as did the Irish Protestants, that the Roman Catholics were increasingly in favour in the royal court, and this encouraged them for in Ireland also a Catholic ascendancy was slowly appearing. In the rather cryptic words of the duke of Ormond: 'the loyal are oppressed; the disloyal in power to possess them'.[95] As more and more concessions were made to the Roman Catholics their leaders rejoiced over the: 'general connivance at the exercise of our religion'.[96] When in 1670 Peter Talbot, the titular archbishop of Dublin, had borrowed plate and hangings from Dublin Castle, in order to grace the splendour of his ceremonial, Lord Berkeley, the viceroy sent them to him with the message that in a few months: 'he hoped to see High Mass at Christ Church'.[97] The climate of conciliation in Ireland remained such, in spite of the Popish Plot hysteria, that when the Irish Catholics presented their demands at the Treaty of Limerick in 1691 what they wanted was a return to the liberties and privileges they had enjoyed in the reign of Charles II.

IV   The Protestant Revolution

James II succeeded his brother as king of England on February, 1685, after Charles died as a Roman Catholic. Trouble soon began. The coronation service for James had to be delayed because he refused to receive communion according to the rites of the Church of England. The last professing Roman Catholic to sit on the throne had been Mary Tudor of unhappy memory, and there was general unease over what James would do now that he was ruling a Protestant people. In his opening speeches he indicated that he intended to protect the established church, and what he probably hoped for was an alliance of the Church of England and the Romanists against the remnant of Protestant extremists. There was an attempt at a Protestant coup by the duke of Monmouth that was bloodily suppressed, and the earl of Argyle tried to raise the Covenanters in Scotland before he was captured and executed. Unease grew as concessions were made to the Catholics; fireworks were forbidden on November 5, Guy Fawkes day; dispensations from the Test Act were made so Catholics could become influential in the army and navy; and a new Court of High Commission was set up to try ecclesiastical cases. Abraham de la Pryme wrote in 1687:

> All the land quakes for fear, the jesuits and papists bear all down before them, and many have been heard to say that they expect to wash their hands in hereticks' blood before next Christmas.[98]

Nothing alarmed the Protestants of England and Ireland more than the Revocation of the Edict of Nantes by Louis XIV a mere eight months after James, his ally, ascended the English throne. Tales of the terrible *dragonnades* caught the public imagination, as did the account of what the French troops were doing to Protestants in the Palatinate, Orange and Piedmont. Now the Protestants realized that wherever French power went the people had to accept Catholicism or face death, the galleys or emigration. French Catholic intellectuals like Racine and La Fontaine praised the Revocation, and though Innocent XI had tried to persuade Louis to mitigate the severity of his handling of the Huguenots, he declared the action 'the finest thing His Majesty had ever done', granted plenary absolutions and had the Vatican illuminated.[99] When Huguenot refugees began to land at southern ports in England people were shocked at their condition: 'and every effort was made to succour and help the poor refugees for conscience sake'.[100] What stirred in English minds was the memory of similar refugees who fled the Irish rising of 1641, and the anger was great among even the common people who still celebrated November 17, queen Elizabeth's accession day, by burning effigies of the pope:

> This was still a credulous age... even educated Englishmen were genuinely and persistently afraid of the black and evil intentions of the papists, the dedicated servants of Anti-Christ. The Great Fire of London, which took place in 1666, was popularly attributed to them. In so far as witchcraft lingered on in rural areas it was associated in people's minds with popery.[101]

James only ruled in England for four short years, during which time he engaged in an increasingly bitter struggle in parliament and with the church as he sought to promote the Catholic cause. When his wife, Mary of Modena, bore him a son, a Catholic heir for the throne, 'seven eminent persons' sent an invitation to William, the Protestant prince of Orange, married to James' daughter Mary, to come and save the nation from Catholic tyranny. William had wanted to bring England into the struggle against Louis XIV begun by the League of Augsburg, a coalition of anti-French nations, and he accepted the invitation. When William landed in England on November 5, 1688, James fled to France and the protection of Louis XIV.

Anxiety over James' plans to Catholicize the nation was even greater in Ireland than in England when he first came to the throne. The king was intent upon establishing the kind of Catholic church that Louis XIV governed in France, and he had every intention of nominating to Irish sees. For this reason he worked not with a papal nuncio, but with Richard Talbot who had long been the leader of the Catholic party at court. An able soldier who had served under Thomas Preston in Irish Confederacy times he was created earl of Tyrconnell, commander-in-chief and virtual governor of Ireland for the king. By 1687 he was lord deputy and began a quiet but relentless displacement of Protestants from positions of power in the army and the administration. Churches were seized, masses were celebrated in them, vacancies were not filled, their income going to Catholic bishops, and a planned reorganization of the land settlement set in motion. Protestant families began to flee to Britain, including some bishops. Also to Britain were sent some 3000 Irish soldiers to help the king, soon after the announcement of the birth of an heir to James. The Irish troops in England were ill disciplined and when they began to riot all the fears of Charles I's reign returned. Louis XIV was paying for the support of other troops raised in Ireland, and in both islands Protestant anxieties were at their height when William arrived in England and James fled to the sanctuary provided for him by Louis XIV at the court of St. Germain.

As soon as news reached Ireland of William's landing Protestant hopes rose enough that Protestants in Munster tried to seize towns such as Bandon and Kenmare. This forced Tyrconnell to weaken his control of the north. It also gave the people of Londonderry courage to shut their gates against a Jacobite force under the earl of Antrim, and Enniskillen also refused to admit royal troops. Protestant organizations sprang up in other areas; William and Mary were recognized as king and queen in England; and Tyrconnell was forced to send a strong army north to join with his forces at Carrickfergus and Charlemont in a suppression of the rebellion. In this he was largely successful; soon only Londonderry and Enniskillen remained in Protestant hands, but the Protestants had been in communication with William and were sure that he would help them:

> The Protestant settlers were well aware of what was at stake. The English revolution had temporarily worsened their position in Ireland, but it gave them the opportunity of reversing the Catholic revival which had taken place since James's access... They were confident that William's government would not abandon the English stake in Ireland and that William could not afford to allow Ireland to provide a base for his rival.[102]

Historians and others have often commented on the anomaly of the strife in Ireland which was not primarily concerned with either Irish or religious affairs. It was part of the struggle of the European powers to contain the expansionist designs of the French absolutist king, Louis XIV. It would have been impossible for James to attempt to regain his throne beginning with the Irish campaign without French military or financial help, and James knew that in accepting French aid he was committing himself to support of the Bourbon cause in the European wars. In no real way was the French intervention in Ireland a religious exercise, and though the French generals might use sectarian exhortation to inspire Irish levies the cause they were promoting was the secular one of supporting the French crown. James also was not primarily concerned with either Irish or religious affairs during his time in Ireland for he realized that to identify himself too closely with the Irish Catholic cause would have denied him any future acceptance in England.

For his part William of Orange was completely absorbed by the problems of his continental war against Louis XIV, and he was for the age a liberal enlightened secularist in ecclesiastical affairs. Though he was personally pious he showed little interest in the bigotry he found among some of his Calvinist supporters, or among his Irish Protestant allies. What he represented was the pragmatism which was appearing among Europe's new generation of nation-building princes. No nations had suffered more than the Netherlands republics during the devastating religious wars of past generations, but by the time of William the Dutch leaders had moved out of an age when national concerns were dominated by the claims of religious ideology. Now the Dutch fought wars with England and Portugal over trade and colonial interests, the affairs of *realpolitik*. At the same time William loathed the French monarch's repressive religious policies which he viewed as 'a crime against the moral order, a sin':

> William was not only a devout Protestant but also one of the few men of his age who had real grasp of the principles of toleration. His lawyers were Catholics, his maitre d'hotel a Jew... the prince's resistance to the designs of France had a firm moral basis.[103]

On the other hand Louis XIV was able to make cynical use of the French church, as he did after the death of Innocent XI in 1689, because the papacy in the eyes of contemporaries lacked a moral base in its policies: 'the place of the Pope as Italian monarch seemed to outsiders to take precedence of his place as spiritual leader among the nations'.[104] Innocent XI was perhaps the outstanding pope of the seventeenth century, but he could not control the practice of nepotism, and his successors were often obliged to contend with attempts to establish open and direct rule by cardinal-nephew. This was tolerated by Alexander VIII (1689–1691) particularly, who invested his family with lucrative benefices, and subsidized his native Venice. Though he did negotiate with Louis XIV and win back the confiscated papal territories of Avignon and Venaissain, this *rapprochement* cost Alexander the friendship of the empire. The next pope, Innocent XII (1691–1700) was much more austere in his control of nepotism, but he was not a strong pope diplomatically, and his compromise settlement with Louis XIV allowed continuance of a Gallican church which was to exist essentially intact until the French Revolution. The pope at the beginning of the new century, Clement XI (1700–1721) represented those Roman authorities who wanted a non-political pontiff, and he was benign enough that his elevation was even welcomed in Protestant countries. By this time it was obvious that the papacy was a spent force in European affairs, however, and the Holy See had no representation in the congress leading to the treaty of Ryswick in 1697. In the territories of even nominally Catholic princes there was now little respect for the authority of the papacy:

> There was almost everywhere something resembling a direct, simple and complete supremacy of the prince over all persons and matters in his dominions. So far as they concerned the relations of states, the far-reaching claims of the papacy were now merely archaic. The Reformation had freed Catholic powers from them as well as the Protestant.[105]

Neither the Irish Catholics, nor the Protestants, realized fully the declining authority of the papacy, however, when the events of 1689 brought about a radical change in government and society. They were not part of the evolutionary progress towards liberalism, toleration and enlightenment that was slowly taking place in parts of Europe. The Irish churches and their adherents remained in an atavistic 'time-warp'; the Protestants nursed their memory of 1641, and the Catholics refused to forget or forgive the excesses of Drogheda or Wexford. So far as the Protestants were concerned during Tyrconnell's rule, they were the victims of 'papal oppression', when in Leinster 'Merryboys' and other Catholic gangs ensured that 'plunder was the order of the day'. The Catholic army camped on the Curragh appeared like a crusading host, its soldiers ordered: 'to confess regularly, and to forfeit three month's pay if they failed to produce a priest's certificate of having received the sacrament at least twice a year'.[106] Protestant alarm increased even more when James landed in Ireland in March, 1689, and his almost completely Catholic parliament issued a bill of attainder charging many Protestants with high treason. Mass was celebrated in Christchurch, Dublin; part of St. Patrick's cathedral was used by the royal army as a stable; and priests began a general take-over of Protestant churches:

> The priests threw off the mask and acted with undisguised audacity; affirming that the king had nothing to do with them, or their churches; that they were immediately subject to the pope; and that they would regard neither the king, nor his proclamations, nor laws, made to the damage of the holy church.[107]

For their part the Protestants resolved to oppose the terror they were convinced was about to be visited upon them once more. Their decisions was helped by the presence among them of continental victims of Catholic militancy, French Huguenots, who had fled to Ireland after the Revocation of the Edict of Nantes in 1685. Charles II, as the grandson of Henry IV, who had originally granted the Huguenots their original privileges in 1598, had allowed some of the refugees to come to Ireland, and though they were few in number they were ideologically important in urging resistance to the threatened Catholic pogrom: 'to the newly arrived Huguenots it must have seemed that the events of 1685 were about to happen all over again in their refuge'.[108] Most Protestants shared their fear and loathing of Catholic tyranny, and James's forces discovered this when they hurried to Londonderry to find the defence of the city organized by the stubborn anti-Jacobite Protestant rector, George Walker, and a militant Scots colonist and cavalryman Adam Murray. When William finally arrived in Ireland his Protestant army of Dutch, Danish and German troops, had as its core French Huguenot regiments whose members like their countrymen already in Ireland, had no love for the Catholic religion or its adherents. The overall commander of the Williamite forces was the Huguenot duke of Schomberg, who had left the French army at the time of the Revocation of the Edict of Nantes.[109]

After his victory at the Boyne William delegated command to his able Dutch general, Godard van Ginkel, who attempted to transcend the sectarian bitterness of the Irish Protestants and to negotiate with the Catholics over the questions of religion and the ownership of the land. This peace initiative came to nothing when the Jacobite command passed to the marquis de St. Ruth, a ruthless persecutor of the Huguenots, who had distinguished himself by his ferocity during the suppression of the heretics in Savoy in 1685.[110] During the preparation for the decisive battle of Aughrim St. Ruth urged the priests to tell the Catholic troops to give no quarter to the heretics. Eighty priests were to fall, crucifixes in hand, urging on the Catholic army, inflamed by the final exhortation given to them by St. Ruth:

> You may be assured that King James will love and reward you; Louis the great will protect you; all good Catholics will applaud you; I myself will command you; the church will pray for you; your posterity will bless you; God will make you all saints, and his Holy Mother will lay you in her bosom.[111]

Ginkel's wish was to carry the Irish campaign to its conclusion as quickly as possible in order to free the Williamite forces to fight the French on the continent and, as a means to that end, he was intent upon conciliating the Catholic leaders. When he tried to persuade Galway to surrender, after the death of St. Ruth at Aughrim and the rout of the Jacobite army, he promised the Catholic clergy and laity full private practice of their religion, and the nobility protection of their property. When Ginkel made terms with the Catholic general Sarsfield, prior to the latter's surrender at Limerick, he did so at dinner parties attended by the Catholic archbishops of Armagh and Cashel. There he assured the Catholics that they could expect such freedom of worship as was: 'consistent with the laws of Ireland, or as they did enjoy in the reign of King Charles II'. Not all Catholics warmed to Ginkel's overtures, however, and in the countryside priests warned of the danger to the souls of young men who might deal with the heretics rather than go to France with Sarsfield, to return later as part of a crusading Catholic army.[112]

The Irish Protestants were equally as intransigent as the priests. When Rinuccini had been in Ireland the cardinal secretary of state had written to him to say: 'the Holy See can never by any positive act approve of the civil allegiance of Catholic subjects to a heretical prince',[113] and most Protestants accepted that the Irish Catholics had paid heed to the Roman admonition, and continued to do so. That most Irish Catholics were disloyal to the crown was self-evident. Many of the Catholic young were absent from the country, training as seminarians in Roman missionary colleges, or serving in continental Catholic armies. These emigrés were resolved as priests or soldiers to return and to liberate their country by any means possible from heretical oppression. There were a minority of Protestant bishops, such as William Moreton of Kildare who were willing to risk *rapprochement* with the papists, and there was even talk of providing payment for the recusant bishops if they submitted to William's rule.[114] Most of the Protestant prelates, however, followed the lead of Anthony Dopping, bishop of Meath who had remained in Dublin as commissary of the archbishop during the Jacobite era. He strongly opposed any concessions to the Catholic church because of its untrustworthiness. In a sermon in St. Patrick's cathedral he argued that such was the proven treachery of Irish Catholics that the government was under no moral obligation to observe even the concessions it had granted in the Treaty of Limerick. Protestant opinion was inflamed over the devastation of the Protestant Palatinate at the time, and sermons, tracts and pamphlets stressed the danger of ever trusting the papacy, the French, or the Irish Catholics.[115] The dean of St. Patrick's, William King, had also remained in Dublin during the Jacobite terror, and in his preaching and writing he concentrated on the evil of the deposing power claimed by the papacy. So long as the Irish Catholics served the Roman ecclesiastical and political authority they had, of necessity, to be held in subjection, for they could not be trusted to serve the commonwealth.

It was this kind of fear, by no means a groundless one, so long as Britain was at death-grips with the power of Louis XIV, which brought about the Irish Penal Laws. There were other reasons for them, as we will see, but theological antipathy was a minor cause. What was paramount in the Irish Protestant mind was the need for protective measures to ensure that neither Rome, nor any other foreign Catholic authority, could force upon Ireland the oppression that it had experienced in 1641, during the years of the Confederates, and lately under James and Tyrconnell. Even though the Protestants had won the battle for the moment, with the help of European and British help, they still felt besieged, not only by the Irish Catholics, but by whatever external power Rome could raise against them.

The enemy remained the court of Rome, not the Irish Catholics. There was never in Ireland, apart from the sporadic excesses of Cromwell's English Ironsides, which were never sustained, the mentality of the *dragonnades* which characterized the Catholicism of France in the time of Louis XIV , or the policy of genocide carried out by French troops, including the Irish, on the continent. The Irish Protestants were part of the increasingly literate and intellectual world of Protestant Europe in the days of Louis XIV, and they were presented with clear evidence of what faced them if, through not being vigilant, they lost their liberty and were at the mercy of Catholic power. Voltaire had become 'the conscience of Europe' from the time he defended the Calas family who were innocent victims of persecution, and then denounced the shocking treatment of Huguenots at Abbeville. These atrocities, which became the concern of Frederick the Great and others, were certainly known by the Protestants of England and Ireland, long before the scandal associated with the Revocation of the Edict of Nantes in 1685. They were appalled by the stories that reached England quickly of the suffering of the refugees, and the rumours that James II was doing all in his power to deny them relief.[116] The Protestants were also distressed by the mind of Bossuet, bishop of Meaux, who had extolled the extirpation policies of Louis XIV:

> You have confirmed the faith; you have exterminated the heretics; it is the worthy work of your reign, which rightly characterizes it. Through you heresy is no more: God alone has been able to work this marvel; King of heaven, preserve the king of earth; this is the prayer of the churches; this is the prayer of the bishops.[117]

Though the papacy was no longer in a position to direct the Counter-Reformation policies of earlier years, the Protestants accepted that in the Catholic world the passionate intolerance of the past had not disappeared. From the Irish standpoint it was recognized that the old 'fervour of righteousness' had not disappeared among the Catholic emigrés, when the seminarians of the Irish College in Seville took, among other oaths, one: 'to defend to the death the doctrine of the Immaculate Conception'.[118] Ireland was still to be cursed with the conflict of the Reformation and Counter-Reformation eras long after the spirit which had first put Catholics and Protestants at each other's throats had begun to wane elsewhere in Europe.

Chapter V

The Age of Protestant Domination

'... though Popery can never become Protestantism, the professors of
Popery may nevertheless become Protestant in principle.'

> Thomas Campbell, *Philosophical Sur-
> vey of the South of Ireland in a Series
> of Letters to John Watkinson, M.D.*,
> Dublin, 1778

I   William King's Ireland

Although the Treaty of Limerick in 1691 ended war in Ireland for the next
six years, until the Treaty of Ryswick William III remained concerned about a
possible Jacobite return invasion of the island supported by French troops. The
latter agreement, however brought an end to hostilities between the great European powers, William was acknowledged as king of England and Ireland, and
Anne as his successor. This effectively ended any immediate external threat to
Ireland and the first act of the parliament of 1697 was the passing of a bill which
banished all: 'papists exercising ecclesiastical jurisdiction and all regulars of the
papist clergy'.[1] The strongest supporters of the legislation were Anthony
Dopping, the bishop of Meath, and the Huguenot, Henri de Ruvigny, earl of
Galway who was a lord justice. The Roman Catholic authorities were not surprised by the intransigence of Dopping who had suffered much under James, nor
by Lord Galway who was encouraging the settlement of the persecuted Huguenots in Ireland. There had been a plot to assassinate William the previous year,
and the Protestants took for granted that whatever official settlements were made
the Roman Catholic authorities would be a menace to peace so long as the
Jacobite threat remained. Everywhere in the country were priests: 'daily stirring
up and moving sedition and rebellion to the great hazard of the ruin and desolation of the kingdom'.[2] Moreover in the north of Ireland were the Presbyterians
who hoped that the Calvinist king might abolish episcopacy in Ireland as well as
Scotland. It should be noted that it was common in the eighteenth century for
the adherents of the Church of Ireland to distinguish their body by assuming for
it alone the name of Protestant.

The strongest objection to the privileged position the Church of Ireland
claimed for itself came from the Ulster Presbyterians. William King, the son of

a Presbyterian and himself a Scot, had been the bishop of Derry until 1703 and he had watched the great influx of his fellow-countrymen into Ulster with great misgivings, for towards the claims of the church they were 'mighty insolent'.[3] When Jonathan Swift was the Church of Ireland clergyman at Kilroot in County Antrim his reaction to the Presbyterians was similar to that of William King. Previous incumbents of Kilroot had been Presbyterian and, in the words of one of King's northern correspondents:

> The nonconformists are much the most numerous portion of the Pro-
> testants in Ulster... Some parishes have not ten, some not six that
> come to church, while the Presbyterian meetings are crowded with thou-
> sands covering all the fields. This is ordinary in the county of Antrim
> especially, which is the most populous of Scots of any in Ulster.[4]

The toleration issue was of great concern in both Britain and Ireland by the time that Anne came to the throne, with the Tories going through 'periodic waves of High Church fury'[5] which was directed against the dissenters rather than the papists. King was convinced that the gift from the crown to the Presbyterians, the *regium donum* was used to found new nonconforming congregations, and it did not please him that some incumbents used Scots curates who could be hired cheaply. Not until the passing of the 1704 act, 'to prevent the further growth of popery', which included a denial of public offices to all who did not take the sacrament according to the rite of the Church of England, were the opponents of the dissenters at all satisfied. A battle for the 'principle of toleration' was taking place, but the infighting between extremists and moderates over the problem of church-state relations was intense, and formed the background for the struggle to strengthen the penal laws in 1707 and 1709.[6] During the last years of Anne's reign, with the high church party in the ascendant in England, the position of the dissenters got worse and the *regium donum* was suspended in 1714, to be renewed when George I came to the throne.

William King had been the actual ruler of the Dublin archdiocese in 1689 because the bishop, Francis Marsh, had fled and King, as dean of St. Patrick's, assumed his duties. He suffered imprisonment, and when his liberation came he enjoyed great prestige among the Protestants. On the day that William III entered Dublin King preached a sermon at St. Patrick's in which he argued that because the Catholic monarch, James II, had threatened to destroy the Protestant church, the faithful had to abandon traditions of non-resistance, or passive obedience, and to resist his tyranny. Other bishops presented 'providential arguments' justifying the Williamite take-over of the throne,[7] but King's *State of the Protestants of Ireland under the Late King James' Government* was considered to be one of the most powerful apologetics for the Protestant rebellion. In it he claimed that the position of the Irish Protestants under James was analogous to that of the Huguenots under his ally, Louis XIV: 'he had as fully determined our ruin as that king had resolved the avoiding the Edict of Nantes when he made his solemn declaration to the contrary'. King's common sense argument was:

> If a king design to root out a people, or destroy one part of his subjects in favour of another whom he loves better, that they may prevent it even by opposing him with force.[8]

King's powerful apologetic won him the see of Derry in 1691 but there were churchmen who believed in the Divine Right of Kings and looked upon the Dutch Calvinist William as a usurper. One of these Non-Jurors, Charles Leslie, chancellor of the Connor diocese pointed out that King believed final authority lay with the people and his viewpoint was that of the 'Commonwealth and rebellion'.[9] Leslie was right inasmuch as King was a Whig in politics, although a strong ecclesiastical Tory who believed that the monarchy and the church existed to strengthen the Protestant nation which was to labour for the good of the whole community, under God. Besides the Non-Jurors there were the Presbyterians who did not accept King's argument that the church was to be governed only by the king and convocation who received their commission to do so from God. King had attended school in Dungannon and delighted in infuriating the Presbyterians whose sensibilities he knew so well. When he was bishop of Derry he produced a work entitled *Discourse Concerning the Inventions of Men in the Worship of God* in which he stated that the Church of Ireland rather than the Presbyterian communion was closest to the religious life demanded by scripture. The Presbyterians, he wrote, failed to attend public service regularly, to read the scriptures at their meetings, or to celebrate the Lord's Supper as often as they should. This brought forth enraged responses from Presbyterian controversialists like Rev. Robert Craghead of Londonderry, and Rev. Joseph Boyse of Dublin, and the ideological controversy continued well after William King's translation to Dublin in 1703.[10] King wanted a Protestant alliance however and he later worried that harassment by the Church of Ireland contributed to the great flood of Presbyterian emigration in the 1717–1719 period, which left land vacant to be occupied by 'popish tenants'. When it came to contending with Rome, King wanted Presbyterian solidarity as he told William Wake, archbishop of Canterbury in 1719, when he denied that established church pressure encouraged Ulster Presbyterian emigration:

> Some would insinuate that this is in some measure due to the uneasiness dissenters have in the matter of religion, but this is plainly a mistake; for dissenters were never more easy as to that matter than they have been since the revolution, and are at present; and yet they never thought of leaving the kingdom, till oppressed by excessive and other temporal hardships; nor do only dissenters leave us, but proportionately

of all sorts, except papists.[11]

King's dislike of the Presbyterians reflected family prejudice, for his father had to flee Scotland when he rejected the Solemn League and Covenant. His dislike of popery, however, represented his direct experience of Roman Catholicism for in 1679 he had been brought to Dublin by his patron, archbishop John Parker, and appointed rector of St. Werburgh's in the Liberties. The area abounded with militant Protestant weavers, who fought running battles with the Catholic butchers of Ormond market, and it was in this milieu that King developed his strongly anti-Roman Catholic sentiments. The 'Liberty Boys' were strengthened by French Huguenots as well as Dutch and Flemish weavers and all of them were 'extravagantly Presbyterian' — especially when reinforced by high-spirited Trinity College students.[12] King's unfortunate experiences during James' reign, including his confinement, did nothing to ease his anti-papal antipathy which, like most attitudes of King's, was well-reasoned and not based on mere emotional prejudice.

King had opportunity to express his anti-papal viewpoint when during the reign of James the dean of Derry, Peter Manby, became a Roman Catholic while he continued to hold his preferment under a 'royal dispensation'. When Manby issued an apologetic for his change of faith King immediately produced a fiery criticism of this apostasy in his *Answer to the Considerations which Obliged Peter Manby to Embrace the Catholic Religion*. Here King displayed his High Church theological position, as he argued that the Catholic church was the whole body of men professing the religion of Christ, and the Church of Ireland was part of the whole. As for the Roman church he decried the lack of morality shown by past pontiffs, and he was scathing in his treatment of the superstitious rites which were tolerated in that communion. Politically he considered Irish Roman Catholics essentially disloyal because of the 'allegiance they owed to the foreign potentate in Rome'.[13] Yet King was no advocate of direct repression of the Irish Catholics which he believed to be counter-productive. The best way to confute 'popery' he told the archbishop of Tuam, Edward Synge, in 1724, was to prepare the Protestant clergy to preach sensibly against Romanism and its manifest errors.[14] Recusancy remained in Ireland, he believed, because of foolish political persecutions in other ages:

> I firmly believe, if all had been treated with the same moderation, with
> due care and proper means, a great part of the Roman Catholics would
> have now joined the reformed religion.[15]

Like other Protestant leaders King's instinctive liberalism was qualified, however, when there was much political agitation before the death of Anne in 1714 and the Hanoverian succession to the English throne proved to be unpopular. James Edward Stuart, the Old Pretender, had landed in Scotland in

1708, with the aid of a French fleet, and though the House of Stuart was not to succeed to the throne, only the Whigs were to support strongly the 'German Georges'. The Stuarts had been granted dispensation by the papacy to make Catholic episcopal appointments in Ireland, and it seemed almost certain that Rome would in some way try to take advantage of the agitation of 1713–1714 when King reported that the country was: 'in a high ferment, higher than ever I saw it except when in actual war'.[16] When the Old Pretender arrived in Scotland again in 1715, King was filled with apprehension as he discussed with his correspondents the 'insolence' and 'presumption' of the papists:

> ... their hopes and expectations seem to be founded on the rebellious and traitorous person called the Pretender, who was bred up and instructed to introduce the Roman superstition and French government into these realms.[17]

Though he had made use of Irish speakers to reach the people when he was bishop of Derry, he found himself torn between his desire to find accommodation with the Irish Catholics and his fear of the Catholic alliance with Roman power. He saw the Irish Catholics to be an astute people, intelligent enough to take advantage of weakness in Protestant society to their own benefit, and he worried as he observed recusants taking over the land with the help of feckless or unscrupulous landlords, and using their continental Catholic connections to become dominant in trade:

> Most of the trade of the kingdom is engrossed by them; and by this covetousness of the landlords they will get possession of the lands; and how the Protestants will secure themselves, or England secure Ireland, when all the community are all papists is surely worth considering.[18]

King's wish was to ignore the religious activities of recusant bishops and priests, so long as their activities did not bring up questions about their political loyalty. Yet he realized that while the Jacobite threat had to be taken seriously, and the exiled Stuarts were supported by the papacy, the Irish Catholics who owed allegiance to the court of Rome as well as the crown could not be fully trusted.

Neither could King ever fully trust the Ulster Presbyterians. His own ecclesiology was like that of the English Elizabethan divine, Richard Hooker in that he saw the Church of Ireland as a reformed body, yet one in continuity with the medieval church, existing in its catholicity to serve all in Ireland, even the Catholics, Presbyterians, or other dissenters who rejected its services. Since King held the Presbyterians in as much suspicion as he did the Catholics he was not persuaded by the writings of men like James Kirkpatrick of Belfast who, in his lengthy *Historical Essay Upon the Loyalty of Presbyterians* of 1712 argued that though at times his people might appear rebellious they were well worth the trust of the authorities.[19] King remembered from his time as bishop of Derry, from 1691 until 1703, how troublesome a people the Presbyterians were, and how difficult it had been to get them out of the church establishment. Indeed King considered the Protestant establishment under attack by both the Roman Catholics, and the militant Presbyterians from Scotland, as he had told bishop Nathaniel Foy of Waterford in 1697:

> The faith of religion is very weak amongst us and the sense of it almost lost and the matter is laid deeper than most are aware of. 'Tis come to a formed conspiracy and agents and emissaries are employed to cry down our religion. In short, we are used as our Master was.[20]

King did not blame the Catholics or the Presbyterians for all that was wrong with the Church of Ireland, however. When he was bishop of Derry he had to deal with the bishop of Down from 1671 to 1694 Thomas Hackett who was known, from his chosen place of residence, as 'the bishop of Hammersmith'. Hackett openly sold livings to the highest bidder, including Catholics to whom he granted false certificates of conformity. His constant companion was a woman named Cole who governed the bishop absolutely and acted as agent in his disposing of preferments.[21] He was finally deprived, together with his dean and archdeacon by a royal commission, but King was aware there were others who followed bishop Hackett's example. The dean of Connor was deprived for adultery, as was Jonathan Swift's successor at Kilroot. In fact, the diocese of Down was in such a state that King believed a follow up of all accusations of immorality made to the authorities would result in the suspending of half the clergy.[22]

King's efforts to reform the Church of Ireland, which was in a shocking state after the long years of warfare, did not come to an end when he was translated to Dublin. We know much about his reforming efforts from the voluminous correspondence he carried on with the archbishop of Canterbury, William Wake, and other prelates concerned about the state of the Irish church. King worked with Jonathan Swift to have Queen Anne's Bounty, which augmented the income of small livings, extended to Ireland, and he did all he could to get back church land from the gentry who had for so long pillaged the church. Nor did he hesitate to make public the dismal state of affairs, even in his own archdiocese where the clergy suffered from the lack of glebes and were forced to be non-resident:

> I have not ten parishes in the whole diocese endowed with glebes, and not six of them that clergymen can live on. I drew out a state of this diocese and laid it before the convocation who were not pleased with it, because, as they said, it too much discovered their nakedness.[23]

King's intention was to oblige Wake and the English establishment to reckon with the true state of the Church of Ireland, and to realize that matters like the paucity of clergymen' was: 'a great obstruction to the conversion of the natives, and a great occasion for the multiplying of sectaries'. Another weakness that had to be remedied, said King, was the lack of pastoral zeal of those ambitious English clergy who came often to Ireland as chaplains of the Lord Lieutenants and then obtained Irish sees through patronage. King boldly described for Wake the career of one of these young men, Simon Digby, whose advancement was assisted by the political influence of his English father, Essex Digby who was bishop of Dromore. The younger Digby owed his preferment to the sees of Limerick and Elphin not only to his useful political connections, but also to his skill as a water colourist which, King believed, 'greatly recommended himself to men in power and ladies'.[24] When he died in 1720 King described for Wake Digby's 'accomplishments' in his last diocese of Elphin:

He generally lived out of his diocese; and though his predecessor left him the shell of a very good house, yet he took no care to finish it, or, by what I can learn, to preserve it from decay. He left the diocese, as I understand from everybody that come from thence, in a miserable condition: churches greatly wanting, and those that are, ill-supplied. I am informed that, though the diocese be large, there are only about thirteen clergymen in it.[25]

King never ceased to complain about the appointment of English 'cast clergymen' to Irish sees, and he poured scorn on William Nicolson of Derry who had been translated from the see of Carlisle, and used his time in Ireland to fill lucrative parishes with his friends and relations.[26] When the Presbyterian Joseph Boyse launched an attack on the lengthy absence from his diocese of St. George Ashe, bishop of Clogher from 1697–1717, King suggested strongly to that prelate that he return to show his critics that his diocese was not a 'pompous sinecure':

There is great exception taken... at your long absence. Your friends murmur at your deserting them, and your enemies excuse their negligence by your absence; and the common enemies of the church conclude that bishops are not necessary since they can be so long spared.[27]

The redoubtable archbishop could do little more than exhort a scholarly but pastorally inept bishop like St. George Ashe, but in his own jurisdiction he made strenuous efforts for reform. The dean and chapter of Christchurch cathedral, for example, had long neglected the twenty-seven churches they were responsible for, and when pressed by King argued that as members of a chapel royal they were not under his authority. Their stance led to a long law-suit which lasted until 1724 but, in the end, they had to submit and begin to change their ways. By the following year King could report a general civilizing of society even in places as notorious as Ringsend and Glasnevin. His success as a reformer was considerable:

> The county of Wicklow was full of Quakers and dissenters; but having got seven new churches in it, and filled them with good men, there is hardly a meeting left in that part... As to the city, the parish of St. Nicholas Without is in my neighbourhood and there was but one church in it, and that a very small one, and seldom filled. On a good minister being there placed, instead of one who was not agreeable, the church immediately filled; and though enlarged with galleries, so as to receive double the number, there wanted room. To help them, service was opened in the cathedral of St. Patrick's which was not officiated before regularly; that was likewise filled. And though it has usually a thousand people every Lord's day yet there was not reception enough for the auditors; on which we got a new parish erected out of the former, and a new church, St. Luke's built, of an hundred and forty foot wide with spacious galleries; which church is frequented every Lord's day with about a thousand hearers, and yet there wants room; so that we are about enlarging the old church.[28]

King's reformation was reinforced by a minority of dedicated Irish bishops, such as Nathaniel Foy of Waterford who had suffered imprisonment in James' reign because he preached against the opinions of a Sorbonne doctor who had occupied the pulpit at Christchurch in Dublin. He used his own income to repair his palace; by his will he endowed a free school, and was foremost among those who were concerned about redressing the many ills in the church.[29] The Synge family who had come from England in the early seventeenth century gave the Church of Ireland five bishops in three generations, and they are to be numbered among the reformers. Edward Synge who was archbishop of Tuam from 1716 pressed parliament to allow him to make over some of his tithe income for the support of poorer clergy.[30] He also called for religious toleration, as did his son Edward, who preached in 1725 before the House of Commons in a service commemorating the rising of 1641, and in his sermon he urged that only 'the inward persuasion of the mind' should be the means to advance the Protestant faith.[31] The Mayo born Theophilus Bolton, a learned man who became archbishop of Cashel in 1730 built a library in Cashel, brought a water supply to the city, and expended large sums on restoring the thirteenth century Cormac's cathedral. Henry Maule, bishop of Cloyne from 1726, organized much rebuilding in his diocese, established a public library and stood up to local Protestant bigots who toasted William of Orange as: 'the instrument in the hand of God for delivering us from popery and arbitrary power'.[32] John Stearne who succeeded Jonathan Swift as dean of St. Patrick's and then became bishop of Clogher was famous for his benefactions and his 'bias towards the disaffected'.[33]

Despite this role call of dedicated prelates the majority of the early eighteenth century bishops in the Church of Ireland appear to have been political placemen, not noticed for their piety, learning or charity. They were, however, united in a common resolve to reject full toleration to the Church of Rome because of its determination in the words of the elder Edward Synge: 'to impose rules or doctrines upon others'.[34] They, of course, with the latitudinarian theological outlook so common for the age, had no desire to impose their way of religious life upon all the Irish people. In this they were realists, sharing the observation which William King made to one of his curates in 1715:

> The bulk of the common people in Ireland are either papists or dissenters, equally enemies to the established church; but the gentry are generally conformable, and the church interest apparently lies in them.[35]

So long as the Church of Ireland prelates maintained the allegiance of the governing classes they were content to leave the majority Catholic people to live and to worship in their own misguided way, though in their accommodating fashion they showed no resistance when Catholic lords or gentry wished to conform to the Church of Ireland. They may not have been zealous promoters of the reformed faith, but neither were they persecutors of the recusants.

Although the Protestant church leaders showed a lack of zeal when it came to promoting mission among the general Catholic population the convocation of 1703 supported the idea of a major mission, in spite of a belief in the upper house that work among the Irish-speaking people was no more than 'commendable': 'useful where it is practicable'.[36] When the convocation of 1709 debated a mission again, both houses 'considering with great compassion the condition of the recusants of this kingdom', expressed their belief that 'many of them may be prevailed upon to join themselves in communion with the established church'.[37] As we have noted earlier, the recusants that the members of convocation referred to were the gentry, for there was comparatively little interest shown in the Irish common people or their language, let alone a mission to them in William King's time.

The kind of concern that Bedell had shown for Irish studies had been maintained intermittently at Trinity College after the Restoration, especially when Narcissus Marsh was provost. An Irish scholar himself he had the Fellows and students attend Irish lectures, supported the study of Irish-born scholars, and worked with Robert Boyle, the great chemist, in publishing the Old Testament in Irish. Marsh and Boyle had a new fount of Irish type cast, and brought out copies of both testaments for mission use.[38] One of the supporters of the idea of mission at this time was Andrew Sall, who had been rector of the Irish College in Salamanca, became a Protestant and was chancellor of Cashel cathedral before he died in 1682. Only an occasional reference is made about Irish studies at Trinity following the Revolution, however. A vice-provost named Hall supported Irish lectures from his own pocket, and a 'certain Mr. Linnegar' was appointed by the provost and Fellows to teach Irish in the hope that: 'if the said work was promoted and encouraged it might prove a means to convert the natives and bring them over to the established church'.[39]

In spite of the luke-warm support given by either the official church or Trinity College there were clergy who carried on the Bedell tradition and tried to work in an eirenic spirit in their parishes and used the Irish language. One of these was Nicholas Browne, a Trinity graduate of provost Marsh's day, who used the Prayer Book in Irish at his services, and translated the first part of Thomas a Kempis' *Imitation of Christ* into Irish.[40] Another was John Richardson, a Tyrone native, who was rector of Belturbet in the Kilmore diocese. Inspired by Bedell's example in previous times he was convinced that the ordinary Irish people, 'who were reckoned the best men in the French army' were the sort of 'virtuous and intelligent people' who would benefit from education in their own language. Coercion would never win them over from the Roman thrall, but only 'gentle usage and Christian treatment':

> When any of them are so happy as to be made sensible of the horrors
> and corruptions of the church of Rome, and to have sound principles
> instilled into them they become very good Christians, very loyal
> subjects, and true friends to our excellent constitution in church and
> state.[41]

Francis Hutchinson, an Englishman and chaplain to the king, stepped outside of the usual immigrant bishop role when he became bishop of Down in 1720 and he and his family immersed themselves in the concerns of their new community. Hutchinson was zealous to bring true religion and civility to the people and in 1723 he had a new church built on Rathlin island with the help of Queen Anne's Bounty, provided a catechism for the five hundred or so Irish speaking inhabitants, and bought a library for the incumbent of the remote parish.[42]

Ideally this is what William King wanted, an episcopal bench filled with dedicated men who would promote the pastoral mission of the church, for the benefit of all Irish society. What he had to work with were the English placemen visited upon the Church of Ireland: 'some chaplain that never served a cure, and will think it ungenteel to trouble his head with the spirituals of his office'. The only hope for the country if the reformed faith was to be brought to the people, he believed, was to fill all levels of the establishment with zealous men: 'the most active, prudent and industrious clergy if we ever expect it should become Protestant'. In an unpublished letter five years before his death, King confessed his disappointment over what was happening in an age when, in reaction to the passions of the preceding century, few churchmen or statesmen thought in terms of mission:

> It is plain to me by the methods that have been taken since the reformation and which are yet pursued by both the civil and ecclesiastical powers that there never was nor is any design that all should be Protestants.[43]

II   The Penal Laws

A very positive side to the latitudinarian spirit of the government was that there was never in Ireland, during the age of European religious penal legislation, the kind of ruthless harrying of dissidents that had been carried out in Spanish territories for so long, and still existed in France. William King was aware that the government was not about to support a major Protestant religious mission, but neither was it going to disturb society by a rigorous suppression of Ireland's majority religion. As King told the earl of Sunderland in January, 1715, when what repression there was was at its height:

> If the same mild hand be designed to be continued over them that they are under at present, it seems to me best to make no noise about them; for inquiries or order tending that way, when no consequence follows, only makes them more secure and daring... there is an expectation in the kingdom that something should be done, and, if it do not begin from the fountain of power, or be not supported and prosecuted with resolution and steadfastness from thence, instead of doing good it will do a great deal of hurt, discourage the Protestants, and animate the papists, as has frequently happened formerly on proclamations against them.[44]

There is little evidence to support the traditional Roman Catholic version of Irish history which represented the years 1711–1726, in particular, as a time of terror.[45] This was when extremists demanded among other measures the branding and castrating of unregistered priests or friars, and the government was judged to have engaged in: 'one of the most persistent legislative efforts ever undertaken to change a people'.[46] Nor can much authority be granted to the folk-tales of hunted priests, mass rocks, and other phenomena: these belong to the Cromwellian age, not the Ireland of William, Anne and the Hanoverian Georges. When mass was celebrated in the open it was more often because of the absence of mass houses, rather than fear of the authorities in a time when:

'Dublin Castle was better informed of the names and activities of the priests than the Vatican'.[47] Dublin juries regularly refused to convict peaceful priests who were unregistered under the penal acts,[48] and the government was greatly embarrassed when a priest-catcher apprehended Edward Byrne, the recusant archbishop of Dublin in 1718.[49] At no time was Catholic worship as such considered illegal, and even Propaganda Fidei in Rome was willing to acknowledge that: 'penal laws were rarely universally applied in their full vigour'.[50] Most contemporary historians acknowledge that the implementation of the penal laws against the Catholics has been much exaggerated.[51]

It should not be overlooked that the religious penal laws, as we have noted, were also used against the Presbyterians and other dissenters to their great annoyance. The Presbyterian ministers especially resented that whereas the ordination of Catholic priests was recognized, their religious position was not. In Ulster, in particular, the leaders of the established church found the Scots who crowded into the north more of an immediate threat than the papists. Some 80,000 of them had entered by the 1690's and those who wanted tough laws to control these turbulent people found the government, as in the case of the Catholics, very reluctant to interfere. The authorities had enough problems to deal with, and they had no intention of using the civil arm to put down sessions and provincial synods which sought to bring Presbyterian authority among the people:

> The Presbyterians of Ulster were not a group of scattered congregations, but formed an organized body with a system of parochial, provincial and general assemblies covering the whole north of Ireland. Not only so but they were in close touch with their co-religionists in Scotland, who within a few years had been able to overthrow and persecute an established episcopal church.[52]

With the Presbyterians, as in most cases with the recusants the government's attitude was to engage in a 'connived or de facto toleration'; which the Irish parliament refused to make legal. The laws against them may have been only irritants, yet they did contribute to the massive Presbyterian emigration to America in the eighteenth century. Greatly resented was the established church claim that only its courts could deal with marriage, education and wills. Attempts were made to have Presbyterian schoolmasters prosecuted; tithes had to be paid to the rector of the parish; and most provoking of all Presbyterians could not bury their dead 'unless the church read over them'.[53]

King and the other Church of Ireland prelates accepted the need to 'connive at toleration' by ignoring the laws and restrictions which sought to restrain Catholic and Presbyterian religious practices. King admitted to the lord lieutenant in 1727 that no other policy was possible. Though the papists were a threat because of their Jacobite allegiance:

The papists have more bishops in Ireland than the Protestants have, and twice (at least) as many priests: their priories and nunneries are publick; it is in vain to pass laws against them, for the justices of the peace are no ways inclined to put such laws in execution; and, to help the matter, there is a notion prevails universally that the government is so engaged with the neighbouring popish powers by treaties and confederacies that they are obliged to connive at the practices of their popish subjects.[54]

Apart from the government, King knew that even among the leaders of the church there was no interest in religious persecution of even the mildest sort. When there was public unease over the recusants, at some time of crisis such as the Jacobite landings, moderate churchmen immediately sought to calm the hysteria of the moment. Typical of the eirenicists of William King's era was the increasingly tolerant Edward Synge, who was still bishop of Raphoe when he preached before the government in the year following the Jacobite rising of 1715. In it he represented the growing liberalism of those churchmen who pleaded for a pluralistic appreciation of the way of life of the Irish people whose religious judgments differed from those of the Protestants:

If they are honest and peaceable men they ought not by the rules of the gospel to be harshly treated, and much less to be persecuted or punished for their dissent.[55]

King shared to a large measure in this spirit of accommodation, but like most European Protestants he was aware that the persecuting spirit had never disappeared in the Roman Catholic world. The treatment of the Huguenots and other Protestant people in the territories governed by Louis XIV could not be ignored: 'the priest combined with the courtier to sanctify the cult of Bourbonism'.[56] Throughout the eighteenth century European Protestantism was to remain in a state of wary apprehension as stories abounded about the continuing persecution of the Huguenots in the French galleys and elsewhere. Voltaire, as we have noted, ensured that Europe knew of merciless treatment of individual Protestant families, and the persecution of Huguenots, which he compared with the worst excesses of the Spanish Inquisition.[57]

The fact that many Irish Catholic families had their young attend continental seminaries, or find employment in the armies of the great Catholic powers, also helped to qualify King's liberal instincts. He was not apt to ignore the providing of an archbishop for the Catholic church at Narbonne, and a general for the French army, by a prominent recusant family like the Dillons of Connaught.[58] He also knew of the connections that consistently Jacobite orders such as the Dominicans and Franciscans had with their continental brethren. However reluctantly, King and other Irish Protestant church leaders shared with the government the conviction that penal laws, which were a pale reflection of those in France, had to be retained on the statute books. The growing latitudinarian spirit within the Irish Protestant community might ensure that the penal laws were lax in their application, but so long as the Jacobite threat remained, they were politically and socially necessary;

> This is the ground of the wise and wholesome laws for the disarming papists...that they may not have in their hands the means of being as cruel and wicked as their religion would make them.[59]

The Irish Protestants prior to 1745 were an anxious people with, they believed, good cause. After the defeat of the Young Pretender at Culloden, where Irish Wild Geese had fought well for the Jacobite cause, the mind of the age was well presented in a sermon by the dean of Kilmore, John Madden, in St. Anne's, Dublin:

> We of this nation particularly (surrounded by popish enemies on every side as numerous as they are zealous for the religion of Rome) look'd every day and hour when the flame would break out among us.[60]

Innocent XI had granted the Stuarts the right to nominate to Roman Catholic bishoprics in Ireland, and this practice was to be continued until 1765.[61] The French were a threatening power throughout most of this period, and Protestant leaders like William King would have agreed with lord Acton's later opinion, that Louis XIV was the real author of the Irish penal system which determined how much freedom the recusants could be allowed: 'personal liberty they must possess; political liberty they must not possess'.[62]

Historians concerned with insular Irish affairs have often chosen to ignore the perceived threat from Rome and France which exercised the Protestants, and have pleaded that: 'the primary concern of the penal code was with property'.[63] W.E.H. Lecky believed this, and it was ably argued by Gustave de Beaumont in his 1839 work, *L'Irlande Social, Politique et Religieuse* of 1839. It is, of course, a persuasive argument because there was obviously little religious fanaticism behind the penal laws, and many Catholic landlords were persuaded to conform to the established church. Another element in the conforming process, however, was the latitudinarian atmosphere of the time which had reduced tensions between the two nations, and made conversions easy. Even in Connaught, 'the most Catholic part of Ireland', social-religious tensions lessened.[64] Although the numbers of Catholics were increasing greatly, while the proportion of Protestants was falling, even matters like mixed marriages which had once caused so much social tension were accepted easily.[65] In the towns where the Catholics were taking over most of the trade discrimination was becoming rarer, and even in Dublin there was clear evidence that: 'Catholics and Protestants were learning to live together'.[66] When so much social consensus was emerging as a Catholic middle class began to appear, and there was little or no attempt to apply the penal legislation of previous times, conformity rapidly increased as the question was asked 'whether the difference between being a Protestant and a Catholic was sufficient to justify putting one's estate in jeopardy'.[67]

The sermons of the period show clearly the waning of sectarian concerns on the part of the Established Church clergy. Henry Jenney, member of an ecclesiastical planter family that had been in Armagh for nearly a century, preached a 'Gunpowder service' sermon before the House of Commons in Dublin in 1731, urging Protestant charity towards the Catholic poor in their 'abject condition'. He also urged toleration for their betters so long as they were law-abiding, not bringing upon themselves the penal statutes that were now only 'empty menaces... so tempered with laxity in the execution that as yet there has been no reason to complain of them':

> We must all agree that such of the papists as are obedient to the government and peaceable in their behaviour deserve some indulgence from us and ought not to be treated with rigour only because some of their religion have formerly not been so.[68]

In the same year the bishop of Killala, Robert Clayton, mildly urged that only those Irish Catholics who chose openly to serve the political authority of Rome should be reminded that the penal laws were still in existence:

> ... as may be necessary to prevent the growth of popery, and to secure us against all dangers from the great number of papists in this kingdom.[69]

William King, however, never lost his abiding anxiety over Catholic resurgence. He had experienced vividly, and was never to forget the brief terror associated with the Jacobite rule in Ireland and, as he told one of his correspondents in 1727, there were grounds to be anxious about the Catholics' reassertion of themselves when the government showed no inclination to hinder their economic and social progress:

> I remember something of Ireland for sixty years... but cannot call to mind that the papacy seemed so much indulged and favoured as at present, excepting in King James time. They insult the king's officers everywhere that are concerned in the revenue. Nobody dare accuse their priests, or hinder their insults; for amongst their mobs they either maim them or knock them in the head... they have proposed themselves, as I understand, two maxims: the first is to underlive the Protestants, as to expenses; and the second is to outbid them for all

farms that are to be new set. By this means they worm out Protestant farmers... As to the trade of the kingdom they have got the best of it into their hands, and have several advantages of the Protestants. A popish merchant is better received in popish countries with which we trade than Protestants; and the generality of farmers and graziers in Ireland being papists, they choose to put their goods into the hands of those of their own religion; and lastly the country assists them in running their goods both out and inward.[70]

William King was recording in his time what has become increasingly clear to many modern historians, that under the penal laws the Catholic church and the community it represented:

> ... had more freedom to work out its destiny in Ireland than it had in many of the countries of Europe where Catholicism was the State religion, and where Catholic rulers constantly intervened in church appointments and in church policy.[71]

King's concern about the government's toleration of increasing Catholic assertiveness was shared in particular by the Huguenots in Ireland who had, like him, directly experienced Roman Catholic oppression in the past.

III   The Huguenots in Ireland

The structure of the penal laws was based, as we have noted, on the model of Louis XIV's repressive measures against the Huguenots, and there have been some Roman Catholic writers who have argued that the same spirit of vicious repression characterized the Irish government's system of religious oppression. In the words of the renowned nineteenth century polemicist, and future archbishop of Sydney and cardinal, Patrick Francis Moran:

> Everything was done by the persecutors that cruelty, or greed, or religious bigotry, or hatred of race could suggest to crush out the very life blood of the Irish peasantry.[72]

When charges of this nature are made it is often suggested that what lay behind any Protestant manifestation of bigotry was the unforgiving hatred of Roman Catholicism which was never abandoned by the Huguenots in Ireland. The 1697 Bishops Banishment Act, for example, had been interpreted as an act of revenge engineered by Henri de Ruvigny, earl of Galway who had been the last deputé général to Louis XIV at the time of the Revocation of the Treaty of Nantes.[73]

There is no doubt that up to 10,000 French and other refugees who came to

Ireland, fleeing from French religious persecution brought with them a deep loathing for the civil and religious authorities that drove them into exile. The earliest group arrived in the second half of the sixteenth century, fleeing the attentions of Catherine de Medici in France, and the duke of Alva in the Low Countries. Others followed the reduction of the Huguenot stronghold of La Rochelle by cardinal Richelieu, and in the 1667 period the duke of Ormond encouraged 500 families of Walloon and French weavers to settle in Carrick-on-Suir. A major migration took place after the Revocation of the Treaty of Nantes in 1685. The last group of emigrés were those who came after the ending of the War of Austrian Succession in 1748. At that time unemployed soldiers joined with the Jesuits in hunting down the members of the few Protestant communities that could still be identified: Dublin newspapers recorded boatloads of Huguenots arriving in the 1750's and 1760's, and some came as late as 1787, shortly before the chaos of the French Revolution put an end to their sufferings.[74]

When the Irish Protestant population was small, especially in the south of the island the influence of the Huguenots was considerable. They came from privilege in France, formed almost a third of William's army,[75] and those who settled with the help of grants from the crown, greatly strengthened the anti-Catholic spirit within both the Church of Ireland and nonconformity. Not only did they maintain their French language and distinct identity, but also a militant Calvinist theology which often brought them into tension with the latitudinarian clergy of the establishment. In a town like Portarlington, which was part of the estate of the marquis de Ruvigny who had commanded the Williamite horse at the battle of Aughrim, the Huguenots remembered their long history of persecution, and horrors like the St. Bartholomew's massacre. One of the reasons why some of them refused to conform to the established church was their conflict with William Moreton, an imperious English 'high church' prelate who was deemed to be overly friendly to the papists. The Huguenots simply could not abide a bishop who could talk of state payment for popish prelates.[76]

Their educational superiority and manufacturing skills brought many of them to Dublin and by 1720 they were about 4,000 in number, about 5% of the city's total population. Some of them were master weavers who moved into the Liberties which became a strongly Protestant area in eighteenth century Dublin. One of the Williamite half-pay officers, the first David Diggues la Touche, helped to persuade other skilled Huguenot artisans to come to Ireland to give their expertise to the building up of the linen and silk trades, as in the case of Louis Crommelin in Lisburn. Other Huguenots, like the La Touche family, or Jeremiah D'Olier emerged as powerful bankers and property developers. They married into the Protestant nobility, and one of the chief means of assimilation into Irish Protestant society was provided by preferment in the Church of Ireland.

Within the Protestant churches and the dissenting bodies maintained by the Huguenots the influence of the emigrés was immense. Peter Drelincourt, for example, who became dean of Armagh in 1691 was the son of a well-known pastor and writer in France. Shortly after his arrival in Ireland he became chaplain to the duke of Ormond, and had published a typically Protestant tract, *Speech Made to the Duke of Ormond to Return Humble Thanks for the French Protestants Lately Arrived in the Kingdom.*[77] This was published in 1682 before the revolutionary crisis, and was typical of the kind of militantly Protestant publications which the Huguenot clergy would produce throughout the eighteenth century. In 1746, following the Jacobite débacle of the previous year, James Sercesi brought out his *Popery Always the Same* which had wide English and Irish circulation as it dwelt on the role of the priests in stirring up bigotry, and promoting violence against Protestants. Their actions, he said, would: 'astonish and amaze an English reader not at all used to such enormous cruelties'.[78] An anonymous work, *Historical Memoir of the Most Remarkable Proceedings Against the Protestants in France, 1744–1751* was published in 1752 with its thesis arguing: 'the spirit and essence of popery to be cruel and persecuting'.[79] In detail it listed the names of those recently degraded from the nobility, banished, flogged, imprisoned in the galleys for life, or put to death. It also included the names of children in Normandy forcibly taken from their parents to be reared as Roman Catholics. Philip Le Fanu, rector of Clonegal in the Ferns diocese was more scholarly in his anti-Roman writings, such as his *History of the Council of Constance* of 1780, as was Daniel Beaufort, rector of Mountrath in the Ossory diocese who brought out his *Short Account of the Doctrine and Practices of the Church of Rome Divested of all Controversy* in 1788.[80]

These scholarly Huguenot writers, with a legion of lesser writers who produced anti-papal broadsides, never let the Irish Protestants forget the memory of the St. Bartholomew's massacre, the *dragonnades* and the galleys where so many of their relatives languished. It was as unlikely for them to do so as for European Jews of the twentieth century to forget the Nazi holocaust. Their influence on the Irish Protestant psyche was immense. There were four Huguenot congregations in Dublin, two of them within the establishment, and involvement in political, economic and intellectual life, as well as intermarriage brought these fiercely anti-Roman people into the mainstream of Irish social development. The first literary periodical in Ireland, the *Literary Journal* (1745–1749) had as its editor the nonconformist Huguenot, Peter Droz. Families like the Le Fanu, Fleury and Maturin became leaders in the evangelical wing of the Church of Ireland; the Saurin family included a dean of Ardagh, as well as the resolutely anti-Catholic Emancipation bishop of Dromore, James Saurin, and his ultra-Protestant brother William who was attorney-general of Ireland from 1807–1822. It is not surprising that when the Huguenot bishop Richard Chenivix died in 1779, after thirty-three years at Waterford, there were then three deans and three archdeacons in the Church of Ireland who were Huguenots. None neglected to remind the Irish Protestants of the genocide of their people, and as late as 1907 Edward Arber's *Torments of Protestant Slaves in the French King's Galleys and in the Dungeons of Marseilles (1686–1707)* was printed for readership in Ireland and England.

It was not difficult for the Irish Protestants to add to their memory of 1641 and of the oppression of the Jacobite era, the remembrance of the sufferings of the Huguenots. Money was gathered at St. Patrick's for the suffering Protestants on the continent.[81] When the pious, prudent and learned Theophilus Bolton, who was to become archbishop of Cashel, preached the Irish rebellion sermon at St. Andrew's, Dublin, in 1721 he said when the papacy could encourage Catholic princes savagely to attack Protestants in French territory, and 'to utterly extirpate' one of the most flourishing reformed churches of Europe:

> It is extremely difficult to believe him serious who asserts that a reformed church may be safe under a prince of the Romish persuasion.

Bolton was considered to be a leader of the 'Irish interest' among the bishops, and his sympathy with the Huguenot cause, like that of so many others in the established church was of great significance in strengthening Protestant resolve about the dangers of Roman Catholicism in an increasingly latitudinarian age.[82] The Huguenot cry for 'freedom for the children of God' was not ignored by the Irish Protestants in the age of the penal laws who remained fascinated by their 'poor brethren in France': 'victims of superstition which are led or rather dragged to the temple of the idol'.[83]

The militant faith of the Huguenots contrasted with the retiring pietism of the almost nine hundred German-speaking Palatines who fled the armies of Louis XIV and settled in Limerick and Kerry. They were in danger of losing their identity until they were revitalized by the preaching of the early Methodists. It was from the Palatine village of Ballingarrane that Philip Embury and Barbara Heck emigrated with others to America to begin the Methodist Church in the New World.[84] They too had suffered severely from the Roman-French persecutions, but they were a simpler people than the Huguenots, very much a minority because of their German language and culture, and their energy was devoted to keeping their communities ethnically intact. Because of their vulnerability they remained religiously and socially introverted, avoiding conflict with their Catholic neighbours, and seeking survival as an end in itself. Some of them, on the Ponsonby-Barker estate at Kilcooley, county Tipperary, were delighted in 1798 to meet Hessian troops who spoke German.[85]

Modern Irish historiography, reflecting the ecumenical ethos of the late twentieth century, has tended to produce a curiously non-sectarian mentality which is attributed to the eighteenth century Huguenots: 'Victims of persecution in their native country, social outsiders subject to constraints in their adopted country, they are improbable promoters of the Penal Laws'.[86] Their 'ideological' writers in both England and Ireland, however, never ceased in their pamphleteering, and it is much more likely that the only reason they did not bring about a strengthening of the penal laws was that the general climate of opinion in Protestant Ireland was against them doing so. When their families were still being sent to the galleys throughout the first three-quarters of the eighteenth century, and their collective memory of past wrongs showed no sign of disappearing, it would have been 'improbable' if they had not 'promoted' wherever possible anti-papal and anti-Catholic sentiments. William Saurin, in later years, was to say that he was nourished on such ideas with his mother's milk,. He had no hesitation when he was attorney-general in advising Robert Peel. the chief secretary, on the danger in 1816 of the Roman Catholics encouraging and directing the 'brutality and savagery' of marauding bands of peasants:

> Advisers such as Saurin... had long counselled that the Roman Catholic religion was the 'grand cause' of their country's evils and disturbances. They were intensely suspicious of a priesthood, estimated to number well over 2,000 which... claimed to be the true and only church of Ireland, and exercised a powerful influence over millions of 'ignorant and ferocious' peasants who evidently regarded the descendents of Protestant settlers as usurpers of their land and enemies of their church and religion.[87]

It is naive and wishful thinking on the part of some historians to consider that when the Irish Protestants never forgot the rising of 1641, and the Irish Catholics nursed their memory of the massacre at Drogheda in 1649, that somehow the Huguenots ceased to recall their continental oppression once they got to Ireland. A clerical family, the Maturins, never forgot that Peter Maturin who brought them to Ireland had been crippled by twenty-six years in the Bastille.[88] Saumarez de Bourdieu, minister of the French church in Lisburn in the mid-eighteenth century took pride that his family had fought with Schomberg at the Boyne, and lamented that the new laws against the Huguenots issued by Louis XV in 1724 brought confinement to the galleys for life if one attended a reformed church service.[89] The Trench family treasured in their family history the story of an ancestor leading Williamite forces through the bog to obtain victory at Aughrim.[90] The sufferings of their compatriots and relatives in France were to continue in the reign of Louis XVI, with freedom assured to them only by the revolutionary Constitution of 1791. After generations of persecution, remembrance of the St. Bartholomew massacre, the *dragonnades,* the Revocation of the Treaty of Nantes and the galleys were difficult to exorcise, and they made their contribution to the evolution of the Protestant mind in Ireland.

IV Ireland and the Enlightenment

The hatred which the Irish Huguenots had for the papacy as well as all things Catholic was not an insular phenomenon. During the eighteenth century in Protestant Europe popular anti-Catholicism joined forces with the irreligious tendencies of the intellectuals like Voltaire and Diderot to show detestation of the Jesuits, the other religious orders, and everything associated with the religious wars of the seventeenth century which had brought so much horror upon society: 'The man in the street was quite convinced that the Pope was Antichrist, or the incarnation of Satan, and that the Roman Mass was nothing else but sorcery'.[91] Even John Wesley who deeply appreciated traditional Catholic spirituality wrote often about the 'papist peril', and objected strongly when the Saville Act of 1778 lifted some of the penal laws. His brother Charles in his hymns could write of the 'blind sons of Rome'.[92] The Wesleyan *Public Advertiser* stressed the Roman peril: the militant ecclesiastical system which had never repealed the canon of the Council of Constance that, 'no faith is to be kept with heretics'.[93]

A complex of cultural and religious developments on the continent, in Britain and in Ireland ensured, however, that the religious animosities of the Huguenots and other militants never again became a dominant issue in either church or state. The age of Europe's wars of religion was past, and both the Roman Catholics and the Protestants were beginning to realize that the mass of people could not be forced into church establishments. Events proved that there would always be dissenters, those who would refuse to conform, and even the most thorough-going of inquisitions could not eliminate them. France had for a long time persecuted Huguenots in the Cevennes, the Camisards, who had fought back against their oppressors, yet by the 1760's the Duc de Choiseul, who dominated the government, supported the expulsion of the Jesuits who had led in the terrorizing of Protestants in the French territories. He also turned a blind eye to the attempt of the few Huguenot survivors to reorganize themselves after so many years of pogrom.[94] Very slowly the traditional Tudor ecclesiastical policy of qualified toleration of religious minorities that were not a threat to the state was being accepted in many parts of Europe. The great Catholic powers of Spain, Austria and France were now less expansionist in their designs and Protestant fears were easing. In England and Ireland by the time Louis XVI was on the throne Catholics were no longer looked upon as a potential French fifth column and when France intervened in the American War of Independence English Catholics prayed for George III in the canon of the mass.[95]

Religious toleration inevitably accompanied the coming of the Age of Reason and in the late seventeenth and early eighteenth centuries the Enlightenment spirit encouraged speculative theologians who far transcended the traditional theologies of either Rome or the Protestant churches. In England, Edward Stillingfleet, the future bishop of Worcester, had published in 1659 his *Irenicum a weapon-salve for the churches wounds* which dismissed forms of church government as unimportant. In 1664 he wrote his *Rational Account of the Grounds of the Protestant Religion,* a latitudinarian tract with a strongly anti-Jesuit bias representative of current sectarian thought. The Quaker, William Penn, issued his *Great Case of Liberty of Conscience* in 1671; and during the years of revolution 1689–1692, John Locke pleaded the case of religious liberty for all who were not a danger to the state. Three years later he brought out his *Reasonableness of Christianity* which was greatly praised by the free-thinking Deists of the age. The influence of this kind of thought in Ireland was represented by a convert to Protestantism, John Toland, whose work of 1696, *Christianity not Mysterious* radically challenged the Irish intelligentsia before Toland was forced to flee to the continent to be feted in many royal courts.[96] It was to take a long time before such ideas of rationalism, ecclesiastical indifferentism, and religious toleration were to filter down to influence the mass of churchmen, but they were in the air, and they did ensure that even in Ireland the sectarian spirit among both the Catholics and the Protestants was now tempered.

The great English divines of the early eighteenth century, like Joseph Butler, a prominent exponent of natural theology and ethics, who became bishop of Durham in 1750, or William Law who brought out his *Case for Reason* in 1731, were not supportive in any way of the sectarian passions of the past.[97] Neither was the great Irish-born bishop of Cloyne, George Berkeley, who was the most tolerant of men. He established a spinning school, a workhouse and a hospital for poor Catholic neighbours; conducted services in Irish, and recommended the admission of Catholics to Trinity College without them attending chapel, divinity lectures or learning catechisms.[98] Very much in the Bedell school of churchmanship Berkeley viewed any call for the implementation of the penal laws as morally reprehensible, an offence to Christian reason.

One of the most influential of Irish Protestant prelates was archbishop Edward Synge of Tuam: 'who for many years exercised a great influence over all Irish policy'.[99] His eirenical *Essay on Catholic Christianity* of 1729 was considered to be a theological masterpiece, and in his writings he urged Protestants to ignore the irrational religion of the Catholics with their absurd worship. He saw no reason 'why they as well as other sects ought not to enjoy the benefit of toleration':

> Where different parties or churches cannot be brought to an agreement touching the circumstantials or religion they ought to treat one another with Christian charity and mutual forbearance.[100]

As for the penal laws, they were to be deplored, offending as they did 'men's consciences' which all men ought to obey for the sake of their salvation. His son Edward, who became successively bishop of Clonfert, Cloyne, Ferns and Elphin shared his father's religious opinions, and had published six sermons (including his remarkable sermon before the House of Commons in 1725 which we have noted); he was an exemplar of his father's popular and decidedly non-sectarian *Gentleman's Religion with the Grounds and Reasons of It,* 'a rational account of religion and Christianity in general' for 'men of reason and understanding'.[101] Synge was cultivated enough that Handel praised him for being 'learned in music'.[102] Like his father he was a prelate of influence.

On one level religious toleration by the Protestants of the established church in Ireland reflected the growing influence of religious latitudinarianism, or even indifferentism, which was increasing among so many of the European churches. Enlightenment ideas of toleration even had affect in Ulster, for there the ministers and others who studied at the Scottish universities imbibed many of the characteristic ideas of the period—such as those of the Declaration of Independence of their American cousins who spoke of securing for all men the right to 'life, liberty and the pursuit of happiness'. More practically, however, the growing religious toleration in Ireland was a reflection of the diminishing threat from the great Catholic powers of the continent, and the end of the Jacobite movement. The 1745 Jacobite rising was not supported by the Catholics in either England or Ireland in any significant way, and it was from that time that the government began to relax its vigilance in the latter country. Five years after the rising Prince Charles Edward visited London secretly and was formally received into the Anglican church. Nine years later he publicized his change of allegiance: 'The Roman Catholic religion... the artfull system of Roman Infallibility... has been the ruin of the royal family'.[103] Charles Edward was to return to Roman authority in his last days, but the papacy avoided the Stuarts from the time the Old Pretender died in 1766, and ignored his son's claim to the English throne. By this time the English Catholics were in disarray. Richard Challoner was the conscientious bishop of the London district for forty years, 1741–1781, yet he could do little to arrest the loss of Catholic morale. The Catholic aristocracy and peerage were both withering away, and the laity were taking control of temporalities from the clergy in the cisalpine movement, a kind of English Gallicanism. Though the Relief Act of 1778 marked the beginning of the dismantling of the penal laws there was still no change in Roman Catholic fortunes as the decline in influence and numbers continued between then and 1790.

The recusants were reminded at this time by riots that broke out on 2 June, 1780 that 'no popery' was still an issue with the English populace regardless of the latitudinarian ideas of toleration of the privileged classes. A mob headed by Lord George Gordon, a Scots eccentric and fanatic, marched on parliament to demand repeal of the Relief Act of 1778. Catholics had their houses pillaged and the city was taken over until the king ordered the military to restore order. About 285 people died as a result of the rioting, and it was vividly clear to the government that the traditional fear and hatred of the papacy was still a factor in English society. During the rioting the Irish who were engaged in trade in

London received special attention from the mob,[104] but in Ireland itself the crisis passed without incident. The English recusants were distraught enough at this juncture to have their bishops, clergy and laity of note sign a 'Protestation' in 1788 drawn up by the radical peer, Lord Stanhope:

> ... they did not believe that the Pope held power to release subjects from their allegiance to George III their lawful king; no obedience was due to the Pope or to a General Council should they be required to take up arms against the government; 'we acknowledge no infallibility'; the Pope could not dispense oaths, nor might Pope or priest pardon perjury, rebellion or high treason... it was not true that faith need not be kept with heretics.[105]

Led by the cisalpines the recusants went along with their 'assimilation instincts', ignoring even the disciplinary decrees of the Council of Trent on marriage.[106] As for the authority of the Holy See: 'to the cisalpines the papal doctrine and Rome itself seemed, although true, extremely uninteresting'.[107] Richard Challoner and his co-adjutor of the London district, accepted much of what was wanted by the Catholic 'chieftest gentry', and lived at peace with a government and social order that sought to redress the extremism of the Gordon explosion. Though the Roman Catholics were to remain as second class citizens until 1829:

> The practice of treating them as pariahs soon ceased to be general and gradually became a symptom of socially inadmissable bigotry.[108]

The weakness of the eighteenth century papacy had been revealed to English churchmen from 1716 when William Wake became archbishop of Canterbury. He had been chaplain to the English embassy in Paris, had met many of the leading Gallican churchmen, and almost immediately after he became primate he began to correspond with them. Two of the Sorbonne theologians, Dr. L.F. Du Pin and Dr. Piers Girardin, were strongly opposed to the papal directed persecution of the Jansenists, and they considered with Wake how the papal authority might be reduced to one of mere honour, and how a union of the Church of England with the French Gallican church might be brought into being. What Wake was suggesting for the French Gallicans was the kind of decisive break with Rome that William Bedell and Paolo Sarpi had considered in Venice in the preceding century. This was needed, they agreed, some form of an ecclesiastical union where:

> ... each church ought to enjoy its own liberties, rights and customs, which ought to continue unshaken and which cannot be infringed by the Roman pontiffs.[109]

Wake realized there was no hope for such a scheme without support of the civil powers in both countries, and the correspondence ended with the death of Dr. Du Pin. The very fact that church intellectuals could openly discuss such an issue, with some support from the archbishop of Paris, however, reveals the loss of authority of the eighteenth century papacy. Within most parts of Europe the conviction was arising that now was: 'the time to shake off an intolerable yoke'. [110]

The pope at the beginning of the eighteenth century was Clement XI, an experienced ecclesiastical civil servant who was ordained priest shortly before the conclave which elected him. He lacked political sagacity, found himself at war with the Austrian emperor and in 1708 his papal army of some 20,000 troops had to surrender at Ferrara. By the time that the War of the Spanish Succession came to an end in the Treaty of Utrecht in 1713 Rome was virtually ignored internationally. In France the Jansenists were openly anti-papal, united with the Gallicans on occasion in opposition to Roman authority, with much talk of appealing to a future general council of the church to hear their case. After Clement tried to silence the Jansenists in the bull *Unigenitus* in 1713 he found that what had been a French debate about religion had turned into a European discussion of the see of Rome as a teacher of doctrinal truth. When the pope tried to persuade the English Catholic bishops to take an oath of allegiance to the Hanoverians, some of the prelates refused to abandon the traditional papal claim to depose heretical monarchs. [111] To add to Clement's trouble a violent earthquake and flood devastated much of Rome in 1703, there was a great shortage of food in the city, sickness became epidemic, and then came a public scandal when senior churchmen were accused of abusing young ladies to whom they had given refuge:

> Hostile opinion made much of the incident, at home as well as abroad, and the authority of the Holy See was affected at a time when its influence almost everywhere was beginning to decline. [112]

The policies of the next two popes were almost as disastrous as those of Clement XI. Innocent XIII (1721–1724) recognized Austrian rule in southern Italy in return for Austrian recognition of his own right as feudal suzerain. He then returned to the policy of supporting the exiled Stuarts, and promised the Old Pretender financial support if he was able to reestablish Roman Catholicism in England. He also managed to divide the curia over his strong opposition to the Jesuits. His successor, Benedict XIII (1724–1730) was a holy and lively old Dominican, the compromise candidate of the cardinals representing French, Spanish and Austrian interests. He was dominated by an unscrupulous man, Niccolo Coscia who pillaged the papal court through bribery and the selling of papal offices after Benedict made him a cardinal. The take-over of church property was scandalous at this time as the rulers in Savoy and Sicily joined with others in the favourite sport of the Catholic monarchs, 'despoiling the papacy'. Elizabeth Farnese, the queen of Spain, was able to wrest from Rome a cardinal's hat for her seven year old son.[113]

The decline continued during the ten year rule of Clement XII, a 'caretaker' pope elected in an exceptionally contentious conclave. Aged, and blind from 1732 he had to endure the overrunning of the papal states by Spanish troops, and a revolt of the Roman population over recruitment of their citizens into the Spanish army. Benedict XIV who succeeded Clement in 1740 was liberal, intelligent, a cultured lover of the arts, much appreciated by the *philosophes*. He had wise advisers but, gentle by nature, he made concession after concession to the secular powers. A concordat of 1753 practically surrendered all church appointments in Spain to the crown. Frederick II was recognized as king of Prussia, though he had taken over Silesia with its large Roman Catholic population. A decree of 1741 exempted mixed marriages from the juridical form prescribed by the council of Trent. Benedict only half-heartedly condemned the 1753 edition of Voltaire's works, and by the time he died the Holy See was granted little authority even in nominally Roman Catholic countries.

Voltaire had argued that 'nothing can be accomplished against infamy until the Jesuit order is destroyed',[114] and the next pope Clement XIII (1758–1769) faced the problem of dealing with the 'grand grenadiers of fanaticism and intolerance' as they were labelled by the *philosophe* d'Alembert. Clement tried to stand up to the fierce attack on the Jesuits and papal authority by the Bourbons who ruled in Spain, France, Naples and Parma, as well as the hostility of the Protestants, the Jansenists, the Gallicans and the *philosophes*. He placed the *Encyclopedia* on the Index in 1759, but the intellectuals and monarchs no longer paid attention to papal anathemas. Portugal expelled the Jesuits in the same year, France followed in 1764, Spain, Naples and Sicily in 1767, and Parma in 1768. France occupied papal enclaves in Avignon and Venaissin. In Germany the pontiff had to battle with Febronianism, the German counterpart to Gallicanism.

By 1773 the next pope, Clement XIV (1769–1774) faced a complete break with Rome, threatened by the Bourbon states, until he issued a brief dissolving the Jesuit order. The Inquisition was abolished in Tuscany and Parma in 1769, in Sicily in 1782, the Index was virtually ignored, and coercion of conscience seemed finally to be recognized as un-Christian and laid to rest. Like his predecessor at mid-century, Benedict XIV, Clement sought to conciliate the spirit of the Enlightenment, and the secular powers:

I prefer to let the thunders of the Vatican rest... Christ would not call down fire from heaven... Let us take care not to mistake passion for zeal, for this mistake has caused the greatest evils to religion.[115]

In his attempt to conciliate Clement XIV virtually abandoned support for the

Stuart cause, and he received hospitably members of the Hanoverian royal family in Rome. These concessions were granted at great personal cost by a pope who was morbidly filled with fear of assassination at this time, when his enemies believed the prestige of the papacy had sunk to its lowest level for centuries.

At the end of the seventeenth century, while Innocent XII had been negotiating with Louis XIV over the issue of Gallicanism in the French church, the Irish had written to Rome to complain that their appeals to the Holy See about their problems were being ignored.[116] An 'exposition sincere' was sent to Rome about 1727, complaining of the penal laws, but this was during the pontificate of Benedict XIII, when the rapacious cardinal Oscia dominated the papal court, and not much attention was paid to the Irish problem. There was an oversupply of ill-trained Irish priests early in the century, 'odious wherever they are';[117] confession, which was so important to the Tridentine reform programme was difficult to enforce; regular religious marriages were often avoided; and fraternization with the Protestants was steadily increasing after mid-century:

> There is a degree of ease in the relations between Catholics and Protestants, and relations continue to be good in many respects for the next few decades, Catholics and Protestants attending one anothers funerals... or Protestants contributing to the building of Catholic chapels.[118]

Most importantly of all was the ease with which the priests who had studied in Gallican continental seminaries fitted in with the latitudinarian religious and social order of Georgian Ireland. Like the English cisalpines the priests tended to ally themselves with the Roman Catholic gentry, rather than with the lower class of people:[119]

> Six or seven years in Paris, Lille or Louvain, did not make living conditions in the south and west of Ireland any easier to contemplate or bear. No matter how gracefully executed, or skilfully constructed, a Louis Quatorze bow and a mud cabin were irreconcilable.[120]

Like their counterparts in the established church the Irish bishops and priests generally identified with the spirit of the age of rationalism and enlightenment, when the bigotry that lingered among some of the Huguenots in the Protestant world, or the regulars in the Catholic, was considered to be atavistic and objectionable. To the great benefit of all: 'despite the popery laws, social relations were easing between Catholics and Protestants'.[121] The Protestants could never afford, as in England, to be indifferent to the Catholics who formed the majority population of Ireland but, as the Catholic gentry was assimilated, the Jacobite threat waned, and the effete papacy of the time showed little or no interest in strengthening its control over Irish Catholicism, it looked as if the age of religious contention was coming to an end. In 1781 the Catholic bishop of Meath wrote to Rome about the Irish Catholics living under: 'the best of kings and an enlightened parliament'.[122] Now the problem for the Protestants of Ireland was how would they react, ideologically and otherwise, to this unexpected easing in traditional sectarian tension.

V   The Protestants and the Easing of Penal Laws

The Presbyterians of Ulster who dominated northern society, especially in counties Down and Antrim, had by the middle of the eighteenth century little or no fear of their Catholic neighbours. This left them free to resent the established church authorities who harried them over matters of marriage, education and inheritance, and even the burial of the dead. They also bitterly resented payment of tithe to the rector of the parish and from the early years of the century a flood of emigrants left Ulster for America for both religious and economic reasons.[123] The majority of those who remained, when they were not expressing resentment of the Protestant bishops and their courts, indulged themselves in internal division within their church as they struggled over the theological issues which have always bedeviled the Calvinist world. Most of them gave their allegiance to the traditional expression of reformation theology summed up in the Westminster Confession of Faith which viewed the pope as the Antichrist, but some Presbyterians welcomed more tolerant latitudinarian ideas of the Enlightenment which came into Ulster from Scotland.[124] The latter group found a leader in Rev. John Abernethy, an eloquent and scholarly minister of Antrim, whose followers were known as 'New Lights' for their welcoming of ideas of the Age of Reason, and their rejection of the formularies of the past. By 1725 those who refused to subscribe to the Westminster Confession had their own Presbytery of Antrim, and another non-subscribing presbytery was also formed in Dublin:

> For many eighteenth century divines, the essence of religion lay in general truths—the existence of a beneficent creator whose worship tended 'to purify and enlarge the human heart' and encourage a benevolent spirit and not in the zealous contention for doctrinal tenets which only did hurt to the cause of true religion.[125]

The quiescence of the Ulster Catholics during the Jacobite invasion of near-by Scotland in '45, encouraged more Presbyterians to relax their suspicion of the papists, and this continued when archbishop Michael O'Reilly of Armagh called on the priests to pray for the king at the beginning of the Seven Years War with France in 1756, and to disavow the contention that the pope could depose heretical monarchs.[126] During the last part of the eighteenth century the Presbyterians tended to ignore the recusants and to engage themselves in their theological in-fighting, as well as to focus on the political issues that were to lead up to '98.

The leaders of the established church could not afford themselves the theological introversion of the Presbyterians according to the primate, Hugh Boulter, who was archbishop of Armagh from 1724 until 1742. His road to preferment had been helped by a remarkable anti-Jacobite sermon which he had preached at Southwark in 1725,[127] and he had served as dean of Christ Church, Oxford, bishop of Bristol, and chaplain to George I prior to his Irish appointment. An intelligent and able careerist he had the confidence of two successive sovereigns and their viceroys, and thirteen times he acted as one of the Lord Justices in Ireland. In his first visitation charge to his clergy, an unusual occurrence in Armagh, he urged his clergy to persuade the Catholic people that only in the crown would be found for them the liberty and security which they wanted. Their Christian duty was to communicate with their parishioners of all persuasions so that:

> ... by fortifying them against the errors of popery you may at least effectively secure them from falling into the snares of the priests who lie in wait on all sides to deceive them.[128]

Boulter knew that the task of persuading the mass of the people to join the established church, to accept 'subordination not servitude'[129] in the words of archbishop of Canterbury, William Wake, was not an easy one. In 1727 he told Wake something of the difficulty facing him when he considered extending the influence of the Church of Ireland:

> There are probably in this kingdom five papists, at least, to one Protestant. We have incumbents and curates in the number of about 800, whilst there are near 2000 popish priests of all sorts here. A great part of our clergy have no parsonage-houses, nor glebes to build them on. We have many parishes, eight and ten, twelve and fourteen miles long with, it may be, only one church in them, and that often at one end of the parish... all agree that no clergyman in the country can live without a moderate glebe in his hands; and... there can be no hopes of getting ground of the papists without more churches and chapels.[130]

As for the papists a report he made to the House of Lords on 'the present state of popery' revealed that popish archbishops and vicars-general regularly exercised ecclesiastical jurisdiction, that there were large and pompous buildings used as mass houses, and 'the papists frequent them as openly as the protestants do their churches'.[131] Apostasies were common: 'in many places the descendants of many of Cromwell's officers and soldiers 'have being gone off to popery'.[132] Among those who became Protestants many of them: 'have popish wives and mass said in their houses and breed up their children papists'.[133] Though Boulter time and again decried the general ignorance and impiety to be found among Catholics and Protestants alike, he affirmed the superiority of the reformed faith and the blessings all the people could receive under the crown. The alternative was that: 'God will give us up to the errors and darkness of popery'.[134]

Boulter was a thorough-going Erastian churchman, but this does not mean he was simply a worldly careerist, without any charitable sensibilities, as his detractors have often portrayed him. His concept of the English 'royal protectorate' included the provision of education for all the people, regardless of their religious persuasions. Back in the days of Wentworth, the archbishop of Canterbury, William Laud, had provided help for schools: 'which might be a means to season the youth in virtue and religion', to rescue a people 'long laid in the silent dark'.[135] Private foundations like those provided by the wealthy Erasmus Smith, and schools set up by individual pious bishops such as Nathaniel Foy of Waterford, or Henry Maule of Cloyne had helped to provide some education for the poor, but what Boulter had in mind was a whole system of education, established by royal charter, to provide education for the poor in Ireland. Sustained by endowments, the education given by the schools was to be free. In them the children were to be 'instructed in the English tongue and principles of true religion and loyalty', and to be given 'a spirit of labour and industry', rather than the 'blind superstition and destructive principles of popery'.[136]

The charter for such schools was obtained in 1733. The bishops and most of the governing class supported the schools, but the catholic priests inevitably opposed their avowed proselytizing purpose, and did all in their power to keep Catholic children out of them. In spite of the great need for education in the country, Boulter's concept of the Charter Schools as the 'great bulwark against popery' had little success in most parts of the country. In part it represented the kind of innocence that an English prelate like Boulter brought into the Irish situation with its traditional sectarian animosities. From the standpoint of the late twentieth century there is considerable naiveté in Boulter telling his clergy of his scheme for 'universal' education:

I must own, for my own part, I should be glad if we could so far prevail on the priests as let us thoroughly instruct their children in those parts of religion about which there is no dispute between our church and theirs.[137]

Those Catholic families who did send their children to the schools complained of social persecution organized by the priests, and soon there were scandalous stories of popish children being transported to other counties, or being apprenticed to Protestant masters in the north.

As a political prelate Boulter had many enemies, and when he died in 1742 he was accused of leaving 'a realm in ruins, and a church in woe'.[138] This is not really fair to Boulter who was judged by Lecky to be 'well-meaning'[139] and Walter Harris, his contemporary, noted his public charities, including extensive relief for the poor during the scarcities of 1727–1728.[140] When he died he left £30,000 to augment benefices, and to purchase glebes; during the shortages of 1739–1740 he was said to have relieved by his own bounty any person in Dublin who applied for help from him. He also pressed the government in London for help to be given to the common people, as in a plea to the Duke of Newcastle in March, 1727:

> Since I came here in the year 1725, there was almost a famine among the poor; last year the dearness of corn was such that thousands of families quitted their habitations to seek bread elsewhere, and many hundred perished; this year the poor had consumed their potatoes, which is their winter subsistence, near two months sooner than ordinary, and already through the dearness of corn, in that want, that in some places they begin already to quit their habitations. I hope we shall meet with so much compassion at the council... that the inconveniences we are at present so frequently exposed to may be gradually removed.[141]

After the death of Boulter another Englishman, John Hoadly, had an undistinguished term as primate. He was followed by another political prelate, George Stone, who became archbishop of Armagh in 1747. A man of boundless ambition, known as 'the beauty of holiness' from his handsome appearance, he had almost no religious sensibilities. He usually acted as head of the commission of lord justices during the frequent absences of the lord lieutenant, and there is much to be said for the comment that he was in reality 'the true Lord Lieutenant' during his primacy.[142] He devoted himself to ensuring that English-men dominated the bench of bishops and, apart from this ecclesiastical function, carried out with the aid of his patron, the duke of Newcastle, brother of Henry Pelham the prime minister, he was not much interested in religious affairs. He did preach a traditional Irish rebellion anniversary sermon in 1741, when he was bishop of Ferns and Leighlin, which spoke of the 'bloody designs' and 'fury of the church of Rome', but once he was primate his tone was suitably modified. In 1751 he urged the Protestants to set a good example for the papists now that repression in an enlightened age was something of the past:

> Without a change of conduct in this and some other particulars all laws for preventing the growth of popery are but mockeries, and were this reformation affected might be unnecessary.[143]

His political enemies were many, and they had many criticisms to make of this 'false, artful, meddling priest'[144] before his death in 1764, but towards the

Irish Catholics and their traditional religion Stone's policy was one of benign toleration. With the war going well against France after Wolfe's victory at Quebec in 1759, with Spain in decline, and the Bourbon powers intent upon pressing Clement XIII to dissolve the Jesuit order, Stone could afford to dismiss magnanimously the need for penal legislation when he preached before the lord lieutenant and the Irish lords:

> The sense of the mildness of the government we live under has extended itself so far that even among those whose religious errors have been the means of their being deprived of the full benefits of a free constitution there have of late appeared dispositions which are extremely laudable, and which surely ought to meet with every encouragement that can be thought consistent with prudence and our own security.[145]

The spirit of Enlightenment religion, which was as apt to concern itself with problems of 'civility' as it was with 'true religion'. was reflected in the mind of the scholarly George Berkeley, bishop of Cloyne, whom we have mentioned in passing. His concern from the time he was a Trinity College student was 'the public good of society'[146], and his ideas were expressed clearly in his *Querist* where he asked questions: 'to make his countrymen think and especially the ruling class among his countrymen'.[147] He particularly asked whether the penal laws against both Presbyterians and the Catholics did not impoverish the whole community, and questioned whether: 'the dirt and famine and nakedness of the bulk of our people might not be remedied'.[148] His concern for the Catholic poor won him the criticisms which William Bedell had known a hundred years earlier, and though the Cloyne Protestants worried about reports of a 'great body of rapparees up in the county of Kilkenny' the crisis of 1745 passed peacefully for Berkeley with the people lighting bonfires at his gate when news came of the young Pretender's defeat.[149] This encouraged Berkeley to address the Catholics in his diocese the following year in an appeal for their loyalty:

> For my dear countrymen of all religions, I shall ask you a few questions... Is not the present mild government planted by law established? And would you hinder the growth of such a flourishing tree under whose kindly shade your lives, your liberties, your estates, and even the Roman Catholic religion has remained unmolested.[150]

Berkeley was very much a peacemaker in his local community, gentle, kindly, eirenic, with a deep love for the Irish Catholic people, but no toleration for the ecclesiastical and political machinations of the court of Rome. When a man in his diocese, Sir John James, indicated in 1741 that he was about to become a Catholic Berkeley suggested he first read Pietro Giannone's *History of*

Naples to see how papal power had been misused. As for papal claims of infallibility Berkeley suggested Plato's allegory of the cave, of men seeing reality dimly and indirectly, should be remembered: 'we dare not take in the high unerring positive style of the Romanists'. Berkeley could not respect Rome's policy of 'silencing her sons and keeping them quiet through fear', and he urged James to balance its system of thought control by joining with others in 'occasional conformity': 'a papist of tolerable reason, though bred up in the Roman church, may, nevertheless, with a good conscience, occasionally join in our worship'.[151]

As for the Roman Catholic clergy Berkeley urged them to join with their Protestant counter parts in service to the poor who looked to them for sustenance;

> Give me leave to tell you that no set of men upon earth have it in their power to do good on easier terms with more advantage to others and less pain or loss to themselves. Your flocks are of all others most disposed to follow directions, and of all others want them most.[152]

His *Word to the Wise* of 1749 revealed a bishop and a man who not only preached an ethic of altruistic love but lived by its precepts. He refused translation to other sees; refused to allow himself to be considered for the primacy; and steadfastly devoted himself to his exhortation of the people of Cloyne, his writings and good works, presenting to his contemporaries in the established church a model for clerical life. During the famine and pestilence of 1741 Berkeley personally doctored the people, served food out of his own kitchen, and gave a bounty to the poor weekly during the terrible winter. There were about fourteen thousand Protestants in his diocese and more than eighty thousand Catholics.

Berkeley's scepticism about papal theological claims was representative of Enlightenment thought generally, and reflected a now traditional Church of Ireland aversion to extravagant religious speculation. In 1709 William King had greatly annoyed the Presbyterians when he criticized their predestinarian ideas, arguing that: 'analogical knowledge of God's nature and attributes is all of which we are capable at present'.[153] Such suspicion of dogma was commonplace among the established church sermons of the period. John Clayton, to whom is attributed the scientific discovery of the possibility of gas lighting, when he was rector of St. Michan's in Dublin regularly criticized the Roman fascination with religious infallibility rather than human reason: 'the mother error... a cloak for ignorance'.[154] Josiah Hort in his time as bishop of Kilmore and Adagh saw one of his primary tasks to be the protection of the minds as well as the bodies of the people of his dioceses:

> ... at this time when the emissaries of the church of Rome are busy in

all quarters of the kingdom to instill their pernicious errors into weak and incautious minds, and to draw them over to their idolatrous communion.

That was in 1729 when the Jacobite threat was still a real one in the minds of many people, but two years later when it was published his *Instructions to the Clergy on the Visitations of the Lord Bishop of Kilmore* urged dismantling of the penal laws:

> Coercive laws may restrain and disable those who hold principles that are destructive to the Church and to the State, but they can never convince nor convert anybody; they may bind men's hands and tongues, but can never reach their hearts. This is only to be done by enlightening their minds, and making proper application to their understandings and consciences.[155]

Enlightening of minds to Hort was to be a quiet process, as he told the clergy of Tuam in his visitation address to them as archbishop of 1742. Even among the Protestant faithful:

> If you should... take occasion to explain and enforce the doctrines of Protestantism and of the established church it might be of great use to fortify your people and prevent apostasies.[156]

As for the papists, the object of preaching among them was to be 'practical', giving them a 'persuasive to a good life', with the Book of Common Prayer presented as an antidote to 'bigotry and high prepossession' in 'this more enlightened and unprejudiced age'.[157]

Proselytizing had little appeal for the clergy or laity of the established church. They agreed with Dr. Benjamim Bacon who assured the Irish House of Commons that what was needed in the country was not sectarian preaching but moral example given by those who represented the Protestant faith:

> Wherever a minister of the established church has been constantly resident, exemplary in his life, and tolerably diligent, he has not failed to gather a decent congregation in time.[158]

A cleric who lived by this philosophy was the dean of Down, Patrick Delany, who regularly visited all in his northern diocese, papist and Presbyterian alike, ignoring sectarian differences while he tried to improve matters like the scandalous condition of the local jail which was of concern to everyone. Most of the clergy were like Delany, tolerant men, not interested in controversy over 'false and erroneous doctrines'. They detested the papacy as a despotic institution which crushed the human spirit, but towards Irish Catholicism as practiced by the people they had little prejudice or animosity. They shared the mind of John Law, bishop of Clonfert (1782–1787) who confessed to a friend that:

> Unable to make the peasants around me good Protestants, I wish to make them good Catholics, good citizens, good anything. I have therefore circulated amongst them some of the best of their own authors whose writings contain much pure Christianity, useful, known and benevolent sentiments.[159]

Sometimes, of course, their liberalism carried them to extremes, and John Clayton's son, Robert, got into trouble when, as bishop of Clogher he wanted to 'rationalize' the traditional faith by removing the Nicene and Athanasian creeds from the prayer book.[160]

One of the better insights into how a Protestant clergyman existed in a remote parish where his flock was a minority of the population was provided by Samuel Burdy, curate of Ardglass near Downpatrick in the last decades of the eighteenth century. Burdy was of Huguenot origin, and he chose to write not of himself but of his friend, Philip Skelton, whom he had first met in 1781. Skelton was in the view of Burdy remarkable for his 'consideration of the consciences of others'.[161] Born in Lisburn in 1706, he was a third generation planter of a family that had survived both the terrors of 1641 and the Jacobite era. He studied at Trinity College, then served in a series of parishes in the wild country around Lough Derg and Pettigo in County Fermanagh. The people generally were rough, uncultured, disorderly, fond of drinking and fighting, and it often stood Skelton in good stead that he was a physically powerful man, although even he on occasion needed a bodyguard. The ignorance of the people was profound whether they were nominally Catholic or Protestant: 'they scarcely knew more of the Gospel than the Indians of America'. Skelton recognized that their advance from barbarism to civility must be a slow and gradual one, but he laboured assiduously among them, 'practiced physic' at Pettigo, and twice he sold his extensive library to obtain food for those starving in times of shortage. He got along well with the Catholic priests, and when news of the Right Boy insurrection in the south leading to the loss of church property reached him his comment was: 'our luxury, pride and neglect of duty must be punished'. This humble cleric when he was leaving Pettigo to go to Devenish after nine years in the wilderness asked the local poor for their blessing when he was leaving. When Skelton died in 1787 Burdy described him as a 'living glory of the Irish church'.[162]

Where even the usually tolerant Skelton displayed a lack of charitableness was in his consideration of the court of Rome. He wrote extensively and intelligently, his works being published in five volumes in 1770, including a large study entitled *Deism Revealed*. In these writings his most penetrating criticisms of Rome appeared in his *Protestant's Manual*[163] where he discoursed on tyrannies like the Creed of Pius IV which had brought so much suffering to the Huguenots and other Protestants, including those who had had to flee to Ireland.[164] Yet the answer to Roman tyranny he argued must be only: 'by reason and Scripture, and not by unchristian retaliations'. He decried how far the Roman church had moved from primitive Christianity through 'novelty and unwarrantableness', but in true Enlightenment fashion he had no intention of using coercion or any other means to force his convictions upon others:

> I give you a full view of popery... and leave you to consider of it... and seriously consider whether it be fit or safe for them to mingle such stuff with their common Christianity.[165]

VI   The Catholics and Protestant Ireland

Two years before his death William King had expressed his belief that the Catholics of Ireland were almost as well off as they had been under James II. It is certainly true that by 1730 the penal laws were of little consequence to the recusants. Catholic businessmen were prominent in Dublin, Cork and Limerick, using their clannishness, wealth and political organization to lobby against discrimination of any kind. A powerful Catholic middle class was appearing which was in no way willing to accept official restriction of its way of life, or its religious preferences. A Jesuit remarked on Catholicism in Dublin in 1747 where a parish system of pastoral care was then firmly established:

> Never was a city better provided with learned and zealous instructors than Dublin is at present, we now begin to have vespers sung and sermons preached in the afternoons. You see hereby how peaceable times we enjoy.[166]

Certain extravagant devotions were curtailed when parliament was in session, but recusant religious practices hardly reflected those of the 'hidden Ireland' mythologized by later nationalist writers. By mid-century the Catholic merchant class was supporting strongly the building of schools, the publication of religious books, and other means of spreading their faith. The privileged members of both the Catholic and Protestant churches seemed to be at ease with one another as they attended one another's funerals, and it was not unusual for Protestants to contribute to the building of Catholic chapels as we have noted. Even the prelates shared in the new spirit of *rapprochement*, with Nicholas Madgett, the Catholic bishop of Kerry agreeing that Catholic servants might attend prayers in Protestant households.[167] George Berkeley, the philosophical Protestant bishop of Cloyne, in his *A Word to the Wise*, called on the priests to transcend traditional religious differences and work with their Protestant neighbours to serve the common good: 'why should disputes about faith interrupt the duties of civil life, or the different roads to Heaven prevent our taking the same steps on earth'.[168]

Many Protestant churchmen, of course, did not appreciate the altruistic ethics of the eirenic Berkeley, and remained unimpressed also by the tolerant spirit of a prelate like Madgett, whose mind had been broadened by his work as president of a college in Paris. They were nervous about the growing power of the Catholics, and remained suspicious of the new spirit of accord in the country. Some believed that the recusant merchants had become wealthy through their contacts with disloyal Irish exiles on the continent,[169] and the great population increase among the Catholics caused them alarm at a time when Protestant emigration from Ulster was constant.[170] Among them also was a deep suspicion of the loyalty of the many converts to the Protestant faith, especially those in the legal profession.[171] They noted that recruitment of Irish Catholics into the armed forces was increasing: by 1775 recruitment was openly encouraged throughout the country, and by the Napoleonic era the Irish were to form up to a third of the regular army's rank and file.

There was less Protestant anxiety in both England and Ireland after the failure of the Jacobite venture of 1745, but as the Gordon riots of 1780 in London were to show there was still among the Protestant populace as a whole an abiding antipathy towards Roman Catholicism. In Ireland, by the 1770's, the confidence of the Protestant ascendancy was such that there was less concern for the political and social influence of the faith of the majority population which was dismissed as superstitious, idolatrous and intellectually degrading. An overbearing paternalism developed among some of the Protestant landlord class who assumed, in the words of the nineteenth century historian, J.A. Froude, that God had left the Irish 'as a race unfinished':

Nature has allotted superiority of strength to superiority of intellect and character; and in deciding that the weaker shall obey the more powerful, she is in reality saving them from themselves, and then most confers true liberty when she seems most to be taking it away.[172]

Unfortunately for those Irish Protestants who thought in these proto-Darwinian terms their complacency was soon to disappear because new ideas of radical egalitarianism began to enter Ireland in the last thirty years of the eighteenth century. Once more the Catholics and Protestants of Ireland were to find themselves in conflict, but not as a result of the intrusion of authority from either Rome or London. The new concepts of the 'rights of man' were to shatter the brief period of religious and political accommodation of the Catholic and Protestant communities in Ireland.

Protestant Ireland was to show itself unprepared for the ideological upheaval which began with the American War of Independence. It was still obsessed with a possible temporal resurgence of papal power, even when the threat of a Jacobite revival was over. When war broke out with France in 1756 the English were concerned as in the past about the recusants taking an oath of abjuration, denying loyalty to the pope or the house of Stuart. In Ireland the Protestants took an intense interest when the Catholic gentry prompted the Catholic primate, Michael O'Reilly, with other bishops to write to the priests urging them to offer prayers for the king and the royal family. The pope disapproved of this action, but from 1760 he made no mention of the Stuart king in his briefs of appointment to Irish sees, and when James III died in 1766 the papacy severed all connection with the Stuart cause. The question of an oath of loyalty remained an issue in Ireland nevertheless and, until 1778 and the first Catholic relief act, the Catholic leaders remained divided over the question of taking or refusing an oath of loyalty.[173]

Insular religious concerns, however, were not as important in determining Catholic-Protestant relations in Ireland as were external developments brought about by the English-French conflict. By the treaty of Paris in 1763 France was obliged to cede a huge territory in America to England, including Quebec with its large Catholic population. London was now faced with the problem of recusancy on a large scale in an area other than Ireland, and by the Quebec Act of 1774 it granted the French Canadians many concessions the imperial government would not grant to the Irish. These concessions greatly alarmed the colonists of the Atlantic seaboard, then meeting in the Continental Congress to protect inequities in British Rule. The Quebec Act greatly extended the boundaries of Quebec southward, and the American colonists feared their own expansion westward would be curtailed. They also resented the favourable treatment given to the vanquished French whom they continued to regard as subjects of a foreign despotic and pro-papist power. The French general Montcalm had been ruthless, as had his Indian allies,[174] in his campaigning against the Americans, and the colonists were furious that the mother country was not only coming to terms with the enemy, but was granting to the Quebecois considerable licence, even in religion. It was not unexpected that shortly after the Quebec Act the American colonists began their War of Independence. The emigrant Protestant Ulstermen among their numbers gave considerable help to what was viewed as a war of freedom.

When the American war began the Catholic leaders in Ireland did all in their power to show their loyalty to the king's cause. Leading members of the Catholic nobility and gentry did their utmost to encourage recruiting, offering bounties to their tenants who enlisted. When a general fast was ordered on 13 December, 1776 for success of the king's arms in America the priests generally encouraged their flocks to observe it. Some Protestants recognized in their proclamations of Catholic loyalty an attempt to win political concessions, and newspapers of the time kept up reminders of the burning of Huss and Jerome of

Prague, the St. Bartholomew's massacres, the Spanish Inquisition and the fires of Smithfield.[175] The Protestant extremists also feared that large numbers of Catholics would enlist; that the regiments which left for America would be replaced by units containing Irish Catholics returning from French service,[176] and that armed papists would become a dominant force in the country. They were also uneasy when the Protestants organized their Volunteer units to defend the country and when from early on Catholics were admitted to them in places like Cork, Kerry and Armagh.[177] Generally, however, the Protestant authorities believed they had little to fear from the Irish Catholics in the early years of the American war; like the earl-bishop of Derry, Frederick Hervey, they dismissed the faith of the people as a 'mild and harmless superstition'.[178]

It is probable that the passive faith of the majority people of the late eighteenth century in Ireland was similar to that of the Irish emigrants who flocked to England at that time, and early in the following century:

> ...for a considerable proportion of Irish catholics their religion was still a folk-religion, barely touched by the counter-reformation, short on formal instruction, and unfamiliar with the obligations of regular religious observance and sacramental practice.[179]

So long as the penal laws were not stringently enforced and the Irish Catholics were left alone to practice their 'folk religion', they were satisfied with religious affairs, 'under the best of kings and the mildest government' as they reported to Rome.[180] Their complaints to Propaganda were concerned with dissensions within the Catholic community, rather than harassment by the government. Their fear was that internal strife or violence might once again expose them:

> ...to the dreadful artillery of penal laws which though never revoked still seems to be almost buried in oblivion in this country.[181]

At every opportunity they attempted to persuade the government, and Rome, of Catholic desire for peace and good order. When a quarrel arose over the Dominican monastery in Mullingar in 1785 the local Catholic gentry hastened to give assurances that this dissension did not reflect disloyalty among either regular or secular priests:

> We the undersigned gentlemen of the county of Westmeath do certify that we have these many years past known the Roman Catholic clergy of Mullingar to be useful to the publick, to have conducted themselves with propriety and amenable to the laws, and that we are sure no gentleman of the established church will at any time molest them or any Roman Catholic clergyman of whatever denomination while they continue to demean themselves as upright and loyal subjects.[182]

As for the papacy of this time, Clement XIV died in the year of the Quebec Act, leaving his successor to deal with the Bourbon states who had bullied the pontiff into dissolution of the Jesuit order. Members of the British royal family had been hospitably received in Rome, and it was now clear that support for the exiled Stuarts had come to an end. In England a Catholic intellectual like Joseph Berington proclaimed bluntly: 'I am no papist, nor is my religion popery'.[183] He had no use he said for those who acknowledged 'the prerogatives of the despots in Rome', and accepted that: 'the flock in the maxims of the Roman court was made for the pastor, not the pastor for the flock'.[184] A popularizer of such convictions was Arthur O'Leary, an Irish speaking Franciscan whom John Wesley found 'not to be wanting either in sense or learning'. He tried to persuade the authorities that those Irish clergymen who had been trained in continental Gallican seminaries would never be disloyal to the sovereign, whatever their spiritual allegiance to Rome:

> The bias of the French-Irish clergyman was strongly in favour of monarchy, and... on his return to his native land...his feelings as a subject underwent no change and he regarded allegiance to the sovereign under all circumstances as a sacred obligation which it would be a political blasphemy to denounce.[185]

There were, of course, cautious men in the Irish hierarchy who were not happy about criticisms that O'Leary and others made about the deposing power of the pope and other prerogatives. The chief of these was the Dominican, John Thomas Troy, who was successively bishop of Ossory and archbishop of Dublin. He had spent thirteen years in St. Clements, Rome, and he opposed the suspected Gallicans in the hierarchy, archbishop James Butler of Cashel, and Patrick Joseph Plunket of Meath. Yet Troy often quoted Bossuet and consistently sought to persuade the Irish that there was no conflict between the loyalties they owed to the pontiff and to their sovereign:

> ...canonical obedience to his Holiness, and communion with the centre of unity was perfectly reconcilable with their loyalty as subjects and the allegiance they had sworn to their gracious sovereign king George III.[186]

These last decades of the eighteenth century were a time of Protestant triumphalism in Ireland. Even before the humiliation of the papacy in the years of the French Revolution it was clear that Roman Catholicism was institutionally a power in extreme crisis. Powerful landlords like 'Humanity Dick' Martin with his vast estates in Connaught became Protestant, as did the father of John Fitzgibbon, the future earl of Clare, and Dr. Patrick Duigenan of Trinity College who emerged as a Protestant bigot. There were also prominent churchmen converts such as Charles Warburton, bishop of Limerick and then of Cloyne who had been trained as a Catholic priest; Thomas Lewis O'Beirne, the very able bishop of Meath, who had been a seminarian at St. Omer; and Walter Blake Kirwan, one time Catholic chaplain to the Neapolitan embassy in London who became one of the greatest preachers in the history of the Church of Ireland. The most spectacular of the converts was John Butler, Catholic bishop of Cork, who renounced his obedience to the papacy, married a protestant cousin, lived with her for thirteen years, and then was received back into Catholicism. At the time when the Irish Protestants were forming their Volunteer regiments, and making a public display of their power in an Ireland largely denuded of regular troops, the Church of Ireland was displaying a remarkable air of assurance which proved attractive to an increasing number of converts.

Another of the noticeable prelates of the time was Richard Robinson, later Lord Rokeby, who was primate of the Church of Ireland from 1765 until his death in 1794. A bachelor, he lived in Armagh with all the magnificence of a prince palatine, dedicating himself to bringing beauty and culture, as well as the reformed faith, to the impoverished city. The handsome stone buildings on the hills of the city reflect his generosity for it was Robinson who endowed the city with a school, a public infirmary, an observatory and an excellent library. He even considered Armagh becoming a university centre for the north, and he was well respected by Catholic and Protestant alike:

> None... of his predecessors resided so constantly in his diocese, nor so punctually fulfilled its duties. None of them gave so powerful a stimulus to the industry of the people or affected such permanently useful improvements in the country.[187]

The most flamboyant of the Protestant prelates was Frederick Hervey, earl-bishop of Derry, the English nobleman and cleric who enthusiastically identified himself with the Protestant patriots, and the Volunteer movement. When the Volunteers held their great convention in 1783, the year following the recognition of Ireland's legislative independence, he strongly pressed for the ending of Catholic disabilities in the debate then taking place in parliament and among the Volunteers. He allowed Catholics to make use of disused protestant chapels, offered financial help to the Catholic bishop of Derry, and in 1771 he called upon Clement XIV when he was in Rome. It was in that city he died in 1803, an object of considerable Irish Protestant suspicion because of his 'popish sympathies' which had led him to be treated with too much consideration by the cardinals. His critics conveniently ignored his generosity which included support to the Presbyterians of Belfast when they built their first meeting house.[188]

A prominent Protestant layman who was the subject of suspicion because of his friendship with Roman Catholics, such as Thomas Hussey, the bishop of Waterford, was Edmund Burke. When he strongly supported the various acts for

Catholic relief he was 'deemed a papist', and Protestant extremists never forgot that his mother, sister and many relatives were Catholics, as had been his wife before she conformed when they were married. However great was his parliamentary reputation, there were those who accused him of being not only a papist but a Jesuit as he persisted in unpopular acts such as welcoming emigré French priests. It seemed almost remarkable that Burke still maintained his conviction that the established church was the best religious institution for those who would accept the comforts it offered to them.[189]

However complaisant the Catholic leaders or sanguine the Protestant élite were about the passing of traditional sectarian conflict in Ireland, there was still a tendency for the lower orders of society to divide over economic, political and social issues, and to identify their group with 'religion'. During the 1761–1765 period there appeared in the south the Whiteboy phenomenon, a peasant revolt against economic oppression in most instances. It happened during the war with France, when Francois Thurot landed at Carrickfergus in 1760 to be met by armed Protestants who repelled the invaders. Despite the victims of the Whiteboy outrages being both Catholic and Protestant, and some of them were priests, there was widespread belief that the unrest was organized by emigré Catholic Jacobites.[190] Although the first outbreak died out in 1766 there was sporadic trouble with Whiteboys for another twenty years, and out of the movement came a martyr remembered in religious fashion with a day set apart for his remembrance, Nicholas Sheehy, parish priest of Clogheen who was hanged in Clonmel in 1766.[191] Sheehy was a folk hero, but generally the Catholic bishops and clergy were not revered by the Whiteboys. In 1775 the Catholic archbishop of Cashel organized the defence of the house of his landlord brother, and the following year the coadjutor bishop of Meath killed a Whiteboy during an attack on his house.[192]

By 1779 John Thomas Troy who had come from Rome two years earlier to be bishop of Ossory solemnly excommunicated the Whiteboys with full 'bell, book and candle', directing the wrath of the Roman Catholic authority against the 'unthinking wretches, their associates and abettors':

> May their days be few, and others take their places. Let their children be carried about vagabond and beg, and let them be cast out of their dwellings. May the usurers search all their substance, and let strangers plunder their labours. May there be none to help them, nor none to pity their fatherless offspring. May their posterity be cut off in one generation. May there names be blotted out and let their memory perish from the earth.[193]

Rome was informed of this solemn excommunication of 17 October, 1770, and how the extreme threat of 'interminable torments' was promised to those guilty of 'nocturnal excursions' and 'unreasonable depredations'.[194]

Few Protestants were aware or appreciative of the resistance that Troy and other Catholic clergy brought against the Whiteboys, and it was widely believed that some priests 'encouraged or at least connived with the levellers', especially in Cork. Fear that a well-orchestrated anti-Protestant movement was taking place in Munster led to the 1786 publication of a remarkable work by Richard Woodward, bishop of Cloyne, entitled *Present State of the Church of Ireland*. In graphic detail the bishop described the threat of burning Protestant churches, the demand that some of them be used as mass-houses, and the suffering of the clergy, deprived of their tithes, whose incomes were so reduced they lived on the edge of beggary. Woodward was convinced that there were sinister directors who encouraged systematic outrages: 'a dark and deep scheme planned by men skilled in law and the artifices by which it may be evaded.'[195] Woodward's work, in turn, brought about a Catholic apologetic which denied that: 'insurrection in the south was a... popish insurrection for the purpose of overthrowing the protestant religion'. The bishop of Cloyne was wrong to resurrect old fears of the 'horrors of blood-thirsty popery', and to propagate calumnies which: 'couple Captain Right with Titus Oates and revive all the old legendary tales of popish plots and popish missionaries'. The fact was that not only Catholic bishops and clergy had spoken out against the Whiteboys, but Lord Kenmare and other Catholic nobility and gentry and asked for government help to contain what seemed to be a spreading insurrection.[196]

Woodward's publication went through many editions and Catholic criticisms inevitably brought forth protestant responses which showed how deep and widespread was the lingering fear of a papal directed Catholic resurgence in Ireland.[197] To try to calm the growing sectarian controversy the liberal Catholic priest Arthur O'Leary published a series of pamphlets addressed to both Woodward and the Whiteboys. In his eirenic fashion he reminded his readers that violence of this nature was not confined to Ireland, as the London Lord George Gordon riots of 1780 had shown. There, he argued, atrocities were committed as great as those of Captain Right in Munster.[198] As for Woodward's charge of sectarian conspiracy and sedition, O'Leary pointed out that a 'crowd of peasants' had begun to attend the Protestant churches because they had: 'shaken off every subordination to their own pastors'. Was this, he asked, the conduct of a people under the influence of: 'agitating friars and Romish missionaries... sent here to sow sedition'?[199] As for the Whiteboys, O'Leary wryly suggested they should appreciate that the tithes they paid went to parsons who: 'trained up from their early days the Protestant nobility and gentry on the principles of morality and virtue'.[200] He could find little to say in praise of those priests who had drawn the wrath of the Whiteboys upon themselves because of their exorbitant exaction of dues from the poor: 'pampered theologians whose God was their belly and whose religion as a hogshead of wine'.[201]

By 1778 it was intimated that the king wished concessions to be granted to the Irish Catholics, and Luke Gardiner, an Irish M.P. who was to die at the hands of the rebels in '98, introduced the first Catholic relief bill. Concerned largely with property ownership by Catholics it granted nothing to the great mass of the people, and left untouched the penal statutes against Catholic ecclesiastics. After Henry Grattan led the Irish parliament into its period of independence, however, other legislation followed, and in the new parliament Gardiner introduced a second Catholic relief act repealing or modifying penal legislation on matters like the residence of bishops and regular clergy, as well as the registration of priests. Yet there remained strong Protestant opposition to the ending of the penal laws, especially when there was so much unrest in the countryside, not least in Ulster where Oakboys protested tithes and Grand Jury injustices, and Steelboys resisted rent rises on Lord Donegall's estates. Though use of the penal legislation was by now very rare its existence provided security assurance for anxious minds. Change was in the air, however, and after the successful American revolution, and with the unrest in France, the authorities were willing to concede much to keep the masses in all parts of Ireland quiet.

Universal hatred of the tithe system threatened to bring even the Presbyterians and the Catholics together, and it was against the background of war with France that Henry Grattan and his supporters pressed for reform of the tithe system in successive bills, and then for further Catholic relief in 1792. This act granted wide concessions, but it still did not deal with the admission of Catholics to the political processes. This demand was only met when a Catholic Convention led by middle class people like the Dublin merchant John Keogh, and the Protestant Wolfe Tone, decided to bypass the Irish parliament and the Lord Lieutenant and to appeal their cause directly to the king. This resulted in the granting of the Relief Act of 1793 which gave Catholics political rights, and most importantly the right to bear arms. The militia units raised after the passing of this act were largely Catholic in composition. Though the oaths they had to take before accepting a seat in parliament kept them out of the legislative process, the middle class Catholic leaders who had taken over from the nobility and gentry were not unhappy with their political progress at this stage. They wanted time to organize themselves further, and in the meantime they shared with their southern Protestant counterparts unease over the liberal and even revolutionary ideas that were developing among the Presbyterians and others in Ulster.

VII   The Ulster Radicals and Catholicism

During the summer of 1789 reports from France took up more and more space in Irish newspapers, and a Belfast paper, the *Northern Star* maintained a correspondent in Paris throughout the revolution. The paper carried in great detail the debates in the French convention; there were seven Irish editions of Tom Paine's *Rights of Man*, and many of the northern intellectuals responded passionately and positively to the ideas of radical liberalism which had appeared in the American Revolution and were now putting an end to the *ancien régime* in France.[202] This revolutionary enthusiasm gave new life to the declining Volunteer movement, and it was the northern Volunteers who began to link the American declaration of independence of 1776, the Irish 'constitution of 1782' and the idealistic determinations of the French revolutionaries. Especially in Antrim and Down, where there was a 'New Light' tradition of theological liberalism, there was not only an upsurge in Volunteering in 1792-1793 but also a movement towards friendly cooperation between Presbyterians and Catholics. The Ulster Presbyterians had also suffered from the penal laws, they too resented being kept out of public life, and they had considerable sympathy for the lot of their fellow 'dissenters' from the established church. Like many other eighteenth century thinkers they considered Catholicism to be a dying superstition, and they no longer paid attention to Rome as either a religious or a political threat.

The Catholics generally did not share the enthusiasm of the Presbyterian radicals for the French Revolution. The French church had suffered much at the hands of the revolutionaries, and by 1794 many of the members of the Irish Brigade in the French army were transferring their allegiance to the British crown. Catholic dislike of continental liberalism helped them to minimize their demands for further concessions after the Relief Act of 1793, and their nobility, gentry and bishops were as hostile to the ideas of the French revolution as were the upper class Protestants. The only real enthusiasm for radical liberalism lay in the democratic Dublin group within the Catholic Committee who were quite prepared to work with the Ulster Presbyterians in the cause of parliamentary reform and civil rights. In 1791 the paid secretary of the Catholic Committee was the young Protestant barrister, Wolfe Tone, who attacked the penal laws that remained in his pamphlet, *An Argument on behalf of the Catholics of Ireland.* Tone wanted to bring together Irishmen of all creeds and to establish complete religious equality. At the same time Tone was no lover of religion, and he especially disliked Catholicism. He sneered at the mass when he was in France, and his hope was that revolution in Ireland would: 'emancipate the catholics from all religious superstition'.[203]

Tone's viewpoint was shared by only a minority of Catholics, such as the physician William M'Nevin who forthrightedly confessed his anti-religious opinions after his arrest, following the rising of 1798:

...the said M'Nevin having acknowledged distinctly that the intention was to abolish all church establishment, and not to have any established religion, and that for his own part he would as soon establish the Mahometan as the popish religion, though he was himself a Roman Catholic.[204]

The tragedy of Tone, M'Nevin and the other United Irishmen who wanted revolution in Ireland was that they never understood the latent power of sectarianism which still bedeviled the great majority of Irish people in the 1790's. It was also the tragedy of the British administration when it sought to strengthen national unity in the face of the threat from revolutionary France once war began in 1793. After the viceroy, earl Fitzwilliam, sought to conciliate Catholic demands for further concessions, Protestant opposition to his policies brought his swift recall. When in the same year, 1795, the Royal College at Maynooth was opened to provide higher education for Catholics other than that provided by the old colleges in revolutionary Europe, Protestant sectarian sensibilities were quickened, and resentment towards the granting of further concessions deepened among the Irish Protestants.

The Irish Protestants generally, apart from the United Irish ideologues in Ulster, knew that in the countryside the tension between Catholics and Protestants was once more steadily increasing. Ideas of 'liberty, equality and fraternity' were in the air, and they had influence among other Irish than the middle class men who formed the United Irishmen. Especially in Ulster there was a great sharpening of sectarian strife among the peasantry in 1795. A climax was reached in September when a pitched battle between Protestant Peep o'Day boys and Catholic Defenders took place at the Diamond in County Armagh. The Defenders who had provoked the conflict were routed, and the victorious Protestants formed what became the Orange Order, to protect their own countrymen's interests, and to protect the Protestant ascendancy.

Many of the objectives sought by the Defenders were those of the Whiteboys of earlier times, but included in the Defender oath of allegiance were ideas reminiscent of the seventeenth century. Among their aims was an intention to: 'plant the true religion that was lost at the Reformation', and for this reason they had been sent on their mission by 'Simon Peter, the head of the church'.[205] There were also in the Defender movement muddled ideas of the Stuarts and the French coming to deliver the Catholics of Ireland. It is still a debatable issue whether the Defenders would have been of significant help to the French, if the expedition of General Hoche to land troops in Bantry Bay in 1796 had been successful. Just before the French arrived the government had agreed to allow the Protestants, who formed the majority of the landlords, to organize units of yeomanry from among their tenants. It was believed that this would balance the power of the largely Catholic militia regiments raised partly by ballot.[206] Ireland was now filled with armed sectarian military bodies, ready to serve as part of the armed nation at war with France. They were obviously more to be reckoned with as fighting units than the Volunteer companies they had replaced, and the problem of the authorities was to keep control of the sectarian tensions in both the militia and the yeomanry in the face of either external or internal threat to the nation.

During 1796 the United Irishmen also developed a military organization, largely in Antrim and Down. Some of the principal leaders were arrested by the end of the year and in 1797 general Gerard Lake was sent to Belfast with extraordinary powers to crush the incipient rebellion of the United Irishmen. His troops were both militia and yeomanry and he intelligently used them in areas where there would be little temptation for them to identify themselves with the rebel cause. It was the Catholic Monaghan militia which terrorized Belfast while the Orange Monaghan yeomanry remained in their rural parishes for the 'policing' of Monaghan.[207] Lake's policy of military repression was so successful in Ulster that it was soon extended with the use of brutal force to Leinster and Munster where large armed bodies of Defenders, now closely linked with the United Irishmen, were openly committed to rebellion. By the end of 1797 in Munster and Leinster the people were suffering from the rival terrorism of troops and rebels alike, the latter seeking arms and intimidating those who opposed them.

The rebel leadership was rounded up in the spring of 1798, but in May Father John Murphy, the Wexford leader of the insurgents, began a month long savage struggle when his forces annihilated a body of the North Cork militia. Other priests provided leadership and, though some Protestant radicals supported the rebels, the insurgents were soon attacking, plundering and slaughtering the Protestant people of Wexford. For many their only chance for survival lay in conversion as the ferocity of the seventeenth century wars of religion swept through the countryside:

> The chapels, both in Wexford and the neighbourhood, and around Vinegar Hill, were crowded with Protestants, who sought to secure their lives, property and liberty, by obtaining from the priests certificates of conformity.[208]

One of the most dramatic of the outrages during the struggle in Wexford took place at Scullabogue where a large group of Protestants had been confined in a barn on the orders of Father Philip Roche 'the mainstay of the whole crusade'. Following 'peremptory orders to that effect' made by a priest the barn was set afire and over a hundred people, including women and children, died.[209] The horror of this event 'left an indelible mark on Irish history', particularly in the memory of the Protestant people. Another image that is recalled by Protestant extremists, on occasion, is that of Father John Murphy (whose bayonet may still be seen in the Enniscorthy museum) leading his troops while holding high his crucifix.

The immediate effect of the Wexford terror was the influence it had in Ulster when news of the 'crusade against Protestants' was received. The Orange Order was by then spreading rapidly and had no trouble reviving old sectarian divisions as tales of the southern 'religious phrensy'[210] were spread, but in spite of this agitation there were in June, 1798 isolated risings by the Ulster United Irishmen who were almost all Protestant. In the one battle of significance, at

Ballynahinch, there were more Catholics in the government forces than among the rebels. The insurgents had hoped for reinforcement from Catholic Defenders but the news from Wexford had influenced the latter, and they were resentful that the leader of the Ballynahinch forces was Henry Monroe, a Lisburn Protestant: 'they even accused Monroe of trying to establish a Presbyterian state'.[211] Many Protestants had already lost any interest in maintaining an alliance with the Catholics. Bishop Percy of Dromore, who was in Dublin when the rebellion was at its height, reported: 'the murder of the Protestants in the south will prevent them ever joining again with them, much less in the present rebellion'.[212]

The last event of '98, the landing of French troops under general Humbert, when the risings had been crushed elsewhere, further alarmed the Protestants. Humbert did manage to persuade a few thousand peasants to join his forces, under the impression that by doing so they were serving the pope and the Blessed Virgin. Though the French forces were defeated, and their poor Irish auxiliaries left to the yeomanry and militia who visited upon them the retaliatory horrors which they had previously inflicted upon the Catholic population of Wexford, the Irish Protestants now lived in a frightened community. They looked upon themselves as wholly dependent upon the British government for protection against future French intervention in Irish affairs, while they considered they were the only authority that could restore law and order in their shattered community: 'they saw themselves on the brink of revolution and regarded their remaining privileges as a thin line of defence'.[213]

Protestant anxiety continued during the winter of '98 when robberies and burnings were reported in Carlow, Waterford and other areas, mail coaches had to be guarded, 'banditti' were reported to be active, and rumours of local risings abounded.[214] They were given little assurance by the government at this time, however, for the new viceroy and commander-in-chief, lord Cornwallis, made clear that he was about to curb the excesses of the military whose manner of bringing peace to the countryside had terrorized even the Quakers of Ballitore.[215] Moreover he showed he was unwilling to countenance any Irish Protestant back-lash against the insurgents. Rather he favoured government relief for the Catholics and announced his intention to rule rationally and justly: 'to overcome religious animosities and the violence of parties' in a country which threatened to fall into a state of anarchy.[216] In the south of Ireland, particularly, there now existed a: 'beleaguered nation of Protestants who felt little more identity with the Catholic masses than George Washington's America with the Red Indians'.[217]

Fortunately for the Protestant community in the south, apart from local agrarian agitation and crime, there was neither leadership nor organization for further revolutionary movement. This was shown clearly when the Protestant Robert Emmet tried to revive the United Irish cause in 1803, and his venture failed after bloody scuffles on the streets of Dublin.[218] The Protestants were also helped by the negative reaction of the Catholic hierarchy to the rising, especially to the ferocity of the Wexford insurrection. The bishops were not happy that the banner of religion had been raised and priests had been in the fore-front of the battle. Their immediate concern after '98 was to ensure that there was no spread of the Wexford contagion elsewhere in the south. William Coppinger, Catholic bishop of Cloyne and Ross, who had nearly lost his life in the rising, urged his 'poor deluded people' to help restore quiet to the country-side: 'your eternal as well as your temporal interests are deeply concerned'.[219] The archbishop of Dublin, John Thomas Troy, denounced the United Irishmen and Defenders, in the same way that he had the Whiteboys earlier when he was bishop of Ossory. On 22 June, 1798 he condemned them as 'a disgrace to Christianity and as the outcasts of society' whose oaths were 'unlawful, sinful, wicked and damnable'—then they were formally excommunicated.[220]

The rising also brought about much soul-searching in Ulster. Although most of the province had been tranquil, and the Presbyterians had defected from the movement of which they had been the main originators, there had existed among the Protestants sanguine hopes, like that of William Steel Dickson, one-time Volunteer officer and moderator of the Synod of Ulster, that the Irish Catholics could share in a new era of civil and religious liberty: 'to prove to the world that the liberality of Protestants had been neither ill-timed nor unsafe'.[221] Yet even Dr. William Drennan, who had been carried along by the aspirations of the American Declaration of Independence, and the proclamations of the French Revolution, had had strong reservations about an alliance with a religious body infamous for 'denouncing knowledge and debate and disquisition'. After the shock of the Wexford rising he confessed his unhappiness that: 'the savagery of the lower Catholics was even greater than the law of retaliation could account for'.[222] Other radicals, like those of Downpatrick Masonic Lodge No. 367 had passed resolutions calling for the admission of Catholics to parliament, but the 'violence of their principles' led them to forget or ignore 'the inherent Protes-tantism of Ulster'.[223] In their extreme liberalism these radicals shared in the error of the United Irishmen leader Wolfe Tone, who was captured and committed suicide shortly after the defeat of Humbert's forces:

> He had embraced... the deistical and republican notions of the revolutionary era, and he so far misunderstood his own countrymen as to believe that they too would readily abandon long-standing animosities of creed and class.[224]

After '98 those Protestants who shared in the liberal hopes of the United Irishmen became a dwindling minority:

> The northern Presbyterians'... revulsion produced a quiet but apparently permanent change in their sentiments. They accepted the Union with Great Britain with very little demur, and never since that day has any

large body of northern Protestants entered into alliance with the Roman Catholics of the south for political purposes.[225]

Chapter VI

Catholic Resurgence After the Union

'...the confessional divide that remained the structural reality of Irish politics'.

R.F. Foster, *Modern Ireland, 1600–1972*, London, 1988, p. 290.

I   The Revival of the Nineteenth Century Papacy

From the time that pope Innocent X was ignored, when he denounced the far-reaching concessions granted to the Protestant powers in the Treaty of Westphalia, the papacy was granted little authority in the world of diplomacy. The leaders of the nations in the age of Enlightenment recognized the outstanding qualities of Innocent XI, who stood up to Louis XIV at the end of the seventeenth century, but there were few other pontiffs who commanded such respect. According to the church's teaching the spiritual authority of each pontiff was unaffected by his temporal activities: 'the waters of divine grace continuing to pass through him unaffected by the possible foulness of the conduit'.[1]   Few historians have been willing to view the popes in this fashion, however, and this was particularly true during the years of the French Revolution.

The successor of Clement XIV, who had been pressured by the great powers to dissolve the Jesuit order, was Pius VI, a politically inept individual, and a rather vain aesthete who bankrupted the papal treasury in his attempts to beautify Rome.   He had one of the longest pontificates in history, from 1775 to 1799, and throughout it he was obliged to offer concession after concession to Catholic rulers who granted little authority to papal claims.   Febronianism in Germany and Josephism in Austria represented the appearance of national Catholic churches, and in 1786 the grand duke of Tuscany supported the synod of Pistoia, presided over by bishop Scipio de Ricci, where the French Gallican Articles of 1682 were adopted, and bishops were exempted from papal authority.   Pius VI was not able to stand up to the leaders of the revolution in France, and after Napoleon invaded the papal states he had to accept humiliating peace terms.   In 1796 he recognized the Republic, ordered Catholics to obey its government, and then had to bow to further demands when the French took over the Eternal City and deposed Pius as head of state.   At the time of the 1798 rising in Ireland Pius VI was being moved from place to place in Italy.   He died a prisoner in France, and was buried in the local cemetery in Valence as 'Citizen Braschi'. It seemed in the last year of the eighteenth century that the demise of the Holy See was to be expected, and the fortunes of the papacy had reached their nadir.

A conclave was held in Venice, however, and the cardinals chose as a compromise candidate a Benedictine monk who took the title of Pius VII. Always open to new ideas, he proved in 1800 to be innovative in his reorganization of the curia, not least in his creation of a layman, Ercole Consalvi, to be cardinal-deacon and papal secretary of state. Consalvi was then only 43 years of age, a man of genius who had been trained in the curia, and he proved to be the aide in diplomatic affairs whom Pius VII so desperately needed in his negotiations with Napoleon. In 1801 the pope agreed to a concordat proposed by the emperor, and though he was also forced to accept the Organic Articles which raised Gallican issues once more, Rome was pleased with the concordat which did much to reestablish papal influence in France, and gave Rome a new position in European affairs. Pius himself was so satisfied with the new honoured position the church was granted in France, where it had previously been persecuted, that he ignored the advice of the curia and took part in Napoleon's coronation as emperor in 1802.

Trouble with Napoleon began again, however, when the pope refused to join in the continental blockade of England, influenced as he was by Consalvi who was a great Anglophile. Pius was forced to have Consalvi resign, and tensions were such that in 1808 Napoleon took over what remained of the papal states, and he occupied Rome. The pope's response was to excommunicate all 'robbers of Peter's patrimony', without mentioning Napoleon by name. This lead to the arrest of Pius and his eventual transfer to Fontainebleau where the emperor bullied the exhausted pope into signing another concordat which included an implied surrender of the papal states. Pius retracted his signature, however and, when military reverses persuaded Napoleon to release the pontiff, he returned to Rome in May, 1814, his moral stature greatly enhanced in the eyes of the English and the other opponents of French power.

One of the pope's first acts was to reinstate Consalvi as his secretary of state, and the cardinal used his diplomatic genius to ensure at the Congress of Vienna that all the pope's temporal domains were returned to him except for the two small enclaves of Avignon and Venaissin in France. Then Pius worked with Consalvi to begin a reform of the papal states, though not along the reactionary lines which were wanted by the *zelanti*, the conservative cardinals. Pius did, however, restore the Jesuits. Then he condemned Protestant bible societies, the religious 'indifferentism' which had been spread by the Enlightenment and the Revolution, as well as the Freemasons who supported the Carbonari, the secret society which was emerging as a revolutionary power demanding Italian unity. By the time that Pius died in 1823 the papacy was once more regarded as a supra-national authority, and the papal office granted respect which it had not enjoyed for generations.

Outright reverence of Rome was revealed in the writings of laymen like the romantic politician vicomte de Chateaubriand who produced, just four days after the concordat was proclaimed in 1802, his intriguing *Génie du christianisme* with its argument that the Christian faith was the main source of art and civilization in Europe, through the stimulus it gave to the intellectual and spiritual creativity of mankind. The work had tremendous appeal to the European conservatives who were caught up in romantic reaction to everything the Enlightenment, and the French Revolution had stood for: 'to summon all the powers of imagination and all the interests of the heart in support of that religion against which they had been armed'.[2] In 1819 the Savoyard Joseph de Maistre appeared as the father of nineteenth century ultramontanism with his work *Du pape* which envisaged a fully theocratic society with the pope its unquestioned head, the supreme arbiter and guide of all peoples and sovereigns. Only one institution, argued de Maistre, had lasted for 1800 years and provided spiritual stability amidst radical flux, and that was the papacy which sought to protect men from the Antichrist of deified man. A contemporary of de Maistre, the Gallican Louis de Bonald in his writings did not give to the pope the pre-eminence granted in *Du pape*, but he too viewed Holy Church as the archetype of all régimes because of its authoritarian structure.

The most influential of these supporters of a revived Catholic church was Felicité de Lamennais, who was also a layman when he began to produce his romantic vision of a social and cultural counter-revolution in Europe led by the papacy. In his early years a devoté of Rousseau, Lamennais was converted with the encouragement of his brother who was a priest and his collaborator in his first work *Réflexions sur l'état de l'Église* published in 1808. In this work he decried reliance on human reason which led to rationalism, intellectual anarchy and atheism, and urged the appearance of a systematic clerical organization to revive the faith. Lamennais was the centre of a circle of like-minded friends who were obsessed with the idea of a clerically-dominated society with the pope as the supreme leader of monarchs and peoples. In 1818 he published the first volume of his *Essai sur l'indifférence en matière de religion* where he developed this theme, and continued it in further volumes in 1820 and 1823. The effect of his writings among many churchmen was tremendous as it seemed to give to Roman Catholicism the promise of a 'second spring', especially when Lamennais argued that without religion European society faced only decay. By 1825 he was extolling the divine right sovereignty of the papacy and the need for it to be recognized:

Rome seems to me nowadays the only motherland of Christians ... No church without the Pope; no Christianity without the Church; therefore no religion and no society without Christianity.[3]

The only hope for civilization lay in the acceptance of the authority of an infallible pope as the trustee of the entire human race rather than some version of the deified state.

From 1820 an important member of the Lamennais circle was René-François Rohrbacher (1789–1856) who was inspired to write his massive twenty-nine volume *Universal History of the Catholic Church* which appeared between 1842 and 1849. He composed the work while he was a professor in the Grand Séminaire, and it was both a sustained argument against the failings of Gallicanism and an apologetic for an extreme expression of ultramontanism. As it was read to an ever-increasing number of seminarians in their refectories its influence was immense. By the end of the nineteenth century it had gone through nine editions, and many of its critics claimed that the influence of Rohrbacher's history brought about the ultramontane victory at Vatican Council I. It was not good history, but the influence of its sustained thesis, which included a shocking misrepresentation of Protestantism, was wide-spread. Controversy of any kind only gave Rohrbacher publicity and the Gallicans found it almost impossible to: 'prevent ultramontane, that is, papist doctrines from spreading among the younger clergy like gangrene'.[4] To the romantic age which it addressed in his religious idealism was to be found:

> ...the idea of what the Vicar of Christ should be like: independent of national, dynastic or other material interests, guided by divine wisdom and animated by Christ's universal solicitude for the whole church and for all mankind.[5]

It was flattering to the papacy to have ideologues such as Chateaubriand, de Maistre, Bonald and Lamennais develop their ideas of a Catholic resurgence, but many conservative churchmen among the *zelanti* preferred to ally the papacy with the reactionary ecclesiastical policies of Metternich and those who wished to resurrect the traditional union of 'throne and altar'. The successor of Pius VII, Leo XII, was elected by the *zelanti* who wanted the church to focus on affairs such as the raising of clerical intellectual, moral and disciplinary standards, and showed little enthusiasm for the church assuming the kind of leadership in the changing of European society urged by Lamennais in his writings, or by a small minority among the cardinals. Leo himself had fallen out with the liberal-minded Consalvi at the time of the Congress of Vienna and, as soon as he became pope, he replaced Consalvi as secretary of state with a much more con-servative cardinal. Then he launched an attack on indifferentism, toleration, and Freemasonry, reinforced the Index and the Holy Office, favoured the Jesuits, and turned his attention to his temporal rule in the papal states. There the feudal aristocracy was given great privileges; traditional ecclesiastical courts were reestablished; a close control of university teaching was introduced; and the Jews were once more restricted to ghettos. Secret police were employed to use the death penalty, if it was necessary, as every sign of resistance to the papal autocracy was ruthlessly crushed. By the time he died in 1829, just before Catholic Emancipation was granted in Britain and Ireland, Leo was widely hated as the pope who had made the papal state one of the most backward in all of Europe.

Leo XII was more conciliatory with the European rulers than he was with his own subjects, and he devoted himself to building up the prestige of the papacy. He announced a Holy Year for 1825, which was a moderate success as pilgrims poured into the Eternal City. He also continued Consalvi's policy of establishing concordats, and did all he could to reinforce the conservative powers who were resisting the ideas of liberalism which the French Revolution had spawned and which were still 'in the air'. He responded positively to the theocratic ideas of Lamennais and received him graciously in Rome. Yet he was not enough of a leader to upset any of the 'legitimate' rulers of the age: a concordat was concluded with William I, the Calvinist king of the Netherlands, when tensions between Catholics and Protestants were great.

Leo XII died in February 1829, a failure to the *zelanti* who considered him too soft in his opposition to liberalism. His physically frail successor was Pius VIII who had ill-health and was destined to rule for only eighteen months. It was almost inevitable that in his weakness he would temporize in his policies, and though he followed the example of his predecessor in castigating indifferentism, Freemasonry, secret societies and Protestant bible societies, he also mitigated somewhat the harsh police regime which Leo XII had established in the papal states. In France he accepted the succession of Louis Philippe when the unpopular Charles X was deposed; but he was unhappy over the alliance of Catholics and Liberals which won Belgium its freedom from Dutch rule. Pius also avoided intervention when the Catholic Poles began their rising against the authority of the schismatic Russian Tsar, Nicholas I. The Catholic Emancipation Act in Britain and Ireland coincided almost exactly with the accession of Pius VIII and a solemn Te Deum was sung to mark the occasion. The papacy had had little direct influence on the events leading up to Catholic Emancipation, however, and Rome was uneasy about the victory of liberal and nationalist ideas in Ireland as well as elsewhere in Europe. It was fascinating for Lamennais and his followers to promote an ultramontane ecclesiology, but Rome was not yet ready to accept the leadership role in religious, political and cultural affairs which these romantics wanted to impose.

II   John Milner, the English Cisalpines and Ireland

'The term cisalpine is associated as closely with the eighteenth century as is that of ultramontane with the nineteenth'.[6] Whereas the latter Catholic movement was deeply attached to the Holy See and looked to Rome for guidance as it served what it perceived to be the universal mission of the papacy, the cisalpines concentrated on the moral obligations they, as Catholics, felt towards the state.

They had a tendency towards anti-clericalism and, apart from dogmatic teaching on spiritual matters, they were suspicious of any meddling in temporal affairs attempted by the court of Rome. The English Catholics at the beginning of the nineteenth century preferred to call themselves cisalpine rather than Gallican, as their French counterparts did; both movements shared the same concern, serving the interests of the state before those of the papacy.

Between 1778 and 1829, when the structure of anti-Catholic legislation was being dismantled, a series of Catholic bodies in England composed of aristocrats and gentry came into being which excluded the clergy from most of their deliberations: 'being quite able to judge and act for themselves'.[7] They particularly wanted a say in the appointment of bishops, some of whom, like Charles Berington and William Poynter showed sympathy for their objectives. The great opponent of the cisalpine spirit was John Milner who emerged as the foremost defender of those English Catholics who wanted a hierarchical government of their community. A protegé of Bishop Richard Challoner he had studied at Douai, served as a priest in Winchester from 1779 to 1803, and then was appointed as vicar-apostolic (bishop) of the Midland district. There he remained for twenty three years, living in Wolverhampton but making frequent visits to London, to Ireland and to Rome. Milner was unflagging in his opposition to the Catholic laity who failed to accept without questioning the divinely instituted hierarchy of the church and to agree with Milner's longing for papal leadership. Inasmuch as the cisalpine Catholic gentry as a governing power were in decay by the time Milner died in 1826: 'one might well be entitled to speak of Milner as the father of the modern English Catholic community'.[8]

Milner's chief cisalpine opponent was the secretary of the Catholic Committee of the 1790's, Charles Butler of Lincoln's Inn, a pious and learned lawyer who drew up the 'Protestation' of 1789 disclaiming matters like the deposing power of the pope, and papal infallibility, which had attracted Protestant censure. This action was taken in the hope it would help Pitt to draft a bill of relief for 'Protesting Catholic Dissenters', but though the 'protestation' was supported by almost all the Catholic clergy and bishops the most interesting result of the proposal was the effect it had on Milner. Naturally pugnacious he devoted himself to combatting everything that Butler and cisalpines stood for, from this time forward.[9] When finally he became vicar-apostolic of the Midlands he was a power to be reckoned with, determined as he was to restore papal authority in the Catholic church in England.[10] He had little sympathy for his colleagues who tried to work with the cisalpine laity, and his castigation of the Catholic Committee with its 'insidious, schismatical proceedings;' was unrelenting.[11] Milner's capacity for intrigue increased greatly when he was appointed English agent for the Irish bishops, a position which allowed him to visit London often, to the great distress of William Poynter, vicar-apostolic of the London district who tried to work with the laity. Milner was convinced that this could not be done; for the cisalpine laity had no intention of accepting either a further exercise of episcopal jurisdiction, or the authority of the court of Rome in ecclesiastical affairs.[12]

Milner knew that in England his was a minority voice, and that most Catholics, clergy and laity alike, joined with Charles Butler and the cisalpines in assuring the government of their loyalty to the crown and to the constitution:

> Their loyalty in the army, and their attachment to the constitution are unquestioned. They have been proved in every part of the globe. They have shared the glory of England in every spot where England has acquired renown.[13]

Butler reminded his readers that the late rebellion in Ireland had been the work of Protestants, not Roman Catholics;[14] that up to two-thirds of the armed forces were Irish Catholics; that the government of the time had not forgotten the atrocities of 1641, or the machinations of Rinuccini but believed that in Ireland: 'the sins even of the vilest actors among them should not be visited on their tenth generation'.[15] As for the terrors of former days when the papacy had used its temporal power so savagely against the Protestant heretics, Butler replied to the accusations of Robert Southey and other writers in 1825 dealing with issues like Bloody Mary, the Gunpowder Plot and the St. Bartholomew's massacre by offering an intelligent and sustained apologetic.[16] Those days he argued are now long past and English Catholics do not accept the right of the pope: 'to absolve subjects from their allegiance to their sovereigns, or to kill an excommunicated sovereign, or break faith with heretics'.[17]

The tensions between Milner and Butler were so great that they were brought to the attention of Rome, but the papacy was in such turmoil with the return of Pius VII to Rome in 1823 that nothing came of the dispute. Milner's attack on Poynter's policies earned him a rebuke from Propaganda, however, and Milner knew that in spite of all his energetic pamphleteering and intriguing his cause was unlikely to be successful so long as it was restricted to only the English church. He became convinced in the midst of this kind of controversy that the way forward for the English Catholic church was to have it organized and directed in the manner that he perceived the much larger Irish Catholic church, with its Roman-influenced hierarchy, then was. He had visited Ireland in June, 1808, and returned to England full of enthusiasm for Maynooth and the spirit which he believed was universal in the country, a love of hierarchical government in the Irish Catholic church with its traditional religious practices and a deep reverence for Roman authority. In his usual polemical fashion he published a 'series of letters to a Protestant gentleman in England' praising the bishops and priests who had through their pastoral wisdom contained the 'conflagration' of the '98 rising, yet managed to keep the confidence of the people. The latter he described as a people ready to cast off their hitherto inferior role in Irish society: 'the Helots and Gibeonites of their native land'.[18]

In the same year that Milner visited Ireland the question of the crown having a veto on appointment to the Irish bishoprics became a public issue, as well as the suggestion of the state 'pensioning' the Catholic clergy. These schemes had first been discussed and agreed to in secret negotiations before the Act of Union when, in 1799, the four archbishops and six bishops who constituted the trustees of Maynooth, had accepted on behalf of the entire Irish Catholic episcopate an unlimited government veto on appointment to vacant sees.[19] They had also given assurances that they would support the union, in the expectation that Catholic Emancipation was about to be granted. All this was revealed in 1808 when motions for Catholic relief were presented by Henry Grattan in the Commons, and the veto idea was once more considered. At that time Milner was willing to approve the idea of a veto, but then, like the rest of the hierarchy he encountered the full outrage of Daniel O'Connell who used the issue to put himself into the public eye, as the tribune of the people who demanded that the bishops not allow themselves to become puppets of a government which wanted not Catholic Emancipation, but Protestant ascendancy in Ireland. In fact, Milner was accused by O'Connell of being on a 'vetoistical mission' for the British government, and he quailed as O'Connell encouraged an agitation among the clergy and the 'many headed mob'. Newspapers like the *Dublin Evening Herald* were full of abuse directed against Milner, the Catholic gentry, and those bishops who seemed to approve the granting of ecclesiastical patronage to the crown. A National Synod was hastily convened in Dublin, and the bishops bowed to the O'Connellite hysteria and rejected every form of crown interference in the government of the church.[20]

Milner was never allowed to forget his support of the veto in 1808, nor were the Irish bishops given any respite by O'Connell who used his political skills to engage the clergy in his pressure for Emancipation. In 1810 the bishops were persuaded to pass sixteen resolutions against this kind of government interference in Catholic affairs,[21] and when in 1814 Rome issued the notorious 'Quarantotti rescript' urging an acceptance of the veto, in reply to an appeal made by the English Catholic Board, O'Connell was given the opportunity to make his famous statement: 'I would as soon receive my politics from Constantinople as from Rome'.[22] A reluctant Daniel Murray, the coadjutor bishop of Dublin, was sent off to Rome to inform Pius VII, newly released from captivity, of the popular revulsion against a Gallican control of the church, and the rescript was withdrawn for further examination by the pope and Propaganda. This did not end the question of the veto, however, and the agitation within the Irish Catholic community continued. Able political figures like Thomas Wyse and Richard Lalor Sheil were not only members of a 'vetoist party' in a divided Catholic community but they were concerned about O'Connell allying himself with those priests who were political agitators. As for O'Connell himself he was later to show that the question of state interference in church affairs was not the issue of principle his rhetoric seemed to imply.

When he was being lionized by the English Whigs in 1825 he appeared willing to consider pensioning of the clergy for the sake of Catholic relief, and this cost him a loss of face. In contrast to O'Connell's stance, James Doyle, bishop of Kildare and Leighlin said he would resign his see rather than accept a stipend from the crown: 'for if my hand were to be stained with Government money, it should never grasp a crozier, or a mitre ever afterwards be fitted to my brow'. 23

This was one of the few instances when O'Connell's political prescience seemed to fail him. The ideas of the French Revolution, liberty, fraternity, égalité, were still influential and had taken root, in an Irish form, among the clergy and others who had been exposed to the ferment on the continent. Added to the brooding and abiding resentment the people held for anything to do with the Sassenach it meant that, in Ireland, an old fashioned Gallican settlement whereby salaried clergy served the state was an impossibility. Alexis de Tocqueville was told by a west of Ireland priest:

> The day I received government money the people would no longer regard me as their own. I for my part might be tempted to believe that I did not depend on them and one day perhaps we would regard each other as enemies.24

At the time of the 1814 rescript from Rome urging acceptance of the veto O'Connell had judged well the mood of the clergy, and the majority of the people when he had made his speech to an aggregate meeting of Catholics on 24 January, 1815. Then he had proclaimed that he was opposed to this exercise in papal temporal authority:

> I am sincerely a Catholic, but not a Papist. I totally deny that... even the pope himself can claim submission... on this matter. My confidence is great in the venerated prelates of Ireland, who fill their sees in a succession unbroken for an hour since the days of St. Patrick. Should they fail, which I cannot believe, there is still the unalterable constancy of the people of Ireland. If the present clergy shall descend from their high stations to become the vile slaves of the clerks of the Castle, let them look to their masters for their support... The people... would communicate with some holy priest who had never bowed to the Dagon of power; and the Castle clergy would preach to still thinner numbers than attend in Munster or Connaught the reverend gentlemen of the present established church.25

In the words of Professor Oliver MacDonagh, this was 'Gallicanism with a vengeance';26 a call to ally the Catholic church with the political objectives sought by O'Connell and his followers, but in the circumstances of 1815, when the whole issue of 'legitimacy' was under discussion, and Gallicanism was associated with the old régime on the continent, no one really understood what was taking place in Ireland. Certainly John Milner did not but, inadvertently, through his interest in the Irish ecclesiastical scene, he had considerable influence in the development of Irish Catholicism. At the time that O'Connell contributed much to the emergence of the priests as popular political figures, it was Milner who encouraged the Irish hierarchy to identify itself with the counter-revolutionary power which was then developing in Rome. Both political populism and ultramontanism have remained as sometimes conflicting, sometimes complementary facets of Irish Roman Catholicism since the time of O'Connell and Milner.

Milner's thought developed as he sought in his writings to disassociate himself from those who had advocated the veto. He was stung by O'Connell's opinion that he was an agent of the British government, a cisalpine missionary, or the idea that he approved of a pensioned Irish Catholic clergy acting as a 'standing army' ensuring England's security.[27] Henry Grattan had voiced this thought in 1810 when he praised the value of a 'domestic nomination' keeping out foreign influence in Irish affairs,[28] and Milner used his replies to the polemics of writers like Dr. Charles O'Conor to clarify his position on the veto. O'Conor was a consistent vetoist, librarian of the marquis of Buckingham, and the author of a series of pamphlets, *Columbanus ad Hibernos* to which Milner replied. In support of the cisalpine position O'Conor argued that the English Catholic church was 'traduced' by those who believed it served ultramontane principles. As for the Irish church it deserved diocesan election of its bishops: 'the pope has no more to do with the Irish church than the bishop of Constantinople has'.[29] As it was the Irish bishops had a qualified authority intimidated as they frequently were, together with the clergy and gentry, by the peasant terrorists who called themselves Carders, Caravats, Shanavests or Threshers. The parish priest's influence was visibly declining, and the only hope for the Irish Catholic church was for it to work with the state to bring order in the country.[30] O'Conor's fifth *Columbanus* publication of 1812 was a large one concerning the correspondence he had had with John Troy, the archbishop of Dublin, where he dismissed censure by that prelate as 'Rinuccini cant'. His sixth, published in the same year, attacked the growth of ultramontane sentiments at Maynooth, promoted by the 'cabals and intrigues of the Roman courtiers... to establish the universal monarchy of Rome'. The cost of this Roman venture was to be great in Irish society for it would radically separate Catholics from their Protestant neighbours:

> I am one of those many Catholics who grieve to see Protestants estranged from us by the revival of the vilest transalpine maxims.[31]

By the time that Milner returned from his Irish visit he was dedicated to ingratiating himself with the O'Connellites, spending much time in trying to explain away his 'uncertainty' when he supported the veto like the Irish prelates had in 1799. The Irish Catholics, he believed, needed the help of O'Connell in temporal affairs, but to combat Protestant heresy their salvation lay in a union with English Catholics in service to the authority of Rome.[32] With his ready pen he was soon busy addressing the Irish problem: calling for a defence of the faith not only in Ireland but in France, in Spain, in Naples, Tuscany, Austria and the Netherlands, wherever it was threatened by the Jansenists, Gallicans and others who rejected the authority of the Supreme Pontiff.[33] He urged English Catholics to be united with their Irish fellow-churchmen in service to Pius VII who had chosen the way of martyrdom in his leadership of the faithful.[34] He also kept Propaganda informed about developments in both England and Ireland. In 1812 he poured out his vexation over the *Columbanus* writings of Charles O'Conor, claiming that O'Conor received support from John Douglass one of the vicars apostolic. Most of his brethren, he reported, because of 'the present unfortunate eclipse of the Holy See' had:

...deserted the cause of the church's independent jurisdiction on one hand, and of her inviolable adherence to the successor of St. Peter as the centre of unity on the other.[35]

Milner's opinions did not ingratiate him with his English colleagues who ousted him from the Catholic Board, and though he was warned by Rome about the complaints which Propaganda had received, Milner knew by the time that the Quarantotti rescript of 1814 reached Ireland that he had the support of the Irish hierarchy.[36] He also reckoned that little real censure would be visited upon such a loyal supporter of papal authority as himself: 'Oh how much we stand in need of the authority of the Holy See to set things right in England and to preserve our little flock from actual schism'.[37] Propaganda's advice to him amounted to a suggestion that he draw less attention to himself by writing under an assumed name. His position was well secure before he died in 1826, however, for he had published a remarkable work of strongly ultramontane apologetic, *End of Religious Controversy in a Friendly Correspondence between a Religious Society of Protestants and a Catholic Divine*. Though the work first came out in 1818 it was still being republished by the Catholic Truth Society at the end of the century, as a valuable guide for those engaged in religious controversy.[38] In 1825 Henry Phillpotts, the future Bishop of Exeter in the Church of England, congratulated Charles Butler and the English Catholics for having nurtured in Milner: 'your own English pope'.[39]

Yet Rome was never at ease with Milner, and when in 1814 he accompanied Daniel Murray to Rome to protest against the rescript in favour of the veto, he was intruding into the diplomatic world dominated by cardinal Consalvi who was seeking to use every bargaining power possible to obtain the return of the papal states. Consalvi was taken aback when he was informed of the 'hatred which the

Irish bore to the English government', and he quickly formed the opinion that Milner was both imprudent, and a troublesome intriguer.[40] Inevitably Consalvi distanced himself further from the Irish cause when he became aware of O'Connell's hostility towards himself: 'Consalvi, the Italian... though a Cardinal... not a priest... a secular Cardinal just fit for any bargain and sale'.[41] The *Dublin Daily Chronicle* of 2 August, 1816 dismissed Consalvi as the 'perfidious minister... the mere agent of the government'. It is little wonder that when the Irish Catholic Board sent a Franciscan, Richard Hayes, to Rome to warn against further negotiations with England Consalvi secured his expulsion after Hayes wasted two years trying to get a hearing. In 1816 the pope wrote to the Irish bishops telling them of the help the English had given him in the struggle to regain the papal territories, and his consequent unwillingness to deny the British rights which other governments already possessed.[42] Rome was not about to offend Britain by championing the troublesome Irish.

III   **The Irish Hierarchy, the Union, and the People**

The importance of Milner in Irish ecclesiastical affairs is that he was an ultramontanist before the papacy was willing to assert itself in the post-Napoleonic era or reconstruction. He was also convinced that his ideas had no chance of acceptance in England, with or without encouragement from Rome, but in Ireland there was hope that bishops and clergy would give him support in his great mission to reassert papal authority among the people on both islands. Milner took seriously his position as agent of the Irish church in England, and rejoiced that he was now the voice in Catholic affairs for the 2000 priests in their twenty-six Irish dioceses, whose powerful religious authority he contrasted with that usually found in the English Catholic church with its 400 priests and four districts:

> He would discuss matters with the English vicars-apostolic whether by letter or by word of mouth as one of themselves, and then would suddenly claim a dominating voice on the ground that he represented nearly thirty bishops in ordinary against three or four vicars-apostolic or coadjutors... religion was in a deplorable state in England and that the only hope of a remedy was in the assistance of the Irish bishops.[43]

Just as O'Connell was intent upon using the latent power of the Catholic clergy, putting them in service to his political goals, so Milner determined to win over the Irish to the service of ultramontanism in England as well as Ireland.

From the standpoint of Rome this was troublemaking indeed; Irish immigration into England was increasing rapidly, particularly after 1820, and the 80,000 Catholics in England in 1770 were to become 'something like three-quarters of a million in 1850'[44]–most of the increase representing the Irish influx. This folk migration meant a change in the English Catholic community; the memory of the Gordon riots was still alive, and neither Rome, the English vicars-apostolic, nor the Irish bishops wanted to be identified with the kind of religious or cultural mission for which Milner longed. Milner wanted Rome to appoint some kind of Irish-type overseer of English Catholicism to control its schismatic, heterodoxical 'diversity of discipline and practice'. He naively believed such a person would be welcomed by the Irish Catholics in England especially, those who: 'look up to the prelates in Ireland... for the rule of their belief and conduct'. Such ideas were very alarming to John Thomas Troy, archbishop of Dublin, who wrote to William Poynter, the vicar-apostolic of the London district in 1810, about Milner's insinuation' that the Irish hierarchy was promoting a pro-Roman expression of the faith. It seemed clear that, in reality, there was little of Milner's pro-papal enthusiasm to be found among the Irish bishops. By 1819 Milner was bitterly complaining to Daniel Murray, Troy's coadjutor that the archbishop avoided him and other bishops did not reply to his letters. Cisalpine sentiments were still strong in both Ireland and England where in ecclesiastical affairs churchmen expressed: 'a most resolute determination to maintain the independence of their temporal sovereignty'.[45] The ecclesiological ambivalence of the time was clearly revealed in the episcopal career of John Thomas Troy.

Troy was an able bishop who had displayed his administrative abilities in Rome where he had served his Dominican order before returning to Ireland to become bishop of Ossory in 1777. His long stay in Rome of twenty years ensured that when he first came to Ossory he saw himself as: 'the guardian of the Roman interest in the Irish church when Gallican sympathies were abroad in Ireland'.[46] Troy found much to criticize in the Gallican attitudes of prelates like archbishop James Butler of Cashel, and Patrick Plunket, bishop of Meath, but many of the other bishops he believed to be singularly lacking in any conviction. He knew much about the state of the episcopate because the primate, Anthony Blake, was senile and he had to act as administrator of Armagh until a new primate, Richard O'Reilly, who had been trained in Propaganda college, was appointed in 1787. O'Reilly had private means which meant that he 'had it in his power to live in a manner becoming his dignified station'. Concerned with maintaining his life of 'modest magnificence' O'Reilly had limited success in controlling the sectarian tensions which plagued his archdiocese:

In 1815, an 'information centre' was established in Armagh, where religious factions posted resolutions containing a list of fairs where catholics and protestants might meet to fight it out.[47]

Catholics were forbidden by public notices to deal with Protestants, and there was deep distrust of the magistrates who were often blatantly Orange in their sympathies. The situation in Armagh improved somewhat only with the appointment of Patrick Curtis as primate in 1819. Curtis had been rector of the Irish College in Salamanca, and then director of military intelligence for the duke of Wellington during the peninsular war. Even this determined man had to bow to social pressure, at times giving cautious support to O'Connell and his movement, although he also demanded his arrest in 1824 as a 'salutary measure'.[48]

The turbulent state of Irish society ensured that Troy, as bishop of Ossory, worked closely with the Protestants to promote 'friendship and attachment'.[49] He had particular trouble with the Whiteboys who objected to what they believed to be extortionate dues demanded by the priests and, as we have noted, he excommunicated with formal religious condemnation those who refused to pay customary fees:

> We exclude them, their accomplices and abettors, from the participation
> and communion of the precious body of our Lord, from the society of
> all Christians, and from the threshold of the church in heaven and on
> earth, declaring them by these presents excommunicated, accursed and
> condemned to the everlasting fire of hell, there to burn with the devil
> and his angels and all the wicked.[50]

During these Ossory years when Troy was obliged to contend with the agrarian unrest in both his own diocese, and in the Armagh archdiocese, he worked closely with the civil authority. By the time the crisis of the 1790's was upon Ireland Troy was viewed as a Gallican by most of his contemporaries who noted his closeness to the government, especially after his translation to Dublin.

In 1793 when Troy issued his *Pastoral Instruction on the Duties of Christian Citizens* he not only scorned the Catholic Defenders as 'the vilest offenders and transgressors of divine and human laws', but in a second edition he praised the British Constitution which protected the people from both despotism and anarchy. As for papal authority he admitted that in spiritual affairs Catholics could not 'consciously abjure' papal direction,[51] but he denied that this in any way made the Irish Catholic church a threat to the establishment. In 1794 Troy presented a memorial to the government: 'expressing the hope that the moral instruction of the people' would be worthy of the crown's consideration.[52] This helped to persuade the state to subsidize Catholic education at Maynooth, and Troy attended a dinner at the Castle on the evening of the official opening of the college. The '98 rising was to Troy a senseless and wicked occurrence, and it brought from him a swift excommunication of the United Irishmen and Defenders,[53] a reminder to the laity of all the political concessions they had won in the last twenty years, and an exhortation for them to reject false guides who would lead them into tumult.[54] As for the clergy, in 1802 Troy reminded them of their need to withstand their detractors by being, like himself, 'a steady royalist': 'the love of our country is a duty prescribed by religion'.[55]

This was the prelate that Milner hoped would join with him in launching a proto-ultramontane mission in both Ireland and England, but in doing so he sadly misjudged Troy who took pride in being judged a peace-maker even by the anti-Catholic convert Patrick Duigenan. Troy knew he had enemies who accused him of harbouring seventeenth century opinions about keeping faith with heretics and deposing heretical princes, as well as believing in papal infallibility,[56] and he wanted no trouble with the Protestant government during the years following '98. He told the English vicars-apostolic what Milner was about, then left the trouble-making agent to be handled by his conciliatory coadjutor after 1809, Daniel Murray. Robert Emmet's ill-conceived rising had shown that revolutionary ideas were still in the air in Ireland, 'the chord that has never failed to madden our populace into rebellion', and Troy knew that this was a time for the Roman Catholic hierarchy to be exceedingly circumspect.[57] Troy could expect no guidance or help from Rome while Pius VII remained the victim of Napoleon's wrath so he tried to remain neutral in political affairs, and his Irish advisers supported his cautious dealings with the government and the Protestants. His duty they saw was to avoid: 'adding fuel to the flame, and in widening instead of trying to heal up a wound already too wide'.[58] This was not easy to do. In 1806 Troy was taken to court by a critic who accused the archbishop of not warning the government about the probability of the Emmet rising which brought about the death of Lord Kilwarden in 1803. Troy won his case against the charge of 'popish perfidy', but only because he could obtain references to his good conduct from leaders of the establishment.[59]

Troy's loyalty was representative of that of the hierarchy of his generation as a whole, and the 'world-view' of the bishops was different from that of priests who dealt directly with parsons, tithe proctors, police, magistrates and landlords:

> The bishops were, after all, the ruling body of a nationwide organization representing some eighty per cent of the population, and at the same time they were involved, as a hierarchy, in the complex world of international diplomacy, which formed the context for the political activity of the Church of Rome.[60]

They were aware, of course, of the opprobrium attached to them when they opposed the 'rise of agrarian secret societies and the spread of terrorism, designed to enforce peasant-made law over the law of the state'. William Coppinger, whom we have noted decried the excesses of the people in the dioceses of Cloyne and Ross in '98, had an apologetic tone in his defence of the inequality of rank and property in Ireland where society seemed to be divided between Protestant 'conquerors' and Catholic 'savages'..[61] Francis Moylan of Cork who had studied and been ordained in France, was one of the most Gallican of the bishops, in the sense of acknowledging the crown's influence in the regulation of ecclesiastical affairs. He issued a pastoral urging 'loyalty, allegiance and good order' when the French fleet appeared off Bantry Bay; he was one of the ten prelates who agreed to a government veto on episcopal appointments in the Maynooth meeting of 1799; but when he chided his people for 'taking false and wicked oaths' at the time of the rising, he felt cause to assure them:

> I never received a pension or emolument directly or indirectly from the government... it was never offered nor promised me.[62]

The bishops knew well that: 'pre-famine Ireland was a violent society in which public order was often precarious and sometimes non-existent'. Affairs could be so bad that, as in a disturbed area of Galway in 1819, priests could join with the magistrates to beg help from the army. In another instance of 'Gallican' cooperation a priest raised a subscription for the rent of a barracks in which soldiers might be stationed. Such efforts at 'social pacification'; were assisted by the bishops, and archbishop Everard of Cashel in 1818 and 1819 gave instructions for each parish to establish an 'association for the preservation of lives and property'.[63] The Catholic clergy, at the same time, reckoned with the counter-measures which might be taken by the Whiteboys, or by those who expressed their dissatisfaction with their clerical leadership by seeking acceptance in a Protestant congregation.[64]

In the light of these pastoral 'realities' it is not to be wondered at that archbishop Troy and the other Irish bishops showed a minimum of interest in the proto-ultramontane ideas of Milner when, with Rome in turmoil, no real support for them could be expected from the Holy See. Wherever possible they wanted 'accommodation' with the temporal power of the state. Milner did receive encouragement from one member of the Irish hierarchy, however, Thomas Hussey who had been for a long time chaplain of the Spanish Embassy in London. He had then become the first president of Maynooth, and from 1797 until his death in 1803 he was nominally bishop of Waterford, although the pope had granted him a licence for non-residency, to pursue 'private business' associated with his Spanish appointment. Hussey had many establishment friends although he was a long time opponent of the liberal Catholic Fr. Arthur O'Leary who was able to live in some style with the aid of a crown pension. When he was appointed to Waterford he tried to continue to act as president of Maynooth, which made him unpopular with his fellow bishops, and it was unexpected behaviour for such an ambitious cleric to produce a pastoral which succeeded in alarming the Protestant authorities who still had: 'a paranoiac dread of the political designs of the Irish Catholic church'.[65] In the pastoral Hussey complained about Catholic soldiers being obliged to attend Protestant places of worship, and he also protested the attendance of Catholic children at schools taught by Protestant teachers.

The Protestant uproar was immense. This hitherto frequent visitor to

Dublin Castle was accused of being 'an inquisitor from a Spanish seminary', a prelate whose 'deliberated attack' on 'reformed religion':

> ...kindles up the flame of religious discord, who exasperates the poor against the rich, who separates the soldier from his officer, who influences the Catholics against the Protestants, who... abuses the whole existing government.[66]

At a time when 'the liberal and enlightened part of mankind of every denomination were labouring to draw a veil' over the 'ridiculous animosities' of Christians in past ages Hussey with his talk of Catholicism being the religion of Irishmen had chosen to:

> ... blow up the dying embers of discontent and kindle afresh in the peaceful breasts of the people committed to his care the unhallowed flame of old animosity... towards their Protestant brethren by the breath of calumny and cruel invective.[67]

From the time of his pastoral Hussey was the object of great suspicion. When prayers for Pius VI were offered in the London Spanish chapel in 1798, a year before his death in captivity, it was noted that Hussey at the altar mentioned the closeness of Britain and the papacy at the time when the Twelfth Light Dragoons had been landed at Civitavecchia in an attempt to protect the pope. Later, however, it was known that Hussey praised the authority given to Catholics by the apostolic succession, and denigrated the sad state of those who served 'the religion of the state'.[68] Like Milner, Hussey was a proto-ultramontanist willing to stand up to the Protestant ascendancy in church and society.

Hussey's tendency to be so 'high spirited' was viewed with dismay by Troy and Moylan and the other Irish bishops who wanted religious peace and considered Hussey's remarks on Catholic soldiers attending Protestant services 'injudicious'. They were especially upset by his telling the clergy to deny the sacraments to those Catholics who allowed their children to attend Protestant schools and, if the parents were obdurate, they were to be publicly denounced. These 'intemperate and inflammatory' directions were reprehensible. As for the soldiers, when William Moylan remonstrated with Hussey the latter said that he had done no more than others who had had protested 'the cruel whipping of the soldiers of the Sligo militia'.[69] Hussey rested his case on the support he received from Edmund Burke and others who appreciated his argument that to drive Irish Catholic soldiers to Protestant services would: 'in time make them indifferent to all forms of worship, and therefore Jacobinize them, upon the French scale'.[70]

The 'Jacobinizing' of the peasantry was the great fear not only of the government but also of both the Catholic and Protestant churches in the early years of the Union. The viceroy and commander-in-chief, Lord Cornwallis had no intention of allowing a Protestant back-lash after the '98 atrocities in Wexford, or any other act of folly which might excite the peasantry and allow the French to once more attempt to take advantage of the social unrest in Ireland.[71] He favoured Catholic Emancipation, so long as it helped to 'overcome religious animosities and the violence of parties', and he knew the potential for violence among the common people with their elemental antagonism towards anything that was Protestant or Saxon–to them interchangeable words. The Catholic clergy in the period before O'Connell began his agitation for Emancipation were not politicized, and Cornwallis and his successors believed that usually they could count on the priests to try to control rural violence; though they always had to reckon with the terrorism of the secret societies who used intimidation against Catholic and Protestant clergy alike. The Carders of Westmeath in 1813, for example, not only regulated the dues of the priests, but threatened the lives of those clergy who interfered with their assassinations and other atrocities.[72] Though the largely Catholic militia was not stood down until 1816, and was used with English militia units to control rural unrest, the overall military establishment was much reduced by 1813. The yeomanry were mostly in Ulster, identified with the Orange lodges, so that during years of food shortage like 1819–1820 and 1821–1823, in places like Munster, parts of the country were on the verge of rebellion. At times like this rebellion was barely contained as in the lower Shannon area in 1815 where there were open marches held by the peasants who were armed and led by fife bands and formed almost a standing army of the disaffected: 'a vast trades union for the protection of the Irish peasantry'.[73]

Religion played a minor role in the activities of these insurgents, most of their victims were other peasants, and they threatened priest and parson alike. From 1810 on the largely Palatine settlement of Kilcooley in Tipperary was in a state of siege, which the yeomanry could not control. In 1822 there were thirty soldiers stationed in New Birmingham barracks to give protection for the Protestants, but there is no indication that the breaking into houses looking for guns, the attacks on mail coaches, or the murder of a tithe proctor reflected other than economic motives.[74] Where sectarianism appeared it was apt to be in Ulster where, in 1815, in Derry a pitched battle between Ribbonmen and Orangemen took place. The former body were sometimes distinguished from Whiteboys, Carders, Rockites, Caravats and others by claiming to be a Catholic protection society, but there was always a confusing overlapping of economic and sectarian motives in such a nation-wide movement. Since the formation of the Orangemen, after their victory against Defenders in the 1795 Armagh battle at the Diamond, the influence of the order had largely been confined to the lower classes in Ulster. It did have its representatives in lodges in the Castle, among the magistrates and the landlords, however, and the government had difficulties with people like the Orange attorney-general William Saurin. Though there was some connection between the Protestant peasants and their social superiors in the

Orange lodges or the yeomanry,[75] the Catholic middle class was widely separated from the peasant masses by income, education and interests. There were times when well-off Catholics would support the priests in their limited success in opposing violence, but generally they avoided involvement to escape the wrath of the peasants, or the suspicions of the government.

Following '98 the constitutional union of Ireland with Britain seemed a logical answer to the Irish problem, though not one initially welcomed by the ascendancy Protestants in spite of their anxiety over the endemic unrest which characterized the early years of the nineteenth century:

> ... a structural answer to the Irish problem, with overtones of 'moral assimilation' and expectations that an infusion of English manners would moderate sectarianism.[76]

At this time, however, the ascendancy Protestants believed there was little likelihood of a sympathetic alliance between the Catholic clergy and the masses as economic depression in many areas brought suffering to the countryside. Sir John Carr in a visit to Clonakilty in 1805 described how the parish priest denounced from the altar a baker who had not contributed to the chapel fund. For this the priest was charged, and a mixed Catholic and Protestant jury awarded damages to the baker. Carr's comment was: 'this trial is of no little consequence to the community, in as much as it clearly exhibits that the influence of the catholic priest, armed with the terrible weapon of excommunication is not so omnipotent over his flock as it is usually considered to be'. Most of the priests, and especially those who were better off, very much wanted the 'repose of the country' and they chose to 'familiarly associate' with their Protestant neighbours and to be distinguished by their 'probity, rank and property'. Priests 'of high rank' regularly visited the Castle to 'be noticed with gracious attentions'.[77]

In fact, in many instances there seemed to be little to distinguish the life-styles of some of the Catholic clergy from their Church of Ireland counterparts. Anthony Blake, archbishop of Armagh from 1758–1787, whom J.T. Troy helped during his senility, had caused 'grave discontent' when he insisted upon living in his family home in Galway. Daniel Delany of Kildare and Leighlin who died in 1814 was:

> ... somewhat dilatory in performing the various arduous duties of episcopal life. Passionately fond of the society of intellectual and sincere friends he often forgot, in the charm of their presence, to exercise some long-advertised visitation.[78]

The life-style of the parish priests was frequently a bit above that of the most prosperous of their congregations, and this won the priests both approval and criticism, usually the former:

It was part of a resurgent Catholicism that the priest should be seen to
have social position and a residence which would compare favourably
with that of his Protestant counterpart.[79]

In some areas bishops and priests were particularly popular with their
Protestant neighbours and when William Egan of Waterford and Lismore, who
had spent many years in Seville, died in 1796 his funeral procession was attended
by most of the principal Protestant gentlemen in the community, including the
Mayor and corporation of Clonmel. The Protestants recognized the social value
of the priest in helping to maintain rural peace, and this was pointed out by the
liberal Catholic Fr. Arthur O'Leary when he addressed the House of Lords in
1800:

Many instances could I adduce in which the peaceful voice of the priest
was more effective to quell riots and disturbances than the thunder of
cannon could have been.[80]

In Tuam the social intercourse was such that when the dean of Castlebar in 1802
claimed he had been suspended by his archbishop, Edward Dillon, because he had
'intimacy with Protestants', the latter let Propaganda know of this 'most
villanous calumny'.[81] In spite of Wexford in '98 there were Protestants who
were eager to point out how few priests had taken part in the rising; and there
was a general embarrassment in the Catholic community over the Emmet rising.
It was accepted that most Catholics shared Daniel O'Connell's opinion that
Emmet: 'merits... the severest punishment'.[82] This was an age when: 'popery
appeared to many to be a thing of the past... superseded by more enlightened
Roman Catholicism'.[83]

The liberal attitudes of many of the Protestants therefore did not disappear in
spite of '98, Emmet's fiasco, the endemic outrages of the *banditti,* and the worry
about a possible French invasion. Hope was still held that once Emancipation
came the Catholics would act like other 'nonconformist' bodies and share in the
blessings that could be provided by a pluralistic Irish society.[84] This thinking, a
reflection of the age of reason, was voiced in the hope of Wolfe Tone in 1793,
that the Catholics would not: 'attend to the rusty and extinguished thunderbolts
of the Vatican'.[85] It was, of course, assumed that the social position of the
Protestant ascendancy would not be challenged in any new settlement.

Most Protestants believed with Henry Grattan in 1808 that the papacy was
no longer a political power, with the pope reverenced by his followers as: 'a
mere interpreter of disputed points of Scripture'.[86] The Irish Catholics were to
be congratulated for eschewing old tenets about the pope having the authority to
depose heretical monarchs, or to dispense Catholics from keeping faith with
heretics.[87] They found reassurance for their convictions when Msgr. Erskine,
who came as papal envoy to the king from 1793 until 1801, received a cool

reception from English Catholics, but was well treated by the crown when he tried to act in as conciliatory a manner as possible.[88] This was the era when Arthur O'Leary was at the height of his popularity and the Union was generally welcomed. Few doubted the insights of O'Leary who assured his contemporaries that among Catholics even the canonical obedience traditionally given to the pope was now minimal, and the decrees of the Council of Trent influenced only 'speculative points' of theology.[89]

Yet unease still remained among those Protestants in Ireland who observed Catholic affairs. The peace-loving Daniel Murray, coadjutor to archbishop Troy from 1809, had begun a building program that was to produce ninety-seven churches in the archdiocese before his death in 1852. The Jesuits had been restored in 1814, and new orders like the Christian Brothers, the Marists, the Presentation Sisters, the Brigidines and others had established themselves after the union. Everywhere there were signs that quiescent Catholicism, which the Protestants had for so long taken for granted was now changing rapidly. What if the ultramontane ideas of John Milner inspired a generation of Thomas Husseys—or, even more alarming, if an unholy alliance was to be made between the priests and their turbulent parishioners in seeking some temporal goal?

On the doctrinal level there had been in the last half of the eighteenth century a small but rapidly growing body of Protestant evangelical churchmen who found in their theological beliefs an exclusivist concept of salvation which put an end to their latitudinarian toleration of their Catholic neighbours. These were the churchmen who were influenced by John Wesley who first came to Ireland in 1747, and found that his preaching on grace, holiness and religious enthusiasm had a great appeal to many Irish Protestants, especially among the lower orders of society, including the military.[90] Wesley also found he was given an attentive hearing when he preached on the failings of Catholicism, which he summed up in a 1752 pamphlet after a tour of Leinster: 'A Short Method of Converting all the Roman Catholics in the Kingdom of Ireland, Humbly Proposed to the Clergy of this Kingdom'.[91]

Wesley had no use for the institution of the papacy which he considered an unfortunate historical aberration in the development of Christianity. He was convinced that Rome was still a threatening and persecuting power, hungry to encourage the kind of atrocities that had given the French the St. Bartholomew's massacre, the English the fires of Smithfield, and the Irish the slaughter of 1641. In his journal of 3 June, 1758, he commented on Catholic religious life in the neighbourhood of Castlebar:

> … surprised to find how little the Irish papists are changed in a hundred years. Most of them retain the same bitterness, yea, and thirst of blood as ever, and would as freely now cut the throats of all Protestants.[92]

When Wesley found social unrest in Bristol in 1778 he commented:

I can compare this only to the alarm which spread through the nation in King William's time, that on that very night the Irish Papists were to cut the throats of all the Protestants in England.[93]

The repeal of the first of the penal laws brought forth his opinion that whereas he wished no man to be persecuted for his religious principles, Wesley believed that because of Rome's teaching that no faith was to be kept with heretics: 'no Roman Catholic does or can give security for his allegiance and peaceable behaviour'.[94] This comment was included in Wesley's pamphlet used by the Protestant Association which contributed to the inflaming of the mobs who caused so much havoc in the alarming Gordon riots of 1780.

Wesley's pamphlet brought into the lists Arthur O'Leary who published in the *Freeman's Journal* a scathing attack on Wesley's tale of a priest who said he would not burn a protestant alive: 'unless it were for the good of the church':

We are but little concerned in the transactions of the twelfth or thirteenth century. We are a new world raised on the ruins of the former, and if hitherto we could not agree as Christians it is high time to live together as men.[95]

Against this kind of bigotry O'Leary argued that the Catholics were not only loyal to the Protestant crown, but it was the priests who had done so much to save the Irish people from 'the contagion of immorality and Jacobinism'.[96] The anti-Catholic message of Wesley was eagerly received by many Protestants, however, and Daniel O'Connell in later years was to describe the Methodists as 'the bitterest contemporary assailants of Catholicism'. He also disparaged the 'filthy slime of Wesleyan malignity'.[97] There was no Catholic accommodation possible with those Protestants who thought like Wesley and most of his followers.

One of the most able and intelligent of the conservative Protestants was Thomas Elrington who had been professor of natural philosophy at Trinity before he began parish work. In 1809, when he was rector of Ardtrea in the Armagh archdiocese, shortly before he returned to Trinity to become provost, he wrote his *Reflections on the Appointment of Dr. Milner as the Political Agent of the Roman Catholic Clergy*. He attributed the change taking place in Irish Catholicism to the pressure put upon its prelates to accept ultramontane direction. He 'detected' the 'augmenting vehemence' with which demands were being made: 'to share equally with the Protestants of the Establish Church the political power of the state'. As the state appeared ready to accede to the Catholic demands Protestant anxieties increased; for history suggested that the Catholics would not be accommodating towards the heretics if they were allied with Rome and in a position of power: 'it yet remains to be determined with what disposition towards Protestants that sect is now activated'. The banishing of 'the philosophic spirit' and its replacement with the 'narrow prejudices of former ages' Elrington associated with the appointment of Milner, his Irish tour, and his provocative description of the Irish Catholics as helots and slaves dominated by Protestant persecutors. Now the Irish Catholic church was to be subservient to doctrines of past unenlightened ages, which Milner advocated though he knew they were 'particularly obnoxious to the reformed churches':

> He had declared that the Roman Catholic laity must implicitly submit their moral conduct to the direction of the priesthood.[98]

Elrington was successively bishop of Limerick, and then of Ferns from 1822, and was considered to be a leading Protestant intellectual, carrying on scholarly disputation with not only Milner but Arthur O'Leary and James Doyle.[99] Many clergy responded to his warning about what Milner was trying to bring into the Irish situation. One of them, a Huguenot, Thomas le Mesurier, rector of a parish in Buckinghamshire, bluntly identified the disputatious Milner: 'as active an inquisitor as any of the most determined members of the Holy Office'.[100] Others recognized that Milner's resurrection of Counter-Reformation ideas associated with his exaltation of the papal office had the potential to divide radically once more Irish society when the people had barely recovered from the excesses of '98. As we have noted, few of the Irish Catholic leaders were happy about what Milner was proposing; neither the vicars-apostolic in England, nor the Irish hierarchy showed any enthusiasm for his love of controversy.

Milner, however, represented the new spirit of ultramontanism that was appearing in the Roman Catholic communion, and it was this movement that was to put to an end the attempts at conciliation between the Irish churches that were appearing in the quarter-century before the crisis of Catholic Emancipation when, in the words of the duke of Wellington, a 'sort of theocracy' governed Ireland with the backing of Rome. 1818 saw the publication of Lamennais's *Essai sur l'indifférence en matière de religion*, and its affect was electrifying among many Roman Catholics, even in far distant Ireland. The young priests coming out of Maynooth were not as socially passive as their continental-trained predecessors. They were ready to assert themselves and to challenge the dominant position in intellectual, religious and cultural affairs assumed by the parsons. One of the first observers of the Irish scene to note the influence that the Roman revival was having was Sir John Hippisley, who had acted as English envoy to the Vatican between 1792 and 1796. He was a strong advocate of Catholic emancipation when he returned to England to become a member of parliament, and he kept up correspondence with friends in the curia. As early as 1806 he recognized that ultimately Rome would have more influence in Ireland than in England, and this would probably lead to trouble: 'the influence of Rome on her hierarchy in Ireland was greater than here, and... it could be more easily

directed to dangerous purposes.[101] He worried about the threat to the authority
of the liberal cardinal Consalvi, and the victory of the *zelanti*. In the year of his
death, 1825, Hippisley sensed the rebirth of papal triumphalism with the
proclamation of a holy year, the condemnation of indifferentism, toleration and
Freemasonry, and the reinforcing of the Index and the Holy Office.

IV   The Irish Ecumenists

Few Irish churchmen, either Roman Catholic or Protestant, had the
advantage of Hippisley's understanding of what was happening in Rome,
however, and many of them remained hopeful that an easing of sectarian tension
was taking place. Joseph de Maistre had published the ultramontane 'bible' *Du
Pape* by 1819, with its religious interpretation of history under Providence, but a
long struggle with the Gallicans lay ahead, and only a few Irish Roman
Catholics shared the proto-ultramontane faith that was important to John Milner.
Daniel O'Connell's faith was deepening after 1816 but his alliance with the
priests was still in the future; as for Rome, as we have noted, he told the
Freeman's Journal of 9 May, 1814 that he: 'would as soon receive my politics
from Constantinople as from Rome'. As for the common people and their oral
traditions, little is known about them apart from the insights into their existence
given to us by priests, parsons, landlords or visitors to Ireland. Their society
was certainly a violent one, but until the rise of the O'Connellite movement for
Catholic Emancipation the Irish peasants were left alone to work out their
own economic and social, if not religious, salvation. What law governed
them was that of the agrarian secret societies, not that of the state. Even the
secret society law was qualified by local factions, and what part sectarianism
played in the struggles among the *banditti* or Whiteboys is hard to know. There
were occasional quiet periods, as in the autumn of 1817, but the population
growth was one of the largest in Europe, it was not to level off until the 1820's,
and there was a great struggle for land and survival in the bad economic period
following the Napoleonic wars. Agitation against priests who pressed for their
dues was not uncommon, and when the peasantry paid tithe for support of the
Established Church there was only too often a religious element in any local
economic dispute. Catholic folk-memory never forgot the stories of how the
heretics had grabbed land in the past, and dreams of deliverance from political
oppression and imperial domination were always just below the surface of
peasant life. Intense excitement about the hope of divine succour accompanied
the reading of 'Pastorini's prophecies' which had been printed in Dublin as early
as 1790. The 'prophecies' were the work of an English vicar-apostolic of the
Western District, 1770–1797, Charles Walmesley, a Benedictine, who published
a commentary on the Apocalypse in 1771 under the name 'Pastorini'. By 1820
a sixth, Irish edition, was published in Cork, with great enthusiasm shown by

churchmen who engaged in millennial speculation; while the Irish peasantry were told about and welcomed Pastorini's promise of divine deliverance from their miserable existence:

> Walmesley's reading of the Apocalypse led him to assert, among other things, that God's wrath would be poured out to punish heretics about fifty years after 1771, thus initiating the sixth age of Christ's church, the last before the second coming.[102]

Catholic-Protestant relations at this time, especially among the clergy, seemed to depend upon the personalities concerned, and the local economic and social situation. In Derry, for example, the custom, from 1788 almost to the eve of Catholic Emancipation, was for the clergy of both churches to walk in procession to celebrate the Protestant rebellion of 1688, with religious dissensions 'buried in oblivion.'[103] In the Limerick diocese it was customary for the priests to guarantee rural peace during tithe collection by bargaining with the parsons for less than the full legal portion.[104] Dr. Thomas Betagh who was a Jesuit, and a devoted pastor to the Dublin poor was so well respected by all that when he died in 1811 he was given a public funeral.[105] Walter Blake Kirwan, who was educated as a Jesuit and was a professor at Louvain before he converted to Protestantism in 1787, gained renown as a preacher in Dublin churches. Five years before his death in 1805 he was made dean of Killala, and his great gifts, praised by Cornwallis, Henry Grattan and others, were appreciated by many notables, and by other people of both communities. It never occurred to Kirwan to engage in religious or ecclesiastical controversy.[106]

One of the most gifted of Protestant prelates who also eschewed controversy was John Jebb of an Anglo-Irish family in Drogheda. When he was in the Abington parish, in the Emly diocese near Limerick he was a great friend of the parish priest who had the pastoral care of the majority of the 'poor barbarians of this parish'. In 1821 he was invited to address the Catholic people from the parish altar at the invitation of the priest, at which time he spoke of their social and economic misery and urged them to avoid tumult. This was a period, in this area, when it was customary for the clergy of both churches to walk arm-in-arm when attending public funerals, and throughout his life, as clergyman and bishop, Jebb had no difficulty with the Catholic clergy. His ecclesiology was that of the Tractarians, who were to express his concepts fifteen years later in the Church of England; for although he venerated the early Christian church, and considered himself a Catholic, sharing in the universal faith of that time, he was no lover of Rome which threatened the integrity of the individual's conscience: 'fetters the judgment by implicit submission to authority'.[107] He firmly rejected: 'the dark unqualified dictation which is exercised by the Church of Rome through her existing functionaries'.[108]

When Jebb became bishop of Limerick in 1823 he continued his friendly relations with the Catholics, and he and bishop Charles Tuohy became good friends. His attitude was shown clearly in his first episcopal charge where he told his clergy:

> Throughout the south... the clergy have the melancholy pre-eminence of being, I had almost said the single class to whom the people look up, for relief in their distresses, for counsel in their difficulties... for common honesty and civility in the ordinary transactions of life... in most parishes the poorer inhabitants feel that the rector is to them the most important individual in the neighbourhood.

In their pastoral work, however, the Protestant clergy were to remember always that they were: 'aided by a band of valuable coadjutors. I mean the Roman Catholic priesthood'.

> Zealous to promote the temporal, and according to their views, the spiritual welfare of their flocks, they have shown themselves not only willing but desirous to compensate for the public advantage with their brethren of the Church of England.

The only competition there should be between the two bodies of clergy was which would become: 'better citizens and better Christians'.[109]

Throughout his life Jebb kept up a correspondence with Alexander Knox, a layman who had been secretary to lord Castlereagh and, though Knox was a friend of John Wesley, he had nothing of the latter's antipathy to Catholicism. Knox saw the Roman Catholics as: 'fallen both from themselves, in their ancient integrity, and from the apostolic churches'. He agreed with Jebb that in their day 'common sense' militated against old tenets such as that of papal infallibility,[110] and he told Hannah More, the English evangelical and philanthropist, that Rome's authority was of the past:

> I have little doubt that a time will come when the Roman Catholic clergy of Ireland will, in a body, propose to conform to our church.

The failing of the Roman system to Knox was that it was a tyranny: 'equally opposed to reason and Holy Scripture'. Its demand for 'total subjugation of every faculty of the inner man in the great business of religion' was not to be countenanced by those whom Providence has blessed with 'mental liberty'.[111] With all this Jebb agreed, and his temperate objection to the Roman court was qualified by his love of the Irish Catholic people whom he also was persuaded would become part of the Church of Ireland 'built upon the foundation of the Apostles and Prophets'. Providence had blessed Ireland with a church where: 'neither Rome, nor Geneva, nor the gates of hell itself may prevail against it'.112

Jebb provided contemporaries with a valuable insight into the religious situation in Ireland when, in a private printing the year before his death in 1833, he had published a biographical memoir of his friend William Phelan. Phelan was born in Clonmel in 1789 of humble circumstances, and he is important because he knew well the sensibilities of the Catholic people. He told of attending a funeral of a youth when a friar took him by the hand to point out of a window:

> Look there, look around you, my boy; those mountains, those valleys, as far as you can see, were once the territories of your ancestors; but they were unjustly despoiled of it. I can never forget the impression. My young blood boiled in my veins. For the time I was, in spirit, a rebel. And... had it not been the good pleasure of Providence I might have terminated my life on a scaffold.113

Phelan was not destined to remain within his Catholic community, however, for he attended an endowed school run by a pious Protestant whom he greatly admired. He was upset when a friend commented that it was said that so good a man 'could not be saved', and from that moment he said he was 'in no good disposition for the creed which could pronounce reprobation'. He 'virtually reasoned myself' out of the Church of Rome, refused a place at Maynooth, was admitted as a sizar at Trinity College, and listed himself as a Protestant when he first entered there. In spite of his change of ecclesiastical allegiance he: 'never ceased to bear the tenderest affection towards his Roman Catholic brethren'.114 In 1815 he took orders in the Church of Ireland, became a fellow of Trinity, and from 1823 he served in the parish of Keady, County Armagh, until his death in 1830. Very scholarly, he was planning a history of the Church of Ireland at the time of his death.

Phelan throws light on much of the religious thinking of both communities at this time, not only because of his own lower-class Catholic background, but also because of the honesty and even-handedness of his insights. In 1817 he published a work entitled *The Bible not the Bible Society* where he described most of the Catholic bishops as 'professional bigots', filled with a deep sense of uncertainty because of their separation from Rome and its discipline. The bishops rejected papal authority when they made episcopal appointments; they called synods without papal authority; yet they were uncertain when social agitators encouraged them to shrug off the Roman yoke: 'the hierarchy seems wavering on the verge of schism'.115 As for the priests, their 'vanity and ambition' seems boundless but they were aware they had lost influence with the Catholic gentry who were: 'in general satiated with the absurdities of their religion, and disgusted with the ignorance of their priests'. But for their natural pride, and their being 'too generous to abandon a priest who depends for his support altogether upon voluntary contributions', these gentlemen were very close to conforming to the

Established Church. The priests had also lost their influence with the peasants who bitterly resented paying dues:

> The clergy have virtually abjured the Pope's supremacy; the agitators are men of no religious peculiarities; the country gentlemen and the opulent inhabitants of towns are in general inclined to reformation, although in several instances lapse into philosophism; and finally the peasantry are every day regarding with more and more disrespect the only persons to whom they have hitherto looked for moral guidance and religious instruction.[116]

Phelan belonged to the same conciliatory school of thought as William Bedell in the sixteenth century, and though, at this time when there was much confusion in Irish Catholicism, he wanted to bring his fellow countrymen the blessings of the bible, which the bishops and priests were now powerless to keep from them, he had no use for the trouble-making Protestant proselytizers of the time. In 1817 he brought out a scathing attack on one of the most unattractive of them, R.J. M'Ghee, who was for many years a minister at Harold's Cross Church in Dublin. Phelan wondered whether M'Ghee's bigotry reflected 'nerveless calumny', 'feeble truculency' or should it be attributed 'to the rancour and malignity of the heart, or the shallowness and perplexity of the understanding'. Phelan's philippic was colourful enough that Daniel O'Connell quoted from it when he himself attacked the Protestant proselytizers, using Phelan's censure of M'Ghee: 'in his representations, malicious—in his quotations false—in arguments, despicable–in assertion, undaunted'.[117]

One result of the Protestant proselytizing of this period that Phelan recognized was that it played into the hands of the priests. After O'Connell and others identified it as a threat to tradition the peasantry once more rallied about their clergy. When select committees of both the Commons and the Lords were set up in 1825 to look into the 'state of Ireland', Phelan was asked to give evidence to the Commons' committee, and there he expressed his belief that a great change had taken place between 1817 and 1825. Now, he said, he feared that the laity were once more tools in the hands of the priests, in part, at least, because of the proselytizers: 'I should not be surprised if indirectly it gave the priesthood a greater degree of power, by exciting a greater degree of fanaticism among the lower classes of people'.[118] As the priests increased their authority among the people again there was evidence that once more Phelan's generation was to see visited upon them in the drive for Catholic Emancipation the thraldom of the court of Rome: 'the political system of popery, or popery politically considered'.[119]

Phelan was concerned about the new spirit of resentment appearing among the priests, which he recognized was an inevitable development as long as Protestant militants like R.J. M'Ghee were so active, and Phelan's apprehension over the trouble they were causing was shared by many churchmen. Evangelicalism was not readily welcomed by the Church of Ireland prelates for it especially brought not only trouble in the countryside but division within the Protestant community. From 1813 there was a steady increase in non-episcopally directed organizations such as the Hibernian Bible Society, the Hibernian Church Missionary Society, the Sunday School Society, the London Hibernian Society, and the Religious Tract Society. These were favoured by evangelical churchmen, and there were others, such as the Irish Evangelical Society which represented the missionary outreach of the nonconformists in Ireland. As well there were several 'training colleges' which were established in Dublin: 'for the purpose of raising up a native agency by the education of young Irishmen who felt called to this work'. Supporting the work of such agencies were powerful evangelical resident nobility such as lord Roden, lord Farnham, lord Lorton, lord de Vesci, lord Powerscourt and lord Mount Cashel. These were the men who supported the Rotunda meetings of the evangelical societies held in April of each year. The Catholics of Dublin were 'affectionately' invited to attend, but any who did were exposed not only to an account of missionary triumphs in the Irish countryside but to ferocious attacks on the court of Rome:

> The staple of the oratory was almost invariably an attack upon the Church of Rome, dwelling chiefly upon its despotism and cruelty, the horrors of the Inquisition, and the dangers to the Constitution and the Throne, as well as to all Protestant churches and institutions, which would be involved in the concession of Emancipation. All the evils ever produced in Christendom by the scarlet 'Mother of Abominations' were collected and poured forth upon the head of the Irish priesthood.[120]

Phelan's dismay over the missionary endeavours of the Protestant zealots was shared by most of the religious leaders of the time. Dr. Delahogue the emigré and Gallican professor of Dogmatic theology at Maynooth encouraged the tolerant belief that heretics were to be excused their 'invincible ignorance' which reflected the beliefs of the society that had nurtured them. Echoes of this tolerant viewpoint was even found in the pastoral address of the Catholic bishops if Ireland on 26 January, 1826 which caused a great stir in Rome for it was accompanied by a denial of papal temporal authority in Ireland, and a questioning of papal infallibility.[121] Churchmen who thought like John Milner could not possibly tolerate the belief that: 'salvation is possible in all religions, provided you believe honestly and sincerely the religion you profess to be the best'.[122] This was a time when it was possible for John Jebb, the Protestant bishop of Limerick, to walk arm in arm with a Catholic priest who, on taking leave of the prelate, knelt as he would to his own ecclesiastical superior.[123] All was in flux, religiously and otherwise, in these decades before the sectarian division of the peoples once more over the issue of Catholic Emancipation, and it does appear that the uncomfortable issue of 'exclusive salvation' was avoided wherever possible.

The religious and ideological confusions of this time help to explain some of the contradictory statements and actions of one of the great Roman Catholic bishops of the pre-famine period, James Warren Doyle who became bishop of Kildare and Leighlin in 1819. A member of the Augustinian order, he had studied at Coimbra and like the Roman Catholic primate Patrick Curtis, he had acted as an intelligence officer for the British during the Peninsular war. He was a life-long friend of both Curtis and Wellington.[124] The boldest, and most intelligent and radical of the episcopate of the time, he kept O'Connell at arms-length[125] and was a master at assuming seemingly contradictory positions. At the height of religious controversy hysteria of 1825–1826 he was not loathe to excommunicate peasants who attended Protestant services, and to boast of converts to Catholicism numbering some two hundred a year in his dioceses. At the same time, as we will see, he could boldly suggest union of the Roman Catholic church and the church of Ireland, regardless of papal authority.

Doyle's ecumenism was probably a reflection of his concern for the turbulence of his people and the problem of social peace. Two years before his suggestion of ecclesiastical union his dioceses were racked by violence which included the burning of the house of the parish priest at Mountrath, and an attempt on the priest's life, probably by Protestant terrorists. Doyle laid much of the blame on the Ribbonmen, who had caused much trouble in the area following the 1821 visit of the king: 'our gracious sovereign has just visited us like a common father'. The people, Doyle said, were to love even their 'brethren in Christ' who were Protestant extremists; he decried the extravagances of Pastorini's prophecies and reminded them of the folly of rural outrage when the year 1798 is 'within the recollection of us all'.[126] This was the time in the words of Doyle's biographer, when the Catholic spirit was 'prostrate'. Then came unexpected deliverance through the arrogance of the newly appointed Protestant archbishop of Dublin, William Magee. Magee was very able, skilled as a theologian, and an unwavering opponent of the claims of the church of Rome, and when he uttered his public challenge to the representatives of both the Catholics and the Dissenters in his primary charge as archbishop of Dublin in 1822 he initiated the furious controversies associated with what he called 'the Second Reformation'. Nothing did more to revive Irish Catholic zeal than the resulting tumult, which accompanied a renewal of social unrest after the famine of 1822 and the beginning of the political agitation of Daniel O'Connell and the Catholic Association.

Magee's charge was delivered on 24 October, 1822 in St. Patrick's, Dublin:

We, my reverend brethren, are hemmed in by two opposite descriptions of professing Christians—the one possessing a church, without what we can call a religion; and the other possessing a religion, without what we can call a church–the one so blindly enslaved to a supposed infallible ecclesiastical authority as not to seek in the Word of God a reason for the faith they possess; the other so confident in the infallibility of their individual judgment... that they... resist all authority in matters of religion.[127]

The Presbyterians were long accustomed to such assertions of established church arrogance and they simply ignored this demonstration of prelatical pomposity. The Catholic Association had not yet been organized to champion the Catholic cause, and it fell to J.K.L. (Doyle) to present himself as the protagonist for the majority church. His reply to Magee's charge displayed his considerable scholarship as he attacked the archbishop's view of the established church:

A church which wisely disclaims infallibility, and whose creed has been composed in part of the traditions of men, and compiled from time to time by lay persons and ecclesiastics whose very names are a reproach to all connected with them.[128]

Doyle's lengthy riposte was reproduced in newspapers and in pamphlet form, and was succeeded by other assertions of Catholic worth which had the intelligent members of both religious communities following the controversy.[129] It was read in England as well as in both parts of Ireland, and it roused the Catholic population strongly to support their newly discovered champion, whose spirited retort to Magee's arrogance was unprecedented.

The next year Doyle took the initiative in the dispute when he addressed a public letter to the lord lieutenant, the marquis of Wellesley, Wellington's eldest brother, who was believed to have 'a strong predilection for the Roman Catholic cause'. J.K.L.'s *Vindication ... of the Irish Catholics* was a closely reasoned work of seventy-one printed pages which argued that the Catholic clergy were willing to support the secular authorities in providing the civilizing of society in Ireland which the Established Church was manifestly failing to provide. Doyle stressed that although he was an uncompromising foe of the church establishment as it was, supported by the evil of the tithe system, he was not an enemy of Protestantism as such. He praised the liturgy of the Church of Ireland; considered its bible 'with all its imperfections' a noble work; and acknowledged the 'esteem' he felt towards its hierarchy. At the same time he suggested that some of the mischief caused by religious enthusiasts in the Protestant church reflected the fact that many of them were 'destitute of employment'.[130]

On 6 May, 1824 the member for Grampound in the House of Commons, Alexander Robertson made a speech urging the union of the churches in Ireland, and to everyone's surprise Doyle addressed a letter to Robertson a week later supporting the idea of a union, which would be a great blessing to the people of Ireland:

The time is favourable for the Government is powerful and at peace; the Pope is powerless and anxious to conciliate; the Irish Catholics are wearied and fatigued exceedingly desirous of repose; the Established religion is almost frittered away... The clergy without, I believe, an exception would make every possible sacrifice to effect a Union; I myself would most cheerfully and without fee, pension, emolument or hope, resign the office which I hold, if by doing so I could in any way contribute to the union of my brethren and the happiness of my country.[131]

He also asked that Mr. Robertson would once more call the attention of parliament to the consideration of this important possibility.

Immense excitement followed the publication of the letter which to Doyle was the: 'only true road to the solution of the Irish question'.[132] Milner was appalled at this 'wrong and productive of mischief' publication by Doyle whom he characterized as 'visionary', as well as 'young and ardent'.[133] Doyle had been the first prelate to join the Catholic Association, and had been hailed as an Irish patriot-bishop but this call for a union of the churches was very confusing for some Catholics, as were the ideas of his *Vindication*. Protestants were astonished also by his suggestion that the pope's authority be considered as one of spiritual power which they could then recognize:

As for the supremacy of the Pope, it seems not improbable that a large majority of the Church of England would readily concede to him such an authoritative primacy among Christian Bishops as should not, in any respect, be inconsistent with the existing laws of the land, the spirit of the constitution, or the King's supremacy in ecclesiastical matters of a temporal nature.[134]

This concept, which still has appeal to many Anglicans in the late twentieth century was examined by Thomas Newenham, one of the Protestants who refused to pour on Doyle the 'coarse abuse and invective' which came from others. Newenham joined with John O'Driscol, the liberal author of *Views of Ireland: Moral, Political and Religious* (1823) and the Ulster layman, Alexander Knox in a correspondence with Doyle about his plan. Newenham admitted that when he first read Doyle's suggestion he thought it 'puerile, visionary, vain and impracticable'[135] but when he recalled attempts in the past to find Catholic-Protestant accommodation, such as that of Sarpi in Venice[136] he gave the idea his serious attention. Knox, on the other hand was openly suspicious of what Doyle was about, for only he himself knew:

...whether the specific object, on the Roman Catholic side, was anything else than by circumstantial concessions to obtain substantial submission to the Church of Rome... a return to that yoke of mental despotism from which it pleased Providence to withdraw us by means of our Reformation.[137]

Nothing came of the idea, which seemed ultimately to reflect Doyle's 'flying a kite' and on 14 June, 1824 Doyle practically ended the correspondence by saying he did not want to say more: 'unless I could perceive a likelihood of the matter being taken into consideration by government'. Only this, he thought, would enable the plan to move forward without 'religious dissension'.[138]

What is clear from this venture, when in the correspondence the names of Pascal, Quesnel, Wake, Bossuet and Leibniz, as well as Sarpi, were thrown up, was that this period, just before the O'Connellite agitation divided the churches and Irish society, appeared to herald some hope of religious peace for the country. Doyle seemed to be suggesting that the Irish Catholics were not only rejecting the extension of Roman authority that Milner and his supporters wanted, but that they were willing to 'part with its essence as an ecclesiastical polity'. The time was not ripe, however, for the pope of Rome to be accepted: 'as merely patriarch, bishop or head of the western church'. In one of the final letters in the correspondence John O'Driscol told Newenham that if he supported a dream of this nature: 'the good and the wise will be with you, but these are few'.[139]

There were many reasons for the ecumenical ideas of these churchmen to fade away quickly, one of the most immediate being the continuance of the bombast of William Magee in a pastoral of 1827. Doyle replied to it on the urging of his friend Sydney Smith who had started the *Edinburgh Review* in 1802, and who now assured the Catholic bishop of his support, although Smith was a Church of England clergyman: 'I will immolate the beast in the *Edinburgh Review*'. Doyle said he was not out to 'inflict wounds' but to stand up to the: 'now reiterated attacks of a Christian Bishop, who claims to discharge an embassy for Christ'. Doyle's reply was published in both Dublin and London, occupying 146 pages, and it won considerable sympathy for J.K.L. who had opposed Magee's 'charge breathing discord and dissension'. Doyle did not dissimulate as he replied to past charges of Magee; he included a statement made in parliament that the religion of Catholics was politics, and politics their religion:

This saying... is true to a certain extent. Not only politics, but education and every right or franchise we possess or claim, is resolved into or connected with our religion; and this religion being the apparent cause and the distinctive mark whereby we are separated from our fellow-subjects, it is found blended with our privations and wrong.[140]

Unfortunately for all, after Doyle had governed himself to respond so equably to the goading of Magee, Protestant defenders like Charles Elrington, Regius Professor of Divinity at Trinity, were able to attack him as 'a papal militant...

ambiguous on the loyalty of Catholics'.[141]

Bishop Doyle died in 1834 and with his passing there was little likelihood of the ecumenical hope of ten years earlier being revived. He represented the generation of prelates who had been nurtured in Gallicanism, which meant that in his dealing with the Protestants in parliament he had a readiness of understanding and communication that made negotiation easy. In the evidence he gave to the Commons and Lords committees on the state of Ireland in 1825 he had no difficulty in informing the committee members that the authority of the pope in Ireland was 'merely spiritual'; at the time of the Clare election immediately prior to the granting of Catholic Emancipation he assured the Protestants that their atavistic fear of popery was ill-founded. Doyle considered that domestic nomination of bishops in Ireland was desirable, and ideally Ireland should have a patriarch: 'a title tantamount to "the Pope of Ireland"', for this would put an end to the fear of the Roman authority which still dominated the government, the press and the churches:

> Since the riots of 1780 the outcry against the Pope had never been so vehement... 'No Popery' was chalked on every wall; the dangers of 'foreign influence' formed the daily theme of a hostile press and platform; an uninterrupted stream of anti-papal diatribe poured from the pulpit.[142]

V   The Crisis Years of Catholic Emancipation

Though the papacy was not yet ready to assert itself in Irish affairs in any significant way in the years immediately preceding Catholic Emancipation, Leo XII's jubilee of 1825 (the first since 1775), marked the renewal of concern for the universal mission of the Roman Catholic church throughout the world. The time for a new triumphalist expression of the one true faith had arrived, and throughout Europe ecclesiastics who shared the longing of John Milner were becoming aware of it. Leo was a firm believer in absolutism in church and state and, although he was not a leader, it was during his pontificate that the *zelanti* established their power base and determined the policies which would extend papal authority, as we have noted, even in Britain and Ireland. The renewed presence of Roman influence in Irish affairs was a slow process, however, and not one that then much concerned the Protestants. When relief bills for the Catholics were discussed there was usually a caution that the priests' 'intercourse with Rome should be confined to ecclesiastical matters',[143] but apart from this, and some suspicion of the Jesuits who were considered to be ideological opponents of Doyle there was little anxiety about Rome—until O'Connell began the recruitment of the priests in his agitation.

The Protestants were always aware of how easily religious offence could be given to the Catholic people, and how quickly sectarianism could appear in any local rural dispute. The Protestants understood the truth of what 'Mgr. Kinsley, bishop of Kilkenny' (sic) told Alexis de Tocqueville in 1835 about his people:

> They have the virtues dear to God, but they are ignorant, violent, intemperate, and as incapable of resisting the first impulse as savages.[144]

Rural parsons, for example, seldom offended against customs of local accommodation by insisting on the use of the established church rituals in burials. The Protestants were not blind to the terrible poverty of the people, which visitor after visitor commented upon, and they realized how easily violence could erupt, as in the 1822 period after famine conditions appeared in parts of the country. When there was so little arable land available to feed a huge population the struggle for survival was never ending, and usually the activities of the secret societies and faction fighters reflected economic tensions within the peasant culture. Yet sectarian overtones appeared only too commonly, as in the gang-rape of Protestant women in county Cork whose husbands served in the Rifle Brigade.[145] Bishop Doyle denounced the idea of a 'total extermination' of Protestants in Pastorini's prophecies, 'a superstitious attachment to fables',[146] but such millenarian beliefs would not go away, as the Protestants knew. Above all the Protestants were concerned when O'Connell defended the Rockites when they engaged in their periodic atrocities.[147]

The Protestants generally were very apprehensive of O'Connell and what he was about, from the time he used the veto issue to bring himself before the public as a political agitator. In his early days he had been a Deist; many of his companions had been Protestants, members of Kerry gentry families; his wife's brothers were impecunious Protestants, offspring of a mixed marriage, and it was a long time before he emerged as a fervent believing Catholic. He had spoken strongly against the union in 1800, but during the Emmet rising he had served in both the Lawyer's Artillery when they patrolled in Dublin, and the Kerry Yeomanry in their peace-keeping activities. He made a passionate speech in 1810, 'a rhetorical set-piece' in which he disclaimed any role as a Catholic protagonist:

> I trample under foot the Catholic claims, if they can interfere with the Repeal... were Mr. Perceval, tomorrow, to offer me the Repeal of the Union, upon the terms of re-enacting the entire penal code, I declare it from my heart, and in the presence of my God, that I would most cheerfully embrace his offer.[148]

In 1817 he was protesting that Ireland was under the tutelage of Propaganda in Rome: 'as if this were a mere missionary country without a national church'. He wanted 'domestic nomination' to the episcopate, and 'national independence' for the Irish church. He then scorned archbishop Troy, 'the pliant Trojan' as well as bishop Daniel Murray for their support of the veto, which reflected new and covert British lobbying in the curia. Yet his religious ideas were still unformed:

> By the second half of 1818, however, his emphasis had changed from the politics of sectarianism to the politics of ecumenism: in between he had striven to conjoin the Catholic cause and that of moderate parliamentary reform. Ceaselessly, backwards and forwards, he probed for some weakness in the government's front which a new agitation might exploit.[149]

This was not a man in whom the Protestants were going to put much faith.

Everything about O'Connell seemed to be contradictory. Richard Lalor Sheil and the other Catholic vetoists were embarrassed, and the Protestants cynically amused by O'Connell's servile obeisance to the king during the royal visit of 1821. On one level he was accepted as a Catholic liberal, and in speech after speech he tried to persuade the Protestants that he was no bigot:

> My political creed is short and simple. It consists in believing that all men are entitled to civil and religious liberty... which, while it emancipated the Catholics of Ireland, would protect the Protestant in France and Italy, and destroy the Inquisition together with the Inquisitors in Spain. Religion is debased and degraded by human interference.[150]

Yet O'Connell was delighted when bishop Doyle joined the Catholic Association, to show the way for the legion of priests who followed his example, though the relationship between the complex prelate and the astute politician was never an easy one. O'Connell by the end of 1825 was complaining of Doyle's hostility, and Doyle, in later years complained of O'Connell's public attacks upon him: 'why does he seek... to weaken my influence with the misguided people whom God has confided to my care'.[151] When crisis arose, however, they worked together in support of the Catholic cause of Emancipation, along with the new Catholic Association which the Protestants found so threatening, for within it: 'every Catholic priest in the country was to be an honourary member *ex officio;* and it was upon them... that he relied to organise the entire democracy'.[152] It mattered little to the Protestants what O'Connell said: it was what he was doing that counted, and from their standpoint he was organizing 'a species of *jihad...* conflating successfully the racial, the tribal and the religious appeals'. To vote other than directed by the priests was to 'betray your God and your country'.[153] Behind the priests was the hierarchy and its members were forced into secular politics by the O'Connellite agitation, in spite of cautions from some of the more Gallican minded bishops, though all of them had joined the Catholic Association by 1829.

By 1828 the Protestants concluded there was no coming to terms with O'Connell who was intent upon destroying the 'Protestant constitution'. Throughout Ireland were established Brunswick clubs to oppose his purpose, and some appeared in Britain. All were prepared for stout resistance if the Catholic Association tried any kind of intimidation to achieve its ends and when Jack Lawless, a radical Ulster journalist, tried to lead an invasions of Ulster by Catholic peasants several thousand Orangemen at Ballybay blocked their progress.[154] There was to be no extension of Catholic Association influence into Ulster and, in fact, there were other areas in Ireland where O'Connell was virtually unknown.[155] Yet in most parts of the country the priests canvassed the electors in the general election of 1826; they managed the by-election in Clare where the Catholic Association machine ensured O'Connell his election; and in 1829 Wellington bowed to the inevitable and brought in a bill for Catholic Emancipation. O'Connell could rejoice over a 'great and glorious triumph', an emancipation bill without either a veto or a pensioning of the Catholic clergy, its only qualification being a weak clause against extension of the Jesuits in Ireland, and a prohibition of Catholic bishops using territorial titles for their sees.[156]

The Protestants, of course, recognized that O'Connell and the Catholic Association, with the help of the Catholic clergy, had successfully mobilized the largely rural Irish electorate and gained a great political victory: 'it secured in 1829 the first great legislative measure forced on parliament through the pressure of a political organization outside parliament'.[157] The Protestants had hardly been passive during the years following the Union, however, and by the time of Catholic Emancipation the thirty year dialectic they had carried on with the Irish Catholics had put them ideologically at least on a war-footing. They knew well that the battle they were fighting was not just a political one. They recognized with apprehension that Rome had become once more a serious authority in Irish affairs, and by the second stage of O'Connell's agitation in the Repeal years, the Protestants were prepared to engage in their long rear-guard battle during the years leading to disestablishment of the Church of Ireland. They knew what was being visited upon them and Lord John George Beresford, the archbishop of Armagh, warned the House of Lords on 2 April, 1829, what encouragement Catholic Emancipation would give to the priests who now wielded power: 'the priesthood are in fact everything; and the people, and even the agitators themselves, are but instruments in their hands'. He recognized their 'never-dying hostility to what is Protestant', and warned that it was inevitable that they would seek 'ascendancy' in Ireland:

Does anyone believe that by these concessions the Church of Rome will be suddenly rendered tolerant, that the Romish priesthood will be content to hold an inferior rank to a clergy, the validity of whose orders they deny, and leave in possession of its privileges a church which they revile as intrusive and heretical–that they will become indifferent to domination the nearer they approach to it, and the greater their means for obtaining it–that they will quit their hold upon the wills and affections, the passions and prejudices of the people, at the very moment that their spiritual despotism may be turned to most account in forwarding their temporal aggrandisement.[158]

This paranoic reaction to the Church of 'Rome was, of course, nothing new, though until Catholic Emancipation it was shared by only a minority of churchmen. Its best representative from the time of the Union had been Dr. Patrick Duigenan, a convert from Catholicism, advocate-general and privy councillor:

... an honest and able man with considerable knowledge of law and ecclesiastical antiquity, but coarse, eccentric, quarrelsome, intolerably violent and vituperative, and much more of the type of a controversial theologian than of a secular statesman.[159]

So far as Duigenan was concerned it was a tragedy that any part of the penal code had been repealed, for no Irish Catholic had ever been, or would be, loyal to a Protestant king and government. The Catholics, led by the priests, were mortal enemies of all Protestants:

Does their recent conduct at Scullabogue, at Wexford, at Vinegar Hill inspire you with hopes of safety, when they shall have you in their power?[160]

However favourably received archbishop Troy might be at the English court he still upheld ideas of papal infallibility; bishop Hussey was trying to persuade Catholic soldiers to turn on their officers; and John Milner was trying to undermine the Protestant monarchy.[161] The people these prelates governed were: 'the most ignorant and consequently the most bigoted in Europe; their hostility to a Protestant British government for the very tenets of their religion is incurable'.[162]

Few other Protestants were as openly anti-Catholic as Duigenan, except for William Hales, a Trinity College professor of Oriental languages who was an ardent enemy of the papacy and the court of Rome.[163] Duigenan, however, became almost a bogey-man to the Catholic intelligentsia, as well as to Protestant liberals. He was associated in the mind of the Catholic nationalists with Major Sirr, the ill-reputed servant of the crown, 'the Fouché of the Irish rebellion' who had captured Lord Edward Fitzgerald in the '98'.[164] To others, who wanted religious peace in the years following the Union, Duigenan presented the worst possible display of Protestant ascendancy arrogance. An 'unprovoked philippic' against Maynooth brought a protest from Peter Flood the college president,[165] while eirenical Protestants denounced him:

> By the Duigenan school were are taught to believe that in a moral point of view the protestant and the catholic are distinct and irreconcilable beings, and, of course, in a political point of view, not to be united by time or circumstances.[166]

After the Union those liberal Protestants who decried Duigenan and his followers as 'hostile to the tranquillity of Ireland', represented a wave of reform that was beginning in the Church of Ireland. Many of its prelates reckoned that now the Irish church was organically united with the Church of England and under review by parliament, sooner or later there was going to be a close scrutiny of how its huge and wealthy establishment could justify its existence. The primate at the time of Union was William Stuart, the determined youngest son of the earl of Bute. His father had been prime minister in 1763, and this scion of a governing family had every intention of reforming the Church of Ireland. To try to keep out of the episcopate the profligate George de la Poer Beresford, who became bishop of Kilmore eventually, the primate used the threat of resignation.[167] To get rid of another bishop, the third son of the earl of Roden, who was charged with homosexual offences, he successfully used an episcopal court that was held at Armagh.[168] The primate had much to reform. Above all Stuart and the other reforming bishops had to cope with the latitudinarian inheritance of the eighteenth century, including languid clerics and decayed facilities. It was costly to use litigation to get back or buy church lands, to repair churches, and to provide glebe houses.[169] It was also difficult to combat a traditional abuse such as non-residence, but slowly reforming bishops had their way.[170] An immediate result was that the drift into Catholicism was checked in areas where the Protestant clergy had been inattentive to the spiritual needs of the people. The efforts of the reformers were helped by the attention that Spencer Perceval, a strongly religious prime minister, gave to the call for the Protestant clergy to: 'set up as lights upon a hill'.[171]

Duigenan and his militantly Protestant associates were upsetting to Protestant liberals who still thought in latitudinarian Enlightenment terms but, together with Milner's ultramontane supporters, they heralded an intense period of religious excitement in Ireland. During the first decades of the nineteenth century among the many evangelical societies which were introduced to Irish society, some were directly concerned with presenting biblical knowledge to the Catholic peasants. The Hibernian Bible Society of 1806 distributed 209,000 bibles in the next twenty-three years: the Irish Society founded in 1818 directed its efforts to give the bible in the native tongue to the Gaelic-speaking Irish. Very intrusive among the Catholic people in both town and country were the agents of the Religious Tract and Book Society, which in ten years distributed over four million tracts, many of them directly insulting to Catholics. The

Sunday School Society for Ireland enrolled a quarter of a million pupils through its three thousand branches after its foundation in 1809. It also gave bibles to poor children. Everywhere in the countryside there seemed to be appearing schools, scripture readers and itinerant preachers, all striving to spread knowledge of the bible among the peasantry.

In some areas there were priests who accepted the use of the scriptures as primers to help the people obtain literacy, but one of the first acts of Pius VII, as we know, when he returned from captivity was to condemn Protestant bible societies generally, and by the time that William Magee was issuing his ecclesiastical and religious challenge in 1822 a fierce ideological struggle was shaping up in most parts of the country.[172] Not only were the bible schools producing converts to Protestantism, but some of the adult converts (including the occasional priest) were actively engaged as missionaries, decrying the religion-steeped culture of the peasants: 'the pestilential predictions of Pastorini and the secret but widely pervading influence of Jesuitism'.[173]

Within the established church one of the best examples of an evangelical clergyman was Peter Roe who had taken his degree at Trinity College in 1798, served in the college Yeomanry, and became an evangelical. Most of his clerical life, before his death in 1841, was spent in Kilkenny where he was perpetual curate at St. Mary's, and was particularly loved by the troops of the garrison. Strongly evangelical in his theology, and a powerful preacher, his vivid sermons fascinated the troops,[174] while his theology was biblical enough that he was one of the few parsons who was granted the approval of Methodist critics, such as Matthew Lanktree.[175] He was not appreciated by the bishop of Ossory, John Kearney, however, for the one-time provost of Trinity College was deeply suspicious of the evangelical clerical meetings Roe organized lest they cause division among the diocesan clergy. Roe was too busy acting as chaplain to the troops, many of whom were Catholic, and engaging in evangelical activities within the church, to engage in direct encounter with the Roman church, though his anti-papal theology was much like that of the Methodist militants, and his sectarian influence in the church was considerable.[176] He helped to launch the Hibernian Bible Society in 1806, and greatly encouraged men like George Hamilton of Killermogh parish who became a prominent Hebrew scholar. Hamilton delighted in controversy over Catholic refusal to allow the laity to read the scriptures without guidance, and not only wrote to Daniel Murray of Dublin on the subject, but took direct part in a large public discussion on the issue in Carrick-on-Shannon in November, 1824.[177]

Though courageous and dedicated Methodist ministers such as Charles Graham and Gideon Ouseley did all in their powers to report to their conferences: 'fresh trophies won from Popery for Christ, as well as the stability of previous converts', much energy was dissipated in internal squabbling between the various Methodist associations.[178] The Presbyterians too, as we shall see, also spent much time on internal internecine dissension. In terms of developing a strategy of mission to the Catholics, the Church of Ireland was most active, especially among its evangelicals who established a tradition of missionary work in Ireland in the 1820's. The father of the evangelicals in the established church is considered to be Thomas Tighe who spent forty-three dedicated years as the rector of Drumgooland in the diocese of Dromore. His family home had been visited by John Wesley several times; Tighe trained at Cambridge under Charles Simeon; and one of Tighe's curates was Benjamin Mathias who went on to the Bethesda chapel in Dublin.[179] Mathias was a powerful preacher, but his theological views seemed so close to those of the dissenters that Trinity students were forbidden to attend the chapel, and it did not get a licence from the archbishop until 1828. He had great influence on men like professor James Singer of Trinity, who later became bishop of Meath, and Caesar Otway who, with Singer, founded the evangelical and anti-Roman *Christian Examiner*. These men were leaders in rediscovering the thought of divines like James Ussher, and the Irish Articles of 1615 became a private standard of belief for many of them. The established church was in the thinking of these people the true Catholic church of Ireland; and this powerful minority of dedicated churchmen developed a way of thought that was both 'high church and evangelical'. On no level were they willing to accept Roman ideas of 'exclusive salvation' religiously or ecclesiastically.[180]

We have already met Thomas Elrington, the learned bishop of Limerick and then of Ferns, who had been provost of Trinity College from 1811–1820. He had reacted strongly to the 'popish pretensions' of John Milner, and had expressed outrage over the claim that Protestants were not fellow Christians because of defects in the consecration of Church of Ireland bishops. Theologically Elrington was more of a high churchman than he was an evangelical, but no one did more to promote missions among the Catholics. He even had the temerity to clash with James Doyle, with both employing 'heavy artillery' in their confrontation.[181] Elrington believed in 1822, when the 'Second Reformation' was launched with William Magee's charge, that 'the fields are white to harvest'. Like one of the famous converts of the time, Samuel O'Sullivan, brother of the even more famous Mortimer, he had long believed the people were rejecting the authority of the priests:

> There is no concealing the matter. Popery in Ireland is tottering to its fall. Its gentry and wealthy traders are beginning to regard the system in which they are brought up as rich men regard poor relations; they may be willing in a quiet way to extend to it a little countenance, but they are by no means proud of the connexion, or willing to be identified with it.[182]

Samuel O'Sullivan was chaplain of the Hibernian Military School from 1830–1857, but a convert who knew well what was going on in the Catholic community in Dublin. Charles Gavan Duffy always considered him a 'furious bigot' but, if any credence can be given to the evidence he presented to his contemporaries in the Protestant world, it does seem that, just before O'Connell won over the priests and the people to his cause, and Rome began to assert itself once more, there was a state of religious and cultural confusion in Irish Catholicism. The Protestants sensed this, and the 'Second Reformation' represented the determination of some of the Church of Ireland leaders to take advantage of what they believed to be an opportunity to encourage a major mission among the Catholic masses.

It is difficult to know how many of the Protestant clergy or their supporters, fully endorsed the 'Second Reformation' controversy campaign. It developed during the years following the famine of 1822, which had brought immense suffering among the people, and prelates of both churches were concerned about how the peasant outrages of the time might be exacerbated by it. In December 1824 lord Clancarty was so worried that he tried to get from Wellington, then master general of ordnance, heavy weapons to defend his estates.[183] From the standpoint of establishment generally this was an unwelcome time indeed to stir up religious trouble between the clergy. Patrick Curtis, the Catholic primate was appalled by Magee's trouble-making charge in 1822, and contrasted its arrogant tone with the 'liberality and decorous moderation' of the Protestant archbishop of Armagh lord John George Beresford, for Curtis recognized that: 'this is not uttered as a mere rant or flourish so usual in a Fifth of November or Powder Plot sermon'.[184] Yet the start of controversy, though vividly revealed by the challenge implicit in Magee's words, cannot be attributed solely to him. From 1820 a new, disturbing, and challenging note was being heard in the writing of 'Hierophilos', John MacHale, who from the fastness of Maynooth poured scorn on bible societies, and accused the Kildare Place society of engaging in proselytizing in its elementary schools which received financial support from the government. His writings were powerful enough that patrons such as O'Connell and the duke of Leinster severed their connection with the society. In 1825 Propaganda moved MacHale from his academic position to make him co-adjutor bishop of Killala, where he proved to be a passionate nationalist and self-appointed 'tribune of the people'. While MacHale was still at Maynooth he had his comments to make on Magee's charge, as might be expected.[185]

In the light of what was to befall the established church during the next forty odd years it seems incredible that William Magee should have been as arrogant as he was when he complained to the chief secretary in 1823 about how the Catholic Association interfered in parish affairs, and criticised the established church which was: 'held up to public contempt... by a set of popish priests'.[186] In 1825 he gave evidence on the state of Ireland to a committee of the House of Lords for a full five days. There he laid stress on the noticeably more spiritual character of the Church of Ireland clergy in his day, and how this 'marked improvement in the character and exertions' was resulting in a great wave of conversions, though some of the new members were but 'ostensible Protestants'.

Yet there was a great need to care for these people and Dublin especially needed new churches for the 'convert poor'. One of the particular problems was how to handle the large number of priests who sought ordination in the established church. Until 1796 there had been legal provision to give each conformist priest £40 a year until a curacy was found for him, but this legislation had not been renewed with the endowing of Maynooth. Such was the problem now, said Magee, with the convert-priests so demoralized, that something had to be done for them. The bishop of Kildare had been forced for two years to keep at his own expense a scripture professor from Maynooth until a curacy was found for him. It was phenomena such as this that persuaded Magee to tell the Lords: 'In truth, with respect to Ireland, the Reformation may, strictly speaking, be truly said only now to have begun'.[187]

One of the converts of the period—though to Catholicism—was W.J. O'Neill Daunt, a secretary to O'Connell and director of his agitation in Leinster. Daunt as a political person considered the 'furious theological excitement' of the 1824–1826 period an attempt to dissuade the people from supporting the O'Connellite movement for Catholic Emancipation, and he has left us a vivid picture of what Magee had unleashed:

> The controversial excitement through the country was actually frightful. The Protestants were taught to look on the religion of the Catholics as a grand magazine of immorality, infidelity and rebellion; while the Catholics, in their turn, regarded their enthusiastic assailants as the victims of a spiritual insanity derived from an infernal source, and as disastrous in its social results as it was bizarre in its exhibition. The kindly charities of friendship were annihilated; ancient intimacies were broken up; hatred was mitigated only by a sentiment of scornfull compassion.

In County Cavan, where lord Farnham enthusiastically encouraged proselytizing, weekly bulletins listing the names of those who had left popery were revealed on men who perambulated the streets of towns, or were placarded on walls.[188]

In the secular society of the late twentieth century it is difficult to appreciate that when, for example, there was a six days debate in April 1827 between the County Leitrim orator, Father Tom Maguire and a Protestant debater, the Rev. Richard T.P. Pope, the whole of Sackville street in Dublin was blocked by crowds who wished to attend the event in the Dublin Institute.[189] What the contest revealed was how much the protagonists and the audience were concerned with attacking or defending the papacy and its authority. Richard Pope who led off devoted most of the first day to the question of the 'infallibility' of the Church of Rome while Tom Maguire defended the teaching authority of Rome as the only protection the faithful had against religious error:

> If the unlimited right of private judgment be recognized, then will a

seven-fold shield be thrown over every error, however impure every heresy, however damnable, every folly, however ridiculous. It will be the origin of every species of madness, violence and fanaticism.[190]

As much reference was made to Christian history as to scripture and as Pope made constant reference to papal authorities such as cardinal Bellarmine, or questioned the thought of the conciliarists of the fifteenth century, the debate kept returning to the question of the authority of the Roman see. As the Protestant attack on Rome proceeded apace the Catholic audience increasingly sided with its defender and his argument regarding the value of papal *magisterium*. There was little mention of the Gallican values that had had appeal to Catholics of earlier times. Rather there was a constant reference to the edicts of various pontiffs, the decrees of Trent, and even the writings of John Milner.[191] In the light of the Europe-wide ecclesiastical revolution which accompanied the appearance of aggressive ultramontanism in Rome at this period, it was to the advantage of those who defended the papal cause that the Protestants kept insisting that the Irish Catholics found their authority in Rome not the Gospels: 'you have founded your church upon Peter and not upon Christ'.[192]

There were, of course, other Catholic champions who represented the Irish rather than the Roman Catholic cause in their struggle with the Protestant controversialists. One of the most powerful of these men as a preacher and a lecturer was Daniel Cahill, a gigantic man six feet five inches in statute who had the kind of popular appeal that Gideon Ouseley presented for the Methodists or Tresham Dames Gregg for the Church of Ireland. He had studied at Carlow College under James Doyle, became a professor there during Doyle's episcopate, then established an academy in Carlow. His academy was not successful but soon he emerged as a public preacher, lecturer and writer, strongly supported by other defenders of the Irish Catholic people, archbishop Daniel Murray, Charles MacNally, bishop of Clogher, and Michael Blake of Dromore. None of these prelates were considered to be strong Romanists. Cahill was a patriot in the sense that he never let his audience forget past stories of 'Saxon perfidy and cruelty' and he could vividly describe John Calvin laughing during the burning of Michael Servetus.[193] Cahill revelled in his role as a controversialist, whether he addressed audiences in Ireland or in America where he was immensely popular:

Today, an article in an Orange newspaper sneering at Purgatory; tomorrow, the Rev. Isaac fulminating against the Mass, Eliza bemoaning the celibacy of priests; or Johanna at a Biblical re-union quoting 'texts' against honouring 'the Virgin'... But hold! A giant enemy suddenly rises up against them—an Irish Sampson rushes forth to smite the Philistines of his country... in the pulpit, the press and the lecture-hall.[194]

On the other hand, in a manner worthy of James Doyle, he could say after the sectarian rioting in Belfast in 1857:

> If any labor of mine could promote the peace of that town, with which I happen to be acquainted, and where I have received kindness from all classes of society, I would cheerfully devote my time and my influence, to promote the union of the Catholic and the Orangeman–to make them forget the past, and to be bound in permanent friendship for all future time.[195]

Without doubt the most substantial Protestant controversialist was Mortimer O'Sullivan, a convert from Catholicism, who had attended Richard Carey's school in Clonmel with his brother Samuel and William Phelan. A man of considerable personal charm Mortimer O'Sullivan had never broken relations with his Catholic relatives who lived in Waterford and Tipperary, and he told the select committees of the Lords and the Commons in 1825 that he knew as much about the state of the countryside and the unrest in it as any man. The previous year he had published his large work, *Captain Rock Detected, or the Origin and Character of the Present Disturbances* in which he expounded his conviction that the agrarian outrages of the time reflected the economic misery of the people rather than religious differences which were of secondary concern to them. As for the Catholic gentry they were, he believed, if they were not Deists, 'in reality Church of Ireland Protestants'. Regarding James Doyle's idea of union, he approved of it in the abstract, though he doubted the value of it in social terms:

> But I am very far from believing that a union, if it were effected, would tranquillize the country... The union of the churches would not lower the rents, nor wipe off the arrears, nor accustom the people to habits of comfort. It is from their miseries the danger of the country proceeds; they are impoverished, and, of course, discontented. The sense of the oppressions and miseries with which they are overwhelmed is strong therefore they are continually assailing the foundations of the government; and whenever they shift their weary side the whole island trembles! Relieve the people from their misery, let in one cheery hope among them, and, in six months they would defy the Romish clergy and the Catholic Association–leave the people in their distress, and every measure of imperfect relief will be only making them more formidable enemies.[196]

In the post-Emancipation period O'Sullivan became rector of Killyman, and then prebendary of Ballymore in the Armagh diocese, and in those years until his death in 1859 he became more of an extreme Protestant as ultramontane authority increased in Ireland. In his *Captain Rock Detected* of 1824, however, and in the evidence he presented to the select committees of the Lords and Commons on the state of Ireland in the following year, he was remarkably objective and persuasive in his religious-sociological analysis of what was happening in Irish Catholic society during the years when O'Connell was first beginning his rise to political power.

O'Sullivan agreed with William Phelan's earlier opinion that in the 1817 period the authority of the priests among the people appeared to be 'notoriously on the decline'.[197] It was not uncommon for the peasants to 'serve processes' upon the priests, and O'Sullivan noted the priests then received little help from the gentry. The latter thought little of the Maynooth graduates especially who often came from small country town shopkeeper families:

> The priests, neglected by the wealthier classes, devoted themselves altogether to the lower orders and to keep up their influence availed themselves of the prejudices of their flock, and fanned their resentments into a flame.[198]

O'Sullivan believed this alliance of priests and people was in many areas becoming clearly apparent by the 1820–1822 period, the time when Magee made his provocative charge because he recognized the loss of influence of the priests among many Catholics of wealth and influence. Then when the famine appeared in many parts of the country in 1822, and rural disturbances increased the people became more and more likely to accept the local leadership offered by the priests: 'they find that the priests, I will not say joined themselves in their plans, but at least sympathized with the passions of the people'. The result of this alliance, which took various forms throughout the countryside was potentially revolutionary O'Sullivan believed:

> This union of the priests with the lower orders has formed and given power to a party which did not exist fifteen years ago.[199]

The shock of famine conditions, in Munster particularly, brought a kind of 'peace' to Ireland in 1822 but by that time O'Sullivan believed the priests with their superior education had managed to assert not only their domination of the people but to organize a sectarian movement. They practised the social censure of 'naming from the altar' those who did not support their 'party', and even engaged in physical chastisement of those who were friendly to Protestants, or allowed their children to attend schools of which the priests did not approve. Tradesmen who tried to stand up to them found they could be reduced to beggary if the priests inflamed the peasants against them. Even the gentry were beginning to bow to the priests lest some outrage be visited upon them. The Catholic bishops knew what was happening, but they too were intimidated by this exercise in totalitarian democracy. O'Sullivan said: 'I could mention instances where people supported the parish priest against the bishops'.[200]

O'Sullivan recognized that when many of the gentry were Protestant the growing division between the peoples had both an economic and a religious cause, but he believed the latter was becoming more important as the priests used their authority to encourage separation of the two communities. He noted particularly that: 'there is a much greater aversion from being present at the worship of Protestants than could formerly be observed'.[201] This development influenced some of the Catholic gentry who were now so dominated by the priests that they kept their own counsel while even some of the Catholic bishops were pressured. One of these was Patrick Everard, a good friend of archbishop Daniel Murray, who had been rector of the Irish College in Bordeaux, and had almost lost his life during the French Revolution. He was for a short time president at Maynooth on his return, then he was appointed coadjutor and then archbishop of Cashel from 1814–1821. A scholarly and conciliatory man, representative of the generation of priests who had had a continental education, he was a dedicated reformer in his archdiocese, and this brought upon him much criticism from the priests. O'Sullivan attributed the ill-treatment he received to his friendship with many Protestants, however, and believed this was the main justification advanced by the priests for their anti-episcopal animus:

> He was very conciliatory in his manners and deportment towards Protestants and I believe maintained a very general intercourse with them and he was, from the time that he became archbishop, continually opposed by almost all the Roman Catholic clergy, and after his death they manifested a kind of disrespect for his memory.[202]

It was now becoming clear to the population generally, said O'Sullivan that trouble might be visited upon anyone who had 'close intercourse with Protestants', and the 'notion of exclusive salvation has become the tenet of persons who would have formerly rejected it with abhorrence'. Sectarianism was now a probable element in any 'outrage':

> The strong part which the Roman Catholic clergy took in keeping the people separated from the Protestants, and the decided part which they also took in accommodating themselves to the feelings of irritation, which the people cherished against the landlords and against the clergy of the Church of England had considerable influence in communicating a religious character to the disturbances.[203]

So long as the people used their power of intimidation against those of whom the priests disapproved, then as in times of religious strife in the past: 'they called it a war and the act is a crime no longer... when it militated in the interests of the church'.[204] O'Sullivan stressed how much he knew, admired and loved the Irish people; but he was now beginning to be concerned that they were serving the alien authority of Roman religion rather than the welfare of Ireland. At the same time he acknowledged that the priests who identified with the 'rancour' of the people were in danger of being carried along by forces over which they had no control, and he was very pessimistic about the alliance of Catholicism in Ireland with radical democracy. The priests he believed were in a very uncomfortable position for they feared in many instances that the people might turn against them, and ignore their power to bully at stations, or to 'call from the altar' and, most threatening of all, refuse to pay dues:

> The people of Ireland are prone from the state of wretchedness and mis-
> ery in which they live to disorder, and there is a sort of prejudice taken
> up against the Roman Catholic priest if he engages himself on the side
> of order, and endeavours to mitigate the violence of the people.[205]

O'Sullivan questioned whether the priests really understood what they were about when they allowed themselves to become overly identified with some of the causes of the peasantry, for the people were now influenced by secular ideology as well as the traditional religious faith of past centuries:

> I am perfectly convinced that from the time of the rebellion in 1798 per-
> sons who were outlawed then, and who were sheltered by the poor in
> the remote parts of the country had infused into the minds of the people
> their own disaffected notions; and I am also aware that at various times,
> persons professing to be, or really having been concerned in the
> rebellion of 1798, passed through the county of Tipperary and the
> county of Waterford, and I think, by this means the minds of the people
> were prepared for communicating a political character to any disturbance
> which arose.[206]

O'Sullivan wondered if the priests had the innate authority to control a mob influenced by revolutionary sentiment. In any case he took a gloomy view of what was appearing in the Irish countryside as political leaders and social agitators appeared: 'who confuse the bigotry of the priesthood with the principles of democratic radicalism'.[207]

There seems little to fault in O'Sullivan's observation of the state of religion in Ireland in the 1824–1825 period, but it was essentially an insular viewpoint that was soon to be overtaken by the intrusion once more of Rome into Irish affairs. Leo XII's first encyclical, *Ubi primum* was published in May, 1824 as a sop to the conservative *zelanti* who had elected him. In many ways it was a precursor of *Quanta cura,* in the pontificate of Pius IX, as it strongly opposed the dangerous teachings that were appearing in the church and sought to raise the intellectual, moral and disciplinary standards of the clergy. It was published in the same year in Ireland, where it encouraged the bishops to give pastoral instructions to their people warning them of the dangers of 'latitudinarianism or indifferentism'. It also warned the bishops about the dangers which faced the faithful if they accepted scriptures in the vulgar tongue from members of the bible societies:

> Turn away your flock by all means from these poisonous pastures... if the sacred Scriptures be everywhere indiscriminately published more evil than advantage will arise thence on account of the rashness of men.[208]

The Irish bishops said in their pastorals that they 'fully concurred' with the papal instructions, and they ordered that tracts and pamphlets given out by the Protestant societies were to be destroyed; bibles were to be returned to their donors, or deposited with the priests. Most importantly of all the encyclical put an end to the speculation about Protestants being worthy of salvation in spite of their 'invincible ignorance': 'we profess that out of the Church there is no salvation'.[209]

In 1826 a pastoral address from the Irish hierarchy seemed to soften this statement about 'exclusive salvation', with talk of 'Protestant fellow subjects whose good opinion' was valued, needing to know that: 'wilful and obstinate opposition to revealed truth as taught in the Church of Christ excludes from the Kingdom of God'. The address was mostly concerned, however, to deny the traditional Protestant slanders that Catholics could murder heretics; need not keep faith with them; and were disloyal to the crown. These accusations were denied, as well as the belief that the pope sought: 'temporal or civil jurisdiction, power, superiority, or pre-eminence, directly or indirectly within this realm'. Also denied was a pious belief which caused the Irish hierarchy a great deal of trouble when news of it reached Rome, as we noted earlier:

> It is not an article of the Catholic Church, neither are they thereby required to believe that the pope is infallible.

Furthermore the bishops said that they did not hold themselves:

> ...bound to obey any order in its own nature immoral, though the pope or any ecclesiastical power should issue or direct such an order: but on the contrary that it would be sinful in them to pay any respect or obedience thereto.

The address was signed by thirty bishops, including Patrick Curtis the primate, Daniel Murray archbishop of Dublin, and James Doyle.[210] Ultramontanism had not yet taken root in Ireland, but during the pontificate of Leo XII it was clear that Rome was going to war with 'liberalism' in all its forms, and had every intention of taking over direction of the Irish Catholic church as part of that strategy.

Neither Rome, nor the Catholic Association, nor even the established church, had any major influence on what was developing in Ulster where, as usual, the Presbyterian church sought its ideal of having its authority co-terminous with that of civil society. At the time of the Union Alexander Knox suggested to chief secretary Castlereagh, who had a Presbyterian background, that this was the time for the government to make concessions in Ulster:

> The republicanism of that part of Ireland is checked and repressed by the cruelties of Roman Catholics in the late rebellion and by the despotism of Bonaparte. They are therefore in a humour for acquiescing in the views of government beyond which they ever were or (should the opportunity be missed) may be hereafter.[211]

The government did seize the opportunity, inasmuch as it massively increased the *regium donum,* the state payment for Presbyterian ministers. Many of the Presbyterians still had ultra-liberal sentiments, like those of the United Irishmen before '98, and the Synod of Ulster remained faithful to its resolution of 1793, in favour of Catholic Emancipation, when the issue was debated again and approved in 1813. The leader of the religious conservatives in the later discussion was Henry Cooke who wanted to agitate for greater safeguards to ensure the preservation of the Protestant character of the British state.[212] Cooke also emerged in the 1820's as a vigorous champion of orthodoxy, as the Presbyterians were radically divided between those who subscribed to the Calvinistic Westminster Confession of Faith, with its view of the pope as the Antichrist, and those who were in favour of non-subscription and doctrinal pluralism. The latter party were deemed Arians in their theology, and led by Henry Montgomery they put up a tremendous battle in the annual meetings of synod in the years just before Catholic Emancipation. This internecine squabbling ensured that the Presbyterians paid little attention to the Catholic or Roman threat which was of so much importance to the rest of Ireland.

If the Ulster Presbyterians tended to ignore southern Ireland, and concentrate upon their own affairs, the O'Connellite movement showed no real interest in extending its influence in Ulster. When O'Connell himself gave evidence before the Lords committee on the state of Ireland in 1825 he admitted his lack of knowledge of affairs in the province, which he had only visited in transit.[213] It was this uncertainty about Ulster affairs, and northern Protestant sentiments, which lay behind the 'mission' of John Lawless in 1828 of which O'Connell approved, and to which we have already referred. Sir Thomas Wyse, the author of *A Historical Sketch of the Catholic Association* spoke of Lawless's failure of nerve, which led him to turn back and avoid battle at Ballybay, as providential:

A defeat of the crowd who accompanied him would have been followed up by a carnage; the carnage, by a massacre of the Catholics of the north. Their brethren of the South would not have looked on–hundreds and thousands would have marched from Munster–a counter massacre, a Sicilian Vespers, perhaps would have taken place.[214]

The Catholic Association later circulated a large placard in Ulster, addressed to 'our persecuted brethren in the North', which urged a closer association with southern Catholics, but the Lawless fiasco had persuaded the O'Connellites that no dramatic help from the south was to be offered again.[215]

It was as well from the standpoint of law and order that O'Connell did not seriously try to extend his influence in Ulster. From the time of the Defenders and the Orangemen clashes in the late eighteenth century sectarian tension in Ulster never eased. Orange ballads recorded victories like the 1818 'Great Fight at Aughnacloy' when at the time of the local races Orangemen and Yeomanry had joined forces to drive the Catholics of Monaghan over the Tully bridge.[216] Only two were killed in that skirmish, but more died in a battle between Orangemen and Ribbonmen in the fair at Maghera in county Londonderry in 1823.[217] On the eve of Catholic Emancipation the Protestants made very sure in the Clones area of Monaghan that their ascendancy was recognized:

An Orange flag was always hoisted on the Twelfth of July, from the steeple of the Protestant church. On the occasion... of the first of the 'fighting fairs', as they came to be known, after the streets had first been cleared by the Orangemen and the Yeomen, the former paraded them in all directions and in large bodies, waving their bludgeons over their heads and calling for the face of a Papist or a Penny Boy (i.e. supporter of the Catholic Association). When this act of drama had closed, the Yeomen were drawn up in rank and file on the Diamond, and Dean Henry Roper, a magistrate and head-parson of the place reviewed them on horseback.[218]

This threatening atmosphere was less in Belfast, though the parish priest of the city from 1812, William Crolly had to endure outrages such as the breaking of his presbytery windows by the Orangemen. He remained on good terms with the Protestant middle classes, however, and when in 1815 St. Patrick's on Donegall St. was consecrated thanks were given for the financial help of Protestants and Dissenters.[219] It was not until the end of the first quarter-century that noticeable sectarian incidents began, at the same time that the Catholic population of the city increased enormously. When Crolly was appointed bishop of Down and Connor in 1825 public dinners were held to celebrate the occasion and they were well attended by Protestant well-wishers. Crolly appointed as parish priest of Belfast a friend, Cornelius Denvir, and Denvir continued his predecessor's eirenical gestures. When Crolly was translated to Armagh in 1835 his clergy drew up a petition to Rome asking that he be allowed to stay with them in Down and Connor lest: 'religion might be injured by his departure'.[220]   In later years, as we will see, neither the Irish Catholic nationalists, nor the Roman authorities, were to appreciate either Crolly or Denvir who practised the art of the possible in religious matters in Ulster.

Chapter VII

The Struggle for Catholic Ascendancy

'If Catholic injury demanded redress, the Protestant fear required security'

> Anon. *Fiction Unmasked or a Letter to the Roman Catholics of Ireland on the Conduct of Certain Men Who Compose the Catholic Junta.* Dublin, 1815, p. 9.

I   Ultramontanism and Revolution

Although Catholic Emancipation was not granted in Britain and Ireland until after the death of Leo XII in February, 1829, the assurances of Consalvi that such relief was inevitable had meant that Rome did all it could to encourage the process. In most matters, however, Leo XII was narrowly clerical in his outlook and when he died he was profoundly unpopular; considered by the *zelanti* to be too soft, and by the liberals a tyrant. His successor, Pius VIII, was dominated by his pro-Austrian secretary of state, Giuseppe Albani who had brought about his election, and he showed considerable unease over the threat to the rule of 'legitimate' monarchs which appeared in Belgium, France and Poland in 1830. Cardinal Albani was disgusted with the alliance of Belgium Catholics with the anti-clerical liberals to win freedom from domination by the Calvinist Dutch King William I of the House of Orange, and he described this exercise in expediency as 'monstrous'. Neither was Rome entirely happy with the take-over of the French throne by Louis-Philippe, although the church under the deposed sovereign, Charles X, had been increasingly Gallican in its sympathies. When the Poles began their struggle for independence from the rule of the Orthodox Tzar, Rome was again ambiguous in its response to the tyrannical rule of a Catholic people by a schismatic sovereign. At the same time that the Poles were striving for their political independence the Italian *Carbonari* were trying to establish a state for themselves at the expense of the papal states, Modena and Parma. When Pius died in November, 1830 he left these ecclesiastical and diplomatic problems to be solved by his successor: that very day conspirators tried to seize the castle of Sant' Angelo, and the French ambassador warned that Louis-Philippe would expect the new pontiff to be liberal and to ensure: 'the independence of those provinces which he would be called upon to govern'.[1]

Once more, however, the *zelanti* had their way in obtaining the election of a conservative pope who would stand up to such liberal pressures. Their lobby was supported strongly by the Austrian statesman, Metternich who also wanted an absolutist-minded pope who would not bow to the revolutionary spirit of the age. The pope who emerged from the difficult fifty-day conclave of 1830–1, with the backing of Metternich, was a Camaldolese monk, a strong upholder of papal infallibility and the temporal authority of the papacy, who took the name Gregory XVI. During the imprisonment of Pius VI in 1799 he had published his ideas in a book entitled *The Triumph of the Holy See and the Church against the Attacks of Innovators*. Almost as soon as he was enthroned his reaction to risings in the papal states and Rome itself was to call in the Austrians to crush the revolts ruthlessly. The unrest could not be controlled, however, and France also entered the scene seizing the town of Ancona and putting the papal states under military occupation for seven years. With the aid of two reactionary secretaries of state, Bernetti and Lambruschini, Gregory arranged for the hiring of a papal army but throughout his reign the states of the church simmered with revolt. What kept the situation from being even more desperate was the contention between the republicans who followed the young Mazzini and other groups of nationalists. By the time this obstinate and narrow-minded pontiff died in 1846 he had revealed his reactionary incomprehension of the changing world by banning the railways in papal territories, and by filling the papal prisons with liberals, nationalists and others who opposed the tyranny of a pope who was regarded as an Austrian vassal.

It was under Gregory XVI that the ultramontane movement first became a force to be reckoned with both inside the curia and in the universal church. Leo XII had revived the practice of proclaiming the *magisterium* of the church with full solemnity in *Ubi primum,* his encyclical which denounced those modern errors of liberalism and indifferentism which brought about the de-Christianization of society. Gregory XVI continued this tradition in his important encyclical *Mirari vos* of 1832 which fulminated against the notions of freedom of conscience, freedom of the press, and the separation of church and state. The substance of the encyclical reflected the pope's response to the call by Félicité de Lamennais for Rome to lead in a crusade for 'liberty' directed by the papacy.

Lamennais had been distressed by the July revolution of 1830 in France. Anti-clericalism had appeared during the uprising, and under the new ruler Gallicanism appeared as strong as ever in the French church. His response was to found a journal, *L'Avenir* whose motto was 'God and Liberty'. One of the leading writers who emerged in its pages was vicomte de Montalembert, a young man of twenty who had just returned from Ireland, convinced that he had witnessed in the Catholic political movement led by O'Connell a sacred cause which could inspire liberal Catholics everywhere. Like Lamennais he presumed that the western world was in a flood-tide of transformation, evolution of

European society was inevitable, and the church had to choose to work with or against this new spirit of freedom. Another writer in *L'Avenir* was Henri Lacordaire, a young barrister, who suggested that Lamennais, Montalembert and himself go to Rome, as 'pilgrims of God and liberty' to have their movement blessed by Gregory XVI.

Unfortunately for the three idealists, who talked of 'the cry for deliverance' of the Belgians, the Poles and the Irish, Gregory XVI was alarmed by the excesses of local and popular freedom-seekers in the Romagna, where his troops were struggling to contain the Italian nationalists. Ideas of the separation of church and state, such as Lamennais suggested, were anathema to him, and though he was gentle in his reproof he let the three men know through his intermediaries that they had revived controversies that were very dangerous. They were to return to France and await his decision after their ideas were examined fully. When Lamennais insisted upon remaining in Rome he was finally granted an audience with Gregory who was kind and affable, offered Lamennais a pinch of snuff, but said nothing about the ideas which had appeared in *L'Avenir,* and which he found so disturbing.

Instead, the pope's answer to Lamennais and his followers was *Mirari vos* which condemned all the main causes of *L'Avenir,* liberty, the separation of church and state, and union with 'liberal revolutionaries'. Support for Polish nationalism was to be abandoned. Lamennais in turn produced his *Paroles d'un croyant* of 1834 in which he admitted the authority of the church in faith, but not in politics. This work was also proscribed by Rome and though his two companions remained in the church, Lamennais left it never to seek reconciliation. Gregory XVI had set the face of the papacy against liberalism in all its forms and, if Lamennais was a precursor of the Modernists of later years, Gregory's *Mirari vos* set the tone for the conservative *Quanta cura* and the Syllabus of Errors of Pius IX. The mentality of *Mirari vos* also ensured that Rome took an extremely cautious view of O'Connell and his Repeal campaign yet, as O'Connell took care not to involve the Holy See in his political activities, Gregory was able to maintain silence about affairs in Ireland. The pontiff could not be silent about Poland, however. In 1832 the papal brief *Superiori anno* stigmatized in Poland:

> ...those authors of lying and trickery who, under cover of religion, defy the legitimate power of princes, break all the ties of submission imposed by duty and plunge their country into misfortune and mourning.[2]

O'Connell viewed the Belgians and the Poles as a people who by striking for liberty, showed the world that: 'one nation cannot continue with impunity to wrong and oppress another'.[3] At the same time he never identified himself closely with their struggles. By the time that Young Ireland began to assert itself within the Repeal movement O' Connell realized that he had to be careful with Rome, for the new organization had Protestant leaders, spoke of the use of physical force and was strongly influenced by the Italian nationalist movements. Gregory's suspicions of O'Connell's liberal Catholicism would have been justified if he had lived to hear the praise O'Connell received from the leaders of the Italian *Risorgimento* in later years.

Gregory XVI may have had grave reservations about O'Connell's *agitazione*, but he had every intention of extending the spiritual authority of the papacy in Ireland. For ten years before his elevation to the papal throne he had worked in *Propaganda Fidei*, acting as Prefect of the congregation from 1826. During this time he formed a friendship with the young seminarian Paul Cullen, attending the disputation of his doctoral thesis, and consulting with him often about Irish affairs. It was Gregory who arranged for Cullen's appointment to the chairs of Greek and Oriental languages in Propaganda college, and the closeness of the two men deepened from the time that Cullen advised the pope about new regulations to govern episcopal nominations in Ireland. During the period that Cullen acted as rector of the Irish College in Rome after 1832 his intimacy with the pope deepened even more, to continue until the death of Gregory in 1846.

His acceptance into the ecclesiastically conservative organization of Rome in this period, ensured that Paul Cullen became a committed ultramontanist, sharing in the convictions of the ideologues, de Maistre, Rohrbacher and others who idealized the papacy:

> It is not based primarily on Scripture or strict theological reasoning, nor on the empirical record of most actual popes... The Ultramontanes tended to project onto the distant Holy Father the qualities they found lacking in their own bishops near at hand. Thus they naturally sought to promote the general acknowledgement in the Church of the Roman Pontiff's supreme authority and to maximize the actual exercise of this authority by him over the day to day life of the Church.[4]

Cullen and the other Roman ultramontanists, were not just idealists, however, for they were at the centre of Roman power, and willing to work with the conservative Gregory XVI to extend the power of the papacy wherever they could— including Ireland. It was an uphill battle. In 1826 fourteen French archbishops and bishops had signed a joint pronouncement qualifying the papacy's right of intervention in political affairs for spiritual reasons. The division between Gallicans and ultramontanists was extreme in France, with the former displaying a spirit of suspicion, almost of hostility towards Rome. What helped the ultramontanists was not only the ideological support for them provided by Rome but, as in France, intimidation by Gallican-minded governments that positively encouraged native hierarchies to look over the Alps for deliverance by the Holy See. The Catholics of the Rhineland had trouble with the Prussian monarchs who wished to unify Germany: in 1837 the aged archbishop of Cologne was imprisoned for his obdurate resistance to the state, and this 'Event of Cologne' became a European scandal. In Switzerland in 1842 Gregory XVI declared null and void measures taken against the rights of the church in Catholic cantons, and within three years they had formed a defensive confederacy ready to fight a civil war.

The ultramontane advance was most clearly revealed in France during the pontificate of Gregory XVI for it was then that the faithful were most divided. A quarrel over control of education, however, helped conservative Catholics to rally support for the ultramontane cause which was greatly assisted by the appearance of *L'Univers* a new Catholic journal, and a gifted propagandist, Louis Veuillot, its editor who seemed to many to be a new but ultra-orthodox Lamennais. He had had a sudden enlightenment in Rome in 1838, and from the time he joined *L'Univers* two years later he was a fervent ultramontanist whose views were so extreme that in 1844 he was imprisoned. He was to continue as editor of the journal until his death in 1883, and during Vatican Council I he was so much a confidant of the paper that *L'Univers* became almost an official organ of the papacy. A great defender of the temporal authority of the papacy, as well as of papal infallibility, he was a renowned intellectual champion of ultramontanism in the secular world. Within clerical institutions as we have seen, the great work of propaganda was the multi-volumed *Universal History of the Catholic Church* by the priest-historian René-François Rohrbacher, a romantic defender of Roman authority:

Every Christian nation which breaks with this center breaks with itself, with its past which it renounces, its present which it tears asunder, with its future which it throws to the winds.[5]

The great weakness of ultramontanism lay in its stubborn support for retention of the pope's reactionary temporal authority in the papal states. Cardinal Consalvi and some liberals may have wanted reforms to be carried out in the papal territories, but cardinal Albani and the other conservatives in the curia resolutely turned their backs on the new spirit appearing in Italy and throughout Europe. The feudal aristocracy were given back their old privileges, the Jews were confined to the ghetto once more, and the papal states emerged as one of the most backward territories in Europe. This ultra-conservative reaction to the liberalism of the early nineteenth century ensured that there was little Roman sympathy for the nationalist causes in Belgium and Poland, and an abiding suspicion of Daniel O'Connell's activities in his role of 'lay pontiff' in Ireland. Whenever liberalism became militant in the papal states Gregory XVI did not hesitate to use ruthless measures against the Italian nationalists, with the help of Austrian and French troops.

The uncomfortable political 'reality' did not deter the fealty which the ultramontanists offered to the pontiff as the supernatural universal spiritual authority, standing over and against not only national hierarchies with all their weaknesses, but even secular political powers when they threatened either the pope's spiritual or temporal rule. The pope was the spiritual leader of the faithful, the guarantor and guide of civilization, the oracle of wisdom, the leader of nations. Thanks to the authority revealed by a series of strong-minded popes a re-birth of Christendom was in the making: the church was about to quicken the world: 'Thou art Peter, and upon this rock I will build my Church and the gates of hell shall not prevail against her...'.

Certain writers, who were not always sound theologians, vied with one another in explaining the attributes of the papacy. Some went so far as to substitute the Pontiff's name for that of Christ in the breviary hymns, and even to describe him as an 'extension of the Incarnate Word', or 'the third Incarnation of the Son of God'.[6]

The ultramontanes of the nineteenth century Roman Catholic church were those churchmen who looked to the papacy to lead the needed opposition to the threatening theological and political liberalism of the age.

II   England and the Catholic Second Spring

In the last years of the eighteenth century the cisalpine Catholics of England had insisted that the laity, in effect the aristocracy and the gentry, should have a say in the appointment of bishops, and were inclined to view the Roman authority as an enemy prepared whenever possible to interfere in ecclesiastical affairs in England. The French Revolution lessened suspicions of Rome, however, and the Irish Act of Union confused the insular opinions of the cisalpines. The Catholic schools and colleges, so long established abroad, were brought back to English soil, and the recusants benefited from the wave of vague benevolent sentiment that welcomed the enormous invasion of French royalist clergy. The passions of the populace at the time of the Gordon riots seemed to be forgotten. Pius VII in captivity and bullied by Napoleon was hardly an authority to be feared. Many of the emigré clergy were convinced Gallicans: some even followed the Abbé Blanchard who had been suspended for his writings against the pope. John Milner, on the other hand, as we have seen, ensured that the English Catholic hierarchy had to reckon with their new relationship with the much larger Catholic church in Ireland.

Partly as a result of the 'Irish deluge' after 1790 the domination of the English Catholic church by the aristocracy and gentry lessened, and by the time a new Catholic Board was constituted in 1808 the laity seemed ready to accept reluctantly the right of Rome to appoint the vicars-apostolic. The last attempt at lay control was Henry Grattan's bill of 1813 which would have vested a veto in a royal commission consisting of Catholic peers and gentry. At that time William Poynter, vicar-apostolic of the London district was willing to negotiate on this suggestion so long as there were as many bishops as laymen on the committee. By 1829 the appointment of Catholic bishops was left to the Holy See.[7]

Milner never wavered in his opposition to the cisalpines, and continued to stress the authority of the divinely instituted hierarchy as a matter of Catholic principle. He could not abide a situation such as that in St. Patrick's, Soho, where until about 1813 a committee hired the priests, and defied diocesan efforts to change the situation.[8] In the last years of his life he was more temperate, however, for Propaganda, probably on the urging of cardinal Consalvi, rebuked him for the language he used in some of his writings.[9] From the time of Milner's death in 1826 until the coming of Nicholas Wiseman to England, as coadjutor of the Central district and president of Oscott College in 1840, the Catholic church in England was remarkably calm. O'Connell not only received little acclaim for bringing about Catholic Emancipation, but he was denied membership of the Cisalpine Club when he tried to join it.[10] The romanticism of the age which produced a fascination with things medieval brought about a general toleration of the Catholic community and the quiet and dignified vicar-apostolic of the London district, Dr. James Yorke Bramston, made certain that the Catholic question was not drawn to the public's attention during the period of agitation that accompanied the passing of the Reform Act of 1832. Liberal Protestant churchmen like Edward Stanley of Alderley, soon to be bishop of Norwich, defended the Irish Catholics who suffered a 'most galling inferiority... exasperated by hope deferred and insulted by the most atrocious calumnies'.[11] Even the evangelical Edward Bickersteth was willing to remind his contemporaries that in the country were: 'thousands of truly benevolent, amiable, moral men among the Papists, who abhor from their hearts cruelty and tyranny'.[12]

The voices of Stanley and Bickersteth were not representative of the opinions of most Protestants in the years following Catholic Emancipation. So long as the English Catholic community kept to themselves the majority of Protestants were indifferent to the affairs of what was considered to be an ancient form of dissent. From about 1835, however, the *Times* took up the cause of the Established Church clergy in Ireland who were then suffering greatly during the Tithe War. What was happening in Ireland was described as an inevitable result of popery seeking its unchanging ends and purposes, a 'Roman plot hatched at Maynooth'.[13] O'Connell was linked with this popish conspiracy which sought constitutional subversion, and his name was always accompanied by invective which scorned his corrupt political practices. When Mortimer O'Sullivan and Robert M'Ghee, the Irish Protestant campaigners, made an English speaking tour denouncing popery the *Times* acclaimed them. The paper solicited public subscriptions for the impoverished Irish parsons, and earlier it had encouraged the tercentenary celebrations associated with the publication of Miles Coverdale's English bible dedicated to Henry VIII. This outburst of Protestant nationalism the *British Critic* dismissed as an exercise in 'Papophobia'.[14]

It was actually a minor outbreak of Protestant hysteria, but it was important as it revealed a wide-spread bigotry and a popular resentment of the privileges granted to the Catholics by the government in 1829. Old fears were rapidly being rekindled:

> Popery, both at home and abroad, is in the possession of immense strength, and has been, and is now, marching forward with giant strides to its old ascendancy... in Ireland, for years the proportion of Roman Catholics to Protestants has been gradually and steadily increasing through the former laxity of the Established Church, the zeal of Popery, and the recent bitter persecutions which have tended so much to the encouragement of Protestant emigration.[15]

The excitement continued until 1841, and without doubt Peel and the conservatives encouraged this outburst on the part of the *Times,* supported by the Orangemen and the Evangelicals.[16] 'Popery' became the principal issue in the by-elections of the time, and the government was made aware that the Catholic Emancipation legislation which had been carried by the parliamentarians had not changed the cultural, religious or national attitudes of the populace as a whole.[17] The English had only to look at the violence in Ireland during this time, and fear arose that somehow the sufferings of the Protestants in Ireland was about to be visited upon them:

> If Popery be absent, there are prosperity and peace. Wherever there is turbulence—wherever there is anarchy—wherever there is national excitement or civil war, Popery is the sole author and agent.[18]

Throughout the nineteenth century evangelical Protestants in England were to continue to arouse the latent fear in the populace by resurrecting the memory of the St. Bartholomew's massacre and other horrors of the age of religious wars perpetrated by Roman Catholicism:

> Let us then hold up the inhuman system to merited execration, let parents teach their children, and children teach their children to dread and to oppose this abomination of desolation.[19]

Neither the *Times* nor the evangelical zealots would have had the success they had in stirring up popular feelings against the papists, however, if it was not apparent to people in many parts of the country that the numbers of these suspect people were rapidly increasing. During the first quarter of the nineteenth century steam power ensured regular and fast crossings between Ireland and the mainland, and with much competition fares were cheap. Liverpool was immediately affected by the Irish influx, while settlements of the new arrivals were rapidly established throughout the midlands, in the area around Glasgow and in the metropolis. By mid-century it was estimated that there were over 500,000 Irish born in the country, out of a population of eighteen million, and local communities were very aware of the numbers and the strength of the new arrivals. In Liverpool which had the greatest density of population in the country in the first half of the nineteenth century the Irish were bold enough to attack an Orange Order parade as early as 1819. In 1824 the Catholic newcomers then organized a huge St. Patrick's day parade of between 10,000 and 12,000 which the Orangemen did not dare attack. A great fight, however, occurred on the 12th of July parade of 1835, and from this time an Orange parade often provided a 'religious row' confrontation.[20] In fact it looked as if the whole gamut of Irish sectarian rivalries had been brought across the Irish sea. Powerful Protestant leaders appeared like Hugh McNeile, the Antrim born clergyman of St. Jude's in Liverpool, or Hugh Stowell, an evangelical Manxman, and their message was a familiar one in Ireland: the pope was the Antichrist, the Roman church was the enemy of Christianity, and the papists sought political power for the sake of crushing heresy. During 1839 and 1840, Stowell and his supporters in the working class Operatives Societies were putting on great demonstrations in Manchester:

> We have to a great extent got up in Manchester again that wholesome horror and antipathy of popery that, I am sorry to say, was fast sinking in the public mind. I say wholesome horror of popery, because though in many minds it is little better than a prejudice, yet a prejudice founded on truth is the next best thing to a principle.[21]

Following Catholic Emancipation there was a constant stream of Irish labourers into England because of depressed conditions in Ireland,[22] and many of the Irish who came were sophisticated in their understanding of trade union organization.[23] They had had experience labouring not only in operative societies in Dublin and elsewhere, but were accustomed to working closely together in the kind of secret society organization which they had known in Ireland. The result of this was that very quickly the immigrants, who had first been dismissed as 'blacklegs', began to assert themselves in militant labour organization. It is no accident that so many of the Chartist leaders, especially those urging physical force, had Irish names, and there is much evidence to suggest that it was the Irish who did most to mould Chartist policies and outlooks in the 1840's:

> ... the participation of the Irish contingent strengthened the 'physical force' element and helped to commit the movement to a policy of

revolutionary change which was far beyond its resources at the time. The Cuffey conspiracy in 1848, which may be regarded as the last spark of the 'physical force' group was led by William Cuffey, Thomas Fay, William Lacy, and William Dowling, all of whom seem to have been Irish.[24]

The Irish even produced a radical leader in Feargus O'Connor who had once sat as the O'Connellite member for Cork in 1833–1835. O'Connor broke with the Liberator, however, and by 1835 had identified himself with Thomas Murphy, Thomas Cleary and other members of the Marylebone Radical Association. He supported the Poor Law struggle, contributed to the radical *Northern Star* and encouraged agitation in West Riding communities where he became a kind of folk hero who tried to identify the sufferings of the English proletariat with those of the Irish peasantry. O'Connor was as much a blustering demagogue as O'Connell, and in the minds of many English critics typical of the kind of unwelcome and troublesome Irish who were causing so much social unrest on both sides of the Irish sea.[25]

English Protestant anxieties were disturbed not only by the growing number of Irish papists who were flooding into the country but, even more alarmingly, by the seeming fascination that a small but very vocal minority of Church of England clergy showed for the theological and ecclesiological ideas of popery. Theological controversies modelled on those held in Ireland became very popular, and in 1830 the daughter of a vicar described one five day marathon:

> The interest it excites is intense and a thousand or more every day–the Papists have got a young Jesuit, a noisy vulgar man from Cork, a priest from Birmingham, Sheenan, and a few more. On our side is a Mr. Armstrong from Ireland, an amazingly powerful speaker who cuts them up terribly and Archdeacon Digby... Mr. Percival was chairman for four days... when he said... I do believe that the Papacy is the Babylon spoken of in Revelations.[26]

One of the largest of these Irish-inspired controversial meetings was held at the Roman Catholic college at Downside, lasting for six days in February and March, 1834. At that time the Tithe War was raging in Ireland, the government appeared to be placating Irish Catholic opinion by the suppression of Protestant bishoprics, and it seemed clear to the evangelical Protestants in both islands that the Reformation cause was being undermined from within. Then came the explosion of the Tractarian movement in the Church of England.

John Henry Newman and the Oxford Tractarians were intent upon reviving signs of apostolic holiness within the Church of England, which had not yet emerged out of the latitudinarian lassitude of the eighteenth century, when they began to publish their tracts. None of them were good historians and, as they immersed themselves in the task of reviving among the clergy a sense of apostolic commission, they ignored England's long history of anti-Catholic bias. The readers of their tracts, however, had their minds well prepared about the dangers of popery and Newman's 1836 lectures in Oxford on 'Romanism and Popular Protestantism' did not receive sympathetic acclaim. When Hurrell Froude's *Remains* appeared in 1838, with its denigration of Protestantism, passionate controversy erupted.[27] This was the time when a public subscription was raising funds for erection of the Protestant Martyrs' Memorial in Oxford.

Newman's lectures on 'Romanism' had been preceded by a series on Roman doctrines and practices delivered in London during Advent 1835 by Nicholas Wiseman the visiting rector of the English college in Rome. A member of an old Irish family, though born in Spain, he was a great favourite of Gregory XVI, and was *Romano di Roma* in his romantic devotion to the ultramontane cause. When he was in Rome he had become close to a recent convert, George Spencer son of earl Spencer, who was consumed by the vision of converting England once more to the Roman Catholic faith. Spencer was part of a romantic movement in Cambridge which included young men like the wealthy landowner, Ambrose de Lisle, and the architect Augustus Pugin who was passionately involved in the Gothic revival in church building.[28] Wiseman shared in their enthusiasm for the conversion of England, and in 1838 he published an article in the *Dublin Review* comparing the position of the Anglicans concerning papal authority with that of the heretical Donatists in the early church. This article was very upsetting to Newman,[29] and when he wrote the most famous of the Tractarian movement's publications, Tract XC, in 1841 he argued that not only could the Thirty-Nine articles of the Church of England be interpreted in a 'Catholic' manner, but that Rome had not seriously deviated from the true faith in the definitions of the Council of Trent. One of Newman's intentions in the tract had been to dissuade men like W.G. Ward, fellow of Balliol, and later editor of the *Dublin Review* from seceding to Rome, but in this he was unsuccessful. Ward was but one of the wave of defectors, opposition to the Tractarians increased, and soon Newman found his fascination with ecclesiastical authority had brought upon him episcopal censure. A great personal crisis developed for him, and in October, 1845 Fr. Dominic Barberi, a Passionist missionary in England accepted his submission to 'the Roman obedience'.

In 1840 Wiseman was appointed coadjutor to the vicar apostolic of the London district, but he found on his arrival in England that he was not well received by many of the Catholics who did not easily accept: 'the great sweep of his ideas, the trailing clouds and the cherubs of Roman glory'.[30] Neither were they interested in the coterie of Anglican clergy who followed Newman into the Roman church. As the number of notable converts from Anglicanism increased however, at the same time that the influx of Irish Catholics into England showed no sign of ebbing, it was obvious to many English Catholics that a new spirit of revival was appearing in their minority religious community. After a memorable sermon by Newman at the Oscott synod of 1852 many English Catholics talked of the 1840's as a time of 'Second Spring'.[31]

Wiseman himself was scandalized by the lack of support he received when he promoted the idea that there might be a great return of the English people to Roman authority should the conversion movement be maintained:

> For Catholics to have overlooked all this, and allowed the wonderful phenomenon to pass by, not turned to any useful purpose, but gazed at till it died it, would have been more than stupidity, it would have been wickedness.[32]

He had cause for rejoicing, however, when a Roman mission by Rosminians and Passionists prospered in England, and the wearing of the Roman collar, and the appearance of Italian devotions in the chapels heralded the development of ultramontane influence within the church.[33] He was pleased when the vicars-apostolic showed interest in his acting as their Roman agent, which they agreed to because they did not trust Propaganda. Slowly the English Catholic church was changing, with about sixty Irish priests working in the north and in London by 1840, and more of the vicars-apostolic showing interest in the mission work of the regulars. Newman viewed the events at mid-century as the coming into being once more of an English expression of the Roman Catholic church which had been in abeyance since the Reformation. Wiseman's presence contributed much to this revival, and his labours were strengthened by those of the Benedictine William Bernard Ullathorne who was to be a strong supporter of the Roman cause as vicar-apostolic of the western district from 1846. A firm ultramontanist he did much to help Wiseman to fuse the Old Catholics and the recent Oxford converts and the Italian priests in a common mission. Not all the vicars-apostolic, or the Old Catholic clergy were willing to go along with Wiseman's militant conversion ideas, and most probably shared the opinion of the western vicar-apostolic, Peter Baines, who strongly opposed this 'novel and extraordinary project'. At Easter in 1840 Baines issued a flattening pastoral letter which described the conversion of England as 'morally impossible, and therefore not to be made an object of public prayer'. There should be no treatment of Protestants as heretics, nor should there be the cultivation of devotional or dogmatic excesses like that of the Immaculate Conception which would offend even friendly Protestants.[34]

It was as well that sober prelates like Peter Baines encouraged the English Catholics to keep a 'low profile', even when the *Times* and other detractors began to flag in their 'no popery' assault. From about 1843 Sir Robert Peel considered that the only way to deal with the O'Connellite Repeal agitation in Ireland was to ensure that there was as little civil injustice in Ireland as possible.[35] He determined to rid the country of all obvious grievances in the hope that he could win the Catholic prelates and priests, in particular, back to the support of law and order. One of the ways he attempted to do this was to pass legislation that would make available to the priests, with a minimum of administrative trouble, money left to Catholic religious bodies in wills. This brought into being the Charitable Bequests Act of 1844 which caused a great storm in Ireland, as we will see. The other legislation which enraged the ultra-Protestants in England, was the enlargement of the annual grant of the British government for the Catholic seminary at Maynooth from £9000 to £30,000.[36] The resulting uproar was immense: half of Peel's own conservative party voted against him in parliament, and though the Whigs, Liberals and Radicals supported the grant they took political advantage of the furore.[37] As for the grant itself the tumult showed how much anti-popery feeling still existed everywhere in the country.[38]

The furore was great indeed: in Macaulay's memorable phrase: 'the Orangeman raises his howl and Exeter Hall sets up its bray'.[39] The latter referred to a favourite meeting place for missionary and other societies, where the Protestant Association held gatherings to unite all the bodies opposed to the Maynooth 'concession'. Out of this agitation came the Central Anti-Maynooth Committee chaired by the zealous Sir Culling Eardley Smith which made clear the danger now threatening the nation and the empire:

> Popery, under the guidance of the Jesuits, is making a convulsive and desperate effort in every quarter of the world, and now also, it is besieging the Protestant bulwarks of the British Crown and Constitution.[40]

Excitement increased when a book by Charles Greville, Clerk of the Privy Council appeared arguing that not only were the Catholics in Ireland being deliberately pacified but: 'the grant to Maynooth is the first and most striking recognition of the principle of concurrent endowment'.[41] Now the established church itself was seen to be under attack, and powerful speakers like the Hon. and Reverend Baptist Noel opined that: 'the present measure was only the commencement of a system of legislation which would inevitably terminate in the endowment of the Romish church'.[42] Much of the effective protest of the Anti-Maynooth Committee was dissipated by tensions between churchmen and dissenters, but most Protestants recognized that the appeasement of the Irish Catholics by the government was now an on-going process and sooner or later the established church in Ireland was to be abandoned. Gladstone was prophetic when he told Henry Manning in April, 1845:

> I have always looked upon the Maynooth measure as what is called buying time–a process that presupposes the approach of the period of surrender.[43]

III   **Ireland and the Will to Catholic Ascendancy**

At the time of the Irish rebellion in 1798 Alexander Knox, with his usual perspicacity, wondered if, beyond the reinforcement of class hatred by religious fanaticism among the Catholics, there was not a natural form of assertiveness by a people who resented Protestant assumptions of superiority:

> It is not affront to the Irish Catholics to suppose they are but men; but more than men they must be if, after having gained their point by intimidating the Ministry in England, they would have rested satisfied with anything short of absolute ascendancy in Ireland. Heaven knows I bear the sincerest goodwill towards the Irish Catholics but I cannot give them credit for what is not in human nature. Like all other bodies of men that ever existed they must be under the influence of that potent principle which has not unjustly been called the *Esprit de Corps;* they must ever in their mildest temper, and under the most conciliating circumstances desire not merely equality but superiority for their own party and would necessarily consider as rivals those who should seem to stand in their way to that attractive pre-eminence.[44]

Writer after writer in Protestant society in the years following the union echoed this same concern, though seldom in the philosophical manner of Knox:

> They will never be satisfied until they establish a Catholic ascendancy on the ruins of Protestant ascendancy... to set their pretensions at rest you must sacrifice to them Church and State, the mitre and the throne.

At the heart of the Catholic demands would be found bishops like the 'ambitious and intriguing' Hussey serving the legatine office as if he was another 'fiery spirited Rinuccini' ever ready to drive the people once more into 'religious madness'.[45]

By 1812 the war against France was at a critical point; and with the army and navy filled with Irish recruits, and the papacy once more winning international sympathy, even the Protestants of distant Roscommon expressed their fear of what was happening in the country. Catholic disabilities were apparently to be further reduced by the government, while the Irish Protestants were: 'persuaded by the conduct of the Catholic leaders that they sought Catholic Ascendancy':

> They... now speak more the language of a national convention than petitioners seeking by constitutional means a redress of alleged grievances.[46]

When the parliamentary committees were holding their 1825 hearings on the state of Ireland Protestant pamphleteers of the period urged parliament to recognize that what was sought now was 'Popish Ascendancy': 'the ultimate object of the priesthood is to become the establishment in Ireland'.[47] In the same period William Urwick, an English Congregationalist who had settled in Sligo, and was a great controversial preacher, returned to England and reminded his fellow countrymen that in Ireland there still existed 'the huge impostures which prevailed in the days of Huss and Jerome, Wycliffe and Luther':

> The notion that Popery had changed, and become civilized, had cast away its persecuting and intolerant spirit, was then beginning to spread in the fashionable belief of the educated; and this was the notion which paved the way for the Tractarian movement.[48]

It seemed clear to Urwick and others that by the time the Protestants were organizing their political Brunswick Club amidst cries of 'No Surrender' on the eve of Catholic Emancipation,[49] they were already admitting that in the struggle of the time they lacked the spirit to maintain their ascendancy: 'Protestants do not acknowledge the same obligation to their agitators which Catholics acknowledge to theirs'.[50]

The threat of ultimate Catholic ascendancy always was a source of anxiety to the Protestants under the union, but of more immediate concern to them, if not of fear, was the growing resentment of the Catholic peasantry over the payment of tithe for support of the Church of Ireland. Tithes paid to the Catholic clergy had been assigned at the time of the Reformation to the ministers of the established church, but it was not until after the Protestant revolution of 1690 that they were regularly levied on the Irish people. Each area of the country developed custom with regard to payment, but almost everywhere tithes were a source of friction between the clergy, the people, and the landlords.[51] At the time of the union the primate, William Stuart, and the archbishop of Cashel, Charles Brodrick, had sought to redress the wrongs in this system of church maintenance, but they had limited success, and after the fall of agricultural prices in 1815, the tithe issue became a crisis situation.[52] When widespread unrest accompanied the famine of 1822 the agitation against tithes became severe, with many gentry encouraging the people to protest against payment of tithes rather than rents.

As the disturbances spread in 1822 Thomas Elrington, the Protestant bishop of Ferns and Leighlin, argued that they were not religious but were a reflection of the economic grievances of the peasants who suffered from exorbitant rents.[53] Particularly hated by the peasants were tithe proctors used by the clergy to collect the tithes. Grattan described them as 'a subordination of vultures': the English historian J.A. Froude said they were 'of all the carrion birds who were preying upon the carcass of the Irish peasantry the vilest and most accursed'.[54]

In the environs of Dublin the tithe rate was set by the proctors on New Years day and a contemporary has described the scene in the Killiney area:

> A scene of clamour and contention ensues that defies description; the proctors sometimes terrifying the unfortunate parishioners with threats of processes and citations for the arrears of tithes still due... till at last the agitated wretch not infrequently consents to give much more than he had been charged in the field book.[55]

Many of the parsons accepted a twentieth or a thirtieth rather than a full tithe; in some parts of the country potatoes were not tithed; and usually a local accommodation to avoid strife was attempted, sometimes with the parish priest acting as mediator. On the other hand there were avaricious Protestant clergy, and when the landlords had to pay for tithes on grasslands after 1824 they only too often had a hand in disturbances: 'the anti-tithe movement... was strongest in those parts of the country where large farmers were most numerous, primarily Leinster and Munster'.[56]

One of the ways of remedying the hated system, which everyone wanted to change, was to have a tithe composition act passed which would enable the Protestant clergy to substitute a fixed money payment for the tithe, thereby getting rid of the tithe proctors. The Protestant primate, Lord John George Beresford did not like this suggestion, however, for it went against the scriptural idea of tithe, he thought; the result was that the tithe legislation was not made compulsory. While the establishment in church and state sought to find an answer to the problem of the tithe the tensions between the clergy, people and the landlords continued.[57] The outrages that followed did little to enhance the popularity of the Church of Ireland, and the *Edinburgh Review* suggested to its Whig readers that the tithe was no more the property of the Protestant clergy than taxes raised for the army were the property of the troops.[58] As tensions rose it was inevitable that sectarianism would enter the debate and even James Doyle, who sought conciliation with the government wherever possible, showed no toleration of the tithe system: 'May our hatred of tithes be as lasting as our justice', but at the same time he tried to quell the terrorism of the secret societies, and to decry excesses of the Orangemen.[59]

The struggle over tithes was also taking place in England, where the agitators discovered that a quarter of the tithe received by the parsons had originally been set aside for support of the poor.[60] Doyle made use of this information in his protests against the tithe system in Ireland, and to the Protestant clergy his role was seen as a reinforcement of those who were using 'the artillery of calumny and vituperation' against them: 'inviting the peasantry to a perseverance in their attacks upon the properties of the clergy'.[61] Even Doyle, who had hitherto been held in great respect by the Protestants for his resistance to the secret societies, was held suspect before his death in 1834.

Everywhere about them the Protestants saw conspiracy. The pamphlets of the time are concerned with tithes but also abound with accounts of Catholic bishops and priests 'anathematizing' the circulation of the bible, while at the same time they tolerated the republication of the sectarian 'prophecies' of Pastorini. They also told of priests teaching Catholic children that the Protestants were the descendants of robbers and plunderers:

> Certain it is that the priests throughout Ireland have done and are doing their utmost to excite against the Protestant incumbent the hatred of his parishioners. With the fearful influence which they possess over their minds it would be strange indeed if they were not in general successful.[62]

Some, however, thought the Tithe War was not in a real sense sectarian, though the priests tried to take advantage of the tensions between the two peoples. Henry Cotton, the archdeacon of Cashel, argued as Thomas Elrington had ten years earlier, that the Tithe War was essentially economic, the beginning of a long term struggle with the holders of property.[63]

Whether the unrest reflected religious prejudice, or economic resentment the *Dublin University Magazine* of 1833 claimed that since Catholic Emancipation a total of 94,000 Protestants had left Ireland. The exodus they said was so great:

> ... it were almost impossible to state fully, and if so stated would not be credited. It is not from this or that neighbourhood alone. Panic and disgust have seized upon the Protestant yeomanry throughout Ireland. The country is not bleeding merely, it is sweating blood.[64]

The result of the great struggle between 1831 and 1838 was a further tragic separating of the people, religiously and socially. The Protestants were convinced that behind the agitation were the same priests who had helped the O'Connellite movement before 1829, and were now skilled agitators. In the Palatine community at Kilcooley in county Tipperary, one of the most restless areas, a Catholic mob gathered outside the Protestant church at the time of service, and intimidated by entering and stamping their feet. An Orange lodge was formed on the estate by the landowner, William Barker, as well as an armed Protestant Defence Association, and though actual violence was avoided the tension in the community was great. Until the government forced the suppression of the Orange Lodge on the estate it had sent financial aid to Orangemen in gaol in Downpatrick waiting for the assizes.[65]

Sectarian tensions increased in southern Ireland as the countryside was cursed with endemic violence, for this was the turbulent age of peasant faction fights, and the collection of tithes with the aid of the army or constabulary, often resulted in violence and death. At Rathcormack in Co. Cork occurred one of the most infamous of these events when soldiers and tithe agitators clashed, with deaths and injuries the result.[66] The rector of Rathcormack obtained his tithe on this occasion, but from that time he had to have his house garrisoned, and the expectation was that he would have to leave the country. Elsewhere many incumbents were: 'reduced to absolute indigence... only preserved from starving by the bounty of the British public'.[67] The suffering of the parsons was much less in the north where commutation of the tithe was widely accepted, and the Catholics were neither through numbers nor spirit in a position to intimidate. At the same time, as Mortimer O'Sullivan prebendary of Ballymore in the Armagh diocese revealed, the Protestants everywhere were now under threat, their only hope unity in the face of a drive for the 'extermination of Protestantism' in Ireland.[68]

Many shared the anxiety of O'Sullivan in England as well as Ireland, for the tales of the intimidation of the Protestant clergy were readily accepted in Exeter Hall and elsewhere in the country. Daniel Murray, the Catholic archbishop of Dublin, protested a charge made by the bishop of Gloucester in the *Gloucester Journal* of 12 December, 1835 that the Irish hierarchy had encouraged priests to denounce from the altar Protestant clergy who were subsequently murdered. The English bishop replied to Murray's protest by denying what the press had attributed to him but, in the process, revealing the disgust felt by the English hierarchy over affairs in Ireland:

> In enumerating the sufferings of the Irish clergy I said that some had been murdered; others brutally assaulted; and their lives threatened... I observed that they were unable to obtain their dues, the payment of which had, in some instances, been forbidden by the priest from the altar. I next remarked that their consequent distress had been made a subject of ridicule and insult by certain of the highest of the Roman Catholic hierarchy.[69]

By the time the Tithe War came to an end with the Tithe Rent-Charge Act of 1838, which was of little help to the peasants who now had to pay the tithe to the landlords who were not apt to reduce it as the parsons once had, the division between the churches was sad. The parson now received part of what was collected for him by the landlord; but he had a diminishing contact with the people, and a greater identification than ever with the landlords. After 1838 many of the Protestant clergy were persuaded by the Tithe War confrontations to listen to the extremists among them who pointed out that there was as much crime in popish Tipperary as in all of Ulster:

> The papists, maddened by success, are thirsting for Protestant blood, and the priests are active for the spoil. The whole empire is disorganized and overrun by the machinations of popery.[70]

However justified by experience Protestant fears may have been the fact was that the Tithe War was not the clerically-directed campaign of terror that some Protestants believed it to be. Following the victory of Catholic Emancipation the desire of the bishops was to get the priests back into their presbyteries. What the hierarchy wanted was made clear in the statement of public policy issued in February, 1830:

> ... a steady attachment to the constitution and laws of your country, as well as the person and government of our most gracious sovereign will be manifested in your entire conduct... let religious discord cease, let party feuds and civil dissensions be no more heard of...[71]

'Civil dissension' was endemic in this age when faction fighting was prevalent, however, and so out of clerical or any other control that in 1824 a select committee of the House of Commons was set up to report on the phenomenon, especially in county Tipperary. In 1837 there were eighteen faction fights and 157 riots reported by the constabulary, all of them extremely violent. In one of the bloodiest encounters, between the Cooleens and the Black-Mulvilhills on 24 June, 1834, the army stood by helplessly, as did priests, unable to stop the brutal carnage.[72] Catholic and Protestant leaders alike were alarmed for the ferocity of the people in the Whiteboy era had not been forgotten; the agitation then had been as much against the payment of dues to the priest as the giving of tithes to the parsons. Though the 'detested impost' of tithe collection was removed in 1838 the priests were aware that the tithes were still: 'unfortunately associated in the popular mind with dues'.[73] The Catholic clergy generally in pre-famine Ireland were only too aware of the potentially dangerous power of the peasantry, and they knew how easily that force could be channelled into a political movement which they were loathe to be too closely identified with, let alone to try to control. James Doyle understood the mentality of the peasantry during the Tithe War: 'their distress, their hatred of Orangemen, their love of religion, their faith in prophecies, their hope of seeing Ireland free'. Yet he also remembered what the fury of the peasants had brought upon Irish society in the not distant past:

> The year 1798 is within the recollection of us all; at that fatal period, Protestant and Catholic, and Dissenter of every class and description... combined to overthrow the government. You witnessed their failure... and many of you experienced their fatal consequences.[74]

Doyle was not the only Catholic bishop of his generation who was disturbed by the hatred of everything Protestant that was being promoted by some of his episcopal colleagues, and by many of the graduates of Maynooth.[75] Sectarian folk Catholicism was dividing society, begging the kind of directing authority that Rome provided only with the coming of Paul Cullen as papal legate at mid-century. The anti-Protestant sentiment of the time was noted by Alexis de Tocqueville in 1835 when he attended a dinner given by Doyle's successor as bishop of Kildare, Edward Nolan, which included among the guests an archbishop, three other bishops, and several priests:

> The feelings expressed were extremely dogmatic. Distrust and hatred of the great landlords; love of the people, and confidence in them. Bitter memories of past oppression. An air of exaltation at present or approaching victory. A profound hatred of the Protestants and above all of their clergy. Little impartiality apparent. Clearly as much the leaders of a Party as the representatives of the Church.[76]

Not all Irish Catholic prelates were as sectarian minded as those that de Tocqueville encountered, fortunately, and it was widely recognized that encouraging popular agitation against 'everything Protestant' was counter-productive when it increased support for the Orange Order. When Lord Bandon and his son joined the Grand Orange Lodge of county Cork in November, 1834, he said it was for the cause of 'Protestant defence' that they made their commitment:

> The circumstances of the present times have roused the spirit of all true Protestants throughout Ireland and have made them feel the necessity of uniting more closely together than formerly...[77]

Those Catholic ecclesiastics who wanted to use the church in the cause of Repeal, as they had in the campaign for Catholic Emancipation, remained a minority, most bishops tried to control the spread of agitation, and in 1831 the priests of the ecclesiastical province of Leinster were forbidden to use churches for political purposes.[78] Doyle privately opposed Repeal in 1831, and worked against Repeal candidates the following year. Daniel Murray was joined by the bishops of Ossory and Ferns when he opposed Repeal, and in January 1834 he persuaded the bishops in synod to reaffirm the injunction of 1830 forbidding priests to engage in political activity.

There were, however, politically radical bishops like MacHale of Tuam, Keating of Ferns, Blake of Dromore, and Browne of Galway who simply turned their heads when the priests in their dioceses engaged in political activity:

> One priest considered it part of his duty as a priest to give general 'encouragement' to Catholic electors from the altar, to instruct the people in their moral duty and to notice publicly those who did not take his advice; and parish priests used to attend registry sessions and elections, riding to the polls at the head of their parishioners.[79]

Francis O'Finan of Killala, who opposed political priests, and was driven to the verge of a breakdown by MacHale,[80] wrote to Propaganda in March, 1836:

> It is no longer the zealous pastor of souls who receives popular applause... but rather the bold and intriguing priest who makes himself the leader of the people in political matters.[81]

The result of complaints like this was that cardinal Fransoni of Propaganda wrote two letters to primate Crolly to complain in 1839 about MacHale and other bishops exciting popular passions at political banquets where the government was denounced. The letters were not made public, though the bishops knew of them, but they were ignored by MacHale and his followers who threw themselves wholeheartedly into the Repeal campaign when it was re-launched by O'Connell in 1840.[82] Nothing more was to be heard from Rome about this issue for five and a half years.

During the Tithe War, and whenever there was an outbreak of local rural 'outrage' the Protestant minority expected help from the state as the guardian of law and order. This was an age of political reform in Britain, however, and under the union the established church, in particular, found its ecclesiastical role in Ireland under increasing scrutiny in distant London. The sufferings of the parsons in the 1830's inevitably drew Ireland to the attention of the legislators who, quite reasonably, considered whether a form of social engineering might be attempted in Ireland which would ease the tensions between its peoples. Out of this concern came various commissions of inquiry into Irish affairs which begged an end to traditional ways of social organization that appeared to contribute to the social friction and violence found in most parts of the island. As the commissions and committees published their reports the Protestants concluded that the state could no longer be looked upon as the protector of their way of life; rather it seemed to them intent upon granting any concession to the Catholics which was demanded.[83]

The most important of the changes brought by the state was the introduction of the National System of Education in 1831 which ultimately made the Irish peasantry one of the best educated rural people in Europe. In the eighteenth century the Protestants had greatly criticized the parish priests for their failure to 'instruct the people in Christian education' leaving them 'for the most part in stupid ignorance'.[84] The obvious remedy was for the Protestant church to build up a 'society of free schools' where the bible would be introduced to Irish children, and at that time it was taken for granted that the schools would be openly proselytizing bodies:

> ... that the poor Popish natives may be the more easily induced to suffer their children to be brought up in a religion different from their own.[85]

In the years following the union various evangelical visitors from England came to Ireland[86] and urged that the desultory educational experiments of the past should be absorbed into a large-scale attempt to promote education in the Irish language, making use of the bible, but avoiding sectarian or denominational comment. This demand brought into being in 1818, the Irish Society for Promoting the Education of the Native Irish Through the Medium of their own Language. This Irish Society grew to be a substantial organization which, its adherents believed, not only educated its pupils but 'wrought changes in the moral condition of the peasantry':

> A powerful instrumentality does exist in Ireland by the use of which her very exciteable native population may be controlled, and their passions and their energies directed into useful channels.[87]

According to the Second Report of the Commissioners of Irish Education in 1826 various Protestant societies were providing elementary education for over half a million students. Some, like those of the Protestant Charter School Society, or the Association for Discountenancing Vice and Promoting the Knowledge and Practice of the Christian Religion were accused of consistent proselytizing. The largest body, the Kildare Place Society, was at first supported by Doyle, who was in favour of interdenominational education, and even by Daniel O'Connell, but by 1824 it too was accused of proselytizing. This was a great challenge for the government which placed so much faith in education as a means of civilizing the ever-turbulent peasantry; for the Catholic schools were few in number, and the Catholic church was without the resources to create the denominational system of education it would have liked to have. So there came into being the National System of Education from 1831, under a board representing several denominations, where pupils were to study together, with separate periods of study set aside for religious instruction by clergy of their denominations. None of the churches liked this, however, and by mid-century the system had evolved into schools, especially in the Catholic areas, that were, in effect, denominational. The papal delegate, Paul Cullen, as we will see, fought to obtain state support for Catholic denominational schooling but, as a compromise, he reluctantly accepted the largesse of the National System and made use of it in most areas of the country where Catholics filled these schools:

> ... very dangerous when considered in general, because its aim is to introduce a mingling of Protestants and Catholics, but in the places where in fact there are no Protestants this mingling cannot be achieved.[88]

The leaders of the established church were appalled at this legislation for it took away from the church its traditional role as educator of the people, which they considered to be an integral part of establishment. It also upset the evangelicals who crowded Exeter Hall in meeting after meeting to protest this giving in to popery, by a government which apparently agreed to deny the people of Ireland knowledge of the bible. Now 'official interference' was reinforcing the 'excommunication' tactic which the priests had used to deny the people the Holy Scriptures: 'they enforce a spiritual prostration of intellect and principle at the shrine of a corrupt and degrading superstition'.[89] The primate lobbied the government strongly for financial help for Protestant schools that were set up under the Church Education Society, but by 1845 Robert Peel bluntly told Beresford that the government would not agree to the:

> granting of public aid to at least three different societies in Ireland by each of which secular instruction should be combined with religious instruction in the particular doctrine of each communion... all hope of mixed education must be extinguished and a line of demarcation would be drawn between the children of different religious persuasions more marked than has hitherto existed at any period.[90]

Without state aid the Church Education Society could not survive, and in the 1850's more and more Protestant schools accepted government aid in joining the National System–which the Catholics had cheerfully made use of for a long time. Finally in 1860, amidst cries of 'Judas', the primate acknowledged what was happening and informed churchmen that if they could not keep up their schools they should join the National System to ensure education for their young.[91]

The attitude of the Ulster Presbyterians was just as negative towards the National system for it was seen by them that if the priests would have access to schools paid for by the state and if bible reading took place the priests would ensure that Catholic children would be forbidden to attend. Inevitably this kind of sectarian action took place, which prompted a Protestant response. In spite of the hopes of a minority of liberal Protestants, such as the Presbyterian commissioner of education, James Carlisle of Dublin, who had agreed with the government's belief that the new national system would help to heal the divisions in Irish society, Henry Cooke, the great champion of Presbyterian orthodoxy from the 1820's, easily persuaded a majority of members of the Synod of Ulster to oppose non-denominationalism from 1834 onwards. The synod began to establish its own schools while at the same time it pressed the state for financial support. The government soon wavered in its resolve about insisting upon non-denominationalism in Ulster, which had remained relatively quiet during the years of the Tithe War, and in 1840 public funds were granted to a school which was not to be run in strict accordance with the board's regula-tions.[92] In effect, no priest was to be allowed in the school, and this marked the end of the hope for integrated education in Ulster. Denominational education was recognized in

Ulster as a reality which had to be accepted if the province was to remain quiet.

There were, of course, some 'civilizing' state interventions which the Protestants welcomed, such as Robert Peel's revision of the police acts of 1786–1787. Ireland had paid policemen long before England, and the more centralized state control meant that the lord lieutenant could proclaim any part of town or country as being in a 'state of disturbance' and govern it accordingly. The Protestants also welcomed the infirmaries and dispensaries which appeared in the 1830's, giving the Irish peasants a health service which was unusual for the age. The workhouses, modelled on those built in England under the 1834 Poor Law Act also met Protestant approval generally as an attempt to deal with the appalling poverty in the countryside. From the standpoint of the established church especially this was how the Irish problem should be handled, with the state reinforcing the efforts of the church to bring not only true religion but civility to all the inhabitants of Ireland. Whereas the priest was often viewed as a servant of disorder and unrest, as well as religion, in the Protestant mind the parson was the agent of Christian civilization when he performed his ecclesiastical and social role as 'the resident gentleman' in his parish. This role was praised by a government inspector who was investigating the state of the country during the Tithe War:

> I must as a public officer, whose duties call me into close contact with the clergy throughout the most remote and (by all others of the highest classes) deserted parts of the kingdom, declare that were it not for the residence, and moral and political influence of the parochial clergy, every trace of refinement and cultivation would quickly disappear. Putting religion out of the question, the Establishment clergy are a means of supplying an educated and resident gentry in Ireland.[93]

In spite of the rejection of their services by the great mass of the people the Protestant clergy still served the ideal role that lay behind the concept of establishment. In the words of Power le Poer Trench, the evangelical archbishop of Tuam in 1835:

> I consider a parochial minister is responsible for every living soul within his parish... the clergy of the Established Church are the ministers of Christ to the Roman Catholics no less than to the Protestants, and as such they are not unfrequently called upon.[94]

The ideal of establishment was not going to survive intact the scrutiny of the reforming zeal of parliament, however, and the Tithe War ensured that a restructuring of the Irish church was inevitable. During 1832 there were 242 homicides, and innumerable robberies, burglaries, burnings, houghing of cattle, assaults, riots and offences against property as the people resisted payment for the upkeep of the Protestant church. The revenue of the church was some £800,000 to support 22 bishops, including four archbishops, and a legion of dignitaries. The entire church had only 852,064 members, less than there were in the see of Durham alone.[95] Change had to come, yet some observers felt that reform of the church was a useless venture because, ultimately, what the Catholic population wanted was its abolition as an establishment.[96]

The government was willing to consider almost any solution to the Irish church problem, including: 'a suggestion, seriously made, that the Church should engage its own soldiers to cooperate with Crown forces in the recovery of the tithes'.[97] Parliament knew that whatever was attempted would bring about a hysterical reaction on the part of those who would see suppression of any part of the church's temporalities as 'a direct disavowal of the sovereignty of God'. Finally in 1833 it acted by introducing the Church Temporalities Bill which called for a reduction of the Irish sees from 22 to 10 as vacancies occurred, and the suspension of 66 sinecure parishes where no service had been held for three years. The predicted uproar was great, in England as well as Ireland, as we have noted, for churchmen saw in the Irish bill a programme by the state to view the church in an utilitarian way: if the establishment was not of social benefit it would be reduced or eliminated. To English High Churchmen, like the Oxford dons who began the Tractarian movement, the Irish bill was: 'a first and a mild instalment of a programme which would reduce the Church of England to a department of the Civil Service'.[98]

The Irish Protestant response to the legislation was, predictably, presented in sectarian terms. The archdeacon of Cashel, Henry Cotton interpreted the Irish church bill as a catastrophe, a step towards:

> ... erecting a Roman Catholic establishment in Ireland upon the ruins of the Protestant church; and empowering the tenets of Rome once more to overshadow and oppress the purer faith of Protestantism.[99]

The reaction of R.J. M'Ghee of Harold's Cross, Dublin, was so extreme that in a series of writings he hinted at a rejection of the state legislation by churchmen.[100] This greatly annoyed archdeacon Edward Stopford, who became bishop of Meath in 1842. He told M'Ghee in a public letter that his talk of 'renouncing all claims to apostolic authority' and his calling upon the clergy to choose whether 'the Bible or an Act of Parliament is to be the standard according to which our church is to be governed' was irresponsible. Of matters of church and state M'Ghee 'knew nothing' and he was mischievous to call upon the clergy: 'to rush into the evils of dissent and schism, and overwhelm the Established Church in Ireland in confusion and ruin'.[101] Stopford, who was close to the primate, knew how vulnerable was the established church in an age when parliament was focusing its attention on Ireland and reform was in the air. There was little with which to defend the anomalies that the *Edinburgh Review* and numerous other critics pointed out:

> There are 157 benefices in Ireland, in which there is no resident
> clergyman, and no service is performed in a place of worship; and there
> are 41 in which there is also *no* member of the Established Church.
> Thirty-six benefices of this latter class, in the whole of which there is
> no church, no resident clergyman, no member of the Established
> Church, derive incomes from tithe alone, exclusive of glebe lands, to
> the amount of £4142.[102]

M'Ghee's anxieties were not to be easily exorcised, however, and following
the Church Temporalities Act he claimed that the Church of Ireland had a crisis
of identity. First, said M'Ghee, the state had initiated the National System of
Education, 'to banish the Word of God from the education of our country', and
now the Protestant clergy had their characters 'calumniated and held up,
blackened by Popish falsehood in the very midst of the British senate'. Instead
of its craven Protestant bishops M'Ghee wished the Church of Ireland had leaders
with the boldness of John MacHale who had boasted of the bishops of the
popish church:

> We are not weeds that may be planted or plucked up at pleasure–we are
> not these corporate functionaries whose titles depend upon a royal
> patent.[103]

Even without the episcopal leadership it deserved the Church of Ireland had to
fight against the clergy of Rome who sought to impose on the people of Ireland
anarchy, barbarism and the despotism of Roman superstition. Within a year of
the passing of the Irish bill M'Ghee had found the cause that he was to serve for
the rest of his life: the summoning of the Protestant people of Ireland to resist
the advance of the Antichrist in Rome who sought to impose his authority, his
religion and his culture upon the people of Ireland.

M'Ghee was influential in what he preached and wrote because he spoke to
the deep anxieties of the time, when no one seemed to be in control of the
anarchy that appeared to be spreading throughout southern Ireland. His
'detection' of a Counter-Reformation conspiracy behind the turbulence directed
by the priests received a ready hearing not only in Ireland but in Exeter Hall in
London. M'Ghee based his message on Roman publications which he said had
been approved by the Catholic hierarchy in Ireland and secretly used to foment
discord among the people. The most important Roman directive was contained
in the theology of Peter Dens, who had been president of Mechlin Seminary
from 1735 to 1777, and he produced a fourteen volume work of systematic theology based on the teachings of St. Thomas Aquinas. Included in Dens' work
were Counter-Reformation ideas such as the putting to death of heretics.

M'Ghee also claimed that a bible had been produced in Cork in 1818, MacNamara's bible, with a commentary by Dens in it. The bishops of the Leinster province had secretly approved Dens' theology, and, though the laity knew nothing of this, a Roman directed anti-Protestant policy was now operative in the Catholic church.

When M'Ghee, in his usual highly excitable way, introduced this discovery at Exeter Hall in June, 1835 the platform was filled with evangelical Irish leaders such as the earl of Roden, and the earl of Bandon, as well as influential clergy-men like Mortimer O'Sullivan, Robert Daly, Joseph Singer and Caesar Otway. M'Ghee told his audience that although archbishops Troy and Murray had assured parliament that no anti-heretical directives were operative in the Irish Catholic church, Dens' theology had been adopted as a standard guide for the priests since 1808. The *Freeman's Journal* of 27 June, 1835 launched an attack on the 'antics of the prime mountebank' who performed for the 'new menageries of Exeter Hall', and denied the use of Dens at Maynooth, or its being read by the clergy elsewhere. The newspaper was ill-informed, however, for Dens' 'course of theo-logy' had been printed for use at Maynooth in 1808, and it had been agreed 'that each prelate should take a certain number of copies' of the work.[104] When the bishop of Exeter brought up the question of Dens in the House of Lords Daniel Murray wrote to Melbourne the prime minister to say that although Dens' theo-logy had been printed and was in circulation, and it contained some 'obsolete opinions' there could be no fear that now any 'heretic' need feel threatened.[105] This by no means satisfied M'Ghee who continued his attack and even invoked a letter on the issue from O'Connell in the *Morning Chronicle* of 2 August 1836. He told another large gathering at Exeter Hall that what the whole affair showed was the determination of the Irish Catholic bishops to have the canon law of the Roman court rule the people in Ireland, not the common law of Britain.[106]

M'Ghee is credited with some fifty publications on the theme of a secret Roman campaign to take over the Catholic Church in Ireland and in his writings he stressed that 'our poor Roman Catholic countrymen are not the authors but the victims of papal iniquity', and the mission of Irish Protestants should be the deliverance of the people from 'the cruel yoke that bows down them and our church and our nation'.[107] He paid particular attention to Maynooth as a bastion of ultramontanism, and chided the established church clergy for their unwilling-ness to call the people out from their allegiance to: 'that apostasy, that Mystery, that Babylon the Great, the Mother of Harlots and abominations of the earth'. He left to take up a parish in England in 1846, but he continued to write on Irish affairs, and often returned to Ireland to lecture in his typical manner which was: 'frenzied and rapid when he gave forth his views of the Canon Law of Rome clashing with and trying to overcome the Civil and Constitutional Law of England'.[108]

More colourful than M'Ghee was the great champion of the Protestant work-ing class Tresham Dames Gregg, 'Trash 'em Gregg' in its folklore. He attended

Trinity while the great religious controversies were being held, then after a short time in an industrial parish in Yorkshire he returned to Dublin to be elected by the churchwardens and 'poor parishioners' as chaplain of the chapel of St. Mary in the parish of St. Nicholas Within the Walls. Archbishop Whately tried his best to oust the trouble-making Gregg from this medieval sinecure but the ecclesiastical law was so complex that he was unsuccessful. Safe in this position, the fanatically Protestant Gregg referred to himself as 'Chantry Priest' of St. Mary's, while he carried on an ideological war with the Catholics of Dublin. He openly quarrelled with Whately when the archbishop tried to get at Gregg by using the medieval tactic of laying the chapel under interdict. Gregg was defended by the astute Isaac Butt in this contest which Whately failed to win, and he had to endure the jibes of Gregg who considered him not only an 'indifferent scholar' but 'soft on popery'. Gregg also dismissed as a 'Puseyite' the scholarly James Henthorne Todd of Trinity College who refused to admit the pope was the Antichrist.

Gregg himself was a considerable scholar in Old Testament studies, receiving a Doctor of Divinity degree from Trinity in 1853, and he showed his intellectual abilities in a five day controversy with Fr. Tom Maguire in 1839. Maguire retired from the contest on the last day of the marathon and the Protestants considered Gregg the winner. The usual 'authenticated report' of the debate was duly published in the same year, and throughout its 361 pages of the marathon and the Protestants considered Gregg the winner. The usual 'authenticated report' of the debate was duly published in the same year, and throughout its 361 pages Gregg promoted his thesis that the Roman Catholic church served the Antichrist. The following year he published a bulky work which summed up his thought, *Protestant Ascendancy Vindicated,* with the argument that only in Protestantism could the Irish people find the freedom which would deliver them from the 'degrading influence of popery' which depressed Italy, Spain, Portugal and South America. Now the Irish people were still in bondage:

> I believe Ireland to be the most miserable country in the world, and that
> it is rendered so by popery... that nothing less than the complete
> prevalence of Protestantism can make Ireland happy and prosperous.[109]

As the years passed Gregg's polemics never weakened. In 1846 he attacked Whately as a product of Oriel College, Oxford: 'that notorious hotbed of heresy, popery and folly, sent over to us in judgment for our sins'. As for the Irish Catholics they were to be pitied for their servitude to Roman tyranny which kept them:

> ... in a state of such perfect bondage that like the brute animals they
> shall be governed by their superiors, and swayed by them, as though
> these governors had made their reasons captive.[110]

In later life he developed some 'peculiar ideas' as he involved himself in prophecy, publishing in 1872 a drama, *Queen Elizabeth or the Origins of Shakespeare* which sought to show how Mary, Queen of Scots, was used by the Antichrist, but in the 1840's he was at the height of his powers, and his influence among the Protestant workers was considerable.

The extreme anti-Romanism of Gregg was a dominant expression in the Irish Protestant mind during the O'Connellite years. W.J. O'Neill Daunt believed it did more than anything else to keep the Protestant working class in Dublin from supporting Repeal, as 'the fanatical bellows were kept in full blast':

Preachers, orators and writers, whose idea of Christianity appeared to be confined to the duty of hating the Papists and shouting 'To hell with the Pope!' now bellowed about Antichrist, romanced about apocalyptic numerals, ranted about the Inquisition, and threatened that if Repeal were obtained the Papists would ride roughshod over the Protestants.[111]

A succession of publications, the *Protestant Penny Magazine,* the *Watchman,* the *Penny Watchman,* and the *Protestant Penny Journal,* kept up the paranoia over the advance of the Antichrist of Rome. It was a time of economic depressions, especially among the hand-loom weavers and other 'operatives' of the Liberties, but the anti-Roman agitation of Gregg ensured that there was no Catholic-Protestant alliance to serve the needs of the working class.[112]

In actual fact there was remarkably little direct influence from Rome during these pre-famine years, and when the papacy intervened in Irish affairs, the first time since the veto controversy, it was when Propaganda in the spring of 1839 sent two letters to primate Crolly reproving the political agitation of the priests in support of O'Connell, as we have noted. This was unknown to the Protestants and, indeed, to most of the Catholic clergy for the letters were kept private. It is unlikely that the Protestants would have appreciated the papal action if the letters had been made public. By 1839 they were convinced, following Catholic Emancipation, the National System of Education, the Church Temporalities Act, and the terror of the Tithe War, that powerful forces were arrayed against them, determined to destroy Protestant ascendancy in Ireland. When, like archdeacon Henry Cotton, they asked *Cui bono?* by all that was taking place, their immediate and simplistic answer, which reflected their historical experience, was–the court of Rome. A great battle was shaping up in Ireland to put an end to British-Protestant authority: to leave the Irish people dominated by the papacy and by Canon Law. This the Irish Protestants were determined to resist to the utmost of their power:

We will demand and we will insist upon downright Protestant ascendancy and nothing less–the ascendancy of God's word, of God's law, and of God's people...nothing short of carrying out these views will save the British Empire from destruction.[113]

In the immediate pre-famine years there was more to Irish Protestantism than the shrill polemics of R.J. M'Ghee, T.D. Gregg and their supporters, however. Although the Church of Ireland, in particular, was becoming more evangelical, it had by no means abandoned its traditional staid form of Calvinistic theology.[114] Nor was it intellectually dormant for it showed great interest in the millenarian speculation of the age,[115] and out of the Church of Ireland came controversial figures like John Nelson Darby, the founder of the 'exclusive' Plymouth Brethren.[116] At the same time the Church of Ireland maintained a 'high' doctrine of the church as a Catholic body in the apostolic succession, over and against the claims of the Presbyterians and other dissenters, and the exclusivist doctrines of the Roman Catholics.[117] There was little interest shown in Tractarianism, however, which primate Beresford in his charge of 1842 attributed to the Irish Protestants meeting with the most malignant form of Catholicism on a daily basis:

> In this country where we have constantly before our eyes a practical exhibition of the superstition into which the principles of the Church of Rome lead, and must ever lead, the simple-minded and ignorant poor of that communion...[118]

Nor was there any sense of despair over the Protestant mission to the whole of the Irish people in the years just before the famine. In spite of the forces which threatened them, including the political priests who served O'Connell, and the still feared foreign power of Rome, the Irish Protestants saw plenty of evidence that cultural Protestantism, at least, was making a considerable advance in the country. However much the Catholic and Roman militants might protest, by the early 1840's the God of the Catholics was: 'the God of Victorian Puritanism, a British and Protestant God most unnaturally superimposed upon a Latin church'.[119] Sir William Wilde commented in 1849 that the cultural influence of Protestantism was such that even the folk observances of the people were changing:

> The tone of society in Ireland is becoming more and more *Protestant* every year; the literature is a Protestant one, and even the priests are becoming more Protestant in their conversation and manners. They have condemned all the holy wells and resorts of pilgrims, with the single exception of Lough Derg, and of this they are ashamed; for, whenever a Protestant goes upon the island, the ceremonies are stopped.[120]

Whatever impression the Tridentine reforms had had upon the countryside observance of them seemed to have waned, or not to have taken root, and apparently even traditional liturgical observances were being ignored by a considerable number of the people outside the towns, especially in Gaelic-speaking areas of Connaught. Modern scholars debate the religious strength of Irish traditional Catholicism at this time,[121] but there seems little doubt that the Protestants generally believed that if there was a period of peace in Ireland the Protestantizing of Ireland was yet possible. They encountered enough nominal Catholics who had no use for ideas of exclusive salvation that they remained hopeful of enlarging their community culturally, if not religiously.[122] The Protestants retained their conviction that their place in Irish society was a providential one: 'more and more Irish Protestants felt themselves to be the only repositories of social order, true morality, and individual independence'.[123]

IV O'Connell, the Priests and the Protestants

Although the Protestants may have thought, in moments of social and political calm, that they were the creators of 'a distinctly Protestant political culture... during the first forty years of the Union',[124] yet their minority position was such, and the attack upon them persistent and fierce enough, that their mentality tended to be increasingly anti-Roman Catholic rather than pro-Protestant:

> The actual state of the Church of Ireland bore little relation to the fervent ideal of a civilizing mission in the steps of St. Patrick (who was appropriated by Protestant antiquarians as an avatar of the Reformed Irish Church). As with Protestant politics, the psychology was that of a minority on the defensive.[125]

The situation was different in Ulster, of course, where there was a majority Protestant population, and when Henry Cooke urged at a large gathering at Hillsborough in 1834 that the Presbyterians and the Church of Ireland should unite to oppose the common threat of Roman authority few of his listeners thought such an unwelcome alliance was necessary. Henry Cooke and others were alarmed at the government's seeming desire to do only what Rome approved,[126] but they were not intimidated by the Repeal of the Union campaign of Daniel O'Connell and the priests. When the Liberator came to Belfast in 1841 he was immediately challenged to debate by Cooke, and when he refused, Cooke, at a gathering to celebrate the 'repulse of the Repealer', reminded his listeners of the material and other blessings which Protestantism and the Union had brought to Ulster. [127] The Presbyterians were prone to blame the plight of Protantism elsewhere in Ireland on the lack of spiritual resolve of the parsons:

'much of the boasted growth of Romanism might be attributed to the gross neglect of the Episcopalian clergy'.[128]

When O'Connell began his Repeal agitation after his Catholic Emancipation victory, the character of the movement he had long led began to change. He lost the strong support of Thomas Wyse, Richard Sheil and others who sought more conciliation with the Protestants, while others were not sure what O'Connell wanted in Repeal. His goals were never defined but it was accepted that what the Repealers were saying was that the union was illegitimate and there had to be a new negotiated settlement in Ireland that would bring about a devolved government which would inevitably be Catholic in membership and ethos. O'Connell himself was not by nature a bigot and in principle his eighteenth century liberalism wanted freedom of conscience for all Irishmen. At times, as in 1832, he deliberately tried to win the Protestants to his cause but, according to W.J. O'Neill Daunt, his secretary when he was lord mayor of Dublin, his religious views shifted as the years passed. Daunt was a convert to Catholicism, whose interest in this aspect of O'Connell's life reflected his own troubled religious development. In the Repeal period O'Connell employed Protestants to serve his personal affairs but, as we will see, he had increasing difficulty in communicating with Thomas Davis and the other Protestants in Young Ireland who accused him of leading a party seeking Catholic ascendancy.

It was almost inevitable as a 'tribal chieftain', as he was viewed when he was at home in Kerry, that he would applaud converts to Catholicism, approve the divisions that the Puseyites were making in the Church of England, and find satisfaction in the growth of Catholic self confidence.[129] Beyond his 'folk' Catholicism, however was a deepening respect for the authority of the Holy See. The liberal who had once proclaimed that he was no papist,[130] as the years went by confessed ever more readily his submission to the spiritual authority of Rome. To him 'there was no salvation outside the church':

> I revere in all things the authority of the Holy See... there is not a single person who pays more sincerely than I do, and with all my heart, the submission—in the widest sense of the word–to the Holy See which the Catholic Church demands of her children. I have never said and I shall never say a single word which I would not subject to her authority with profound obedience. I am attached to the centre of unity with the most ardent desire never to separate myself from it either in thought or word or action... my submission to the authority of the Church is complete, whole and universal.[131]

Though O'Connell himself strongly denied striving for Catholic ascendancy there is no doubt that some of his lieutenants did; his public utterances were more and more clerical as he tried to please the priest-organizers of his campaign; and he did 'bend a little to the ultramontanist wind'.[132]

The Protestants as well as Young Ireland accused O'Connell of leading a 'priest's party', and in 1836 they accused him of supporting Dens' theology. By the time of the 'monster meetings' of 1843, and attendance of up to a half million supporters of Repeal reported, the Protestant fears of a Catholic *jihad* seemed justified. Though a handful of Catholic bishops held back from giving full support to the campaign, they refrained from showing open opposition to O'Connell. Rome had obliquely reprimanded Ireland's political priests in 1839, but of this the Protestants knew nothing. They did know, however, that there had been no overt papal condemnation of what O'Connell was about, and they suspected some kind of collusion. They remembered that in 1830 the Belgian Catholics had rebelled against their Dutch Calvinist king; a revolution had just taken place in France; and the Catholic Poles had tried their hand at revolution in 1830–1831. The southern Protestants shared the increasing anxieties of the Ulster Presbyterians as the O'Connell agitation moved to its climax:

Under the influence of O'Connell a system of agitation was inaugurated which changed the whole tone of society in Ulster. A newspaper called 'the Vindicator' was established in Belfast, whose chief mission was to inflame sectarian passion, and stir up Roman Catholics against their Protestant fellow-countrymen. Unfortunately, the Catholic clergy became the tools of O'Connell. Catholics were reminded of their vast numerical preponderance. They were told they had a right to pro-portional influence, power and representation in all government, local as well as imperial. Protestants were denounced as heretics, usurpers, aliens. It was shown how they had taken Ireland by the sword; how they had driven out or murdered its patriotic or native chiefs; how they had enslaved their brave and attached subjects. ... its effects upon an excitable people was lamentable. Most of them believed it to be literally true. They groaned in agony when addressed as 'Hereditary Bondsmen'. They were inspired with intense hatred of Protestants.[133]

So great was the sectarian division raised by the Repeal campaign that Wellington seriously suggested that the northern Protestants should be armed and trained as a yeomanry or volunteer force which would maintain the law:

Ireland is in truth no longer a social state. There is neither property nor safety for life remaining except for those in the ranks of the repealers of the Union.[134]

O'Connell played his dangerous game, using the people disciplined by their clerical handlers as he held meeting after meeting, mixing demand for appeasement with veiled threat, and the public excitement mounted. In May 1843 O'Connell at Mullingar tried to interrupt William O'Higgins, the Catholic bishop of Ardagh, time and again when the prelate shouted his defiance of those who would inhibit the political work of the priests:

> I defy any minister in England to put down agitation in the diocese of Ardagh. If they attempt to rob us of the daylight we will retire to the chapels... If they beset our temples we will prepare our people for those circumstances... and if for that they bring us to the scaffold, in dying for the cause of our country, we will bequeath our wrongs to our successors.[135]

O'Connell's interruptions of O'Higgins' peroration in effect only echoed and emphasized the prelate's words, and by this time in the Repeal campaign it was not clear who was using whom as the movement seemed now to have a life of its own. When O'Connell shouted his strongest 'defiance' at Mallow he was 'playing with slaughter' as he brought with his words the huge gathering to the point of taking to the field: 'you may soon have the alternative to live as slaves or die as freemen'. He suggested Peel and Wellington were 'second Cromwells' as he invoked the horrors of the religious warfare of the seventeenth century, including the slaughter in Wexford of 'three hundred inoffensive women of all ages and classes... collected around the cross of Christ'. This he shouted would never happen again for the 'English ruffians' now had to contend with nine million defenders if they tried again to use Cromwell's 'blunted truncheon' against the Irish and their aspirations.[136]

The 1843 Repeal campaign was really O'Connell's last great hurrah for he was sixty-eight years old and events over which he was to have no control were soon to overwhelm Ireland. Yet a gathering like that at Tara, county Meath, on 15 August, 1843 drew a disciplined crowd that the *Times* estimated to be about a million in numbers. Throughout the site six altars were erected for the saying of mass all morning; two bishops and thirty-five priests sat on the platform with the Liberator, and the people bowed to this display of ecclesiastical and political authority in an almost mechanical obedience. The whole campaign obviously now depended upon the commitment of the Catholic prelates and priests to the agitation, and by mid-summer 1843 the Home Secretary Sir James Graham openly identified it as such:

> It is a religious struggle directed by the Roman Catholic hierarchy and Priesthood, on which we are about to enter; and I very much doubt whether any political considerations enter much into the causes or objects of this strife, which will lead to blood-shed and convulse the empire.[137]

The situation changed from the time that O'Connell, carried away by his rhetoric when announcing a monster meeting at Clontarf, talked in terms of an assembly of 'Repeal cavalry' and used other military allusions. The meeting was banned, and the army occupied the Clontarf field. At the beginning of 1844 O'Connell was charged with seditious conspiracy, he and his fellow-defendants were found guilty, and O'Connell was sentenced to a year's imprisonment. He remained in Richmond penitentiary in comparative luxury from May until September. During his time in prison he made one of his few political blunders when he attacked Robert Peel's charitable donations and bequests bill, on the grounds that it was not only a 'pernicious' threat to the religious orders but a secular intervention in the domestic concerns of the Catholic episcopate.

This legislation is important because it brought Rome into Irish affairs once more, and led to a significant division between the bishops. The papacy was not happy over the reports it was receiving from Ireland, but they were mediated through Paul Cullen, rector of the Irish College in Rome, and Cullen at this period was over-identifying himself with John MacHale and the other pro-O'Connell bishops. Metternich, the Austrian Chancellor had made representations to Rome concerning the Irish unrest, but Cullen was able to tell MacHale that, when he saw the pope, he came away assured that he was not going to be swayed by any outside pressure:

> The Pope is still quite well, though getting close to eighty. He is still much attached to Ireland and always inquires most anxiously about Repeal. The English government made an attempt to get him to write to the Irish bishops and clergy to desist from taking part in that movement. But he declined to do so, alleging that those who were on the spot must best know what was to be done in so difficult a question.[138]

When the charitable donations and bequests bill was introduced in 1844, however, the pope soon discovered, to Cullen's great discomfort, that 'those who were on the spot' had differing opinions about the legislation. Until 1844 Irish charities had been administered by an almost exclusively Protestant board set up by the old Irish Parliament. Peel's legislation suggested a new board of thirteen, including five Catholics, and Catholics in parliament and many in the country recognized: 'the bill was a considerable improvement on the existing legislation on charitable and religious trusts, being more liberal in its treatment of Catholic interests'.[139] The bill, which the Home Secretary said had been 'framed in the spirit of peace', was immediately attacked by John MacHale as an indication of the government's 'deadly hate' of the Catholic faith. From prison O'Connell decried this insidious attempt to influence 'the doctrine, discipline or usages of the Catholic church'. On the other hand William Crolly, the primate, Daniel Murray of Dublin and Cornelius Denvir of the Down diocese all agreed to serve on the new board. By the last months of 1844 the Repeal movement, and much of the country, was convulsed over a new agitation which opposed the bill, and the rumoured appearance of a concordat between Britain and Rome.

There was some satisfaction within the government that bishops like Murray and Crolly stood up to the intimidation by MacHale and his followers-,[140] and it took the opportunity, through its unofficial representative in Rome, William Petre, an English Catholic, to persuade the Holy See that the new legislation was of benefit to the Catholic church in Ireland. It also persuaded the papacy to issue a rescript saying that in spite of the injunction sent to the Irish bishops in 1839 the Catholic clergy were still involved in political affairs and were failing to inculcate subjection of the people to the temporal authority in civil matters. The rescript particularly condemned the popular political excitements directly created by the priests, and instructed Crolly to admonish all ecclesiastics who defied this teaching.[141] 1843 had seen major disturbances in Rimini, both Gregory XVI and cardinal Lambruschini, the papal secretary of state were filling the papal prisons with Italian nationalist agitators, and the year before Gregory died in 1846 the whole of the Romagna was seething with disaffection. MacHale, O'Connell and all who engaged in *agitazione* in Ireland over a relatively innocuous parliamentary bill were not appreciated in Rome. Though the rescript was deemed by the MacHaleites not to apply to circumstances in Ireland, 'being purely hypothetical',[142] and Rome continued its policy of not censuring O'Connell, Paul Cullen himself was put in a vulnerable position.

In September of 1844 Cullen had been congratulating MacHale for 'such decided war against the new "charity bill"', and he promised MacHale the next month that he would inform the pope about the MacHaleite and O'Connellite opinion of the bill. Then his tone changed in his letters to MacHale. By January he was begging MacHale: 'for heaven's sake exert all your powerful energies to restore peace in the Church!' Shortly afterwards, a frightened man, he wrote to one of the chief MacHaleite agitators, bishop John Cantwell of Meath:

> I am not at all well and... I was wrong in taking any part in the proceedings publicly... I do not know what they will do here...God grant that nothing bad may occur in Ireland. Things are gone to a terrible state. Every effort should be made to preserve or restore union. For God's sake exert yourself! It is bad to push things to extremes... There is not a word of truth in the report about concordats... What an awful calamity it would be to have any rupture with the Holy See.[143]

The reference to 'concordat' which Cullen mentions in other letters suggests that he was identified with those who were spreading the rumour of an official link between London and Rome.

The result of the crisis over the Charitable Bequests Act was that from this time onwards there was tension between Rome and O'Connell. O'Connell himself did all he could personally to identify himself with those who were cautioned by or submitted to Roman authority. He had some misgivings, moreover, about the MacHaleites who were prone to identify Catholicism with traditional nationalist values as the Irish church became ever more aggressive, confident and even triumphant. He also had continuing difficulty with Thomas Davis and others in the Repeal movement who were concerned that MacHale and the priests were taking over the agitation to have it serve a Catholic rather than a secular nationalist cause. The Protestant Davis was: 'neurotically suspicious of popery and quick to detect schemes of priestly tyranny'.[144] The crisis also ensured that henceforth Paul Cullen would never allow himself again to be caught up in Irish nationalist agitation, to become a 'vassal of a popular party'.[145] The letters between the Irish bishops at this time reveal their recognition of what O'Higgins of Ardagh called 'Dr. Cullen's terror', and his distancing himself, so long as their support of the O'Connellite cause continued. Rome now realized, in the words of *The Times:* 'the people follow their pastors; their pastors are guided by the prelates; the hierarchy are devoted to O'Connell... the great secret of O'Connell's success must be found in the religious accompaniments of his agitation'.[146] Rome was not happy about religious affairs in Ireland over which it seemed to have less and less control.

Rome's attitude towards the Irish agitation was also conditioned by external developments in England. In order to win from O'Connell some of his moderate Catholic support, another of Peel's acts of conciliation, after the ill-received Charitable Bequests Act, was the endowment of Maynooth, and as we have seen, the authorities in Rome as well as Britain were shocked by the ferocity of the 'No Popery' agitation. 1845 was the year of Newman's defection, and the hysteria in the country was intense. In Ireland also the Protestants expressed their resentment of the Maynooth grant as yet another concession to the papists in their march to ascendancy. The *Dublin Evening Mail* believed that the 'guardianship' of Protestant liberties was being abandoned by an uncaring government:

> Let our friends reflect upon the state of the Protestant party in Ireland and ask themselves what have they left to fight for? Their Bishops abolished. Their Church doomed. Their clergy insulted... Their petitions disregarded. Their lives sacrificed. Their property confiscated. They themselves suffering under the operations of a penal code. The Religion antagonistic to that of the State endowed. The leaders of the Protestants mocked. The representatives of their gentry sneered at. Their old and sacred institutions made a subject of mirth.... Their confidence in public opinion destroyed.[147]

This was not the time for Rome to be identified with the concessions that Peel was making in Ireland. Another reason for Rome to distance itself was the growing vendetta between the Protestants in the Young Ireland movement and the clerical supporters of O'Connell's agitation. The situation was an uneasy one, with O'Connell concerned that he might lose Thomas Davis by reason of his 'Protestant monomania'.[148] O'Connell protested that he did not want the Repeal Association to become an exclusively Catholic one, but his almost total dependence on the clerical organization he had built up, and the ethos of Catholic exclusivity that went with it was finally to lead to Young Ireland's secession. Rome wanted nothing to do with a religiously plural political association that might degenerate into an Irish expression of the Young Italy movement; this had been formed by Giuseppe Mazzini in 1831, who took over the anti-papal role of the Carbonari with its demand that the papacy surrender its temporal authority in Italy. Like many observers of the Irish situation the authorities in Propaganda must have wondered how much real control O'Connell had over the masses even with the help of the priests: 'O'Connell and his party are rather the hand than the head; they rather express the feelings of the people than direct their opinions'.[149] At the same time they wondered how much control even the priests had and, like Paul Cullen, from this time forward they were concerned that Irish *agitazione* might produce its own Mazzini.[150]

V   The Great Famine

Rome's concern over Young Ireland eased greatly by the summer of 1846 when its secession from the Repeal movement took place, and the Catholic church leaders chose to maintain their support for O'Connell. In the words of *The Times* of 13 August, 1846: 'Old Ireland has beaten its young rival. The priests have done it'. The passion went out of Irish politics at this time, however, for everyone became aware that the country was suffering its second, and this time total, failure of the potato crop. The Young Irelanders withdrew from the public arena to seek: 'that intellectual and moral discipline that best fits men for freedom'.[151] O'Connell was greatly concerned by the economic situation and what its affect would be on the Repeal movement by the end of 1846 but, like the government he underestimated both the extent of the food failure, and the complex administrative problems that had to be solved if Ireland's huge and impoverished population was to be provided with sustenance. The rigid *laissez-faire* principles of Lord John Russell's Whig government were criticized by few in Ireland.[152] Though the crisis of 1846–1847 was a national one, this was not at first recognized because the authorities sought to keep relief on a local basis so that the landlords would be forced to carry much of the relief burden. The government produced a particularly hard-working and dutiful administrator of relief policies in Charles Trevelyan of the Treasury Department, but it was not until the terrible spring of 'Black '47' that the government admitted that direct outdoor relief provided by the state was necessary if the calamity was not to be even more shocking than it was. Free distribution of food to the poor eventually eased some of the worst evils of the famine, but it came too late to help about a million who died of disease or malnutrition, or another million who were forced to emigrate.

On many levels the great famine of 1845–1848 proved to be a watershed in Irish history. The political situation altered with the death in September, 1846 of Thomas Davis who, in the words of O'Connell was: 'an example... to the Protestant youths of Ireland'.[153] On 15 May, 1847, O'Connell himself died on his way to Rome and his heart, as he had requested, was sent on to the Eternal City. Among the people generally interest in nationalist politics waned as a desperate struggle for survival continued, and in their bitterness many echoed the sentiments expressed by Paul Cullen in Rome in May of 1847: 'our rulers are such Turks, or worse than Turks, they would not let so many thousands die of pure starvation'.[154] Evidence now suggests the unfairness of such judgments, but they were widely made. A man like Sir Robert Kane, a Catholic agricultural scientist on the official relief commission, was wholly dedicated to finding some way to ease the suffering of the people. So was the high-minded and evangelical Trevelyan, whose bureaucratic mind could not grasp that in an area like Erris in Mayo there were no public-spirited and educated squires, as in England. And there were few of the much needed priests, parsons, doctors and yeoman farmers who would accept that it was their social duty to serve on relief committees. Such 'realities' were beyond the comprehension of the suffering masses, however, and from the time of the famine the Protestant ascendancy people allied with the government authorities found themselves confronted only too often with a deep and abiding resentment:

> It was out of the sufferings of 1846–1847 and its aftermath, that a new and harsher attitude towards the British government found its way into the thoughts of Young Ireland, and thence into the common fund of Irish nationalism.[155]

The sense of bitterness and betrayal among the people added significantly to the defensiveness of the Protestants, especially those of the privileged classes, in the post-Famine years. Stories abounded of ill-treatment of the people by government authorities, and even by the Protestant clergy. As in many cases in Irish history, there was to be found some truth in any situation referred to, but the way the suffering was relieved varied greatly in different parts of the country. The picture of Belfast in the famine, for example, shows bishops and clergy of both denominations labouring heroically to serve the people side by side, with relief committee members carrying on their work without flagging even after the government made its offer of financial help.[156] Studies of rural parishes again indicate how diverse was the suffering of the people, the spread of disease, and the efficiency of relief committees, as well as the amount of outside help that was received to help the poor. Dom Mark Tierney in his detailed study of the remote parish of Murroe and Boher in county Limerick says of the famine in that area:

> Taken all in all, the Famine in Murroe has not left memories of any excessive misery or universal suffering.... The famine years were ones of mere survival. The people held on in grim determination, knowing that it could not last forever. They valued their lands and their home-steads almost more than life itself. And since the landlords did not exact any rent during these famine years, the majority of the people stayed where they were and hoped that the future would bring them better days.[157]

In Kilcooley in neighbouring Tipperary there was no evidence that many died from food shortages and cholera, which was common in Cashel and Kilkenny, for disease did not spread to the country districts. The workhouses in Killenaule and Kilcooley were full, but relief administration worked well in the New Birmingham committee which was supported by the local gentry. To give employment one of them, William Barker, sold the family jewels to pay for the building of five miles of demesne wall by the local poor. On the other hand the behaviour of the Killenaule Relief Committee was scandalous. The chairman was the Protestant curate, John Latouche who was ignored, and because of the absence of resident gentry what help there was came from the curate's banking family. The local Palatines were not noted for their generosity.[158]

By the time the famine was at its height in the 'black years' of 1846–1847 a strong sense of defensiveness and even communal guilt was appearing among the Irish Protestant landlord class. The shameful evictions by a Mrs. Gerrard of county Galway brought forth condemnation by Lord Londonderry in the Lords and Daniel O'Connell in the Commons, and the denunciation of the sufferings in a place like Skibbereen by the press increased the unease among the members of the governing class.[159] It was recognized by most of those attempting to alleviate the situation that the catastrophe was beyond the capabilities of the government, or the churches, or any organization of the time to cope with:

> What does seem clear is this: serious economic and social problems existed, of a sort that landlords were not primarily responsible for creating, and with which even the most sympathetic of them could not adequately deal.[160]

Among those who directly engaged in relief operations, such as the Society of Friends, it was recognised that the landlord class, most of whom were Protestant, were often themselves victims during the emergency:

Many of the landlords evinced conspicuous self-sacrifice and individual heroism; one-third of their number were absolutely ruined by the famine. The owner and the occupier too often sank together in a common ruin. It was stated in Parliament that there were persons of position who, at the outset of the famine were members of the relief committee, and before it was over were reduced to begging for a dole of Indian meal wherewith to support life. The period was indeed one of those 'which revealed the mingled baseness and heroism of human nature'.[161]

Yet the landowners, as well as the clergy and other Protestants, were aware that sectarian talk about the 'genocide' of the Catholic population being tolerated was commonplace, and inevitably their siege mentality was reinforced. They understood the opprobrium that could be visited upon them whenever anyone was charged with 'evictions through caprice and religious bigotry'.[162]

On the whole the clergy, both Catholic and Protestant were exemplary in their service to the people. Early in the famine the Quakers of London and Dublin had formed relief committees, and members of these bodies such as the aged William Forster, James Hack Tuke and Marcus Goodbody travelled through the snows of Donegal and south to Mayo in the terrible winter of 1846–1847. Their comments on the state of the people, and the heroic labours of the clergy show how sacrificial and necessary was the rôle the clerics played. Tuke's address to the Dublin relief committee in 1847 told them of the 'peculiar misery' of the barony of Erris in Mayo, and the parish of Belmullet: 'Human wretchedness seems concentrated in Erris, the culminating point of man's physical degradation seems to have been reached in the 'Mullet''. In a second edition of the report on his visit Tuke took to task evicting landlords,[163] and he and his fellow Quakers are as reliable and objective observers of the famine as any to be found. As to the clergy who ministered in a desolation like Erris the Quaker praise was unqualified. The Quakers could bring relief supplies to a place like Erris, but they had no infrastructure for its dispersal to the starving. One Quaker, Edmund Richards, came to Killybeggs in the Mullett to drop off two boilers for cooking Indian corn: 'but there was no one available locally, to set up a food station, the boilers could not be operated and the people died'.[164] In most other cases, however, the Catholic and Protestant clergy worked together in their desperate attempts to keep the people alive, organizing distribution of relief as it came in, and often taking on the job themselves. Without their efforts the people were lost.

The chief organizer of relief in Erris was the rector of Kilcommon Erris parish, Samuel Stock, who had been there since 1816 and was closely identified with the people. He worked well with the parish priests, wrote to Lord John Russell in person, and begged from the commissariat officer in Belmullet aid from the major supply of food kept there by the government. The Quakers trusted him implicity, and worked directly with him. Stock joined with the local priests to bring pressure on absentee landlords, as well as on the Church Commissioners who held much land in Erris. The work of these men was even praised by the penetrating social critic and traveller, Asenath Nicholson who remarked on the absence in Erris of religious tension during the emergency.[165]

Samuel Stock was not accused of 'souperism'—giving soup or other relief supplies only to those Catholics who promised to become Protestant—but the charge was widely made. The Quakers chose to have the parson administer relief, not only because that was the accepted social role of the Established Church clergyman, but also because it was believed that he would be just in his distribution of food. His own flock was so small that, even if he first favoured them, he would be without bias afterwards in his general distribution, whereas it was feared that if the priest gave out the food he would give first to those who paid their dues. In most cases the priest was not available for the immediate task of distribution, however, for his particular task in the catastrophe was to provide sacramental blessing to the dying. The trying job of actually giving out the stirabout or other food was often delegated to the wives and daughters of the Protestant clergy. The mortality rate among them from 'famine fever' was high.

The charge of 'souperism' of course was not a new one and Samuel Stock, and other older clergymen who had suffered through the famines of 1822[166] and 1831, knew well the problems that would arise if any recipient of relief chose to identify himself with his benefactor or his church. A good landlord might escape censure, such as John Hamilton of St. Ernan's island, near Donegal town, who was constantly among the poor, personally alleviating their wants and using his means to buy grain and potatoes. His grateful tenants built a causeway to thank him for his efforts, and the inscription plaque recorded 'the mutual love between John Hamilton and the people'.[167] But let someone like W.B. Stoney, the evangelical rector of Newport, work with the local priest in helping the poor, as he had in 1831 with his loans of money for seed potatoes and his manning of 'two stirabout boilers of immense size', and all his heroic actions were viewed with deep suspicion.[168]

Proselytizing did exist, inevitably, and in certain instances it was rampant.[169] Whether the converts in places like Dingle and elsewhere in Munster became Protestant out of religious conviction or were bribed by offers of educational opportunity or other temporal betterment is impossible in any instance to prove. If they 'took the soup' in a time of famine, however, and subsequently converted to Protestantism there was no doubt in the minds of the priests, and of the Catholic people as a whole, that cause and effect were obvious to behold. Once a Catholic individual or a family was identified with such apostasy the local resentment was usually so fierce that they were forced often to emigrate, either to England, to America, or a Protestant 'colony' in another part of Ireland. The socially disruptive problem of 'Rice Christians', and the need for missionary compounds to shelter them, was to be experienced in many other parts of the world during the nineteenth century—even by the Roman Catholic church.

One of the most troublesome of the Protestant settlements was that of Rev. Edward Nangle on Achill Island, in John MacHale's territory. He had been converted to evangelicalism by William Krause, the 'moral agent' on Lord Farnham's Kingscourt estate in county Cavan, and shortly afterwards he dedicated himself to working among the 'Irish-speaking population'. When he heard of the terrible suffering of the Achill island people during the famine of 1831 he visited the area, leased land from the proprietor, and determined to establish a Protestant settlement there. In this project he was given the whole-hearted help of Power le Poer Trench, the last Protestant archbishop of Tuam, Robert Daly, the future bishop of Cashel, Joseph Singer, the future bishop of Meath and polemicists like Caesar Otway, editor of the evangelical *Christian Examiner*. In July, 1834 with his wife he took up residence on the island. Almost immediately he established a school where, within a year, he had 420 children, and used the services of a local Irish scholar, Michael McGreal as a teacher.

This led to an immediate reaction by the Catholic clergy who then set up two national schools in the vicinity of Nangle's, although MacHale in other circumstances opposed the National System. MacHale visited the island in 1835, and harassment of the Protestants began. 'Exclusive dealing' separated the supporters of Nangle from their neighbours; priests 'called from the altar' the names of those who frequented the Protestant settlement; parents of children attending Nangle's school were cursed; one of the Protestant clergy was badly beaten up and scarred for life; a coastguard was killed in a fracas, and the government was obliged to station constabulary in Achill. Nangle was a pugnacious man, however, and he used the attacks upon the settlement as a means of raising money in Exeter Hall and elsewhere. He also set up a printing press, and was soon turning out controversial pamphlets attacking Roman liturgical practices, including 'the idolatry of the Roman Mass'. He accused the Roman priests of being agents of a foreign temporal power, and defended the Church of Ireland clergy as 'the true inheritors of the cloak of St. Patrick'. By 1837 Nangle was producing a monthly publication, *The Achill Missionary Herald and Western Witness,* and soon the island was being visited by travellers, not all of them, including S.C. Hall and Asenath Nicholson, showing much appreciation of what Nangle was about. Inevitably the charge of 'souperism' was levied against Nangle when the famine of 1846 arrived, and by June 1847 the English Catholic paper, *The Tablet,* was in full cry against his use of bribery to obtain converts.[170]

Whatever the truth or otherwise of 'souperism' being systematically practised on Achill there is no doubt that the people gained by Nangle's experiment. They benefitted from the Protestant schools, and they even won the attention of John MacHale, who was often regarded as a political rather than a pastoral bishop. Following a successful confirmation visitation by archbishop

Trench in 1848, MacHale, not to be outdone, followed his example in 1850, and promised the building of more schools and a monastery on lands he had purchased from the Encumbered Estates commission.[171] Moreover, there is no doubt that Nangle kept alive people who would otherwise have perished during the famine. Practical philanthropy also accompanied the labours of a Protestant medical doctor, Neason Adams, who had come from Dublin in 1834 and spent his whole life on the island devotedly serving the people until he died in 1859. Nangle himself was made the rector of Skreen parish in Mayo in 1852, and from that time the colony declined as its work was taken over ineffectually by a series of evangelical agencies.[172]

The other significant Protestant colony experiment in the pre-famine period was at Dingle in county Kerry, and there also the charges of 'souperism' were made. The colony was supported by strong-minded men like the convert Moriarty brothers, Mortimer and Samuel, and to the Catholic leaders in Munster the colony was looked upon as not only a religious outpost but also as a much resented model 'Protestant community'. It failed to survive beyond the famine years, however, and the challenge it presented was, like at Achill essentially a local one.

'Souperism' of the famine years was a complex issue because the traumatic effect of the horror the people experienced meant that they lost faith in much that had once sustained them religiously and culturally. Paul Cullen visited the west of Ireland during the famine and he found several parishes abandoned by the priests in MacHale's territories because: 'no priest can be found to accept them on account of the dangers of death from starvation or fever'. He was shocked also to hear that MacHale for some reason had returned to Rome money sent for the aid of his starving people, saying there was no need for charity in his province. Cullen was inclined to agree with another bishop who remarked upon MacHale's action he: 'must have lost his reason, his veracity or his religion'.[173] Nor was MacHale's lack of pastoral judgment unusual in the famine years. Cullen's uncle, the militantly nationalist James Maher, expressed his scorn in the summer of 1847 of the comfortable life style of the priests in the midst of want: 'bishops travel about in their carriages, our priests in their gigs as comfortably as in the most abundant of seasons'.[174] In the Gaeltacht areas where it has been estimated that mass attendance ranged between 20 and 40 percent, any failing in clerical zeal added to the confusion of identity felt by many of the people.

An example of this was provided by the experience of Rev. William Allen Fisher of Kilmoe, county Cork. An Irish speaker, he was a devoted pastor in his remote parish from 1842 until his death from famine fever in a food crisis forty years later. During the great famine the population of his parish decreased from 8000 to 3000, and Fisher's task during these years was to obtain food for his people from Cork. The only clergy who might have helped him, Robert Traill of Schull and Richard Townshend of Skibbereen both died of famine fever, and the task of begging food from England and setting up soup kitchens fell upon himself alone. During this ordeal he fell ill with fever himself and almost died. During his illness the Catholic people were greatly demoralized because their priest had left them, and Fisher found himself acting as pastor for the whole community. He was trusted enough to receive remittances sent home by emigrants to their families, and soon his church was filled with converts. He even heard their confessions, using the authority of the Irish canons of 1634.[175] As his congregation grew he built a chapel of ease at Toormore, or Altar, contributing much of his own income to the building of the chapel, two large school houses and a house for a curate when he arrived.[176]

Inevitably he was accused of being a 'souper', and a Catholic missionary, Fr. John Murphy, was sent to stem the tide of conversions, using the intimidation tactics that were common at the time. Contemporary writers have disputed the story that the Catholic clergy abandoned the parish for long but it is unlikely that Fisher could have engaged in his building programme if they had been around.[177] What happened in Kilmoe parish is still a live issue in Cork even in the last years of the twentieth century, and Mr. Eoghan Harris has produced a historical play *Souper* about these events for use on the stage or on television.

On the eve of the famine one of the trustees of the Dingle colony described the community, whose aim was to revive the linen trade and to encourage farm-husbandry, in terms of its being a cultural as well as a religious alternative for the people: 'these poor souls who are willing to escape from worse than Egyptian bondage, and who desire to come to the light of God's holy word'.[178] Unconsciously at least in the Catholic Irish mind this is what 'souperism' represented: the perennial temptation to abandon traditional Irish culture and folk religion, and to live in the world of the Sassenach with all its alien values. Whether the Irishman served in the imperial army, emigrated to Britain or to one of the British colonies, attended a Protestant church, or 'took the soup', he was abandoning 'bonding' with his tribe. From the religious standpoint Edward Maginn, coadjutor bishop of Derry, who had told Paul Cullen that John MacHale was 'more than a brother—a father to me', described what happened to any young Catholic who entered the Protestant world of Trinity College:

> We have ... never yet known a Catholic youth to have spent any time at Trinity College who did not return home shipwrecked in faith and in morals, wholly profligate. In faith latitudinarian, Protestants, in morals, are no less so.... Laxity in morality has ever been the consequence of laxity in religious belief.[179]

To Irish nationalists, then and now, the famine has been described in terms of genocide; a deliberate reduction of the overpopulated[180] island whose people were so troublesome to govern:

... this wholesale depopulation has been confined to the Catholics; a mere fraction of the other creeds suffered from fever and cholera, while they were wholly exempt from the merciless infliction of extermination, the poor house and emigration... the depopulation of the poor persecuted Catholics of Ireland... the result of the burning and unquenchable hatred of their race and their creed.[181]

The legacy of the famine in Irish ecclesiastical affairs was a bitter division between the Catholic and Protestant clergy and laity. The Catholic clerical viewpoint was well presented in the works of the Rev. John O'Rourke who spoke of the majority Irish people standing firm in the faith after 'fierce assaults', 'three centuries of terrible conflict'.[182] His viewpoint was echoed in the outbursts of MacHale who decried the various emigration schemes of the time as 'a devilish plot to exile the bone and sinew of the country'. Edward Maginn, bishop of Derry, threw away all restraint when he joined in the attack:

Why have the bare-faced impudence to ask me to consent to the expatriation of millions of my co-religionists and fellow-countrymen? You, the hereditary oppressors of my race and my religion... you, who have made the most beautiful island under the sun a land of skulls, or of ghastly spectres... you never, gentlemen, laboured under a more egregious mistake than by imagining that we could... have any, the least confidence in anything proceeding from you.[183]

The Protestant leaders, in their turn, often attacked the priests for denying aid to the starving people: 'they preferred to hoard it up for the building or repair of chapels... to promote the glory of their own denomination'.[184]

By the end of the famine the Catholic people of Ireland were so demoralized, in such a state of 'culture shock', and in the minds of some of their leaders in danger of becoming 'West Britonized' (in the parlance of modern historians)[185] that they were prepared to welcome once more direction from Rome. The Roman *imperium* which had been so limited in both England and Ireland from the time of James II was ready to launch the 'papal aggression' in England, and in Ireland to begin its prolonged mission to establish religious and cultural ascendancy. The spirit of the Counter-Reformation was once more to be nurtured in Ireland, under the guise of nineteenth century ultramontanism. The agent of the process, the director of the new Roman mission, was Paul Cullen, one-time rector of the Irish College in Rome, who came to Ireland as primate and papal delegate in 1850.

Chapter VIII

The Ultramontane Advance

'The Pontificate of Pius IX... has reached over the whole extent of the Church with greater power than that of any other Pope in the whole succession'.

Purcell, E.S., *Cardinal Manning*, London, 1896, II, p. 551.

I   Pio Nono's Counter-Revolution

When Gregory XVI died in 1846 the conclave to elect a new pope chose a compromise candidate, cardinal Mastai-Ferretti bishop of Imola, rather than the reactionary secretary of state, Lambruschini, favoured by the *zelanti*. An indefatigable pastor, who had made some gestures of support to Italian nationalism, the new pope Pius IX early showed some signs of liberalism, but once he encountered the difficulties which had produced the reactionary policies of the previous pontificate his own response was intemperate. Although gaslighting was introduced on Roman streets and the Jews were allowed out of the ghetto as gestures towards modernization, his first encyclical of 1846 criticized intellectual liberalism, and the dangerous secret societies of the time which promised the ruin of religion. When revolutions broke out in Europe, and the pope refused to ally himself with the Italian nationalist movement, his reaction to the assassination of the papal prime minister, Pelegrino Rossi, was to flee Rome and seek refuge in Gaeta north of Naples. There he remained for seven months, becoming greatly dependent on his secretary of state cardinal Antonelli.

Giacomo Antonelli was a throw-back to the Renaissance: a flagrant nepotist, his brother ran the bank of Rome, and he himself was criticized by his contemporaries for his love of money, of jewels, and a moral behaviour that was considered to be questionable. The pope greatly appreciated him, however, for Antonelli was able, a pragmatist, a realist, and courageous as a politician. He handled the French government adroitly after its troops had driven Garibaldi and Mazzini from Rome and he was responsible for the papacy's temporal policies, which presumed that the government in the papal states would have the backing of French bayonets. Antonelli's abilities ensured that the papacy emerged once more as a political power in much of Europe as he astutely handled Rome's foreign diplomatic affairs from the time of the papal return in 1850 until his death two years before that of Pius. Pius realized that he was personally not astute as a politician, and though he was never a tool of the cardinal he always heeded Antonelli's reminder of the fate of Rossi after concessions had been made to the revolutionaries. Following the events of 1848 Pius was very conservative:

> If it had ever been possible to describe Pius IX as 'liberal' he was so no more, and would never be so again. Thenceforward he sought the salvation of the church and of society in the restoration of doctrinal truths, and disciplinary authority.[1]

The result of Pio Nono's concentration upon 'dogma and discipline' was a series of enactments that prepared the papacy to lead the universal church in direct opposition to the revolutionary spirit in secular European culture and society that was then evolving. One of the great papal declarations of his reign which characterized the ultramontane revival was that of the immaculate conception of the Virgin Mary, a dogma proclaimed without a council being summoned, or the pope acknowledging advice from theologians or prelates: Pius had exercised *de facto* the privilege of infallibility. Ten years later the pope issued an encyclical known to history as *Quanta cura,* with a 'Syllabus of Errors' attached to it, listing those doctrines, theories, ideas and statements of which the papacy did not approve. The encyclical proclaimed authority in areas beyond those of faith and morals as it condemned indifferentism, rationalism, naturalism, pantheism, utilitarianism, liberalism and Gallicanism. Throughout Europe from this time it was to be expected that questions of discipline and forms of worship were to be referred to Rome, priests were encouraged to appeal to Rome against decisions of their bishops, and published works deemed by Rome to be favourable to Gallicanism were placed on the Index. Bishops throughout the world were expected to visit the pope at regular intervals; the laity were to be introduced to doctrinal 'truths' through journals like *Civiltà cattolica* of the Jesuits; the clergy were urged to imitate the Roman order (after 1850) of wearing a long soutane instead of breeches and frock coats. A new order in the universal church was to be enjoined at all levels of religious and ecclesiastical life.

To those who did not serve the ultramontane cause it seemed that the pope was declaring war on his age. Protestant newspapers in Germany spoke of a return of the papal inquisition; in Naples and Palermo there were solemn burnings of the papal pronouncements; and in France Napoleon III forbade their publication, and promised prosecution of bishops who had them read from the pulpit.

Pio Nono was not only at war with his age ideologically: from 1850 until 1870 his papal army was used to oppose the state of Piedmont which was trying to unify Italy, and the faithful from all over the world were summoned to the defence of the pope's temporal sovereignty in the states of the Church. From 1852 the Piedmont cause was led by the formidable statesman, Count Camillo Cavour, who was determined to make his king the master of a united Italy. To do this he had to enlist the support of Mazzini, Garibaldi and other patriots, and to drive the Austrians from Italy. This task was beyond Turin's resources so Cavour sought the armed help of Napoleon III and appealed to liberal sympathies throughout Europe. The result of his diplomacy was an attempt by France to drive the Austrians out of Italy, and the whole of Europe was shocked by the resulting bloodshed in the battles of Magenta and Solferino. In the following year Garibaldi took over Sicily and the Neapolitan territories, and when cardinal Antonelli refused to disband his papal army of 'adventurers', the Zouaves, the Piedmontese invaded the papal states. The papal forces were virtually annihilated at Castelfidardo, and following this victory the Piedmontese met with Garibaldi's forces coming up from the south. In 1861 the kingdom of Italy was proclaimed, but Rome itself remained free, defended by French troops. Though they were for a short time withdrawn, a new offensive by Garibaldi against Rome led to a French return in 1867, and the defeat of Garibaldi's Italian troops by a papal-French force at Mentana. The French remained in Rome until the time of Vatican Council I when the Franco-Prussian war of 1870 necessitated their withdrawal.

Criticism of the papal determination to hold on to temporal rule in the states of the Church was intense; not least among Irish Zouaves who, 'relying on the golden promises of their priests at home',[2] had gone to Italy enthusiastically and then suffered greatly during their service in the papal army. Catholic conservatives rallied to the support of the pontiff in his difficulties, however, and intense sympathy was shown by them for the beleaguered Pio Nono. He asserted his spiritual authority by proclaiming a whole series of canonizations and beatifications, and crowds flocked to the Eternal City to pledge their allegiance to the Holy Father. The result of this was a reaction by Catholic liberals in almost all countries, and in the universities. In Germany a remarkable effort had been made since the beginning of the century to rethink the Catholic faith with reference to philosophy, history and theology. At the university of Munich a powerful voice was that of Josef von Dollinger who spoke of 'the national German Church' while he denied the need for the papacy to have any temporal power. A pupil and friend of Dollinger was Lord Acton in England whose review, *The Rambler,* defended the need for intellectual freedom in the church, and the rights of the laity.

The answer of Pio None to the division within the church was to assert papal authority in an unexpected way, through the calling of a general council in Rome: 'to seek with God's help the remedies necessary for the evils which afflict the Church'.[3] Pius himself was determined to have the council produce a definition of papal infallibility, and did all in his power to influence the attending prelates: 'I, Giovanni Maria Mastai, believe in and accept the infallibility, but as Pope I ask nothing of the Council. The Holy Spirit will illuminate it'.[4] When opposition within and without the Council mounted Pius remained undaunted, proclaiming that he had the Blessed Virgin with him in his cause. After one cardinal implied that the charisma of infallibility operated only for the pope when he taught traditional doctrines an emotional scene followed by Pius declaiming: 'I am tradition'. Ireland's contribution to the Council was considerable for about a tenth of the bishops there were either Irish or of Irish descent while the definition of infallibility finally accepted was the creation of Paul Cullen.

The dogma of papal infallibility was pushed through the council during the summer of 1870 with a great sense of urgency, for the French were about to withdraw their garrison forces and Rome would be defenceless if the Italian nationalists chose to occupy the city. With the defeat of France in the Franco-Prussian war the Piedmontese take-over of the city was carried out and the Italian government recognized limited papal temporal sovereignty in a Law of Guarantees. A papal encyclical rejected this attempt at conciliation and the pope and his court retired within the Vatican. Catholics were told not to vote, accept election, or to take any other part in the government of the Italian state. Pio Nono also put under major excommunication any who had taken part in the despoiling of the papal territories. As for himself, he had chosen in political affairs to die as the 'prisoner of the Vatican'.

The tragedy for Pius and the ultramontanes was the irrelevance of the church from this time forward in many areas of cultural and social change throughout Europe. The authority of the papacy had been greatly enhanced within the Catholic church, but not the influence of the church as a whole among the masses of the people. Apart from Ireland and Poland, the people showed decreasing interest in the ministrations of the Catholic church, and were carried along by the state-directed 'revolution' that was anathema to the ultramontanists. Throughout the nineteenth century the Catholic church in nation after nation found itself ushered out of education, control of the family, and any acknowledged place in the state:

> It was clear that Christianity as represented by the Roman Catholic
> Church was less prominent in the political, economic, intellectual, and,
> in general, cultural life of Europe than it had been in the thirteenth or
> even in the fore part of the eighteenth century.[5]

During the last years of his pontificate Pius IX saw religious communities dispossessed in Rome, faculties of theology abolished in the universities, and Freemasons assume high positions in government. France suffered the excesses of the Commune, including the execution of Darboy, the archbishop of Paris and other priests and religious. In Germany Bismarck waged his Kulturkampf, getting rid of religious orders and otherwise harrying Catholics. In Switzerland the priests found themselves subject to civil and sometimes Huguenot authority. In Bohemia the liberals burned the pope in effigy. In Belgium tension between Catholics and liberals intensified. Only in Poland where the Russians had broken off diplomatic relations with the Vatican in 1866, charging the pope with fomenting rebellion, was the influence of Rome a strong social force among the people. The other exception to the loss of popularly acknowledged papal authority was in Ireland.

II   The Papal 'Aggression' in England

The rise of Roman authority in British Catholicism reflected in large part the emergence of an Irish 'nation' on the mainland. By 1851 the Irish-born population was about half a million, double what it had been in 1840,[6] and these impoverished sometimes trouble-making newcomers were seldom welcomed wherever they settled, even by the old English Catholic families who had long shunned publicity. Though the Catholics as a whole never formed more than a tenth of the population until after World War I, Propaganda Fidei which governed Catholic affairs in Britain had concluded by the middle years of the nineteenth century that the growing English-Irish Catholic community needed a new administrative organization to help it in its pastoral mission. The old vicariate organization was to be superseded by a government of bishops in regular dioceses: 'not as a matter of triumph, or a measure of aggression, but as a simply administrative provision'.[7] Nicholas Wiseman, the Spanish-born Irish vicar-apostolic of the London district, was to become a cardinal, and the first Catholic archbishop of Westminster.

The uproar over the government grant to Maynooth had barely subsided, and this re-establishment of the Roman hierarchy in England prompted an immediate tumult once it became public knowledge. Wiseman did not help his cause when he issued on 7 October, 1850 a pastoral letter entitled grandly 'Out of the Flaminian Gate of Rome'. In it every possible papal claim for authority was presented in a baroque triumphalist style, which seemed to imply that now the Roman pontiff was the 'ordinary' for the whole population of England. This was the occasion when Queen Victoria was reputed to have asked: 'Am I Queen of England, or am I not?'[8]

In what appeared to be a revival of the hysteria of the Gordon Riot days of 1780, the cry of 'No Popery' was widespread when the news of the 'papal aggression' became known: 'the mobs of British were out against Catholics. They were afraid of cheap Irish labour, and therefore they knew nothing and believed everything'.[9] Wiseman's pastoral was read in churches, printed in almost all newspapers, and on Guy Fawkes night hundreds of effigies of the pope, Wiseman, and the Jesuits were burned throughout the country. Attacks were made on Catholic chapels as well as some of the 'ritualist' or Puseyite churches. *The Times* described the restoration of the hierarchy as: 'one of the grossest acts of folly and impertinence which the court of Rome had ventured to commit since the Crown and the people of England had thrown off its yoke'.[10] Lord John Russell as prime minister wrote to the Protestant bishop of Durham an open letter decrying not only the papal affrontery but also the machinations of the 'Puseyites' in the Church of England, those Tractarians who had remained within the establishment rather than follow Newman to Rome.[11] A new periodical was produced in Scotland, *The Bulwark, or Reformation Journal* which warned against the evils of the inquisition, monasteries and convents, Maynooth, and Paul Cullen's legatine machinations in Ireland:

> It is now beyond all question that the entire power and policy of Rome is being directed against Britain, with a view to its being subjected again to the degrading slavery of the Vatican... Rome has also of late received great encouragement to turn the whole resources of the Propaganda in this direction. The grants of money given to her agents in all the colonies — the endowment of Maynooth, by which 500 priests are under constant training at the expense of Britain — the defection of multitudes in the Church of England — the influx of Irish Papists into all British cities... all these have no doubt been so many encourage-ments to the Man of Sin to play every effort to reconquer Britain.[12]

The Irish Protestants had their own problems with papal aggression, as we will see, and they played little part in the English agitation directly. In Liverpool, however, Hugh McNeile who was Antrim born, and a Trinity College Dublin graduate, organized 'No Popery' meetings, as did the popular Manxman canon Hugh Stowell in Manchester, and as the turmoil continued parliament had to act. The marquess of Kildare brought up the issue in February, 1851, and a bill forbidding the assumption of Roman Catholic episcopal titles in the whole of the United Kingdom was quickly approved. *The Ecclesiastical Titles Act* was immensely popular in England but the time for penal legislation in religious affairs was past. The Dissenters showed little enthusiasm for state legislation governing ecclesiastical affairs, Gladstone and others never supported the measure, and after twenty years he removed the act which had done little but greatly annoy the Irish Catholics. In Ireland Paul Cullen, the apostolic delegate, used the act to launch a counter-strategy through the agency of the Catholic Defence Association which was founded in 1851: 'to have the interest of our religion properly represented in Parliament'.[13]

The English Catholic Church in the period between the reestablishment of the hierarchy and Vatican Council I was influenced by the presence of its two great converts, John Henry Newman and Henry Manning, both of whom became cardinals. The former was never at ease with Wiseman and his concerns for ecclesiastical strategy, and remained as he always was an academic at heart, primarily concerned about intellectual questions. Newman became an Oratorian, founded the Oratory in Birmingham in 1848 and, except for his unfortunate attempt to act as rector of the Dublin Catholic University between 1854 and 1858, he passed the rest of his life in quasi-retreat. He had little interest in Wiseman's mission, or the priests of the Milner tradition who supported it, displaying instead: 'an instinctive and rather insular distrust of the processes of ultramontane thought'.[14]

Newman's attitude towards the ultramontane question was as complex as the rest of his thought, but in general he always remained a 'liberal' Catholic. He was certainly not the devoté of papal temporal authority which to Manning was: 'the keystone of the Arch of Christendom'.[15] Rather he was sympathetic to the thought of Lacordaire and Montalembert, and still more of the bishop of Orleans, Felix Dupanloup, who later opposed the Infallibilists in Vatican Council I.[16] He certainly rejected the ideology of Veuillot and the writers in the *L'Univers* which saw the church as radically opposing the world, and he objected to the ultramontane pressure for the declaration of papal infallibility which was encouraged by 'an aggressive and insolent faction'. His private letters reveal his anxieties about the Jesuits, and Catholics like his fellow convert, W.G. Ward who said he would welcome a new papal bull every morning with his *Times* at breakfast.[17] Newman certainly had his own view of how an encyclical like *Quanta Cura* and the Syllabus of Errors should be received by the faithful:

> Newman insisted that whatever the animus of the Pope, the Encyclical and the Syllabus were technical documents, not at all on a level with the uninstructed opinion of the chance newspaper reader, that they needed an understanding of the received rules of interpretation of such documents which theologians alone generally possessed. Hence Newman claimed, what Manning and Ward in effect denied, that 'None but the *Schola Theologorum* is competent to determine the force of Papal and Synodal utterances, and the exact interpretation of them is a work of time'.[18]

Henry Manning was a man of action rather than an intellectual. He submitted to Rome in 1851 in the midst of the papal aggression hysteria, seeking to find in papal authority the decisiveness of direction which he had found lacking among the latitudinarian prelates of the Church of England. Single minded and strong willed, he instinctively shared in the spirit of the ultramontanes, projecting, as we have noted, 'onto the distant Holy Father the qualities... found lacking in their own bishops near at hand',[19]—even when he was still an Anglican. From the time of his conversion Manning was warmly welcomed in curial circles, for the relationship he had with Pio Nono was a close one: 'fate willed that it was this archbishop, whom Pio Nono had first seen kneeling in the piazza di Spagna, kneeling still as an Anglican dean—to receive his blessing, who should console the last weeks of his life'.[20] Manning also established a close relationship with Nicholas Wiseman who had poor health and increasingly turned to Manning for help and advice. Within seven years Manning was provost of Westminster Cathedral and from 1861 until Wiseman's death in 1865 he was virtual ruler of the archdiocese. When the cardinal died Manning was appointed his successor through Pio Nono's direct intervention. A strong infallibilist at Vatican Council I he was made a cardinal in 1875, and until his death in 1892 he was renowned for his devotion to the Holy See. By the time that Pio Nono died Manning was clearly the most powerful political figure in the English Catholic church. He was always, however, regarded with great suspicion by Paul Cullen who did not welcome his 'meddling' in Irish affairs, on the excuse that he had an increasing number of Irish priests serving in his archdiocese.[21]

Cullen's suspicion of Manning was largely political, not ideological as it was with Newman in the years following the Vatican Council. This was when Newman continued his friendship with the Bavarian church historian von Dollinger who had been excommunicated for not accepting the conciliar decisions. Cullen, of course, had recognized in Newman what he believed to be deplorably liberal sentiments when he was rector of the Catholic university in Dublin, willing even to employ Young Irelanders on the faculty. Cullen, like Manning, was temperamentally unable to understand Newman, but in the aftermath of the Vatican Council his suspicions of Newman were confirmed, and he concluded that he was actually a threat to the ultramontane cause. Newman's opinion was that the ultramontane party 'exalts opinions into dogmas, and has it principally at heart to destroy every school of thought but its own'. As for the conviction which meant so much to Cullen and Manning, Newman reckoned that: 'history gives little support to the ultramontane view of Rome as a kind of oracle of truth'.[22]

By 1874 Newman was in a bout of self-doubt, saddened that he had written only two books in fifteen years, and wondering: 'what have I been doing with my time'. He knew he was out of favour with the political powers in Rome, and he worried especially about the Jesuits:

> They... think my line too free and sceptical, that I made too many admissions etc. On the contrary I cannot at all go along with them and since they have such enormous influence just now, and are so intolerant in their view, this is pretty much the same as saying that I have not taken, and do not take what would popularly be called the Catholic line.[23]

When Newman did take up his pen again it was to enter the lists against Gladstone in a manner which confirmed Cullen's worst suspicions.

Following publication of the Vatican decrees on infallibility Gladstone decided to express his opinion of the ultramontane movement. Ultramontanism had become of public concern in both England and Ireland when a Catholic priest, Robert O'Keeffe, who had been censured by both his diocesan bishop, and cardinal Cullen, engaged in a series of civil lawsuits and finally engaged the attention of parliament where Roman authority in Britain was questioned: 'one of the largest questions... now agitating every part of Europe, namely, how far ecclesiastical authority was or was not to be supreme over the civil'.[24] This problem greatly bothered Gladstone, as well as rumours of Rome-directed ultramontane intrigue, such as the activities of the Catholic Union of Great Britain, which had been founded in London in 1871 to promote, among other matters, opposition to any civil interference with the spiritual authority of the church. In 1874 Gladstone dedicated to von Dollinger a pamphlet entitled *The Vatican Decrees in their Bearing on Civil Allegiance*. In it he discussed the 'peculiarity of Roman theology... thrusting itself into the temporal domain'. Gladstone believed the universal mission of the Catholic church under Roman direction now threatened every secular political authority: 'Individual servitude, however abject, will not satisfy the party now dominant in the Latin Church: the State must also be its slave'.[25] This theme of continuing Roman aggression was continued in his second pamphlet of 1875, *Vaticanism:*

It is, in my opinion, an entire mistake to suppose that theories like those of which Rome is the centre are not operative on the thoughts and actions of men. An array of teachers, the largest and most compact in the world, is ever sedulously at work to bring them into practice. Within our own time they have most powerfully, as well as most injuriously, altered the spirit and feeling of the Roman Church at large; and it will be strange indeed if having done so much in the last half century, they shall effect nothing in the next.[26]

When Newman replied to Gladstone's anti-ultramontane philippic his work received wide attention, though his defence was so filled with nuance of meaning that it was unsatisfying to many Catholic leaders. His main argument was that Gladstone had misinterpreted the language used in the ecclesiastical pronouncements of 1870, which could not be understood without interpretation by theologians. He also attempted to explain his own position on infallibility. Nothing of what he wrote was appreciated by Paul Cullen. He had been shocked by Gladstone's opinions, 'most wicked and malicious' and 'animated with the spirit of Bismarck'. From this time Cullen was very cool towards Gladstone, and he showed little appreciation of the gentlemanly line taken by Newman in his *Letter to the Duke of Norfolk on the Occasion of Mr. Gladstone's Recent Expostulation*. Cullen confessed that he had to agree with the *Times* which interpreted Newman's scholarly endeavour as in essence a defence of Gladstone's views. Not only was it lacking in spirit but it: 'lays down principles or makes assertions which are calculated to weaken the authority of the Vatican Council'.[27] When Gladstone visited Dublin a year before Cullen's death the cardinal refused to dine with him at the Lord Mayor's table. As for Manning, his reply to Gladstone's 'slanders' was his identical title *Vatican Decrees in their Bearing on Civil Allegiance* where he denied Catholic disloyalty to the state. Communication between Manning and Gladstone was very strained from this time forward and, like Cullen, he treated as an enemy a statesman who could consider that Rome would still use violence to accomplish its aims.[28]

Newman's role in this intellectual skirmishing was important inasmuch as his approach indicated that the ultramontane take-over of the Catholic Church in England was not to be easily managed. His *Apologia pro vita sua* had convinced some Protestants at least that the Catholic Church cared for truth, and that Roman priests might be human, English and large-hearted. His writings on the conciliar decrees enhanced his growing popularity, and in the English Catholic Church his intellectualism offset the cruder and more legalistic mind of the ultramontane Manning, however influential his authority in practical affairs may have seemed: 'Catholic posterity has rated Newman's mind so high that it cannot think Manning even comparable'.[29] Newman continued to fascinate churchmen, both Catholic and Protestant, and by the time that Leo XIII finally made him a cardinal in 1879, a year after Pio Nono's and Cullen's deaths, he was almost a popular figure in the Anglican as well as the Catholic communities.

Ultramontanism did not facilitate acceptance of Roman Catholicism in England where many people felt uncomfortable with the devotions introduced by the 'Italian mission', relics, miracles and pilgrimages. Nor did the Protestants appreciate *Apostolicae curae,* the 1896 encyclical of Leo XIII which decreed Anglican orders to be invalid. Many were upset by the oppression of the Catholic 'modernists' like the convert Irish theologian George Tyrell, who had become a Jesuit and was intellectually and ecclesiastically harried, and they had no difficulty in identifying with Tyrell's disillusioned attacks on 'Vaticanism', or accepting the view of Lord Acton that the principle of ultramontanism was un-Christian and immoral. *Punch* regularly caricatured Newman as sinister, sly, and underhand, and in the English Protestant mind this was 'the widespread though hazy impression of Roman Catholic priests'.[30] By the end of the century religious apathy rather than any spirit of tolerance was to weaken the forces of English anti-Catholicism, but the lingering suspicion that the papists served a foreign authority with temporal as well as spiritual ambitions was slow to disappear in the English popular mind. The *Daily Chronicle* viewed cardinal Vaughan's 1893 reception of the *pallium* in London rather than in Rome, and the renewing of the homage of the English Catholic church to the Holy See as a 'palpable triumph' for the ultramontanists. It was understandable why sympathy for the Irish Protestant view of Rome's ultramontane authority was as widespread as it was. Like the Irish Protestants, the English generally had no difficulty in believing the savagery of the Fenians, and the excesses of the Land War had support from the external and 'sinister power of the papacy': there was some form of connection between 'the superstition of peasants, and the tyranny of men in power'.[31]

III   Paul Cullen's Legatine Mission

The problem for Rome when it attempted to establish its authority and discipline in Ireland was that following the victory of Catholic Emancipation the whole Irish Catholic church was in turmoil, with the people 'entirely devoted to religion'.[32]   As O'Connell's Repeal movement began the people were increasingly assertive, demanding ever greater political, cultural and religious concessions, and the right of triumphal display.   The phenomenon was noted by the German librarian and traveller Johann Kohl in 1842:

Now that the Catholics have been admitted to Parliament... although some of the old distinctions have been preserved (he noticed that in many towns there were separate inns for Roman Catholics and Protestants and was even assured there were Protestant and Roman Catholic cars and stage-coaches), they were beginning to lift up their heads and even to look with contempt upon their Protestant brethren. He saw several handsome Catholic colleges and many new Catholic churches, and these with steeples higher than those of the Protestants—a piece of pardonable pride.[33]

The Irish Protestants were naturally alarmed over the growing Catholic assertiveness, but so were the authorities in Rome who feared what might transpire if the O'Connellite agitation was not brought under control, and its energies sublimated in the universal mission of the church.   Reorganization of the church was to be a formidable task, not least because of the lack of clerical and financial resources to serve the population which continued to increase right up to the years of the famine.   There was considerable unease because official mass attendance varied from diocese to diocese, in spite of the reforming activities of earnest prelates like Daniel Murray, but apart from such religious concerns Propaganda was alarmed about the politicization of the priests.   Rome was well informed about their political activities because the Irish bishops revealed much concerning the turbulence within their dioceses as they engaged in the kind of 'Rome running' not significantly different from that of their medieval ancestors.   Most of them made use of Paul Cullen as their Roman agent, and by the time he came to Ireland as papal delegate and primate he already knew the state of clerical life in most parts of Ireland.   He was particularly well acquainted with the state of the archdiocese of Tuam (which was always to resist his pressures for reform):

> Accounts of the condition of Tuam in the late 1870s recall the
> problems encountered elsewhere forty years before: priests engaged in
> factional squabbles; preaching, supervision of local schools and other
> pastoral functions widely neglected; the best parishes monopolized by
> relatives of the archbishop.[34]

When Cullen first arrived his intimate knowledge of Irish affairs had
prepared him somewhat for what lay before him in his reform mission, but the
actuality of Irish religious life shocked him when he surveyed it.[35]   In
September, 1851 he let Propaganda know of the situation in the provinces of
Armagh and Tuam:

> In this province (Armagh) there are at least three bishops who are hardly
> up to fulfilling their duties. The aged bishop of Raphoe has been
> through this town in a state of intoxication, and is also given to talking
> rather injudiciously. The bishop of Ardagh, Mgr. Higgins, shuts
> himself up for months at a time in his house and receives no one, either
> priest or layman. I believe he is letting himself be conquered by drink,
> and his diocese is greatly neglected... in the province of Tuam also
> there are three bishops who do nothing at all. The first is the bishop of
> Achonry, who for three or four years has been very ill, and I believe a
> little feeble-minded at intervals. He is about eighty years old. The
> second is the bishop of Kilmacduagh, very old also and infirm.... He
> was of Protestant family, and after his conversion he was ordained priest
> and then bishop without receiving conditional baptism in the Catholic
> Church. I have been assured that he has not made a visitation of his
> diocese for fifteen years.... The third bishop is that of Galway, an old
> man and without activity. In that diocese there have been many
> apostates.[36]

The English liberal Catholic Joseph Berington at the end of the eighteenth
century had believed the essence of ultramontanism was the belief that: 'the
flock, in the maxims of the Roman court, was made for the pastor, not the
pastor for the flock'.[37] Paul Cullen certainly believed that the church existed in
Ireland, and elsewhere, only to obey the universal pastor in Rome, and from the
moment he arrived in Ireland he was at war with those who would oppose the
authority of the Supreme Pontiff. Cullen had few complaints to make about the
pastoral activities of a prelate like the diligent Daniel Murray, archbishop of
Dublin, who had brought into being 97 new churches by the time he died; had
supported the labours of the Vincentians, Sisters of Mercy and Sisters of
Charity; and held the first reforming synod by an archbishop of Dublin for three

centuries. On the other hand Cullen did not appreciate Murray's willingness to work with state authority in ventures like the National System of Education, the Charitable Bequests Board, and the 'godless colleges'. As for the other bishops, Cullen as papal delegate had no intention of tolerating the scandalous abuses he found in so many places and brought to the attention of Propaganda. This was what Cullen had come to Ireland to do, to carry out a Tridentine reform of the Irish church, and whether he did this from Armagh or Dublin was of little concern to him. Cullen always viewed himself as a pro-consular official, never a servant of the Catholic church in Ireland. Paul Cullen was the court of Rome in Ireland.

Cullen's strength in his legatine mission rested not only on his ecclesiastical authority but also on his diplomatic skills. Shrewd, secretive and calculating he was a natural politician who quickly grasped the 'art of the possible' in his dealings with the Irish bishops as well as with the British government. He immediately recognized that the catastrophe of the famine, with its decimation of the poorest section of the Catholic community, could prove to be a blessing to the church in terms of reorganization, and the clerical resources of the church, in particular, could be more effectively utilized: 'before the famine any effective service on the part of the clergy was severely limited by the sheer weight of lay numbers'.[38] He also observed that the famine had been disastrous for most members of the landlord class, many of whom lost their encumbered estates to Dublin attorneys and other shrewd Catholic investors. With the whole of Irish society so in flux Cullen showed he was only too willing to give leadership to the majority of bishops who turned to him for guidance, to make the church more 'progressive'. As for the government, Cullen watched closely its uncertainty over the anti-Maynooth and 'papal aggression' agitations, and he reckoned that to deal with Irish nationalism, and the social unrest represented by the Chartists, the idea of a British unofficial concordat with Rome for the sake of peace-making in both the mainland and Ireland was not inconceivable. Lord John Russell had raised the old question of the government's paying the priests in 1848, as well as providing for Catholic churches and glebes. There was also talk again of curtailing the revenues of the Church of Ireland, and it looked as if the nonconformist churches might even make an alliance with the Catholics to bring this about. Everything was changing, the state was apparently in a mood to grant concessions to the Catholics in Ireland, and Cullen was determined that whatever developed he would represent the Catholic cause through the exercise of his legatine office.[39]

To the relief of Cullen Russell's idea of a general endowment of the Catholic church was allowed to die and it did not become an issue again until the time of the disestablishment of the Church of Ireland. Cullen, along with the Irish bishops, sensed that a new era of ascendancy was possible for the church when the state was guiltily compliant after the catastrophe of the famine, and the priests were in control still of the political machine that had been built up in the countryside in the years since Catholic Emancipation. Cullen's instinct told him that if only he could persuade the government that the Roman authority he represented was sufficient to control the priests and their activities among the people, then the government would be inclined to grant him more and more concessions, and indirectly to support his legatine mission. Cullen's encounters with MacHale, however, had already impressed upon him how difficult it would be for him to assume any significant degree of political direction of the Irish nationalist movement, even in its demoralized state after the debacle of the Young Ireland rising. Cullen's use of Roman power to try to undermine the popular authority of Charles Gavan Duffy and other nationalist leaders was not his immediate concern when he first arrived in Ireland, however, for the government had put in motion a higher education policy that put the country into a state of turmoil.

For some time the idea of provincial colleges which might have more attraction to Catholics than the predominantly Protestant Trinity College in Dublin had been considered and, in 1845, Robert Peel put forward a bill for their establishment in Belfast, Cork and Galway. O'Connell and others immediately identified them as 'godless colleges', open institutions without religious safeguards, which would encourage secularism rather than religion. There was also the outcry that the Catholics were being relegated to the provinces. The Catholic hierarchy divided on this issue, as they had on the Charitable Bequests Act, with the opposition led by MacHale and others who denounced this 'infidel, slavish and demoralizing scheme'. Archbishops Murray and Crolly led those Catholics who were prepared to accept the legislation if amendments were made to ensure that Catholics were well represented in appointments, state-paid chaplains were appointed, and teaching was regulated so that the faith of the students was not threatened. Cullen opposed these Queen's colleges as an attempt 'to mix up Protestants and Catholics as much as possible',[40] and he urged MacHale 'to get up a good agitation' against English lobbying in Rome on the college issue, even after the bill was passed. Lord Minto, the English envoy to the Holy See, was to Cullen an enemy not only of the Irish hierarchy, in his efforts to have Rome censure any opposition to the colleges scheme, but also because of his intrigue with the continental liberals:

> There is a vile infidel party throughout Italy ready to pounce upon the Pope. This party rejoiced in the overthrow of the Catholics in Switzerland. They are publishing most diabolical attacks on religion. They are ready to massacre the Jesuits. This party is supported by Minto and the English. The good statesmen of England would gladly see Italy in the condition of Spain and Portugal.[41]

Twice in the early years of the nineteenth century the Holy See had refused to approve national synods which the Irish bishops had requested, but Cullen now had the full backing of Rome when he held his 1850 synod at Thurles, using his legatine authority to summon the prelates. One of the most important subjects on the agenda was the Catholic response to the Queen's Colleges. Daniel Murray led the opposition to Cullen's demand that, instead of supporting the Queen's Colleges, the Irish people should have their own Roman Catholic university. Murray strongly supported the 'godless' institutions as an alternative to Protestant Trinity College and with his followers ignored Cullen's Roman instructions to condemn the colleges which Cullen produced at the synod. Cullen got his way in obtaining a condemnation of the colleges but by only one vote in a badly divided synod, and from this time the Catholic demand for a university of their own began. The MacHaleites had kept quiet while Cullen wielded his legatine authority to deal with Murray and his Gallican followers and, by the end of the synod, the tight procedural control Cullen exercised, as well as his personal strength of character, showed the Irish Church clearly that a new order was about to be imposed upon them by the 'staunchest of all the ultramontanes.[42]

Roman authority was not easily accepted, however, and the Synod of Thurles represented only the beginning of Cullen's vicissitudes as he sought to impose Roman discipline upon the divided church. Some 400 Catholics were soon attending the Queen's Colleges, and Murray and his followers showed that they were not about to oppose others who might want to join them. Until the idea of a Catholic university took substance Catholic young men could attend only Trinity or the Queen's Colleges, if they stayed in Ireland, and those bishops who supported Cullen were not optimistic about the proposed institution actually coming into being. By September 1851 Cullen was almost in despair as the Gallican supporters of Murray continued to promote Catholic attendance in the Queen's Colleges:

They are determined not to yield an inch to the Synod of Thurles, nor to the Pope himself... Is it not an awful thing to have the education of the Irish clergy depending on those men? They can make all Ireland Jansenistical in a dozen years. There is no means of removing them.[43]

With the furore going on in England over the 'papal aggression' Cullen knew that he could look for little support from Rome. Any further display of triumphalism, beyond the 'glory' of Thurles,[44] would only bring upon him the wrath of the English Protestants. As for the Irish Protestants, they saw in Cullen's activities Roman imperial designs. The Belfast News Letter warned of an incipient 'Ultramontane plot': 'since the pope's legate, Dr. Cullen, came over to Ireland, riding roughshod over prelate and priest and people, to teach them obedience to His Holiness'. Ireland in its editorial view was 'in danger of becoming a papal fief'.[45] Mortimer O'Sullivan in his *Plea for Inquiry into the Political Constitution of Romanism* interpreted Cullen as the political organizer of Maynooth's 'fierce intemperance' and 'disaffection to the state'.[46]

Cullen did not share O'Sullivan's belief that Maynooth was a supporter of his ultramontane mission, however. The reports on Maynooth that he had received during his years in Rome, while acting as Irish agent for the hierarchy, gave him sympathy for the views of an observer of 1824 who had said:

> The students who enter it are peasants. They leave it with as great an ignorance of the world as they brought into it, but they acquire in it an *esprit de corps* which it is impossible to describe of which a taste for religious controversy and a keen anti-British feeling are the leading features. They are just the men to influence the people and be led themselves by a bold demagogue.[47]

Cullen was determined that the Maynooth priests were to be 'led' by himself as papal delegate, rather than the Young Irelanders, the radical rump of the O'Connellite movement who had favoured the Queen's Colleges, had Protestant members, and were no friends of ultramontanism. So far as Cullen was concerned the Young Irelanders were as dangerous as the followers of Mazzini in Italy. He was not planning to surrender the Maynooth graduates to the influence of such men who 'promoted a spirit of distrust against Rome... among the young priests recently ordained in Maynooth'.[48] He was not in the position to do much about Maynooth when he first arrived, however, for he knew the government was also considering how to deal with the disaffection among its graduates. By 1853 he learned that a commission of inquiry was being set up and he rejoiced that some of the dissident anti-Romanists in the college might be dismissed. He told Propaganda that he could do little about the deplorable situation himself for: 'there is a sort of republic established there which is almost independent of the ordinary'.[49] After Cullen got the evidence of the commissioners which suggested some of the seminary authorities were 'determined to crush Ultramontanism'[50] he used various pressures to bring them to heel, and he never ceased to watch Maynooth closely for signs of disaffection from Rome.

Cullen's handling of the Maynooth situation was typical of his astute management of the Irish Catholic church. He had no hesitation in encouraging the state to do his work for him, but in everything he did personally he sought steadfastly to ensure that it contributed to the extension of papal authority in Ireland. His mission was never an easy one, especially when he tried to impose Roman order which was in conflict with traditional custom. The Munster bishops, for example, strongly opposed his attempt to 'regularize' customary sacramental usage, such as the holding of 'stations' or house masses. Cullen was not unduly upset when the Munster bishops appealed to Rome on this issue, for even though they received a limited toleration of 'stations', they had appealed to the Holy See. Cullen was determined that on every possible issue the Irish hierarchy was to be encouraged to appeal to the Holy Father who alone could protect them from the dangers of infidelity and heresy: 'they who resist the prelate of the first see, resist the ordinance of Christ, and unless they repent, will have to undergo the punishment of their contumacy'.[51]

Throughout his life, as we will see, Cullen was intent upon making use of the state in the area of education, however much he would ideally have liked all instruction of the people directed by the hierarchy and the priests. Mixed education to Cullen was anathema, so his manoeuvring with the state was always complex, and he had deep suspicion of the liberal Catholics of the Young Ireland movement who did not appreciate the separation of the people along religious lines. He knew how the followers of Thomas Davis had protested about the growth of popery and priestly tyranny in Ireland, and shared their leader's determination: 'not to be the tool of a Catholic ascendancy'.[52] Yet this was what Cullen was convinced was the way of salvation for the Catholic people of Ireland, their submission to the spiritual guidance of the Holy See, in all aspects of their lives. Cullen had no doubts about what his mission was to seek to accomplish—the establishing of Roman authority in Ireland.

Cullen was relentless in his campaign: 'to bring Ireland into line with the discipline directed from Rome',[53] and his direction of it was greatly helped by the death of Daniel Murray and the opportunity it gave the papacy to move him to the centre of power in Dublin. Cullen knew that Murray's death marked an end to the establishment hope that a new church-state accord might arise in Ireland: 'a fatal stroke to all the plans of government', and from the time of his translation to the metropolis the Protestant press showed that it was aware of what was to be expected from this 'bold despot priest' with his 'crafty and hypocritical policies'.[54] Cullen's long sojourn in Rome had helped to make him an astute politician, and he had no intention of allowing the Young Irelanders and their successors excuse to dismiss him as a 'castle bishop'. Until he was made a cardinal in 1866, and then could openly engage in diplomatic activity as the representative of the Holy See, he avoided direct contact with the government administration. At the same time, in every possible way, he kept up pressure against the state, making use of the tested O'Connellite tactic of making demands, with the implied threat that failure to negotiate would bring upon the government trouble with the turbulent people who would heed only the authority of the priests. He also used his Dublin advantage position to encourage throughout the Catholic community practice of a kind of apartheid. So far as Cullen was concerned, a Catholic either served the Roman authority, or opposed it by communicating and consorting with Protestants:

> Catholics who mix with Protestants are all hostile to us... As for me, I never dined with a Protestant. Once years ago I went to a Protestant house in the county Louth to a *dejeuner* and I was asked to say Grace. I afterward discovered that the gentleman was one of the leading Freemasons.[55]

Cullen admitted to monsignor Barnabo in Propaganda that unlike the Protestants of England who were fanatics, the Irish Protestants, in the wake of the famine, were 'extremely discreet and restrained'. As much as possible, however, he was determined to have nothing to do with them. Cullen was not renowned for his sense of humour, and it is difficult to know what to make of a hotel entry he made in 1858:

> Paul Cullen and Fr. Blake of Galway are middling pleased with this place. They principally object to the beds having a Protestant feel and hope that all good Catholics will help to remedy this evil by frequenting this hostel more than they do.[56]

Trouble with MacHale began when Cullen avoided joining in the castigation of two members of parliament who in 1852 broke ranks with the Irish 'independent opposition' group at Westminster so they might take office in the government. This convinced MacHale and others that the journalist Frederick Lucas was right when he believed that Cullen was covertly using his ecclesiastical authority to hamper the independent opposition in parliament. Charles Gavan Duffy knew that Cullen viewed him as 'an Irish Mazzini' who would ultimately 'make war on religion', and there is little doubt that Cullen was much opposed to Duffy and the other nationalists whom he lumped together as 'Young Irelanders'. Matters came to a head when Cullen, MacHale and Lucas were all in Rome in 1854 for the definition of the Immaculate Conception dogma. Rome showed little sympathy for Cullen's opponents; Lucas died shortly afterwards, a disappointed and exhausted man; Duffy left Ireland, leaving it to Cullen 'to Italianize the old sod';[57] and MacHale became an implacable enemy of Cullen which he remained until the end of his days. It has been argued that Cullen's ruthless treatment of Lucas and the others reflected only his anxiety over their appeal to Rome, but it was part of his abiding suspicion of the nationalist movement which might impair the ultramontane mission of the church. Patriotism could be appreciated by him, but only if: 'sanctified by religion and guided by prudence, justice and charity',[58] which only the Roman Catholic church could provide. Cullen's supra-insular 'political vision... was that Irish Catholics would convert the world-empire of Protestant England to the true Catholic faith'.[59]

Cullen's primary political concern outside Ireland was the defence of the papal states against the incursions of the Italian nationalists. He noted what Cavour called 'the benevolent neutrality of England on the side of Sardinia', speeches by men like Lord Clarendon on 'the reprobate papal state', and the British agent Odo Russell talking about 'brutal mercenaries and greasy priests'.[60] When MacHale refused to allow a collection in aid of the papal cause in his diocese, which Cullen had ordered, he let Rome know of this treachery,[61] and throughout the winter of 1859–1860 his letters show his unflagging support for the beleaguered pope's temporal power:

> Were Rome delivered up to the domination of infidels, were the aspirations of Lord Shaftesbury and the evangelicals realized, and Gavazzi and Mazzini enthroned in the Vatican, who can contemplate the consequences without being sorely afflicted.[62]

The anti-papal evangelicals were shown no mercy in his public letters, and nationalist bishops like John Cantwell of Meath who showed himself unenthusiastic over the plight of the pope soon knew of Cullen's displeasure. Even the Catholic laity were harried: Sir John Pope Hennessy, M.P. for King's County, was scorned as a Queen's College graduate and as an apologist for Orangemen when he did not support Cullen's crusade.[63] The Protestant press watched with wonder Cullen's urgent fund-raising from the Catholic poor, and lost no time in pointing out that the money was to be used to support a despotic power which would refuse to consider a constitution for the people of Italy.

Irish volunteers were sent to Italy in 1860, and casualties were considerable in the fighting at Castelfidardo and elsewhere. A great deal of money was also raised through a papal lottery and other schemes to support the papal cause, as well as Peter's Pence, in spite of the distressful economic conditions which prevailed in Ireland in the 1863–1864 period. When Irish young men once more volunteered to serve in the Zouave regiments raised in the last stages of the papal war Cullen was in a state of apprehension. Not only had the Irish begun to refuse to support Peter's Pence, as they had in the past, but it was clear that the war was now unpopular in Ireland at the very time that the papal army was making its last stand before Rome. The new Irish Zouaves were proving to be as ill-disciplined and turbulent as the volunteers of 1860 had been, and Cullen was worried that when they returned they would reinforce the anti-Roman feelings in the country, as their predecessors had done:

> They all went out enthusiastically for the Pope, what way will they come home? Probably filled with hatred of everything Roman. They will produce a bad impression and this imperfection will be widely felt as the men are from every part of the country.[64]

All of this was noted by the Protestant press which had much to say about Cullen showing his 'true colours' as a papal functionary, not a pastoral bishop, as he fleeced the pockets of poor Catholics: 'in his real character as Legate of the pope'.[65] None of this criticism fazed Cullen who saw the Zouaves fallen in the papal cause as defenders of Catholic civilization, resisting the spread of the errors that the pope had denounced in 1864. A solemn mass was held in the pro-Cathedral in Dublin on 17 December, 1867, for those who had lost their lives in the battle at Mentana, and Cullen's discourse praised them:

The cause for which they bled was the cause of justice, authority, civilization and religion. They fought against revolutionists determined to overthrow every lawful government; against socialists and communists, intent upon plunder and robbery, against the adepts of secret societies, leagued together for the destruction of religion... they fought against the infidels and unbelievers, resolved to overthrow the Gospel of Jesus Christ.[66]

Long before Cullen's support of the papal cause in Italy, however, his critics recognized clearly his intentions. After his first decade as papal delegate in Ireland the Protestants were convinced that what he was about was, in the words of the *Belfast Telegraph* of 18 November, 1861, the establishment throughout the island of Roman 'ascendancy and domination'. The government seemed willing to surrender to the demands of his 'Ultramontane insatiability', and what the Protestants faced in the future was 'universal serfdom'. It was not only the Protestants, however, who objected to Cullen's legatine objectives; John MacHale and his nationalist supporters quickly showed that they were not appreciative of the 'universalist' outlook of Cullen which far transcended the insular political world of Irish Catholicism. MacHale, for example, was far from happy by Cullen's appointment of English convert, H.W. Wilberforce, to act as secretary of the Catholic Defence League in 1852. Nothing came from this short-lived body to protect ecclesiastical interests, but it confirmed MacHale's suspicions that the insular political objectives he sought through the use of the 'priest in politics'[67] were not to win the support of the papal delegate whose paramount concern was the ultramontane mission of the universal church. MacHale was not in favour, or in tune, with what was developing in Rome from the time he was humiliated in Rome in 1854 for suggesting that: 'the church was a democracy and not a monarchy'.[68]

The Irish nationalists of all schools of thought Cullen tended to dismiss as 'Young Irelanders', and they included any Catholics who showed any support for the Queen's Colleges. Many of them were disgusted when Cullen chose as the first rector of the Catholic University the convert Englishman, John Henry Newman, with the implication that: 'we have no educated Catholics ready to do anything' for the educational advancement of the faith.[69] What Cullen wanted ideally for the Catholic university was it to emerge as a kind of Roman seminary, but in the event this did not happen. John Henry Newman thought the new university should be rather like the Oxford colleges he had known, he got along well with the Young Irelanders on the faculty, and to Cullen's great disappointment Newman's rectorship was a short one.[70] Cullen was never to build up a Roman Catholic institution which would be intellectually triumphant over the Protestant Trinity College: an accomplishment which he had hoped was possible with the brilliant Newman as rector.

The Cullen-Newman relationship reflected the lack of appreciation of what the papal delegate was about on the part of many of his contemporaries in Ireland. Cullen had decided to appoint Newman to the Catholic University after Newman delivered his *Lecture on the Present Position of Catholics* in 1851, and dedicated them to Cullen. In them he had said: 'the violence of our enemies has thrown us back upon ourselves and upon each other'.[71] but, as Cullen soon discovered, the 'enemies' of Newman were not necessarily those of the ultramontanists. The narrowness and militancy of vision of the papal delegate was never to appeal to the complex mind of John Henry Newman. Neither was it appreciated by the Irish Protestants who soon discovered that ecclesiastical compromise on any issue involving inter-church relations had no appeal to Cullen. It is little to be wondered at that, after his death, the *Dublin Evening Mail* of 25 and 26 October 1878 accused him of trying to establish in Ireland a reign of 'sacerdotal Caeserism' under direction of the Vatican. The editors said that most Irish nationalists who shared in the tradition of Wolfe Tone or Thomas Davis could see little to applaud in the policies of this 'narrow rigid devotee', 'a Roman of Romans' who acted as 'a thoroughgoing champion of war to the knife against the heretics', as he served his 'external commission' to set hitherto conciliatory Catholics against their Protestant neighbours.

For his part Cullen throughout his time in Ireland had little or no serious confrontation with the Protestants whom he found, as we have noted, to be 'extremely discreet and restrained'. Such self-effacement on the part of the Protestant hierarchy, in particular, reflected their reluctance to support militant evangelical societies in their struggle with Roman Catholicism, as we will see. Another reason for Protestant diffidence was their awareness that Cullen's ultramontane policies were strongly opposed within the Irish Catholic church. They knew that the papal delegate was going to have a great struggle with John Mac-Hale and his supporters, who resented almost as much as the Protestants the foreign authority which was visited upon them. In the circumstances the Protestant tactic was to sit back, and watch how the Cullen-MacHale struggle evolved.

By the late 1850's Cullen was almost in despair as he reported to Rome on what the MacHaleite priests were doing in their 'Mazzinian' agitation on behalf of the 'Young Irelanders'. Regularly, he said, they beat up old priests who resisted them, voted for Orangemen, and had bishops publishing pastorals calling for agitation. They ignored sectarian differences, tolerated political allies who were Protestant, and behind them Cullen feared was the sinister power of continental liberalism and Freemasonry—the force that threatened the pope's temporal territories. In 1862 there came the Fenian crisis which Cullen was convinced was encouraged by the Orangemen who wanted an excuse to bring back penal laws. The chief agitator, Patrick Lavelle, was one of MacHale's priests who came to Dublin to carry on an irritating warfare with Cullen in what was interpreted as 'Mazzinianism and hatred of the church'. Rome's response to the appeals for understanding from both Cullen and MacHale was to urge caution.

MacHale ignored such advice, however and opined that the more the papal delegate's authority grew the more the esteem of the people of Ireland for Rome declined. This was at a time when Poland was about to explode in nationalist rebellion, the papacy had just lost its states, and it assumed a 'wait and see' policy.

While Cullen 'waited' he kept Rome informed of the anti-ultramontane spirit that was growing in Ireland. The Fenian paper, the *Irish People* was not only more Protestant than Catholic but it was 'very hard on priests, bishops and the Pope'.[72] Lavelle was stirring up anti-Roman hatred by claiming the papal legate was extorting money out of the starving people to support the papal war against the Italian nationalists. In the *Connaught Patriot* Cullen found 'Jansenistical' articles rubbishing papal authority, and in desperation he organized a National Association at the end of 1864, to be concerned with disestablishment of the Church of Ireland, as well as with educational reform, and tenant rights. The *Dublin Evening Mail* of 10 January, 1865 dismissed the new body as 'a fresh attempt to Ultramontanise the Irish people', and Cullen himself soon recognized that this was not the way to win the people to the Roman cause.

When the state began to move against the Fenian leaders in 1865 Cullen brought out a pastoral on 10 October urging the people not to support Fenianism which was a creation of Orangemen and enemies of the faith, like the English Protestants who were supporters of Garibaldi. He took satisfaction with the arrest of one particular Fenian Thomas Luby and expressed his belief that he was not only the son of a parson, and the nephew of a Fellow of Trinity College, but probably an atheist. After the risings of 1867 the rebels were dismissed as: 'reckless madmen who would rob us of the only treasure we have, our religion'. At the same time Cullen praised those soldiers who had gone to confession before taking part in the arrest of rebels at Tallaght, and bluntly revealed his own political philosophy:

> This ought to convince our rulers that education without religious control is well calculated to promote revolution.[73]

Such a provocative utterance reflected Cullen's determination to use O'Connell's tactics, of threatening to withdraw control of the masses, unless the government gave in to the papal legate's never ending demands for concessions which would enable Rome to extend its authority over Ireland's Catholic people.

It was Cullen's relentlessness in seeking to establish Roman authority in Ireland, culturally as well as religiously, which most alarmed the Irish Protestants. With every opportunity he told the Poor Law Commissioners, or the various parliamentary committees to which he gave evidence, that Roman Catholic ascendancy eventually had to be recognized. Whereas MacHale was seen to represent the pre-famine insular world of O'Connellite nationalism,[74] Cullen in his pro-consular capacity served the ascendant authority of militant

ultramontanism. This was an imperial power to be reckoned with the Irish Protestants realized by the time of disestablishment of the Church of Ireland: they
were faced with an implacable enemy. When Cullen gave evidence to the Powis
commission on elementary education in 1869 his sectarian animus was clearly
revealed: 'I think the principles of the National Board are the principles of the
Reformation'. A state-controlled educational system would not readily be tolerated by Cullen who referred to the commission given to the Roman Catholic
church to teach 'divine truth', and all that followed from this belief: 'We require
control so as to be able to prevent the spread of error. We ask nothing more'.[75]

So far as most of the Irish Protestants were concerned, it was clear that the
papal delegate wanted in religious and cultural affairs the ascendancy that had
long been theirs. Once the state recognized this usurpation, the Protestants
would face the kind of inquisition which Cullen had carried out among the
Roman Catholics, for the Roman court still:'threatens persecution to all
Protestants when opportunity serves'.[76] The Roman prelate who could threaten
with excommunication young ladies who attended a Masonic ball, and could identify Fenians with Freemasons, was a force to be feared should he ever be in a
position to exercise his authority fully.[77] In Ulster eyes he was 'the very
embodiment of ultramontane intolerance',[78] but in Dublin his being made a cardinal gave the Catholics, according to one of their newspapers, a great sense of
pride in their identification with papal imperial power: 'the Roman purpose and
the cousinship with emperors and kings which it infers'.[79] At the same time the
Freeman's Journal of 21 August, 1866 called for the end of every Catholic
disability, and the passing of every sign of Protestant ascendancy which still
existed in the laws of the land:

> They submit to those things though there are in the whole land of
> Ireland but 700,000 souls for the pampering of whose unholy pride
> these iniquitous laws are maintained.

The Protestants knew, of course, that Cullen's authority was in reality
limited to those who submitted to ultramontane direction, and the mind that the
Fenians represented would not easily accept the Roman *imperium:*

> We can only look on and wonder that a people who are perpetually
> shrieking against the laws of England as incompatible with their ideas
> of liberty can howl a jubilate over the infliction of such a real tyranny
> as the Pope and Dr. Cullen have forged between them.

There was bound to be liberal opposition to 'the emissary who has utterly dena-
tionalized their church' and ensured that 'the national voice in the selection of
Irish bishops has been peremptorily silenced'. Yet at the time that Cullen
received his cardinal's hat he seemed to be, from the Protestant viewpoint, very

much in command:

> The papal church in Ireland is no longer Irish but in the strictest sense
> Roman... the Irish Catholic church of forty years ago has vanished and
> the people have got an inexorable and mysterious tyranny in its stead.
> We have never heard that they like the change and there are symptoms
> tending to show that they hate it... in the process of stripping it of its
> ancient national character Dr. Cullen has been the great instrument of
> the court of Rome. And for this memorable and odious exploit he now
> receives the scarlet hat.[80]

Cullen's great year was 1870, when he attended the Vatican Council to give
leadership to the infallibilists, and to organize opposition to MacHale and the
other prelates who opposed the decree. It was also the year when he tasted the
fruits of sectarian victory in Ireland following the disestablishment of the Church
of Ireland. This was an almost inevitable development in an age of institutional
reform, for as early as 1857 Nicholas Wiseman when writing on Irish affairs had
scented that conquest which was first necessary to obtain ultramontane ascendancy—the downfall of the Protestant Church of Ireland:

> We believe that its existence, not merely tolerated, but protected and
> justified by liberal and clever men, is as foul an anomaly, and as inex-
> plicable an enigma to the minds of enlightened publicists and statesmen
> abroad, as is the defence of slavery in the United States.[81]

From the standpoint of utility a legion of people Catholic, Protestants and
Dissenters, in both England and Ireland, questioned the value of the ecclesiastical
establishment, but the problems associated with both disestablishment and disendowment of the Church of Ireland were so complex that political leaders hesitated
to act. Lord John Russell tentatively even approached Rome in 1865 to discuss
what might be done with the wealth of the Protestant church if it was dis-
endowed.[82] The English Nonconformists added their voice to the clamour, and
when the Irish cardinal supported them *The Times* of 16 November, 1868,
commented on the strange 'union of Cullen with Knox'. Cullen resented
Manning and other English Catholics who interfered in the Irish situation, however, and he was firm in rejecting the idea of receiving any aid from the state
when the wealth of the Church of Ireland was redistributed. His correspondence
in 1867 and 1868 show his satisfaction that disestablishment seemed inevitable,
and that the Protestants were so depressed at the prospect. The *Dublin Evening
Post* reported how poorly attended was a meeting of the Protestant Defence Association on 5 February, 1868; and Cullen noted that the *Dublin Evening Mail* a
year later, on 30 January, 1869 commented resentfully that the jubilant
Catholics of Ireland would gain 'little for the church which the pontiff rules',

even with the Church of Ireland brought low. Cullen by then was so self-assured that he suggested to Gladstone just before the first reading of the disestablishment bill that an exception might be made with regard to rejecting Protestant property in the case of Christ Church cathedral in Dublin. Nothing came of this suggestion, but the *Dublin Evening Mail* of 19 November, 1869, ascribed to Cullen a desire for complete Roman ascendancy in Ireland:

> ... not alone over the Protestants of Ireland, but over the legitimate authority of the state itself... Mr. Gladstone must kiss the dust at the feet of the pope's representative or he does nothing.

Gladstone had his own reservations about Cullen and Roman power, as we have seen, and the Liberal support of the cardinal's ambitions was temporary. Disestablishment of the Church of Ireland was considered to be a victory for Cullen, however, and he could not resist holding a *Te Deum* for this humbling of Protestantism. A grand dinner was held at Clonliffe where Cullen 'gave the health first of the Pope, then the Queen... Mr. Gladstone and all who contributed to pass the church bill'.[83]

The other triumph of Cullen in 1870 was the astute rôle he played in the passing of the dogma of Papal Infallibility at the Vatican Council. The Irish Protestants paid little attention to what was reported of the council in the press, but from what they could gather it was clear that Paul Cullen was one of the most powerful and influential of the ultramontane cardinals who formed the inner circle of Pius IX. In fact, recent research indicates that Cullen's conciliar contribution was such that: 'it led contemporaries to consider him as a potential papal candidate in the event of Pius IX's death in the early 1870's'.[84] In the view of curial officials he was 'absolutist and reactionary', 'a Syllabist and Infallibilist', and his authority was such that it was Cullen with cardinal Bilio who produced the infallibilist formula that became dogma. The Protestants of Ireland had the ill-fortune to have to contend with this powerful personality of Cullen when they fought their rearguard action against the pressure from the court of Rome in distant Ireland: 'a prelate in the Roman mould... a valiant defender of the temporal power, primatial jurisdiction, and personal infallibility of the pope'. With the support of Pius IX, and the curial representatives Cullen had: 'transformed the Irish church from something of a mission church into one of the most effectively organized (national) churches in Europe'.[85] The ultimate authority in this church, however, was to remain from the time of Paul Cullen that of Rome—and the Irish Protestants were never to cease to fear the alien authority (to them) which had been visited upon Ireland.

IV   The Protestant Retreat

It was during the years of the 'Cullenization' of Ireland that the Protestant siege mentality became fully developed. Some of it can be attributed to the slow realization by the Protestants that they were not to receive from England either the political or religious reinforcement of their way of life that they would have liked. This was, as we have seen, a continuous complaint throughout Irish Protestant history but in the last half of the nineteenth century during the ultramontane take-over of Irish Catholicism many Protestants, as at the time of disestablishment, were to regret bitterly what they considered was abandonment of their cause by the English authorities. The British tactic in missionary work was to leave direction of spiritual affairs to religious societies. Their members were to encourage individual converts to bring themselves, justified by their faith, before God, and for them to then help other individuals to find their salvation: 'the first principles of Protestant missions had been that Christians should have the bible in their hands in their own language at the earliest possible date'.[86] Roman missionary strategy, on the other hand, had been for the church to work with states to bring whole populations to accept the faith as interpreted by the Council of Trent. At first the papacy had worked with the monarchs in Spain and Portugal, but from the time of the founding of the Sacred Congregation for the Propaganda of the Faith in 1622 France had sought with the Roman authorities for the mass conversion of peoples. In Protestant memory this had meant the use of coercion through 'inquisitions' like the *dragonnades* in France. From the time of Elizabeth, however, the state in England had shown no enthusiasm for a policy of supporting directly Protestant missions among the Irish Catholics.

There were always, of course, some churchmen who argued that British temporal power should support the Protestant church in Ireland, using force, if necessary, to protect it. This had been the view of Gladstone in the 1830's when he engaged in theorizing about ecclesiastical affairs, but thirty years later he had engaged in his great *volte face* and considered disestablishment of the Church of Ireland. His argument for this was pragmatic as he told Nonconformist friends: 'as a missionary church it was an obvious failure because the proportion of Protestants to Roman Catholics had been greater during the sixteenth century than it was during the nineteenth'. Not only was there no utilitarian argument for the establishment but the church had become a 'menace to religion, to civil justice and to peace'.[87] Gladstone was echoing a conviction that had been slowly growing among English churchmen that there was really no defence for such an anomalous institution:

> Few, we think, will now maintain, that it is essential for the religious welfare of Ireland that the Established Church of that country should exhibit in long array 2 archbishops, 10 bishops, 139 dignitaries, 187

prebendaries and canons: or that there should be 1333 incumbents of benefices, and 752 curates.[88]

On the eve of disestablishment *The Times* in its leader of 4 September, 1868 opined that there were few disinterested observers of the Irish established church who would argue the need for its survival as it then was:

The benefit of a splendid and high-titled Establishment is very much confined to places, to classes, to cliques, and to families, to the owners of patronage, and the possessors of influence.

The religious census of 1861 showed that members of the established church formed just over 11.9% of the population; there were almost as many Presbyterians, just over 9%; and 77.6% of the Irish people were Roman Catholics.[89] By the latter years of the 1860's it was clear to any thoughtful Protestant that not only was there to be no succour by the state for the church to encourage its mission work among the Roman Catholics, but the climate of secular reform in parliament threatened a radical change in the prevailing relationship between the Protestant churches and Westminster.

Because of what Cullen had accomplished the Irish Protestants faced the future with a great deal of trepidation on the eve of disestablishment of the Church of Ireland. Fifteen or so years earlier they had been almost sanguine as they considered the state of their church, in spite of many heavily-encumbered Protestant estates having fallen into Catholic hands, and there being considerable disturbance on the land connected with the tenants' rights issue.[90] Such was the identity crisis among the people following the ravages of the famine, that in the 1850's there seemed no fear that the priests could organize the kind of anti-Protestant protest movements that had characterized the tithe war or repeal movement years. Just before Cullen held his legatine council at Thurles the Congregationalist preacher, William Urwick, who was a shrewd social observer, wrote: 'it is the opinion of many who ought to be well acquainted with the religious state of the country, that the Roman Catholic system is being seriously shaken'.[91] Some evangelically minded churchmen, as we will see, even thought that the time was ripe for a massive mission by religious societies among the people who seemed ready to abandon their traditional Catholic faith. On the other hand establishment figures, such as Richard Whately, the Protestant archbishop of Dublin, made it clear that people like himself had no interest in trying to bring the majority population over to the Protestant faith.[92] At the most, prelates like Whately were willing to tolerate the continuation of intellectual religious controversies, such as the evangelicals had delighted in before the famine. Meetings of Protestant Catholic clergy engaged in theological point-scoring could do little harm, and if individual conversions followed such encounters they would be satisfied; the social contention that would accompany

any policy of organized proselytizing had no appeal to them.

In the post-famine period, however, the English evangelicals were at the summit of their influence. They were in a militant mood after the anti-papal hysteria, associated with the Maynooth Grant and the reestablishment of the Roman hierarchy had revealed the anti-Catholic and anti-Irish feelings of much of the populace. The zealots in Exeter Hall, the headquarters for the various missionary societies, were ready to launch a major campaign to win the dispirited Irish Catholics over to the reformed faith: 'while Sumner was still archbishop of Canterbury, while Lord Palmerston presided over the cabinet, and while Shaftesbury the noble head of evangelical laymen was stepson-in-law to the prime minister'.[93] Reports from Ireland convinced them of the disarray in the Catholic community there, and they were determined to help the 'spiritually impoverished' peasantry who were trying to free themselves from 'priestly tyranny'. William Urwick, for example, reported on the new openmindedness shown by the Kerry country people who were less superstitious and displayed:

> ... less slavish subjection to the priest, less dread of his ghostly frown...less concern for the missionary and his message unless they expect some temporal boon from him... Popery in many parts of Ireland is becoming less like that of Spain and more like that of France.

The Orange order was so moribund that the priests, 'positively low both intellectually and morally' with less and less influence over the people, could not even warn about that institution's Protestant oppression to rally support to their cause. In fact many of the people spoke openly of Protestant generosity during the famine, and realized that for too long they had been 'dupes of designing demagogues'.[94]

There was, as we have noted, no way for the Protestant militants to realize that from the time of the synod of Thurles, the greatest of ecclesiastical 'designing demagogues' had already begun to assert Roman authority over the Irish Catholic church and its demoralized people. The *Edinburgh Review* of January 1851 in a general overview of Irish affairs virtually ignored the authority of the Catholic church in the country. It did comment, however, on the 'agitation of the ultra-montane section of the Roman Catholic hierarchy against the Queen's Colleges', and the change in tone from 1845 when the colleges had been sanctioned, and that of Thurles where the agreement to work for the good of the country was 'violated'. The expectation was that the Catholic laity would reject 'a decree like this which proceeds from a bare majority of a divided tribunal':

> We shall expect to see the Roman Catholic laity in this instance vindicating their church from the reproach to which the Synod of Thurles has exposed her; defending the past conduct of their bishops against their present doctrines and pretensions.[95]

The analysis of the *Edinburgh Review* might have been accurate if archbishop Daniel Murray had lived to rally support for the 'godless colleges' and the concept of united education, but with his demise Cullen, whose power was not yet fully appreciated, was free to extend Roman domination among the laity as well as the priests. A year later some of the Irish Protestants had begun to be aware of what was taking place in the Catholic church. They noted correspondence in the *Dublin Evening Post* of 12 June, 1852, lamenting the changes taking place now that Daniel Murray had departed, and how his curates were being 'culled'. The *Irish Ecclesiastical Journal* had much to say about 'Dr. Cullen's Proceedings in Dublin':

> Strange reports are prevalent in Dublin respecting the spirit which he has already exhibited as the Pope's Vicar-General or Legate a latere... bringing into due submission our luckless fellow-subjects, the Roman Catholics of Ireland.[96]

The problem for the Protestants was that they did not have an able leader who could contend with Cullen. Primate Beresford was elderly and representative of an age that had fought hopeless battles like the cause of the Church Educational Society as an alternative to the National System of Education—which Cullen had accepted in lieu of denominational education in order to have Roman Catholic education provided and paid for by the state. Richard Whately, the archbishop of Dublin, was no match for Cullen who persuaded the Dublin province Catholic bishops to condemn scripture lessons which the Protestant prelate had drawn up for the National schools. The Board of National Education gave in to Cullen's pressure, as we have noted, the books were removed from the schools, and Whately resigned. Cullen worked seven days a week, up to eighteen hours a day during his long legatine mission, ever seeking for some educational or other vantage point to advance Roman authority. When there were abuses at the expense of Catholics in the military Cullen immediately made the matter a public issue, with a demand for 'redress of grievances'.[97] Any local act of prose-lytizing in a state institution was immediately brought, in great detail, to the attention of the lord lieutenant, discussed in the Catholic press, and raised in the House of Commons.[98] The state as well as the Protestant church felt at times under siege and, from the time Cullen became a cardinal, Dublin Castle saw more and more of him, not merely seeking political or social approval, but demanding concessions which would increase Roman control in the Catholic community. Whenever he met with British officials Cullen resolutely seized the opportunity to attack the proud Protestant clergy:

> ... whilst breathing nothing but hatred, and desirous to oppress, these preachers hold themselves forth as models of toleration and liberty and condemn all others as models of despotism and tyranny.[99]

To understand what Cullen accomplished in his 'Cullenization' of the Irish Catholic people and their church (as his critics called his legatine mission) it needs to be recognized that Cullen was indeed an ecclesiastical general. Frederick Lucas said he was always at war with something,[100] and in his battles he was strongly supported by the Roman authorities at Propaganda and elsewhere in the curia who trusted him completely. He was determined to bring about a revolution in Ireland, to bring its people totally under domination of the Roman *imperium:*

> It is hard to find anything in Thurles that had not been laid down at Trent. Hitherto the full Tridentine pattern had been difficult to implement in Ireland. Now it was to go the way of Catholic Europe.[101]

When Cullen deplored the advance of Protestant missions in Connaught he was in constant communication with Propaganda about the situation. The war he was fighting on that 'front' was but one battle in the on-going struggle of the universal church against the powers of darkness in this world. While he directed the Irish campaigns he had the Irish bishops send letters of support to the archbishop of Freiburg when Catholics were persecuted in Baden. He also collected money for this cause, which was sent to Louis Veuillot, editor of the ultramontane French newspaper, *l'Univers,* whom he thanked for: 'the signal services which you have so frequently rendered to the cause of religion and charity in Ireland'.[102] Of particular help to him were the Roman directed religious orders which came to Ireland from the continent, such as the Passionists in 1848, the Oblates of Mary Immaculate in 1851, and the Redemptorists in 1853.

British policy in Ireland was from the standpoint of the Protestants one of benign neglect. The government was embarrassed by the huge establishment which supported such a small proportion of the total population, and was under much attack by the Roman Catholics, the Nonconformists and the radicals. In an age of increasing secularism it could not have done anything substantial to support the policies of the Church of Ireland, let alone encourage its mission activities, so the defence of the Irish Protestants was conducted as usual by the religious societies of the time in traditional ways. Unfortunately for the Protestants, the strategy the societies developed was ill-conceived and directed, and long before disestablishment it was clear that Cullen's ultramontane forces were to be victorious. From the standpoint of the Protestants the state did nothing for them in the years between the famine and disestablishment. On the other hand 'inch by inch' the government yielded ground to Cullen and the Roman authority he served as his power became dominant in Ireland. Even the disestablishment victory brought no respite: 'The Royal Assent was scarcely given to the Irish Church Act until Cardinal Cullen and his confrères raised a howl of religious discord'.[103]

The Roman cause was helped by the most important Protestant religious society in the post-famine years being English in origin, in organization, and in financial backing. The Irish Church Missions to the Roman Catholics was the creation of Alexander R.C. Dallas, a Waterloo veteran who thought in terms of a strategic mission to convert the Irish people to the reformed faith. After the Napoleonic wars he was ordained and spent forty years as rector of the parish of Wonston in Hampshire.[104] An extreme evangelical, and a friend of many of the leaders of that party he first visited Ireland in 1840:

> Every subsequent visit strengthened his conviction that the minds of the Roman Catholic population were prepared for a more open exhibition of the Gospel, and a more extended system of missionary aggression upon the gross delusions and superstitions in which they were enthralled.[105]

In January, 1846, he began to deluge Irish Catholic households with evangelical tracts using the post, then with the help of Exeter Hall zealots he raised a great deal of money and formed his society. The society focused on MacHale's province of Tuam which the *Dublin Evening Post* of 11 November, 1851 accepted as 'good generalship' for it was here that the people suffered most from a lack of pastoral care:

> They knew that Education was put under ban and anathema in these parts. They knew that the National Schools were denounced by the highest ecclesiastical authority in the place...

By 1853 Dallas was able to announce that he had over three hundred agents working in his society, with five thousand children receiving scriptural instruction. By Dallas's own account he was more apt to preach to the dying rather than give them temporal help,[106] but soon the charge of 'souperism' was being applied to explain every conversion to Protestantism. This was the accusation that soup, stirabout, or other help was given to the needy only on the condition that they accept the version of the Gospel faith that Dallas and his followers brought from England. Both O'Connell and Lord Brougham raised the issue in parliament, and the majority of Irish Protestants were dismayed when they realized a new round of religious-cultural struggle was to be visited upon people who had barely recovered from the strain of the Tithe War.

Dallas fought his war in both England and Ireland. Very tough minded, he was not as easily intimidated as were the Irish parsons by belligerent priests, and every one of his Scripture Readers who suffered an indignity was soon relating it to the huge crowds who flocked to Exeter Hall. The English evangelicals found in the Irish Church Missions a way to hit back at the ultramontanists who had brought the 'papal aggression' to England. Dallas was delighted when his fellow

Englishman, the convert Henry Wilberforce, used the Catholic Defence Association of which he was secretary to attack Dallas and his missionary efforts. This battle helped Dallas not only to raise further funds, but to gain valuable publicity. *The Times* of 7 October, 1851 gleefully reported:

> It seems now pretty clear that something like a reformation is taking place in the province of Connaught... In the missions of the Irish Protestant Church which had achieved such signal success, we recognize a just and fair reprisal for the arrogant aggressions of the Pope.

The *Dublin Evening Post* of 11 November, 1851 admitted: 'We learn from every unquestionable Catholic authority that their success is in almost every part of the country'. Three days earlier *The Tablet* had noted that the contagion had taken root in Dublin. *The Nation* of 20 November, 1852 reported sadly:

> There can no longer be any question that proselytism has met with an immense success in Connaught and Kerry. It is true that the altars of the Catholic Church have been deserted by thousands born and baptized in the ancient faith of Ireland.

The period 1849–1854 was a golden age for the Irish Church Missions and Rome was very disturbed by what was taking place.

As soon as Cullen arrived in Ireland he was engaged in the task of re-organizing the church, to have it throw back any further advance by the prose-lytizers. On 16 June, 1851 he sent a long and detailed 'battle report' to Propa-ganda, where he admitted that in MacHale's territories the Protestants had estab-lished well-financed strong points. Oughterard was no longer a Catholic parish as it was completely taken over by 'Jumpers and Bible Readers' and the people had been abandoned by their parish priest, William Kirwan, who had become pre-sident of the Queen's College in Galway. Hundreds of 'perverts' were being con-firmed in the area. [107] To Cullen the situation was a desperate one for MacHale refused to admit there was anything seriously wrong in his province. Yet, when the suggestion was made by the pope that MacHale might visit him, the arch-bishop pleaded reluctance to leave his people when they were under attack. By 18 February, 1852 the *Dublin Evening Mail,* a Protestant paper reported over 10,000 converts in Connemara.

Cullen and Propaganda had to move carefully because they feared that the mercurial archbishop of Tuam was quite capable of raising the issue of Roman imperialism and appealing to the passions of the people. The tactic the legate used was to isolate each of MacHale's suffragans, and persuade them to accept ultramontane coadjutors with rights of succession. This was a slow process, however, and as late as 1869 John MacEvilly who had been made bishop of Galway, and was to succeed MacHale in Tuam, was telling Rome that Protestant orphanages, schools and churches still abounded and were sustained by English funds. How many converts there were is impossible to say for the conversion of individuals, or of families, inevitably meant their separation from their community. 'Soupers', 'Jumpers', 'Perverts' had a hard time and their natural progress was to emigrate, often with the help of a proselytizing agency. A great many Protestants deplored the animosity that arose through the proselytizing campaign which some astute observers argued was a help to Cullen and the ultramontanists:

> ...the antagonism between the two creeds is greatly increased, and the Roman Catholics have received a stronger and more exclusive organization under the priesthood.[108]

This was certainly so, for Cullen used the Rosminians and other continental orders to launch a counter-attack, and the religious and social tensions between the peoples was great, especially over the issue of 'taking the soup'.

This alleged practice was especially resented by many Protestants. It was, of course, difficult to prove that bribery was used in conversion but the charge was made by men of substance. One of these was George Webster, chancellor of the diocese of Cork who accused the Irish Church Missions in 1864 of this offence in Dublin:

> Under your society a Roman Catholic child receives his bed and breakfast, he is housed and clothed on the express condition that he listens to Protestant teaching and attends a Protestant place of worship.[109]

Other Protestants showed great unease over the bad publicity accorded Thomas Plunket, bishop of Tuam, 1839–1867. He was one of the three clerical sons of the first Baron Plunket, the champion of Catholic Emancipation, but he showed none of his father's political astuteness. He was an enthusiastic supporter of the Irish Church Missions, as well as Edward Nangle's Protestant colony on Achill island, and with the help of his nephew and domestic chaplain, W.C. Plunket, the future archbishop of Dublin, he did his utmost to advance Reformation principles in Mayo.[110] This inevitably brought him into conflict not only with John MacHale but also with astute political priests like Peter Ward of Partry, and then Patrick Lavelle of Fenian fame. The press was fascinated by rioting in Tuam when Plunket attempted to take over a building once used by the Christian Brothers, and by 1854 the *Daily Telegraph* of 13 December was listing the names of Catholic families evicted because they would not send their children to Protestant schools. The *Mayo Constitution,* in particular, filled its pages with stories of the outrages of the 'burglar bishop', and the events in Mayo were even raised in parliament. *The Times* of 27 November 1860, said that although nothing the bishop had done was illegal: 'it does not look well'.

By 1860 the bishop of Orleans was raising money for Catholic victims of the 'war in Partry', and Catholic outrage would have been extreme in its condemnation but for the fact that Plunket's opponent was Paul Cullen's enemy and detractor, Patrick Lavelle. A great agitator and skilled journalist Lavelle had in his student days organized a revolt in the Irish College in Paris which effectively destroyed the ecclesiastical career of John Miley, who had accompanied O'Connell on his last journey to Rome.[111]   Still, Plunket found himself condemned in parliament; both Ward and Lavelle did well out of raising funds for the 'war in Partry'; and Cullen watched with grim satisfaction as the embarrassment of the Protestant proselytizers grew with every attempt of the bishop to justify himself.[112]

The failing of the Irish Church Missions was its inability to win over the support of most Protestants. By 1863 the society was slowly in retreat, trying to ally itself with the Irish Society which gave bibles in Irish to the people, and by then was willing to admit that some Protestants simply refused to help the mission.[113]   The parsons generally had no desire to bring the wrath of Cullen, MacHale, or a Patrick Lavelle upon them, and they knew that where the society was well dug in as in Dublin there was a continuing attack upon its institutions which were viewed as: 'a component part of an aggressive mission to the Roman Catholics'.[114]   Richard Whately, the archbishop of Dublin, was a liberal who had no instinctive sympathy with the proselytizers, but when there were a remarkable number of conversions around St. Michan's and other evangelical parishes he did licence an Irish Church Missions house on Townsend Street, and the Birds Nest orphanage for destitute children. Soon, however, he became convinced that the society's leaders were not wise men.[115]   By 1857 he realized that the proselytizers were doing 'irreparable mischief'. George Webster was then a curate in Donnybrook, and he presented Whately with a great deal of evidence of the moral failings of the proselytizers.[116]   Whately was not about to tolerate such unchristian and ungentlemanly behaviour, including the use of bribery, and he was soon a great critic of the Irish Church Missions. By this time, however, Cullen had decided that Whately was a proselytizer, helped no doubt by the devotion to Alexander Dallas shown by Whately's immediate family—Dallas preached Mrs. Whately's funeral sermon. Cullen had little respect for his Protestant counterpart who, as an educator and a promoter of proselytizing, tried to 'wean' the Irish from 'the abuses of popery'.[117]

Tactically there was much wrong with Dallas's campaign. Controversial religion no longer caught the public imagination as it had in the more insular world of the pre-famine period. Daniel Cahill, one of the Catholic champions of that time now refused to engage in controversy, saying he would 'only debate if ordered to by Rome'.[118]   When the Irish Church Missions distributed pamphlets and put up placards that Cullen and others found so distasteful, they may have won response from disgruntled individuals in the Catholic community, but their message was more apt to offend than to please the majority. Dallas, for example, barely concealed a note of condescension when he published a public *Letter to the Roman Catholics of Kilkenny* on 4 April, 1856:

> It is for your own sakes, more than for the sake of the Scripture-Readers, that we are taking so much pains, and that I am addressing this letter to you. It is a sad and degrading thing for intelligent men to be debarred from the exercise of their reason, and forbidden to receive the information that God himself has communicated to man.

Attached to this letter were replicas of six posters which had been set up in the community:

THE NEW DOGMA ONE YEAR OLD
Whereas
THE ROMAN CATHOLIC BIBLE
Does Not Contain
1st. Any revelation from God
2nd. Any declaration from Christ
3rd. Any epistle from an Apostle
To teach the
NEW DOCTRINE OF THE IMMACULATE CONCEPTION OF THE B.V.
MARY;
And Whereas
The Koran of Mahomet Does Contain This Doctrine
IT IS A TURKISH NOT A CHRISTIAN DOCTRINE!

At most a placard like this would annoy Paul Cullen, who had an intense devotion to the Virgin,[119] but it is unlikely it would influence many of the Catholic townspeople of Kilkenny, except to provoke their 'violent opposition', which the proselytizers welcomed as a step towards conversion.[120]

The Irish evangelical party was passionately anti-Romanist, of course, and ideologically it supported the English-based Irish Church Missions as its journal *The Christian Examiner* clearly showed. It carried on the traditional polemical writing of the period, promising to help the Irish Catholics: 'to burst the chains which the hierarchy have bound upon them'.[121] It also deplored the use that Rome made of the priests, and of Maynooth to ensure that 'the students are saturated with the hatred of English rule and hostility to the British connexion... preached by Roman priests and re-echoed by Roman demagogues'.[122] The court of Rome was constantly decried, as was the encyclical *Quanta cura* and its Syllabus of Errors:

> In every line of the boastful and blasphemous encyclical we can trace the iron heel that would, if it could, or dared, trample down the civil and

religious liberty of our race.[123]

As for Cullen, he did 'everything possible to degrade our people', by trying to deny them education unless it was under Roman direction, his pastorals 'a burden and a permanent insult to this Catholic country'.

At the same time the Irish evangelicals were unhappy over the dissension caused by the Irish Church Missions. Struggles like the 'war in Partry' gave Cullen and the other ultramontanists the excuse to bring further continental reinforcement into the country. It also meant that the English public as a whole was revolted by the excesses and scandals associated with the proselytizing campaign, with the result that there was little sympathy shown to the Church of Ireland generally. Articles which were written in *The Times:* 'might have emanated from Dr. Cullen or Dr. MacHale'.[124] Above all the Protestants were concerned that while the government seemed inclined to grant endless 'concessions to Romanism' in the drift towards disestablishment, the country was racked by the unrest of the Fenian years. Nothing disturbed the Protestant landlord class more than: 'the terrible bogyman of the nineteenth century all over Europe, the priest in politics'.[125] The Tithe War years were not forgotten, priests like Patrick Lavelle were rightly feared, and the threat of outrage seemed always imminent.

The honourable Mary Plunkett, daughter of Lord Dunsany and a novelist has described the dismal services in the Church of Ireland in Kilcooley, county Tipperary in this period, its tiny congregation 'bigoted, intolerant and obstinately low church'. Deeply imbued with the doctrine of justification by faith alone they were apt to consider 'all good works to be avoided as belonging to the Devil'. Outside the gate of the estate where she lived were lounging 'large limbed indolent people, pleasant to deal with, impossible to trust', all of them convinced by the priests that they suffered from the injustice of a stolen birthright. In 1867 there was much talk of rebellion, of Fenians coming from America, secret oaths, forging of pike-heads, and coming mayhem.[126] This sense of siege existed almost everywhere, except in Ulster, as well as the conviction that at the heart of the unrest was the Roman demand to establish its order or system in Ireland:

> It is the system we protest against—a system which is assuredly not
> English, and most certainly, and we thank God for it, is not Irish, but
> is essentially Italian—a system which is a weight on the bosom of our
> noble green isle which we all love so truly.[127]

When there was not actual fear, as in the Fenian period, there was always anxiety, such as that felt by bishop John Gregg of Cork, Cloyne and Ross during his youth. Though his mother was a Catholic he was: 'the orphan child of the only Protestant family in one of the obscurest parishes in the most neglected county (Clare) in Ireland'.[128]   From an early age he knew that, regardless of the ecclesiastical or social assurances given to the community he belonged to, as in the Tithe War period violence against it was a possibility. This anxiety, which so easily translated into fear, was understandable for the rural Protestants belonged to a minority which knew that its constitutional position had been undermined in the O'Connell years, and the process was continuing. Force, threatened or actual, operated in Irish society, even in church affairs, and this was a fact that few disputed:

Historians are apt to reduce to terms of cause and consequence matters about which contemporaries felt in terms of challenging, uplifting, desolating or terrifying personal experience. Destruction, violence, fear, intimidation... to the generation which experiences it, the effects of force upon their lives are real and tangible.[129]

Not all the violence reflected political tensions for the years following the famine were the years of numerous evictions, the memory of which was carried to America by so many of the emigrants. Inevitably this kind of landlord violence led to agrarian outrage, and often homicide. *The Times* of 30 May, 1850 said of murder in Ireland:

It is but too often a proof of some great social disease — of some terrible and wide-spread mischief which is undermining the strength of society itself — portending anarchy, and all the terror and misery with which anarchy is inevitably attended; and thus not only exciting horror at the crime itself but also raising most painful emotions of alarm for the future safety of the social and political institutions under which we live.

Many of the Protestants were concerned for their future safety, and believed during times of social unrest: 'that the Catholic clergy were in some compromising way involved with Fenianism'. Their memory harkened back to the days of the Ribbonmen, and they were reminded in a pamphlet of 1858: 'there is nothing in Ribbonism that is not Romanism; the gun of the Ribbonmen is one with the canon law of Rome'.[130]   They paid attention to the opinion of O'Connor Morris, a well-informed observer of Irish affairs who informed the *Times* of 4 November, 1869: 'the agrarian murders of the last eighteen months have struck terror into the hearts of thousands, and influenced the administration of hundreds of estates'. The Protestants generally were reassured by a severe censure of the Fenians by David Moriarty, bishop of Kerry, but they would have been uneasy if they had known the fury of Cullen over Moriarty's sermon, which he decried as 'Gallican', 'pro-Protestant', and 'open to popular criticism'.[131] As for Cullen's actions in the National Association, which he founded in an attempt to take over direction of the nationalist movement, the Protestant press at least saw it as another example of ultramontane intrigue:

> It will be generally regarded as only a fresh attempt to Ultramontanize
> the Irish people... It is Ireland's misfortune that she cannot find leaders
> who are able to rise superior to sectarianism.[132]

What the Roman Catholic prelates were about was of little immediate concern to
the Protestants, however, for their real fear was an outbreak of local terrorism,
and the dread that it was inspired by some clerical influence.

Apart from violence the Protestants found that increasingly there was no
compromise possible over matters like education. When George Butler, the
Catholic bishop of Limerick, who was considered to be 'well-disposed' towards
dialogue with Protestants, took over his diocese in 1864 one of the first issues
he had to deal with was that of mixed education in Kilscannel school, the
manager of which was the son of Smith O'Brien of Young Ireland notoriety.
The local priests considered there were 'dangerous tendencies' in the school, and
the Catholic bishop had the children of his community withdrawn. Edward
O'Brien then tried to negotiate a management of the school that would be acceptable to both Catholics and Protestants: 'that it may be of the utmost possible
benefit to the neighbourhood'. O'Brien promised he would give to the bishop
guarantees 'sufficient to insure the Catholics against any undue influence', but
Butler refused to consider anything but a total surrender of the school to Catholic
authority: 'your school must share the fate of all National Schools in the south
of Ireland: it must be practically denominational'. If this was accepted there
could be 'mixed education' in the sense that Protestant children would not be
kept out:

> A National School under the management of a Catholic priest or
> laymen should be open to Protestant children if they choose to enter;
> but the manager is not bound to compel them to come, nor is he guilty
> of any dereliction of duty by allowing the Catholic children to fill the
> school, if they alone present themselves.[133]

In the face of this kind of intransigence in educational affairs, and it was
common throughout the countryside, the Protestants had to reckon with a *de
facto* assertion of Catholic ascendancy in one of the most important of social
organizations. Butler, incidentally, was not favoured by Cullen who thought him
too involved in local clan affairs and financial scandals.

It was not only in the field of education, however, that the Protestants had
to acknowledge that the Roman Catholic church was demanding and obtaining
'ascendancy' in the south of Ireland, in effect replacing the Church of Ireland as
the ecclesiastical body which could win concessions to assist its mission from a
now compliant government: 'the Roman Catholic clergy strike higher for the

earthly honours which are dropping out of her feeble hands, and which they intend to seize'.[134] What was taking place in the words of the Nonconformist clergyman, James Godkin was an open display of Roman Catholic 'triumphalism':

> That the multitude might see how completely the tables had been turned upon the Protestants, and how the evil spirit of ecclesiastical domination was passing out of one body into another.[135]

On the eve of disestablishment it was clear to the leaders of the Church of Ireland that their role in Irish society was being radically challenged. Archbishop R.C. Trench of Dublin in his 1868 charge noted the 'simmering discontent of the Catholic hierarchy', and their demand for ascendancy. They showed no interest in correcting the real need of Ireland, persuading Catholics and Protestants alike to forget the great wrongs of the past such as the massacres of the seventeenth century:

> It is for both, for Celt and for Saxon, for Roman Catholics and for Protestants alike, to forgive and forget what of wrong they or their forefathers have suffered.

Under the leadership of the ultramontane bishops, however, the hope for conciliation between the churches was not likely to come about:

> I am not wronging the Roman Catholic Church as represented by its hierarchy when I say that in its judgment not to have everything is to have nothing; that so long as it is not supreme all which it has gained, will only be regarded as stepping-stones to some further acquisition.[136]

'Acquisition' was to include 'concurrent endowment' in the thinking of some Roman Catholic leaders such as bishop Moriarty of Kerry, and the convert from the Church of England, Aubrey de Vere, who presented his ideas in a series of pamphlets and in letters to the *Times*. Cullen wanted total disendowment of the Church of Ireland, however, after consultation with cardinal Antonelli, and the whole campaign for disestablishment and the break-up of the Protestant body was directed by him with help from the Roman authorities. His role was identified by Alfred T. Lee, rector of Ahoghill, in his widely published 1868 pamphlet, *Facts Respecting the Present State of the Church in Ireland,* as a campaign to destroy utterly the established church because it was: 'the chief impediment to the religious and political supremacy of Rome in Ireland'. One of the papal delegate's tactics was to denigrate the Church of Ireland by denying its Irishness: 'they are strangers amongst us; unlike our forefathers in the faith, they hold not the communion of the see of Peter'.

This singular institution (the Established Church) was originally established, and has always been maintained by force, in opposition to reason and justice, and in defiance of the will of the great majority of the Irish people. That we therefore resent it as a badge of national servitude, offensive and degrading alike to all Irishmen, Protestant as well as Catholic.[137]

Cullen also claimed that the Protestants had no claim to Holy Orders because they were not under Roman authority:

The Catholic church regards their ordination as invalid, and when any of them return to her fold, they are received only as laymen; or they are re-ordained, should they wish to be ranked among her Clergy.[138]

This charge had long been used against the Church of Ireland, but substantial Protestant scholars like James Henthorn Todd of Trinity College argued that St. Patrick had had no commission from Pope Celestine as the papists claimed. This claim which Todd made in his historical study, *The Life of St. Patrick,* of 1864 implied that the Church of Ireland traced its foundation back to St. Patrick, and that the Roman Church not the Anglican was the institution that was un-Irish.[139] The argument was taken up and enlarged by Church of Ireland apologists: 'The Irish church was a spiritual institution as the Church of Christ before the English invasion, or the intrusion of the papacy'.[140] This controversy was developed at some length by Alfred Lee who argued that popery only came into Ireland with the Roman ecclesiastical representatives who accompanied the Norman invasion in the reign of Henry II:

Foreign bishops consecrated in foreign lands assumed to themselves the position of the lawful bishops of Ireland, and from these foreigners, and not from the bishops of the church of St. Patrick does the present Roman Catholic episcopate in Ireland derive its succession.[141]

The Roman case was put by William Maziere Brady, a Church of Ireland clergyman who converted through the agency of Cullen's nephew, P.F. Moran, and spent the last years of his life writing voluminously in the Eternal City. Skilled in controversy his point scoring endeared him to Cullen who thought little of the Protestants laying claim to St. Patrick.[142]

Regardless of Church of Ireland pretensions Cullen knew from the census of 1861 that its political humbling through disestablishment and disendowment was imminent. The census showed that the members of the established church were then only one eighth of the population; the Catholics were ten of every thirteen people in Ireland.[143] After all the work of the Irish Church Missions and other agencies, and with massive Catholic emigration, since 1834 there had been about a two percent increase in the population of the Church of Ireland, relative to other denominations.[144] When the Fenian crisis drew British public attention to Ireland John Francis Maguire, M.P. for the city of Cork, moved for an enquiry into the state of Ireland, and it was then that Gladstone decided that the time for disestablishment of the Church of Ireland had come. He read the mind of parliament which generally agreed with the assessment of the Church of Ireland made by the Radical member, Robert Lowe:

> You call it a missionary church. If so, its mission is unfulfilled. As a missionary church it has failed utterly. Like some exotic brought from a far country, with infinite pains and useless trouble, it is kept alive with difficulty and expense in an ungrateful climate and ungenial soil. The curse of bareness is upon it; it has no leaves; it bears no blossoms; it yields no fruit: 'Cut it down; why cumbereth it the ground?'

The nonconformist preacher Charles Haddon Spurgeon was reported to have said that turning the Irish parsons into the street would be only an act of stern justice.[145]

In spite of their defensive pamphlet war it was soon clear to the Irish Protestant leaders that there could be no saving of their anomalous institution in this age of reform. The archbishop of Armagh spoke of 'Gladstone's declaration of war to the knife', and the sense of vulnerability among members of the Church of Ireland:

> Some think if Disraeli will... raise the no Popery cry—put the question as one of Popery or the Gospel in Ireland he would defeat Gladstone. We are no doubt in a perilous position... I feel in rather a weak and lonely position.[146]

When the Protestant prelates petitioned the queen they indicated their dismay over what the Irish situation revealed about Irish Catholics:

> The majority of the inhabitants of Ireland prefer submitting themselves to the ecclesiastical laws of a foreign prelate and potentate rather than to the ecclesiastical laws sanctioned by their own sovereign and they refuse to acknowledge your Majesty's Supreme Authority.[147]

The most hopeful voice raised in the crisis belonged to W.C. Plunket, then treasurer of St. Patrick's Cathedral, and the archbishop of Dublin to be. He urged the Protestants of the Church of Ireland not to look upon their church as 'a mere subordinate appanage of the English crown', as its enemies described it, but rather 'that ancient church of St. Patrick, St. Brigid and St. Columbkill', a purely spiritual body:

Let there not remain a shred of state connection to give a shadow of excuse to those who would still wish to describe it as an alien church.[148]

V   Ulster and the Catholic Resurgence

Ulster, as usual, responded uniquely to the ultramontane campaign in a way
that was a puzzlement to Cullen and to Propaganda. In every part of the
province there seemed to be a different response to the increase in Catholic
power, depending on the local history of the community. In the border diocese
of Clogher, for example, when J.W. Murphy the Catholic bishop reported to
Propaganda on the state of his diocese in 1804 he had noted that its prosperity,
such as it was, reflected the generosity of the local Protestants:

> We have lately got many good chapels erected and covered with the best
> of slate... six more nearly finished, and if God in his mercy is pleased
> to grant this empire an honourable peace shortly I hope, with his
> assistance, and that of our Protestant neighbours, for indeed they have
> been very kind to us on these occasions, we shall get chapels around the
> whole diocese in a few years.[149]

Murphy's successor was an Enniskillen native, Edward Kernan, who had received
his education in Salamanca after attending the Royal School at Portora. He had
a heavy cross to bear in the form of clerical cabals, and these increased from the
time that he was given a coadjutor, Charles MacNally, a great builder of
churches, but also a MacHaleite. MacNally succeeded as bishop in 1844, but
from the time that Cullen arrived he found himself under censure for his pastoral
failings. These he excused by telling the papal delegate that he could do little in
his diocese because of Protestant bullying. Cullen, however, thought little of
MacNally, not least because he too easily assimilated into the Protestant
ascendancy culture of Clogher, of which town he was a native.[150]

Cullen let Rome know of MacNally's many failings, and he remained
suspicious of any prelate who seemed to be able to 'accommodate' himself to the
Protestant society of Ulster. The papal delegate could not understand the
situation in Raphoe which enabled Daniel McGettigan, the future primate, to tell
Rome that locally there were 'no crimes, no processions, no secret societies'.
On the other hand Cullen believed he understood the situation in Dromore
diocese where the aged and passive Michael Blake approved of both the National
System and the Queen's Colleges. Not that Cullen wanted confrontation, for he
was uneasy when he heard of a new assertiveness shown by the burgeoning
Catholic population of Newry. He wanted an ultramontane advance, but not at
the cost of open sectarian warfare, which was certainly threatened in Down and
Connor as the Catholic population in Belfast rapidly increased.

The Catholic population peaked in the urban area by 1861, when it was up to about 34%, and as the Catholics increased in numbers so did the hostility of the Protestants towards them. The parish priest of Belfast from 1812–1825 was William Crolly, an ecumenically-minded cleric but in the eyes of later ultramontanists always an intimidated one. When he became bishop of the diocese in 1825 Protestants attended dinners in his honour, and when he was made primate ten years later, and supported the National System, the Charitable Bequests Act and the Queen's Colleges Cullen was in despair. His successor as bishop of Down and Connor was Cornelius Denvir who also tried to get along with the Protestants. In fact, during one of the debates in the controversy era he had even expressed his personal belief that Protestants could be saved.[151]

When Denvir was criticized by Cullen for being too conciliatory the bishop wrote to Rome to explain the problems of acting as a pastor in the face of 'Orange animus' and 'the diabolical spirit of antipathy prevailing here'.[152] A strong-minded Catholic prelate was obviously needed to stand up to Protestant bullying, and this was provided by the appointment of Patrick Dorrian to the see of Down and Connor. A native of Downpatrick, Dorrian was young, energetic and ready to engage in religious confrontation. Cullen had suspicions of his nationalist tendencies, but in spite of this Dorrian was imposed on Denvir as coadjutor in 1860 and five years later he took over administration from the aged Denvir. Immediately he launched a general mission in Belfast, and at the end of it he was reporting the conversion of some Protestants who had previously taken part in sectarian rioting. By the end of 1865 Dorrian was under attack as an authoritarian ultramontane representing: 'the grinding tyranny under which Rome holds her unhappy children',[153] but, however much his 'despotism' was deplored the Protestants had to admit his ability as sectarian leader. He was a great builder of churches, convents, hospitals and schools; during his episcopate the Catholic priests trebled in number, and he was resolute in pastoral care of the burgeoning Catholic population in his diocese, especially in the 1860's when Belfast grew rapidly in size. His abilities as a controversialist brought him reluctant respect even from some Protestants when he dispassionately and capably denied accusations of Catholic bible-burning made by the rector of St. George's, Belfast, William McIlwaine.[154]

Dorrian's confident militancy was a reflection of a new spirit of assertiveness that was appearing among the Roman Catholics in Ulster. When a new primate, Michael Kieran, was consecrated in Dundalk in February, 1867, the recently created cardinal Paul Cullen officiated, attended by several of the Catholic nobility and gentry, including the member of parliament for the city, Sir George Bowyer, who wore a uniform with the decorations of a Knight of Malta and the Cross of St. Gregory on his chest. Catholic festivals, such as the feast day of the Assumption were regularly celebrated and, especially in the years between 1857 and 1886, 'papist' processions, effigies, banners and party tunes encouraged the Protestants to riot. James Godkin attributed such use of pageantry to the new spirit inculcated through the organizational genius of the papal delegate, Paul Cullen. Cullen was now completely in charge of ecclesiastical affairs in Dublin, and from his headquarters he was directing a revolution which promised a new religious ascendancy in the land: 'we cannot contemplate without astonishment the results produced by the system during the last twenty years':

> Christian doctrines fraternities, and mutual benefit societies are almost innumerable... Their lay managers are kept in hand so well by Cardinal Cullen, that a word from him to his private secretary can set them all in motion at the same moment, in such a manner as to direct and control the whole mass of the Roman Catholic population for any political object in which the Church is for the moment interested.

This Roman take-over of the traditional Irish Catholic church was to be deplored, according to Godkin, for: 'to resist the Church in *any* thing which the Pope commands, is now to fight against God—to become a rebel and a renegade. Papal infallibility leaves no footing in the universe for private judgment'.[155]

It might have been expected that disestablishment and the new spirit of Roman assertiveness would have brought about a significant response in Ulster but, until the Home Rule crisis, which we will look at shortly, the Presbyterians and other religious bodies in Ulster tended to focus on theological and religious concerns in the 1870 period, and to ignore ecclesiastical and political affairs. It is true that Henry Cooke, who always kept a close eye on Rome's 'aggressive usurpation' which was a 'threat to civil and religious liberty',[156] tried to rally the Presbyterians to support the Church of Ireland during the disestablishment crisis, but he was given little support. In England the Baptist preacher, Charles Spurgeon could assure Gladstone that Nonconformist prayers were offered to support him in his work, but the Ulster Presbyterians simply ignored the humbling of the state church and its long-detested prelacy.[157] The Presbyterians regretted the loss of the *regium donum,* of course, but in 1868 the General Assembly was concerned primarily with internal religious matters such as the use of instrumental music in public worship. This mentality of religious introversion continued, even though they all recognized that the Catholic community in Ulster: 'from being a disinherited, impoverished, and oppressed minority... have grown to be the majority of the population'.[158] The Ulster Protestants were also aware that as a result of Cullen's efforts: 'the Church of Rome was virtually endowed in Ireland by the State'.[159] What lay behind such insouciance was an arrogant belief that there was no real threat of Roman Catholic ascendancy ever being established in Ireland; in 1870 in Ulster the Protestants of all denominations still believed they could safely disregard their Roman Catholic neighbours who were governed by their priests and secret societies, 'subject to the rule of common nonsense'.[160]

There were, of course, many spontaneous clashes between Catholics and Protestants at various 'flash points' throughout the province from time to time. One of the most shocking of these was in Belfast in 1857 following a Sunday, 12 July impassioned sectarian sermon by Thomas Drew at Christ Church:

> Of old times lords of high degree, with their own hands, strained on the rack the limbs of the delicate Protestant women, prelates dabbled in the gore of their helpless victims. The cells of the Pope's prisons were paved with the calcined bones of men and women cemented with human gore and human hair...[161]

The pulpit occupied by Limerick born Thomas Drew, who had been in Belfast since 1833, was on the boundary of the Pound and Sandy Row, Catholic and Protestant enclaves. As the Orange congregation came out of the church they were met by a hostile Catholic crowd, shots were fired that night and ten days of continuous rioting followed. Then there were the innumerable local confrontations which led to an increase in sectarian bitterness. One has only to read the *Realities of Irish Life* of W. Steuart Trench which was published in 1868 to realize this. He tells of the murder of a magistrate and land-owner named Mauleverer in Crossmaglen, county Armagh, and his own stratagems to confound the local Ribbonmen. Behind the conspiracy which condemned Trench, who was 'an intelligent and humane land agent', but had stood up to the Ribbonmen, lay a sectarian historical conviction: 'if the boys had held out well when they rose in 1641 they could have had the country to themselves, and driven every Saxon out of it'.[162]

A most important development in Ulster between the famine and disestablishment was the religious 'revival' of 1859. This phenomenon began in local movements for spiritual enlightenment in places like Ballymena and Ahoghill, then spread rapidly throughout the province, climaxing with mass meetings in Belfast Botanic Gardens in June of 1859. Some of those affected by the charismatic excesses which accompanied the movement abandoned the Church of Ireland and Presbyterian bodies, to reinforce more exclusive associations like those of the Brethren and the Baptists.[163] In these bodies the new members engaged in a wholesale retreat from the world where they struggled against the flesh incessantly and often dramatically. Each man, with his bible, stood before God to receive His Grace which would determine both his salvation and his temporal way of life. Almost inevitably the converted rejected those who still clung to the way of religion dogmatically pointed out by priests or other clergy, while some converts who were Catholics became fundamentally opposed to Rome and all it stood for:

> In this great awakening Rome has encountered a new adversary... In the liberation of so many of her unhappy votaries without the

immediate intervention of any human agency, may we not see an earnest of that day of triumph, when her knell shall be rung out in the hearing of exulting Christendom, and when heaven shall re-echo to earth the shout of jubilation that shall rise over her irrevocable doom.[164]

Those re-awakened by Grace who were Roman Catholics were a small minority, but their conversion, often to a mainstream church, ensured that the revival was not condemned outright by the Church of Ireland and the Presbyterians. Edward Stopford, the archdeacon of Meath, spent considerable time watching the revival, including the religious hysteria associated with it in some places. His considered conclusion was that it was a 'good work': 'it widely awakened serious attention to religion in the minds of thousands who never thought seriously of it before'. This he believed would greatly strengthen both the Church of Ireland and the Presbyterians who were most affected by the phenomenon, for the times were trying for Protestantism generally. Purged of hysteria the zeal of the new converts would help the Ulster churches in the days ahead.[165] As for the Ulster Roman Catholics most of them looked with bewilderment upon the charismatic phenomenon:

They could not make out what it was all about. They had always considered their Protestant neighbours as prudent, sensible men, and, as a class, generally better educated, and quite as moral as themselves, and the puzzle to know what new thing had seized upon their imagination was very sincere and perplexing.[166]

The 'puzzlement' of the Catholics reflected the significantly different religious 'imaginations' among folk who had for so long worked separately, bred separately and nurtured quite different religious expressions of faith. Their religious differences had become increasingly important to them during the debates over education, when the Roman Catholic hierarchy had made clear their determination to press for 'exclusivity' in social as well as religious affairs. There are many interpretations of the Ulster revival phenomenon, but a likely one is that the Ulster charismatics, standing, bible in hand, like their Reformation era ancestors, *coram Deo,* were making a powerful statement about the essence of their Protestant faith. They were affirming their community's perception of itself as 'God's people in Ireland surrounded on all sides by antichristian idolatry and superstition'.[167] In the revival was a note of reassurance among a people long dismayed by recurrent social, political and religious upheaval, who were now being challenged by a powerful external authority:

To view the revival from a wider perspective, modern studies of popular revivalism suggest a direct relation between revival and societies whose identity or cohesion is perceived to be under threat... in the case of Ulster, the emergence of a self-conscious and more powerful Roman Catholicism.[168]

Chapter IX

The Protestant Resistance

'The Pope's... infallibility bears upon the domain of thought, not directly of action, and while it may fairly exercise the theologian, philosopher or man of science, it scarcely concerns the politician'

> J.H. Newman, *Newman and Gladstone: The Vatican Decrees*, Notre Dame, 1962, p. 199.

I   Leo XIII and British Catholicism

Paul Cullen died in October, 1878, just eight months after the death of his friend and patron Pope Pius IX, with whom he had maintained a deep suspicion of contemporary European culture. Not everyone in the Roman curia had fully supported the intransigence of Pio Nono, nor the Jesuits associated with the ultra-conservative *La Civiltà Cattolica,* nor a prelate like Cullen, however, and they waited anxiously to see who the next pontiff might be. Before his death in 1876 Antonelli, the cardinal secretary of state, had been convinced that the papal desire to maintain temporal authority in the states of the church was not helped by continuing religious and political tensions with liberal régimes, and very slowly other curial figures began to believe that a rapprochement between Rome and contemporary culture was now called for. One of these men was cardinal Pecci, who had been held suspect by Antonelli, but was generally considered to be an intelligent moderate. Although he was then sixty-eight, and fragile in health, he was the choice of the conclave and, as Leo XIII, he was to give a strong leadership to the church for over twenty-five years.

Leo wanted the papacy to emerge once more as the 'arbiter of nations' but he had to move slowly within the reactionary ambience which his predecessor had built up. At first he strongly denounced socialism, communism, nihilism and Freemasonry and worked hard to increase Roman power at the expense of national episcopates. Like Pio Nono he was obsessed with plans for recovery of the papal states, and his ban on Catholic participation in elections sacrificed any influence the papacy might have had in the new Italy. For the twenty-five years of Leo's pontificate a sterile antagonism between the Vatican and the secular government existed, and in the process an openly anti-clerical movement in Italy took root.

Anti-clericalism was also a major problem in France where in the 'week of blood' which had ended the short-lived Paris Commune of 1871 many clergy died. A kind of *kulturkampf* with the Roman church followed, as it also did in Germany, Austria and Switzerland, and when the French premier, Leon Gambetta, began his bid for power he issued his famous battle-cry: 'I am only expressing the inmost thoughts of the French people when I say—Clericalism, there is the enemy'.[1] Leo obtained a diplomatic triumph when internal pressures persuaded Germany to bring its anticlerical laws to an end in 1886, but he was not successful when he tried to persuade French Catholics to accept the revolutionary régime of the time and to work from within to modify the anti-religious laws of the state. His call for 'ralliement' merely outraged the strongly royalist French Catholics, when anti-Catholic legislation was intensified, and it was made clear to the pontiff that France was not interested in helping him in his political dealings with the Italian government over the occupation of Rome.

Although Leo's political encyclical of 1885, *Immortale Dei*, which argued that the 'vicar of Christ' had the right to counsel human societies, fell on deaf ears in most parts of Europe, his 1891 social encyclical *Rerum novarum* was accepted by many European intellectuals as a major manifesto which upheld the rights of private property, just wages, workers' rights, and trade unions. At the same time Leo retained an innate caution about the church's relationship with secular movements, and in 1899 he censured in America a movement which sought to adapt Catholicism to contemporary ideas and practices. Though Leo wanted to end the political and spiritual isolation built up under Pius IX, he found that the granting of international prestige to the papacy was slow to come. It was a bitter disappointment to him that Italian intervention ensured that the Holy See was excluded from the first Hague international peace conference in 1899. Lord Acton made a shrewd assessment when he said of Leo XIII:

> I think he is the first pope who has been wise enough to despair, and has felt that he must begin a new part, and steer by strange stars over an unknown sea.[2]

One of the 'new parts' he considered was the reestablishing of concord with Britain, in the hope that this might give him leverage with the Italian government, which steadfastly refused to countenance return of the papal states and the temporal authority of the Holy See. At the same time the papal letter, *Ad Anglos,* of 1895 revealed Rome's desire for the return of the 'separated brothers' who embraced heresy in Britain, and it was clear that Leo XIII was going to have a difficult time in his religious and political dealings with the greatest imperial power of the age. Rome continued to fascinate a minority of the privileged classes who became converts, but most of the population associated Catholicism with either the distant authority of the Vatican, or the faith of the immigrant Irish. The Roman Catholics were considered by many to be an alien religious and cultural body in Victorian England.

It was a commonplace for the English to refer to the Roman Catholic church in England as 'the Italian mission', and cardinal Nicholas Wiseman's 'papal aggression' at mid-century was able to succeed, with less uproar than was expected, because the great mass of the people did not take the Roman envoy seriously. One newspaper commented, with considerable wonder, that the papal dignitary who had come from distant Rome was 'thoroughly English in feature and accent'.[3] One of the most difficult things that Henry Manning had to bear with after his conversion, and his identification with Rome and Wiseman, was a kind of cultural ostracization, in spite of his connection with so many of the governing class in England. The evangelical party was still in ascendancy at mid-century, with the archbishop of Canterbury, J.B. Sumner a member of their school of thought, and they were convinced that it was their mission to Christianize the English people: 'nothing short of a nation united in the fear of the Lord was their aim'.[4] They were not likely to show much tolerance towards a body which offered a religious alternative to their gospel—especially when its worship was 'idolatry' and its leader 'the Antichrist' in Rome.[5]

Manning did win some grudging respect for his involvement as a conciliator in the dock strike of 1889, when he intervened in a situation where up to half the dockers were first generation or immigrant Irish Catholics.[6] Protestant suspicions of Roman Catholicism did not abate, nevertheless but were reinforced by a spurt in the rate of conversions from 1868. Protestant unease increased as the law, the diplomatic service and other professions increasingly tolerated Catholic entrants, and the 1891 elementary education act allowed Catholic schools to become an integral part of the educational system of the country. At the end of his life Manning, a cardinal since 1875, could say with some satisfaction:

> The public feeling and goodwill of England towards the Catholic Faith
> and Church is notably changed for the better. Give it another fifty years
> and... relations with the Vatican will be easily formed.[7]

Manning's successor was his friend and dedicated fellow ultramontanist Herbert Vaughan, a member of an old Catholic gentry family, a grandnephew of a cardinal, who was brought up by the Jesuits. He was no social reformer and his 'ardent chivalrous devotion to the Holy See' brought from one of his critics the wry comment: 'Cardinal Vaughan thinks we can only enter the haven of social salvation in the barque of St. Peter of Rome'.[8] Vaughan was always primarily concerned for the advancement of the faith, was as defensive as Paul Cullen had been over proselytizing, and was deeply suspicious of city missions, ragged schools or soup-kitchens which might 'pervert' the Catholic poor.[9] His sectarian aggressiveness was shown when he chose to receive the pallium in London in 1892, rather than Rome, when he became archbishop of Westminster:

'too good a trump-card against the Anglicans to throw away'.[10] A splendid ceremony took place before a large congregation of dignitaries. The *Daily Chronicle* recognized the event as a triumph for the papal church, while the *Times* viewed the occasion as a mark of a more tolerant public attitude towards Roman Catholicism. It was the first such ceremony in England since the investiture in 1555 of cardinal Pole, in the reign of Mary Tudor.[11]

Several scholars have attributed to Vaughan the rise of the spirit of 'ultramontane triumphalism' in England, and it is true that he looked upon the nation as the 'Dowry of Mary', and his approach to Protestantism was one of demanding 'unconditional surrender to the one true Church'.[12] It was Vaughan who consulted with cardinal Merry del Val when the bull *Apostolicae curae* declared Anglican orders 'utterly null and void' in 1896. As he told one of his correspondents:

> Our missioners will go out as Roman as any Roman and as specially devoted to the Pope. It seems to me that the times and the character of England, and her position in the world, make it clear that the woof must be laid upon the papal warp. In England a strong papal adherance is growing up... it is the safeguard against national tyranny and spiritually it is the building of the Religion of Christ upon the Rock which He has set in Himself.[13]

It is little wonder that Vaughan showed little interest in the talks on reunion begun by the Tractarian lord Halifax and the abbé Fernand Portal.

Viscount Halifax had been an undergraduate in Oxford where he was greatly influenced by Pusey, and his discussions with the abbé Portal were of great interest in Rome, and among Anglican churchmen. When Portal visited England to discuss matters such as the validity of Anglican orders with the archbishop of Canterbury, E.W. Benson and other church leaders, the Anglican primate stressed that at that time the idea of corporate reunion between the Church of England and Rome was entirely out of the question.[14] When Vaughan, who had become a cardinal in 1893, was brought into the conversations he made it clear that his idea of union was a total submission of the Church of England to papal authority. He was, in a speech at Preston, particularly offensive in his remarks about the Tractarians and others who engaged in 'Catholic practices': 'reminding them that St. Jerome had said that the devil was *Simia Dei,* the ape of God'.[15] Vaughan's temper was not helped when, as we will see, the Protestant archbishop of Dublin consecrated a bishop to build up a non-Roman episcopal congregation in Spain.

Roman influence in English Catholic affairs was particularly strong at this period, where the tradition of Manning was reinforced not only by Vaughan but by powerful Roman prelates such as Francis Aidan Gasquet and the future cardinal secretary of state, Merry del Val. The former who was English born and educated was to become a well known scholar of the Reformation, and was made a cardinal in 1914. Merry del Val was also English educated, and their influence in England, through Vaughan: 'so affected the clerical mind that the older tradition of the English Catholic clergy almost disappeared in an act of collective amnesia'.[16] Under Vaughan, not only was there no enthusiasm for religious or ecclesiastical *rapprochement* with the Church of England, but the exclusivity ethos nurtured within English Catholicism ensured that the next cardinal archbishop of Westminster, Francis Bourne, carried on ultramontane policies that were described as 'parochial Romanism at its worst' by the Anglican archbishop of York, Cyril Garbett.[17]

Apart from a minority of Anglo-Catholic intellectuals, the encyclical *Apostolicae curae* condemning Anglican orders as invalid had little affect on the Church of England, although the archbishops of Canterbury and York issued a 'Responsio' which pronounced that its ordination conferred the Office instituted by Christ in all its fullness. There was no hint of apologetic on the part of the Church of England which had given much thought to what constituted 'Catholicity'. Although the evangelical party was now past its time of greatest influence English churchmen, as a whole, were sturdily Protestant and had little sympathy for those among them who showed 'Roman' sympathies. When the archbishop of Canterbury, A.C. Tait, in 1874 drafted a parliamentary bill to suppress the growth of ritualism it was drastically amended in a more Protestant and erastian direction by Lord Shaftesbury, and under its provisions four priests were imprisoned for contumacy. The Church Association, led by evangelical churchmen, was influential enough to have the bishop of Lincoln, Edward King, brought to trial in the court of the archbishop of Canterbury over liturgical abuses, such as using lighted candles in the eucharist and making the sign of the cross. This religious in-fighting within the Church of England, which cardinal Vaughan dismissed as an erastian body was a sign of vitality, and ecclesiastical resurgence. Congresses were held annually until the eve of World War I and they helped to nurture what was a time of flourishing intellectual endeavour. The first Lambeth conference was held in 1867, and every ten years afterwards at the invitation of the archbishop of Canterbury. An increasing number of bishops of the Anglican communion attended the conferences, and ecclesiastically the Church of England entered the twentieth century on a rising tide of expectation. It was now the mother church of a world-wide communion, its influence great among the empire builders of the age, with genius enough to hold together a variety of religious parties, ranging from ultra-Protestant evangelical to extreme Anglo-Catholic. It had a quiet strength. As a church it was conscious of how little it was influencing the working classes which had emerged in the cities of the new industrial age, but its bishops and clergy were displaying an increasing pastoral vitality. Anglican scholars such as F.J.A. Hort, J.B. Lightfoot and B.F. Westcott had an international reputation. Great respect was shown for the Anglican attempt in *Lux Mundi,* the 'advanced' theological study of 1889 to cope with the intellectual and moral problems of a rapidly changing society. In the same year, the founding of the Christian Social Union reflected the deep pastoral concern of a socially relevant church.

Strongly reinforcing the Protestant ethos of the Church of England were the British nonconformist churches, as well as a spirit of revival which both appeared in Wales and helped to heal old divisions within Scottish Presbyterianism. A Methodist divine like Hugh Price Hughes had great social influence, and the Congregationalist preacher R.W. Dale was one of the intellectual leaders among evangelicals. While Christianity faded in influence among some of the intellectuals of the age, a legacy of moral earnestness ensured that a concern for the remoulding of British society according to traditional Christian values was not abandoned. Though the church had more impact on the higher social groups: 'it is quite mistaken to hold that the working classes as a whole were largely untouched by the gospel'.[18] To a remarkable extent late Victorian Britain was influenced by Christian and Protestant values, and the churches still maintained much of their authority of mid-century: 'from the pulpit, whether in church or camp meeting... public opinion was largely educated'.[19]

The nonconformist churches in particular still had great social influence in the lives of the masses of the great industrial centres of Britain, and their missionary societies ensured that many people were helped both religiously and socially, in spite of the growing number of secular social agencies which threatened to supplant them in importance.[20] In Scotland the social importance of Presbyterianism was great between 1860 and 1920 not least because: 'all of the Scottish universities and most of the theological colleges were blessed with theologians of great distinction'.[21] Even the established church which was so frequently the object of nonconformist scorn showed no sign of immediate decline in the years preceding World War I, according to C.F.G. Masterman, a shrewd observer of English affairs:

> In 1830 'the acutest characters of the time' says Mr. Wilfrid Ward, 'considered that the Church of England was on its death-bed'. 'It was folding its robes' was Mozley's verdict, 'to die with what dignity it could'. 'The church as it now stands', wrote Arnold, 'no human power could save'. But today on any impartial judgement the 'Established Church' whatever gains or losses it may have received in the long struggle with indifference and unbelief, would never be threatened with any such suggestions of immediate destruction'.[22]

Although the contending Protestant bodies had their ecclesiastical differences, they were helped to maintain their social authority by presenting a similar version of the gospel which was remarkable for its conservatism, according to some modern critics: 'the ideology of moderate Evangelicalism rationalized and defended the existing social and economic structures of society'.[23] No one could deny the widespread religious and social influence of the gospel in Victorian Britain, however, not least the Irish whose political development was shaped to a significant degree by the religious convictions of someone like W.E. Gladstone, the instigator of both disestablishment of the Church of Ireland and the Home Rule crisis.

II The Church of Ireland Reformed

When in 1868 his mission to disestablish the Church of Ireland became a cause of high moral purpose to Gladstone, most Irish Protestants chose to believe he was bowing to Roman Catholic pressure. Manning had long lectured Gladstone on the iniquities of the Church of Ireland and, just four days before Gladstone announced his intention to proceed with disestablishment, Manning had written a passionate letter to Earl Grey on the subject. His uncompromising ultramontanist viewpoint had been expressed earlier:

> It is not a Church: it is an anti-Catholic religion; it perverts the action
> of the civil power; it has persecuted the Catholic faith; it insults it now
> by lording over it; it poisons and embitters all social life; it is a badge
> of ascendancy...[24]

Cardinal Cullen was believed by the Protestants to be the leader of the Roman 'sacerdotal conspiracy' in Ireland, intent upon humbling the Church of Ireland as a first step towards destroying Irish Protestantism generally and curbing civil liberty.[25] Many Irish Presbyterians were not unhappy to see the dethronement of prelacy, but others shared the belief of Henry Cooke that there was value in establishment inasmuch as it was a sign of the State's commitment to Protestantism, and they viewed Gladstone's decision as a Roman victory if it was implemented:

> The religious supremacy of Rome in Ireland would be assured for the
> Roman Catholic priests are the political as well as the religious leaders
> of the people; the Protestant population would rapidly diminish,
> absenteeism would increase, and the landlords, who are mostly
> Protestant would wherever it is possible become non-resident... and if
> time-honoured institutions are thus swept away, where will the spoiler
> stop?[26]

Cullen sounded almost arrogant as the support of the English nonconformists and some of the Irish Presbyterians promised passage of Gladstone's legislation without much outcry. He told Tobias Kirby in Rome that the disestablishment process had 'shaken Protestantism to its very foundations', and believed that Irish Protestantism: 'has no other hold on its followers than the mere temporal endowments. The great motive is money. Remove this inducement and they will become followers of Rome'.[27] Cullen's opinion of the Church of Ireland was that of most of his Irish Catholic contemporaries, who were sure that soon the Roman communion would emerge as the *de facto* ascendancy church, as papal authority was fully extended in all parts of the island. This was certainly the view of the Dominican preacher, Thomas Burke, who had been a theologian at the Vatican Council, and had preached a series of sermons in Rome. A great favourite of Cullen's, his convictions were those of the cardinal:

> His definition of Irish nationality excluded anything not Catholic and everything English: it banished not only the Protestant but the Anglo-Irish. And it sought to give Ireland's attitude to the relationship with England the aspect of a crusade against the infidel and the heretic.[28]

In the columns of the Catholic-owned newspaper *The Anglo-Celt* on 18 July, 1868 the Church of Ireland was described as 'founded and maintained by swords and bayonets'.

In the build up to disestablishment the Protestants became more and more defensive. In February, 1868 a declaration was signed by nearly a thousand Irish Catholic laymen 'of good social standing' to protest their sense of grievance over the Established Church.[29] So far as the popular press was concerned the British general election of 1868 which brought Gladstone to power was a 'religious' one. The *Gazette* described Roman Catholic priests as subjects of a foreign power.[30] The *Saturday Review* wondered if an ultramontane university was about to be funded by the state, or if the next indignity for the tax-payer would be a demand to help sustain the French garrison in Rome.[31] The *Times* had caustic comments to make on the invitation of Pius IX, at the time of preparation for the Vatican Council, for all non-Catholics to return to the fold.[32] On the eve of the 1868 election a Wicklow parish priest declared the contest 'one purely religious that is to secure the equality on religious grounds of the Catholic millions against a handful of Anglicans'.[33] The Protestants waited anxiously for Gladstone to carry out his 'mission to pacify Ireland'.

It seemed clear to most observers in the 1868–1870 period that Cullen's ultramontane mission was having remarkable success. Even the demand for Fenian amnesty was overshadowed by the enthusiasm of the Irish Catholics for their French co-religionists prior to the Franco-Prussian war.[34] New social legislation, such as the passing of the Industrial Schools Act in 1868, was interpreted as government concession to the Catholics who were 'clawing back power and influence'.[35] A prominent layman of the Church of Ireland poured scorn on talk of seeking 'justice' for the Roman Catholics. What lay behind the changes taking place in the island was the desire to 'conciliate' the majority people, and to surrender them to Roman domination and Catholic ascendancy. This he believed would be a disaster:

> Protestant ascendancy is no doubt bad. But Roman Catholic ascendancy
> is no better... If a great triumph is to be given to one side or the other
> it is not human nature that peace should be the result.[36]

The reaction of the Church of Ireland Protestants to the shock of disestablishment was shaped by their determination to resist the Roman Catholic
movement towards ascendancy, as well as by their own continuing position of
economic and social strength. In their communion were nearly all the great Irish
landowners, the bulk of the landed gentry, and a high proportion of the
professional and business classes. Most of their strength was in Ulster and
Leinster, but the influence of the Church of Ireland was considerable in most
parts of the country. Its clergy were almost all university graduates who took
seriously their role as resident gentlemen, and often they were connected by
family ties with the landed gentry. They had sustaining them ideologically a
'high' doctrine of their church, which they stoutly maintained had its origins in
the mission of St. Patrick.[37] At the same time the Church of Ireland generally
was strongly evangelical in its ethos, intent upon 'saving souls' through the
liberating power of the gospel; offering to the people a spiritual alternative to
what was imposed upon them by the papacy: 'a servile submission to authority
in word and action'.[38] In terms of its clerical manpower the Church of Ireland at
the time of disestablishment was blessed with leadership that, in the eyes of contemporaries, was dedicated and effective. The primate was the cautious but well-
respected M.G. Beresford; the archbishop of Dublin was the scholarly New Testament prelate, Richard Chenevix Trench; William Alexander of Derry was
renowned as a preacher and a poet; C.B. Bernard of Tuam, brother of the earl of
Bandon was judged to be an exemplary pastoral bishop; and the respected
scholars of the time included Samuel Butcher, bishop of Meath, William Lee,
archdeacon of Dublin and strongly Protestant George Salmon, famous for his
lectures on the *Infallibility of the Church* which were published in 1888 as a
defence against the tenets of the Church of Rome.

The Church of Ireland was at the time of disestablishment also fortunate that
the economic situation in the country ensured that the relatively affluent
Protestant landlords and gentry were able to contribute both money and time for
its support. The tensions which were to bring about the Land War and Home
Rule had not yet begun to disturb the countryside, and they were in a position
and a frame of mind to give generous support to what was to remain the most
influential and enduring of all the institutions of the old ascendancy—if only
because the Church of Ireland claimed allegiance from its people in all thirty-two
counties. Moreover its members shared in a unifying deeply felt communal
resentment of what Gladstone and the British government had inflicted upon
them. William Connor Magee, who had been dean of Cork, as bishop of

Peterborough expressed their prevailing sentiment well when he told the House
of Lords during the disestablishment debate:

> Irish Protestants will say that though they have been ever the faithful
> and devoted servants of England... you are now about to cast them off
> without even a kind word of gratitude for... faithful and devoted
> loyalty.[39]

In spite of this kind of rancour, which was common among churchmen during
the period between the royal assent to disestablishment on 20 July, 1869 and the
act coming into effect on 1 January, 1871, the Church of Ireland set about
showing what it could do with its new-found freedom from state control.

Setting its constitutional house in order began with a united synod of the
two provinces, Armagh and Dublin, in St. Patrick's Cathedral on 14 September,
1869 in what was in effect a revived Convocation. This was followed by a
General Convention beginning the following February, and it was here that the
vast majority of the clergy commuted the annuities due to them by disestablishment, thereby giving the newly established Representative Church Body
additional capital with which to operate. With this and other matters of a
temporal nature decided, the convention faced the real problem for the Church of
Ireland—the form of religious and ecclesiastical identity it was to assume. The
early 1870's were a trying time in England as well as Ireland as the anti-Ritualist
forces engaged in bitter strife, and archbishop Trench and other strong churchmen
feared a purging of the Church of Ireland of what some of its ultra-Protestant
laity considered to be the taint of subversive popery within it. On 18 July, 1870
the dogma of papal infallibility was defined and promulgated at the Vatican
Council, and there was considerable anxiety that the ultra-Protestants, such as
William Brooke, master of the Court of Chancery, might demand a reorganization of the Church of Ireland that would separate it from the rest of the
Anglican Communion. Master Brooke, in particular, wanted a 'declaration of
our common principles':

> We declare our adherence to the principles of the Reformation, and our
> resolution, so far as in us lies, to maintain the Church of Ireland as a
> Scriptural, Protestant, Episcopal and undivided National Church...[40]

Brooke and his followers wanted also in the first meeting of General Synod in
1871 to 'declare the doctrines' of the Church of Ireland on matters like 'real
presence' in the eucharist, auricular confession, and priestly absolution.

Many churchmen were concerned about division between north and south in
Ireland, as well as a straining of relations with the Church of England if the
militant Protestants had their way in reforming the Church of Ireland. There had
already been a public outcry over liturgical changes introduced in three Dublin

parishes. William Maturin of All Saints, Grangegorman had been admonished in the court of the archbishop of Dublin for saying public prayers with his back to the people, intoning the service, and bowing to the Lord's table. In England a leading Ritualist, and contributor to the *Church Times* was an Irish priest, R.F. Littledale; one of the saints of the Ritualist movement in England, Robert Dolling, was Irish born;[41] and it was genuinely feared by some that a 'popish' fifth column threatened even the Church of Ireland. While Irish churchmen deliberated the future of their church a series of legal actions were taking place in England against the 'advanced' liturgical practices of Rev. W.J.E. Bennett, and the Irish revision of the Prayer Book committee held up its proceedings until the Bennett judgment was delivered.[42] Attendance at committee meetings was large, a reflection of laity having the time and interest to attend, as well as the resolve not to leave the shape of the church to be determined by the bishops and the clergy. Feelings ran high in the many meetings held until 1877, and as some evangelicals like J.N. Griffin praised the 'protestantism' of the Prayer Book of 1552,[43] more liberal churchmen such as George Salmon became very concerned as they realized the comprehensiveness of the Church of Ireland was 'in serious peril'.[44]

The passion of the time was revealed by the attacks made on archbishop Trench in what became known as 'the Maberly affair'. Just before the revision committee began its deliberations Trench had been asked to condemn a manual for confirmation preparation which had been given to a servant girl of a partisan Protestant. When he refused to do so, on the grounds that would make him: 'the ignoble instrument of narrowing the limits of our church', the uproar was immense. The Protestant concerned was L.F.S. Maberly, a Dublin layman, who had once worshipped in Christ Church, Belfast, notorious for the anti-Catholic activities of its rector, Thomas Drew. To Maberly and other ultra-Protestants Trench's 'comprehensiveness' was a 'vile assimilation to the fallen Church of Rome'.[45] Vestry meetings were held throughout the country to discuss the affair, with their deliberations widely reported by the press, yet few churchmen were critical of the stance taken by the archbishop.[46] Although his close work with Catholic priests during a cholera epidemic resulted in his being described as 'a satellite of Cullen's',[47] few Irish churchmen doubted his Protestant credentials. Not only was he of Huguenot descent, and a student of the Reformation and the seventeenth century wars of religion, he had also met with Garibaldi at Gladstone's house. He had vigorously opposed disestablishment, and the real reason for the antipathy shown towards him by the ultra-Protestants was his 'tactlessness throughout the debates' when the Prayer Book revision process took place.[48]

The debates revealed much about the formation of the Protestant mind among the leaders of the Church of Ireland at this time. Leaders appeared like Colonel F.J. Saunderson, an Orangeman and a Unionist M.P. who was married to the daughter of the evangelical lord Farnham. A flamboyant individual he was constantly before the public, once in 1893 for calling a priest a 'murderous ruffian'. He was supported by Charles Reichel, who in 1885 became bishop of Meath. Reichel had a Moravian background, and had had his life threatened after trouble with the Roman church when he was rector of Mullingar in the 1860's. He had sympathy for many of Saunderson's opinions, but in the debates he showed himself to be a highly intelligent moderate although: 'he strove with all his might to have deleted from the Prayer Book any words which might seem to give sanction to the revival of the confessional'.[49]   Other moderates in the Prayer Book discussions were Sir Joseph Napier and Arthur MacMurrough Kavanagh. An important clerical figure on the conservative traditionalist side was Richard Travers Smith who as rector of St. Bartholomew's, Dublin, was to win considerable notoriety for his Ritualist sympathies. A skilled and respected theologian he did much to persuade the 'high church' party to accept the 1878 Prayer Book when it was finally approved and produced.[50]

To an amazing degree the Church of Ireland following disestablishment put its house in order, not only in temporalities with the establishment of the Representative Church Body but in spiritual concerns following lengthy debates over liturgy and theology, and the appearance of the revised Prayer Book of 1878. In fact, after an exercise of common sense leadership by *via media* churchmen, there were few significant changes in the doctrinal and liturgical expressions of the Church of Ireland, though generally its form of worship became less austere. The extreme Protestants did have success in curbing the authority of the clergy, however, and in matters such as clerical appointments the laity in the Church of Ireland emerged with a strong voice. Yet lay tyranny, feared by some of the bishops,[51] was avoided, as was a division between churchmen of the north and of the south. Nor was there any movement for the church to identify itself wholly with an Ulster-based pan-Protestant movement. The 'high church' ideology of William Fitzgerald, bishop of Killaloe and Samuel Butcher, bishop of Meath had great influence during the debates,[52] and by the end of the century the ethos of the Church of Ireland was a paradoxical one of 'high church' and evangelical sentiment.

Another ecclesiastical bogey laid to rest during the post-disestablishment period was the possible development of a significant Ritualist movement within the Church of Ireland, which had been long dreaded by the ultra-Protestants: 'the evil leaven of Anglican popery is surely though it may be slowly extending its influence in our Irish Church'.[53]   The dedication of the laity instead found expression in a great surge of church activity, with cathedrals built or refurbished in Cork, Kildare, Derry, Connor and Dromore, and a new interest to improve traditional worship. Cross-channel customs inevitably had influence on the Church of Ireland and innovations began to appear in worship:

> Three-deckers were swept away, the black gown well nigh altogether abolished, the holy communion more frequently celebrated, the psalms

chanted, the holy days of the Church better observed, public worship more reverently conducted—all these and other more important advances.[54]

There was some anti-Ritualist protest, of course, inspired by the restoration of Christ Church Cathedral in Dublin, which was financed by a wealthy distiller, who also paid for the building of the Synod Hall. His architect was an enthusiastic medievalist and soon the ultra-Protestants were protesting about: 'pictures, crosses, rood-screens and other paraphernalia of the Church of Rome... symbols of idolatry'.[55] The ultra-Protestants did help to ensure that the distiller was not elected to general synod, and so he was deprived the pleasure of sitting in the hall he had built.[56]

The most prolonged anti-Ritualist protest was carried out in the parish of St. Bartholomew in Ballsbridge, Dublin. The church was opened in 1866, at the time when followers of the Protestant fanatic, Rev. Tresham Dames Gregg, were trying to prohibit the introduction of a semi-choral service in St. Bride's, in Dublin.[57] This was at the height of the Fenian era when 'popish plot' hysteria heightened Protestant sensibilities, and from the beginning of its existence St. Bartholomew's services were under scrutiny by those who viewed the new church as the 'barque of ritualism... in our archepiscopal see'.[58] Richard Travers Smith, who had emerged as a conservative theological leader during the Prayer Book revision battle, became vicar in 1871, and it was during his time at St. Bartholomew's that a prolonged struggle was carried on over the place where a brass cross might be placed in the chancel without it being seen as an object of adoration 'in true Roman fashion'. The correspondence columns of the Dublin daily papers were filled with comment on the 'Outrage in St. Bartholomew's Church' until the turn of the century,[59] not least when a sisterhood for education of girls was associated with the parish from 1876. In England in the same period there was the same agitation over the practices of the Ritualists which most churchmen ridiculed:

> The Anglo-Catholics were constantly accused of being the Holy Father's fifth column within the Anglican citadel. The accusation was silly but believed.[60]

Surrounded as they were by a large and generally unsympathetic Roman Catholic population such a charge against the Ritualists was considered 'silly' by very few Protestants in Ireland. There was never much enthusiasm for the development of Ritualism in the Church of Ireland, when fear of cultural and religious assimilation was great.

The middle ground in churchmanship was held by Dr. George Salmon, one of the great provosts of Trinity College, Dublin between 1888 and 1904, who had previously been regius professor of divinity. The year he became provost he produced his most famous work, *Infallibility of the Church,* a profound work which had great influence among many churchmen. A defence of Protestant principles against the Church of Rome the work showed his convinced Protestant beliefs which influenced whatever he engaged in. He objected, for example, to a transfer of the divinity school at Trinity to the Representative Church Body, lest it lead to the creation of a 'Protestant Maynooth'. He also consistently opposed Home Rule which, he feared, would advance the cause of Rome in Ireland. In many ways he represented the essence of Irish Protestantism in his generation: 'a strong protestant, averse to sentimentality, quick to scrutinize the claims of ecclesiastical authority and contemptuous of ritualism'.[61]

At times the anti-Roman Protestant Church of Ireland was a trial to Anglo-Catholics like lord Halifax who was 'exasperated' by the interest taken by Irish churchmen like W.C. Plunket in ecclesiastical affairs in Spain, at the time that he was attempting to promote an improvement in Anglican-Roman relations, during his communications with the abbé Portal in the last decade of the century. W.C. Plunket, who had become archbishop of Dublin in 1885 had worked in Protestant missions in the west of Ireland, and was a friend of Alexander Dallas the founder and director of the Irish Church Missions. It was Dallas who introduced him to the existence of a small reformed episcopal church in Spain which had begun to emerge following the revolution of 1868 and the granting of religious liberty. One of the leaders of the Spanish Reformed Church was an ex-Roman priest, Juan B. Cabrera. Plunket became the patron of Cabrera and the Spanish Reformed Church translating its liturgy into English, and promoting its cause in England, Ireland and America.[62] In 1894 Plunket with two other Irish bishops after consultation with the general synod, went to Spain to consecrate Señor Cabrera as bishop. He had earlier ordained a priest for the Lusitanian church, a Protestant body, in Portugal. From the time of Plunket until 1963 when the Spanish Reformed Church and the Lusitanian Church were received into full communion with the Church of Ireland a kind of general oversight of the Iberian Protestant bodies was maintained, much to the annoyance of those who opposed any movement which by its very existence underlined the 'evils of Romanism'.[63]

Even the 'high church' prelates at the time of this 'Spanish scandal' showed clearly their Protestant bias, however unhappy they might be in theory over bishops wandering into dioceses with which they had no legal connection. William Alexander of Derry would only say that the proposed consecration was a 'very difficult and delicate one', while Robert Knox, the primate expressed what was probably the feelings of most Irish churchmen when he said:

> I cannot bring myself to turn my back on any movement which results
> in coming out from the Church of Rome, especially in Spain, steeped
> in ignorance and superstition.[64]

At the heart of the Irish Protestant response to Roman Catholicism was a deep-seated suspicion of what Rome might perpetrate in Ireland if ever there it obtained the free hand that it had known in places like Spain and Portugal. W.C. Plunket admitted in 1870 that one of the reasons he wanted Romanists to attend Trinity College was his fear that the state would set up an alternative Roman Catholic institution which: 'would... quench free thought and poison the fountains of truth by its Ultramontane influences'.[65]

III   The Land War and the Plan of Campaign

The great classical scholar, J.P. Mahaffy, who became provost of Trinity College in 1914, lived in County Monaghan as a boy and held a warm regard for 'the delightful sympathetic Roman Catholic peasants' whom he contrasted with Protestant tenants on his mother's estate. Yet he found himself inevitably siding with his own people, their culture and religion, in a country where the people were radically divided:

> As long as Roman catholics and protestants exist in Ireland it marks and emphasizes the contrast not only of two creeds, but two breeds, of two ways of thinking, of two ways of looking at all the most vital interests of men. The whole temper of the two is totally at variance —the one based on authority, the other on the right of private judgment.[66]

Mahaffy's mind was typical of that of the Protestants of his generation and class which accepted the inevitability of conflict between the two peoples who, because of mutual suspicion, and perennial struggle over matters like land and religion, felt themselves perpetually estranged from each other:

> The pure Celt, who is always a Catholic, has less regard for truth than the Protestant, with his touch of Saxon breeding. Secondly, the long oppression of the Roman Catholics, and their enforced separation from Protestant society, has created a clan feeling, which in times of what one side translate as faith towards country and religion, the other call traitorous betrayal of friends and relations.[67]

The division between Catholics and Protestants were clearly shown during the period of the Land War of 1879–1882. Gladstone's Land Act of 1870 revealed that the British government could be persuaded to intervene in the land question on the side of the tenants, and when he was returned to power in 1880 he indicated he was willing to prepare another land bill. This was at a time when landlords were active in evicting tenants who had defaulted in their rent, the political Home Rule movement was allying itself with rural agitation, and the Protestant landlord and gentry classes felt as threatened as they had during the Tithe War years of the 1830's. Under the leadership of Charles Stewart Parnell who pressed for agrarian reform as well as Home Rule in parliament, and the social agitation promoted by Michael Davitt in the countryside, ordinary law was paralyzed. Davitt formed a National Land League in 1879 to direct his rural campaign, and from the beginning it was: 'predominantly a Catholic-based organization, and... Protestants often tended to shun or oppose it'.[68] By 1880 a Clonakilty landlord, William Bence-Jones got Orange workers from Bandon and county Cavan to help him survive the 'boycott' of his farm operations by the Land League, following the precedent set by Charles Boycott, land agent for lord Erne's estate on Lough Mask. Most of the Catholic bishops and priests had doubts about the moral aspect of the land campaign, although archbishop Walsh of Dublin and Croke of Cashel were hailed as 'patriot bishops', and to the Protestant landlord class what they faced was a campaign in which sectarian influences were clearly at work. A propaganda war against the agitation was led by the *Dublin Evening Mail,* and an Orange Emergency Committee was set up by the Grand Orange Lodge of Ireland. In spite of such defensive organization many Protestant families decided to leave Ireland.

There was little panic among the Protestants of Ulster, however, and wherever the Land League tried to establish itself in the north it was faced with the resolutely adversarial stance of the Orange Order. Violent incidents in Monaghan and Fermanagh in 1883 where the Land League tried to establish their programme in several areas, led to confrontation by Protestants determined to put themselves on a war-footing. By 1883 violent incidents in the Ulster border counties was common:

> Politicization formalized the old divides; rural violence called upon the ancient reactions of local vigilante groups; landlords organized frontier patrols and proclaimed their right to 'drill'.[69]

Especially during the last quarter of the nineteenth century Ireland was greatly divided by the issues of land and religion which had always separated its contending peoples. Home Rule was the dominant political issue of the time, and its affect on the shaping of the Protestant mind of the time was enormous, as we will see when we consider next the challenge of Parnellism. The political struggle was largely fought in Westminster, however, and to the Irish Protestants their immediate concern was the strife over the land. So far as they were concerned the rural agitation which was to culminate in the Plan of Campaign from 1886 was obviously directed on the local level by the priests: 'no deputation to the "big house" was complete without at least one priest'.[70] When the Land League first established itself in Barnstown, county Wexford, the farm labourers complained bitterly over their neglect by the priests who were overly involved in land demonstrations. The Protestant landlords, remembering the pressure tactics which O'Connell and Cullen had used so successfully in previous generations, recognized the tactic of the 'priest handlers': grant the concessions we demand on behalf of the people or face the wrath of the peasantry. What was promised the landlords by their recalcitrant tenants was now more sophisticated than the rick-burning intimidation of the Whiteboy era, but because it was organized it was more threatening. Under the Plan of Campaign the dissatisfied tenants on particular estates combined to offer the landlord their version of a fair rent. If this was refused, they paid him nothing; instead they contributed the proposed sum to an estate fund which would be employed for the protection of tenants in the event of landlord retaliation.

There was now no Paul Cullen to control the political activities of the priests who formed a third of the Land League's country conventions. The unrest of the 1880's allowed the Catholic clergy to reveal their anti-English prejudice and their scorn of contemporary authority including the magistrates, the police and the military. In Tipperary no less than 77% of the total priesthood played some public part in politics from 1850 to 1891.[71] An occasional bishop in the 1880's like Edward O'Dwyer of Limerick, or Pierse Power of Waterford, opposed the Plan of Campaign but most were willing to go along with the rural unrest, convinced that what they tacitly supported were 'measures essential to the religious interests of the nation'.[72] Amidst the unrest some threatening clerical figures emerged, and most Protestants of the landlord class directly experienced some form of intimidation. Lord Ernest Hamilton recorded the actions of the local priest 'the bitterest Nationalist of all North Tyrone' who crossed himself and spat when any member of the Hamilton family passed him.[73] Militant Protestants naturally reacted, and most would have agreed with Dawson Massy of Carlow who had earlier argued that behind the religious intransigence was a well-organized campaign by the Roman Catholic bishops who were intent upon a 'land-grab':

> They wield their millions of ignorant devotees by hopes of regaining their lost lands; so that agrarian violence underlies the whole history of Irish agitation, often local, sometimes swelling into dangerous outbreaks, or rising to the dignity of civil war.[74]

Unfortunately for peace in the land the *engagé* priests did much more than cross themselves or spit on the ground when they met protestant landlords. In 1869 the Fenian influence had been such in the church that Odo Russell, the unofficial English representative to the Holy See, had evidence enough to press cardinal Antonelli for the suspension of two priests, Lavelle and Ryan. The latter had *inter alia* allegedly said: 'The people must kill the landlords as one kills partridges in September'.[75] This was at a time when the papacy was about to lose its temporal power in Italy, and though he had no sympathy with revolutionaries Pius IX chose to leave Cullen to use his legatine office to chastise the turbulent Lavelle and Ryan. The situation was different in the 1880's when the Roman Catholics in England were being increasingly tolerated, and the Vatican was generally worried about how to control the political activities of the Irish bishops and clergy, although it was still willing to use the Irish unrest as a diplomatic bargaining power. Leo XIII wanted a diplomatic relationship with London that would bring him help in his campaign to win back the papal states, and a great concern for him was how to apologize for the statements of outspoken 'patriot' bishops such as archbishops William Walsh of Dublin, or Thomas Croke of Cashel. As the agrarian agitation continued, however, and it became clear how much the Roman Catholic clergy were involved in the unrest, the pope and the Roman authorities had to give priority to the moral implications of what was happening in Ireland.

Leo could not ignore the 'irrefutable proof', passed on to Rome by members of the English hierarchy, of outrages such as the assassination of people 'named from the altar' by priests, and the Irish hierarchy's apparent toleration of a widespread use of threats and violence which amounted to organized terror. Rome's fear was that the outrages in Ireland would inevitably bring about an English protestant backlash—a reaction suggested by Mgr. Laird Patterson who was close to the government:

> Lord Salisbury himself, the descendent of Cecil and Burleigh, stated only two years ago most generously that the English are ashamed of their persecution of the Catholics in the past. That is the general attitude in England today. But now, with this behaviour of the Irish priests—how long will this favourable attitude continue? It is a long time since we heard in England the fanatical cry, 'Down with Popery'! But if these Irish Catholic priests go on behaving as they do, we may well hear it again.[76]

Some of the Irish hierarchy were also alarmed over the turmoil in the countryside, and both John Healy of Clonfert and Edward O'Dwyer complained to Rome about the evils of boycotting and other priestly activities in the Plan of Campaign. Finally, when an English mission arrived in Rome headed by the duke of Norfolk, seeking Roman intervention, Leo XIII decided that he had to bow to the growing demand for some kind of mediation.

The papal intervention when it came was a well-considered one, reflecting the insights produced by the legatine mission conducted by Mgr. Ignatius Persico, a member of the Capuchin order, who had been for many years a leading figure in Propaganda Fidei. He arrived in Dublin on 7 July, 1887, stayed a week, and formed an impression of William Walsh, and other 'patriots', that was passed on to Rome in one of his despatches:

The public meets the Archbishop daily—not in person, but in the news-papers, either in the form of letters to the editor, or in articles. The latter deal mostly with political and literary matters, rarely with religious ones.[77]

Persico visited Belfast which he found quiet and orderly, with respect and deference shown to his person. Wherever he went he had criticism to make of the bishops: the bishop of Waterford and Lismore he found to be an alcoholic; the bishop of Dromore, aged, paralyzed and not in his right mind; the bishop of Killaloe was decrepit, a permanent invalid living in Paris; the bishop of Cloyne was totally deaf; the bishop of Clonfert displayed 'mental aberration'. Con-sidering such physical limitations suffered by so many members of the hierarchy Persico could well understand how a strong bishop like Walsh could dominate proceedings: 'Woe to any bishop who does not think like the Archbishop of Dublin'. When he got to Cashel he found Thomas Croke to have a 'mania for politics', a bitter resentment of the English, and to be the patron of a junior curate, Matthew Ryan who had published a popular work entitled *The Sacred Duty of Revolution*. By the end of 1887 Persico was able to send Rome his general report which portrayed the priests as the dupes of secular nationalist leaders:

The Fenian leaders make no secret of their hostility to Catholicism. However, as long as the priest is prepared to march with them, they take advantage of him and use him; but the moment he hesitates they execrate him and dismiss him as unpatriotic.

So far as he could determine: 'the Episcopacy which, largely out of timidity, makes no attempt to swim against the current' was, like the rest of the clergy, 'following not leading the people'.[78]

By the time Persico's mission was completed the legate decided that the bishops were 'cold and hostile' towards him. The *Freeman's Journal* of 17 December, 1887 accused him of collaborating with the English government in return for the establishment of diplomatic relations between the Holy See and the Court of St. James, as well as an endowment of a Catholic university in Ireland. *The Pall Mall Gazette* opined on 16 December, 1887:

The English government is using the Papal Legate as a coercionist catspaw. In short, the English Government's aim is to prevent Home Rule by Rome Rule.

Few of his critics who anticipated what he would report to Rome were surprised when a papal rescript condemned the violence in Ireland with a wealth of detail that could only have come from the legate. The decree was unequivocal in its condemnation of both the Plan of Campaign and the tactic of boycotting. It was a tremendous shock to the Irish 'patriots', reminiscent of O'Connell's tensions with Rome over the question of the Veto: 'the nationalists accused the government of "drawing a veil" over the pope's eyes in order to succor rack-renting landlords'.[79] As for Persico's direct contribution to the making or issuing of the decree historians have had conflicting opinions,[80] but the legate himself was horrified when a suggestion was made that he return to Ireland. He told cardinal Rampolla bluntly:

> There is absolutely no point in my returning. It would only arouse further suspicion against the Holy Father. They would say I am interfering again and it would, I am sure, produce a conflagration. The representative of the Holy Father would be exposed to a thousand insults. In fact they would stone me.[81]

The problem for the Irish hierarchy was how they would respond to the papal rescript. The leadership was given by William J. Walsh who had become archbishop of Dublin in 1885 after serving as president of Maynooth where he was considered to be a natural leader and an intellectual with many talents. A 'firm nationalist' he had quickly established an ascendancy over the other bishops, and he was welcomed by the Parnellites and the people generally. It was early rumoured that George Errington, the British emissary in Rome, had opposed his appointment and this gave him immediate credentials with the nationalists. In fact the major influence in the pope's decision seems to have been cardinal Manning who had reminded the pontiff of Irish reaction if he had even seemed: 'to be swayed by English influence'.[82] Walsh was in Rome at the time the decree appeared, and he was in a quandary when he heard of it, after it was given papal approval: 'the whole thing is deplorable. It is hard to say what ought to be done'.[83]

The response of the nationalist clergy was developed by T.W. Croke the redoubtable archbishop of Cashel. Although his mother had been a Protestant, and she and Croke's sisters resisted conversion for many years, Croke and two brothers became priests. He studied at the Irish College, Paris, then the Irish College in Rome where he was influenced by Paul Cullen. He wrote a thesis entitled 'The Moral Power of the Pope', strongly supported papal infallibility in 1870, and during the short time he was bishop of Auckland he displayed suitable ultramontane discipline in ordering diocesan affairs. When he was given the Cashel appointment in 1875 Rome ignored the names suggested by the Irish church in its *terna,* and when he arrived in Ireland he was the object of considerable suspicion as the friend of cardinal Simeoni of Propaganda, and of Paul Cullen. Croke was aware that he should not put a foot wrong, and for the two years after his appointment he remained very much under the shadow of cardinal Cullen. His strongly nationalist sentiments were brought out by the Fenian question during the last year of Cullen's life, however, and he had good things to say about the impoverished Fenian poet and author, Charles J. Kickham.

With the death of Cullen Croke felt free to express his ardent nationalism, and he entered more and more into the public eye from the autumn of 1879 onwards. When he did so he filled the Protestant landlords with alarm over his open support of rural agitation, and he also caught the attention of the authorities in Rome, particularly in 1883 when he wrote a letter to the *Freeman's Journal* on 8 January, supporting the patriotic editor of *United Ireland* in a Mallow election campaign. His political activity was brought to the attention of Propaganda by George Errington in Rome shortly afterwards, and Croke was rebuked by cardinal Simeoni: 'to refrain in future from such activities, otherwise the Holy See may have to take more active steps to obtain obedience to its instructions'.[84] That Croke did not take the Roman admonition seriously became clear when in the *Freeman's Journal* of 17 March, 1883 he advocated raising a tribute to Parnell, who was then in financial difficulties. The Protestant landlords had by now identified Croke as the most nationalist of all the Catholic bishops, and the authorities made sure his venture was brought to the attention of the Vatican, where the question was reportedly asked: 'whether the Pope or Dr. Croke is to rule in Ireland'.[85] By the time the Plan of Campaign began Croke encouraged political agitation openly and he particularly supported one of his priests, the revolutionary-minded curate of Hospital, Matthew Ryan whose militant activities and writings earned him the sobriquet 'The General'. When this 'lieutenant in the church of Christ' was sent to Kilmainham prison Croke was unswerving in his defence of the bullying Ryan who: 'boasted of the alleged fright and financial ruin of the landlords, a belief strongly supported by Croke himself'.[86] There is no doubt that in the period of the Plan of Campaign the Protestants of many parts of Ireland did share both 'fright' and the fear of 'financial ruin', and their sense of being in a state of siege deepened.

Cardinal Manning used his influence to help Croke in Rome, but the authorities there were uneasy when it was reported that another of Croke's priests, Arthur Ryan, openly praised revolution in terms which might have been used by Mazzini, Garibaldi and other leaders of the *Risorgimento:*

Rebellion against tyrannous misgovernment is, the wide world over, a sacred duty. Irishmen bless it, and Irish priests and Irish bishops bless it, and declare it to be high and unassailable morality—a holy war in the cause of the poor and oppressed... We give our glad 'God speed' to what promises to be, at long last, a successful Plan of Campaign.[87]

Even before the rescript was considered for publication Rome was preparing a dossier 'Concerning the Latest Affairs in Ireland',[88] and the impressions given by Persico concerning Walsh, Croke and other nationalist bishops, as well as the ferocious intimidation throughout the country confirmed what was already known in Propaganda. When the papal decree arrived, and Walsh confessed he was not sure how to respond to it, Croke began an exercise to vindicate himself. He urged 'filial respect for the Sovereign Pontiff'; forbade the clergy to attend meetings supporting the Plan of Campaign or boycotting; and he told Matthew Ryan to shut up. His great fear was that the Irish church would come under the: 'apparently sinister influence of the Holy Office or the Secretariat of State'.[89] The result was a decline in the number of boycottings, although the Plan of Campaign continued unabated in Croke's dioceses. When he wrote Propaganda Croke suggested that through interference by the papal secretary of state Roman officials were now deciding Irish affairs of which they were ignorant.[90] Rome had thoroughly dampened the growing clerical involvement in the Plan of Campaign. In Ireland bishop O'Dwyer of Limerick risked the vilification heaped upon him by the nationalists and proclaimed the Plan of Campaign morally wrong. He also withdrew from priests of Limerick the authority to absolve penitents who continued to support the Plan.[91] The nationalists, of course, protested and John Dillon in a speech at Drogheda scoffed at the idea that the papal rescript indicated Rome rule in Ireland:

> We owe it to our friends in England, we owe it to the ancient traditions of our country, we owe it to our Protestant fellow countrymen who expect they are about to share with us a free Ireland... that it will not be an Ireland that will conduct its affairs at the bidding of any body of cardinals.[92]

The Roman authority in Ireland was in Protestant eyes always a threatening force, however, and they saw in the Persico mission a confirmation that the authority of the papacy in Irish Catholic affairs was now permanently established. The revolution carried out by Paul Cullen in his long legatine mission was not about to be overthrown by any Irish ecclesiastical authority. Irish nationalists sometimes refer to the Persico era as a 'Roman interlude' which in no significant way interfered with the control of insular Irish affairs by the hierarchy. To the Protestants, however, the periodic explosions of patriotic passion were the real times of historical 'interlude'. The British government in 1920 was to be assured enough of Roman authority in Ireland that it requested from the Holy See another replay of 1887, with the coming of another 'Persico mission' to control the crisis of that time. After Cullen Roman authority was an abiding reality in Irish affairs that no one could afford to ignore. Certainly Parnell and his followers paid heed to it in the late 1880's. The Plan of Campaign continued for another two years, as a complicating and exasperating political issue but its influence was limited. Parnell disassociated himself from the land question, at the cost of division with his chief supporters John Dillon and William O'Brien.

IV   Parnellism and Protestantism

Paul Cullen would not have been surprised at the appeal of someone like Dillon to the Protestants; he was apt to lump together as threats to the Roman Catholic authority any revolutionary movement, such as that of the Garibaldians or Fenians. When the Fenians were driven 'underground' he told Tobias Kirby in Rome:

> The Fenians are coalescing with the ultra-Protestants. Their cry now is that we should give a share in all public Catholic institutions and in their government to Protestants. Here in Dublin they made an attempt to put in five Protestants as managers of a Catholic hospital... They are also joining the Protestants in favour of mixed education.[93]

When Home Rule ideas began to emerge Cullen interpreted Isaac Butt and others as Tory Orangemen trying to get into parliament by playing the patriot game. They were not the men who would serve Catholic causes: denominational education, closing of the Queen's colleges, obtaining a charter for the Catholic University, or supporting Pio Nono in his battle with Bismarck in Germany. To Cullen the early Home Rulers threatened to revive the chaos of the Young Ireland era, when anti-Roman figures like Edward Lucas and Charles Gavan Duffy had been guilty of: 'promoting a revolution against religion by trying to undermine the bishops' authority to discipline their priests'.[94] Cullen did not fail to notice in Butt, his next-door neighbour on Eccles Street in the 1868 period, an anti-Roman prejudice which was common among his Protestant contemporaries: 'he was the very type of ultra-domineering narrow-minded Protestant ascendancy'.[95] As he told Manning: 'the principal leaders in the movement here are professors of Trinity College and Orangemen who are still worse'.[96] Cullen had no intention of allowing some secular-directed *agitazione* to appear in Ireland if he could help it, to produce perhaps some Protestant nationalist leader who would contest the Roman control which Cullen was so successfully imposing on church and culture. When W.J. O'Neill Daunt became secretary to the Home Rule association in 1873 he said of the cardinal:

> ... not only does he not help, but actually thwarts the home rulers. Not a priest in his diocese except two has ventured to join our association up to this time; and of these two, one has withdrawn his adhesion.[97]

From Cullen's ultramontane standpoint there was much to justify his suspicion of the Home Rulers. He was able to curb the political proclivities of the clergy under his immediate authority, but in the general election of February 1874, which returned fifty-nine Home Rule members, the priests frequently ignored the influence of their bishops and were very active in the election. Sometimes the clergy divided over the choice of candidates, and in one heated meeting in Mayo, which even John MacHale could not control, the clergy were groaned and cheers were given for Bismarck and King William.[98] It was at this time that Gladstone brought out his anti-Roman *Vatican Decrees in their Bearing on Civil Allegiance* where he vented his criticism of what had been accomplished in Vatican Council I: 'the Rome of the Middle Ages claimed universal monarchy. The modern Church of Rome has abandoned nothing, retracted nothing'.[99] A bitter controversy with Manning followed over the question of Roman Catholic civil obedience. At that time the O'Keeffe case was also coming to an end in Ireland, and the contention of Fr. Robert O'Keeffe that ultramontane doctrines taught in Ireland were incompatible with civil loyalty, seemed to agree with what Gladstone was saying.[100] The 1874 period to Paul Cullen was a time of ideological confrontation, and he saw nothing in the new Home Rule movement which would give heart to the ultramontane cause which was the basis of his whole existence.

Fortunately for Paul Cullen he knew comparatively little about Charles Stewart Parnell who only entered parliament in 1875 and three years later, the time of Cullen's death, he was not yet ascendant over Isaac Butt. If Cullen had known of the anti-Catholic background of the Protestant landlord who was to emerge as the 'uncrowned king' of Ireland he would have been greatly dismayed. The family had come to Ireland at the time of the Restoration, and been influential enough in the late eighteenth century for Sir John Parnell to become chancellor of the Irish Exchequer. No friend of the Catholics prior to when they got the franchise in 1793 he had even defended the penal laws. Charles Stewart Parnell's grandfather who had been a member of parliament for Wicklow just before the rise of O'Connell had considered: 'the Popish religion as the most formidable source of slavery and superstition that has sprung from the abuse of religion'.[101] The influence of the Plymouth Brethren was strong in the next generation and C.S. Parnell's father, especially when he visited Mexico, showed an: 'attitude to Roman Catholicism' which was 'hostile in the extreme'. The religious impulse seems to have disappeared among Parnell's siblings, except for his sister Fanny who embraced a peculiar attachment to ultramontanism which led her to write adulatory poems to the pope, archbishop T.W. Croke and other Catholic figures.[102] As for Parnell himself, the most reserved and laconic of men, the judgment of his contemporaries was that any religious tendency he had was well concealed: 'the only religion Parnell himself has is to believe that Friday is an unlucky day'.[103]

It is probable that his recognized agnosticism allowed the Catholic hierarchy to treat with him in a way they could not have if he had displayed any degree of Protestant religious fervour. Parnell's dealings with the Catholic bishops were 'shrewd and distant',[104] but tension could not be avoided whenever the educational issue came up, and: 'the emergence of a parliamentary party with independent ideas of its own was not one which gave the Irish bishops unmixed satisfaction'.[105] Perhaps his lack of religious sensibility was most important in his contacts with Ulster, where he never seemed to appreciate the religious fears of its Protestant people. The idea of giving Ulster any special treatment, because of its socio-religious culture, had little appeal to the Wicklow gentleman, who had no intention of tolerating an Ulster withdrawal that would weaken or make insecure the existence of the southern Protestant society that had nurtured him.

Parnell was certainly in no position to identify the party enthusiastically with the Catholic masses in the way that the episcopal nationalists would have wanted. When Parnell was at the height of his power archbishop Walsh told cardinal Manning:

> The seventeenth century had not passed away, that the people were still struggling for their religion and their land, and that the permanency of the one depended to no little extent on the possession of the latter.[106]

When the land war raged in the 1879–1881 period Parnell was uneasy about popular opinion, such as the Catholic belief that any eviction was part of a Protestant plot. As he watched the agrarian agitation grow to the point where chaos threatened the countryside he determined to put all his efforts into constructive parliamentary pressure in the cause of Home Rule. From 1882 he totally repudiated any identification with agrarian agitation, and he particularly rejected the Plan of Campaign. Parnell knew well that many of the nationalist clergy were willing to look upon the land war as a crusade against oppressive Protestant landlords, and he took care to ensure that he was not swept along in a movement whose atavistic passions he could not control, or empathize with. On the land question Parnell was content to accept and take credit for the concessions made by Gladstone in his Land Act of 1881, and to avoid giving leadership to a movement whose identity came from its battle against: 'urbanization, landlordism, Englishness and—implicitly—Protestantism'.[107]

By the time that Parnell returned from his fund-raising successful tour of America in 1880 he was viewed by his Home Rule supporters as the greatest political leader since O'Connell. Yet so many variable forces were at work in the Catholic religious scene that his authority there was sometimes a qualified one. Though many of the priests were unenthusiastic supporters of the Parnell alliance with the rural unrest that produced the Land League of 1880, only five of the twenty-eight bishops supported it.[108] Parnell deliberately distanced himself from the Roman controversy in Ireland when there arose so much resentment of the Vatican's desire to have diplomatic relations established with Britain, and the nationalist bishops expressed their suspicions of the Holy See's motives.[109] After the rescript condemning boycotting and the Plan of Campaign appeared Parnell carefully left his Catholic colleagues to deal with the issue. It was John

Dillon who made an ideological stand:

> In the conduct of our national affairs, the defending and asserting of our
> rights, we Irishmen—Protestants and Catholics alike—should be free
> from any interference; whether it comes from Italy or any other country.
> That is the principle of Irish liberty, and I say without fear that if
> tomorrow, in asserting the freedom of Ireland, we were to exchange for
> servitude in Westminster, servitude to the cardinal who signs that
> document or any body of cardinals in Rome, then I would bid good-bye
> for ever to the struggle for Irish freedom.[110]

Dillon and the other nationalists had cause to be concerned about the curbing
of Irish freedom, at least in ecclesiastical affairs. Although both archbishops
Walsh and Croke were furious in 1889, when Rome made appointments to the
dioceses of Kerry and Waterford that ignored the wishes of the Irish church, there
was nothing they could do about it. As Walsh commented bitterly: 'The
recommendation of ecclesiastics for the office of Bishop, has now, beyond
question, been raised out of the hands of the Irish bishops.' It seemed to the
nationalists as if they were experiencing 'the Veto revived'.[111] They strongly
suspected a political motive behind Rome's unusual episcopal appointment
policy, and Dillon, who was personally devout but very independent in his
thinking on clerical affairs, protested strongly about what he feared was taking
place:

> I say woe to the Catholic Church in Ireland if the priests are driven by
> the Court of Rome from politics, and woe still more if we know it has
> been done at the bidding of a corrupt English ministry.[112]

The nationalist party had no intention of accepting Roman control of Ireland's
political life, and Dillon expressed a popular opinion when he told the *Freeman's
Journal* of 19 December, 1887: 'although they revered the Pope in Rome as the
head of their religion, they would no more take their political guidance from the
Pope of Rome than from the Sultan of Turkey'.

The question of Roman interference in Irish political affairs which bothered
the nationalists was also of interest to the Protestants, who were convinced that,
whatever the tensions of the moment, Home Rule would ultimately mean Rome
rule in Ireland. They had been savaged in the south during the land war of
1879–1882, as well as by the boycotting and other excesses of the Plan of
Campaign. So far as they were concerned they were under direct attack by
agitators supported by the priests, and sustained by funds provided by American
Catholics. They feared what faced them if the Parnellites were successful. They
were sure that under Home Rule they would be discriminated against in public
affairs, and their ascendancy with its cultural attributes would disappear. Few of

them doubted that if the Roman clergy were given a free hand in education the results at Trinity College would be disastrous: 'Ireland would become as intellectual as Ashantee'.[113] Whether there was a quarrel between Rome and the Irish hierarchy over immediate control of the Catholics of Ireland or not, the Irish Protestants knew they were under attack whichever general, Roman or Irish, clerical or lay, directed the strategy of the day. The historian W.E.H. Lecky, for example, had a romantic longing for the restoration of an Irish parliament, like that about which he had written so much. The Fenian and Land League crises however turned him into a convinced unionist. He wrote to the *Times* 5 May, 1886 about the threat of rule by 'priests and Fenians', supported by the votes of an 'ignorant peasantry' and subsidized by 'avowed enemies of the British empire' in America. He justified his strong unionist stance, which influenced him when he was M.P. for Dublin University from 1896 to 1903, by saying that: 'Henry Grattan himself would have been on my side'.[114] Lecky's views were shared by most Protestants, and 'fervid unanimity' against Home Rule was expressed in the General Synod of the Church of Ireland in April, 1886.

The anti-Home Rule position of the Ulster Protestants was clearly revealed from the time that the Land League displayed its nationalist colours, and brought about wide-spread violence in the counties of Monaghan and Fermanagh.[115] Just as they had turned back Jack Lawless and the other O'Connellites in the 1840's, so the Ulster Protestants were determined to keep Home Rule agitation out of the north. By 1885 a strong alliance between Orange lodges and the Conservative party had sprung up; riots that were clearly sectarian took place in the Belfast shipyards, and a powerful and well-integrated political machine to resist a southern take-over was organized. Parnell was obtuse in his reaction to the Ulster rejection of the movement he led, and seemed to give no credence to the uncomfortable fact that: 'many Ulster Protestants did really believe that home rule meant Rome rule'. His dismissal of them was patronizing in the extreme: 'on the whole they have shown themselves to be a selfish and inconsiderate race mindful only of their own interests'.[116] Parnell was very much a southern landlord, capable possibly of bringing about some reconciliation between Catholic democracy and the southern Irish ascendancy minority, some of whom believed they could control Ireland better than the incompetent English administration. The Northern Protestants, on the other hand, never received his sympathy for he never understood them:

> He found it difficult to identify with them, and for most of his career his views on their role and problems were uninformed and ill-conceptualized... he was virtually the captive of Catholic nationalism during the entire period when he was supposed to be its unrivalled autocratic leader.[117]

It was not only the Ulster Protestants whom Parnell failed to understand.

When the scandal of his relationship with Katherine O'Shea became a public issue from Christmas 1889, Parnell apparently did not reckon with the moral outrage of the churches, Catholic and Protestant alike, and he believed that: 'he would emerge from the ordeal without a stain on his honour'. He was unprepared for a climate of opinion that would judge him: 'not merely as a proven adulterer' but as one who engaged in continuing 'squalid intrigue'.[118] The Ulster Protestants shared the moral outrage of the English nonconformists when the scandal broke, but Parnell's influence in the north was so small that their opinion was not of great political importance to him. The situation was different in the south. In 1881 archbishop Croke had assured cardinal Simeoni of Propaganda that though Parnell was: 'unfortunately for himself a Protestant, he is nevertheless a man of high honour and unimpeachable moral character'.[119] The uproar that accompanied the divorce proceedings greatly embarrassed Croke and other prelates, but it also brought out among some of the rank and file nationalists a latent resentment of their leader, who had chosen to spend little time in Ireland after the failure of Gladstone's 1886 Home Rule bill. On occasion he had shown what was evidently a natural disdain towards the mass of his followers whom he once described as 'a cowardly set of papist rats', according to William O'Brien.[120] Distressing to many of his followers was his continuing indifference to the moral indignation which the divorce raised, and was so important to the age. It seemed as if Parnell did not really comprehend what all the fuss was about.

Parnell's policy of allying himself with the Liberal cause after 1886, and his focusing on British parliamentary affairs, ensured that the immediate outcry took place there. The age was one where moral laxity was frowned upon, there was great interest in public morality, and once Parnell admitted adultery he was viewed as 'a deceitful and thoroughly untrustworthy man'. The great Methodist preacher, Hugh Price Hughes thundered: 'if the Irish race deliberately select as their recognized representative an adulterer of Mr. Parnell's type, they are as incapable of self-government as their bitterest enemies have asserted'.[121] In Ireland, however, the bishops were comparatively circumspect in their comments, for the issue of the divorce was shattering to them, and the political implications of the scandal immense. This was not true of the priests, and an 'endless, monotonous vituperation' began[122] which was as savage as the condemnation of the nonconformists in England. One of the more moderate judgments was made by the *Irish Catholic* of 29 November, 1890:

> Mr Parnell has wounded deeply the moral and religious sense of our people; he has probably sinned nearly as much against Ireland as against morality.

Writing privately to archbishop Walsh from Milan, archbishop Michael Logue snidely expressed his personal shock at the moral laxity of the leader who had been so respected: 'A man having the destinies of a people in his hands and bartering it away for the company of an old woman is certainly not a person to beget confidence'.[123]

The fall of Parnell brought into focus in a way that was reminiscent of the mass movement of the O'Connellite and Fenian years the problem of the priest and his authority among the Irish people. Back in 1871, when the issue of Fenianism was still alive, a Protestant landlord commented shrewdly on the position of the Irish Catholic priest in the midst of civil unrest (as Mgr. Persico did in his 1887 report):

> I believe the priests have never before had so hard a game to play. The interests, or supposed interests of the Roman Catholic church have hitherto been bound up with their own personal power. This power has been very great, and is prized by them above everything. On the other hand, it is certain that the Fenians positively hate priestly interference of any sort. Their leaders love power as much as the priests do, and they are eaten up by an insatiable vanity of self that never will submit to the rule of the priests or anyone else. If they ever had the upper hand, there would be an end of the powers of the priests, and the priests know it.

W. Bence–Jones went on to say that, as in Limerick, the Fenians and the priests might seem to work together: 'but this will not do generally, it would soon issue in the loss of most of the personal power by the priests'.[124] Such a concern for clerical authority, of course, was always present during the Home Rule agitation era, when Rome and the Irish hierarchy were deeply disturbed by the popular political campaigning, as well as the outrages during the land war and the Plan of Campaign. In the fall of Parnell, and the confusion among some of his anti-clerical followers, the Irish hierarchy saw the opportunity of a rapprochement with Rome, as well as a new assertion of priestly authority among the people.

Need of reconciliation was especially true of archbishops Walsh and Croke, whose continuing support of the nationalist movement had put them under scrutiny in Rome. They knew this well for, at the time that Persico was drawing up his report, Walsh was in Rome, kept there by Leo XIII and cardinal Rampolla, the Vatican secretary of state, both of whom wished to 'advise' the Irish prelate about the 'final pacification of Ireland'.[125] At the same time archbishop Croke in Ireland was making clear to Mgr. Persico how unwelcome any form of Roman interference would be in Irish affairs:

> I gave him my mind very plainly. I told him that we distrusted everyone and everything Roman... if the Pope sought to substantially check the action of either the priests or Bishops in Ireland, the Irish race

over the world would resent such interference and disregard it.[126]

In his *ad limina* visit of 1885 Croke had brought the same Gallican spirit to Rome when he had told one high placed Vatican official:

> If the Italian bishops and priests took the same course that we in Ireland had taken, the Pope would be a free man, instead of being a prisoner, and the Italian clergy respected and loved by the people, instead of being hated and despised.[127]

Such intemperance made Croke and Walsh many enemies as they soon found out. Complaints against the extreme nationalism of Walsh and Croke had already been made by bishops such as Edward O'Dwyer of Limerick and John Healy of Clonfert as we have noted, and with the Parnell crisis, the nationalist prelates knew they had to move quickly to protect their flanks from any Roman disciplinary measure.

The way of reconciliation with Rome, and reassertion of hierarchical authority in the midst of the debacle in Ireland was shown by cardinal Manning. To Manning's critical and still English eye 'Parnellism' had always seemed to be a kind of Reformation-age 'Tudorism': 'the Tudors had turned the priests out of their due influence in English life and left the laity in command'.[128] From Manning's ultramontane viewpoint the evil of the Parnell phenomenon was that leadership was principally in the hands of laymen, and therefore the divorce scandal should be seen by the Irish hierarchy as a divine blessing: 'a great opportunity for the bishops to regain control of the movement'.[129] This never came about for Parnellism, as a movement, died with the loss of its leader. The nationalist party within the Irish Catholic church also disappeared when archbishops Walsh and Croke began to retire from politics: 'and took their cold comfort in a silence that was both an admonition and an example to their episcopal brethren'.[130]

The clerical leader who was emerging during the final years when Parnellism dominated the country was Michael Logue, a Donegal native, one time professor at both the Irish College in Paris and at Maynooth, translated from Raphoe to Armagh in 1887, and made cardinal by Leo XIII in 1893. He had no use for Parnellism, 'a mere tail to the Radical party in England' and he analyzed for archbishop Walsh on 31 July, 1890 why he resented the movement with its anti-clerical lay leadership:

> They have climbed to their present influential positions on the shoulders of Irish priests and Irish bishops. It was the priests who worked up the registers for them, the priests who fought the elections, yes and it was the priests who contributed the sinews of war... They now think they are secure enough to kick away the ladder by which they

mounted. I fear we are only in the beginning of the trouble. These gentlemen have now got the priests into their hands, and in a little while they will be able to attack the bishops, priests and the Pope himself with impunity.[131]

With Logue's encouragement the Roman yoke was grudgingly accepted once more, after the hierarchy met and considered the situation while the crisis continued. On 16 October, 1890 they issued a 'Pastoral Address of the Archbishops and Bishops of Ireland' condemning hasty or irreverent language which might be used against the 'Sovereign Pontiff, or to any of the Sacred Congregations through which he usually issues his Decrees to the faithful'. As Walsh told Manning the pastoral was a clear assertion 'of the authority of the Holy See... a quiet rebuke to those who have been so ready to proclaim that we had ignored the Decree'.[132]

The bishops were enabled to act upon their new approach to the Irish political situation when Parnell chose to fight to retain his leadership of the party he had largely created: 'there can be no doubt now that the bishops and their priests were the largest single factor, and indeed the decisive factor, in the struggle for political power after Parnell was deposed by his Party'.[133] Archbishop Walsh led in the mobilizing of opposition to Parnell, and when a by-election was held for North Kilkenny episcopal pressure persuaded the candidate Parnell had counted on to step down.[134] Care was taken to ensure that the defeat of the Parnell candidate would be a crushing one:

In every polling-booth in the division a priest sat at the table as personation agent. The people were instructed to declare that they could not read and the voters came in bodies with their priests... declaring they were Catholics and would vote with their clergy.[135]

All the crusading instincts which had once been used to sustain the Parnellite party were now turned against it. The people were told by the *Irish Catholic* of 13 December, 1890:

It is a conflict... into which our priests might well descend crucifix in hand; for it is a struggle in which are ranked powers of light and darkness, of Heaven and Hell, of Virtue and adultery.

The Protestants who witnessed the near-hysteria which accompanied the destruction of the Parnellite movement noted that there was only one possible victor when: 'the clan feeling for a chief clashed with the native obedience to the Catholic Church'.[136] Parnell did not go easily, however, and he was supported by the *Freeman's Journal* which was anti-clerical enough in tone to bring upon it the censure of T.W. Croke and others. Croke told Michael Davitt, founder of the Land League, that the trouble in the land reflected the intransigence of Parnell who refused the advice of the hierarchy to go quietly:

> We are in a dreadful mess in this unfortunate country. I do not see how we are to get out of it. This maniac is rushing through the country every week, setting Irishmen at each other's throats, belauding himself, and flinging filth and abuse on all who dare to differ from him.[137]

Croke's response to the activities of the Parnell rump party was to rally his priests to oppose by violence, if necessary, the followers of the morally reprobate Parnell. He told Walsh plainly that 'the blackthorn will be mercilessly applied' in defence of an anti-Parnellite demonstration.[138] He did not hesitate to urge Michael Ryan of Murroe parish to 'draw the sword' if necessary to break up a Parnellite meeting. Fr. Ryan was one of the most notorious clerical agitators in County Limerick, 'the sworn enemy of Irish landlords', and the Parnellites in November, 1891 had a taste of the kind of intimidation so many landlords had experienced in the past.[139] In July, 1892 bishop Thomas Nulty's pastoral described Parnellism as a direct threat to the Catholic faith:

> Parnellism, like Paganism, impedes, obstructs, and cripples... the fruitfulness of the preaching of the Gospel and of the diffusion of the Divine Knowledge without which our people cannot be saved.[140]

The pastoral was published just before the general election.

V   Protestantism and Ulster Unionism

Irish nationalist history is filled with the names of great Protestant leaders such as Wolfe Tone, Robert Emmet, Thomas Davis and Charles Stewart Parnell, but none of them in their time was representative of the political aspirations, or even the confessional sensibilities of most of their co-religionists. This was particularly true of Parnell whose cause was supported by only a small minority of Protestants, few of whom were Ulstermen. When Gladstone was about to introduce his first Home Rule bill a special meeting of the Church of Ireland General Synod passed resolutions protesting against what was seen to be a threat to the union between Great Britain and Ireland. A similar protest was made over Gladstone's second Home Rule bill of 1893, and by then the voice of the Ulster Protestants was clamant in its opposition to the idea of Home Rule. The Presbyterian General Assembly of March 1886 had no dissentient voices raised when a series of resolutions declared that Home Rule would not safeguard the 'rights and privileges of minorities scattered throughout Ireland'.[141] Few northerners thought there was much likelihood of the majority Catholic people of Ireland shrugging off the Roman yoke in the manner of the people of Italy or France. Not unlike their seventeenth century ancestors most Ulster Protestants believed that without resistance to the political and religious goals sought by the Catholics they would be lost as a people:

> They believed that Rome would be able to dictate policy to the Irish parliament and that policy would be the extirpation of Protestantism in Ireland. Even if Protestants were not actually persecuted and burned, Roman Catholicism would be made supreme by placing education in the hands of priests and by compelling Protestants to attend Catholic schools... Protestants would be deprived of all wealth, privilege and influence and those that were not driven out of Ireland would be impoverished and made hewers of wood and drawers of water for their Roman Catholic masters.[142]

Many southern Protestants thought in a similar way, particularly those who had suffered from intimidation during the Parnell years, but as a small minority, vulnerable because it was so scattered, even in the days of ascendancy such Protestant conviction was kept under restraint and not openly expressed in the blunt manner it was in Ulster. When Charles Gavan Duffy was editor of the *Vindicator* in Ulster he commented in 1839 that although some Belfast Catholics were wealthy respected merchants, and others were traders and professional men:

> ... to be a Catholic in Ulster is not merely to be the object of Orange hatred and Tory enmity... but the despised, ill-treated and disregarded political dependent of Protestant reformers.[143]

Ulster formed the ideological heartland of Irish Protestantism and, whatever the situation elsewhere in Ireland, its response to any political development was sure to be unique. O'Connell had had no success in extending his agitation to the north, and it was almost inevitable that, when Protestant unionism developed in reaction to the Home Rule crisis, Ulster's response was going to be strong and defiant. Though the northern Protestants may not have formed a 'nation' they shared in a sense of community and common interest that enabled them to combine in a mass movement of opposition to Irish nationalism. They also formed the majority population in the north eastern part of Ireland, were governed by a sense of 'territorial imperative', and had no intention of tolerating a Catholic claim to pre-seventeenth century possession of the land.

Gustave de Beaumont in his 1839 study of pre-famine Ireland, *Ireland, Social, Political and Religious* viewed Ulster as the Scotland of Ireland, where all the anti-papist passions which the colonists of James I had brought still flourished, reinforced as they had been by newcomers at the time of Cromwell and William III.[144] There seemed to be a general conviction on the part of the

Protestants that either they had to be in control of society, or the papists would take over as they had between 1641 and 1649. The Orange Order, which had begun as an instrument for persecution of Catholic farmers by Protestant farmers in the late eighteenth century, was viewed a hundred years later as a valued means of social control by Protestant landowners and the merchants and industrialists of the towns.

When Henry Cooke, as moderator of the General Synod of Ulster, gave evidence to the parliamentary committees on the state of Ireland in 1825 he said that most Protestants did not trust their Catholic neighbours whom, they believed, were inclined to treason. Cooke reckoned that Catholics still shared the mentality of 1641, convinced as they were that Protestants could not be saved, and he did not believe the Catholics were fit to govern a state.[145] Cooke's response to O'Connell and his Repeal agitation was to call for an end to tensions between the Presbyterians and the members of the Church of Ireland. At the great Protestant rally at Hillsborough in 1834 he urged such an alliance without much success, but he won the applause of the thousands of Orangemen and others who were present when he denounced 'Romish agitators' who sought to obtain 'Popish supremacy' from a 'weak and vacillating government' which gave in to O'Connell's tactics of intimidation. Repeal, said Cooke was but 'a discreet word for Roman ascendancy and Protestant extermination'.[146] On 20 August, 1837 he gave a famous sermon in which he argued that God not only permitted but commanded ministers to engage in political activity, like the reformed ministers of old who had been 'the real liberators of Europe'. He said he would:

> Charge upon this generation to beware of the leaven of Rome ecclesiastical, which teacheth self-righteousness as the Pharisees; and to beware of the leaven of Rome political, which enforceth a yoke, as Herod.[147]

Cooke was a Protestant zealot ahead of his time, however, and when he tried to found a Protestant Defence Association in the same year it met with lukewarm response and was short-lived.

What kept a Protestant alliance from developing was traditional resentment of the established church by the Presbyterians, rather than any lessening in suspicion of the Roman Catholics. The Catholics in the south could afford to ignore the Protestants, apart from government, but in Ulster the minority was so large, especially in Cavan, Donegal, Monaghan, Fermanagh and Tyrone that the Catholic world was of morbid fascination to many Protestants. Generations of children were taught about 'tyranny of Rome': 'a religio-political system for the enslavement of the body and soul of men'.[148] In the 1860's Ulster landlords were quite prepared to arm 'sound' tenants with 'very superior rifle arms',[149] and they regarded the beginnings of the Home Rule movement with great suspicion; especially when it attracted a renegade Protestant like the Belfast provision merchant J.G. Biggar, who rose to the Supreme Council of the Irish Republican Brotherhood and later converted to Roman Catholicism. Parnell treated the Ulster Protestants with 'sophisticated cold disdain', and they reacted negatively when he continued to treat them: 'as though they constituted a solid but insignificant bloc of bigotry and reaction'.[150] The Protestants were sure enough of their power in Ulster, however, that it was not until 1883 that they recognized fully the power of the Home Rulers, after the winning of a Monaghan by-election by Tim Healy, a Dublin journalist and later a barrister. In the words of his defeated Protestant opponent:

> The priests in the county were his sponsors, his canvassers, his personation agents, and his poll clerks. I do not speak merely of the younger clergy... I include the older clergy, the parish priests, the canons, and the higher dignitaries... To no one is Mr. Healy so much indebted for his success as to the Very Rev. Canon Hoey... At Carrickmacross he never for a moment relaxed his exertions, aiding to the booths the weak and helpless creatures who were to go through what was for them a mere unmeaning form. Indeed so complete were his arrangements that one agent seeing the deathlike pallor on the faces of these independent electors, asked the reverend gentleman if, having exhausted the poorhouses and the hospitals, he had now taken to the graveyards.[151]

In the same year the worst fears of the descendants of the Planters were realized when Michael Davitt, former Fenian, and founder of the Land League boasted: 'we have seized Irish landlordism by the throat, forced it to disgorge some of the plunder which it took from the farmer in Ireland in the past'.[152] This to the Ulster Protestants, combined with the new assertiveness of the priests, was a declaration of war.

Their resolve to defend themselves quickened when in the 1885 general election the Home Rulers won 85 of Ireland's parliamentary seats, sweeping all areas except eastern Ulster and Trinity College, Dublin. Though Gladstone's Home Rule bills of 1886 and 1893 were defeated, and the threat of Ireland having limited self-government within the empire faded, the kind of defence alliance of Protestant power that Henry Cooke had once considered now seemed more attractive. Whatever the cost Ulster Protestantism was to keep the union with Great Britain, and to have nothing to do with 'disloyal Ireland':

> They agreed with Burke that without England Ireland would have been 'the most wretched, the most distracted and the most desolate part of the habitable globe'. ...the settlement of Ulster had been entirely justified 'by antecedent conditions and by results': from being 'the worst of the provinces, socially and morally', a 'sink of murder, misery and vice', as

well as 'the most backward in industrial enterprise', Ulster was turned into a 'land of smiling prosperity'.[153]

The Ulster Protestants were fortunate to have emerge as one of their leaders at this time colonel E.J. Saunderson, a large landowner of County Cavan, who first appeared in the public eye when he vigorously opposed disestablishment, as we have seen, and distinguished himself in Church of Ireland affairs during its period of reconstruction. A convinced Orangeman and able speaker he lost out in a candidacy contest in the 1874 election because of the campaigning against him by bishop Nicholas Conaty, a renowned controversialist,[154] and the Kilmore diocese priests. Saunderson was successful in the 1885 campaign, however, when sectarianism dominated the election process: 'the Orange spirit is aroused, and now it is victory or death'.[155] When Saunderson was criticized for ordering arms, drill and uniforms for the Orangemen he denied that this made him and his followers in any sense a threat to society:

> The usual idea of a revolutionist was a man who proposed to pull down the institutions of the country; they, on the contrary, desired and intended to maintain intact the institutions of the country under which they had thriven.[156]

It was Saunderson who brought lord Randolph Churchill to Ulster in 1886, to 'play the Orange card' after Gladstone announced his conversion to Home Rule. No reinforcement could have done more to bolster Ulster Protestant morale at this time for Churchill not only urged all-out resistance to Home Rule—'Ulster will fight and Ulster will be right'—but he assured them of support if the hour of trial came:

> There will not be wanting to you those of position and influence in England who are willing to cast in their lot with you—whatever it may be—and who will share your fortune.[157]

Saunderson rejoiced when in 1893 Arthur James Balfour, former Irish chief secretary, and future unionist prime minister, watched a parade of 100,000 loyalists in Belfast. Balfour also told a Dublin audience that if Home Rule was ever pushed upon them the Ulster Protestants would have no option but to fight: 'the last refuge of brave men struggling for their freedom cannot be denied them'.[158]

Saunderson represented the landowning section of the Ulster Protestant resistance movement, which also had a folk hero in William Johnston of Ballykilbeg, County Down. Born in the year of Catholic Emancipation, educated at Dungannon Royal School and Trinity College, Dublin, he entered the Orange Order in 1848. Briefly imprisoned for leading an Orange procession at

Bangor, Johnston became M.P. for Belfast and, although he was a minor landowner in county Down he stood, he said, for the 'protestant working men of Belfast'. He urged tolerance towards Catholics,[159] but by 1874 he was firmly committed to opposing Home Rule which by then was widely identified as a Catholic cause:

> Home Rule is simply Rome rule and, if home rule were accomplished tomorrow, before that day week Rome rule would be evident. The 'enthusiastic Catholics' would do in all Ireland as they are doing in Belfast... they would tell you loyal men that you had no rights at all, no voice at all, no claim to the country at all.[160]

Financial difficulties obliged him to accept a post as inspector of Irish fisheries, but he was returned as M.P. for South Belfast in 1885 as an independent Conservative and a militant Orangeman. He made the usual anti-Home Rule noises, defending Protestantism, the union and the empire, but he also encouraged Saunderson and others who wished to bring in supporters from outside Ulster to form a strong unionist movement. He hesitated over the question of arming the unionists but when Gladstone pressed on with his second Home Rule bill Johnston gave his approval to: 'such steps as may be necessary to maintain the union... and the security of the Protestant faith'.[161]

It was not until 1904–1905 that the most comprehensive and effective organization, the Ulster Unionist Council, was formed, but from the time of Gladstone's Home Rule campaign of the early nineties the Ulster Protestants were determined to fight what they feared was to be an extension of the power of Rome in their heartland. Most Catholics were inclined to dismiss as a kind of historical paranoia the 'siege mentality' of the Protestants:

> The opening of a College-green Parliament would mean the inauguration of an era of revolutionary activity... the despatching of an Irish Armada against England, the storming of London by an Irish army, and the decapitation of Queen Victoria by an Invincible specially hired by means of 'American dollars'.[162]

Yet, as one astute modern historian has observed: 'a siege mentality does, however, require besiegers and besiegers there were for Ulster Unionists in the nineteenth and early twentieth centuries'.[163] The Gaelic Athletic Association from 1887, and the Gaelic League from 1893 sought in sport and literature to promote a culture which most Ulster Protestants found alien. In parliament the nationalist M.P.'s busied themselves with Belfast affairs:

> ... not on their merits but in order to win political and other concessions for Belfast Catholics, thus increasing the Protestant

suspicion that ethnicity and not ability would determine the social
stratification of Home Rule Ireland.[164]

The concerns of the unionist movement would not have existed, of course,
unless they reflected the destructive sectarian division between the peoples which
the rioting in Belfast and elsewhere revealed as the Catholic nationalists asserted
themselves. The first riot was in 1813 when Catholics clashed with Orangemen
during a procession of the latter, and two deaths occurred. Then during the
century the rioting slowly increased, as in the clash at Dolly's Brae, in both
intensity and frequency.[165]   On 12 July 1857 there was a new escalation in
ferocity when rioting lasted for ten days, and called for a parliamentary inquiry.
In 1864 the rioting went on for eighteen days with twelve killed, and this led to
the replacement of the mainly Protestant local police force with 450 men,
mainly Catholic of the Irish, later Royal Irish Constabulary.[166]   1872,
unusually, saw the Orange parade on the 12th of July pass without serious
incident, but then on 15 August the Catholics, led by J.G. Biggar, the extreme
nationalist, held their first large parade, calling for the release of Fenian
prisoners. This set off nine days of rioting, leaving five killed, 243 injured, and
Belfast having: 'the appearance of a place that had been sacked by an infuriated
army'. The rioting led to large-scale evictions of the people of both communities, with new lines of religious divide appearing.[167] The annual outrages
accompanying 'the marching season' then lessened somewhat and in 1880 only
two were killed in four days' rioting. By 1884 only eight were injured in a
single day of unrest.

The political situation greatly aggravated the sectarian division in the city.
After the Home Rule bill of 1886 was defeated there was great rejoicing in the
Protestant conclave on the Shankill road, with bonfires and a torchlight
procession. When the constabulary interfered their barracks were attacked, and
the sporadic rioting continued from July to September with thirty-two people
killed, 371 injured, and tens of thousands pounds of property damage.[168] From
1864, when attempts had been made to drive all Catholics from the shipyards,
Harland and Wolff's premises had been a Protestant stronghold, but in 1886 there
was another purging of the minority of Catholics left in the workforce there.
The R.I.C. reported at the time that it would have taken 1000 soldiers to protect
the Catholics on Queen's Island where the shipyards were. Rioting, though of a
lesser degree, accompanied the failure of the 1893 Home Rule bill. The
Protestants were determined not to accept any move towards rule by a
'tyrannical' Catholic majority guided by Rome.[169]

The Protestants reckoned themselves to be completely justified in their fear
of the Roman clerical system which would put them in what they believed to be
the dreadful bondage they saw all around them. In the villages and towns they
knew:

> Nothing is more firmly fixed in the minds of many shopkeepers and
> their peasant customers than that the prosperity or destruction of their
> business is at the will of the priest... every national schoolmaster... is
> the creature of the clerical manager, promoted and dismissed by him at
> will.

The greatest fear of the Catholic peasant was that if he really crossed the priest
he and his family would suffer 'one of the greatest calamities that can overtake a
person', dying without the consolations of religion.[170] From what the
Protestants saw of the rule of the priest in the rural community especially he
was practically 'a tribal chief',[171] who: 'rules with more pomp than ever did any
landlord'.[172] Such priestly tyranny the Ulster Protestants would never accept,
and in the words of a leading Presbyterian layman just before Gladstone's second
attempt to bring Home Rule to Ireland: 'we will have nothing to do with a
Dublin parliament. If it be ever set up we shall simply ignore its existence'.[173]
On the other hand their unionist sympathies were unflagging as the Presbyterian
moderator of 1890 stressed: 'the sentiment of loyalty towards and pride of the
British inheritance and commonwealth of peoples has been common to us all'.
In the British link lay their political strength, in spite of what Gladstone was
attempting, and they had no desire to accept Rome's imperial rule, rather than
that of Britain.

Ulster's liberal Protestant tradition had not completely disappeared, of
course, and there was a small but sturdy minority of Presbyterians who
supported the idea of Home Rule, when Gladstone introduced his 1892 bill.[174]
Most of the Presbyterians, however, in the post-disestablishment period had no
desire, having escaped one ascendancy, to embrace another only fifteen years
later.[175] The ascendancy which they feared then was that of the traditional court
of Rome which was described by lord Farnham of the Church of Ireland in 1899
for the Conference of that year:

> The intolerable dogmatism of the Church of Rome, with the alleged
> infallibility of her head, and her stern and unbending discipline, under
> which, in all matters, individual opinion and freedom of conscience,
> must be surrendered to the keeping of the Church.[176]

It was fear of this Roman power which finally put an end to the old rivalry
between the Church of Ireland and the Presbyterians. When the Catholic bishops
in 1885 petitioned Gladstone to make the Church 'of' Ireland change its name,
and Tim Healy argued the bishops' case in parliament, there was no support
from the Presbyterians who at an earlier time might have wished for such a
humbling of Anglican pretensions.[177] Nor did they display any enthusiasm for a
paper like the Belfast Catholic paper *Weekly Examiner* which dismissed the
Church of Ireland in 1886 as an 'alien church'.[178] In the face of what they

perceived to be a common enemy with imperial ambitions the Protestants of Ulster had closed ranks; they presented a united defence to what they saw as a major Roman offensive which was to be visited upon them. They were aware, as were the increasingly triumphant Catholics, what the future promised: a major attempt to bring the Irish Protestants back to the Roman obedience:

> The time has arrived for action. The day of Ireland's missionary heroism is at hand, and to be utilized first of all in our own country... To bring into the bosom of Holy Church the million of our separated brethren is a most attractive programme, and there is in it enough of the heroic to claim the hearts of Irish Catholics.[179]

Chapter X

The Road to Partition

'The dividing line (between nationalists and unionists) is essentially a religious one'.

> Rt. Rev. Maurice Day, Bishop of Clogher, *Fermanagh Times*, 10 October, 1912.

I   Pius X, Benedict XV and the British

In spite of his letter, *Ad Anglos* of 1895, calling for a conversion of England, and his denial of the validity of Anglican orders in his encyclical *Apostolicae curae* of the following year, Leo XIII had sought a new relationship between Rome and Westminster, if only for the hope that the English might yet assist him to recover the papal states. The year before his death he had even spoken in conciliatory terms about the British rule in Ireland: 'they who oppressed her of old are now ashamed of their dealings with her, and they desire to make amends by beneficent and friendly legislation'.[1] Leo had begun to lead the papacy out of the isolation it had experienced under Pio Nono, but when he died in 1903 Italian Catholics were still estranged from their secular government; France was intensifying its anti-Catholic legislation; and the church in Germany still experienced the consequences which followed the ending of the Kulturkampf. When the conclave met to choose his successor, the Austrian emperor, Franz Joseph vetoed election of Leo's cardinal secretary of state, and the cardinals decided they wanted a pope who would not follow Leo's policy of trying to appease secular governments.

Their choice was the relatively unknown patriarch of Venice who took the title Pius X. The new pontiff chose as his secretary of state cardinal Raphael Merry del Val, who was Spanish, although he had been born in England. Then he set about to demand a universal acceptance of the ultramontane authority of the Holy See. The immediate result of Pius's new assertion of ecclesiastical and religious intransigence was a diplomatic break with France leading to the end of the concordat of 1801, as well as the transfer of the church's property to lay associations. Elsewhere on the diplomatic front Pius protested the separation of church and state in Portugal in 1911; refused to receive the ex-president of the U.S.A., Theodore Roosevelt after he had given lectures in a Methodist church in

Rome; and angered Russian and British authorities by protesting the treatment of Catholics in Poland and in Ireland. His one concession to accommodation with the new social order that was appearing in Europe was his toleration of Italian Catholics taking their part in national elections. Pius feared greatly that socialism was growing in its influence in Italy. His major political trial was in France, however, and there his stubborn refusal to agree to the separation of church and state emphasized Roman authority, but at the cost of estranging the church from much of the population.

Pius had apologized for his political activities in his first encyclical, *E supremi apostolatus* where he had argued that: 'the Supreme Pontiff cannot separate politics from the magisterium he exercises over faith and morals'.[2] It was in the field of 'faith and morals', however, that Pius X was to use the 'magisterium' in a particularly heavy-handed way as he strove to drive underground, or out of the church, those Catholic intellectuals who sought to adapt the dogmas of the faith so that they would be intelligible to their secular contemporaries. Throughout his pontificate the Roman Catholic church was to be convulsed over this problem of controlling 'modernism' among the church's theologians, and in the process the discipline of the Roman court was enhanced, but many of the best minds in the church were alienated by what was considered to be an 'obscurantist' inquisition. The encyclical *Pascendi* of 1907 condemned certain liberal propositions which were labelled heretical, an oath disavowing 'modernism' was forced upon the clergy, and scholars throughout the church were closely examined about their theological beliefs. This process was supplemented by a thorough revision of the canon law during the last years of his pontificate, and Pius X was recognized by the time of his death just after the outbreak of World War I as one of the most conservative of popes. He was to be canonized during the pontificate of one of his equally conservative successors, Pius XII, in 1954.

After Pius X's 'reign of ideological terror',[3] and the outbreak of World War I, the cardinals knew that the church could not afford another division, spiritual or political, and their choice for Pius's successor was an experienced diplomat, albeit a newly created cardinal who took the title Benedict XV. Benedict did an able job of keeping the Holy See neutral during the conflict. He also tried to conciliate, proposing to the Allies and the Central Powers a seven point peace plan, based on justice, rather than military victory. This venture was ignored, however, and when peace did come Italy insisted that the pope had no part in the settlement. In spite of these diplomatic set-backs the Holy See did manage to extend its influence, and by the time that Benedict died in 1922 there were twenty-seven representatives of the nations at the Vatican, including a British chargé d'affaires who had arrived in 1915.[4] Tension still remained with the Italian government, and in spite of the movement towards *détente* of his predecessor, Benedict was unable to see a solution to the Vatican's problem, a *rapprochement* with the secular government in Rome. On the other hand, his first encyclical called a halt to the bitter animosity which had built up between traditionalists and modernists, and Benedict never abandoned the missionary work which he hoped would include a return to papal authority of all those who still kept the mystical body of Christ, 'rent and torn'.

> The plans of the Roman Pontiffs, their cares and their labours, have always been specially directed to the end that the sole and unique Church which Jesus Christ ordained and sanctified with His divine Blood should be most zealously guarded and maintained, whole, pure and ever abounding in love... and open wide its door for all who rejoice in the name of man and who desire to gain holiness upon earth and eternal happiness in heaven.[5]

During the pontificates of Pius X and Benedict XV the Protestants in England (and Ireland) were aware of a continuing 'Romanization' of the Catholic Church in Britain. As we have seen, the English Roman Catholic church was under firm Roman guidance during the rule of cardinal Manning's chosen successor, Herbert Vaughan who was archbishop of Westminster from 1892, and became a cardinal a year later. A member of a very devout Catholic family he had studied at Rome and was ordained there. He had six brothers who were priests, and six sisters in convents. During the years of controversy just before the Vatican Council he had purchased the *Tablet* to promote the ultramontane cause, and to counter English sneering at Roman religious extravagances such as devotions, pilgrimages, relics, and the miracles of Irish folk religion. Although Vaughan showed little interest in affairs in Ireland,[6] he was very concerned with the Irish immigrants in England, as well as the 'leakage' of the faithful who, he believed were lured from the true faith by Protestant proselytizers and through mixed marriages.[7]

Vaughan wanted as his successor cardinal Merry del Val, who was nominally a priest of the Westminster archdiocese, but the appointment went to Francis Bourne who was to occupy the see for thirty-one years from 1903 till 1935. Bourne had an Irish mother, but he was a Londoner by birth, was always attached to that city, and profoundly English in his preferences. He never had the contacts with the curia that Vaughan had had, and at times he was suspicious that in Rome cardinals Merry del Val and F.A. Gasquet were conspiring against him.[8] Whatever the case, there was no doubt that through the Venerabile, the English college in Rome, a very strong allegiance to the Holy See was still being cultivated in the English church, and it was to foster among the English clergy a vigorous 'Roman spirit' which included a: 'very strong commitment to the conversion of England':

> The English College was ... but one part of the steady pressure of ultramontanisation which was transforming English Catholicism,

subordinating ever more absolutely the local church to papacy and laity to clergy while at the same time segregating Catholics, so far as possible, from the dangerous influences of other churches and modern ideas. It was a combination of the papal monarchy of Pius IX's reign and the anti-modernism of Pius X's, and it was at work at every level of episcopal appointment and clerical formation, spirituality, doctrine, law.[9]

The ultramontane Catholicism of the age was legally impressed upon the English church through the anti-modernist oath, which demanded of priests about to be ordained that they rejected liberal interpretations of scripture and history, forcing upon those who took it an almost fundamentalist orthodoxy of Catholic theological thought. The new code of canon law governed matters like liturgical observance and sacramental life, imposing a uniformity of observance that greatly assisted a centralized control of pastoral life. Most importantly, from the standpoint of English and Irish Protestantism was the *Ne Temere* decree of 1908 which promulgated in a new universal way the marriage regulations of the church. Now no marriage was valid in the eyes of the church if performed by a Protestant minister, or merely by civil contract. A mixed marriage was valid only if celebrated before a parish priest, the Ordinary, or some one delegated by them. This legislation produced a great sense of injustice among many Protestants, reinforcing existing social tensions between themselves and their Catholic neighbours.

Among intellectuals nothing was more divisive than the 'white terror'[10] imposed upon the clergy by Rome during the pontificate of Pius X. Many Protestants regarded with apprehension the harassment of Catholic scholars who questioned the belief of the conservatives that: 'whensoever any doctrine is contained in the divine tradition of the Church, all difficulties from human history are excluded'.[11] The Roman action was a trial for someone like lord Acton whose posthumous work *History of Freedom* appeared in the same year, 1907, as Pius X's encyclical *Pascendi* condemned the modernist movement. Another dissident was Baron Friedrich von Hugel, whose mother came from Scottish Presbyterian stock. He had as his friends members of the modernist movement in the Catholic church, and in 1905 he founded a society for the study of religion which brought him into touch with thinkers of diverse views. He wrestled with the problem of the relation of Christianity to history, and had much sympathy for the speculations of thinkers like the French biblical scholar Alfred Loisy, and the French philosopher Maurice Blondel. Because he was a layman, and possibly because he was a baron, von Hugel escaped formal condemnation of his opinions, but this was not the case of his lifelong friend the Irish modernist theologian, George Tyrell. Tyrell had been a member of the Church of Ireland, a friend of one of the saints of Anglo-Catholicism, Robert Dolling, when in 1879, fascinated by its 'sense of tradition and continuity' he had converted to Roman Catholicism and became a Jesuit. He soon found the Roman curia to be an enemy of intellectual reform in the church, however, and an authority that would not tolerate his attempts 'to make room for the "Protestant principle" within the substance' [12] of his newly adopted faith. Outspoken in his condemnation of the 'evils of Vaticanism' he died in 1909, and was refused Catholic burial. Following his death there was: 'almost no clerical theological work going on in the English church'.[13]

This Roman obscurantism appalled the Protestants, of course, but the Protestant churches were still strong enough in the early years of the twentieth century that they did not feel seriously threatened in anyway by the growth of ultramontanism in the Roman Catholic church in Britain. There were some converts, and Irish immigration continued to swell Catholic numbers, but by 1900 total adherents numbered no more than 1,300,000 in a total population of 32,500,000.[14] There was still an atavistic suspicion of popery in all its forms, but no longer the kind of anxiety about Rome that someone like the poet Edmund Gosse felt in the 1860's:

> I never doubted the turpitude of Rome. I do not think I had formed any idea of the character or pretensions or practices of the Catholic Church, or indeed of what it consisted, or its nature, but I regarded it with a vague terror as a wild beast, the only good point about it being that it was very old and was soon to die.[15]

There was unease whenever the Romans engaged in any triumphal display in succeeding years, such as a Corpus Christi procession in Leeds in 1876 when the papal flag flew from St. Mary's church, the Blessed Sacrament was carried by a guard of twelve men with drawn swords, and the Guild of the Immaculate Conception marched in blue cloaks.[16] Though the liberalism of the age denied public protest when in 1895 a May festival in Holbeck included a crowning of the Virgin Mary [17] there was enough latent hostility that the London Eucharistic Congress of 1908 brought forth: 'an almost paranoid gust of popular hostility, evoking memories of gunpowder, Titus Oates and the Gordon Riots'.[18]

There were areas like Liverpool, however, where the Roman Catholic population was over four hundred thousand, constantly reinforced by Irish immigration, and it nurtured a robust working class culture. Sectarian warfare in Liverpool was perennial because:

> Over a hundred years of Orangeism in Liverpool had, by 1919, produced a strong working class culture, with its own music, songs, traditions and social organization of benefit clubs, burial societies, and quasi-religious ceremonies. It continued to be faced by a huge Catholic population, increasingly well-led, still identified with Ireland, poverty, charity, a burden on the rates, competition for jobs etc.[19]

Sectarian tensions surfaced elsewhere on occasion, where the Roman Catholic population was becoming strong, in the area around London, and on Tyneside. The Roman church was still considered to be an alien institution, and its critics still asked the traditional British Protestant question: 'ought we to allow Catholicism in Britain'.[20] Irish Catholic behaviour such as the persecution of Jews in Limerick by the Redemptorists was immediately brought to public notice by the ultra-Protestant press, together with a warning that the priests were ready to 'subjugate, to bend, or to break the will of an imperial race':

> Rome's hatred of Protestant Britain is so intense that she pants for the ruin of this land, which has been foremost in spreading the light of the Gospel.[21]

The Presbyterian scholar, Rev. Alexander Robertson, who prided himself on an intimate knowledge of Roman affairs after a long sojourn in Italy, warned of the papal threat in a series of works. In one of them he reminded his readers of what Gladstone had said in his first Vatican pamphlet about Rome's presumption:

> She alone arrogates to herself the right to speak to the state, not as a subject but as a superior, not as pleading the right of a conscience staggered by the fear of sin, but as a vast Incorporation, setting up a rival law against the State in the State's own domain, and claiming for it, with a higher sanction, the title to similar coercive means of enforcement.[22]

Whenever an anti-Roman polemic appeared it inevitably recounted evidence of papal aggression as experienced in Ireland, where the ecclesiastical *imperium* of the Vatican threatened the Protestant population. Vivid accounts were rendered of the effects of *Ne Temere*: 'on one Sunday in August twenty Protestants joined the Roman Catholic church in Limerick, all converted with a view to marriage'.[23] A great uproar accompanied the exposure of the case of Alexander McCann in 1910 who, encouraged by his priest it was said, left his Protestant wife in Belfast and took away his children. Joseph Devlin, the nationalist M.P. for West Belfast, described the McCann affair as: 'the greatest asset of the Ulster tory party since the days of King William III'.[24] Sectarianism of this nature in Ireland continued to make an impression upon English Protestants and to increase the intellectual and psychological gap between themselves and their Catholic neighbours. Hensley Henson who became bishop of Durham in 1920 was convinced that the 'continuing conflict' with Rome remained 'the governing ecclesiastical issue' facing the nation.[25]

II The Irish Catholics and Sectarian Cultural Division

From the ultramontane standpoint what had been disastrous in the Parnell years was the reassertion of Ireland's form of Gallicanism, an overt alliance of the Catholic church with a nationalist movement led by a secular-minded layman, in this case a nominal Protestant. Leo XIII just before Parnell's death in 1891 expressed hope, according to Tobias Kirby:

> ... that the present crisis may bring about in the end a wholesomer state of things, and break down the lay dictation of the past years and restore the Bishops and the clergy to their proper influence with the people, which the past agitation has been gradually undermining.[26]

Rome was not dismayed when Irish bishop after bishop expressed relief that there had been a providential deliverance from 'a bold unscrupulous despot' whose ambitions would ultimately have made him a 'detestable persecutor of the Church'. Archbishop Walsh of Dublin took credit for the leadership he and archbishop Croke of Cashel had taken in the assault on Parnell and his followers. Croke also expressed shock that among some politicians: 'the authority of the Holy See even within its own sphere of moral teaching has been repudiated'.[27] On the other hand Rome was not about to put much trust in Walsh or Croke in the future, and it was inevitable that the cardinal's hat was given to the archbishop of Armagh, Michael Logue in 1893, rather than to Walsh whose credibility in Rome had been undermined, not least by some of his episcopal colleagues.

Mgr. Persico had appreciated Logue's allegiance to the Holy See in his appendix to his report of 1887 where he commented on the state of individual dioceses:

> This holy prelate... is a man of scrupulous conscience, a lover of ecclesiastical discipline, humble and unaffected by human respect. The Holy See can count on him and therefore it would be opportune that he be called to Rome to make it well understood to them (the Bishops of Ireland) of the necessity to introduce a new ecclesiastical life in Ireland.[28]

Two other prelates who commended themselves to Rome by disassociating themselves from the agitation of the late 1880's were bishop Edward Thomas O'Dwyer of Limerick, and bishop John Healy, coadjutor of Clonfert, who became archbishop of Tuam in 1903. Both these prelates were labelled 'Castle bishops' by the nationalists, but in both London and Rome they were viewed as representative of: 'the moderates in the Irish hierarchy who were anxious to throw off the yoke of archbishop Walsh and his political friends'.[29] They steadfastly heeded the monition of Leo XIII in 1888:

Let your people seek to advance their lawful interests by lawful
means... without prejudice to justice or to obedience to the Apostolic
See.[30]

They were convinced that the Parnell party was not a Catholic one, neither in personnel nor spirit; it did not seek to establish a Catholic state, run by Catholics,
motivated by Catholic principles, and in the long run it would be a threat to the
traditional authority which the priests had held among the people.

O'Dwyer, in particular, had put his emphasis on the mission issue that was
so important to the ultramontanists, the controlling of education. Schools were
under the nominal jurisdiction of the National Education Board but the administration of schools was, in fact, controlled by local 'managers' who were almost
always clergymen. They had the right to appoint and dismiss teachers, and the
board rarely interfered when a manager was dissatisfied with a teacher. By 1860
the board was reconstructed and, by convention, it was accepted that exactly half
the seats were reserved for Catholic appointees. The National System was still
nominally 'nondenominational' but O'Dwyer could tell a Birmingham audience
in 1900 that in three-quarters of Ireland secular education was denominationally
segregated as thoroughly as was religious education.[31] The board had given up
any serious efforts to promote 'mixed education' and was allowing each denomination to create its own segregated system with the financial aid of the state.
Similar arrangements existed for intermediate schools after 1878 and by the end
of the century O'Dwyer and others could take satisfaction that the Catholic
young were being protected religiously in their educational opportunities up to
the university level.

When it came to university education archbishop Walsh was as equally
committed to the cause of protecting the Catholic young from secular and Protestant influences. He bargained hard for a Catholic institution of higher
learning with the Chief Secretary, Augustine Birrell, who recognized Walsh's
envy of the site and the wealth of Trinity College:

To live in a Catholic city, as a Catholic Archbishop, with this Protestant Elizabethan Institution for ever staring you in the face, was no
doubt galling to a proud prelate, who had, besides, made a serious study
of University education in Ireland.[32]

There was, of course, the Catholic University which had been founded on the initiative of Paul Cullen in 1854 but, after its notoriety when J.H. Newman was
briefly its rector, the institute had struggled in poverty without making much
impact on the educational world around it. In 1882 it had assumed the name University College, Dublin and passed under control of the Jesuits who ran it for
thirty years. Its numbers remained small, however, and it did not qualify for
public money because it was privately founded and exclusively a denominational

institution. Walsh and the rest of the hierarchy were not happy when Trinity College, which had admitted students to degree courses without religious tests since 1795, in 1873 opened its fellowships and scholarships to non-Anglicans. Any temptation to assimilation into Protestant culture was to be strongly resisted. The thirty-year attempt by the government to have degrees awarded by a purely examining body, the non-sectarian and comprehensive Royal University, which came into being in 1879, was not a success. The Roman Catholics wanted a fully denominational university of their own, aided by the state.

At the turn of the century higher education was still an educational, religious and political question, with the Protestants particularly concerned lest Trinity College be merged into some form of a University of Dublin. This persuaded Protestant leaders like Edward Carson and the historian W.E.H. Lecky to become strong supporters of a Catholic university when various merger schemes were floated, and Trinity's traditional Protestant identity was maintained when a settlement was reached in 1908 whereby the National University of Ireland was to be set up as a federation of the colleges at Cork, Dublin and Galway, with Maynooth linked to them as a 'recognized college'. This satisfied the Catholics, and the Protestants were pleased with a restructuring of the Queen's University of Belfast, the old Queen's College of that city, writ large. Nominally the National University was to be 'undenominational' but from its beginning it was a Catholic university, receiving substantial government funds. This compromise solution to the university question was, in the words of a later historian: 'in a profoundly significant sense the prelude to the partition of Ireland in 1921'.[33]

The early years of the twentieth century witnessed the sublimation of the political sectarian spirit of the Parnell era into a movement to stress the cultural differences between Ireland's Catholic and Protestant peoples. In 1893 Douglas Hyde, the son of a Roscommon parson had founded the Gaelic League with the help of a young Catholic scholar, Eoin MacNeill from the glens of Antrim. The League wanted to arrest the decay of the Irish language, by encouraging study of it as well as the development of Irish crafts, music and art. The movement received the cautious approval of the hierarchy, by June 1900 the teaching of Irish in primary schools was endorsed, and the priests began to see the League as a means of cultural de-anglicization, one of the ways for the Irish people to free themselves from 'West Britonism'. By September, 1900 a Waterford Catholic, D.P. Moran was editing a new weekly paper, *The Leader* which associated revival of the language with a re-assertion of traditional Catholic and Gaelic values of the Irish people:

> Among the symptoms of West Britonism which were attacked in its early issues were 'Gutter Literature' and the 'imported amusements' offered in Dublin's theatres and music halls. Needless to say, such concern with sexual morality coincided with the preoccupations of

many Catholic clergymen. The conception of 'the Irish mind' as 'chaste, idealistic, mystical' sullied only by the 'invading tide of English ideas', particularly those ideas embodied in 'trashy' periodicals, was attractive to many clerics.[34]

By this time the Gaelic League was being taken over by the Catholic nationalists, with Moran in *The Leader* urging: 'if a non-Catholic Nationalist Irishman does not like to live in a Catholic atmosphere let him turn Orangeman'.[35] Although the Gaelic League's non-sectarian rule was not effectively abandoned until 1915, it: 'like the Irish Parliamentary Party before it, was gently taught that it could enjoy rewards from the Church if it tacitly accepted responsibilities'.[36]

On the popular level of sport this cultural struggle, which brought into being the Gaelic Athletic Association, made no effort to be other than socially divisive. Two thousand G.A.A. hurlers marched at Parnell's funeral, to represent, with Gaelic footballers, those who sought to promote an uncompromising hostility to all who played foreign games, especially those of Britain. The first patron of the Gaelic sports' movement was the militantly nationalist archbishop T.W. Croke who recognized in the G.A.A. a means of rejecting an important popular medium of British culture:

> If we continue travelling for the next score years in the same direction... condemning the sports that were practiced by our forefathers, effacing our national features as though we were ashamed of them, and putting on with England's stuffs and broadcloths her masher habits, and such other effeminate follies as she may recommend, we had better at once, and publicly, abjure our nationality.[37]

On another level this anti-British cultural spirit produced the longings of the Protestant Douglas Hyde, which inspired other Anglo-Irish writers such as W.B.Yeats, to develop a literary movement that would transcend the values and concepts of the West Britons. In his remarkable 1892 lecture to the National Literary Society in Dublin Hyde called for a 'de-Anglicizing of Ireland', a turning away from things English:

> Irish sentiment... continues to apparently hate the English, and at the same time continues to imitate them; how it continues to clamour for recognition as a distinct nationality, and at the same time throws away with both hands what would make it so.[38]

The divisions between the Catholic and Protestant peoples were certainly revealed at the time of the Boer War but, as in the First World War, they are difficult to interpret. The nationalist interpretation of Ireland's response to the conflict has been to argue that almost all Irish Catholics sympathized with the Boers as representatives of a small nation struggling to be free. They rejected the dreadful 'jingoism' of the time, especially that which arose in Protestant Ulster, and spontaneously applauded Boer victories and British defeats. Tales of Irish soldiers cheering Kruger as they departed for the Cape abounded (though even these need interpretation)[39] and much has been made of the two very small Irish brigades of John MacBride and Arthur Lynch who fought on the Boer side. On the other hand there were a great many Catholic Irish who served the crown in various capacities, and they and their families were as enthusiastic about the Irish regiments and their accomplishments as were the northern Protestants.[40] Pride was taken in the Victoria Crosses won by the Irish, and the bravery before Ladysmith and elsewhere that won the queen's acclamation of 'her brave Irish'. There is no doubt about the wide enthusiasm for the newly formed Irish Guards shown by the people of Dublin when the regiment accompanied the royal visit of 1903.[41]

In general it can be said that, 'for a generation before 1910 there was no sectarian strife outside Ulster' and peaceful relations prevailed though 'actual social fusion was still infrequent and intermarriage was rare'. There was a hardworking minority at work, however, intent upon a 'silent, practical riveting of sectarianism on the nation'.[42] Chief among the anti-Protestant, anti-British dissident movements was, in the eyes of many Protestants, the Ancient Order of Hibernians. American in origin it was not important in Ireland in the nineteenth century, but from 1902 onwards it began to have influence. Cardinal Logue did not like what he saw of the new movement and he spoke out strongly against the order: 'a pest, a cruel tyranny, and an organized system of blackguardism'.[43] He forbade his priests to give absolution to any who attempted to coerce people to join the A.O.H., and even threatened a general excommunication of all the organization's members in his Armagh diocese. To Logue the movement represented a lay agitation over which the clergy would have little control, but his attempts to find a constructive approach to the A.O.H. were not successful. It continued to prosper. When the new Home Rule agitation began after 1906 bishop O'Dwyer of Limerick echoed the cardinal's suspicions of this organization which could cause so much trouble if Home Rule became a reality. He would 'dread the existence of such an irresponsible power'.[44] Neither the constitutional nationalists, nor the Catholic bishops were pleased when a Hibernian demonstration in 1912 at Castledawson in County Derry led to a clash with local Presbyterians, and triggered off serious rioting in Belfast. Easy to be identified with Defender or Ribbonmen antecedents, the A.O.H. seemed to be exactly the sectarian movement which the Orangemen wanted to justify their own excesses. With the spirit of republicanism re-emerging in the form of Sinn Fein, the creation of the Dublin journalist, Arthur Griffith in 1905, the Catholic bishops were uneasy over what was developing politically in the country, and their power to control it.

Apart from the reappearance of revolutionary sentiment the episcopate was also concerned with a small number of dissident Catholics who were not happy about the cultural tyranny of the priests. The most annoying of these men was the prolific writer and lecturer, Michael McCarthy, a T.C.D. graduate, a barrister, who was unremitting in his attack upon Ireland's ultramontane church. His writing was rather dull but his first work *Five Years in Ireland, 1895–1900* which came out in 1901 went through eight editions, though dismissed by the Jesuit *New Ireland Review* as: 'a virulent and sustained denunciation of the Catholic clergy of Ireland'.[45] McCarthy's brief was the thraldom in which the Irish Catholic people were held by a Rome-directed clerical organization. Its devotees outnumbered those who served the imperial and local governments combined. He criticized the 'black chilling shadow of the sacerdotal brigade' which kept young Catholics from attending an institution like the college at Galway, where most of the academic prizes were taken by Ulster Protestants while Catholic youths had to emigrate.[46] The national schools of Ireland were dismissed as 'sectarian hatcheries… an asset of emolument and patronage in the hands of the priesthood as much as the churches, monasteries and convents'. The priests, 'and the Italian plotters behind them' gave Ireland its tragic 'priest-sodden history'. These priests are 'enemies of Ireland… bullies and cowards, terrifiers of weak women and undeveloped children'.[47] McCarthy's polemics were such that it is remarkable that they were read at all, but the many editions they went through showed that they were, and that a respectable publishing house like Hodges Figgis found it financially profitable to publish them. It is also unlikely they were read only by Protestant militants, praised as they were by papers like the *Spectator*.

III   The Protestants and the Third Home Rule Bill

Until the beginning again of agitation over Home Rule the Protestants rejoiced in a hiatus of calm in their traditional and essentially defensive struggle (as they saw it) with the papists. The Irish Catholics in the years following the Parnell crisis were engaged in clerical and political in-fighting that appeared at times to be all consuming.[48] The Catholic clerical *New Ireland Review* of April, 1895 remarked on the phenomenon of the national political movement not being led by Protestants, as in the past. The now exclusively Catholic political movement was divided between the Parnellites who nursed a sense of betrayal by the priests; the anti-clerical party led by John Dillon that was linked to British radicalism; and the followers of T.M. Healy who were most favoured by the bishops if only because they were least likely to 'tolerate anything hurtful to the church'.[49] Much of Healy's support was encouraged by the *Irish Catholic*, a popular paper in the presbyteries, but one so immoderate in its opinions that archbishop William Walsh threatened to denounce it publicly.[50] The Protestants had every intention of keeping themselves out of this savage political turmoil which consumed the Roman Catholics in the last years of the nineteenth century.

Gone now among the Anglicans was much of the old spirit of ecclesiastical superiority which had once so infuriated the Presbyterians and other nonconformist churches. In the annual conference of the Church of Ireland held in Belfast in 1893, the professor of ecclesiastical history at Trinity College, Dublin, G.T. Stokes, gave a summary of Irish Protestant history from the time of St. Patrick who, he said, had never accepted the authority of the pope, through the time of the Reformation, when the Protestant churches had been cleansed, purified, reformed, to the present day when Irish Protestants were united in defence against papal power:

> We recognize and embrace every orthodox Presbyterian, every sound Wesleyan, Congregationalist, or even Plymouth Brethren who hold fast to the great central truths of Christianity, as by his baptism a member of Christ's Holy Catholic church.[51]

The shared faith of the Irish Protestants would protect them from the: 'foreign sway and jurisdiction as embodied in papal claims and domination'. What now was wanted was a firm pan-Protestant alliance which would, as in the past, enable reformed churchmen to withstand the assault of tyranny.

It seems clear that what was still feared by the Protestants was not the traditional or folk Catholicism of the majority Irish people, but the papal governed and directed clerical organization which, they believed, was still consumed by the desire to drive heresy out of Ireland, to bring the Protestants once more under Roman obedience. As for the Irish Catholic people themselves, most Protestants would have shared the sentiment of the Presbyterian scholar, W.D. Killen, who in 1902 confessed his sympathy for what the Irish Catholics had suffered in history:

> They have long been taught to regard themselves as a persecuted people—though in some respects they have suffered less than the Presbyterians; but whilst the Presbyterians, rather than submit to unjust laws or landlord oppression, emigrated... to the western world, the Romanists crouched under the yoke and continued to exist in poverty, ignorance and disaffection.

The tragedy of the Irish Catholics was that in their misery they turned for succour to the imperial institution of the Roman church which did nothing to set them free, but used them to serve Roman designs:

> They are connected with a system of church government which is rotten

to the core... an example of the purest despotism—opposed alike to Scripture and to common sense, as well as antagonistic to that liberty wherewith Christ has made his people free.

Killen's hope for the Irish Catholics was that they would follow the example of Italy by keeping the essence of their faith, but shrug off their submission to papal power. This he considered unlikely and he finished his religious auto-biography with a *cri de coeur*:

> God save Ireland. O save the land of my fathers from the yoke of the bishop of Rome... from mischievous agitators... and from blind guides who are leading her from bad to worse.[52]

Some Protestants in the south did not fully share the mind of the venerable Dr. Killen whose academic position as president of the Assembly's College in Belfast had kept him from any direct experience of what went on in the country-side during the land war era. Some of his fellow Presbyterians who had, how-ever, were less anti-papal than Killen, and witnessed to their having been 'treated with great kindness' by the great mass of the people 'among whom their lot is cast'. Even their attitude towards the priests was ambivalent, and the Pres-byterians both hoped and feared that the control of the people by the priests might be waning:

> A great change has undoubtedly taken place in the attitude of the Irish people towards their priests. There have been not merely indications, but many strong manifestations of revolt against priestly and even Papal authority. Fulminations from Rome against the Land League and recent agrarian movements produced little effect upon the Roman Catholics, except to draw out a spirit of insubordination to the ecclesiastical power. Whether this will prove an unmixed good remains yet to be seen. There is a danger of revolt against all authority, of casting-off all religion, and of utter infidelity and lawlessness as the result.[53]

The Anglicans also were uneasy about the social situation, regardless of the defeat of the Home Rule bill of 1893 which general synod had totally rejected as, in the words of archbishop Robert Knox of Armagh: 'a bill to suppress the Pro-testant faith'.[54] They agreed with the conviction of the Belfast Quaker, John Pim, that Home Rule would: 'surrender Irish society to the invisible and visible tyranny of the Romish clergy'.[55] On the parish level, as reports of select vestries to synod show clearly, the Church of Ireland felt under siege even though the threat of attack led by the priests was not imminent and such religious apprehension was a reflection only of general social anxiety.[56]

There were, of course, exceptions to the general Protestant reaction to the threat of Home Rule. Sir Horace Plunkett, for example, was a very liberal unionist who believed that Protestants should join with the Catholics in 'rebuilding Ireland from within'.[57] Sectarianism plagued his work to build up his cooperative movement, and though he straddled the religious divide, coming from a family that had Catholic branches, he found himself accusing his fellow Protestants in Ulster of bigotry, and the Catholics as being more concerned with authoritarianism and church-building than with the shocking economic realities facing the people.[58] Plunkett's lack of tact, at times, probably contributed to his failure to do much more than re-organize the dairy industry, but more important was his inability to appreciate the religious-political tensions which were about to consume Ireland once more:

> In the very years when he was launching his movement the whole political situation was in ferment and out of that ferment would come a mood and temper sharply inimical to the well-meant efforts of Protestant landlords to lead their fellow-countrymen by cooperative paths to quiet pastures.[59]

Another idiosyncratic Protestant was the nationalist J.O. Hannay, rector of Westport who won fame as the novelist, George Birmingham. He too had criticisms to make of both Roman Catholicism which aggressively sought worldly power, and the Church of Ireland for thinking of itself as the chaplaincy service for the English garrison. At the same time, however, Hannay praised the work of individual Church of Ireland clergymen,[60] and his being a Protestant clergyman effectively barred him from being welcomed in the Gaelic League, which in the 1906 period was still officially non-sectarian and non-political. The parish priest of Tuam used his position as chairman of the local branch to drive Hannay out of the league on the grounds that in his writings he attacked 'catholics and Irishmen as such'.[61] Other Protestants who joined the Gaelic League through a love of the Irish language were also made to feel uncomfortable in a society where extreme nationalist views were widely held and Protestants had a hard time to accept: 'the narrow views of life and literature that seem to be the creed of the Gaelic League'.[62]

An aspect of this 'narrow view of life' was revealed in Limerick in 1904. In the city was a small Jewish community, largely Lithuanian in origin, of less than two hundred persons. On 12 January, 1904 a Redemptorist, John Creagh preached a sermon accusing them of shedding Christian blood, and of threatening to 'kidnap and slay Christian children'. He was supported in the pages of the *United Irishman* by Arthur Griffith the Sinn Fein leader who demanded 'freedom for the Irish peasantry from the international moneylenders and profiteers'. The result was the economic ruin of almost all the thirty-five families when Creagh demanded the people 'not to deal with the Jews'. The Protestants of the city defended them, and raised relief for them, but they suffered insults and intimidation on the streets and their lives were generally made miserable.[63] Although most Catholics also condemned Creagh's 'narrow-minded bigotry', the Protestant Standish O'Grady in the *All-Ireland Review* of 23 April commented: 'it is difficult to believe that the priests and the Bishop of Limerick could not put an end to it if they tried'. The Limerick Jews were also defended against the 'blood libel' by Michael Davitt in the *Freeman's Journal* of 18 January, 1904, and by John Redmond, but the boycott lasted two years, and eighty Jews were driven out of the city. Fr. Creagh was finally moved from Limerick and later emigrated to New Zealand.

Another issue that disturbed the Protestants prior to the Home Rule crisis of 1912 was the Roman *Ne Temere* decree, mentioned earlier, which came into effect on Easter Day, 1908, and was viewed by the Irish Protestants as part of the papacy's: 'declared war upon modern thought and liberty'.[64] So far as the Protestants were concerned the decree totally nullified any talk of the protection of the Protestant minority in Ireland if Home Rule became a reality. The Presbyterian journal, *The Witness*, said bluntly on 2 February, 1912: 'Under home rule... the parliament and executive alike are certain to be controlled by a majority subject to the direction of the author of the *ne temere* decree'. Great meetings were held in Dublin and Belfast to protest the decree, and it was roundly condemned by the bishops of the Church of Ireland.[65] What shocked the Protestant community was the open admission by the papacy that Roman law took precedence over the Common Law in the issue of marriage, and that it had little respect for Protestant rights:

A mixed marriage performed according to law in a Protestant Church, although it is legally valid, is declared by the Roman Catholic Church to be no marriage, and the wife is said to be living in concubinage. On the other hand, if the parties opt to be married by a priest in a Roman Catholic church they will not be married before the altar, but in some less consecrated place, and a document has to be signed by each of the parties saying that any children of the marriage will be baptised, educated and confirmed in the Roman Catholic faith.[66]

The *Ne Temere* decree further persuaded the overwhelming majority of the Protestant population that, if Home Rule came about, Rome rule among the majority people would bring pressure on the Protestants to assimilate into the Catholic faith, and Catholic culture. It was not difficult for them to foresee how their numbers might be decimated, especially in the south of Ireland. Though there was always a minority of nationalists, political and cultural, who remained energetic and outspoken, the overwhelming number of Protestants agreed with the 1912 general synod of the Church of Ireland when, in a special meeting, it affirmed: 'unswerving attachment to the legislative union now subsisting between Great Britain and Ireland'. Only Hannay of Westport and four others opposed the resolution.[67] In Trinity College an attempt was made to have the university exempt from the jurisdiction of any future Irish parliament.[68]

The *Ne Temere* decree put an end to the era when the Irish Protestants had been content to sit back and watch the government's attempt to kill Home Rule by kindness, following the failure of the second Home Rule bill of 1893. By 1912 when the third Home Rule bill renewed the threat that Britain would allow a Roman Catholic majority people to rule in Ireland, the focus of Protestant attention shifted to the north, the intransigent stronghold of Ulster. Monster rallies had been held there opposing *Ne Temere*;[69] the pulpits were filled with declamations against religio-political conspiracy,[70] and the newspapers reminded their readers that what was under threat was not just their Protestant faith:

> The Ireland of the south was discontented and miserable, whereas the Irish of the north were prosperous and happy.[71]

No sacrifice was to be too great to protect the Protestant heartland, where alone reformed churchmen had the power to withstand those who would destroy their faith and their culture. Doggerel popular verse called for them to be vigilant:

> For 'happy homes' for 'altars free'
> For freedom, truth, and for our God's unmutilated word,
> These, these the warcry of our march,
> our hope the Lord on high,
> So put your trust in God, my boys
> and keep your powder dry.[72]

The clergy of the various churches showed no hesitation in joining with the popular movement to withstand Home Rule and to protect Protestantism when on Easter Tuesday, 9 April, 1912, 100,000 men marched past a platform holding Andrew Bonar Law and seventy English, Scottish and Welsh M.P.'s. The solemn proceedings had been opened with prayers by the Church of Ireland primate, John Baptist Crozier, and the moderator of the Presbyterian Church had led in the singing of the 90th psalm. Bonar Law's father, briefly a Presbyterian minister in Coleraine, where he was born, had a great love for Ulster, and this he passed on to his son the future prime minister of Great Britain.[73] Caught up in the passion of the time also was Charles Frederick D'Arcy bishop of Down, Connor and Dromore who addressed the men and dedicated the colours of various detachments of the Protestant Ulster Volunteers. He replied to his critics by pointing out that in Ulster it was the Volunteers who were:

> ... the great means of keeping peace and preserving order, while demonstrating to the world their unalterable opposition to the change

they had determined to resist.

D'Arcy vehemently denied he had seen Maxim guns in the hands of the Volunteers or blessed them. He was also criticized for signing the Ulster Covenant on 28 September, 1912, together with the Presbyterian moderator, Rev. Henry Montgomery, and 200,000 other men. His defence of his allying himself with this popular demonstration was to say that it was necessary: 'to give such control to the leaders and such power to the people of Ulster that no politician, no matter how violent, would dare to use force'.[74] On another occasion he is reported to have said: 'there are things worse than civil war',[75] and he would have agreed with the judgment of the *Times* the following year: 'the Covenant was a mystical affirmation... Ulster seemed to enter into an offensive and defensive alliance with the Deity'.[76]

There were, of course, the minority of Protestant churchmen, like the Presbyterian J.B. Armour of Ballymoney, who could fill the local town hall with some 500 Protestant home rulers of one sort or another.[77] There were also the radical, dissident, and nominal Protestants like Alice Stopford Green, Captain Jack White, and Roger Casement who were passionately anti-British, and supported armed struggle by the nationalists[78] and ignored the religious questions of the time. Though they were appreciated by the nationalists, in the churches their influence was small indeed. Most churchmen listened to admonitions by their leaders to show 'calmness and restraint' and to 'promote peace and good order in the community', but they were prepared to take up arms if they faced 'enforced subjugation to an alien Irish parliament'.[79]

The Roman Catholic response to the threatening situation in Ulster was to make light of it, and even the truculence of Edward Carson the unionist leader, or the build up of the Ulster Volunteer Force was not taken seriously by cardinal Logue and others.[80] The people who took the Ulstermen seriously, on the other hand, were the southern Protestants. They were greatly apprehensive over the intransigent spirit which they knew was sweeping the province, and they feared greatly the threat of partition, though they answered in 1913 in the negative when Carson asked them: 'If I win in Ulster am I to refuse the fruits of victory because you have lost'. From the autumn of that year there tended to be a divergence between the two sections of Irish unionists; and though Carson was a southerner he put more and more of his efforts into ensuring that at least six of the nine counties of Ulster would refuse to accept Dublin rule, if Home Rule became a reality. The southern unionists were not to be counted upon to do much to defend themselves, especially if partition was to be reckoned with: 'they are so different from the north of Ireland'.[81] What neither the Roman Catholic hierarchy, nor the northern and southern unionists knew, however, was that in November 1913 Patrick Pearse had reached a crossroads in his thinking as he revealed in an essay entitled 'The Coming Revolution'. Like the Ulster Protestants he had come to the conclusion: 'that nationhood is not achieved otherwise than in arms'. During the year that saw the outbreak of World War I the speeches and writings of Pearse were to be filled with an obsessive theme of bloodshed, a 'crusade' for Ireland's people seeking freedom: 'Ireland will not find Christ's peace until she has taken Christ's sword'. Thomas MacDonagh and Joseph Plunkett were two other leaders of the 1916 rising who were: 'Catholics with a strong inclination towards religious, or quasi-religious mysticism'.[82] When the Easter rising took place, there was little doubt in the minds of most Protestants, especially in Ulster, that:

> In appearance the rebellion was amenable to reconciliation with the Irish Catholic religious world, and was heir to, and indeed an aspect of much of Irish religious tradition... which took aggressive pride in holiness, hated the enemy... with a holy hatred, and pursued, without counting the cost, holy sacrifice and holy death.[83]

IV   The Irish Churches and World War I

Patrick Pearse did not have long to wait for the time of blood sacrifice to come. Nothing did more to contribute to the sectarian divisions in Ireland, both north and south, than the crisis of World War I and the responses of the churches to it. John Pentland Mahaffy, who became Provost of Trinity College just after the beginning of the conflict, and had a son in the forces, recognized the seriousness of Pearse and his followers when he denounced them for their 'traitorous views' in opposing enlistment in the army.[84] When the war began in August, 1914, many churchmen and others believed civil war was not far off if the government attempted to bring in Home Rule for all the country, including Ulster.[85] This particular 'temper of variance' eased with the beginning of the great European conflict, however, and in response to the war in the early months there did not seem to be any significant difference shown by either the Roman Catholics or the Protestants. In Ulster most of the passion of the Protestant extremists was poured into the organization and dispatch overseas of the 36th (Ulster) Division. The Catholic hierarchy was distracted by the death of pope Pius X in August, 1914, and when cardinal Logue returned from Rome the press made much of his comments on German excesses, with headlines declaiming: 'Loyalty of Ireland—Cardinal Logue and the War'.[86] His words also appeared on recruiting posters, and John Redmond the Irish parliamentary leader seemed content with what he believed to be 'encouraging' episcopal support for his strong commitment to the imperial war effort. A police report at the end of 1914 stated that the Catholic clergy generally supported the policy of Redmond's party towards recruiting and service. In this the priests, as usual, followed the sentiments of the people. Up to 20,000 cheered the first reservists who left the North Wall in Dublin for the war on 5 August, 1914.

In the August to December 1914 period some 43,000 men enlisted in Ireland, and a further 37,000 joined up in the January to August 1915 period. Then came a slump in recruitment as news of the slaughter of the Munster and Dublin Fusiliers in Gallipoli reached Ireland, as well as the losses of the Connaught Rangers, the Royal Irish Fusiliers and other units in the second battle of Ypres. Recruitment was becoming a source of division as the proportion of Ulster volunteers remained comparatively greater than in the other provinces. More ominously was the realization after the slaughter of 1 July, 1916 on the Somme that the decimation of the 36th (Ulster) division had strengthened the power of the rebellious 'Irish' volunteers who had remained in Ireland. As the public opinion towards the war began to shift, so did the attitude of the priests, and in a recruiting conference at the viceregal lodge in 1915 the Catholic bishops were notable by their absence.[87] A police memorandum of 10 April, 1916 remarked: 'The Roman Catholic clergy as a body are, on the whole, lukewarm on the subject of recruiting'.[88]

It has been argued that compared with other parts of Britain a disproportionately small number of recruits were obtained from Ireland[89] and, if this is so, it is likely that the attitude of the clergy may have influenced the Irish response to the war. Part of the answer for the shift of the priests' support for the war effort from 'general' in 1914 to 'lukewarm' in 1916 may have reflected the ultramontane sympathies of the Irish Catholic clergy. Bishop O'Dwyer of Limerick who held a 'simple hatred of heresy and unbelief, and a scorn tempered with pity for all outside the pale of the catholic church' certainly had ideological objection to support of the allied war effort:

> ... his sympathies were altogether with the great Catholic Empire of Austria and the sixty million Catholics of Central Europe as against infidelity and Protestantism as represented by the allies.[90]

When Irish emigrants were trying to leave Liverpool for the USA in the autumn of 1915, and were attacked as shirkers by a mob, O'Dwyer said: 'their crime is that they are not ready to die for England. Why should they? What have they or their forbears ever got from England that they should die for her?'[91] T.M. Healy told William O'Brien that: 'the young priests hate the French anti-clericals and talk of Austria's Catholicity', and he probably based his judgment on an increasing number of priests who sought to give respectability to the Irish Volunteer movement and 'inhibited' zeal for the war effort.[92]

It is probable that like so much else in Irish history recruitment varied greatly at different periods in various parts of the country. Nationalist historical memory has been such that remarkably little attention has been paid to the Irish contribution to the allied cause in World War I, but when local studies have been made the results have been unexpected: 'The Wexford experience suggests that even in an overwhelmingly Catholic and Nationalist region of Ireland, the general response to the war was neither hostility nor indifference'.[93] Studies of recruiting posters indicate that: 'many posters embodied either verbal or pictorial appeals from... (contrary to common belief) Catholic clergymen... most numerous were the excerpts from statements made by Catholic bishops and priests'.[94] Yet after the war most Catholic churches and schools had no memorials to the Catholic fallen (St. Mary's, Haddington Road, Dublin, being a notable exception as well as Clongowes Wood in Co. Kildare).[95] The most unfortunate example of nationalist Ireland's denial of its war-dead was the 'mean spirited ruination' for so many years of the great national war memorial at Islandbridge.[96] Apart from Ulster it has been very difficult to gauge the Irish Catholic popular attitude to the war.

Within the forces sectarianism was minimal as the 36th Ulster and the 10th and 16th Irish divisions fought alongside each other, as well as British divisions which had many Irish in their ranks. The chaplains helped to break down old divisions, especially when they served together in the front lines. In theory Anglican chaplains were not to serve in the same advance positions as their Catholic counterparts (who were there particularly for the administration of Extreme Unction) but casualties among them (88) compared with the Catholic (30) suggest that the ban was ignored.[97] Most chaplains heeded the advice of the famous Geoffrey Studdert Kennedy, who had trained at Trinity College, Dublin: 'Work in the front line and they will listen to you'.[98] There was universal admiration by Protestants for the heroism of Fr. Willie Doyle, S.J., who fell in 1917 in the Third Battle of Ypres where the 36th Ulster and the 16th Irish divisions were decimated. Recommended for the Victoria Cross he was loved even by the Orangemen.[99] The *Irish Catholic Directory* of 1919 claimed that over 500 Irish Catholic priests had served as chaplains during the war.[100]

The great crisis for the churches arose with the rising of 1916, which the press clearly condemned as a 'German-managed Irish rising', not unreasonably, with Roger Casement landed by German submarine, and the Germans sending the supply ship, *Aud*, filled with arms. During the insurrection the vague suggestion had even been advanced that a German prince should become king of Ireland,[101] and the popular rumour was that the Rising was the prelude to a German invasion. To that part of the population, in Ulster and elsewhere, who had members of their families serving in the forces, or were otherwise engaged in the war effort, the rising was an act of unforgivable treachery. The Church of Ireland archbishop of Dublin J.H. Bernard, who was in the thick of the battle with his palace overlooking St. Stephen's Green where rebels were entrenched, passionately condemned the insurrection. He had a son and a daughter engaged in the war, had lost a son who was in the Dublin Fusiliers during the Gallipoli landing, and in a short letter to the *Times* he said: 'this is not the time for amnesties and pardons, it is the time for punishment swift and stern'.[102]

The feelings of archbishop Bernard were without doubt shared by the other Church of Ireland prelates who were in Armagh for the consecration of a new bishop of Derry when news of the insurrection first came to them.[103] The Ulster Presbyterians saw in the Rising confirmation of their belief that Irish nationalism of any kind was 'ultimately anti-British'.[104] The reactions of the Irish Catholic bishops were ambiguous, and when they became known they did not help to encourage the brief Catholic-Protestant detente of the early war years. The first to hear of the seriousness of the situation was archbishop W.J. Walsh of Dublin, when a law officer urged him to appeal to the rebels to lay down their arms. All that Walsh would do, however, was to urge people to keep off the streets: 'in this time of unprecedented excitement and danger'.[105] His general attitude seemed to be that the fault lay with the government which, with its ample resources for social control, had allowed so much blood to be spilt. His main concern was that he not be made a 'catspaw' of the government.[106] When cardinal Logue received a telegraph from pope Benedict XV requesting information, and expressing hope that conflict would cease, Logue gave a non-committal assurance that everything was under control.[107]

After the execution of the leaders of the Rising took place there was an extreme revulsion of public opinion, and though the British government was seen to be misguided: 'the number actually executed was very small by comparison with that usually following a revolt in such circumstances'.[108] All of the insurgents who were put to death were Catholics, except for Casement who converted shortly before his execution, and all except the old Fenian Tom Clarke made peace with the church.[109] The rebel leaders had also sought through Plunkett's father, a papal count, the pope's blessing on the rising; one of the pro-cathedral priests had acted as a chaplain to the Post Office garrison; and soon tales of the great piety of those executed were in circulation. Masses were said for the fallen, including the executed rebels, and part of the Catholic press sought to identify Pearse and the others as not only national heroes but martyrs of the Roman Catholic faith.[110] In Ulster, about to experience the slaughter of the old Ulster Volunteer Force on the Somme, and with most of the population supporting the war effort, the reaction to this act of 'Catholic' treachery was resolute. The Ulstermen noted the moderate tone of the British newspapers towards the Rising; on 4 May the *Nottingham Journal and Express* expressed its regret for the deaths of four officers and 216 other ranks in the Sherwood Foresters, yet believed that the crisis had: 'demonstrated beyond the possibility of cavil the loyalty and enthusiasm for the common cause of Britain and her allies of the Irish nation in the mass'. Such moderation for Ulster was not possible, as analogy was made with the rising of 1641, and the Protestants refused to accept the opinion of the 26 April *Manchester Guardian* that the insurrection was but: 'the wild act of a small and violent faction'. Psychologically at least, from the time of the Rising of 1916, partition was a reality in the mind of most Ulster Protestants.

When the idea of the Irish Convention, to produce a scheme of Irish self-government, was introduced in July, 1917, at a time when the British were preparing for their bloody Passchendaele offensive, the British press was sure there was at last light at the end of the Irish tunnel: 'it is now solely and wholly in the hands of the Irish themselves'. [111] The problem was that the Irish in Ireland were radically divided along sectarian lines. The majority population had already begun to revere the Catholic rebels of 1916: 'an intrinsic component of the insurrection (for all the pluralist window-dressing of the Proclamation issued by Pearse) was the strain of mystic Catholicism identifying the Irish soul as Catholic and Gaelic'. [112] The Ulster Protestants in turn remembered the Somme when the 36th Division suffered on July 1 5,500 casualties and had to be taken out of battle the next day. On July 12 of 1916 Belfast had a five minutes silence instead of a parade. [113] Lost was the flower of Ulster's Protestant youth: 'unparalleled for its kind since Cromwell's "Ironsides" in enlisting stern religious fervour and political enthusiasm in a fighting phalanx'. [114] This same spirit lived among the members of the Convention, and they had no intention of surrendering to the well-meaning pressures put upon them by Sir Horace Plunkett and others who sought conciliation:

> The Conventions outcome... illustrated Ulster's intransigence: heavily committed to the war effort, with their champions strongly entrenched in Lloyd George's government, the prospect of entering a nationalist Ireland that had tried to stab the Empire in the back was less alluring than ever. [115]

The Irish Convention finally disposed of the myth that there could be, as things were, a united Ireland which would be self-governing. The Ulster Unionists were not bluffing, and when they said they would not be party to any scheme of Home Rule they meant exactly what they said. The government, however, was loath to recognize the Ulster intransigence. Up until April, 1918, when he introduced the issue of conscription, Lloyd George was hoping that the Irish Convention would produce recommendations which would allow him to introduce both military service and Home Rule. Home Rule, however, was by then an improbable development, and the big issue for the Irish Catholics and Protestants alike in the spring of 1918 was that of conscription. There was also the problem of partition, for it seemed clear that the Protestants in the province of Ulster would have nothing to do with rule from Dublin.

Conscription had been introduced amidst great controversy in Britain in March 1916, but it was not extended to Ireland. John Dillon told Parliament that up to 15 December, 1915, the numbers of new Irish recruits to the British Army had been 91,549 of which 50,196 were Catholics and 41,353 Protestants. [116] Then came a slump in recruitment as the war situation worsened, as we have noted, emigration to America continued, and disappointment with the failure to obtain Home Rule depressed Irish youth. Nevertheless there were still 14,013 voluntary recruits from Ireland in 1917, without there being any particular recruiting campaign.[117] Even when the conscription crisis arose and Sinn Fein mounted anti-recruitment rallies more than 11,000 joined the forces during the first eleven weeks of 1918.[118] The idealism of John Redmond and his followers had not disappeared and the Sinn Feiners were increasingly identified as 'pro-German' by many Irish.

Crisis came in the spring of 1918 when the German army was able to move troops to the West after the collapse of Russia. America had entered the war but its armies had not yet arrived in great force, and in a sudden massive offensive the Germans began to overrun allied armies. Casualties were massive, particularly in the 16th (Irish) and 36th (Ulster) divisions, which were already weakened and war-weary.[119] By 6 April the situation was grave and Lloyd George concluded: 'we cannot go to the House of Commons and ask our people to make sacrifices, sacrifices which the Irish in America are making, and leave the Irish at home out'.[120] To mollify Irish opinion it was agreed that, whatever was decided by the Irish Convention, Home Rule would be introduced, as matters of principle were set aside in support of the war effort. On 16 April the conscription bill was passed and the Irish nationalist party left the House of Commons and returned to Ireland. In the event, conscription never was extended to Ireland for the German army after reaching the Marne, only 37 miles from Paris, met with stiffened resistance, including American troops in June and the German final retreat began. In the meantime the Roman Catholic church had thrown its weight behind the Sinn Fein party which bitterly opposed conscription and wanted: 'to consider the advisability of establishing an all-Ireland Covenant on the subject'.[121] Most people realized, however, there was no chance of Ulster Protestants working with Sinn Fein for they heartily despised everything that de Valera and his followers stood for.

The blood spent at Thiepval, Passchendaele and in the bloody retreat of 1918 had given Ulstermen a new martyrology. They could admire, indeed revere the Catholic Irish of the 16th division who fought alongside them; and kept alive the idealism of John Redmond that brought over 200,000 Irish into the field by the end of the conflict. For the nationalists who tried to serve—as the Ulstermen saw it—the German cause in the Rising of 1916 and who had refused to enlist while the Ulstermen and Redmond's supporters were slaughtered in the trenches, they had nothing but contempt. This contempt was shared by many of the returned soldiers in the south. In the last weeks of the war the Holyhead mail boat was sunk by a German submarine with the loss of four hundred Irish lives, and two nights after Armistice night a mob, including many Irish soldiers, totally wrecked Sinn Fein headquarters in Dublin. In the north the Protestant hostility towards the Irish nationalists was inevitably extended to the Catholic church when it began to respond to Sinn Fein's attempt to win clerical support for its anti-conscription campaign.[122] De Valera called on archbishop Walsh who was a Sinn Fein sympathizer, and having obtained his opinion, led a delegation to the hierarchy who were easily persuaded to give their support to the anti-conscription cause:

> We consider that conscription forced in this way upon Ireland is an
> oppressive and inhuman law which the Irish people have a right to
> resist by every means that are consonant with the law of God.

On the following Sunday worshippers were to be given opportunity to take a
pledge opposing conscription and, after mass, subscriptions to support the anti-
conscription cause would be collected outside the church gates.[123]

This resurrection of the clerical-nationalist form of alliance of the O'Connell
and Parnell periods persuaded even liberal southern Unionists that acceding to
Home Rule would result in massive civil unrest, at a time when Britain had its
back against the wall. It was then reported in the *Irish Times* of 29 March, 1918
that Protestants were threatened on the streets, and forced to sign the anti-
conscription pledge. Edward Carson, the Ulster Unionist leader, in a letter to the
same paper on 2 May, 1918 said it would be folly:

> ... in the midst of the gravest crisis of the fate of European civilization,
> hurriedly to impose some new solution which will place Ireland under
> the joint rule of Sinn Fein nationalists, and the Roman Catholic
> hierarchy.

Everywhere there were rumours about the priests urging insurrection: 'they have
been told in chapel to fight for Ireland, that Germany will help them, and that
when the Germans come all things to Ireland will follow'.[124] Sir John French,
the lord lieutenant, saw the Catholic bishops teaching 'absolute rebellion';
others believed the inspiration for the Sinn Fein and Catholic church revolt had
come from Rome.[125] In fact, Rome urged the Irish bishops to act with moderation[126] but, as in the agitation of earlier years, there were priests who openly
urged armed resistance if conscription was enforced, the excommunication of
Catholic members of the Royal Irish Constabulary, and even their assassination
if they tried to enforce conscription. A whole infra-structure of resistance blessed
by some of the priests was coming into existence, to give Sinn Fein members a
new respectability:

> ... the Church could not avoid being associated with them in the minds
> of most people. For many, the Irish national struggle also became a
> struggle between Catholics and Protestants.[127]

A vivid insight into what the Church of Ireland prelates thought of the
action of the Catholic Church in the conscription crisis was given by John
Henry Bernard, the archbishop of Dublin. In April, 1918 he was asked for a
briefing by the archbishop of Canterbury, Randall Davidson, about the actions of

the Irish Catholic bishops:

> You ask a difficult question. What do I think of the Roman Catholic
> bishops? I think very badly of them... It is argued that they do not
> really desire Home Rule, although they always pretend they do desire it,
> because they wish to be on the popular side... I cannot accept such a
> view... It is suggested that they take their marching orders from the
> Vatican, and that the Vatican desires Germany to win the war and thinks
> she will win it... This, again, is plausible, but I doubt (a) if the
> Vatican would give such orders to Ireland, without giving them to
> England as well, (b) at one moment of the war, at least, two or three of
> the Roman Catholic bishops spoke in favour of recruiting... but that
> all the R.C. bishops are really pro-German, and are so, because they
> take their orders from Rome, is very doubtful. My own view... is...
> they would forfeit their influence now, if they did not fall in with the
> popular dislike of conscription... another is that I believe them
> honestly to desire to prevent bloodshed. Undoubtedly many lives would
> be lost, were any serious attempt made *now* to impose compulsory
> service on Ireland... they denounce it now, because they are afraid of
> losing control of their people.[128]

Bernard's cautious assessment of what the Catholic hierarchy was about was
probably shared by most thoughtful Protestant leaders, especially in the south.
They knew well that with the priesthood condemning conscription it would be
very difficult for the Royal Irish Constabulary to enforce it. They recognized
that the rebels of 1916: 'were a handful then' but had grown 'to a host now with
the priesthood at their back'.[129] For the sake of civil order they hoped the
Catholic hierarchy could control the situation.

Ulster's approach to the conscription crisis was different from the rest of the
country, and reflected local tensions between Catholics and Protestants which increased as soon as the issue arose. From the time the conscription crisis first
began the great concern of Ulster was that of partition; Lloyd George when he
tried to appease the nationalists by making an offer of Home Rule did so on the
basis that north-east Ulster would not be part of the new political arrangement.
This was anathema to Ulster's Catholics who feared that with the withdrawal of
the protection of Westminster they would find themselves at the mercy of their
'hereditary foes'.[130] In the words of Charles McHugh, the Roman Catholic
bishop of Derry, such a change in political authority had to be resisted as
strongly as possible: 'to become serfs in an Orange Free State, carved out to
meet the wishes of an intolerant minority, is a position to which we will never
willingly submit'.[131] The Protestants, for their part, had no intention of yield-
ing an inch to the demands of McHugh and the other nationalists of Ulster.
They viewed the Catholic minority in Ulster as a body fully committed to direc-

tion by the imperial and foreign power of Rome, intent upon using any means to force the Protestants into assimilation into Catholic culture. When Edward Carson returned to Ulster for a tumultuous welcome in February 1918 he listened to sermons on his first Sunday in the province that were delivered by both Presbyterian and Church of Ireland clergy on the theme: 'Ulster was as firm as ever and would not climb down', accompanied by the then favourite Ulster hymn—'O God our help in ages past'.[132] So far as the Protestants of Ulster were concerned, if the hated Home Rule forces were victorious, they would have nothing to do with rule from Dublin. Their long state of siege was to continue—but from now on they would be on their own, at last able to put their house in order.

Immediately following the end of the war, and the signing of the Peace Treaty with Germany, the Ulster Protestants were concerned lest the Home Rule Act of 1914, which was still on the statute book might automatically come into operation, without an amending bill to exclude north-east Ulster from its provisions. At this time Sinn Fein was carrying out its campaign of terror in the south, including an attempt to assassinate lord French the lord lieutenant. Britain was war-weary and, as Carson surveyed the scene he feared that all of Ireland would be surrendered to the nationalists and to the priests. A fortnight after the signing of the peace treaty he issued the words of warning to a huge assembly in Belfast:

> If there is any attempt to take away one jot or tittle of your rights as British citizens, and the advantages which have been won in this war of freedom, I will call out the Ulster Volunteers... We are loyal men, the Government and the Constitution and the British Empire are good enough for us, and the man who tries to knock bricks out of the sound and solid foundations, if he comes to Ulster, will know the real feelings of Ulstermen and Ulsterwomen.[133]

Chapter XI

The Confessional Republic

'The constitution was worthy of a Catholic nation and brought nearer the promised land of a united republic'

Sean T. O'Kelly, *Irish Press*, 24 June, 1937

I   The European Peace and Papal Resurgence

The papacy had no direct role to play in the treaties signed at Versailles following the end of World War I, but in strategic terms it had some cause for satisfaction. Strongly Catholic nations like Lithuania and Poland came into being, and three years after the settlement the overwhelmingly Roman Catholic Irish Free State was recognized by Britain and the other European nations. The treaty between Britain and the Irish Free State did not come into force until ten months after the death of Benedict XV in 1922, but it represented in the thinking of contemporaries a significant advance in Roman influence. The traditional tensions with Britain seemed to be fading; and when the peace negotiators dealt with the future ownership of Roman Catholic missions in German colonies, Balfour, the English foreign minister, was one of those who supported the move to grant them to the Holy See, thereby, in effect, recognizing the supranational authority of the pope. From the Roman standpoint, however, there was considerable offence taken when the Holy See was excluded from the League of Nations. In Catholic eyes it was always to remain the 'Protestant and Masonic' institution at Geneva.[1]

Nevertheless, successful diplomacy helped to ease difficulties between Rome and Paris; Mussolini praised the papacy, even before he came to power in Italy; and in Germany, the nuncio, Eugenio Pacelli, the future pope Pius XII, worked to promote peace among contending factions of the Catholic church, and to prevent the victorious allies from further humiliating Germany. After the Netherlands appointed an ambassador to the Vatican its prime minister, Van der Linden, a Protestant, when speaking of Benedict XV, said:

Today no political centre wields more influence in the cause of peace than does the Vatican. The Pope is truly one of the great powers.[2]

Pius XI, who had been the nuncio in Poland, when he became pope in 1922 determined to follow the way shown by Benedict XV, striving by diplomatic means to extend the authority of the Holy See in the chaotic Europe of the post-war period. Breaking with the tradition of his predecessors the new pope gave his blessing, *Urbi et Orbi*, from the exterior balcony of St. Peter's instead of from an interior gallery. With the help of cardinal Gasparri, his secretary of state, Pius set out to work diplomatically to restore rights and authority to the Holy See, in the fashion of cardinal Consalvi after the Congress of Vienna. Sometimes his task was comparatively easy, as in the case of Portugal where there was a veritable Catholic revival following the apparitions at Fatima in 1917. Rome supervised closely the work of the patriarch of Lisbon, cardinal Cerejeira, who was an old friend since student days of professor Oliveira Salazar, who became prime minister in 1932. Salazar's Portugal emerged as a strongly clerical state, based upon Catholic principles, although in theory there was independence between church and state. The concordat established with Germany in 1937 was more difficult to obtain, but it did gain for Rome significant rights and prerogatives at the same time it won for National Socialism international prestige. The most important concordat of all from Rome's perspective was the 'conciliazione' with the Italian government of 1929. The pope recognized the House of Savoy as sovereign of Italy, and renounced all claims upon the kingdom's territory. For its part the Italian government accepted the papacy as a sovereign state, with an autonomous government, rights and prerogatives, and its territorial base of Vatican City. Catholicism was recognized as the official religion of the Italian state, and it was agreed that when there was a dispute in politics which might involve religion the laws of the church were to prevail. The Lateran Agreements were immensely popular, and the triumph of Pius XI was complete when the Italian sovereigns made an official visit to the Vatican. A visitor who congratulated Pius XI on his diplomatic success was told: 'It's not a diplomatic act, but an act of Our priestly magisterium'.[3]

Inevitably it was said that the Vatican had become a mere organ of fascist propaganda, and the pope was greatly embarrassed by the invasion of Ethiopia, and by the terror tactics used by the state against Italian youth who served in Catholic Action, an organization which Pius had encouraged since 1922. Similar intimidation took place in Germany with episcopal palaces ransacked, and Hitler's press giving vent to scandalous anti-Catholic calumnies. Yet diplomatic relations were maintained, the pontiff issued warnings against the excesses of the fascist and nazi regimes, and crisis was avoided because both the totalitarian states and papacy were dedicated to the overcoming of international communism. The threat of marxism fully surfaced in Spain after 1931 when the king went into exile and the struggle between the political right and left became intense. Among the marxists, anarchists and socialists of the left were extreme anti-clericals and in the new republic there soon were mobs attacking convents and churches, the Jesuits were suppressed, and church property was confiscated.

The papal response was an encyclical of 1933 denouncing this great scandal, of Catholic Spain turning its back on God, but it had no influence on a situation which became worse from 1936 with the lynching of nuns, the burning of dozens of churches and the hunting of the clergy through the streets of the cities. What protection for the church there was came from the forces of General Franco who, with Italian and German allies, was to bring oppressive order to Spanish society after a thirty month bloody struggle. Clerical casualties in the civil war were numbered in the thousands. So far as the Vatican was concerned the church in Spain was now engaged in a crusade against atheistic communism. In the words of the Vatican periodical, *Osservatore Romano* of 8 January, 1937: 'To a militant conception of life, struggle for a doctrine is a holy war... only liberal agnosticism with its conception of tolerance in theory, as well as in practice... can be shocked by ideological struggles'. Arthur Hinsley, archbishop of Westminster who was created cardinal in 1937 declared the Spanish Civil War as: 'a furious battle between Christian civilization and the most cruel paganism that has ever darkened the world'.[4]

The Roman ideological struggle was highly successful in Protestant England in the years following World War I. In 1920 there was a Catholic community in England and Wales of over two million, the great majority of either Irish birth, or Irish descent. The number of priests had doubled in thirty years to almost 4,000, and in certain areas, such as Liverpool and around London the Irish enclaves were significant in political and social terms. The Catholic community was resented for being Irish; its priests, often foreign trained, were held in some suspicion still by a Protestant population which had tried to invoke the spirit of the Gordon Riots during the London Eucharistic Congress of 1908. On the other hand, like the ultramontanism of the nineteenth century which caught the imagination of so many European romantics after the Napoleonic era, the disillusioned of World War I were sometimes fascinated by the proclamations of certainty which came out of the Vatican. On the average between 1920 and the eve of World War II about 12,000 converts a year were received by the Roman Catholic church in Britain, including prominent literary figures such as Compton Mackenzie, and G.K. Chesterton and intellectuals such as Ronald Knox and Christopher Dawson. The fame acquired by eminent Catholics such as Gerard Manley Hopkins or Hilaire Belloc, gave the church in England a strong feeling of confidence, which was reinforced by a great growth in churches, chapels, seminaries and religious houses.

At the heart of this Roman Catholic resurgence was an illiberal ultramontane spirit, built around the *Ne Temere* decree, the anti-modernist oath, and the new code of canon law which had been promulgated in 1917, to eliminate any peculiar English customs in favour of Roman uniformity. It was not a time of intellectual growth, little of theological importance appeared after the death of Newman and Tyrell, and the modernist sympathizers like Baron von Hugel were passing away. When cardinal Bourne died in 1935 after presiding over the Catholic Church for more than thirty years, his successor as archbishop of West-minster was the Roman educated and very ultramontane Arthur Hinsley, a pro-tegé of cardinal Gasquet. Though Hinsley proved to be surprisingly 'English' in many of his sympathies, the Roman ethos of the church of England continued to develop with its spiritual home the *Venerabile*, the English College in Rome—in spite of the considerable excitement shown in Anglo-Catholic circles during a series of conversations from 1922 to 1926 in the Belgian town of Malines, between the Belgian primate, cardinal D.J. Mercier, and the elderly lord Halifax. Pius XI set straight his views on ecumenism, when in 1928 he issued his encyclical *Mortalium animos*: 'all true followers of Christ... will believe... the infallibility of the Roman Pontiff in the sense defined by the Oecumenical Vatican Council with the same faith as they believe the Incarnation of our Lord'.[5]

In the Church of England, and within nonconformity, the evangelicals seemed moribund from the 1920's onwards, and as Roman authoritativeness con-tinued to attract converts of the calibre of Maurice Baring, Evelyn Waugh, Graham Greene and Frank Pakenham, churchmen other than the Anglo-Catholics were uneasy. The government had clearly decided it was not going to have con-flict with the Vatican and its well-organized forces in so many parts of the empire, if it was possible. It seemed to one contemporary that there was a:

> ... tacit convention that the Roman Catholic minority in this country, which plays so little part in public life, even in proportion to its numbers, should be treated with an obsequious deference such as is not awarded to any other Dissenting body or even to the National Church.[6]

The confident spirit of the Roman Catholic church in Britain was well presented by the convert A.C.F. Beales whose heavily ultramontane view of the papacy, *The Catholic Church and International Order*, was published in 1941. In it Beales even praised the 'astonishing foresight' of Pius IX's 'Syllabus of Errors'. This ecclesiastical assurance was so characteristic of the English Catholic mind that one observer of his first Orange parade in Liverpool expressed astonishment that Protestantism in such a vigorous form still existed:

> I had always been brought up to believe that Protestantism was a dying cult and its adherents cowards and easily frightened; but this mob up here, led by that magnificent white horse, bearing a little boy dressed as a perfect duplicate of Prince William, did not look frightened at all.[7]

Nor was it: as late as 1958 the Roman Catholic archbishop, John Heenan, was stoned by Orange women and children on the streets of Liverpool. In 1985 an Orange parade could still bring about violent confrontation.[8]

II   Protestants and the Irish Free State

The sectarianism of Liverpool was a reminder to the British government that Irish troubles which posed a seemingly insoluble problem in both parts of Ireland, could easily extend themselves to 'the mainland'. The Catholic Irish in Britain were still considered in some praemunireal sense as an alien body who owed allegiance to the foreign authority of Rome. On the other hand the Protestants in Ulster, or those who had settled on the mainland were also in some sense alien, an uncomfortable legacy of the seventeenth century. The government felt uneasy when these Protestants appealed as in times past to the power of Westminster for protection from the aggressive papists who attacked them so often. In spite of the Irish nationalists' interpretation of history, once World War I was over the British government seemed to want nothing more than to be free of the Irish problem once and for all. The difficulty was, however, that the peoples of the two islands in the archipelago had had such intertwined histories for so long that separation seemed impossible, however tempting it might be to allow the Irish to 'sort themselves out'.[9] Failure to recognize this on the part of politicians and governments in the Irish Republic, in Ulster and in Britain was to contribute to the spilling of Irish and British blood for the rest of the century.

The radical division between Irish Catholics and Protestants in the twentieth century began with the rising of 1916, the terror of the war of independence, the civil war, partition and the differing interpretation put upon these events by the two 'nations' in Ireland. We have noted the burning resentment of archbishop Bernard, at the time of the 1916 rising, who believed then, with most of the population of Dublin, that the action of the rebels had been a seditious 'stab in the back' of a people at war:

> The Fourth and Tenth Dublins kept the glorious anniversary of their regiment's heroic landing at Sedd-el-Bahr by defending their own city against the blind self-devoted victims of the hun.[10]

All but a very tiny minority of southern Protestants agreed with Bernard's sense of outrage, which was much deeper than a mere wartime patriotic outburst. It was a reflection of the widespread sense of trauma experienced by the Irish Protestants who were shocked by the depth of hostility shown to all things British by an unknown number of the majority population. They realized they were living in a society where some of the population at least were willing to engage in the deepest of betrayals in a time of European crisis:

> This rebellion was certainly no mere desperate adventure of a few hot-headed youths, which was from the first foredoomed to failure. It had been carefully planned with the aid of the best military brains in Europe, and but for a series of accidents—fortunate or unfortunate

according to the point of view—it might well have succeeded in effecting all that the Germans expected of it, namely, the enforced withdrawal of a very large body of British troops from the western front at a very critical period of the war.[11]

It was impossible for the Protestant people to romanticize what Pearse and the other rebels had begun. Nor could they appreciate the vacillation of the British government which seemed willing to consider the political implications of the treacherous insurrection to please the American Irish lobby. In the words of Bernard: 'no one who lives in Ireland believes that the present Irish government has the courage to punish anybody'.[12]

'Punishing' was carried out, however, as we have seen, but in such a way that a radical division of the Irish people developed, although there was little violence in the country between May, 1916 and early 1919. When the Irish Convention began in July 1917 it seemed as if the social discord in the country had not seriously affected the church leaders who attended. The Catholic and Protestant episcopal delegates spontaneously took adjoining seats, but early in the debates the nationalist northerner, Joseph MacRory, then bishop of Down and Connor, made a disastrous sectarian speech: 'raking up the past and awakening some bitter memories of the Anglo-Irish conflict in the nineteenth century'. He was replied to by Col. R.H. Wallace, Grand Master of the Orange Order, bringing up the issue of the papal *Ne Temere* decree. Their clash was but a reflection of the division in thought which was now ominously appearing in the country. The Protestants believed that more and more of the young priests were beginning to support Sinn Fein,[13] and it was known that among the Catholics there was considerable clerical discussion of the ethics of rebellion.[14] As early as the beginning of 1918 it was clear that a rebellion was taking place in some areas; with big houses raided for guns, cattle being seized, and land ploughed up in the name of an Irish Republic. Long before the conscription crisis which drew together the republicans and the Catholic hierarchy the Protestants knew that a clash was coming between the peoples which would be more than ideological and where sectarianism would play its part for: 'in the end the priests were but the populace writ large'.[15]

When the violence erupted the Catholic hierarchy equivocated until the end of 1920 when the savage struggle between the I.R.A. and the police reinforcements, the Black and Tans, reached its zenith. Then two priests were killed, an attempt was made on the life of bishop Michael Fogarty, the nationalist prelate of Killaloe, and the country was shocked by the slaughter of Bloody Sunday, 21 November. The British by this time had attempted to bring Rome into the conflict, but the Vatican decided not to send an envoy to Ireland, as it had Ignatius Persico during the Plan of Campaign: 'the despatch of a legate to Ireland would not be opportune but might, on the contrary, help to create excitement and hinder a pacificatory action on the part of the pope'.[16] In the face of what Sir

Horace Plunkett and others regarded as the demoralization of Irish society which affected Catholics and Protestants alike, some of the Irish bishops were gravely alarmed at what was taking place. Others, however, recognized that in war-weary Britain there was a growing resentment of the excesses of the Black and Tans, and an increasing sympathy for the cause of Irish self-determination. This persuaded some like Michael Fogarty of Killaloe to become openly partisan in their political opinions. When there was a criticism of his Clare people bishop Fogarty defended them and their 'pure and intense religious life' in contrast to 'the filthy compound of burglary and murder, sodomy, bigamy and infidelity, child murder, divorce and sexual promiscuity that covers the standing pool of Saxon life':

> In Fogarty's mind the Anglo-Irish war consisted of the struggle of Holy Ireland against the filth and sacrilege of persecuting Saxons: no censure of the Irish could be expected from such a quarter.[17]

The Protestants were not unaware of the thought-processes of bishop Fogarty, and of so many who agreed with him. They grimly noted that when attempts to secure peace were first made one of the intermediaries was Fr. Michael O'Flanagan, a vice-president of Sinn Fein.[18]

The now elderly William Walsh of Dublin led in distinguishing between politicians and gunmen within Sinn Fein, and by 1920 cardinal Logue, although he continued to denounce both guerilla and government atrocities, was at one with the rest of the hierarchy in roundly condemning the government for the state of the country.[19] His comment on the carnage of Bloody Sunday, when the I.R.A. killed fourteen in the morning, and the Auxiliaries and the police twelve in the afternoon, was: 'If a balance was struck between the deeds of the morning and those of the evening, I believe it should be given against the forces of the crown.'[20]

When the war with the British came to an end with the signing of the Anglo-Irish treaty on 6 December, 1921, the Irish Protestants had no inclination to rejoice. The Ulster Protestants could look after themselves, as we will see, but in the south the harrying of the Protestant gentry began. It has been argued that the Protestant experience might have been even worse if the civil war, waged by Republicans who accepted or rejected the Anglo-Irish treaty, had not so exhausted the forces of Michael Collins and Eamon de Valera that they had little time or energy to harass the Protestants systematically. Nevertheless there was a significant burning of the 'big houses' during the struggle of 1922–1923, and the *Morning Post* of 23 March, 1923 listed 192 Irish Protestant residences and clubs burned in this period. Even the home of Sir Horace Plunkett of Irish cooperative movement fame went up in flames. Few southern Protestants would have failed to agree with his bitter comment on the Treaty and the British government's agreeing to 'a cowardly and treacherous surrender' to the rebels who had

won their victory 'at the point of the revolver'.[21] In the words of one southern
Protestant: 'England has cast us off and given us to the murderers'.[22]
Considering the savagery of this time, when the divided rebels killed off old
comrades by ambush or firing squads, it is perhaps remarkable that the
Protestants in the south did not suffer more than they did:

> Altogether in just over six months the new Free State government
> executed seventy-seven Republicans by shooting, more than three times
> the number executed by the British government in the two and half
> years of the Anglo-Irish war. Thirty-four of the Free State's executions
> were in the month of January, 1923 alone.[23]

The Protestant homes were easy targets, and whatever the motives of their
attackers, sectarian or otherwise, Protestants were reduced to a state of apprehensive terror: 'with their ostentatious loyalism, their ascendancy backgrounds,
and their isolated residences in the countryside they stood out as helpless
symbols, and as convenient targets for anti-British sentiment.'[24]

When Michael Collins indicated that he never considered the Anglo-Irish
treaty as a final settlement with his famous statement: 'The Treaty gives us freedom, not the ultimate freedom that all nations desire and develop to, but the freedom to achieve it',[25] the Ulster Protestants took for granted that force would be
used by the Free State to try to bring them under Dublin rule. The southern Protestants, in their turn, as they watched the savage hatred of the combatants during
the civil war, and the waning of it through mutual psychological exhaustion,
knew that a hard time lay ahead for them: 'like a house wrecked during a wild
party, Ireland had to be cleaned through and restored'.[26] They wondered, in the
light of their history, what toleration they would receive in a country where so
often their traditional enemies, the priests, had openly identified themselves with
and directed violent solutions to problems of 'cleaning and restoring'. A great
exodus of southern Protestants took place; many of the refugees went to the
north to reinforce the intransigent Protestantism of Ulster. Though many landed
families 'stayed on', others left after witnessing the destruction of their own
estates or those of neighbours. In county Clare alone, seventy of the eighty
landed Protestant families departed after 1919.[27] In other areas such as Westmeath, or around Ballinasloe, Protestants of all classes were advised to get out of
the country,[28] and in Leitrim the departure of the Protestants was hastened by the
burning of the Lurganboy school and teacher's residence.[29] Most disturbing of
all was the situation in West Cork where in 1922 seven Protestants were
murdered in the Dunmanway district, and there was a general belief that an
attempt was underway to drive them off their land.[30] Such were the Protestant
fears that in May, 1922 J.A.F. Gregg, the archbishop of Dublin, led a delegation
from General Synod to meet with officials of the provisional government to
inquire: 'if they were to be permitted to live in Ireland or was it desired that they

should leave the country'.[31]

In the midst of the troubles, when fires were set in county Clare Protestant churches,[32] the local Protestants had no time to consider what lay behind such harassment. All they knew was that there was probably no division between the nationalist terrorists and the priests who, they sometimes suspected, were directing the campaign of intimidation. Anticlericalism was rare among the revolutionaries:

> In Ireland, because of the peculiar half-ally half-opponent relationship between the Catholic Church and the nationalists, a full-blown nationalist anti-clericalism was scarcely possible, although a supine and occasionally extreme clericalism was.[33]

The Protestants knew how difficult it was for the priests to stand up to the people when their political passions were inflamed, and that even priests with good intentions: 'wilted, turned tail and shouted with the mob'.[34] Their abiding worry, however, was that some of the priests at least might be serving a sectarian cause, directing a kind of pogrom against the Protestants for religious not political reasons. This they had always feared, in the days of the Whiteboys, the Tithe War, and the Plan of Campaign, and such thoughts greatly engaged them as their houses were burned. Was there behind the onslaught a mentality like that of the Dominican preacher of Cullen's day, Tom Burke, who thought in terms of: 'a crusade against the infidel and the heretic' when he called for the banishing of everything Protestant and Anglo-Irish?[35] Protestant fears mounted when they heard of the murder of the aged and locally popular dean of Leighlin, John Finlay, and the throwing of a bomb outside the Protestant Representative Church Body office in St. Stephen's Green. On the whole, they considered that the suffering visited upon them was the work of Republican, rather than Roman Catholic, extremists, but they realized that this was a time of moral crisis for the majority people. This was shown by Gregg, the Protestant archbishop of Dublin when he warned of the danger to the whole of Irish society if the outrages were continued:

> If Ireland employs terrorism it must pay the penalty. And the penalty is that the country's own moral sense becomes terrorized—terrorized into silence, if not complicity. Ireland will sink into being a country without character. It would be a poor satisfaction to be a Free State and to have lost moral freedom...[36]

Gregg in April 1922 sought help from the Roman Catholic archbishop of Dublin, in making a public statement against the 'deplorable blood-shed', but he was told that archbishop Byrne was already, with the lord mayor of Dublin, attempting to mediate between the Free State and Republican leaders, and he did not think it wise to bring other pressure to bear. When news of further murders in Munster came in, Gregg in a sermon made a direct appeal to the authorities:

> I call upon the government of this country to take the necessary steps to protect a grievously-wounded minority, and to defend the Protestants of West Cork from a repetition of these atrocities, and to save the Protestants there and in other parts of the South from threatened violence and expulsion from their homes.[37]

It was a month later, as we have noted, that Gregg called on Michael Collins and William Cosgrave on behalf of General Synod to see if the government wanted a general expulsion of the southern Protestants. At that time hundreds were streaming across the Irish sea, as well as to the north, many of them having been burned out, and the British government was establishing a relief organization to help them. When the war finally ceased and the Free State came into being, Gregg, in an interview for the *Irish Times* on 6 December, 1922, suggested that all churchmen should unite in creating once more respect for the law as 'a sacred and inexorable thing':

> The teaching of obedience to law is the task imposed on the parent, the clergyman, the schoolmaster, and the statesman. In the moral as in the material sphere, years alone can restore what it has been the work of years to undo.

The Protestants in the first decade of government by the Free State began their policy of 'keeping a low profile' to avoid trouble in the community— especially that which might be stirred up by a priest. The Irish writer Sean O'Casey was raised in a strongly Protestant family where his father's literary diet was the bible, controversial sermons and Foxe's *Book of Martyrs*. So long as the Protestants 'kept to themselves', he said, there was no trouble with their Catholic neighbours:

> It was not too difficult for Protestants to be on decent neighbourly terms with Catholics—as clearly most of them did—while retaining a wholesome dread of what these same Catholics might do if they were mobilized to action by their priests.[38]

The Protestants made sure they were not brought into controversies over religious matters that arose during the government of William Cosgrave, who sought to placate the Roman Catholic church in every way possible. He had trouble, however, over the issue of divorce for under the English law inherited by the Free State it was permitted through private parliamentary bill. The Protestants approved of this arrangement which allowed them freedom of conscience, and in principle Cosgrave wanted to accommodate them, although he was him-self a very conventional Catholic. Archbishop Byrne of Dublin took seriously the imperial authority of the Roman church, however, and argued it had: 'a right to decree marriage laws for Protestants no less than for Catholics because all members who had been baptized are members of the Church and under its juris-diction'.39 Byrne even argued that it would be contrary to natural law to dissolve the marriages of the unbaptised. When Cosgrave gave in to such episcopal pressure and had divorce through private bills eliminated, the southern Protestants said little, but the Ulster Protestants noted how this example of Roman authority denied freedom of conscience.40

The unease among the southern Protestants persisted, and the problem of even a nominal conformity to the heavily Catholic environment of the 1920's remained for them a difficult one. One Protestant wrote to archbishop Bernard late in 1921 to protest the attack on his 'traditions, belief, customs, mental furniture and all that':

> Why I mainly fear and draw back from the new order, which I suppose will flood in upon us sooner or later, is not so much the material loss and annoyance as the tendency to cut us away from our roots, our civilization which is bone of our bone, flesh of our flesh.41

The Protestants in general showed little interest in the post-partition Irish cultural and language programmes. In 1923 the Church of Ireland's board of education complained of the Roman Catholic doctrine found in primary school phrase books, and objected to books by Padraic Pearse used in the teachers' training course. It also regretted that Irish was a compulsory school subject, as it was not the language spoken at home, and study of it denied pupils time which would be spent on more profitable subjects.42 C.F. D'Arcy, the future Anglican primate, who took great pride in his family's Anglo-Norman ancestry, appreciated what he called 'the intense self-consciousness of the Irish and their desire to assert themselves against the overwhelming strength of another people'. On the other hand he had no love for the authority of Rome which he believed crippled the Irish longing for self-determination. He wholly agreed with the opinion expressed by a friend while on a walking tour:

> Once standing on a hill-top in a populous Irish countryside we noted the great barrack-like buildings which the Roman Church had erected for her various orders. 'Those people', he said, 'would like to have us all under lock and key'. The saying expresses the genius and history of the Roman Church almost perfectly.43

The result of this feeling of forced cultural conformity to what was becoming an overwhelmingly Catholic state was a continuing emigration of Protestants from the south of Ireland. The number of Irish Anglicans declined from 1911 to 1926 by 34%—the greatest decrease was in Munster where the decline was 44%. Middleton's Protestant population fell by 60%; that of the Fermoy rural district by 50%.[44]

There was little overt discrimination against Protestants in the private sector of the economy where there were many Protestant employers who, according to Irish custom, 'looked after their own'. Such advantages, of course, were often the envy of local Catholics. Sometimes the charge of discrimination could be raised when it came to local government appointments, as in the celebrated case of Leititia Dunbar-Harrison who in 1930 was appointed county librarian for Mayo by a newly established central committee of local government. The Mayo library committee rejected her nomination on the grounds that she was lacking command of the Irish language, and soon the issue became of national concern with the accusation made that what really barred her from the job was the fact that she was not only a Protestant, but a graduate of Trinity College. Many Catholics, as well as Protestants, were dismayed by what was considered to be an obvious case of bigotry:

> To declare her unfitted by religion or by the fact that she holds a Trinity degree is to recreate under the cloak of Catholicism the spirit of ascendancy which cursed this nation for three hundred bitter years.[45]

At this juncture some of the Catholic clergy, led by dean E.A. D'Alton of Tuam, charged discrimination against a local Catholic candidate,[46] and the Mayo Catholic press hurled itself into what was perceived to be a renewal of sectarian struggle:

> Trinity culture is not the culture of the Gael; rather it is poison gas to the kindly Celtic people... At the command of the bigoted and Free-mason press, Catholic rights are ignored... We are the connecting link between the past generations of our great Catholic dead and the gener-ations yet unborn. We are the spearhead of the far-flung empire of Erin's exiled sons and daughters... Tolerance is synonymous with slavishness.[47]

This was a time for Protestants to keep their heads down. Cosgrave told the Roman Catholic archbishop of Tuam, Thomas Gilmartin that the constitution of the state forbade his interference directly: 'as I explained to Your Grace at our interview, to discriminate against any citizen... on account of religious belief would be to conflict with some of the fundamental principles on which this state is founded'.[48] In the event, however, Dunbar-Harrison was given another appointment which was considered to be: 'fair to the lady, soothing to the Mayo bigots, and good for the government'.[49] De Valera seemed ambiguous on the issue arguing rather wetly, from the standpoint of the *Catholic Mind*, that the people of Mayo were justified in seeking a Catholic librarian if the job called for entry into Catholic homes. To the *Catholic Mind* the uproar had resulted in a complete victory for the one true church: 'We do not mind good honest slaughter. In fact we delight in the profusion of scalps which adorn our wigwam.'[50] The *Standard* agreed that de Valera and others were in peril if they made bargains with the enemies of the people's faith who: 'resent the desire of Catholics to live the full Catholic faith'.[51] Archbishop Gilmartin was so heartened by this outburst of anti-Protestant zeal that in 1933 he formed, on behalf of Connaught children, the Catholic Protection and Rescue Society of Ireland: 'for the maintenance of 600 who but for its efforts would have fallen into the hands of proselytizers'.[52]

III   De Valera's Irish Society

In the minds of some people de Valera was considered to be anti-clerical because, during the civil war when the anti-treaty irregulars battled with the Free State government, the Irish hierarchy in a pastoral of October 10, 1922 sternly denounced what was 'morally a system of murder and assassination of the National forces'.[53] The bishops excommunicated those who persisted in carrying on the war, and among many followers of de Valera there was considerable bitterness towards the church. Particularly was this so at the time when the Free State carried out its executions of Erskine Childers and other members of the anti-treaty forces, and many continued to think like de Valera's supporter Sean Lemass who was to tell the *Irish Independent* on 14 March, 1925:

> We are opening the campaign now against the political influence of the Church. If we succeed in destroying that influence we will have done good work for Ireland and, I believe, for the Catholic religion in Ireland.

De Valera himself, on occasion, made extravagant statements about the Fenian cause but when it came to the church he shared nothing of the nineteenth century anti-clerical spirit of that movement. At the darkest hour for his cause, in the spring of 1923, when de Valera had to deal with a papal envoy sent on a fact-finding mission, his personal reply to a friendly message from the departing Mgr. Luzio was docile in the extreme:

> Please give to the Holy Father my dutiful homage. Though nominally cut away from the body of Holy Church we are still spiritually and mystically of it, and we refuse to regard ourselves except as his children.[54]

As a young man at Blackrock College in Dublin, where one of his closest friends was John D'Alton, the future cardinal archbishop of Armagh, de Valera had considered becoming a priest and was a regular participant in religious exercises.[55] He remained in a very religious environment when he taught at the Jesuit Belvedere College, and the Carysfort College of the Sisters of Mercy. When he was teaching at Maynooth he met many priests who were to become members of the Irish hierarchy, including the remarkably nationalistic Joseph MacRory. A great friend who had influence on his personal development was John O'Hagan, rector of the Irish College in Rome; while towards archbishop William Walsh he held 'the intimate personal affection of a son for a father'. De Valera was not exaggerating when he said in 1917–1918 in an election campaign that he was neither an anarchist nor an atheist, and assured the crowd that he had 'all his life associated with priests'.[56] De Valera was long known as a daily communicant and, in later years when he was installed as President, he had a private oratory, with the sacrament reserved, which he visited five times a day. His veneration of Rome was great; he met in private audience with four popes, attended three papal coronations, and was decorated with the highest papal decoration, the Supreme Order of Christ. Controversies such as those which finally appeared in Vatican Council II never disturbed de Valera: 'in all that concerns faith and morals he might fairly be called docile'.[57]

His religious beliefs influenced greatly his direction of domestic affairs when he came to power as the leader of Fianna Fail in 1932. The Free State that he inherited from William Cosgrave was already well on the way to becoming a confessional society where the government was reluctant to encroach on the entrenched position of the Roman Catholic church in areas such as education. Neither did it do anything to offset the 'preoccupation of the church with sexual morality'[58] which produced in the Free State a singularly puritanical social order. The bishops were obsessed with the evil of dancing among young people, and Thomas O'Doherty of Galway urged fathers 'to lay the lash upon their backs' if daughters came in late from a dance.[59] This was a time when, in the words of Sean O'Faolain: 'the Catholic church was felt, feared and courted on all sides as the dominant power'.[60] A host of lay auxiliaries, like the Knights of St. Columbanus directed a witch-hunt against Freemason influences in Irish society, supported by militant articles in periodicals such as the *Catholic Bulletin*, the *Catholic Mind* and the *Irish Rosary*. This oppressive social order, which was so repellent to Protestants in the Free State, as well as in Ulster was not uncongenial to Eamon de Valera:

> With his religion went a puritanical morality... He himself neither drank nor smoked... His strictures extended beyond the evils of drink to the evils of jazz, the evils of betting on the races, the dangers of indecent books.[61]

De Valera, when he came to power in 1932, had every intention of carrying on the religious policies of a state which was not a fully developed 'theocracy', but one in which: 'the Church has had considerably more influence than any ordinary interest group'.[62]

Fianna Fail had argued for some time that the Cosgrave government was supported by the Freemasons, and accused it of snubbing the hierarchy when diplomatic relations were being arranged with the Vatican.[63] Once he took over the government de Valera did everything in his power to ensure that there would be a minimum of friction with the Catholic church, in Ireland or in Rome. Soon after his government was formed in March, 1932 the pope received from de Valera a letter of 'respectful homage and good wishes' which stated: 'our intention to maintain with the Holy See that intimate and cordial relationship which has become the tradition of the Irish people'.[64] The cordiality of the relationship was clearly revealed in the Eucharistic Congress of 1932 in Dublin where de Valera served as one of the canopy bearers of the papal legate, cardinal Lauri. A million people reportedly attended the legate's mass; a half million were present for benediction at the O'Connell bridge and: 'Irish Catholicism was made into a world show-piece'.[65] Within Ireland it was now accepted that papal blessing had been bestowed upon Fianna Fail, and the tensions of the civil war period could be forgotten.

The following year de Valera made a Holy Year pilgrimage to Rome, and from this time his speeches show an inclination to equate 'Irish' with 'Catholic', when references were made to: 'our people, ever firm in their allegiance to our ancestral faith'.[66] This spirit of triumphalism was shared by his old friend archbishop Joseph MacRory of Armagh who had been made a cardinal in 1929. An Ulsterman, he had been bishop of Down and Connor during the riots of 1920–1921 when the Catholics had suffered grievously at the hands of Protestant mobs, and he was always a clerical 'defender of the faith' passionately opposed to partition. In the summer of 1932 he produced his: 'egregious utterance that the Protestant churches did not form part of the true Church of Christ'.[67] This led to a furious controversy in the columns of the *Irish Times* between MacRory and the formidable J.A.F. Gregg, the Protestant primate.

> On the Cardinal's side the correspondence ended somewhat abruptly; and a rumour got abroad (unauthentic but not inherently improbable) that His Eminence had received a peremptory message from the Vatican to this effect: 'Stop! This man knows too much'.[68]

De Valera himself qualified MacRory's militant Catholicism when in 1936 the cardinal was calling for Ireland to help 'poor Spain' by joining a Catholic crusade in the Spanish Civil War. The cardinal's analysis of the Spanish war was a simple one:

It is not a question of the army against the people, nor of the aristocracy plus the army and the church against labour. Not at all. It is a question of whether Spain will remain as she has been so long, a Christian and a Catholic land, or a Bolshevist and anti-god land.[69]

Ireland, however, did not break off diplomatic relations with Spain and, although Eoin O'Duffy led an Irish Brigade to fight for Franco, a non-intervention act kept Ireland from involvement in what was really the beginning of the 1939–1945 European war.[70] It is probable that through his Roman contacts de Valera knew enough about atrocities on both sides of the struggle to judge that involvement would engage Catholic Ireland in activities 'manifestly opposed to Christian principles'. Like pope Pius IX he: 'adopted an attitude for which he was sometimes blamed'.[71]

Though de Valera had begun the policy of Irish political neutrality European Catholic conservative intellectual thought had tremendous influence in all parts of society. The ideologues of the Irish ultra-right wing Blueshirt movement, Professors James Hogan and Michael Tierney, for example, had argued that their thought was based on the social encyclical of Pius XI, *Quadragesimo anno*, which had been published in 1931. They wanted for Ireland a kind of 'corporatism': 'the medieval guild system brought up to date'.[72] Other clerical extremists also played with similar ideas, such as Fr. Denis Fahey, a Holy Ghost father, who venerated the religious and social order of the thirteenth century based on the concept: 'there was one correct social order, willed by God, which it was the duty of all mankind to strive to attain'. The enemies of the Catholics who served such a vision were the Freemasons, the Jews and the Communists. Another who thought in such terms was one of de Valera's advisers, Edward Cahill, S.J. who wrote on *Freemasonry and the Anti-Christian Movement*, a work which was commended by J.C. McQuaid who became archbishop of Dublin in 1940. The *Standard*, a weekly newspaper founded in 1928, had much to say about: 'the creation of a united public opinion in the cause of Catholic reconstruction'. It also praised the social orders of Petain, Salazar and Franco during the years of World War II.[73] Protestantism generally was not directly attacked, but the strongly Republican bishop of Clonfert, John Dignan, who praised the constitution of 1937 as 'the Christian charter of a Christian people' saw fit to make an 'onslaught' against Trinity College in a lecture at Maynooth in 1933.[74] Many Protestants interpreted the attacks on Freemasonry as a threat to themselves by a Catholic society that had begun to heal the divisions of the civil war, and was now about to impose upon all citizens: 'the civil equivalent of Christian theology, the logical implication of its teachings'.[75]

As one of the foremost Catholic social writers of the time, the Jesuit Edward Cahill, in 1936, sent to de Valera a summary of Catholic principles upon which a new Constitution might be based. In reply de Valera asked Cahill to draft a preamble to such a measure, and this was done in a document which incorporated teaching from papal encyclicals, and articles on the constitutions of Poland in 1921 and Austria in 1934. John Charles McQuaid, who was then president of Black Rock college was consulted also by de Valera, as was the papal nuncio, Pascal Robinson, cardinal MacRory, and the archbishop of Dublin, Edward Byrne. Finally de Valera eased the anxieties of the Protestants and Jews by seeking the approval of archbishop Gregg, and the leaders of the Presbyterian and Methodist churches. The result of these discussions was article 44 of the 1937 constitution which recognized 'the special position of the Holy Catholic Apostolic and Roman church' but also 'recognized' the major Protestant churches, the Quakers and the Jews. It was admitted by de Valera in the Dail that some Catholics were disappointed in such a move towards pluralism, and later reports indicated that neither the pope nor cardinal MacRory were enthusiastic over what de Valera had produced.[76] The steadily declining Protestant population of the south was in no position to do other than express its relief that some measure of constitutional protection was now assured them. The zealous Catholics who might have caused trouble over this token of benevolence were silenced only when it became clear that the pope was not about to oppose the constitution, but the religious minorities remained uneasy throughout the period prior to and during World War II. In the *Irish Times* of 7 March, 1950 the theory of toleration expounded by the Catholic zealots was summed up with candour by the secretary of the Maria Duce movement which had come into existence during the war years. It was formed by the associates of Fr. Denis Fahey, the Holy Ghost religious, whose first book *The Kingship of Christ according to the Principles of St. Thomas Aquinas* had been praised by archbishop McQuaid after it came out in 1931. Maria Duce believed that 'intolerance of error is the privilege of truth':

The ideal (as outlined in the Syllabus of Pius XI, *Ubi Arcano* and *Quas Primas* of Pius XI) is that the Catholic State, while extending full liberty and official recognition to the Catholic Church alone, should not only not connive at the proselytism of non-Catholic sects, but should suppress them as inimical to the common good.[77]

At the very time that Maria Duce was making its statement of principle regarding religious toleration it was also trying to get up a petition to amend article 44 to encompass its beliefs.[78] This was also the occasion when the Knights of St. Columbanus tried by a packed-meeting coup to take over government of the Protestant Meath Hospital,[79] and a Catholic judge hearing a *Ne Temere* problem case ruminated that: 'possibly the constitutional recognition of the special position of the Catholic Church would authorize our Courts to take judicial notice of Canon Law'.[80]

Though cardinal MacRory may have had his reservations about article 44 of de Valera's constitution he publicly described it as 'a great Christian document...

a splendid charter—a broad and solid foundation on which to build up a nation that will be, at once, reverent and dutiful to God and just to all men'.[81] The problem was, as with any constitution, it was going to be interpreted in different ways by different men. When those who thought like the adherents of Maria Duce believed that the toleration expressed in the religious articles was a 'temporary expedient', then the Irish Protestants were more than concerned. The Ulster Protestants particularly asked themselves if their religion might not be suppressed, if it was decided at some future date in a united Ireland that Protestantism was 'inimical to the common good'. When the preamble to the constitution spoke of 'our Divine Lord, Jesus Christ, Who sustained our fathers through centuries of trial', the Protestants were bound to ask 'whose fathers': 'If there was only one Irish people, must the Protestant people jettison their heritage and deny their own fathers before they could become truly part of "the people of Eire?"'[82] When the Protestants considered further articles 2 and 3 which claimed that the constitution was to apply to the whole of the national territory, including Northern Ireland, then they felt threatened indeed. They did not have to be religious zealots to choose to reject what the close alliance of church and state had produced in de Valera's Eire: the bullying arrogance of the priesthood in controlling the sexual mores of the people, the controlling of conscience through the Censorship Act, the poverty of the lower classes which seemed often to be ignored by those in authority, and a stifling conformity in society. All these were to the Ulster Protestants, and to some Catholics anathema:

> The clergy, strong farmers in cassocks, largely voiced the concern of their most influential constituents, whose values they instinctively shared and universalized as 'Christian'... Rarely has the Catholic Church as an institution flourished, by materialistic criteria, as in the Free State. And rarely has it contributed so little, as an institution, to the finer qualities of the Christian spirit.[83]

De Valera legislated as a kind of lay legate: 'not as a son of the church, but as one of its fathers, albeit without actual ordination'.[84] In early years he had to rule out taking over the north by force: 'were it feasible, it could not be desirable'. The only answer he saw was the building up of a society which would be so attractive that the six counties would want to become part of Eire:

> The only hope that I now see for the re-union of our country is good government in the twenty-six counties, and such social and economic conditions here as will attract the majority in the six counties to throw in their lot with us.[85]

The problem was that once de Valera came to power, and devoted himself to working with the Roman Catholic church as closely as possible, he reinforced a church-state system of government which the Protestants found wanting in every possible way: 'it is not easy to see where and why Eamon de Valera drew the line between Christ and Caesar'.[86] De Valera copper-fastened partition through his success in nurturing in Ireland a religious culture, a clerical-ridden society, which the southern Protestants had no choice but to endure, in considerable anxiety, and at times fear, as in the case of a nasty local oppression in Kilmallock, county Limerick in 1935. There protestant churches, homes and businesses were attacked, until a protest from the Church of Ireland brought protection and restitution from the government.[87] Protestants generally became anxious whenever clerical force was mustered, as it was when the priests managed to shut down a publication, *Ireland Today* on the grounds that it supported the republican cause in Spain,[88] and also tried to intimidate the editors of the *Irish Times*.[89] The Protestants of Ulster for their part became ever more determined to resist irredentist pressures for a united Ireland. They saw nothing in de Valera's state that would attract them to become part of it. They believed George Bernard Shaw's prediction of 1928 had come true: 'having broken England's grip of her she slips back into the Atlantic as a little green patch in which a few million moral cowards cannot call their souls their own'.[90] They agreed with writers like Frank O'Connor: 'every year that has passed, particularly since de Valera's rise to power, has strengthened the grip of the gombeen man, of the religious secret societies like the Knights of Columbanus, of the illiterate censorships...'[91] Ireland had indeed thrown off the thrall of what it had chosen to view as foreign domination but, in the minds of many people, at the cost of accepting the oppressive domination of the court of Rome. What had been subservience to church authority, which was praised as piety, brought to the people of the southern provinces but a depressing freedom-denying rule where life was: 'lying broken and hardly breathing'.[92]

> Instead of de Valera's Gaelic Eden and the uncomplicated satisfactions of Ireland free, the writers revealed a mediocre, dishevelled, often neurotic and depressed petit-bourgeois society that atrophied for want of a liberating idea.[93]

IV   Ulster's Protestant State

The Ulster Protestants congratulated themselves that, long before the bitter realization of writers like O'Faolain and other liberal Catholics, they had foreseen what Rome rule would visit upon the Irish people. They accepted that, in the words of an Orangeman in 1869: 'Popery is something more than a religious system. It is a political system also. It is a religio-political system for the enslavement of the body and soul of man'.[94] They, of course, welcomed

Lloyd George's plan to give them their own separate rule, which benefitted the British by removing the Ulster problem from their direct control from 1922 until 1972. In actual fact what the formal opening of the Northern Ireland parliament in Belfast City Hall on 22 June, 1921 represented was the appearance of a Protestant dominated government determined to keep Rome rule out of Northern Ireland. I.R.A. attacks began in the same month and within a year communal sectarian violence had claimed over 2,000 victims, killed or wounded. Bigotry, sectarianism and violence was to continue to plague Ulster, which remained the most disadvantaged part of the United Kingdom, and behind the savagery of the street fighting lay the fear that the Free State would use the Catholic minority to help to take over the north. The Northern Ireland prime minister, James Craig, did make overtures to the nationalists, but they looked south to Michael Collins whose 'interest in the North's affairs was spasmodic and even hysterical and certainly took little account... of the likely impact of his actions on Unionist opinion'.[95] The Protestants displayed hysteria of their own when a pitched battle between the I.R.A. and police in Belleek and Pettigo on the Fermanagh-Donegal border reduced local inhabitants to a state of panic.[96]

The 'hysteria' which still lies latent in the minds of many Protestants throughout Ireland, as it has for so many generations, in Ulster took the form of Protestant anxiety that eventually the southern Catholic government would use force against them, with British connivance, to bring them into the 'confessional' state of Eire. The official biographer of James Craig, St. John Ervine, believed like others that acceptance of the position of prime minister of Northern Ireland was to Craig a vocational call: like Martin Luther he 'could do no other' than accept what God was calling him to do—to save Ulster from Roman tyranny:

> I am aware that this statement of Ulster belief will excite derision among the nervous degenerates who nowadays call themselves intellectuals... but it is enough to say that his countrymen believed, and continue to believe, that James Craig was, under God, chosen to perfect a task that must have baffled, if not defeated, any other person.[97]

In Catholic eyes he was a bigot, an Orangeman who had served as grand master of the county Down lodge, and he certainly showed great insensitivity and lack of imagination in dealing with the Catholic minority. Yet it has been argued that his régime was 'neither vindictive nor oppressive', and Craig was at most tactless when he made his famous statement to a nationalist critic when they discussed affairs in Dublin, where, he said, they: 'still boast of Southern Ireland being a Catholic State. All I boast of is that we are a Protestant Parliament and a Protestant State'.[98]

From the beginning there was no foundation of trust between the two communities in Northern Ireland, where 'the tyranny of the dead' influenced the people of both communities. When James Craig married his English wife in 1905 and brought her to Ireland she entered a world almost beyond her comprehension:

> The Pope had previously been to her a remote and irrelevant figure... who declined to leave the Vatican because he had had some trouble with the King of Italy... In Down she discovered he was a menacing figure whose precise place in the hereafter was a constant preoccupation of many minds... It might seem to her that His Holiness had little to do with the business of Holywood Urban District Council or the system of land tenure in Tyrone, but there were thousands of Ulster people who could tell her very different. A vote this way or that, and the entire College of Cardinals might be prancing in red robes around Donaghadee... Her knowledge of William III had been slight. He was, perhaps, she knew, a Dutchman who had dethroned his father-in-law. What she did not know was that he remained as actual in Ireland as if he were still inhabiting Whitehall.[99]

She soon discovered that in Ireland the word 'chapel' referred only to a Roman Catholic church. Simple people were confused and alarmed when they read that she and Craig had been married in 'the Chapel Royal'.[100] Such popular anxiety reflected Protestant vigilance over what were considered to be continuing papal machinations to bring them under Roman imperial rule:

> Under home rule... the parliament and executive alike are certain to be controlled by a majority subject to the direction of the author of the *ne temere* and *motu proprio* decrees against whose domination all safeguards designed for the protection of a Protestant minority... would be wholly valueless.[101]

When the Irish hierarchy bestowed its blessing on the nationalist resistance to conscription in 1918 the Ulster Protestants had all the proof they needed to convince them that home rule indeed would mean Rome rule, and this they vowed would never be extended to Ulster.

The anxiety of the Ulster Protestants reflected from the beginning some doubt that their six county state would be able to survive as a political entity. They realized that British sympathy for them was waning as the minority Catholics inevitably suffered the most in the sectarian warfare of 1920–1922. The government and republican forces in the Free State were savaging each other in the civil war, and had no energy to interfere in northern affairs where, as Protestant mobs carried out their intimidation tactics, the critical tone of the British press increased. The *Westminster Gazette* of 2 September, 1920 had a cartoon of Carson 'watching the Orange glow in Belfast'; the unionist

Birmingham Post of 12 July, 1921 warned that ill-treatment of Catholics was losing Ulster sympathy; and the *Daily Herald* was blunt in its condemnation of Protestant terrorism:

> The bloody harvest of Carsonism is being reaped in Belfast... The gangs who have organized the reign of terror are the very people who protest they are afraid that they would under even partial Home Rule be persecuted and denied religious liberty.[102]

Joseph MacRory, then bishop of Down and Connor, kept the government aware of what threatened to be a Protestant 'pogrom'[103] and Ulster's refusal to negotiate with the south was widely condemned as well as the bullying tactics of the Protestant mobs. The *Daily Telegraph* of 14 November, 1921 reminded its readers of the concessions Sinn Fein had made to bring the Anglo-Irish war to an end, and expressed hope that the government would persuade: 'Ulster that some concessions to the all-Ireland principle may be made without compromising her safety or essential interests'.[104] The Northern Ireland Protestants believed, however, that if their state was to survive they had to protect themselves, in the face of the determination of the forces arrayed against them. They never forgot Michael Collins' well-known dictum: 'the Treaty gave Ireland the freedom to achieve freedom'.[105]

So far as the northern Protestants were concerned every clash with the northern Catholics was a reflection of the desire of Dublin to bring them under its authority, and to dragoon them into the Roman religious community. When the first minister of education, lord Londonderry had a happy vision of nonsectarian schools, many Catholic schoolteachers and school managers looked to Dublin for moral support of their refusal to accept the 1923 education act. An inevitable movement then began which resulted in Ulster education being maintained on a partly sectarian basis.[106] So it was elsewhere in Ulster society. The hope was, originally, that up to a third of the police force would be Catholic, 'an untypically conciliatory move', but the Catholics because of I.R.A. intimidation, as well as Protestant bigotry, did not enlist in the way they had in the old Royal Irish Constabulary.[107] By 1936 the Ulster police were about 83% Protestant. Within the civil service hiring practices had long been sectarian, and so they continued. On the eve of World War II the argument that Catholics were 'disloyal' to the state ensured that the upper ranks of the civil service were almost totally Protestant, and the lower echelons 90% so: 'the minority's reluctance to serve a "foreign" government and the attitude of the government ensured that the civil service would not be representative of society at large'.[108] Election by proportional representation was abolished 'to clarify the issue between unionism and nationalism', to distinguish between 'men who are for the Union on the one hand or who are against it and want to go into a Dublin parliament on the other'.[109] Likewise gerrymandering, the alteration of elector boundaries was tolerated by James Craig, in order to maintain Protestant domination of local politics. Though it may be argued that Craig did contain the bigotry of some of his supporters, who would have gone to extreme lengths to determine that no Roman Catholic nationalist fifth column had any authority at all in Ulster: 'in the last analysis Craig consistently used the power of the state to further the interests of Protestantism and Unionism'.[110]

How justified were the Protestant fears in the pre-World War II period? Probably not great in the Cosgrave years when the nationalists in the south were concerned with finding reconciliation after the horrors of the civil war. The coming of de Valera to power in 1932 increased Protestant anxiety, however, for throughout his early political life he had made singularly threatening noises about the Ulster unionists. So far as he was concerned in 1917 they were 'not Irish people' but a 'foreign garrison'. He could find no theological argument which would deny the use of force against them,[111] and on his American journey he argued that he was sure that once they had been brought into a united Ireland the Ulster Protestants would gladly acquiesce in rule by Dublin.[112] Even their religious antipathies would fall away for he was sure that they reflected a framework of thought imposed upon the Ulster Protestants by the not-to-be trusted British:

> It was de Valera's constant assertion that Britain had originally fomented religious tensions in Ulster in order to divide Irishmen; that the culmination of this policy was partition; and that her motive throughout was to secure her strategic interests in the Atlantic.[113]

He remained convinced that eventually even the Orangemen would come to their senses and abandon their 'No surrender', 'Not an Inch' mentality:

> Sinn Fein is the only power to deal with the Orangemen. Let the Orangemen fall back on... their fortress of partition—that has no terrors for us. Let them fall back on it... It is after all only an old fortress of crumbled masonry—held together with a plaster of fiction.[114]

Yet de Valera was a distant figure compared to the immediate threat of the I.R.A. militants within Ulster. Hugh McAteer, who was to become the I.R.A. Chief of Staff in 1941, described the 'formation' of his generation in the late 1920's and 1930's when he was interviewed by a journalist in later years:

> All the boys in McAteer's area joined the Fianna, the boy Republican's scout movement, as children in happier areas would join the Cubs to become scouts later on... schooling by the Christian Brothers, attendance at Gaelic League classes (then controlled by the I.R.A.)... To the young men of McAteer's youth it was a toss-up whether they

joined the I.R.A. or became missionaries. Religious fervour and Republicanism were completely entwined.[115]

It was this 'complete entwining' which kept alive the fear of the Protestants that they were threatened with folk oppression. In the early years of the century, when the father of the poet Louis MacNeice was the Church of Ireland rector in Carrickfergus, the Ulster Protestants shared in a kind of communal anxiety as the threat of Home Rule once more threatened to become a reality:

> And I remember, when I was little, the fear
> Bandied among the servants,
> That Casement would land at the pier
> With a sword and a horde of rebels.[116]

Paradoxically the Casement they feared was in no way then enamoured of the 'priest-ridden' Catholics: 'the Irish Catholic, man for man, is a poor crawling coward as a rule. Afraid of his miserable soul and fearing the priest like the Devil'. In fact, Casement then thought that if freedom came to Ireland it would be 'only through Irish Protestants, because they are not afraid of any Bogey'.[117] Few Ulster Protestants ever had any longing for the kind of freedom that Casement wanted, nor could they consider their Catholic neighbours without some apprehension; if you were a rebel you were a Catholic, a servant of Rome, a threat to religion, and to Protestant culture. When they considered Casement's actions during the Easter Rising the Ulster Protestants responded like the young Basil Brooke, then home on sick leave after the horrors of the Gallipoli campaign. Just before he returned to his regiment, to serve in the holocaust of the Somme, he confessed his shame over this 'stab in the back', while so many other Irishmen were performing heroically on the field of war.[118]

There seemed to be no way to rid Ulster of its sectarian struggles which caused so much suffering when the new political entity of Northern Ireland came into being. Some historians accept that James Craig; 'genuinely wished to reconcile Catholic and Protestant in Northern Ireland'.[119] He was personally not a bigot, and was open minded enough to consider the possibility of a united Ireland in his own lifetime, but the division of the two peoples was too extreme for social peace to be legislated. As part of an agreement between Craig and Michael Collins in the spring of 1922 it was agreed that, in return for a complete cessation of I.R.A. activity in the six counties, a committee under the chairmanship of bishop Joseph MacRory was to choose Roman Catholics who would serve in the Ulster constabulary and patrol in nationalist areas. Through mutual suspicion nothing came of this venture.[120] A scheme to promote integrated education failed, partly because Michael Collins offered aid to Ulster teachers and school managers who would not recognize the northern govern-ment.[121] The failure of political and religious leaders to promote social reconciliation policies which the sectarian factions would accept contributed much to the carnage of the time. So far as the Protestants were concerned the Catholic forces were not only supported by the evil genius of Michael Collins, but by the sinister authority of Rome. When the Vatican sent to Ireland the one-time Maynooth student, Mgr. Salvatore Luzio, on a fact-finding mission during the southern civil war, a veritable howl was raised in Ulster where the Protestants were: 'honestly afraid of papal interference in the secular affairs of Ireland'.[122]

The independent-minded politician and journalist, Frank MacDermot, spoke in the Dail in the 1930's about the hope of a united but pluralist Ireland[123] but, as we have seen, the development of radical confessionalism tolerated by the authorities in Dublin ensured that there was no peace between the two parts of Ireland, nor reconciliation between the contending Catholic and Protestant peoples in Ulster. During the dreadful summer of 1935 when eleven people were murdered and over 600 were injured the Roman Catholic bishop of Down and Connor, Daniel Mageean, appealed to Westminster for help, and sought to work with his liberal Protestant counterpart, bishop J.F. MacNeice. Both prelates called on their flocks to live together in a spirit of Christian toleration.[124] This was the time when de Valera was about to prepare the Republic's new constitution with its claim to the northern territories, however, and the southern spirit of revanchism negated any hope of conciliation between Ulster's Catholic and Protestant peoples. By 1938 bishop Mageean was appealing to de Valera to press hard for the ending of Northern Ireland as a political entity: 'partition is an evil which only its removal can remedy'.[125] In the same year Mageean demanded a total separation of Catholic children from Protestants in the educational system: 'our motto is Catholic children to be taught in Catholic schools by Catholic teachers under Catholic management and in a Catholic atmosphere'.[126]

For Ulster's Protestants de Valera's constitution of 1937 ensured that their support for partition of the island would be unflagging. They had watched closely the development of the southern religious and political alliance during the 1930's, and what to them were confessional and irredentist clauses in the new constitution confirmed their worst fears. De Valera had done little to ease their anxiety throughout this period:

> His statement that Ireland 'remains a Catholic nation' reads very much like a declaration of intent. This was in 1935; and his declaration took on an ominous significance for the northern Protestants two years later, when a new constitution claimed for the Dublin government de jure authority over the six county area.[127]

Their sectarian sensibilities had hardly been soothed when, in the year the constitution appeared the southern Catholic politician, Sean T. O'Kelly said that: 'Fianna Fail policy was that of Pope Pius XI'.[128] Three years earlier O'Kelly had been decorated by Pius XI with the Grand Cross of St. Gregory the Great, and he was to be made president in 1945. Any talk of southern Ireland being a Catholic nation was tendentious to the Ulster Protestants.

When World War II came the Ulster Protestants expected that in the words of the old maxim, 'England's difficulty, Ireland's opportunity' there would be a resurgence of I.R.A. activity. After de Valera forestalled cross-border raids by interning leading I.R.A. members, allowing some to carry hunger strikes to the death, and shooting others, the Ulster Protestants watched with ironic detachment.[129] They were intrigued when cardinal MacRory had to be called upon to straighten out an ideological embarrassment when some I.R.A. prisoners in the north proved to be communists rather than good Roman Catholics.[130] They took for granted that, as always in Irish history, the priests would be identified with any social movement among the people, even when it came to rebellion. When 'militant spirits periodically turned to physical force', the Catholic community, including the priests, would not reject them:

> ... the majority of the Catholic population sometimes supported them, sometimes opposed them, but always accorded them a certain legitimacy, the logical conclusion of their rejection of the state and especially its security forces.[131]

The Ulster Protestants believed that in most cases, in both parts of Ireland, the majority of priests whether they supported violence or not were nationalists in their politics. At the very least they gave some encouragement to the anti-partition drive of the I.R.A. Some ultra-Protestants were even convinced that they did so under some form of Roman direction. The minority of southern political leaders who understood the Ulster mind, like Ernest Blythe and Tom Johnson, who had a long acquaintance with the northern Protestants, and neither of whom were Catholics, realized what the reaction of the northern Protestants would be to any southern statement of political policy, if it had a religious overtone. They knew what the northern Protestants would make of a statement by the southern Labour party:

> The Labour Party's policy is based on the papal encyclicals and they proudly acknowledge the authority of the Catholic Church on all matters which related to public policy and public welfare.[132]

If the Labour party thought in these terms, and Fine Gael had helped to spawn the ultra-conservative Blueshirts who flirted with ideas of Catholic corporatism, and Fianna Fail was led by de Valera, what would the Ulster Protestants do but shout again and again, 'no surrender', 'not an inch'.

To most outside observers in the years just before and following World War

II, or indeed since, the solution to Ulster's sectarian culture and the tensions between the Republic and Northern Ireland, has seemed deceptively easy: conciliate, and recognize a pluralistic development of peoples radically separated from each other in religion and in culture. In the words of one British civil servant:

> If the government of Northern Ireland wish partition to continue, they must make greater efforts than they have made at present to win over the Catholic minority, just as on his side Mr. de Valera if he wishes to end partition can only do so by winning over the northern Protestants. At present both sides are showing a lamentable lack of statesmanship and foresight.[133]

The problem for the leaders of the divided communities in Ireland, north or south, was that they, just as much as the people they represented were 'prisoners of history'. In the north it was a history that had produced the self-created 'ghettos' the people lived in, particularly in a city like Belfast, and a way of life which was a long struggle to maintain religious and cultural identity. A working class area like Sandy Row in Belfast had always been a strong Protestant enclave: 'not merely a confessional ghetto but a mill ghetto too. Its working population was effectually separated in all its roles from the population at large'.[134] Particularly was it separated from the Roman Catholic working class population in areas like the Falls Road which had its own strongly different way of life: 'in order to survive, in order to retain its vitality under discrimination, Catholicism tended to retreat into its ghetto and to maintain rigidly its side of the apartheid mentality'.[135] Life for the Belfast Catholics, which was not much unlike that of their southern co-religionists, was equally a reflection of their own history, religion and culture:

> It is a set of values, a culture, a historical tradition, a view on the world, a disposition of mind and heart, a loyalty, an emotion, a psychology—and a nationalism.[136]

As for the question of Irish unity, so long as its ethos was confessional most observers have believed that the Ulster Protestants would never willingly have agreed to become part of Eamon de Valera's Ireland:

> Partition was formidable, not because it was the last remnant of an outmoded colonialism, but because it was rooted in a variety of historical and contemporary circumstances which made the south abhorrent and an object of dark suspicion to the northern Protestant. The power of the Roman Catholic church in education, welfare and society in general; the lingering influence of the civil war in the public

life of the twenty-six counties and the ambiguous attitude of responsible politicians towards the I.R.A.; the restrictions on family life and on the freedom of the individual implied in the denial of divorce, the ban on contraception, and the operation of the *Ne Temere* decree which in effect dictated that the children of mixed marriages should be brought up as Catholics; the censorship of books (and, to a lesser extent, of films); the emphasis upon compulsory Irish—all this conveyed to the northern Protestant mind an overpowering impression of Catholicism, Gaelicism, and authoritarianism, triumphant and triumphalist.[137]

In Ulster, at the same time, there was a very large proportion of the Roman Catholic population which bitterly resented the economic, political and social ascendancy of the Protestants which characterized the years when Sir Basil Brooke was prime minister from 1943–1963. The era was increasingly defined by what one scholar has described as 'government without consensus'.[138] In Roman Catholic eyes consequently the 'unremitting way of politics' of the Protestant majority did much to further sectarian strife, and ensured that 'the barriers between protestant and Roman catholic were virtually unbreached'.[139] Yet during the post-war years new ways of thinking, and new forces were coming into existence, and it was inevitable that the old orders were about to change in both parts of Ireland.

Chapter XII

The Struggle for Pluralism

'There is a spiritual dimension to the problems of Northern Ireland. If the churches are part of the problem—they must be part of the solution...'

Rt. Rev. Robin Eames. Pre-Synod
Sermon, 1981, St. Patrick's Dublin

I   The Papacy Since World War II

There was no indication of the ecclesiastical revolution that was to take place in the Roman Catholic church during the pontificate of Pius XII from 1939 to 1958. The last representative of the age of ultramontane triumphalism he was a canonist who had had long service as a nuncio in Germany. Pius had shown his authoritarian temper and diplomatic abilities during the 1930's when, as papal secretary of state, he carried through the concordats with Germany and Austria. Inevitably, he was elected because of his diplomatic experience on the eve of World War II, the first secretary of state to be made pope since Clement IX in the late seventeenth century. Strongly anti-communist, he was accused by his detractors of showing pro-German sympathies, of maintaining 'silence' over matters like the persecution of the Jews,[1] and of tolerating the crusade carried out by the Roman Catholic Croatians against the Orthodox Serbs and others in Yugoslavia.[2] However Pius XII may be judged, the papal authority was not enhanced during World War II, as Albert Camus told the Dominicans of Latour-Marbourg in 1948:

For a long time during those frightful years I waited for a great voice to speak up in Rome... It seems that the voice did speak up. But I assure you that millions of men like me did not hear it... It has been explained to me that condemnation was indeed voiced. But that it was in the style of the encyclicals which is not at all clear... What the world expects of Christians is that Christians should speak up loud and clear... that they should get away from abstractions and confront the bloodstained face history has taken in our day.[3]

Theologically Pius XII was confrontational: his encyclical *Humani generis*

of 1950 warned against the accommodation of Catholic theology to current intellectual trends, while his *Munificentissimus Deus* and *Ad coeli reginam* of 1950
and 1954 defined the dogma of the bodily assumption of the Blessed Virgin Mary
to the dismay of ecumenists. Pius canonized thirty-three persons, including
pope Pius X, created an unprecedented number of cardinals, and blessed millions
who flocked to Rome for the Holy Year of 1950 and the Marian Year of 1954.
He displayed his diplomatic skill through accords, advantageous to the church,
with Dr. Salazar's Portugal and General Franco's Spain. His appointment of
new cardinals reduced the Italian element in their college, and Pius acted as his
own secretary of state from 1944 while he increasingly diminished the numbers
of those who were allowed to advise him. In his later years there was resentment
within the Vatican over the narrowness of the circle close to Pius, and though
there was general satisfaction with the triumphalism of his pontificate his authority was probably greater outside Rome than it was inside the curia. He was
the first pope to become widely known because of radio and television, and his
authoritarian conservatism caused considerable unease among many Protestants
who considered *Humani generis:* 'the last gasp of unchecked "integrism", the
charter of ultramontanism'. His 1951 encyclical *Sempiternus rex* included the
decidedly unecumenical statement: 'Is it not holy and salutary and according to
the will of God that all at long last return to the one fold of Christ'.[4]

In the immediate post-war years when the Vatican's policies were easily identified with the anti-communist crusade of the 1950's, Roman influence was at its
height in England. The dominant ethos among the Roman Catholic bishops
was that of the *Venerabile,* the English College at Rome where the attitude
towards Protestantism was defined in the 1930's by William Godfrey, who was
appointed Britain's first apostolic delegate in 1938, and became archbishop of
Westminster and a cardinal before his death in 1963. One of Godfrey's students,
when Godfrey was rector at the college dryly noted the ecumenical spirit of the
time in his diary:

> Rector put up notice about Protestant bibles. No one should buy or
> retain same in the college. All centres of Protestant propaganda in
> Rome must be avoided.[5]

Arthur Hinsley, who became cardinal archbishop of Westminster in 1935 and
had been a rector of the *Venerabile* as we have noted, though he proved to be at
times accommodating in his religious expression, and did pray with separated
brethren during the crisis of the war years, always maintained a theological
outlook that was consistently and clearly Roman. The most ultramontane and
able of the English Catholic leaders, however, was archbishop and cardinal John
Heenan. Of an Irish background, he once confided to Malcolm Muggeridge that
he had 'never had a serious doubt in his life'.[6] In 1950, the Holy Year of
Humani generis he was directing a mission to 'bring back the mass to every

village in this isle', and was to be appointed bishop of Leeds in what was to be looked back upon by the ultramontanes as a time of 'high euphoria'.[7] When Heenan became archbishop of Liverpool in 1957 he was a strongly conservative churchman, unhesitatingly maintaining the positions he had assumed as a student in Rome. Yet even he in the year that Vatican Council II began had organized a conference on ecumenism at Heythrop College with cardinal Bea as the principal speaker. The great revolution was about to begin.

The successor of Pius XII was the most famous of all the pontiffs of the twentieth century, John XXIII. He had had a varied career, working during the war years in Greece and France. In the former country he had devoted himself to relieving distress, as well as protesting the deportation of Jews, and as nuncio in France had dealt firmly with the many bishops accused of collaborating with the Vichy régime. At the time he became pope he was patriarch of Venice, noted for his pastoral zeal and informality. Seventy-seven years old when consecrated, this pastoral pontiff, who revered Charles Borromeo, the reformer of the sixteenth century, set about revising the canon law, holding a Roman diocesan synod, and summoning the great ecumenical council, Vatican Council II. The calling of the latter he attributed to a sudden inspiration of the Holy Spirit. The objectives of the council were to be a regeneration of the church, through a revision of its teaching, discipline and organization, as well as a consideration of means for a reunion with separated brethren in both the east and the west. The prelates at the council were urged to expound truth positively, without relying on the anathemas of times past. Eighteen non-Roman observers were invited to the council and, though John XXIII did not live to see the end of the process, what he had initiated proved to be an ecclesiastical revolution in terms of opening the universal church to dialogue with the world. From the standpoint of inter-church relations his most important encyclical was *Ad cathedram Petri* of 1959 with its reference to non-Roman Catholics as 'separated brethren and sons'. It set the spirit for what developed in the conciliar meetings between 1962 and 1966.

Few pontiffs have so captured the imagination of the non-Roman Catholic world, or so stirred the many bishops who sensed that the unyielding spirit which had characterized the Roman church for so long was at last being challenged. 'Good pope John' was succeeded in 1963 by one of the prelates who had assisted him in the planning of the council cardinal Montini, who took the name Paul VI. The new pope found himself very much under the spell of what John XXIII had begun, and though he was generally considered to be much more conservative than his predecessor he brought the council to a conclusion, and began the difficult task of implementing its revolutionary decrees. In pursuit of ecumenical understanding he met with Michael Ramsey, archbishop of Canterbury, in 1966 and held discussions with the Ecumenical Patriarch. To try to ease tensions with the Protestants his public pronouncement *Matrimonia mixta* permitted modest relaxation of the regulation for mixed marriages, but it did little to please the separated brethren. Even more disturbing to his own flock was *Humanae vitae* of 1968 which condemned artificial methods of birth control. The pope was profoundly shaken by the international rejection of the stance he had taken in this encyclical, and among those who criticized his viewpoint were the Anglican bishops who met in the Lambeth Conference of the year the pontiff made his stand. Anglican sensibilities were also disturbed by Paul VI canonizing forty English and Welsh Roman Catholic martyrs of the age of religious wars in the sixteenth and seventeenth centuries.

Paul VI had many critics among those churchmen in his own communion and among the separated brethren who believed he would consider only those reforming measures which did not impinge upon the pope's primacy, or the teaching authority of the church, the *magisterium*. He was willing to meet with the evangelical archbishop of Canterbury, Donald Coggan in 1977 and pledge united work towards reunion, but no mention was made of intercommunion, which the archbishop had suggested. Paul VI was a pontiff who much of the time found himself in a state of siege. One of the leading English Roman Catholics at the council had been the open-minded Benedictine Christopher Butler, abbot of Downside. Thoroughly loyal to the papacy, he was yet clearly not of the traditional school of English ultramontanism. Just after the council he was appointed auxiliary bishop of Westminster. The new bishop revealed the deep disquiet felt by many English Roman Catholics over *Humanae vitae* in a remarkable interview he gave to the *Sunday Times* on 6 October, 1968 which was entitled 'The Dictates of Rome'. In the article Butler referred to what he believed was an unfortunate development in England, the virtual though reluctant rejection of the encyclical by people of otherwise 'good conscience': 'at the very point where authority fails to communicate its message to the conscience, it fails to be effective authority'. It seemed that this encyclical alone was encouraging, perhaps even among churchmen like bishop Butler, a new mentality which Paul VI would have a difficult time to control. The distress of the pontiff when he had to deal with outspoken critics of Rome, such as professor Hans Kung of Tubingen, was perhaps even greater than that of cardinal Heenan who confessed in later years:

> He simply could not understand how transubstantiation, the Virgin Birth, or papal infallibility might worry a good priest. Ecumenism was a matter of friendly gestures; it could not have occurred to him that it might involve the recognition that in some things traditionally controverted, Rome could have been wrong, Protestantism right... His ultramontane training never questioned, left him helpless.[8]

When Paul VI died in August, 1978 his successor was one of John XXIII's episcopal appointees who had become, like his patron, patriarch of Venice. John Paul I was a conservative theologically who defended *Humanae vitae*, but when he found after his election that the majority of the cardinals wanted a curbing of the power of the curia, he announced his intention to press on with the reforms which had begun with Vatican Council II. Unfortunately, John Paul I was denied the opportunity to promote any change for only three weeks after his simple inauguration, rather than the traditional papal coronation, he was found dead in his bed, the unfortunate victim of a heart attack.[9]

The new pope, John Paul II, was the unprecedented choice of the conclave inasmuch as he was the first Slavic pope, the first non-Italian pontiff since Hadrian VI in the early sixteenth century. Archbishop of Kraków from 1963, and cardinal from 1967, he was a formidable adversary of the communist government of Poland as he strongly supported the Polish primate, Stefan Wyszynski in his struggle for freedom for the church. He was also prominent in Vatican Council II, and in the service of the Vatican became a familiar figure in many parts of the world. Resolutely conservative in theological matters he had influenced Paul VI in the creation of *Humanae vitae,* and his many personal missions to distant parts of the church usually resulted in an extension of Roman authority at the cost of the concept of collegiality among the bishops which had been evolved in Vatican Council II. John Paul II showed that he was intent to reassert the concept of papal primacy and the authority of the *magisterium* wherever he went, as he sought to maintain distinction between the sacred and the secular, the clergy and the laity, men and women, and the church and the world. Theological speculations which had abounded since the end of the council were to be curtailed, lest he has said they confuse the faithful: 'It is the right of the faithful not to be troubled by theories and hypotheses'.[10]

In the opinion of Roman Catholic conservatives John Paul's great sense of certainty and mission has been heartening, for many of them believed the church was losing a sense of direction during the last days of Paul VI's pontificate. They have appreciated his encouragement of Opus Dei, that very conservative religious body, and his opposition to most forms of 'liberation theology'. Conservative curial figures like cardinal Joseph Ratzinger have been allowed to use the Sacred Congregation for the Doctrine of the Faith as a form of 'holy inquisition',[11] in the opinion of liberal Catholics. The same people have been dismayed by the growing criticism of national and regional councils of bishops expressed by Ratzinger and other curial functionaries who view them as undermining Rome's authority. The Vatican has deliberately appointed conservative prelates in sensitive areas of the church such as Holland, where the spirit of liberalism was considered to have gone too far. Attempts have been made to bring to heel earnest reform-minded theologians, and the foremost of them all, Hans Kung, has been viewed by the Roman authorities as a kind of modern intransigent Luther.[12] When Dr. John Magee, who had been secretary to Paul VI, John Paul I and John Paul II, was appointed to be bishop of Cloyne in Ireland, his elevation encouraged much media comment. Rome's action was seen by some Irish churchmen as political, a deliberate attempt to centralize authority at the expense of local diocesan concerns:

This is alarming, not only for the laity in the Church who lost their
theological dignity long ago, but also for the clergy in a diocese who
have now been barred as well from participating in episcopal election,
and thus are reduced to rightless servants of any Roman appointee.[13]

Protestants generally have watched with interest and concern the attempt of
the papacy to reassert its authority against the collegiality movement which has
had appeal to so many Catholics. What they have seen of John Paul II has persuaded them on the whole that Hans Kung is right when he speaks of Rome seeking not dialogue with the faithful but submission.[14] Nor do they appreciate
Rome's: 'return to the tradition which said the world had nothing to teach the
church, but should adapt to the monolithic world view propounded by the present
Vicar of Christ'.[15] When the Protestants of Britain looked at the final report of
the Anglican-Roman Catholic International Commission (ARCIC) of 1981,
with its blithe assumption that primacy and conciliarity could be balanced within
a single communion, they were willing to admit that 'under the Holy Spirit our
churches have grown closer together in faith and charity'.[16] At the same time
they saw little in the style of authority favoured by John Paul II to convince
them that Rome's idea of 'conciliarity' would be attractive to them in any future
united church. They did not fail to notice, for example, that when it came to the
Roman Catholic moral teaching in sexual matters, a conservative teaching was
forced upon all churchmen, and implacably reasserted by the court of Rome
month by month. Most Protestant churchmen were pleased when the pope
visited Canterbury cathedral, and they recognized that his pastoral concern
included a very real desire for union with other Christians such as the Protestants
of Britain. Nevertheless they realized that John Paul II's concept of reunion
would demand their unconditional surrender to a very authoritarian form of papal
government:

> Only slowly did it become painfully clear that the direction he was
> taking the Church was such as to make reunion with anyone quite out
> of the question, an absolutism just a little reminiscent of the Stalinism
> he had fought so hard against.[17]

From the beginning of his pontificate John Paul II has made it clear, as in
his encyclical *Redemptor hominis* of March, 1979, that his approach to separated
brethren would be a missionary one. This has been conveniently overlooked by
some ecumenists, but the reality of the pope's 'missionary' attitude was an issue
during the visit of the archbishop of Canterbury, Robert Runcie, to the Vatican
in the autumn of 1989. In an interview with the Italian magazine, *Il Regno,* the
Anglican primate expressed his belief that his co-religionists were: 'beginning to
recognize and welcome a Petrine, universal, primacy in the office of the Bishop
of Rome.[18] Criticism of Dr. Runcie was immediate on the part of ultra-Pro-

testants who described him as a 'crypto-papist', while Ian Paisley, the Ulster
Free Presbyterian compared him unfavourably with Judas Iscariot. Other critics
pointed out that the archbishop's call for the pope to be accepted as leader of a
universal church conflicted with the queen's position as supreme governor of the
Church of England.[19] To the press, at least, it appeared as if Dr. Runcie, be-
witched by the pomp and power of Rome, had been so submissive in attitude
that he had even agreed to sign a common declaration warning that the issue of
women priests was a threat to any unity between the churches.[20] As for the
pope, his missionary attitude remained strong, and he ignored the suggestion that
he consider some ecumenical 'primacy of honour'. In the words of Conor Cruise
O'Brien:

> In receiving Dr. Runcie, John Paul II definitely has had conversion in
> mind: nothing less than the return of England to Rome. For the pope,
> Anglicans are not people of another religion, they are of the same
> religion—the true and Rome one—who fell from grace in the 16th cen-
> tury. They must be restored to grace, with civility and tact, amid
> expressions of 'esteem, respect' and so on.[21]

II   'Rome Rule' in Ireland

Winston Churchill wrote of 'the dreary steeples of Fermanagh and Tyrone
emerging once again' after the cataclysm of World War I, when the 'integrity' of
Ulster's quarrel with the Catholic south of Ireland was relentlessly continued.[22]
Eire's neutrality during World War II did nothing to ease the tension between the
two parts of Ireland. In contrast to the south, Ulster strongly supported the
allied war effort, played host to hundreds of thousands of American servicemen
before D-Day, experienced thousands of casualties through German bombing
(922 killed) and deepened its unionist sentiments, causing Churchill to praise the
north for its loyalty: 'the bonds of affection between Great Britain and the people
of Northern Ireland have been tempered by fire and are now, I firmly believe,
unbreakable'.[23] Though a great many Irish Catholics from both Ulster and the
south served in the allied forces, there was among the northern Protestants a
resentment that northern Catholic bishops opposed from the beginning of the
conflict any form of conscription in Northern Ireland. Sectarian issues were the
subject of debate in the northern parliament where Craigavon's successor, J.M.
Andrews, an Orangeman and a unionist, constantly displayed his fear of 'the
embrace of Dublin'. His successor from 1944, Sir Basil Brooke, shared this
deep-seated conviction that Dublin was intent upon extending its authority to the
north by any means possible.[24]

To the Ulster loyalists Eire's neutrality was considered, on the popular
level, to be pro-German and, to a people at war, unforgivable. When the I.R.A.

launched a bombing campaign in Britain in 1939, and made overtures to Hitler, the Protestants gave little credit to de Valera for his use of the Emergency Powers Act which was used against them the following year. There was briefly a drawing together of Catholics and Protestants during the Belfast Blitz where, except for London, there were more casualties in one night than in any other British city until that time. The whole community were grateful for the help of southern fire brigades which came from as far away as Dublin.[25] The Falls Road escaped attack, however, and not one Catholic Church suffered: 'people afterwards attributed this to the fact that God was a Catholic'. On the other hand Protestant areas suffered much and: 'rumours circulated... that Catholics had helped to guide German bombers by shining torches from the roof-tops'.[26] Anti-Catholic antipathy quickly reappeared in the Protestant community as the I.R.A. continued its sporadic outrages, and war workers came from the south to benefit from the booming war economy.[27] The northern Protestants noted that censorship in the south ensured that there was no active criticism of German excesses in the press[28] and, of course, they thought ill of de Valera's visit to the German embassy to offer condolences on the death of Hitler. Except for the 50,000 volunteers from the twenty-six counties who supported the war effort, the division between north and south, Protestant and Catholics, would have been even greater than it was. Yet even the great number of southern volunteers did not ease the separation of the peoples which by the time the war was ended was a bitter one: 'the six counties, by the magnitude and devotion of their war effort, had done more to perpetuate the partition of Ireland than a whole generation of Twelfth of July demonstrations'.[29]

The religious ideology nurtured by 'the dreary steeples of Fermanagh and Tyrone' also played its part in the separation of the peoples, as did the mentality that emerged in the south during the 'emergency' of the war years. Psychologically Eire's neutrality determined that the southern Irish people were in almost total isolation from what was developing elsewhere, so that the creativity and new thinking about the future that developed following the conflict influenced her hardly at all. Eire remained in a kind of intellectual time-warp produced by an 'ourselves alone' mentality that appeared at times to be singularly unattractive. In the midst of the war against the Nazis a Dail member, Oliver Flanagan, was 'coyly anti-semitic' when he called for regulatory orders: 'directed against the Jews who crucified our Saviour nineteen hundred years ago and who are crucifying us every day in the week'.[30] Such an outburst of ethno-religious intolerance was disturbing not only to most Irish Catholics and Protestants but also to the many liberal writers who from 1940 contributed to Sean O'Faolain's periodical *The Bell*. O'Faolain and the others were sharp in their criticism of the nationalist cant and hypocrisy of the time, and he reminded his readers that wherever the southern Irish were accepted as 'part and parcel of the general world-process' their writings were seen to have a 'distinct English pigmentation'.[31] O'Faolain's credentials were such that he could not be dismissed as just an ascendancy free-thinker writing to the *Irish Times,* and he was ably supported by other contributors to *The Bell.* They made clear that they had no use for an insular confessional culture which would: 'exploit the worker, or assail the Jews, or outlaw the Protestants, or gag the writers'.[32] They particularly refused to countenance in Ireland Rome's direction of a Catholic society reduced to acting as 'a Charlie McCarthy to the Vatican's Edgar Bergen'.[33]

In the post-war years there was no doubt among many of the Protestants of both north and south that the hand of Rome still lay heavily upon the Catholic people of Eire. When an inter-party government replaced that of de Valera in 1948 the new taoiseach, John A. Costello, begged that the authority of Rome be deepened and extended in Eire as a means of 'spiritual fortification': 'when the dark forces of materialism are threatening the foundations on which the great Christian nation of the earth endeavoured to build for their peoples'.[34] One of the first acts of Costello was to send a message of fealty to the pope:

> ... to repose at the feet of your Holiness the assurance of our filial loyalty and of our devotion to your August Person, as well as our firm resolve to be guided in all our work by the teaching of Christ, and to strive for the attainment of a social order in Ireland based on Christian principles.[35]

When Rome declared a Holy Year in 1950 Eire was represented by the minister of External Affairs, Sean MacBride who was remembered by the Ulster Protestants as an I.R.A. leader when a major bombing campaign in the mid-1930's was threatened and caused great alarm.[36] The government was also officially present when the dogma of the assumption of the Blessed Virgin Mary was proclaimed in November of the same year. Protestant unease was great by this time for they recognized that:

> Forces were at work to make Ireland a more totally Catholic State than it had yet become: more totally committed to Catholic concepts of the moral law, more explicit in its recognition of the special position of the Catholic Church.[37]

So far as the Irish Protestants were concerned the worst 'Home Rule means Rome Rule' fears seemed to be realized, as we have noted, during the 1950's when the ultramontane Maria Duce movement was pressing for the Roman Catholic church to be recognized by the state as 'the one true church' in the Republic. Its extremist members had an atavistic interpretation of the limits of religious toleration that was redolent of the age of the *dragonnades:*

> For a Catholic, religion is a matter of dogmatic certitude. For him there is only one true religion. In consequence all non-Catholic sects,

as such, are false and evil, irrevocably so... Toleration for a Catholic always implies that what is tolerated is an evil...

Most readers of the *Irish Times* of 7 March, 1950 who read the Maria Duce statement dismissed it as fanatical cant by an extremist minority. Many Protestants, however, were dismayed when the article also suggested that the state had the obligation in a Catholic nation to work with the church in converting or suppressing 'non-Catholic sects'.[38] This was a time when Catholic militants chose to 'recover' children of the majority faith from Protestant orphanages when they were believed to be threatened by proselytism.[39] It was also the time when public interest was focused on the famous Tilson case which was finally brought before the Supreme Court, and brought a flood of angry letters in papers like the *Irish Times*.[40] Ernest Tilson, a Protestant had married a Catholic girl in a Catholic church, and had made the usual promises that the children of the union would be brought up as Catholics. When the marriage broke down in 1950, however, he lodged his three eldest children in a Protestant home to be raised as Protestants. The Supreme Court finally agreed with a lower court judge that the boys concerned be returned to their mother, but in this widely reported case there was considerable discussion of articles of the constitution which might influence the judicial decision. The only Protestant in the Supreme Court dissented from the majority decision, which many of his co-religionists believed underlined the power of the Roman Catholic church in a clerically-dominated state.[41]

The attempt of the Roman Catholic church to separate its young people from possible Protestant influence at university had led the hierarchy to discourage Catholics from attending Trinity College from as early as the 1920's. After John Charles McQuaid became archbishop of Dublin in 1940, however, a full ban on any kind of 'educational miscegenation' was established:

> The Church forbids parents and guardians to send a child to any non-Catholic school, whether primary or secondary or continuation or university. Deliberately to disobey this law is a mortal sin, and they who persist in disobedience are unworthy to receive the sacraments.[42]

By 1956 this Dublin archdiocesan ban was supported by all the other bishops. At the same time conservative bishops such as Cornelius Lucey of Cork were decrying socialism and other political evils on the grounds that the church as the divinely appointed guardian and interpreter of the moral law had the right to act as the final arbiter in matters of rights and wrong, even in the political arena.[43] Few Protestants of the 1950's as they witnessed the growing militancy of the Roman Catholic church in the Republic would have argued with the judgment that there was everywhere in the nation abject capitulation of the secular to the spiritual power:

It is the church that rules Ireland today, and no politician, however anxious to differentiate himself from his followers would dream of challenging that basic fact.[44]

Even the southern Labour party acknowledged, as we have noted, the authority of the Catholic church on all matters relating to public policy and public welfare. Organizations like the Legion of Mary were ensuring that there was a 'permeation of the community with Catholic principles and Catholic feeling',[45] continuing the earlier work of the *Catholic Mind,* and the *Catholic Bulletin,* which had excoriated Trinity College and the remnants of the old ascendancy at the same time they demanded greater censorship to protect the faithful from evil.[46] Most southern Protestants accepted that their lot was to live in: 'some kind of theocratic state, in which a government formally answerable to the Dail and the people could in some way be manipulated by the church behind the scenes'.[47]

The exposé of hierarchical power in the Republic that the Protestants were never to forget was made when, in the words of the historian John Whyte, the minister of health in the coalition government of 1951 Noel Browne 'blew the gaff' in the notorious 'mother and child' controversy.[48] Browne was an object of suspicion by the church for he had attended Trinity College, married a Dublin Protestant, had been seen shaking hands with the Protestant archbishop of Dublin, and had slandered old Republicans and I.R.A. men.[49] What Browne wanted to bring into being was a state maternity health scheme without a means test, and the hierarchy interpreted this as a direct attack on its organization and control of hospitals and other parts of the health system. The Catholics of Northern Ireland had not objected when Westminster extended Britain's national health service to Ulster in 1947, but the southern bishops quickly showed they were not going to tolerate what Browne hoped to introduce, lest state intrusion into maternity affairs might lead to birth control and other evils. Browne consulted with a theological adviser during the contretemps who cautioned him he was risking denunciation: 'as a Catholic who no longer accepts the teaching authority of the Roman Catholic church'.[50] The one bishop who befriended him, John Dignan, who was knowledgeable about health matters warned him: 'you cannot win against the Catholic hierarchy... look what happened to Parnell'.[51] Nor did Browne win. Forced to hand in his resignation at the request of his fellow cabinet ministers, he was made to realize that the 'Roman Catholic church would seem to be the effective government' in the Republic.[52] In the words of one member of the Dail:

> The most disquieting feature of this sorry business is the revelation that the real government of the country may not, in fact, be exercised by the elected representatives of the people as we believed it was... but by the bishops, meeting secretly and enforcing their rule by means of private interviews with Ministers, and by documents of a secret and confidential

nature sent by them to Ministers and to the head of the alleged government of the State. As a Catholic I object to the usurpation of authority of the government by the bishops.[53]

Sean O'Faolain in an article entitled 'The Dail and the bishops' expressed his understanding of what the Catholic people of Ireland faced when threatened with the 'weapon of the sacraments'. The taoiseach, each Dail member, or even the ordinary Catholic dare not defy the episcopate: 'if they disobey they may draw on themselves this weapon whose touch means death'.[54] Even the southern Protestants found that they had to be careful in what they said during the crisis. The Supreme Knight of the Knights of St. Columbanus bluntly issued a warning to the *Irish Times,* at that time considered to be a Protestant paper:

> The organ of the Protestant minority, he said, missed few occasions to discredit the doctrines and leaders of the Catholic Church, and this year it had openly attacked the religious leaders of the people... One aspect of the attack by the *Irish Times* was the confidence with which those who represented the Cromwellian traditions in Ireland were attempting to drive the Catholic Church out of the life of the country.[55]

Roman Catholicism had no intention of surrendering its social, political and cultural authority in Ireland, however, as Michael Browne bishop of Galway argued in the first issue of the Maynooth sociology journal, *Christus Rex.*[56] The church was not to be confined to 'confessional, sacristy and armchair' for it had a vested interest in all that took place in Irish society. His argument was reinforced during the 'mother and child' crisis by archbishop Jeremiah Kinane of Cashel who said that in any political or social issue concerned with faith and morals, only the Roman authority would be heeded by the Irish hierarchy:

> Subject to the supreme magisterial authority of the Holy See, bishops are the authentic teachers of faith and morals in their own dioceses, and their authority includes the right to determine the boundaries of their jurisdiction, in other words to determine, in case of doubt, whether faith and morals are involved, so that one cannot evade their authority by the pretext that they have gone outside their proper sphere... subjects should not oppose their bishops' teaching by word, by act, or in any other way, and positively they should carry out what is demanded by it...[57]

When a Roman Catholic archbishop could summon a secular minister of health to his residence it was clear to most observers that in Ireland the bishops had 'more power in practice than those of any country in the world'.[58] It was certainly evident to the Irish Protestants, and those of Northern Ireland in par-

certainly evident to the Irish Protestants, and those of Northern Ireland in particular, that 'in any matter' where the Roman Catholic authority chose to intervene: 'the Eire government must accept the church's policy and decision irrespective of all other considerations'.[59] When the hierarchy did give their approval to health legislation in 1953 it was noted that: 'the bishops got virtually everything they asked for and, in effect, rewrote as much of the bill as they wanted to re-write'.[60] What happened in 1951 was never forgotten by the Protestants of Northern Ireland who concluded that it showed for all time what unification into a state with 'a Catholic parliament for a Catholic people would mean':

> If ever there were a clear, crude case of a state being subservient to ecclesiastical influence this was it. Indeed it has not been just a subservience, it has been grovelling.[61]

The southern hierarchy, as was to be expected, argued that when it came to political matters: 'the Church has no competence to control public affairs itself', and the most they could do was to admonish and direct the people as a whole in the way of righteousness. In the words of Cornelius Lucey of Cork in his lenten pastoral of 1957:

> The power of the Pope, the bishops and the clergy, though great, is limited. In the first place they do not so much lay down the law as interpret the law that God has laid down; thus their power really amounts to little more than pointing out to people the obligations that are already theirs... the Church has no physical means of coercing governments, the professions or anyone else.[62]

On the other hand bishop Lucey had told a *Christus Rex* congress in Killarney in 1955 that: 'the bishops were the final arbiters of right and wrong, even in political matters'.[63] This brought an angry rejoinder from a member of the Dail in the *Irish Times* of 16 April, 1955 who chose to write under a pseudonym: 'because I do not want to finish my political career before it starts'. The Protestants of the south knew very well what the Dail member was talking about. In everything they did in the church-dominated society in which they lived they reckoned with the 'ultramontane disciplinary character' of the hierarchy which formed the 'educated, guiding (almost governing) class of the country'. The Roman Catholic church may have denied it had coercive power, but there were many besides the Jews and Freemasons who were uneasy over the threat of violence if they offended ecclesiastical sensibilities, to draw upon themselves the resentment of Maria Duce or the Legion of Mary, or other guardians of conservative Roman Catholicism.

This was particularly the situation in the largest diocese, that of Dublin, where from 1940 John Charles McQuaid ruled authoritatively. Very much an ultramontanist, from his earliest days McQuaid believed that:

> The first duty of the priest and the bishop was the maintenance of order
> and continuity and the preservation of the great Latin tradition in
> Europe.[64]

He modelled himself upon 'silent, magnanimous, far-seeing Cardinal Cullen',
and like his famous predecessor he was intent upon protecting his flock from
evil influences. At an early time in his Dublin rule he got rid of the Mercier
Society, an offshoot of the Legion of Mary, which began dialogue with Protestants and Jews. In 1941 he attacked the non-denominational Civics Institute
of Ireland for: 'no activity of life may be withdrawn from the guidance of Faith',
and to an amazing extent he succeeded in forming the Dublin archdiocese as a
Catholic 'state within a state'.[65] The cardinal secretary of state, the future Paul
VI, visited Dublin in 1951 to praise McQuaid's see as a perfect example of a
Catholic diocese. In the religious society McQuaid had developed there was little
room for Protestants, and scant toleration of their non-Roman Catholic culture:

> McQuaid's attitude to Protestants was rather similar to the attitude of
> academic apartheiders in South Africa to the Bantu, though more
> enlightened. The archbishop was not a Protestant-hater, still less a
> Protestant-baiter; he was simply determined to preserve his flock from
> religious miscegenation which might tempt them to heresy or, more
> probably, to the sin of 'indifferentism'... Papal teaching had expressly
> repudiated coercion as a means to conversion. Catholic and Protestant
> must, therefore, live alongside one another. But he wanted Catholics to
> be taught to preserve and cherish their separate identity.[66]

Sometimes the religious-cultural separateness that McQuaid encouraged
expressed itself in Maria Duce pamphlets decrying international Jewry and
Freemasonry, or in a retreat by Catholic students in Westland Row in 1956
which ended with a march on a 'Communist' bookstore whose windows were
broken by a statue of the Virgin.[67] In such a society it was understandable that
the Protestants maintained a 'low profile'.

There was relatively little Protestant comment, for example, over the ban
placed on Catholics attending Trinity College, which was only lifted with
Roman approval in 1970.[68] Nor was there a major protest when there was a
Catholic boycott of Protestant businesses after a Protestant woman went to
Belfast with her two children, leaving her Catholic husband and their home at
Fethard-on-Sea in county Wexford. Many local priests supported the boycotters,
and the Catholic bishop refused to denounce it, though he was appealed to by his
Protestant counterpart. Michael Browne, bishop of Galway, preaching before
cardinal D'Alton, the primate and other bishops described the boycott as a

'peaceful and moderate protest', and when the boycott finally ended it was more the result of agitation by liberal politicians like Noel Browne, and the intervention of de Valera, than it was from Protestants calling for an end to what was clearly, in the words of the taoiseach 'a deplorable affair'.[69]

Influences from Vatican Council II were slow to appear in Ireland with its 'particularist form of Irish Catholicism, papalist, authoritarian, and brick-and-mortar oriented'.[70] On the eve of the council in 1961 archbishop McQuaid was at the height of his power and in the celebrations of that Patrician Year Ireland was treated to 'a glittering, bejewelled spectacle' as nine cardinals and over two hundred bishops and abbots arrived in Dublin for a triumphal expression of the faith. Radio Telefis Eireann opened in the same year and one of the first problems it had to deal with was the demand by McQuaid that two of its leading broadcasters be removed because the archbishop objected to their viewpoints.[71] He had earlier dominated Radio Eireann. When he was not consulted before a football match was played between Ireland and communist Yugoslavia he tried to have the game cancelled, and he did succeed in keeping government figures from attending the event, the army band attending, or a radio broadcast being made of the game. In 'prestige and esteem' McQuaid's authority was supreme in Dublin.[72]

When the Vatican Council II began McQuaid and the other ultramontanes in the hierarchy refused to take it seriously, and it became clear that no Irish bishops expected wide-scale reforms to take place, let alone a promotion of the ideal of Christian ecumenism. At the end of the council, during which McQuaid had maintained a stately silence, he announced to the faithful in Dublin on his return:

> You may have been worried by much talk of changes to come. Allow me to reassure you. No change will worry the tranquillity of your Christian lives.[73]

The days of intransigence were passing, however, and even in Ireland religious affairs were to change more quickly than in any period of similar length since the Reformation. Catholic liberals compared McQuaid with cardinal Santos, one of the arch-reactionaries of the council, and he was severely criticized for not allowing Gregory Baum or John Courtney, two ecumenically minded priests to speak in the Dublin archdiocese. McQuaid suffered from considerable embarrassment when an ecumenical gathering at the Mansion House somehow resulted in the Protestant primate, Dr. G.O. Simms, sitting in the front row while on the platform presided McQuaid and the Papal Nuncio beside an empty chair. When McQuaid issued his 1968 Lenten Pastoral which seemed to over-exalt the hierarchical authority of the Roman church the Protestants suspected that the once redoubtable archbishop of Dublin dwelt in a theological world that was no longer appreciated—even by his own flock:

When therefore a bishop, in union with the pope and all the bishops of the church, in virtue of his pastoral office, declares to his flock the authentic teaching doctrine of the church, it is as if Jesus Christ were teaching again upon earth.[74]

At the very end of his episcopate McQuaid revealed his interpretation of magnanimity and how it should govern those who approached the Protestants of Ireland in an ecumenical spirit:

They who have entered into such a heritage may not justly be blamed for adhering to such tenets that, in error, they sincerely believe to be true. Only the light of God, the Holy Ghost, and the courage of His grace can bring our separate brothers to understand and accept the claims of the one true church founded by Jesus Christ, the Catholic Church.[75]

The southern Protestants, by then much reduced in numbers through *Ne Temere*, and other factors, had little sympathy for McQuaid's version of ecumenism—neither had their northern brethren. They remembered that de Valera had said in a St. Patrick's day broadcast to America, two years before he produced the 1937 constitution, that Ireland had been and remained a Catholic nation.[76] Articles two and three of the constitution claimed the right of the Dublin government to exercise jurisdiction over the whole of Ireland, the 'reintegration of the national territory', and the majority people of Ulster were convinced that should a Dublin rule of the north ever take place, they would face some form of oppression to persuade them to 'understand and accept the claims of the one true church', as well as the government of de Valera's Catholic republic. The Ulster Protestants paid little heed to the Catholic bishops when they directed the faithful not to express approval of nationalist physical force organizations that wanted to take over Northern Ireland. After the I.R.A. made a New Year's day attack on Brookeborough police barracks in 1957 and two I.R.A. members were killed, one of them proved to be an ardent Roman Catholic, a one-time member of the Legion of Mary and Maria Duce. His cortège drew large crowds on its way to his home town of Limerick, and priests were prominent in their attendance.[77] McQuaid visited an I.R.A. leader when he was on hunger strike and the northern Protestants were further convinced that if they weakened their defences Roman Catholic 'persuasive authority' would be in some manner forced upon them.

When John Charles McQuaid died in 1973 the religious and secular press seemed to convey hope that his 'antipathy to ecumenism' and his support for censorship of the arts, together with other manifestations of a tight ecclesiastical direction of religious affairs in the Republic, were of the past.[78] Liturgical changes initiated by Vatican Council II, such as the abandonment of the Latin mass and many prohibitions such as the eating of meat on Friday, were easily accepted by the faithful. Change was in the air, and nowhere was this more apparent than in the debate about social concerns which began among the laity. Birth control was of particular concern, and rejection of the directives of *Humanae vitae* of 1968 was widespread. Until 1966 the number of ordinations to the priesthood had remained stable, at about 400 a year, but this number was almost halved in the next few years, at a time when the population was expanding.[79] 1972 saw a referendum which approved the deletion from the constitution of the clause giving the Catholic church a special position in the Republic. Maynooth had opened its doors to lay students since 1967 and soon they outnumbered the seminarians. The visit of the pope in 1979 was a triumphal one, with over a million people attending mass in Phoenix Park, with: 'virtually no crime and little drunkenness for the three days of his visit'. The murder of lord Mountbatten, and the slaughter at Warrenpoint ensured that the pontiff did not go to Northern Ireland, however, and the I.R.A. bluntly rejected the pope's call for them to abandon their campaign of terror.[80] There was a slight pause in the downward trend in vocations, but this phenomenon did not last long with the total number of church personnel declining by roughly a quarter between 1970 and 1985. At the same time, McQuaid's successor, the conservative 'man of great charm and intellect' Dermot Ryan,[81] built over fifty new churches during his first decade in office, and from 1974 devoted himself to attacking the evils of sexual immorality, as well as abortion.

When the northern Civil Rights marches of 1968 were succeeded the following year by the spectacle of Protestant mobs rioting in Belfast's Ardoyne area, and British troops were introduced in the Bogside district of Londonderry, the southern Protestants sensibly kept their heads down as nationalist anger increased in the Republic. They watched with concern the religious-political furore which followed the Bloody Sunday killings in Derry, and then the burning of the British Embassy in Dublin in 1972. When Protestant violence was succeeded by the savage I.R.A. campaign in Ulster, the Protestants did not discuss matters like Articles 2 and 3 of the Republic's constitution where claim to the northern territories reflected the same ambition as the northern terrorists. They left that task to courageous people like the politician and writer, Conor Cruise O'Brien who claimed that: 'the Republic's claim on Northern Ireland was a variety of imperialism'. At the most the southern Protestants were willing to agree that: 'O'Brien's denunciation of nationalist self-delusion, posturing and hypocrisy was unanswerable'.[82] An intimidated minority, when they read the increasingly nationalistic editorials of the once friendly *Irish Times* they tried hard not to be identified with the political posturing of the Northern Protestants. They had no comment to make when archbishop Dermot Ryan of Dublin complained about the increasing number of Roman Catholic children attending Protestant schools.[83] The southern Protestants were also quiet when the British ambassador was murdered by the I.R.A. in 1976 and a state of emergency was declared in the Irish Republic. Nor had they much to say when, at the end of the

1970's, the taoiseach, Charles Haughey, ignored Protestant sensibilities to produce his 'Irish solution to an Irish problem' by working with the Roman Catholic hierarchy to produce the Family Planning Act of 1979.[84]

The courage of the southern Protestants began to return in the 1980's, however, when it became clear that in the north their brethren were going to prevail in spite of the I.R.A.'s terror campaign and the government's toleration of an 'acceptable level of violence'. They began to take heart when they became increasingly aware of the break-down of the Republic's cultural and religious insularity. Young Irish people returning from travel and work in Britain, Europe and America brought with them new ideas and influences, as did the wide-spread use of television. It was clear that on many levels the Republic was becoming more anglicized than it had ever been during the years of British occupation. The Irish young particularly were impatient with their nationalist and Catholic elders and their insular 'ourselves alone' mentality. In secular affairs the young were inheriting a bleak future, and they had little appreciation of the concept of a prelate like Jeremiah Newman who still argued that in areas of 'moral concern' the state should recognize church authority:

> If a church can say in truth that its leaders have a divine right to speak for the religious and moral welfare of their people; if, moreover they are in a position through their system or organization, to be able to plumb that people's needs with fair accuracy... and if, furthermore, the people together constitute the vast majority of the population.... However unpalatable it may be to some, the Catholic Church in this country, embracing as it does the vast majority of the people, has a right to have its views attended to by the government.[85]

Ideologically the young found such quasi-theocratic ideas 'unpalatable' and even threatening when an attempt was made to implement them following the papal visit of 1979. The Pro-Life Amendment Campaign became a rallying cause for Catholic conservatives over the abortion issue, yet it had far from universal support.[86] Although abortion was already legally banned in the Republic the P.L.A.C. wanted a referendum to give authority for the ban to be written into the constitution. The issue became such a passionate one that the southern Protestants once more engaged in self-effacement. Nothing was heard from either of the two Protestant Dail members during the debate,[87] though one theologian warned mildly that: 'the majority of Protestants would feel somewhat alienated in this State if the Amendment goes through'.[88] The protest against the campaign came largely from liberal Catholics, like Mary Robinson, soon to be president of the Republic, who spoke of alienation of the country from the rest of Europe, and warned that acceptance of the amendment might be a breach of the European convention on human rights. The *Irish Times* of 31 August, 1983 opined that a successful referendum would further alienate the Ulster

Protestants, and that it would please only those religious zealots who wanted a confessional state, rather than the kind of pluralism union with Northern Ireland would bring:

> ... their often ill-concealed desire to keep the North out of the present twenty-six county state is going to be voted on with some satisfaction by many who want things to remain as they are: who want indeed to move even further away from the society across the Border.

The *Observer* of 4 September, 1983 believed the abortion debate would put an end to the hopes of Garret Fitzgerald and others that pluralism was a possibility for Ireland: 'it will give the lie to any fond notion that Wolfe Tone's "island of Catholics, Dissenters and Protestants" can come into being in the foreseeable future'. Liberal Catholics said the 'coercive tactics' then used by the bishops and others reflected the 'ineffective Catholic teaching, preaching and conversion policies' which so many young Catholics, ex-Catholics and non-Catholics had rejected. In spite of its alliance with the state the myth that Catholic policies still dominated Irish life was being exploded.[89]

The electorate carried by a majority of two to one the amendment which the conservatives wanted, however, and many of them must have responded to the demand of bishop Kevin McNamara of Kerry that the faithful Catholic: 'must consider the Irish bishops' statement in order to make a responsible decision of conscience'.[90] The result of McNamara's 'strong articulation of the papal line during the referendum'[91] was his appointment by Rome to the Dublin arch-diocese after Dermot Ryan, who had been elevated to the curia, died unexpectedly in February, 1985. Rigidly orthodox the new archbishop who had been appointed at the express wish of pope John Paul II was not the popular choice of the Dublin clergy,[92] and he estranged many young Catholics almost immediately by launching a campaign against proposed new contraceptive laws.

Archbishop McNamara soon found that the popular press had little sympathy for his traditionalist views when it came to the issue of contraception, and his stance was widely dismissed as: 'wrong in fact, in logic and in principle'.[93] A tragic case of sexual misadventure involving the deaths of babies in Kerry made the public debate a heated one, and McNamara believed that the nation had arrived at a 'moral crossroads'.[94] The Republic had one of the highest abortion rates in Europe, most of the abortions conveniently taking place in Britain, and the young especially did not appreciate Rome's hard-line demand that the sexual ethics of *Humanae vitae* were to be observed in Ireland. The teen-age pregnancy rate was increasing, the traditional teaching on the indissolubility of marriage was being ignored, 'by a substantial proportion, perhaps by a majority of the relevant age groups'.[95] The ultramontane domination of Irish society was being challenged by the young, especially the 'narrow and puritanical attitude to sexuality' which had existed from the time of Paul Cullen.[96]

The change in public attitude was revealed when a Family Planning bill was introduced in February, 1985 which proposed to make contraceptives more freely available. McNamara immediately launched an attack on politicians who seemed ready to opt out of their Christian duty to legislate for the common good. Bishop Jeremiah Newman of Limerick argued that the proposed change in the law was not acceptable: 'on the grounds of public morality, whether or not the majority of the people might think otherwise'.[97] Newman developed his traditionalist argument in a pastoral letter which stated that politicians were strictly bound to take account of what the bishops taught where the teaching touched on faith or morals.[98] Cardinal O'Fiaich, on the other hand, merely said that no change in the law could make the use of artificial contraceptives right.[99] Bishop Cahal Daly, who had assured the New Ireland Forum that the hierarchy did not want a 'Catholic state for a Catholic people', remained silent. When the legislation was finally passed it was realized that for the first time since the foundation of the state the Roman Catholic church was on the losing side in a trial of strength with an elected government on a matter of public morality.

The year 1985 also saw the government attempt to challenge the Republic's conservatives by changing the wording of article 41 of the constitution which forbade the dissolution of a marriage. Opinion polls initially favoured the initiative, and only McNamara and Newman among the bishops pursued the issue with any vigour, equating once more 'the common good' with the position of the Roman Catholic church on marriage and divorce. The former, in an oblique reference to the taoiseach, Garret Fitzgerald, criticized 'prominent advocates of pluralism' who wished 'to get into step with the permissive ways of our neighbours'.[100] The priests objected to the proposed measure from their pulpits, however, and helped by conservative groups like the Knights of Columbanus and Opus Dei, and wealth and campaign advice from American Irish, the government initiative was defeated. In its final days the suggestion had been made that a lack of safeguard for property entitlement for the divorced would follow any new law, and this had a great effect in rural areas where there was great concern over inheritance of the family farm.[101]

By 1985 it was clear that in the battle to control the sexual mores of the people the bishops had won a victory of sorts over abortion, although about 4000 Irish girls, in a conservative estimate, went every year to Britain for abortion. It had also won on the divorce issue, though polls continued to show that the population wanted some limited form of divorce.[102] The 'condom war', however, was a clear defeat for traditional authority. Articles began to abound in the popular press, and on television there appeared programs concerned with the growing popularity of 'do-it-yourself Catholicism', together with a questioning of beliefs about heaven, hell, and the need for confession to a priest. Criticism was made of the priest's prurient concern about sexual morality, with almost no concern for a transgression such as excessive drinking.[103] A general but gentle scepticism followed the more than thirty reportings of 'moving statues' in the countryside in the autumn of 1985.[104] There was considerable grumbling over the requirement for teachers in national schools to make clear that they were practicing Catholics. No one forgot the sad death of a teenager, apparently abandoned by the community, who tried to leave her baby on the steps of the parochial house in Granard, county Longford.[105] A newspaper survey reported in the *Irish Times* of 2 September, 1987 found that less than half of the young (between 18 and 24) still considered religion to be very important in their lives. Religious authority in the Irish Republic was very much on the defensive by the end of the 1980's.

From the standpoint of the hierarchy, open criticism about matters like the appointment of bishops by Rome also became of concern. Many churchmen were unhappy about the appointment of John Magee, an important curial functionary, to the diocese of Cloyne.[106] When Kevin McNamara died there was much public speculation about his possible successor, and widespread concern as to whether Roman authority would again set aside any local selection: 'Local preferences and needs, as expressed by the clergy and the laity, have been superseded in very many instances by Rome's fiat'.[107] Priests joined in the general anxiety by protesting their 'grave pastoral concern' over the manner of Rome's policy of episcopal appointment.[108] This spirit of unrest over clerical appointments extended to the parish pump level when a priest appointed by an unpopular bishop was 'jostled' by an abusive crowd in Baltimore, county Cork.[109] More and more books began to appear: 'about the tyrannical power of the Catholic Church colonizing the simple minds of simple peasants'.[110] Respect for Roman authority was presumably weakened also by journalistic probings into the circumstances of the discovery of the body of pope John Paul I, the rumoured relationship of the Banco Ambrosiano with the I.R.A. and the role of Opus Dei in the Vatican.[111]

The southern Protestants were aware of the unrest among their Catholic neighbours, of course, but they kept their own counsel. The Protestant dean of St. Patrick's cathedral in Dublin, among others, chided his people for their timidity, but they generally chose to avoid the kind of intimidation some of them unfortunately experienced. A Church of Ireland rector on the outskirts of Dublin found that a local dispute over a mixed marriage resulted in a threatening telephone campaign, breaking of church windows, and abuse by children who: 'let it be known that they didn't think Protestants had any more right to live here than lice or rats or any other vermin'.[112] Other Protestants regularly reported similar experience of name calling and stone throwing when they were young.[113] It took considerable bravery for someone like Catherine McGuinness, when she was a senator, to complain about the attempted imposition of Roman Catholic ethics in public hospitals.[114] Slowly, however, the courage was found to stand up not only to pressure from the Roman Catholic extremists but also from a government which passed social legislation with a 'like it or lump it' attitude towards the southern Protestants and their sensibilities.[115] On issues like the maintaining of a Protestant ethos in certain hospitals, a new assertiveness began to appear, as in the policy: 'to give preference to Protestant applicants at the Adelaide Hospital because of the lack of opportunities elsewhere'.[116] However difficult the battle ahead was to be, what the Protestants wanted was the end of confessionalism, and the recognition of the need for a pluralist society in both parts of Ireland.

It is difficult, of course, to speak for the 'Protestant mind' at any one period of Irish history but it seems clear that, as liberal Catholicism became ever more critical of the ecclesiastical and religious values of the 1970's, the southern Protestants also began to quietly press for a more pluralistic, a less 'confessional' society. They did so quietly because they knew how difficult it would be to bring about the change they wanted. In the words of the *Church of Ireland Gazette* of 26 July, 1974:

> The deliberate establishing of conditions for a multi-religious state, in an admittedly plural society, would mean saying 'good-bye' to a whole range of sectarian embellishments which are woven into the very fabric of the present Republic.

Most Protestants in the Republic wanted a pluralistic state, such as Dr. Garret Fitzgerald and other liberal Catholics desired, which: 'would have to be based on some system of community rights; and the traditional concept of majority rule, would have to be abandoned'.[117] There were some Protestants who were long conditioned to avoid display of any form of religious or ecclesiastical assertiveness, and they had no desire to 'beg trouble', knowing from bitter experience that the Roman Catholic authorities had no intention of abdicating from their ruling position in society. At the same time, most southern Protestants who anguished over the northern 'troubles' knew that the acceptance of pluralism in the south would help to weaken the intransigent attitudes of some of the northern Protestants.

The great majority of southern Protestants were very aware of pressures put upon them to be assimilated into the Roman Catholic society in which they tried to keep their identity. Between 1911 and 1926 the southern Protestant population had suffered a massive decline of 34%. Many factors accounted for this phenomenon, but one of the most important of them was the ruthless insistence that the *Ne Temere* decree of Pius X was to be observed. This ensured that out of each generation a sizable proportion of Protestant young people, with their offspring, were absorbed into Roman Catholicism when they married girls or boys who belonged to the majority community. Garret Fitzgerald has calculated that in the early 1960's about 30% of Protestant men and 20% of Protestant women married Catholics in the Republic.[118] In the Dail in 1985 he said that whereas members of the Church of Ireland, the largest Protestant body in the Republic, had in 1926 comprised 5.5% of the population their proportion was then only 2.8%. Presbyterian and Methodist populations had been halved since the 1920's. The *Belfast Telegraph's* religious correspondent of 6 July, 1985 commented that when nearly half the marriages of the Church of Ireland were then with Roman Catholics, and when Pope John Paul II speaks of reconciliation in Ireland, yet 'remains stony-faced before all appeals to relax the rules', the disappearance of religious tension in Ireland was unlikely:

> Though the Irish Catholic bishops quoting the letter of the law, seek to deny it, the rules have been relaxed if unofficially, in most other countries. In effect, where there is a will, there will be found a way. Imperialism, then, is very much a pan-Irish phenomenon.

From the 1970's the southern Protestants have become ever more vociferous in their condemnation of this Roman intransigence which was bringing about 'the leaching of the Protestant community'.[119] The *Church of Ireland Gazette* spoke of 'slow communal genocide' and said that government talk of the need for 'Protestant witness' was 'monumental hypocrisy'. John Barry, the clerical journalist, commented on the plan of a southern government minister to help Protestant schools:

> ... while at the same time his church is pursuing a deliberately chosen policy which will have the ultimate effect of ensuring that there will be no children to go to them.[120]

Five years later, on 14 June, 1977, in the *Church of Ireland Gazette,* Barry said bluntly that, so far as the Protestants were concerned, Home Rule really meant Rome Rule in their day because their children were lost to them. By this time, however, others besides Garret Fitzgerald and Mary Robinson were strongly pressing for a pluralistic society. Anthony Spencer, a Catholic from Queen's University, Belfast, described the mixed marriage regime, imposed by the Irish bishops, as 'cruel, arbitrary and erratic'.[121] When in 1983 the revised rules of the hierarchy on mixed marriages still included a demand that all children from such unions be baptized and raised as Roman Catholics the disappointment of the southern Protestants was intense.[122] The reaction of the northern Protestants was a reaffirming of their determination to resist what they viewed as Roman aggression:

> On the Catholic side, the mixed marriage syndrome is basically a defensive imperialist relic matching the more strident anti-Popery of the Protestant extremists. It is possible to deck out the Catholic rules in an impressive legal framework; but in view of the flexibility of Catholic practice outside Ireland that will fool no one.[123]

One result of the 'troubles' in the north, which many Protestants have interpreted as a struggle for freedom from Dublin rule and the yoke of Rome, is that
the southern Protestants' voice of protest has become louder as they have responded to the goading of their Ulster co-religionists. In an article of 31 October,
1975 headed 'No Petty People' the editor of the *Church of Ireland Gazette* said:

> Protestants in the Irish Republic have become accustomed to receiving
> more kicks than kudos, particularly in recent years. They have been
> reproached by their Roman Catholic fellow citizens for not taking their
> proper share in affairs of state and by their co-religionists in the North
> for submitting too meekly to a regime inspired from Rome. They have
> been labelled as West Britons by nationalists and as crypto-Fenians by
> loyalists. They have been accused on either side as being timid and
> self-effacing, devious, and concerned only to make the best of all
> worlds. Worst of all, and perhaps hardest to bear, they have been
> written off as a permanent feature of the Irish landscape. They have
> been pitied as the dying remnants of a former ascendancy.

In the same publication of 31 March, 1978, the prominent Belfast clergyman,
Eric Elliott, wrote on 'the most welcome shift of emphasis among southern
Protestants in General Synod': 'a greater concern about public issues, a great
willingness to enter into public debate in the Republic—to assert their legitimate rights and position within Ireland as a whole, and the Republic in
particular'. The long silence of a submerged intimidated people was coming to
an end.[124]

III   **Within Protestant Ulster**

The attitudes of the Protestants of Ulster varied greatly when they considered
the experience of their brethren in the Republic. After Neil Blaney, the Donegal
member of the Dail, told a B.B.C. audience that there had never been discrimination against the minority in the Republic, the *Church of Ireland Gazette*
of 21 January, 1972, with its wide northern readership, remarked that he must
never have heard of incidents like the boycott at Fethard-on-Sea. On the other
hand, against the prejudices of many of its readers, it wondered if the Roman
Catholic hierarchy, which was so secure in the confessional south really wanted
to take over Protestant dominated Ulster: 'the hierarchy do not want the sort of
"Ireland" which Ireland must become if a million infidels are to be brought into
it'.[125] The Presbyterian church in its 1977 publication, *Pluralism in Ireland:
How People of Different Communities May Live together in Toleration and Co-
operation* mildly noted that the south was hardly a pluralistic society when: 'in
the sphere of sexual morality, the law is dominated by Roman Catholic

teaching'.[126] The *Shankill Bulletin* of September, 1983 was much more forthright in its editorial when the banning of abortion through the constitution became an issue in the south:

> For generations Unionists have been opposed to a United Ireland because it would mean 'Rome Rule' and the suppression of the individual. Their views have been confirmed by the present anti-abortion campaign.

Though the attitude of the northern Protestants inevitably reflected their social class, where they lived and their degree of education, they all paid close attention to the increasing minority of Catholic liberals who voiced their own criticism of religion and culture in the Republic. When Garret Fitzgerald was taoiseach and expressed his opinion about partition in a radio broadcast the northern Protestants appreciated what he had to say:

> I saw this country...initially partitioned by the British, who drew the line and established the Northern Ireland State—but also being partitioned by constitutions and laws being passed here, which were alien to the people of Ireland as a whole, to the whole people of Ireland, the different communities who live in this island.[127]

The northern Protestants followed with interest the recurrent southern political scandals of the 1970's, and the scholarly criticism of what was taking place in the confessional state they abhorred and feared:

> Not until the 1970's did the idea take root, and then only precariously, that public morality could concern anything other than the sexual lives of public men. The morality of violence, the morality of perjury, the morality of deceit in commercial and legal transactions, all tended to be relegated in popular consciousness to reassuringly venal status in the hierarchy of moralities.[128]

They found satisfaction in the Republic's minister for defence calling, in the *Irish Times* of 17 December, 1983, at a time of a kidnapping by the I.R.A. for the hierarchy to: 'say unequivocally that membership of Provisional Sinn Fein was wrong, if it is wrong'. With the Ulsterman's sense of rather grim humour they probably enjoyed the *Irish Times* of 11 February, 1984 commenting on Gerry Adams, the Sinn Fein leader, taking up 'the bishop's collection' from the faithful in a west Belfast church, and the *Republican News* defending his action:

> Rumours that the faithful felt obliged to make more than the usual generous donations, from which protection money was then deducted,

have been dismissed as black propaganda.

Not only have the Ulster Protestants appreciated criticisms of the failings of Irish society when they have been made by the Catholic liberals, but they have many times, as we have noted, been bold enough to suggest that the Protestants in the south could do more 'to make it the sort of place which would commend itself to the Protestants of the North'.[129] As the troubles have gone on, however, they have shown less and less interest in coming to terms with the Republic on the political level. The only time they have shown concern for Dublin affairs has been when they have suspected that covert help was coming from the Republic to assist the activities of the I.R.A. or other terrorist groups. They have turned a resolute face against any southern blandishment, insisting that 'No surrender' was not an 'empty catch-cry', not a 'Protestant bluff'. In the words of one Presbyterian clergyman in one of the most sectarian and strife-torn parts of Belfast in 1975:

> My part of Belfast is not a place where there is much of a market for white-flags—or for white-wash if it is intended to cover up the ugly reality of the I.R.A.[130]

They have made clear to the Dublin authorities that, in the words of cardinal Conway, there is no way that the Ulster Protestants can be bombed into a united Ireland. Ten years after their defensive struggle began, the Presbyterians expressed the resolve of other Ulster Protestants when they let pope John Paul II know on his visit to Ireland, he should consider their 'fears and grievances', their state of siege because of: 'the political ambitions prevailing in the Roman Catholic community'.[131]

Fear governed almost every instance of Ulster Protestant intransigence, when they reacted to the never-ending violence towards them from the Catholic community which threatened to out-breed them and ultimately to become the majority population.[132] Ecumenism has been held suspect as a means of weakening Protestant resolve, and there have been sad occasions, like that of the peace-making Presbyterian minister of Limavady, the Rev. David Armstrong, who was forced to leave his charge, the province, and his church.[133] Many northern Protestants had misgivings when the Presbyterian General Assembly refused to delete from its statement of faith references, inherited from the seventeenth century, which spoke of the pope as the Antichrist, and poured scorn on 'popish monastic vows', and the 'popish sacrifice of the Mass'.[134] Neither have they felt happy about sharp criticisms of the Catholic hierarchy made by the Orange Order and other Protestant militants. Yet when the Roman Catholic bishop of Derry, who had opposed the I.R.A. making use of his churches, was embarrassed by a paramilitary cortège arriving while requiem mass was being celebrated, the bishop's criticisms of the I.R.A. were dismissed as 'mere platitudes', as were those of his episcopal brethren:

> There is no meaning or sincerity in their condemnation of the I.R.A. and their fellow-travellers... the security forces and the law abiding people of Ulster can expect no support from the Roman Catholic hierarchy in their fight against the republican terrorists.[135]

The Roman Catholic hierarchy has protested against such charges, pointing out that the I.R.A. has been formally condemned by them in 1931, in 1956, and several times since 1972, but to no avail: even the plea for peace made by the pope in 1979 has been ignored by the terrorists.[136] Inevitably, however, the more extreme Protestants, such as the followers of the Rev. Ian Paisley, have chosen to accuse the Roman Catholic church of being 'soft' in its condemnation of the I.R.A., which has killed six times as many people as the security forces in Northern Ireland, and many more than the Protestant paramilitarists.[137] The great majority of the Ulster Protestants have continued to believe that there is little likelihood that the Roman Catholic church will find the courage to condemn as it should, what they believe to be the I.R.A.'s atavistic campaign of violence when Protestants are the usual victims in what so often appears to them to be a sectarian conflict. They note particularly that much of the killing along the border appears to be genocidal, the victims suffering because of their religious identity rather than some connection with the military or the police. Although the I.R.A. killing fields are all north of the border, many of the incursions against members of the Protestant community are from the Republic. So sustained and savage is the campaign against them that the Protestants take a kind of moral pride in the restraint they show in reprisals, when they point out that their paramilitarists do not kill Catholics in the Republic.

It would be strange indeed if after a prolonged defensive war the Protestant community in Northern Ireland did not share in a 'sense of siege'. It would also be expected that the Protestants would, in some sense, view their trial as part of a sectarian campaign. It is often argued that: 'it is invalid to portray the religious/Christian dimensions of Ulster's problems in simple sectarian terms'.[138] Protestant experience has been such in Irish history, however, that ancient memories persuade those close to victims of sectarian outrage that the forces that oppose them serve religious as well as political causes. It is very difficult for Protestants to view other than clearly sectarian an outrage such as the Republican raid on a Gospel Hall in 1983 in the predominantly Catholic village of Darkley near the Monaghan border, where three of the worshippers were killed and many more of the congregation wounded. Their reaction was predictable when the military shot dead eight heavily-armed I.R.A. gunmen who were carrying out a raid on the police barracks in Loughgall in county Armagh, and nationalist priests questioned 'the legal, moral, and political aspects' of the event. Unfortunately, few Protestants would have been aware that the congregation of the Catholic church in Booterstown, Dublin, walked out of the service when their curate criticized the 'brutality' of the killings.[139] It took a tragedy like the killing in 1987 of eleven Protestants attending a cenotaph service in Enniskillen to bring out a sense of communal horror which transcended the sectarian divide.[140] Another occasion on which Catholics and Protestants united in a sense of moral outrage was when press photographs showed a priest trying to minister to the naked wounded 'Christ-like' body of a British soldier killed by a mob in West Belfast. The murder was denounced by cardinal O'Fiaich as 'brutal and obscene'.[141]

Cardinal O'Fiaich was, however, in the eyes of many northern Protestants the epitome of the political prelate, in the language of east Belfast, 'the Sinn Fein archbishop'. This was not really fair to O'Fiaich who was a warm-hearted man who had a deep pastoral concern for the people in the area where he came from, Crossmaglen on the border with the Irish 'republic. It was almost inevitable that he would sympathize with the local people who resented the strong military presence in their neighbourhood which often disturbed their common pursuits. On the recommendation of the papal nuncio, Gaetano Alibrandi,[142] he had been nominated by pope Paul VI to the see of Armagh in 1977, the first time in 110 years that a priest not already a bishop was elevated to the primacy.[143] An outstanding historian, the author of a biography of the martyred Oliver Plunkett (1975) he had been president of Maynooth, and though he rejected the charge that he was a 'political prelate' he did little to conceal his strong nationalist sympathies. The editorial of the *Church of Ireland Gazette* on 27 January, 1978 noted that at the time of the Octave for Christian Unity meetings that year he called for a British withdrawal from Northern Ireland. This 'appalled' the Protestants because it reflected his 'total failure' in understanding people who immediately cast him in a 'Makarios-type role':

> He has played right into the hands of Paisley. Together they stand—political ideology and religion nakedly intertwined.

The Protestants had not overlooked his silence when the Provisional I.R.A. made an armed attack on the Belfast home of the Catholic member of parliament, Gerry Fitt, who was one of their most persistent critics.[144]

When Republican prisoners in the Maze Prison began their 'H-Block' protests which brought them world-wide publicity O'Fiaich chose to reveal his 'actively nationalist viewpoint' by his public condemnation of the government tolerating unsanitary conditions in the cells of the inmates. The Catholic primate also caused a stir when, in an interview with the editor of the *Irish Press* he: 'came out in favour of Irish unity'.[145] When O'Fiaich from the time of his first visit to the Republican prisoners referred to them as 'the lads' the Protestant community generally interpreted his expression as one of political identification rather than a pastoral appreciation of their suffering.[146] Following the cardinal's visit to Rome to present the Vatican with his interpretation of what was happening in Northern Ireland many of the Protestants were convinced that Rome also had a say in what O'Fiaich and the Republican dissidents were trying to accomplish.[147] Then, when the hunger strikes began, the Protestants believed that O'Fiaich resorted to open intimidation of the government which, he said: 'would face the wrath of the whole nationalist population if it did not compromise on the hunger strikes'.[148]

Tomas O'Fiaich had few diplomatic skills and perhaps his worst gaffe was in his interview with the Catholic publication, *The Universe*, which was referred to in the preface of this work. His argument there that Protestant bigotry was religious, Catholic bigotry was political, won him few supporters among either the Protestants or the liberal Catholics.[149] Earlier he had refused to condemn membership in Sinn Fein, the political wing of the I.R.A. as 'morally unacceptable',[150] and in the *Universe* interview he said hat he did not believe: 'the majority of those voting for Sinn Fein are voting for violence'.[151] Conor Cruise O'Brien who had earlier commented on the cardinal's contribution to the Irish 'tolerance for intellectual dishonesty',[152] was scathing in his criticism of what O'Fiaich had said to the *Universe*, when he seemed to deny that the I.R.A. was a sectarian body:

> I don't think that even a group as cruel and ruthless as the IRA will kill Protestants as Protestants. They are killing many members of the RUC, UDR and so on, who happen to be northern Protestants. But they are killing them because they are members of the security forces, not because they are Protestants.[153]

So far as O'Brien was concerned statements like this were 'sickening semantics', 'unctious niceties about motivations for murder', 'glib insensitivity to the feelings of endangered—and bereaved-neighbours, of another religion and allegiance', which only added to the sectarian tensions in the province. The Protestant bishops of the Church of Ireland, and the president of the Methodist Church agreed that O'Fiaich had, at the very least, been guilty of 'insensitivity in tone and content'.[154] The blunder was all the more noticeable to the Ulster Protestants for the cardinal had been noted in the north for the partiality of his political sentiments:

> He becomes emotional about the death of an I.R.A. man, but cannot apparently bring himself to attend the funeral of one policeman, even when the dead man is a Catholic.[155]

Perhaps the most penetrating criticism of O'Fiaich's nationalist politics came from a Belfast Catholic magistrate, Tom Travers, whose daughter was killed by the I.R.A. as she shielded her father during an assassination following their attendance at mass. If you served as a policeman, prison officer, or in the judiciary in Northern Ireland you were not, he said, 'cherished by the Church or by other Catholics':

> I fear that this attitude is all too common in priests of the cardinal's diocese, so that those who kneel at the altar of God betray us to the gunman and think it is no sin.[156]

There were, of course, many occasions when cardinal O'Fiaich denounced killings which produced great public outrage, as in the case of the Enniskillin cenotaph slaughter, or the horror of the mob killing of the two British soldiers in west Belfast in 1988, but the Protestants of the north remained convinced that he was one of the chief contributors to sectarian animosity in their war-torn province. Guilty also of this offence, the Protestants believed, were two politically active priests of Armagh diocese, Denis Faul of Dungannon and Raymond Murray of Armagh whose 'language of consolation' only too often carried 'the seeds of provocation' in the words of Gerry Fitt, the one-time Belfast M.P. Fitt particularly expressed his disgust when Raymond Murray compared the killing of an I.R.A. bomber with the death of Christ.[157] Denis Faul's nationalist politics were often so strongly expressed that his otherwise commendable work for improving prison conditions was treated with reserve if not suspicion. As for O'Fiaich, his stance was so uncompromising that he was even rebuked sharply by the Dublin government for his failing to condemn support for Sinn Fein.[158]

In the years before his death in May, 1990 Tomas O'Fiaich remained a partisan nationalist who did remarkably little to support the promoters of law and order in the province. In December 1986 he said that the time was not yet right for Catholics to serve in the Royal Ulster Constabulary. This led to lord Brookeborough calling him an 'evil prelate', and the *Church of Ireland Gazette* comment of 20 February, 1987, on the cardinal's 'dissimulation':

> Whatever he did say he did not say that the people to whom he gives spiritual leadership should support the police.

In 1987 O'Fiaich announced that Catholics would feel betrayed if the Dublin government agreed to extradition of terrorists to the U.K.,[159] and he drew an implied rebuke from Dr. Robin Eames, the Church of Ireland primate, when it was reported that O'Fiaich had: 'called on the government to say it would not remain forever in Northern Ireland'.[160] His many obituaries inevitably shared the same theme—his political identification with the cause of the nationalist extremists:

> All too often he was seen as the Provo cardinal, as a man in tune with the IRA, who did not entirely disapprove of their methods, despite his

standing as a church leader. One of his last battles was against integrated education enabling Catholic and Protestant children to share the same schools, and be educated side by side.[161]

In the minds of most Protestants what was regrettable in the primacy of cardinal O'Fiaich was that his partisan political stance played into the hands of his Protestant counterpart, the leader of the Free Presbyterian church, Ian Paisley. Paisley was intelligent, an astute demagogue, who made instant use of every public relations blunder of the cardinal, telling Protestant Ulster what it believed in its heart: that it was surrounded by enemies who wished to destroy its culture, and that within Northern Ireland was a 'fifth column', working with Rome, the Republic, and some parts of the British government to bring this about. Time and again, Paisley stated that he had no animosity towards the Catholic people of Ulster, but he deplored their exploitation by prelates like O'Fiaich who kept them in spiritual and cultural bondage: 'misguided helots dominated by demonic priests'.[162]

Romanism is more properly a government than a worship—a vast and complicated secular organization including, under the style and externals of a devotional system, all the elements of a civil polity... well calculated to bring both subjects and civil rulers under the sway of the pope... at one period or another almost every state in Europe has been obliged to banish from its territories this army of conspirators against the independence of sovereigns and the civil and religious liberty of subjects.[163]

Paisley's birthplace was Armagh, where his father was an evangelical Baptist preacher, and by the time that Ian Paisley was beginning his preaching career he reflected his father's fundamentalist theology, the traditions of the Scots Covenanters, and the mass conversion techniques of American revivalism. From 1950 he was moderator of the Free Presbyterian church of Ulster, a sect composed of disaffected mainstream Presbyterians, with a mission hall on the lower Ravenhill road in Belfast. From the beginning Paisley proved to have genius in stirring up sectarian passions among the Protestant working class people of Belfast. In January, 1958, for example, he brought to Ulster a converted Spanish Catholic priest, to parade him around in ultra-Protestant churches, and to entertain their congregations with stories of life within convent walls, and the inside workings of Rome. When, in Ballymoney, the local Catholic priest, supported by some Protestant ministers, objected to this anti-Catholic agitation, the local council refused the Paisleyites the use of the town hall for their meeting. Paisley immediately used the occasion to denounce what he saw as the rejection of Protestant and Unionist values by the councillors, and in his publication *The Revivalist* he thundered against the Ballymoney priest who had organized the resistance:

> Priest Murphy speak for your own bloodthirsty, persecuting, intolerant,
> blaspheming, political-religious papacy, but do not dare to pretend to be
> the spokesman of free Ulster men. You are not in the south of Ireland.
> Ballymoney is not Fethard and the flag of this land is not the tricolour
> but the glorious red, white and blue of the Union Jack. Go back to
> your priestly intolerance, back to your blasphemous masses, back to
> your beads, holy water, holy smoke and stinks and remember we are the
> sons of martyrs whom your church butchered and we know your church
> to be the mother of harlots and the abominations of the earth.[164]

The following year Paisley used his oratorical skills to excite a Protestant mob
on the Shankill road which engaged in some of the worst anti-Catholic violence
seen in the city for years.

When the civil rights movement began in Ulster Paisley quickly became a
political leader in opposition to it. He was briefly imprisoned for opposing the
march of the civil rights supporters in 1968; became the Unionist M.P. for
Bannside in 1970; and founded his Democratic Unionist Party in 1971. Since
1979 he has been a member of the European parliament. As a politician he has
been consistently successful in re-election as he has made use of his: 'expertise
in tapping, articulating, and challenging all the deep fears and ignorant prejudices
of northern Protestants'.[165] The majority of the Protestant population may
reject Paisley's 'antics' which reflect his background as a backstreet preacher of
bigotry, but like Daniel O'Connell in the early nineteenth century he has the
ability to appeal to folk historical memory, and to invoke the Ulster Protestant
traditional antipathy to Roman authority. When the pope visited the European
parliament at Strasbourg in 1988, and Paisley raised a banner of protest, some
Protestants found it symbolic that it was wrenched from his grasp by Dr. Otto
von Habsburg, a descendent of the old Roman Catholic and imperial family.[166]
His genius at invoking atavistic responses from the Ulster Protestant masses is
given great respect by political leaders. Few have forgotten the anguish that
Paisley caused Terence O'Neill in 1963 when the leader of the Ulster Unionist
party sent a letter of condolence to cardinal Conway on the death of pope John
XXIII. When the mayor of Belfast then had the Union Jack on City Hall
lowered to half-mast,[167] Paisley launched a passionate attack against both
traitorous Protestant politicians and churchmen in a speech in the Ulster Hall.
He scorned especially the apostate churchmen who tolerated:

> ... the lying eulogies now being paid to the Roman antichrist by non-
> Romanist church leaders in defiance of their historic creeds.[168]

Ecumenical gestures of any sort were part of the 'Romeward' march of churchmen who succumbed to the Roman tactic of winning Protestants back to the authority of the monolithic and aggrandising church'[169] which had brought so much suffering to Ireland for so long. However 'simplistic' the explanation may seem to 'politically correct' liberal scholars:

> The Ulster Protestant population defies any explanation other than the obvious one: evangelicalism provides the core beliefs, values, and symbols of what it means to be a Protestant. Unionism is about avoiding becoming a subordinate minority in a Catholic state. Avoiding becoming a Catholic means remaining a Protestant.

'Not an inch' was, and is, the answer to those who would consider surrendering religious or political freedom, in the face of the onslaught to bring the Protestants of Ireland back to the Roman obedience.[170]

Ian Paisley had no doubt that 'Home Rule was Rome Rule' when he looked at the Republic 'the vassal state of the papacy'. It was an identifiable enemy because of its claim and determination to take over the north so that it could extinguish Protestant liberty:

> Protestants love their liberty too much to put themselves into a state where there is censorship, a state where you can't have a divorce, a state where even the elementary liberties of husband and wife are severely curtailed by the law. When one looks at the south of Ireland one can see the genocide that has taken place. When the country was divided it was something like 10 percent Protestant in the south of Ireland and now it's something like 3 percent. So you have a complete annihilation, almost, of the Protestant population in the south of Ireland.[171]

In the historical imagination of Paisley Ulster remains as it always has been since the time of William the Orange, a Protestant fortress holding the far flank of what was once the line of northern nations resisting the steady encroachment of Roman imperialist power:

> The struggle to destroy Ulster Protestantism cannot be viewed in isolation. Ulster is the last bastion of Bible Protestantism in Europe, and as such Ulster stands as the sole obstacle at this time against the great objective of the Roman Catholic See: a United Roman Catholic Europe.[172]

The mainline churches in the era of ecumenism find themselves in a quandary whenever they express their disapproval of Paisley's hectoring attitudes, or his utterances about 'judicial murder' being 'God's law'. Confronted with such dismaying statements the moderator of the Presbyterian church, John Girvan, said that what was going on in the midst of the political strife was a battle for the heart of Unionism and the soul of Presbyterians.[173] In the same period an editorial in the *Church of Ireland Gazette* of 13 February, 1981, on the Paisley excesses, urged a peace-making role for the Church of Ireland during the troubles:

> This church's history proclaims a vision of a church which is independent of a political philosophy, and which is determined to survive not for its own sake, but for the sake of the proclamation of the gospel of reconciliation between God and man, and man and man.

Yet all Ulster Protestants feel some degree of uneasy acquiescence whenever Paisley points to the close religious-political alliance in the Republic which suggests that his thesis of Roman imperialism has some basis in fact. When the Republic failed either to prosecute or to extradite the nationalist priest, Patrick Ryan, who had been said to be guilty of terrorist activities, Paisley warned that there were 'far wider contours' to the case than his fellow Protestants wanted to acknowledge: 'the European community is a Roman Catholic dominated community and the canon law of the Church of Rome holds that priests are not really subject to the law of the land'.[174] When he makes statements of this nature Paisley has an audience, for the Protestants of Ulster have for two decades suffered from a sustained attack on their culture and, only too often, Roman Catholic priests have been believed to share the intentions of Patrick Ryan:

> To be a Protestant in Northern Ireland is to feel defensive and insecure, and there is an instant warmth towards anyone who gives voice to those fears preferably in the most outrageous terms.[175]

The defensive sensibilities of the Ulster Protestants were certainly tuned when the nationalist leader John Hume, a close friend of cardinal O'Fiaich from his days as a Maynooth student, took a leading part in the meetings of the New Ireland Forum in early 1984. When the Roman Catholic hierarchy made its written submission to the Forum the intransigent tone of the document shocked many people on both sides of the border.[176] It was a blunt statement of Vatican doctrine without any concern for reconciliation of the two traditions on the island, or the acceptance of minority rights in a united Ireland of the future:

> A Catholic country or its government, where there is a very substantial Catholic ethos and consensus, should not feel it necessary to apologize that its legal system, constitutional and statute, reflects Catholic values. Such a legal system may sometimes be represented as offensive to minorities. But the rights of a minority are not more sacred than the

rights of the majority.

The document also indicated that the Roman mind did not think in terms of pluralism if a thirty-two country united Ireland came into being, as we noted in the preface:

> Where the offence to the moral principles of the majority of the citizens would be disproportionately serious, it is not unreasonable to require sacrifice of minorities in the interests of the common good.[177]

In February 1984 the hierarchy reacted to the uproar following this written submission by making an oral one, delivered by Cahal Daly, bishop of Down and Connor, who tried to reassure the Protestants: 'The Catholic Church in Ireland totally rejects the concept of a confessional state. We have not sought and we do not seek a Catholic state for a Catholic people'. The Protestant response to this, as well as that of many liberal Catholics was frankly sceptical:

> Churlish Northern listeners were left to wonder why, if the church was so concerned about Protestant rights in the thirty-two counties, it could not be equally concerned about the rights of the 3 percent of Protestants in the twenty-six counties.[178]

The Church of Ireland was the only Protestant church to make a formal submission to the Forum, and in it it complained bitterly about the heavily Catholic bias in the Republic's family laws. When Cahal Daly was asked to give assurance to the Forum that if an attempt was made to drop the Republic's constitutional ban on divorce the Roman hierarchy would not intervene he declined to do so.[179] It seemed to most Protestants that the preference of the Roman Catholic bishops was contentedly to accept the twenty-six counties as they were, with Catholic values well protected, and a thirty-two county alternative, only if their authority in the new society was similarly assured. Other critics thought the hierarchy was saying that its attitude towards a minority depended upon its strength within the social order:

> Given a minority of 20% it would appear to drop its demand for a Catholic ethos in the constitution, but it is unwilling to do so when the minority is 4%. But... surely the principle of civil and religious liberties transcends the numbers involved.[180]

On the whole the Roman Catholic bishops did nothing to persuade the Protestants of either the Republic or of Ulster that the hierarchy was ready to think in pluralistic terms and abandon: 'what they saw as tyrannical tendencies to deprive them of liberty of conscience'.[181]

An unfortunate postscript to the New Ireland Forum was the comment of cardinal Tomas O'Fiaich, after prime minister Thatcher's negative reaction to the report, that he not only deemed it arrogant, but opined that no progress would take place in Northern Irish affairs so long as she remained in charge of the government. He also spoke of the growing 'alienation' of the nationalist community. The *Irish Independent* of 24 December, 1984 remarked that these comments: 'might have been reinforced if the cardinal had delivered the same kind of verbal blows to the Provisionals'. In any case the New Ireland Forum did nothing to lessen the 'alienation' the Ulster Protestants felt towards the case for unification as it was presented by the Roman Catholic hierarchy. At the end of the day, as they love to say in Ulster, the evasiveness of some of the statements made by the bishops left a 'credibility gap'.[182]

IV   The Era of the Anglo-Irish Agreement

An attempt to build on the spirit of discussion which brought about the New Ireland forum was revealed in the suggestion that the governments with authority in Ireland, Westminster and Dublin, should form a 'dual protectorate' to govern the socially divided province of Ulster.[183] Mrs. Thatcher, the British prime minister, rejected firmly suggestions which came directly out of the New Ireland Forum, but the 'dual protectorate' concept was gestating and in November, 1985 there came into being the Anglo-Irish, or Hillsborough Agreement which recognized the Irish Republic as having a 'legitimate interest' in the future government of Northern Ireland. During the talks leading up to the agreement the Vatican's secretary of state, cardinal Casaroli was kept informed of developments by the government of the Republic.[184] Prior to the Reformation it was possible for Rome and London to attempt to impose a dual *imperia* in Ireland, but from the moment this agreement was announced, without the approval of the majority Protestant unionist people, there was a great uproar in Ulster. The perspicacious Belfast journalist Barry White summed up what had happened four months after the agreement came into force:

> We proved our incapacity to govern ourselves, or to stop the rise of the republican movement, so our Westminster paymasters decided to call in a country which felt equally threatened by the I.R.A.—the Irish Republic—to see if a form of government by London, aided and advised by Dublin could work the miracle. It is only four months old, but I think it is clear that the miracle won't be worked.[185]

The agreement did mean that when local events, like tensions over flag-flying in Bessbrook, county Armagh, resulted in a call for a boycott of Protestant shops by Roman Catholics, even the representatives of the most popular Catholic nationalist party, the S.D.L.P. moved in to quell serious trouble.[186] Such local initiatives for peace were strongly supported by public opinion,[187] but on the whole the agreement served only to increase bigotry within the province. So far as the Protestants as a whole were concerned their right of self-development was now curtailed by the two potentially oppressive authorities in Westminster and Dublin. By the spring of 1987 the Church of Ireland primate, archbishop Robin Eames, when opening the General Synod, called for a plan to supersede the Anglo-Irish agreement which had given hope to the Irish nationalists, and nothing to the unionists. His sentiments were applauded by Ian Paisley and other unionist political leaders.[188] There was much talk about devolved government and the usual political posturing by the parties concerned, but by 1990 it was clear that the importance of the Hillsborough agreement was becoming marginal. The reality seemed to be that there was a steady trend towards social parity between Northern Ireland and the rest of the United Kingdom which was now so extensive it amounted: 'to integration by statute'.[189]

The Ulster Protestants remained unhappy about the Hillsborough agreement, but they had withstood what they chose to view as a twenty year war to force them into accepting rule by the confessional republic, and they remained confident of keeping their freedom. They also saw hope of more self-determination for their southern co-religionists. The lot of the latter was improving as enlightened 'secularism' modified greatly the loyalty the Republic's Catholic people had once given without question to their ultramontane hierarchy. Ireland as a whole still had the highest birthrate in the E.E.C., which may have reflected the ecclesiastical opposition to contraception, but the Irish young were consistently questioning the authority of the Catholic church, especially in matters of sexual morality. The *Irish Times* of 2 February, 1989 carried a lengthy report on the new wave of liberalism within the church's seminary system, a reflection of a catastrophic fall in vocations: 'the priesthood—a way of life on the wane'. When the inter-church Irish Council of Churches' conference held its annual meeting in Limerick in 1989 it was reported that in Dublin: 'only seven percent of Roman Catholics under 25 now attend Mass'. The Protestant reporter of this unlikely sounding statistic, which he claimed came from trustworthy Roman Catholic sources, was clearly concerned about this development, and entitled his article: 'a report too serious for any triumphalism'.[190] Not only was the Roman Catholic church in the Republic experiencing the decline in church attendance which was by now almost universal in the western world, but there were signs that the laity were becoming resentful about ecclesiastical matters such as episcopal appointments. When the conservative bishop of Kerry, Kevin McNamara was translated to Dublin, following the appointment of Dermot Ryan to a curial post in Rome, *Magill* magazine of December, 1984 interpreted the action as a clear example of Rome rule in Ireland. McNamara's successor in 1987, Desmond Connell, a

Thomist scholar from Maynooth, was believed to have been the choice of the long-serving papal nuncio, archbishop Alibrandi. A year after his appointment he was embarrassed by a picket outside his home formed by protestors who claimed he was detached from the reality of poverty in Ireland.[191] Such an action was an indication that the public authority of the Roman Catholic church had changed radically from the age of John Charles McQuaid. An increasing number of influential liberal Catholic voices were being raised to question the ecclesiastical and religious control which had for so long permeated every aspect of Irish public life.[192]

None of these developments persuaded the Ulster Protestants that they should abandon their deep-seated suspicions about either the intentions of the Roman Catholic hierarchy, or the imperial ambitions of the Dublin government. The Protestants had not failed to notice that during the 'troubles' which had visited upon them so much suffering, the hierarchy, with one or two exceptions, had sounded ambiguous when it commented on their trials. The Protestants understood what Conor Cruise O'Brien was referring to when he spoke of the 'soft' treatment afforded the alleged I.R.A. activist priest, Patrick Ryan:

> Although they never said that the I.R.A. campaign in Northern Ireland 'met the church's criteria for a just war' they haven't said that it doesn't. On this point the bishops seem to be agnostic.[193]

From the North of Ireland Protestant standpoint the Roman hierarchy in the Republic was still a power to be reckoned with. They took a keen interest in the lot of their co-religionists who sought to keep the Protestant identity of the Adelaide Hospital in Dublin intact, when the Dublin government wanted to have it merged with two other institutions on the outskirts of the city. When the Protestants talked of the distinctive ethos of the hospital, the ultra-conservative Roman Catholic bishop of Limerick, Jeremiah Newman, asked what that would mean when the question of abortion arose. The *Irish Times* called the bishop's intervention 'provocative and insensitive', but the *Belfast Telegraph* interpreted Newman's action as a bullying of the Protestant minority in the Republic; while Belfast Catholics were allowed their Mater Hospital, such an expression of pluralism was not possible in the south.[194] The northern view was also given by the *Church of Ireland Gazette* of 15 June, 1990:

> The real problem in the Republic is that too many people there believe that they are very liberal, truly pluralistic, and generous and fair to minorities.

The Ulster Protestants also kept a close eye on the attitude of the Roman Catholic church in Northern Ireland, where sectarian strife showed no sign of lessening. In the summer of 1990 in the predominantly Catholic town of Downpatrick, the Protestant primary school was seriously vandalized, the Orange Hall and the Masonic Hall were both attacked, and several Protestant buildings burned, in what was interpreted as a 'concentrated campaign' to drive the Protestants out of the community.[195] They noted that in the same season that these events took place the Sinn Fein leader, Gerry Adams received, what was said to be, privileged treatment when he attended a beatification ceremony at the Vatican, and that he stayed at the Irish College at the same time as the archbishop of Dublin.[196] Adams was also prominent at the funeral of cardinal O'Fiaich, and the Protestants were not surprised when the call for excommunication of the I.R.A. which was made by some liberal Catholics was ignored.[197] This demand was raised again after the murder of the prominent parliamentarian, Ian Gow, but the Roman Catholic bishop of Clogher defended inaction by the hierarchy on the grounds it would not be 'practical', nor could the denial of Catholic burial to I.R.A. terrorists be countenanced:

> We have explored excommunication as a deterrent and the conclusion is that it would not serve any purpose. As for burials—the Church is an agent of charity and can refuse no one. We are open to exploitation but there is no other way.[198]

Sometimes the Ulster Protestants have been unfair to their southern co-religionists who have, for example, been more hopeful about the Hillsborough agreement and what it might accomplish. Part of the southern 'soft' line may be attributed to the tradition of keeping a low profile when contentious issues arose, but much of it reflects a growing southern Protestant recognition of the need for a deepening religious pluralism in a society that threatens, at least in the cities, to throw off all religious adherence. Religious observers agree that the visit of the pope in 1979 brought no long term beneficial results, and uncomfortable assessments are now being made of the traditional religious settlement in Ireland:

> Pope John Paul may have won some battles but the 1990's may prove that he and the present hierarchy may have lost the war. Ireland may not be predestined to remain *semper fidelis*.[199]

Though 'the power that resides in Armagh' represents still an 'interest group' like no other in Irish society, there are signs that a 'Protestant-modernist transformation of Irish Catholicism' now may be imminent:

> The major pastoral problem of the Irish Catholic Church is that very many people, including clergy, no longer know why they continue to be Catholics... When a papal voice in the Phoenix Park thundered 'It is the Mass that matters' one could almost hear the echoes answer: 'It is that Mass that is the matter'.[200]

As they enter the 1990's, the southern Protestants, who no longer share the sense of alienation from their Catholic neighbours in the way the northern Protestants still do, are aware of the diminishing authority of the hierarchy, especially among the young, in the Catholic church. Vocations are falling, mass attendance is decreasing, particularly in Dublin which is filled with a young population (as in most cities) that is violent, drug-addicted, suffering from the scourge of Aids and other disease, and dismissive of the traditional pastoral work of the clergy whom they view as part of the problem in the society they live in.[201] Church authority seems helpless when a social and religious activist like Dr. Maura O'Donohue stands up to traditional moral teaching in her position as Aids programme coordinator of a prominent Catholic agency for overseas development.[202] Nothing seems to prevail to stem the tide of Catholic children flowing into Protestant schools, their parents convinced that the young are in no danger of being proselytized.[203] A new era of religious pluralism seems probable in the Republic, and hopefully throughout the whole of Ireland, as the hierarchy appears increasingly uncertain not only in its pastoral mission but in its relationship with the Protestant 'separated brethren'. At the end of the Church of Ireland General Synod the primate, archbishop Robin Eames, told the *Irish Times* (18 May, 1990) that he was calling on the Irish government to consider critically the great 'obstacle to north-south understanding' provided by articles 2 and 3 of the constitution which lay claim for the Republic to exercise jurisdiction over the whole of Ireland. He also asserted that thought had to be given to the chief obstacles to true ecumenism, inter-church marriages, and the ideological problems of ecclesiastical authority and papal infallibility. The era of passive acceptance of Roman Catholic domination which had so long characterized their life in the Republic now seems almost a memory to most southern Protestants.

To scan the Irish press in both the Republic and the north in the period since the signing of the Anglo-Irish accord is to realize that, like the rest of Europe, society is changing rapidly. Old insular shibboleths are being radically and increasingly questioned or ignored by the young who want to be part of what is about to emerge in the larger world promised after 1992.[204] Rampant emigration seems to be a constant among the young in the Republic; public demand for sex education for the young, including information on contraception, is increasing; and concern is openly expressed for the legion of women who travel to England yearly for abortions.[205] The conservative views of prelates like Jeremiah Newman of Limerick, or archbishop Desmond Connell of Dublin continue to have little appeal to the Catholic young, who are apt to lend a sympathetic ear to Protestant calls for integrated education.[206] Even in the vexed area of mixed marriages it is clear that a change is taking place. As early as 1983 the Protestant journalist, Sam McAughtry reported being 'startled by a statistic':

The children of 80% of mixed marriages in one diocese of the Republic are being reared in the Protestant churches... in some other dioceses over 50% of such children are Protestant.[207]

For many Irish students, including those in the north, an increasing opportunity for education in 'mainland' universities is proving to be irresistible,[208] and some of them show little enthusiasm for returning to the insular society they have abandoned. Those who do return from Britain, Europe or America show little inclination to continue the 'ourselves alone' mentality of previous generations. They are much less likely to take seriously the *Ne Temere* strictures of the past, and they find the idea of a pluralist religious expression in society nothing to be feared. Many of the young have demonstrated sympathy for the plight of the Protestants who have had to close churches in the Republic and to accept a declining ecclesiastical establishment.[209]

The recognition of religious and cultural pluralism also seems inevitable in Northern Ireland, but there the resistance by the churches to such a development is stubborn. Government initiatives to build up a common school history course have met with resistance, and the Roman Catholic bishops have carried out law suits against education reforms which seek to promote integrated schooling.[210] The proposal for a common syllabus in religious education has met with similar opposition. The representatives of Rev. Ian Paisley's Democratic Unionist Party have decried the enthusiasm of 'ecumaniacs' and warned parents about their children being 'contaminated with popery':

The curriculum which can be agreed with the representatives of the Roman Catholic church is bound to be detrimental to the religious well-being of Protestant children.[211]

The Presbyterian Church has refused to join the newly created Council of Churches in England and in Ireland, because the Roman Catholic church would be a full member of that body. Isolated through its 1978 withdrawal from the World Council of Churches, this action of the Presbyterian Church has upset greatly two out of five of its members who did not want to adopt an inward looking insular approach which isolates the church from the Christian mainstream.[212]

Perhaps hope for religious pluralism becoming a reality in Ulster lies in the appointment of Cahal Daly as the new Roman Catholic archbishop of Armagh. During his installation as bishop of Down and Connor in 1982, which was attended by eleven Protestant representatives, almost all of them his personal friends, Daly called forthrightly for the end if violence and the finding of Christian peace:

There is too much mistrust, suspicion and fear, stemming often from

sheer prejudice, misinformation and misrepresentation. There are some
in our society who foment bigotry, who promote prejudice, who
exploit suspicion and fear.[213]

Consistently and rationally, since that opening broadside against sectarian
extremism, delivered in St. Peter's pro-cathedral in the heart of the Lower Falls
road in Belfast, the heartland of Sinn Fein and the I.R.A., he has attacked the use
of violence used for a political end. *The Guardian* of 21 January, 1984 reported
one of his bitterest attacks on Republican paramilitarist groups who claimed
they waged a 'just war':

> Judged by every single criterion of the traditional 'just war' theology,
> the present physical force Republican campaign is morally wrong and
> the operations to which it obliges its members are morally wrong.

This put bishop Daly into direct confrontation with Ulster nationalists, who
were just as hard-hitting in their reply to his criticisms:

> You are—it is well known—one of the most conservative theologians
> in Ireland as your stance during the abortion referendum made clear.
> Isn't the truth behind your endless homilies and warnings a very real
> but selfish fear that the power and influence of the Catholic Church is
> on the wane and is being directly threatened by events in West Belfast
> and others parts of Northern Ireland, and that your days of autocratic
> sway could be nearly over?[214]

This did not deter Daly who never ceased to attack the I.R.A. and the Protestant
extremists who would deny to fellow Irishmen pride in their culture and their
identity.[215] When the two British corporals, Derek Wood and David Howes were
savagely beaten to death by the I.R.A. bishop Daly said the events of 'black
Saturday' 1988 'unmasked the ugly real face of the I.R.A.': 'the activities of the
I.R.A. are killing the soul of those involved in it or actively supporting it'.[216]

Similar denunciations were made on occasion by other bishops like Edward
Daly of Derry who struggled hard to keep the allegiance of the young in his war-
torn city.[217] Daly had been a consistent nationalist, however, and he was never
accorded the kind of appreciation which Cahal Daly received from the Protestants
of Ulster. Cahal Daly promised he would endorse without qualification the
decision of any Roman Catholic to join the Royal Ulster Constabulary, and
throughout his time in Down and Connor urged Catholics to get out of the
I.R.A. which had: 'covered Ireland with tears and blood'.[218] No other member of
the hierarchy seemed so willing to speak in such clearly pluralistic terms:

> The Northern Irish conflict has a multiplicity of interlocking causes;

but one element of it is certainly the religious factor. Because of this the ecumenical movement has a still greater relevance and urgency here than elsewhere... Catholics have much to learn from Protestants, and Protestants from Catholics. In a growingly secularized world, we must each support the other in resisting the erosion of Christian society.[219]

To Cahal Daly the 'armed struggle' of the Catholic paramilitarists was 'monstrously irrelevant' for it would do nothing to persuade the one million unionists of the north, 'the real British presence in Ireland' to accept that their future lay in a united Ireland. Their existence, their religion, their culture had to be respected, for they were as Irish as any of their detractors. Within Ireland there were:

Irish people of unionist political persuasion and almost all of Protestant religious faith, who identify themselves also as British and yet claim this island as their home by virtue of nearly 400 years of residence and toil and industry by their forbears.[220]

In these comments, made shortly before he succeeded Tomas O'Fiaich as archbishop of Armagh and primate of All Ireland, Cahal Daly reiterated what his predecessor, cardinal Conway, had said in the early days of the 'troubles': 'Who in his sane senses wants to bomb a million Protestants into a united Ireland'.[221] Perhaps the hope for the Irish people lies in accommodation within a new pluralist society, in both parts of Ireland.

Chapter XIII

Ulster's Popular Protestantism

'What soldier of the cross can stand neuter at present, or remain at ease
in Zion?'

Hamilton, G., *Introductory Memorial
... of the Evangelical Society of Ulster*,
Armagh, 1798

I   The Reformation Inheritance

A pluralist society to the Ulster Protestants is one where individuals and
their churches are free from any coercion which would deny them existence and
development religiously or culturally. Until the period of Republican onslaught
in recent years they have viewed their Northern Ireland social order as one that
provided them, through the protection of the British crown, an optimum
opportunity for them to live as they believe God would have them live:

The United Kingdom of Great Britain and Ireland is, with all its faults,
a pluralist state. Its Catholic millions and their Irish co-religionists
who have chosen to live there find no oppression, nor in real terms do
they suffer any social or political disadvantage.[1]

At the same time, their historical experience has made clear to them that the
Irish Republic, which makes constitutional claim to their province, would very
much like to bring them under the authority of the government in Dublin. This
they object to in principle: 'No nation has the right to set limits upon the
development of the individual liberty and unique nature of man'.[2] When they
consider the assimilative process which has so radically reduced the Protestant
population in the Republic since 1922, they make the political judgment that
the kind of religious and cultural pluralism they desire would not be tolerated by
a Dublin government. In a United Ireland the Ulster Protestants would be
subject to the same ecclesiastical, religious and cultural pressures which
decimated the once vibrant southern Protestant way of life.

A recurring problem in Republic of Ireland and Northern Ireland relations
has been the reluctance of some political and other interest groups to take
seriously the religious demand for freedom, which lies at the heart of Ulster

Protestant intransigence, especially when the people feel threatened. Even scholars have tended to shy away from religious issues of this kind, which have been so important in Ulster Protestant history. It has been pointed out, for example, that T.W. Moody's magisterial study of 1939, *Londonderry Plantation*, avoided the religious aspect of what was taking place in the north-west of Ireland in the seventeenth century.[3] The fact is, however, that the great majority of Ulster Protestants in their churches, conventicles or fellowships affirm doctrines which were first formulated during the religious struggles of the Reformation era. They have lived with these precepts for some four hundred years, and they cannot and will not easily abandon them. Chief among them is the belief that Christians find justification for their spiritual lives when they stand *coram Deo*, before God, without the assistance of any ecclesiastical organization acting as intermediary for the individual. 'The Protestant Principle' referred to in the Preface, 'the protest against any human attempt to limit, or circumscribe, or even define for another the will of God', is a concept that is almost universally shared by Ulster's Protestant people, whatever their denominational allegiance, and their denominations are legion.[4]

Professor Moody's diffidence when it came to the issue of religion in Londonderry is understandable. It will have been noticed that although the present study has been willing to engage the concerns of the readily identifiable and politically active churches, such as the Roman Catholic, Church of Ireland, or even the Free Presbyterian, it has avoided assessing the importance of the myriad of Protestant organizations in Ulster. Yet their supporters are many, they share a long history, most of them are directly influenced by Reformation-era theology and, as in the past, they can have a major cultural and political influence in Ulster affairs, when they are moved by some form of 'revival' spirit; 'they are no mean people'.

Though there is great diversity between their denominations the Protestants of Ulster who express what may be called 'popular religion' share an expression of Christianity which developed in Europe and America from the mid-eighteenth century. Referred to sometimes as Pietists or Evangelicals, they are worshippers in voluntary bodies with a deep respect for religious freedom. They have an instinctive toleration of 'diversity within unity', although some 'covenanting' congregations avoid any close association with their Protestant neighbours. There is usually friendly cooperation between clergy and laity in their churches, and when some threat to the Ulster Protestant community as a whole is perceived, they quickly rally to defend against any authority which would threaten what is believed to be a way of life representative of God's calling to a chosen people. They strongly believe in the primacy of individual conscience over authority and tradition. Usually clergy and laity alike find ultimate religious authority in the Bible, they seek to be internally in control of their spiritual life, and they resent any authority that would seek to govern their consciences, or otherwise to coerce them religiously.[5] Ulster's Protestant 'popular religion' in many ways is like its American counterpart, amorphous, and at times badly divided, yet a power to be reckoned with: 'It may be filled with tensions and contradictions, but it works, politically and religiously'.[6]

What is unique in the Ulster Protestant 'popular religion' community is its retention from its historic past of a deep suspicion about the imperial intentions of Roman Catholicism in Ireland. It shares the contentious mentality of some Protestant Evangelical churches that are found in parts of Eastern Europe or South America. The history of Ulster's Protestant peoples has been one of perennial struggle against what they choose to see as a demonic power that would bring them back into a system of ecclesiastical and religious tyranny. The old concept of the pope as Antichrist is still to be found among Ulster Protestants, and it is not difficult for them to see in the increasingly-united Republican forces of the 1990's, the I.R.A., Sinn Fein, the S.D.L.P., the Dublin Government, and American Catholicism a great marshalling of power by their ancient foe. Militant Republicanism which has caused so much suffering in Ulster is only too easily identified with the crusading spirit of ultramontane Catholicism which they have resisted for so long:

> There is a religious-style overtone in the whole movement, and people
> have described joining it in terms of a spiritual experience, and offered it
> a degree of devotion, commitment and self-denial which would be
> appropriate to someone in a religious order.[7]

The largest denomination which may be included under the title of 'popular religion' is that of the Presbyterians, who have been organized in Ulster since Robert Monro arrived in the early seventeenth century and the first presbytery was formed at Carrickfergus. Their religious and ecclesiastical convictions can be traced back to those shared by John Calvin and his followers who attempted in the Reformation years to establish in Geneva a city-state governed by godly reformed church rulers. This 'Protestant Rome', which Calvin wanted to make into a model reformed church community was under continuous threat from enemies within and without, and Calvin himself considered Geneva to be under siege: 'When I consider how important this corner of the world is for the spread of God's Kingdom I have reason to be concerned about protecting it'.[8] Roman Catholicism with the monarchical claims it had made from the time of Gregory the Great was the great external enemy, but the enemies within the city-state had also to be reckoned with. There was always a strong freedom-loving revolutionary spirit in Calvinism, and from the beginning there were obdurate Protestants who objected to Calvin's notions about 'godly discipline' and his 'leadings towards absolutism'.[9] Calvin had his own ideas about the priesthood of all believers, and a high doctrine of the church which allowed him to define in legal terminology what was true Christianity and what was not. He did not hesitate to allow the clerical and lay rulers of the reformed community to use coercion when it was necessary to protect godly rule in Geneva. Especially resented was excommunication of the ungodly: 'a holy and lawful discipline taken from the word of God'.[10]

Calvin's reformed church movement was both expansionist and militant from its beginning, for it had to exist in a world where the papacy was revealing its intent to obliterate heresy by the use of force in France, Germany and England. Inevitably the Calvinist zealots who sought to establish their disciplined communities of the godly beyond Genevan territory, found themselves in conflict with local rulers and their subjects, and they had urgent need to find theological justification for defence when they were attacked. Calvin in theory was a pluralist when it came to ecclesiastical affairs, and he saw tactical advantage in newly-established reform churches organizing themselves according to their local needs: 'for God has prescribed nothing specific about this'.[11] The Calvinist conviction was that when a reformed community was threatened, God, as He had done in the case of Moses, would raise up a defender from among his servants, and He would ensure that an oppressive ruler would be brought to order if he: 'exalts himself to the point that he diminishes the honour and the right of God'.[12] One of these Calvinist champions who was 'raised up' following the St. Bartholomew's massacre in the French religious wars, was Philip du Plessis-Mornay, the probable author of *Vindiciae contra tyrannos*, which is considered to be a landmark in revolutionary literature with its assertion of the right to coerce authority when it is not responsible to God.[13]

At the heart of such Calvinistic intransigence was the idea that if the godly were in covenant with the deity, there should be a similar contractual relationship between reformed churchmen and secular rulers. John Knox wondered: 'whether obedience is to be rendered to a magistrate who endorses idolatry and condemns true religion'.[14] Knox's collaborator in the establishment of Calvinist rule in Scotland was Christopher Goodman who talked of how: 'God giveth the sword into the people's hand, and He Himself becomes immediately their head',[15] when they suffered from unjust and ungodly rulers. The defence of freedom was of passionate concern to the Calvinists who formed their various conventicles in the English civil war period, and opposed resolutely the authority of the Commonwealth, or even the Presbyterian church. John Lilburne, leader of the Levellers, though not an orthodox Calvinist expressed well the longing for freedom among the small tradesmen, artisans and farmers who made up the rank and file of Cromwell's army:

> Sinful, wicked, unjust, devilish and tyrannical it is for any man whatsoever, spiritual or temporal, clergyman or layman, to appropriate and assume unto himself a power, authority and jurisdiction, to rule, govern or reign over any sort of men in the world without their free consent.[16]

Generation after generation of Calvinists were to show that although they reverenced the ultimate authority of Scripture, believed they were justified before God by their faith, and revered John Calvin's magisterial *Institutes of the Christian Religion*, still found their ideas of radical individualism constrained by the disciplines imposed by the courts of the Presbyterian religious system.

It was this system of church government which kept the Presbyterians from following their instincts of radical individualism and antinomianism. Once they were in power a common tactic of control practiced by the reformed churchmen was to form a covenant, a solemn communal pledge before the majesty of God, to commit their lives to the cause of the Word of God, and what it demanded of them. The most famous of these was the Solemn League and Covenant which was signed by the Westminster Assembly of Divines, 1643–1649, and represented the last great effort to establish a Calvinist system in England,with a uniformity of doctrine similar to that in Scotland. It prompted the drawing up of the Westminster Confession of Faith which at once established itself as the definitive statement of Presbyterian doctrine in the English-speaking world, as well as having great influence with other Calvinist bodies such as the seventeenth century Baptist churches.

These antecedents of modern Ulster Presbyterians were arrogantly self-righteous to the point that one of the Scots commissioners to the Westminster Assembly made a vigorous defence of religious persecution in 1648, when in dispute with Jeremy Taylor. Advocacy of toleration he argued could lead churchmen to put conscience in the place of God and the Bible as guiding authorities.[17] It is little wonder that John Milton could speak of 'New Presbyter is but old priest writ large', and Samuel Butler mocked their religious militancy: 'they proved their doctrine orthodox by apostolic blows and knocks'.[18] Their disciplined yet flexible ecclesiastical system, however, enabled the Presbyterians to bring about a successful Calvinist revolution in Scotland, and to carry their militant faith to Ulster, where it soon became a dominant force.

The first Scots in Ulster in the seventeenth century were immediately confronted by the authority of the Church of Ireland to which they had to conform, at least nominally. They had their own ideas of election, however, inherited from their Calvinist forefathers, as well as the concept of the covenant with the deity, and this helped to give them assurance as they settled in an inhospitable land 'with the bible in one hand and the sword in the other'. Their relations with the Roman Catholic population were tense, and from their reformed church tradition they accepted that the Antichrist in Rome was ever ready to lead the 'congregation of Satan' against them. They listened readily to the political Calvinists who warned them to be ready with the sword when 'Antichrist stirreth his tail'.[19] Patrick Adair, historian, and from 1674 minister of the only Presbyterian congregation in Belfast town, viewed the struggle between the Protestants and Roman Catholics in Ulster as one that could only be understood in theological terms, as he interpreted the Irish rising of 1641:

That which mainly instigated them to this wicked course was that they were Papists, under the power and conduct of the Roman Antichrist—that whore of Babylon, and bloody persecutor of all who worship not the Beast, who could never be satisfied with the blood of those who own the truth of Christ against Antichrist.[20]

These Scots Presbyterians who existed uneasily within the Protestant establishment had many anxieties, but their assurance that God was with them deepened greatly in 1625 when they experienced what they believed was a radical intrusion of divine power into their lives. This assurance came through an event which was to be viewed as theologically seminal in Ulster Presbyterian history. Beginning in Oldstone near Antrim, and then spreading rapidly to Protestant settlements in counties Antrim and Down, congregations experienced in their worship an ecstatic excitement which drew much popular comment. Some of them displayed extravagant symptoms as they were 'stricken', made aware of their sins with great suddenness, some of them 'swooning' before experiencing a sense of Grace. When even members of the local gentry were drawn into the excitement the ecclesiastical authorities moved swiftly to stem the contagion, which was clearly not under control of church leaders. The Presbyterian leaders were especially concerned about the phenomenon because Separatists, Baptists and other Protestant sectaries began to show an intense interest in: 'the sudden and extensive manifestation of the power of Divine grace upon a careless people'.[21]

Ecclesiastical control of the Six Mile Water Revival, as the event was referred to, was soon established by church authorities who brought in clerical worthies to preach, and to curb excesses by stressing sound Calvinist teaching. They also organized 'Antrim meetings' where the converted and others could receive instruction in theology, and soon the extravagances associated with this manifestation of popular Protestantism began to disappear. The social and cultural affect of the Revival did not, however, and the Presbyterian clergy were generally impressed with their communities:

So marvellous was the power of God smiting their hearts for sin, condemning and killing; and some of these were none of the weaker sex or spirit, but indeed some of the boldest spirits, who formerly feared not with their sword to put a whole market town in a fray.[22]

Grace was certainly needed by these Protestant 'swordsmen' and others for 1625 was not only the year of the Six Mile Water Revival, but it was also the year Charles I came to the throne. He was to send Thomas Wentworth to Ireland as Lord Deputy, and with the aid of his chaplain and bishop of Derry, John Bramhall, Wentworth systematically harried the Presbyterian ministers out of the Protestant church. By 1637 Bramhall could report that the ring-leaders among the Presbyterian clergy had returned to Scotland. As for the converted 'swordsmen' they were overawed as the bulk of the army in Ireland was moved into Ulster, and those who did not return to Scotland were swept up in the savagery associated with the Irish Rising of 1641.

In spite of the slaughter in so many of the Irish wars which followed the Rising, the Presbyterian population kept rising as waves of immigration from Scotland took place in the late 1690's and early 1700's. By the end of the seventeenth century they formed more than half the Protestants in Ulster, and probably close to half the Protestants in Ireland as a whole. From the standpoint of government they were a difficult people. Well organized through their kirk sessions, with its strong lay leadership, their presbyteries and synods challenged the government which always had to reckon with the political and social power of the Presbyterians and their reformed religion. The perennial question for the authorities in Ulster when they regarded the powerful Presbyterian church was who: 'shall have the greater influence over the people, to lead them as they please'.[23] It was not only their tight ecclesiastical discipline which gave the Ulster Presbyterians strength, however. They had all suffered greatly in the wars against the Stuarts, and the Irish Rising of 1641 was so seared in the folk consciousness of the Ulster Protestant that it existed there as a kind of 'occult force'. Whenever the Roman Catholics displayed a spirit of aggressiveness in Ireland, the Ulster Protestant folk shibboleth inevitably invoked has been '1641':

> Sooner or later in each successive crisis the cry is raised of '1641 come again'. The fear which it inspired survives in the Protestant subconscious as the memory of the Penal Laws or the Famine persists in the Catholic.[24]

In Ulster Presbyterian history the Six Mile Water Revival is viewed with respect and a degree of wonderment, but at the time it occurred church leaders concerned with discipline were very uneasy with what might proceed from it. The scholarly among them knew that their own Presbyterian system, well-regulated and rational, was not the only form of Protestantism that had come out of the Reformation. They recollected what Luther, Calvin and the other early reformed churchmen had to endure when they encountered the first of the Protestant 'enthusiasts', the Zwickau Prophets, John of Leyden and the other Anabaptists who led peasant movements in the sixteenth century. It was widely believed that these anarcho-millenarian groups with their claim of direct enlightenment by the Holy Spirit had helped foment discord during the bloody Peasant's Revolt of 1525, When they were savagely put down by religious authorities, including those of the reformed churches, their survivors had fled to the Low Countries and elsewhere, bringing their concept of a spirit-guided faith with them. The Mennonites, radical 'independents', were among these refugees, and they greatly influenced the earliest British Baptists whose first 'separatist' congregation had been brought to the Low Countries by John Smyth. When he died in 1612 some of his followers returned to England to found there the Baptist Church. Roger Williams a radical seeker of religious freedom founded the first Baptist church in Rhode Island in 1639, and when the first Quakers came to America in 1654 Williams granted them sanctuary. The Ulster Presbyterians recognized the Protestantism of such sectaries, but always had a dialectical relationship with those who rejected the need for 'godly discipline'.

Their tensions developed especially during the Commonwealth when Presbyterians and Independents were often at odds. Cromwell himself was an Independent who thought little of the ecclesiastical system of the Presbyterians. His sympathies lay with those sectaries who argued that Christ had institutionalized only individual churches, communities of saints in continuous reformation: 'without tarrying for anie'.[25] Convinced that they were guided immediately and directly by the Holy Spirit, the Independents were strong in defence of freedom of conscience, and the protection of what they believed to be mankind's fundamental liberties. Many of them so feared the papacy because of its religious and political tyranny that they regarded the extirpation of Roman Catholicism as necessary, and even spiritually rewarding. Others, however, were such passionate defenders of freedom that they even had the temerity to stand up to Cromwell when he was about to invade Ireland. Their argument was that the rising of the Irish in 1641 represented a struggle for freedom by a conquered people, who should not be punished for their defiance. Some of them paid with their lives for their obduracy, and though most of Cromwell's army in Ireland was composed of Independents, or Anabaptists, who gladly served in the ruthless campaign to break Roman Catholic power in Ireland, the Puritan Cromwell always had trouble with the Levellers, and other sectaries, who were obsessed with the cause of religious and other freedoms.[26]

Some of the Presbyterians had a covert admiration for how the Lord Protector, as Cromwell was officially recognized from 1653, managed to control these spirit-filled sectaries. The church system they had inherited from their Calvinist ancestors had little room in it for 'enthusiasm' or 'spontaneity' in worship, let alone variation in doctrinal belief, and this became a problem for the Presbyterians in the years following the end of the religious wars in Europe. A new movement to revive the Lutheran church was led by P.J. Spener, whose independent outlook led him to call for the laity to have a greater part in church life by providing leadership in emotional evangelical worship. Spener's followers, known as Pietists, quickly brought about a major revival in continental Protestantism, influencing the founding of the university of Halle, and providing by the end of the eighteenth century one of the greatest theologians of the age, Friederich Schleiermacher. The Pietists also influenced Count Nikolaus von Zinzendorf, a wealthy landowner who invited persecuted Protestants from Roman Catholic territories to settle on lands he owned near Dresden. These Bohemian Brethren, or Moravians, named their colony the

Herrnhut, and it soon became a place of pilgrimage for many Protestants.

One of the pilgrims to the Herrnhut was John Wesley who was to have so much success in reviving a more enthusiastic and emotional form of Protestantism in Ireland, and not least in Ulster. He first met Moravian missionaries when he was on his way to Georgia in 1735, and he was haunted afterward by their emphasis on 'feeling' in religion, their conviction of personal salvation of their absolute dependence upon God, and their non-dependence on dogma. Shortly after his return to London he met Moravians again, and then on 24 May, 1738, he experienced a conversion which assured him that his sins were forgiven, that he was justified in his faith by the indwelling of the Holy Spirit, and that he was called to 'offer Christ' to the whole world. After his conversion he went to the Herrnhut to be part of the community for some weeks, rejoicing in the religious liberty found there where the faithful 'call no man master', and they venerated the liberty of the individual's conscience: 'this we cannot suffer to be any way limited or infringed'.[27]

When John Wesley with the help of his brother Charles, and one of the great preachers of the age, Jonathan Whitefield, brought their message of deliverance from sin for the individual, and the joy of a new life guided by the Holy Spirit, to a multitude of people in Britain and in Ireland, their 'enthusiasm' was not appreciated by the Protestant churches of the time which were singularly lacking in spiritual authority. Whitefield's preaching power was such that after a tour in Scotland in 1741 there took place at Cambuslang a revival experience remarkably similar to that at Six Mile Water in Antrim over a hundred years earlier.[28] The Methodist emphasis on individual conversion was such that theological differences abounded among them, but by the end of the eighteenth century they had perhaps 20,000 members.[29] No longer were spiritual affairs in the British Isles to be left to the formal and often lifeless ministrations of the major Protestant denominations, or the various charitable societies that affluent churchmen supported.[30] What the spiritual yearning of the masses needed, in the minds of the Methodists, was the warm assurance that God could regenerate even the most depraved of men, and lead them into a new existence through the power of the Holy Spirit.

Though this was the essence of the Methodist message, there was one passion which John Wesley and his evangelists did share with the major Protestant denominations in eighteenth century Britain and Ireland. This was the general antipathy of the Protestants towards the papists, and to some Methodists this was even a virtue in Ireland:

> If an undefined horror of Popery had not placed an insurmountable barrier in the way, the Protestant settlers might have sunk into the lowest depths of Romish superstition.[31]

Wesley himself shared in the general antipathy towards the Church of Rome, and in his *Journal* in 1778 he cast his mind back to the panic in the days of William III when the popular Protestant opinion was that they faced a pogrom carried out by 'Irish papists'.[32] Little that Wesley encountered during his many missionary journeys to Ireland was to lessen his deep and abiding rejection of the Roman Catholic church. The Church of Ireland and the Presbyterians had scant toleration of his missionary ardour, or the pious earnestness of Wesley's followers, but among some of the churchmen there was a qualified acceptance of the Methodists, if only for their sturdy Protestantism. It was clear that the Methodists feared the Church of Rome, and reacted accordingly; there could be no compromise with priestly autocracy.

II   American Formation

It was not until the latter decades of the eighteenth century that the spirit-guided Methodist movement began to make its contribution towards the popular Protestantism that slowly evolved in Ulster. Prior to that Ulster Presbyterianism was visited by a major revival, reminiscent of that experienced by the early settlers who were 'touched by the spirit' in the Six Mile Water Revival. This 'awakening' took place in the far-away mission field of the American colonies where Ulster emigrants had been arriving in great numbers from about 1718. They were part of an on-going folk migration which reached its height in the years just before the Revolutionary War, when up to 6,000 Ulster Protestants entered the colonies yearly:

In 1700–1776 at least 200,000 left the northern province—a massive drain from a Presbyterian community that probably numbered only 400–600,000 during the period.[33]

The emigrants brought with them women and families, and sometimes their clergy, and developed a sense of religious and cultural apartness that encouraged them to stay together as they faced the challenge of life on the colonial frontier. Few of those who came to the new world for a complex of religious and economic reasons were people of privilege, many of them being indentured servants which was the only means by which the poorest could afford to travel. Most of them were sturdy individuals, who refused to accept any longer 'molestation' by the old world's principalities and powers. The arid denominational disputes of their Ulster homeland were now viewed as being increasingly irrelevant, and their attitudes towards clerical control of their lives was ambivalent. God had opened for them a door for their deliverance in America where: 'the most sacred of all rights, that of conscience and private judgment is preserved for us'.[34]

The first Presbyterian church leader in America was Francis Makemie

(1658–1708) who had been ordained as a missionary by the Laggan Presbytery in 1681. He travelled widely, founding churches in Maryland and Virginia, raised funds for his mission in England, and in 1706 he organized the first Presbytery in America in Philadelphia. His lot was not an easy one, however, the colonial congregations were often too poor to support a minister, or build a church, and the 'judicatory' functions of the Presbytery were not universally popular, however necessary they seemed to Makemie and the ministers who supported him. The church courts were constantly involved in cases of discipline, such as the suspension for four sabbaths of a minister who had washed himself 'on the Lord's Day'.[35] In spite of the grumbling of those who had come to the new world seeking religious and ecclesiastical liberty the presbytery flourished. By 1716 it had 19 ministers, 40 churches and 3000 communicant members.

Makemie, of course, was a churchman of his time, and his publications in America reveal his deep attachment to Reformation era doctrine, especially that taught by the Westminster Confession and the Catechism. He maintained a deep antipathy towards papists, such as those he found in Maryland, and was suspicious of the activities of the Quakers in Pennsylvania with their acceptance of direct spiritual intervention in their religious life.[36] The immigrants put up with Makemie's rigorism, however, and it ceased to become an important issue with them after the despotic governor of New York had him arrested in 1707 for the crime of preaching in a private house. He emerged from this ordeal a year before his death as a kind of folk hero. Most of the Ulster Presbyterian immigrants were fierce defenders of religious liberty, but they still cherished their presbyterian structured church which helped them to safeguard and propagate the faith, and to provide Christian nurture, training and discipline in their rough frontier society.

The Presbyterian leaders may not have thought well of the Quakers, but from the time that William Penn had founded Pennsylvania as a welcoming haven for people of all nationalities and creeds, there had been a separation of church and state and this the Ulster immigrants found attractive.[37] Few of them settled in New England where the Congregational Church and the colonial authorities showed them little welcome. Even fewer stayed in New York where Francis Makemie's religious liberty had been inhibited. Most of them chose to make use of the ports on the Delaware river from where they could make their way to the frontier, or go south through the valley land of Virginia and the two Carolinas. A sturdy and self-reliant people, long accustomed to living in a hostile environment, most authorities were willing to hurry them on to the land-grabbing that was taking place on the frontiers. James Logan, the Lurgan born Provincial Secretary in Pennsylvania described his fellow-countrymen as: 'troublesome settlers to the government and hard neighbours to the Indians'.[38] Wherever the Ulstermen went there was apt to be trouble with the colonial authorities over 'squatting', settling on land without any legal right to do so. As in the old world it was said of the Scotch-Irish: 'they kept the Sabbath and anything else they could lay their hands on'.

They had little encounter with Roman Catholics, except for a minority who settled in Maryland, but most of the Ulstermen there had come as indentured servants, and they were not yet in a position to assert themselves. Most of their fellow settlers as they hurried west and south were German, many of them Pietists, and pacifist groups like the Mennonites and the Amish. They caused little trouble for the aggressive Ulstermen.

The general toughness of the Ulstermen might have been widely resented, but in the harsh world of the frontier in the early decades of the eighteenth century their transgressions were readily overlooked. In a world where warfare with the French and the Indians seemed to be endemic the Scotch-Irish were soon viewed as an élite defensive force. Especially in Pennsylvania and Virginia the Ulstermen adapted readily to frontier life, and in their dealings with the Indians they used Indian tactics, scalping and burning villages where necessary. They soon had the reputation of being an excitable people, hotheaded, 'invincible in prejudice', who fought readily and well to defend the lands they had occupied, often with a minister of religion alongside them:

> Scotch-Irish fighters had revealed themselves to be able soldiers, rough, ingenious, adaptable, ready to endure hardship. They could be counted upon to fight all they were worth in a cause in which they believed. Many were soon to demonstrate all their fighting qualities in the larger War for American Independence. More than this they…displayed willingness to take matters into their own hands without waiting for guidance.[39]

The Presbyterian leaders were soon dismayed by the spiritual threat to their Scotch-Irish young men, especially when the Indian wars continued for they knew: 'one of the great evils of war is the corruption of human nature, and hardening of the heart to all the sensibilities of humanity'.[40] Many of them were to be shocked when young Scotch-Irish massacred a whole Indian village community during the Pontiac wars, with the callous justification that by their action they had freed land for settlement by white men.[41] As early as the 1740's, however, the Presbyterian leaders knew they could not persuade their people to change their ways when congregations pleaded poverty, and even when they could afford a minister soon turned their backs on him if he crossed them. Church courts were constantly involved in cases of discipline, and even the clergy were accused of scandalous behaviour.[42] Real authority lay with people like the Irishman, William Johnson who had settled in the Mohawk valley in 1738, persuaded many Iroquois to fight on the side of the colonists, and was successful enough that he was knighted by the government.[43] In this frontier war-culture without any ecclesiastical control in an increasingly brutalized society, without sound preaching or sacramental celebration, the religious among the settlers were almost without hope.

It was at this time, when the pious among the Ulster Protestants were in despair as the whole colonial society seemed to be lapsing into secularism, that there occurred a religious phenomenon which in its effects surpassed by far the Six Mile Water Revival in Antrim in 1625. The first sign of this 'awakening' was in the preaching of a Dutch Reformed minister, Theodorus Frelinghuysen, whose 'enthusiasm' in the pulpit brought alive the congregations he addressed in New Jersey. His message of an 'inner religion' based on a mystical relationship with the deity, caught the attention of two young Scotch-Irish ministers, Gilbert Tennent, and his brother William. What impressed the brothers was Frelinghuysen's warning about 'presumptious security', the false identification of sound doctrine with saving faith. Gilbert Tennent, in particular, began to preach with flaming zeal, demanding his rough, untutored listeners to make decision immediately between everlasting damnation or eternal joy. His congregations were highly emotional in their response to such a confrontation, they grew in number and soon the 'enthusiasm' spread to other congregations. By 1738 so many new congregations had formed in New Jersey that a new judicatory, the Presbytery of New Brunswick came into being.

Gilbert Tennent displayed a particularly pugnacious spirit when he deliberately attacked from the pulpit the bigotry of orthodox Presbyterianism, in a polemical discourse entitled *The Danger of an Unconverted Ministry*. This was a demand that all candidates for the ministry show evidence of 'gracious and genuine religious experience' before they were ordained. He also attacked the 'ungodly Ministry' of his time which 'grieved poor Christians' because they saw: 'how luke-warm those Pharisee-Teachers are in their publick Discourses, while Sinners are sinking into Damnation in Multitudes'.[44] This sermon was widely distributed, with many congregations agreeing that for a clergyman to have a fine education without piety and conviction was to be deplored. Those who supported the revivalist cause after a synod schism in 1741 were known as 'New Side Presbyterians', and their opponents as 'Old Side'. Gilbert Tennent was dismayed by this division among the Presbyterians; fortunately, he wrote a persuasive pamphlet, 'The Peace of Jerusalem' and by 1758 the schism was over. By this time, however, the 'enthusiasm' associated with the preaching of sin, and the redemption through Christ for all who would turn and receive salvation had become a message of missionary zeal which added greatly to Presbyterian congregations in Virginia and the Carolinas, and had an immediate appeal to the Scotch-Irish and their families who were enduring the brutal existence of the frontier.

Another important element in Tennent's preaching which offended the conservative Presbyterians, was his stress on the need to tolerate religious pluralism. So long as Christians shared in the essential core of the faith, they were regardless of their denominations, 'several branches' of 'one visible Kingdom of the Messiah'. At a time when the great majority of people stood outside the churches altogether, there was need to emphasize the essential unity of the denominations, as well as to express appreciation of the spiritual values which accounted for diversity in the church. This conviction Gilbert Tennent shared with the evangelist, George Whitefield, who after an earlier visit to Georgia returned to the Middle Colonies in 1739. There he was enthusiastically received by people of all denominations, and even Benjamin Franklin thought him a 'reasonable' preacher. Whitefield proclaimed himself to be: 'of Catholic spirit, and if I see any man who loves the Lord Jesus in sincerity, I am not very solicitous to what communion he belongs'.[45] Popular Protestantism had become a power to reckon with in colonial America.

The preacher who made what was universally known as the Great Awakening acceptable to the Calvinistic conservatives in both New England Congregationalism, with its Puritan roots, as well as some of the 'Old Side' Presbyterian churches was Jonathan Edwards. Edwards had briefly served a Presbyterian congregation but his fame in New England came from his reputation as a Calvinist scholar who in his preaching attributed the religious indifference of the colonial people to their reluctance to acknowledge their unworthiness before God. Although not a sensational preacher Edwards' use of the pulpit of the Congregational church at Northampton to fill his listeners with a sense of anxiety, born of the fear of God's wrath, fascinated the townspeople, with hundreds of them experiencing conversion. George Whitefield visited Northampton in 1740, and though he and Edwards had their theological differences they worked together to promote the 'Great Awakening' which 'bore fruit in abundance'. Jonathan Edwards' most memorable sermon was entitled 'Sinners in the Hands of an Angry God' which he preached the year after Whitefield's visit, when the revival was at its height.[46]

Edwards was astute enough to recognize in the 'Great Awakening' a phenomenon which the churches would have a difficult time to control. He was uneasy about Whitefield's emotionalism and sensationalism in the pulpit, and the emphasis Whitefield put upon man's hope associated with man's conversion experience and realization of personal salvation., Edwards preached the Bible alone as an infallible guide to faith and practice, but when on the frontier the Baptists in particular, engaged in revival work, presenting a simplified Gospel with persuasive zeal, to strike deep into the hearts of the poor and uneducated, Edwards was perturbed:

> When exuberance broke out among the people and they behaved in a strange fashion, declaring they had been recipients of new truth, he warned them of the Devil who provoked enthusiasm and deludes men into thinking they have received a special revelation. There is a place for emotion, but only if it is born of the sincere joy which comes through the illumination of the Scriptures. This was consistent Calvinism.[47]

Within popular protestantism, and not least among the Scotch-Irish on the frontier, an important theological dialectic was emerging in America. Edwards represented the conservative Calvinist faith in the authority of the church, interpreted by the ministers, which held in deep suspicion the kind of spiritual mysticism beloved of the Quakers and other denominations, which church authorities could not easily control. In 1754 Edwards produced his well-reasoned Calvinist polemic, *The Freedom of the Will*, against the popular assertion that man's will was not bound but free, but the age was less and less interested in 'sound doctrine'.[48]

In the years before the revolutionary war the pulpit was the most important single force in the colonies for shaping and controlling public opinion, and the affect of the Great Awakening was immense. It helped the growing interdependence of the colonies, helped immigrant bodies to become indigenous, aided a growing sense of community, and gave new humanitarian impulse with the freedom-seeking people who shared the restless, optimistic spirit of the frontier. Samuel Hopkins, 1721–1803, an eminent theologian of Rhode Island emerged as the most vigorous opponent of slavery in New England as he preached a Gospel emphasizing the love rather than the justice of God. He stressed that Atonement was not just for the elect but for all men, and man's freedom was such that he could know salvation through his own volition. As Edmund Burke and other astute observers noted a new society which passionately asserted the right of private judgment, and nurtured extreme individualism, with a theology to support their popular protestant opinions, was a power not to be ignored. Guided and fortified by a dream, a sense of destiny, in any conflict it would not be easily overcome.[49]

To the 'Old Sides' among the Presbyterians, or the 'Old Lights' among the Congregationalists the new spirit of popular protestantism was nurturing a form of antinomianism. Gilbert Tennent argued in a 1742 sermon that those who shared in the spiritual gifts revealed in the Great Awakening knew that matters like civility, or even acts of morality, were not of the essence of a true faith in Christ: 'the law could not condemn if God justified'.[50] Concepts such as this were like manna to the Scotch-Irish frontiersmen who in the years just before the war of independence began to move beyond the Appalachians in their determination to wrest new land away from the Indians. During the four years before the war they were reinforced by the greatest tide of Ulster immigrants. They were a ruthless people, who were increasingly resentful of any power that would try to bring them once more under the old authorities of church or state. The Great Awakening had filled them with visions which they, as reborn men, were sure they could make real if they were only free to form a new society.

The Methodists' mission began with an Ulsterman, Robert Strawbridge, who had settled in Maryland, and his itinerant preaching took place before official missionaries were despatched by Wesley to America. By 1775 there was a full blown revival in the south, much of it due to Methodist preaching which ignored the sectarian insularities which had once divided the people.[51]   Coming into being was a powerful expression of popular protestantism, passionate about the issue of religious liberty for the churches, and for the individual. They had no difficulty in expressing their mutual anxieties when the passing of the Quebec Act in 1774 brought Roman Catholic influences uncomfortably close to New England and the Middle Colonies:

> Popery has been established in the vast and unbounded province of Quebeck with the unlimited power vested in a military government, thereby, when fit occasion offered, to intimidate and awe the Protestant colonies into subjection.[52]

The Ulstermen, in particular, were disturbed by the reappearance of the power of their ancient foe, and this helped to shape their political opinions in the pre-war period. They were convinced that God had guided their coming to the new land; they had a deep sense of destiny, and were determined not to lose their new found freedom in both religious and political affairs.

When enlistments were made for the Continental Army up to half of the volunteers were Irish, and among those who were American born a great many were of Irish descent.[53]   The great majority of them were nominal Calvinists, with ideas about the sacredness of a contract between government and people, and the right of God's people to rebel against oppression: 'their national prepossessions in favour of liberty were strengthened by their religious opinions':

> Throughout the revolted colonies, and, therefore probably in the first to begin the struggle, all evidence shows that the foremost, the most irreconcilable, the most determined in pushing the quarrel to the last extremity, were the Scotch-Irish whom the bishops and Lord Donegal and company had been pleased to drive out of Ulster.[54]

There were probably up to 300,000 Ulster settlers in the colonies on the eve of the revolutionary war, most of them settled on frontier lands.[55]   They were in regular communication with their relatives in the old world, and it has long been recognized that they had great political influence among Presbyterian radicals and others in Ireland in the years of the revolutionary war and afterwards.[56]   In November, 1778, an address to the Irish bearing the name of Benjamin Franklin, and pointing out the close connection between American and Irish interests was given wide circulation.[57]   In later years popular histories of Ulster Presbyterianism were proud of the contribution to the war made by the Scotch-Irish: 'we can name twelve Ulster to one English general around Washington':

> It was a colony of Ulstermen in Mecklenburg County that first proclaimed the doctrine of American Independence before Charles

Thomson of Maryland and Thomas Jefferson of Virginia reduced it to writing in Philadelphia.[58]

The Ulstermen in America were so caught up in the passion of freedom that they did not hesitate to use force against the Quaker-dominated assembly in Philadelphia in 1764 when they felt oppressed, and between 1766 and 1771 they 'regulated' North Carolina to control taxation until a Colonial army crushed their protest.[59] The conviction that their new-found liberty in both religious and political affairs was a gift of God increased greatly during the revolutionary war years, and there developed in popular American Protestantism belief in a kind of secular version of 'election'. At the heart of their faith was the kind of 'assurance' that was known by all who were touched by the continuing spirit of the Great Awakening. It was essentially a radically individualistic folk faith, and it transcended the theological constraints of the old denominations, It was certainly understood and appreciated by the Scotch-Irish frontiersmen:

> If many were Presbyterians, that was likely to be considered an accident of birth—which, in fact, did not prevent them from becoming Baptists or Methodists, if these denominations were active in the communities to which they moved.[60]

Though it was never again as intense a religious experience, for so many the spirit of the Great Awakening survived the war years. In Kentucky a Presbyterian minister of Scotch-Irish parentage, James McGready, through powerful preaching in 1800 was able once more to nurture a spirit of revival. His efforts were aided by two brothers, William and John McGee who were respectively Presbyterian and Methodist ministers, and from the Kentucky Revival emerged the American missionary technique of using 'camp meetings' to sustain the people spiritually in their pioneer existence. In the Cane Ridge, Kentucky camp meeting of 1801 more than 20,000 people took part in an exercise of popular protestantism, with Presbyterian, Baptist and Methodist preachers joining enthusiastically in the proceedings. When it came to communion on Sunday no questions were asked the faithful about their denominational affiliation.[61]

It was the Ulster Protestants of the American frontier who contributed much to the appearance of such popular protestantism which sought to retain the rich heritage of the Reformation, yet found in revival a theological assurance which enabled them in peace and war to enrich the culture of the American frontier. Theodore Roosevelt in his popular *Winning of the West* believed:

> They were fitted to be Americans from the very start; they were kinsfolk of the Covenanters; they deemed it a religious duty to interpret their own Bible and held for a right the election of their own clergy...

In the hard life of the frontier they had lost much of their religion... but what few meeting-houses and school-houses there were on the border were theirs.[62]

Interestingly enough, in view of their history, the Ulster Protestants expressed few anti-popery sentiments in the camp meetings. Theirs was a society with few restrictions in terms of civil law, or convention, and little interest in perpetuating old world bigotry. Recent arrivals from Ulster brought with them traditional animosities, of course, for the emigration of Protestants to America continued until the Napoleonic wars. Prior to the massive Irish Catholic immigration of the 1830's and 1840's, however, it was believed the traditional religious foe had little authority to threaten the Protestant culture emerging in America. The popular religious belief, expressed by a Presbyterian minister in Ohio in the 1840's was that Rome need not be feared:

Our country is safe enough, if we instruct the whole people, and especially the immigrant portion of them... teach them the difference between intelligent liberty and mere licentiousness, place in their hands the Bible and the constitution of the Republic.[63]

The Presbyterians at home in Ulster, of course, learned much from emigrant letters of what was taking place in America, and they were as fascinated by the spirit of the Great Awakening and the influence it had in society as they were by the radical political development in what was to them a missionary situation.[64] The Synod of Ulster meeting at Antrim in 1754 responded kindly to the request of Gilbert Tennent for help to be sent to the trustees of 'the infant college of New Jersey' which Tennent hoped would become a college and seminary of learning.[65] In 1761 the Synod held at Londonderry was critical of the small amount of money sent to help distressed American ministers and their families.[66] Two years later the Synod meeting at Lurgan received an address from the Philadelphia city corporation for help for the poor and distressed Presbyterian clergy and their families on the frontier whose 'poverty is truly distressing' with their 'afflictions greatly heightened by a most barbarous and bloody war with the Indian nations'.[67]

III   '98 and Popular Protestantism

During the years following the Great Awakening in America, when the dialectical relationship between the old Calvinist church establishments, and the new frontier spirit of radical individualism in religious and political matters, was giving nurture to popular protestantism, the face of Ulster Protestantism changed very little. There seemed little to fear from Roman Catholicism whose energies were devoted to political emancipation in the years of the Penal Laws, and Presbyterians, in particular, were free to indulge in the kind of theological and ecclesiastical disputations beloved of their ministers. The latter were graduates of Scottish universities, well-educated men who were able to engage in theological polemics in their pulpits, and to carry their passion for divisive religious disputes into sessions, presbyteries and synods.

The chronic controversy among the Ulster Presbyterians was the question of subscription to the Westminster Confession of Faith. Men like John Abernethy, the eloquent and scholarly minister of Antrim, had led a movement from 1719 which argued that only personal persuasion, not ecclesiastical authority, should govern doctrinal decisions made by the individual. Abernethy's followers were labelled 'New Lights', and by 1725 there was a non-subscribing Presbytery of Antrim.[68] Controversy with the Synod of Ulster continued, however, with the non-subscribers being accused of Latitudinarianism and Unitarianism. Then from 1743 there came from Scotland members of the Secession Church, Presbyterians who were men of great scrupulosity and strong supporters of the Westminster Confession. They formed a Secession Synod, then divided their forces over a Church-State issue that only had relevance in Scotland. They were passionate in their discourses, however, and had appeal to the less educated classes:

> Their sermons... were composed of reiterated doctrines of the Confession, intermingled with denunciations, warnings and reproofs, and delivered in forcible and irascible language, had strong attractions for a class disposed to follow those who appeal to terror and excite to rapture.[69]

Not least among the Westminster doctrines brought to the attention of any congregation was the identification of the pope with the Antichrist.

Another Presbyterian body, the Reformed Presbyterians or Covenanters, came to Ireland and formed their own Presbytery in 1792, to add to an Ulster Protestant scene that was fractured, and its churches increasingly ineffective. The Seceders with their appeal to the lower classes had added some congregations, but the main ecclesiastical body, the Synod of Ulster confessed by 1769 that its institution had been in decline for the past twenty years.[70] This was in spite of the Synod having a firm provincial power base, its existence as a self-regulating organization, promoting a legalistic dogmatism which merged religion and politics, making it almost a state within a state. Its spirit of 'cold moderation' was not affected by the influence of the Great Awakening in the American mission church, and when the crisis symbolized by the Volunteer movement stirred Ulster society, and Presbyterian radicals identified themselves with the United Irishmen, it was clear that the major Protestant religious organization in Ulster no longer had the social control of the population that once it had, although the state reluctantly recognized its political importance.

As for the minor Protestant bodies they had only a qualified toleration by the government, though it did appear that for those who had suffered persecution by the Roman Catholics, the French Huguenots, the Palatines, and the Moravians, there was to be no interference with their activities.[71] The Quakers were so few in number that they too were tolerated in spite of their opposition to tithes, the taking of oaths, and their resistance to other ecclesiastical demands.[72] The Moravians had the most influence of these groups in Ulster with thirty or forty itinerant preachers in the province in the 1750's. In the same period John Wesley made his first of twenty-one visits to Ulster which had become the field for almost half of Methodist missions in Ireland by 1770.[73]

The Presbyterian attitude towards the Methodists and other itinerant preachers was reserved, and the Seceders' reaction to Whitefield was to describe him: 'as a wild enthusiast, engaged in the work of Satan'.[74] There was little likelihood of Presbyterian congregations being caught up in the kind of popular emotionalism that had accompanied his preaching in America. Still very much influenced by Scottish Presbyterian affairs, their religious priority was to reinforce the traditional Calvinist theology and legalistic church organization which they had inherited from their forbearers. Their clergy were conspicuous members of the community, proud of their religious formation in Scottish universities, and their capacity to control any form of religious enthusiasm. The Cambuslang Revival in western Scotland in 1742 following revival preaching by Whitefield had little influence in Ireland, and the climate of eighteenth century Ireland was religiously and politically not favourable to any great spiritual wakening.

Part of Irish Presbyterian tradition in political affairs was a lack of deference to secular authority, an inheritance from Scottish covenanting in the past. The ministers had well thought out radical theories about contractualism between God and man, the government and the governed, and it is not surprising that some of them supported the Enlightenment ideas that encouraged the appearance of the Volunteers and other more radical bodies. At the same time few of them were willing to abandon their visceral rejection of Roman Catholicism, the ancient enemy of liberty, enlightened values and religious toleration. Like the members of the Belfast Presbytery of 1649 they viewed themselves as 'well-affected to the Covenant', and at the same time defenders of the Protestant faith, 'Watchmen in Zion'.[75]

> To assume that radicalism and anti-Catholicism cannot exist within Presbyterianism is to misconceive its true nature. Anti-Catholicism is part of that radicalism, and the United Irishmen were less tolerant in religious matters than later nationalist tradition cared to admit.[76]

It does not fit easily into the Irish nationalist canon of history, but at the same time the radical Protestants of Ireland asserted their desire for political freedom, they continued to associate popery with economic and intellectual enslavement, as did most of their Enlightenment contemporaries. The traditional imagery of William, Prince of Orange, who came from Holland to save them from 'Popery, brass money and wooden shoes', was not forgotten.[77] There was general approval of the triumphal sermons preached after the victory of Culloden, such as that of Samuel Delan, minister of Letterkenny who rejoiced that the Ulster Presbyterians were not to suffer: 'the melancholy experience of Protestants under Popish powers'.[78] It is significant that where the United Irishmen had their strength was in areas like Antrim and Down, where there was a low incidence of Roman Catholic settlement, and the traditional Protestant anxiety about security was uneasily put aside in the crisis leading up to '98. There were few Ulster Protestants who did not have qualms, however, when recruitment of Roman Catholics into Volunteer units began in Belfast in 1784.

Much of the stimulation for ideas of religious toleration came from developments in America, such as the libertarian concepts of Thomas Paine which called for political independence. His work of 1776, *Common Sense*, which was inspired by his Quaker youth, helped to give assurance to those Presbyterian radicals who were beginning to think in terms of religious pluralism:

> For myself I fully and conscientiously believe that it is the will of the Almighty that there should be a diversity of religious opinions among us.[79]

The radicals had close connection with the Ulstermen who were so prominent in the events leading up to the American War of Independence. In the words of one Presbyterian minister: 'there is scarcely a Protestant family of the middle classes amongst us who does not reckon kindred with the inhabitants of that extensive continent'.[80] Most of them rejoiced that, in the words of the *Freeman's Journal* of 31 January, 1782: 'Liberty has there erected her throne, and reigns uncontrolled in civil and religious matters'. The Ulster Presbyterian radical leaders as part of their 'Americanizing' viewed themselves as free men whose rights were also restricted by a despotic and corrupt government. With great self-confidence they secularized traditional beliefs, and to them the struggle was no longer between Christ and Antichrist, but between liberty and despotism.

By 1792 a town meeting in Belfast voted in favour of full rights of citizenship being granted to Roman Catholics, whose papal allegiance was no longer to be feared:

> To clarify the question of the political allegiance of Irish Catholics to the pope, the Belfast society of United Irishmen requested the catholic Committee to make a declaration... disclaiming the right of the pope to

interfere in relations between the sovereign and his subject.[81]

The Protestant Wolfe Tone had become secretary of the Dublin Catholic Committee and in his 1791 *Argument on Behalf of the Catholics* said of the pope's authority: 'I look on his power with little apprehension because I cannot see to what evil purpose it could be exerted'.[82] Some of those who set aside their reservations about allying themselves with the Roman Catholics did so because of contemporary revolutionary ideology coming out of France as well as America. Others, like the Presbyterian minister, William Steel Dickson, wanted a biblically based just society to come into being through the practice of 'scripture politics'.[83] Among the radical ministers about half were orthodox Presbyterians in their theology, and the other half were influenced by liberal 'New Light' thought.[84]

The theorizing and idealism of the Presbyterian radicals was akin to that of the Volunteer leaders who no longer took seriously the Catholic-Jacobite menace, and relaxed over their traditional concern for Protestant survival in Ireland. Why not in this new era seek Roman Catholic assistance against a despotic government? Irish Catholics now took an oath of allegiance and made other gestures of acquiescence in the social order, and the papacy was in no position to assert its claim to universal ecclesiastical and religious authority during the era of the French Revolution. Now, to the Presbyterian radicals and the Volunteers, was the time to let high spirits and self-confidence overrule the traditional fear of the Catholic community which, from the standpoint of Belfast, county Antrim and county Down, seemed to have lost any basis for solidarity. The Catholic allies of the Protestant revolutionaries still retained, of course, their own opinions about Protestant movements like that of the Volunteers; in the words of a modern historian, 'to contemporary Catholics they more closely resembled the 'B' Specials than a nationalist movement'.[85] John Wesley's comment on a visit to Cork in 1778 was that the Volunteers: 'if they answer no other end, at least keep the Papists in order'.[86]

The great failure of the Presbyterian radicals and the men who made up the Volunteer corps was that they did not reckon with the popular Protestant viewpoint that was emerging in the countryside. In many parts of the province were members of a Protestant lower class who took for granted they had a law and order duty to perform in the polity. They were too humble to be considered fit to join the Volunteers, but in any case they had little sympathy with the pro-papist policies of this armed force.[87] Many Protestants were involved in a running war with Catholics in areas where the latter were dominant, and their alarm was greatest when, after the end of the Volunteer movement in 1793, the United Irishmen began to try to involve members of papist agrarian terrorist organizations in their movement.

In the 1740's when the Ulstermen in America were experiencing their Great Awakening their countrymen at home lived in a society where 'the cruelty of creeds continued without abatement'. In 1743 it was reported that prominent Protestants listened to the suggestion that they engage in a preemptive pogrom lest they suffer from a Catholic rising like that of 1641:

> So entirely were some of the lower northern Dissenters possessed and influenced by this prevailing prepossession and rancour against Catholics that in the same year, and for the same declared purpose of prevention, a conspiracy was actually formed by some of the inhabitants of Lurgan, to rise in the night-time and destroy all their neighbours of that denomination in their beds.[88]

When Thurot took Carrickfergus in 1760, it was soon known among the northern Protestants that his family name was O'Farrell whose grandfather had fought in Ireland for James II.[89] The northern Presbyterians followed with anxious interest the depredations of the Whiteboys when they began their outrages in County Tipperary in 1761. Among the lower orders reports of sectarian agrarian terrorism were of more importance than the theological problems of Pelagianism or semi-Pelagianism that captivated the minds of their ministers, or even the perennial issues of subscription to the Westminster Confession of Faith. The Protestant lower classes also formed their secret societies in the 1760's, the Oakboys in county Tyrone, and the predominantly Presbyterian Steelboys in county Antrim, both using intimidation to rectify economic grievances. What was appearing in the Irish countryside was a complex of peasant associations, determined to use radical means to obtain their usual limited objectives. Divisions among them were soon sectarian.[90]

Sectarian division was not always characteristic of these protest groups in areas where the Protestants were few in number. The Rightboys in Cork and Kerry in the 1780's, for example, brought in Protestants to their movement, attacked both tithes and priests' dues, and when excommunicated the Rightboys boycotted mass and attended Protestant services. From 1792, however, on the Cavan-Monaghan border arms-raids were carried out on isolated houses, there were rumours of oath-taking, and a new Roman Catholic ideology began to emerge. There was talk about carrying on the Stuart cause, the need for land redistribution and to Protestant observers: 'the underlying cause of conflict was a fundamentally continuous Catholic conspiracy against Protestants virtually unbroken since the age of religiodynastic wars'.[91] The Whiteboys were subsumed into this new conspiracy which spread rapidly, particularly in Armagh, and was given the name Defenderism:

> Defenderism was not definitively a 'peasant' movement: it was strong in towns and centres of rural industry, and was sophisticated enough to, for instance, send arms-buying delegations to London. It also managed

to absorb French ideology even without the help of the United Irishmen—though Defenderism tended to identify the French cause as Catholic and anti-English rather than 'republican'.[92]

In Armagh there was a competitive balance between the Catholic-Protestant populations, land hunger associated with the linen industry, and the conviction among the Protestant lower orders that the landlords, caught up in the Volunteer movement, were not enforcing the penal laws. This task was readily taken over by the anti-Defender Protestant Peep O Day Boys movement, the name reflecting their tactic of dawn raids on houses where arms might be stored, to be used by Defenders.[93] Just as much as the Scotch-Irish in America, the Protestant lower orders felt that as the Defenders increased in numbers and in ferocity they had a God-given right in the ineffectual polity of the time to raise and deploy physical force. By the mid 1790's this coercive power was being used to drive Defenders and their supporters out of Ulster and into Connaught. The Peep O Day Boys were helped to justify their terrorism by the Defenders' use of violence of a nature that was new in the history of Irish popular protests:

In January, 1791 at Forkhill, Co. Armagh a Protestant schoolmaster, Alexander Barkeley, and his wife were both attacked by Defenders. Their tongues were cut out, and some of their fingers cut off; and a brother of Mrs. Barkeley, a youth of fourteen years had his tongue cut out in the same incident.[94]

This level of sectarian ferocity, a precursor of what was to be visited upon Ulster in the latter decades of the twentieth century, stimulated greatly Protestant aggression which from the mid-1790's became increasingly systematized. The Protestants, who were referred to locally as 'Scotch' engaged in pitched battles in broad daylight with the Defenders on the Meath-Cavan borders.[95] The Protestants viewed the Defender assaults as a self-conscious merging of economic and political aims with a religious crusade: 'With some justification loyal Protestants saw the Defenders as a Roman Catholic organization whose sole purpose was to massacre them'.[96] The *Freeman's Journal* of 2 April, 1796 reported that in a cryptic password of the Defenders the first letter of each word represented the phrase: 'every loyal Irish Protestant heretic I shall murder and this I swear'.[97] Another of their cabbalistic oaths, used to produce a sense of awe and mystery, suggested strongly that the Defender movement was ultimately under Roman Catholic authority.[98]

It was out of these armed sectarian clashes that the Orange Order came into being, after a Protestant victory at the Diamond, near Loughall in County Armagh on 21 September, 1795. What was important about the new association was that it was openly supported by the Protestant gentry and the Defenders were now cast as anti-Protestant and anti-state terrorists. From 1794 some of the Defenders had begun to identify themselves with the United Irishmen, putting their own sectarian interpretation on the ideas of 'liberty, equality and fraternity', and in their ideology resurrecting memories of the injustices associated with the Treaty of Limerick and the Battle of the Boyne. It was through the Defender movement that the United Irishmen were able to extend their influence in many parts of the country in an unlikely alliance of Presbyterian middle class radicalism, and Catholic lower class rural agitation. In the countryside the Orange Order, on its way to becoming a national structure, was seen by the Defenders and their Catholic supporters as the Protestant authority to be most and immediately feared.

In the years immediately leading up to '98, and following the crisis, the religious foundations of the Orange Order were established. Meetings opened with prayers, and there was to be no swearing or drinking in the lodge. Outside the lodge the Orangeman was to present an example to his neighbours of temperance, sobriety and steady observance of the Sabbath.[99] The Orange Order did not in the early years of its existence attract the Ulster Presbyterians in great numbers, however, for from the time that a Gentleman's Lodge was founded in Dublin in 1797, and then a Grand Lodge in Ulster, it tended to attract not only gentry but some aristocrats, and many privileged members of the Established Church. The Orange Order was viewed as a valuable body in times of sectarian crises, but wherever a new lodge was formed recruitment for the United Irishmen increased greatly in the neighbourhood, and there is no doubt that the Orange movement added to the religious divisions of the people. It certainly put an end to the United Irishmen's hope of uniting Protestants, Roman Catholics and Dissenters in a great crusade against the power of Britain.

W.D. Killen, in his continuation of J.S. Reid's history of the Presbyterian Church in Ireland, considered that the horrors associated with the rebellion when it finally broke out was a harsh lesson for many of the Ulster ministers in particular:

> The year 1798 forms a crisis in the history of the synod of Ulster. The misery then entailed on thousands and tens of thousands furnished an emphatic and salutary rebuke to that intensely political spirit which had been cherished by too many Presbyterian ministers.[100]

Other writers were blunt in their assessment that the rising of 1798 almost succeeded because the Presbyterians had become so caught up in their theological and political abstractions that they had forgotten the crusading nature of their traditional enemy: 'four generations had come and gone since the massacre of 1641 which was then almost forgotten'.[101]

> It is surely no wonder that Irish Protestants dread the establishment of any Romish ascendancy in the country, when they know that on every

single occasion since the Reformation, at which Popery has gained the upper hand in Ireland, it has persecuted to the death.[102]

The atrocities in Wexford were particularly shocking to the Ulster Protestants. The accounts of Fr. Murphy leading his insurgents, clad in his black cassock, while they piked to death Mr. Burrowes, the Protestant cleric at Oulart, as well as his son and some of his parishioners,[103] invoked memories of the horrors of 1641 once more. What caught the public imagination of Ulster Protestants most, however, were the accounts they heard of the rebels imprisoning nearly 200 prisoners of all ages and sexes, many of them to be piked to death, and others burned to death in a barn at Scullabogue.[104]

> The papers day by day told how the rebels were imprisoning, plundering and murdering the Protestants; how the priests in their vestments were leading them to the fight, as to a holy war, which was to end in the extirpation of heresy; how Protestants were thronging the chapels to be baptized, as the sole means of saving their lives.[105]

When the rebellion was over there was considerable soul searching among the Ulster Presbyterians. Until then the strength of their Calvinist tradition was such that however much they divided themselves into theological camps, they would present a united face to the world in time of crisis.[106] There had been no common purpose served in '98, however, when one minister was executed for his part in the rebellion, a few were imprisoned, or encouraged to emigrate to America. As the General Synod meeting at Lurgan on 28 August, 1798 said in its humble address to the king:

> We are constrained to lament, with the deepest Humiliation, that the most Stable and Sacred Principles of many of our People and of some of our members, have been shaken by the Convulsions of this Sceptical and Revolutionary aera.[107]

A new note of uncertainty had appeared among the descendents of the Covenanters:

> We Beseech the King of Kings, who stilleth the madness of the People... to preserve your Subjects from every fatal Delusion and to convert our follies, Crimes and Miseries into Instruments of Wisdom, Piety and happiness.[108]

There was a belief that the Covenanting tradition had played its part in the unrest, with some members of the Reformed Presbyterian church in Ireland ready to admit no loyalty to an 'uncovenanted' monarch, or a prelatical established church. No one body of theological thought was more involved than another in the rebellion, however, and in spite of much finger-pointing the Ulster Presbyterian community was a much chastened one after '98. There was a general turning away from the revolutionary idealism and the violent nationalism which the French Revolution had inspired. Gone was the hope of the United Irishmen that there could be a unification of all Irishmen, regardless of creeds, in the quest for parliamentary reform: 'to substitute the common name of Irishman in place of the denominations of Protestant, Catholic or Dissenter'.[109] Above all, even among the radical ideologues, there was a general abandonment of hope that the Roman Catholics could be trusted to act other than they had ever done in the past. The letters of Dr. William Drennan even before the Wexford atrocities were full of references to his distrust of Catholic political motives, and he was aghast over the 'savagery' of the rebels at Scullabogue and elsewhere. He did remain 'ardently anti-Orange and pro-Catholic' throughout his life, but his distrust of the Roman Catholics never lessened. His son was to become a strong Unionist opponent to Home Rule.[110] In the popular Protestant mind the atrocities in Wexford, where the papists 'threw children into the flames;' was to be long remembered, and contributed to a new resolve among the 'watchmen of Zion': 'the sons of men who carried pikes at Ballinahinch to overthrow the rector and the landlord now joined the Orange society'.[111]

IV   **The Home Rule Movement and the Ulster Protestants**

At the end of the eighteenth century the division between Protestants and Roman Catholics remained in Ulster, as it had been at the beginning of the century, of basic significance in the life of the common people. The difference in the years following '98 and the Act of Union was that now most Protestants knew how dangerous the Roman Catholics could be. Whatever the injustice of their subordinate position in Ireland it would have been dangerous to try to extend much toleration to them in an age when there was a general revolutionary spirit among the European masses following the French Revolution and the Napoleonic era. There were, of course, some liberal Presbyterians who chose still to regard the Roman Catholics as a species of 'non-conformist brethren', fellow-sufferers under the ascendancy of the landed gentry, the Established Church, and an insensitive government in London. Henry Montgomery, the Arian minister of Dunmurry, who was representative in some matters of the tradition of the United Irishmen, opposed subscription to the Westminster Confession and believed in doctrinal pluralism, which included in politics Catholic Emancipation. It was the retention of this 'liberal' school of thought in Ulster Presbyterianism that prevented a significant expression of popular Protestantism emerging in the nineteenth century sooner than it finally did. Most Presbyterians were radically divided from the Roman Catholics, and even though they were committed after 1800 to serve alongside the members of the Established Church in defence of the Union, they carried with them into the new century a great memory of past grievances, a deep abiding suspicion of prelacy in a Protestant church. As late as 1858, John Edgar, one time moderator of the General Assembly published a pamphlet, *Presbyterian Privilege and Duty*, where a bishop was described as 'a costly excrescence' in a Protestant communion.[112]

Movement towards finding a popular Protestant front against the growing influence of Roman Catholicism once more, increased with the appearance of Henry Cooke as a powerful voice in Ulster Presbyterianism. Within the Synod of Ulster he succeeded in putting an end to the divisive theological conflicts which had for so long plagued the church, by forcing out the members of the Arian party who formed in years to come a Non-Subscribing Presbyterian Church. This 'cleansing of the temple' by the orthodox allowed the union of the Secession Synod with the Synod of Ulster to take place, however, and Cooke to be looked upon as a 'Protestant Pope', a powerful personage who was said to find his authority by 'uniting Evangelicalism with Orangeism'.[113] He appreciated the potential power of a pan-Protestant movement in an Ireland disturbed by the resurgence of a revitalized Roman Catholicism, but when he announced the 'banns of marriage' between Presbytery and Episcopacy in a great demonstration at Hillsborough in 1834, Cooke's enthusiasm for such a popular form of Protestantism was not appreciated by many of the Presbyterians. There was still jealousy among the Presbyterians over the privileges, exclusivism and pretensions to social superiority found in the Established Church. It was only after the 1834 Irish Church Temporalities Act brought Church of Ireland property under state control, and the Tithe Act of 1838 mitigated some Presbyterian grievances, and the Municipal Corporations Act of 1840 deprived churchmen of the monopoly of town government, that the Presbyterians began to have a warmer feeling towards the members of the ecclesiastical establishment which had oppressed them for so long. By the time that Daniel O'Connell tried to extend his Repeal movement into Ulster there was no difficulty in Henry Cooke and others organizing a united Protestant opposition to this ideological invasion of the north of Ireland. A Protestant rally in Belfast on 21 January, 1841, listed in attendance numbers of clergy from the Established Church, the Presbyterians and the Methodists.[114]

O'Connell certainly recognized Ulster as a Protestant stronghold when he spoke of 'invading' the province, to 'rescue our persecuted brethren in the north'. He had earlier encountered the power of popular Protestantism in the north when his mission in 1829 to spread the good news of Catholic emancipation in county Monaghan had to be turned back to avoid a massacre.[115] The Protestant authority that the O'Connellites encountered at Ballybay was that of the Orangemen, but supporting them was a great groundswell of militant Protestantism which was influenced by British evangelicalism. As a popular Protestant movement it had been gaining in strength since the 1730's in

England, where it was variously described as evangelicalism, Calvinism or Methodism.[116] To John Wesley and others in the evangelical school its fundamental doctrines were a new birth in the spirit, following a forgiveness of sins through the atoning death of Christ. Evangelicalism shared in the common British aversion to popery, had no difficulty in accepting the Reformation identification of the papacy as the Antichrist, and had a deep suspicion of any manifestation of priestcraft, such as the practice of celibacy, or the use of the confessional.

The popular appeal of evangelicalism reflected recognition of the spiritual authority within the movement. On the continent its strength lay in Pietism which produced in Friederich Schleirermacher and his *Discourses on Religion to the Cultured Among its Despisers* of 1799, one of the great theological treatises of the age. Schleiermacher's novel emphasis on religious experience not the bible or denominational creeds as the beginning of encounter with the divine in the life of the individual or the community, was to have great influence in the evangelical movement in both Britain and Ireland. Though bodies such as the Congregationalists or Particular baptists chose to call themselves Calvinists until the last decades of the nineteenth century, the evangelicals generally shifted from ideas of predestination to the conviction that all men could be saved through direct religious experience. The generations of evangelical churchmen whose lives were changed by acceptance of the 'scheme of salvation' advocated by Henry Venn in his *Complete Duty of Man* of 1763, or by William Wilberforce's *Practical View* of 1797, bear witness to the popular power and influence of evangelicalism, not least in the campaign to end the slave trade.[117] By the last decades of the nineteenth century there was widespread recognition in the British Isles of the popular Protestant 'Nonconformist conscience' as an engine of cultural, social and even political change: 'the general drift of evangelicalism which stressed feeling and experience more than systematic thinking was towards practical rather than intellectual concerns'.[118]

The 'practical' aspect of Ulster popular Protestantism reflected the industrial and social changes taking place in the province, especially in the Lagan valley, the very heartland of the Presbyterians. As the population grew from 20,000 in 1800 to almost 350,000 a century later there had to be a massive programme of 'church extension'. Inevitably this called for co-operation between the Protestant churches and, as early as 1827 the Belfast Town Mission to care for the poor was organized on interdenominational lines.[119] It was the forerunner of a myriad of mission halls of one kind or another which began to characterize Belfast and other towns. In many ways they were a protest against the traditional churches with their authoritarian clerical direction, for they offered the individual an intense fellowship in a small committed group. There was among the Protestants generally also an intense interest in temperance issues, and in Foreign missions, that form of outreach that brought to an insular provincial people knowledge of movements for revival which were taking place in distant

America and elsewhere. Most importantly from the Ulster standpoint Protestant co-operation began to appear among their 'Home Mission' agents, who with missionaries of the Established Church, faced together the wrath of the priests who resented the Protestant use of Irish-speaking preachers among their people.[120]

The great practical concern of Ulster evangelicals, of course, reflected their historical experience. The Evangelical Society of Ulster founded by Seceding Presbyterian ministers in 1798 independent of their synod, and modelled on American and British precedents, indicated a new state of mind in Protestant Ulster. It revealed the anxious vigilance which was developing in the alarmed Protestant north when the massacres in Wexford showed how vulnerable the Protestant minority people were in a predominantly Catholic society: 'to be found at any time slumbering upon Zion's walls is very inconsistent with the character of a faithful watch-man, but in times like the present it is peculiarly so'.[121] Just as much as the readers of the famous pamphlet of the bishop of Cloyne a decade earlier they were convinced that they lived in a 'precarious situation' and faced 'consequent dangers to the public'.[122] Though John Wesley made his last visit to Ireland in 1799, his followers in Ireland who then numbered about 20,000 were just as apprehensive about the Roman Catholics as were the Ulster Presbyterians. The *Methodist Magazine* in 1804 serialized an account of George Taylor, a preacher who had been imprisoned by the rebels during '98: 'none of the rebels were so blood-thirsty as those who were most regular attendants at the popish ordinances'. So far as the readers of George Taylor's misadventures were concerned Ireland was the very centre of a 'world-wide conflict between heretical catholicism and biblical protestantism'.[123] Because of the seriousness of the battle forced upon them the Ulster Protestants willingly transcended denominational concerns, welcoming even the small evangelical movement which was appearing among the churchmen at Trinity College, Dublin, and the newly founded Bethesda Chapel, a 'voluntary' place of worship within the establishment.

A preacher named Lorenzo Dow who arrived in Ireland immediately after '98 had great success during a mission characterized by the flamboyant methods he had previously used on the Kentucky frontier in America. He toured the country in 1800 and again in 1806, and he was supported by prominent preachers who came from the mainland to proclaim religious certitudes to a people made anxious by the revolution in Europe, and the threat of Roman Catholic resurgence in Ireland. Irish Methodist preachers such as Charles Graham and Gideon Ouseley were listened to by huge crowds that attended their outdoor meetings and heard the message that the problems of Ireland were: 'directly attributable to the pernicious doctrines of a heretical church, and the manipulation of its people by a corrupt priesthood'.[124] Graham, whose previous work had won him the title, 'the Apostle of Kerry', with Ouseley preached effectively to congregations of up to a thousand people in places like Killeshandra in 1801, with the people filled: 'with the new wine of the kingdom'.[125] So far as the Methodist itinerant preachers were concerned the only way that virtue and piety would flourish among the Roman Catholic population was when it was freed from 'the trammels of their religion' through a 'reduction of popery'.[126]

Prior to O'Connell's Catholic Emancipation campaign the more militant Protestants, at least, had some hope of a missionary breakthrough, but it was by then clear that it would be directed from Ulster where the Presbyterians, Methodists, Moravians, Brethren and others had their strength. Only grudgingly, because of their long resentment of the pretensions of the Established Church, they paid more attention to Henry Cooke's call for 'banns of marriage' with the Church of Ireland which he called for again and again, as in his lecture on the 'Present Aspect and Future Prospects of Popery' at the time of Cardinal Wiseman's 'papal aggression' in Britain.[127] As the years passed the finding of denominational peace between the Protestant churches became a passion for him, so that they might present a united resistance to the seemingly relentless advance of Ultramontane Roman Catholicism, so skilfully directed by the papal delegate, Paul Cullen.

Henry Cooke had great influence among Presbyterian churchmen, but there were other northern Protestants who had on the level of folk resistance their own ideas about how to deal with Roman Catholic aggressiveness. The Orange Order's authority waxed and waned during the mid-century years, but had little appeal to Presbyterians except among some small farmers and labourers in the west of Ulster. When there was a clash of Orangemen with Ribbonmen at Dolly's Brae near Castlewellan on 12 July, 1849 with Ribbonmen casualties however, there was a general sympathy for the Orangemen expressed by other Protestants. The earl of Roden, to whose estate they were marching, was recognized as a leading Protestant in Ireland, and there was considerable resentment when he was displaced as Lord Lieutenant of County Armagh. A Party Processions Act was passed in 1850 to curb marching by the Orangemen, but when there was open toleration of nationalist and Fenian parades in the 1860's, and a leader was found in William Johnston from County Down, other than members of the Church of Ireland began to give support to the Orange cause, intransigent as it was:

> If England does not give us justice, I would not care if there was a repeal of the Union tomorrow... we would be far better off under America if we are obliged to submit to the thraldom that is attempted to be imposed upon us.[128]

It was not only in the countryside that popular Protestantism was becoming militant by the late 1850's. The sectarian rioting that had characterized Belfast working class life since 1835 began to threaten civil order in a major way as Orange influences swayed church leaders in the city, such as Thomas Drew,

Vicar of Christ Church, which contained Sandy Row a Protestant stronghold in its parish. One of his daughters was married to William Johnston, he wrote Orange songs, praised the memory of William III, the 'deliverer who had landed at Carrickfergus', and he delighted in open air preaching on provocative anti-Catholic themes. In these activities Drew was supported by William McIlwaine of St. John's, Laganbank, and 'Roaring Hugh' Hanna, the minister of Berry Street Presbyterian church, and later of St Enoch's church in Carlisle Circus. A sermon delivered by Drew on Sunday, 12 July 1857 triggered off sectarian rioting that lasted over a week and brought about a parliamentary inquiry into its origins. As for Hanna, he was to spend all his pastoral life in Belfast, and as the years passed he was viewed throughout the United Kingdom as a symbol of Protestant intransigence,[129] rather like the Rev. Ian Paisley in the late twentieth century.

What lay behind the popular Protestant sympathy for the Orangemen, and even the agitation of clerical demagogues like Drew and Hanna was the apparent willingness of the British government to grant concession after concession to the increasingly militant Roman Catholic church: 'there was no satisfying the papists',[130] On the parish level the Protestants were aware of a great building of churches by the Roman Catholics, as well as schools and religious institutions, and even the beginning of 'popish' missions which inevitably brought about the deepening of sectarian animosities. There was an ugly demonstration by working class Orangemen in Lisburn in 1853 when two Rosminians tried to conduct a mission in the town. An Orange mob threatened the missionaries, the Catholic church and presbytery were stoned, and but for the action by the police and two companies of soldiers lives would have been lost.[131] Neither the local landlord, nor reluctant local magistrates sought to control this kind of sectarianism, and Protestant church leaders were concerned about their own apparently declining authority among the working classes in this time of religious and social unease.[132] This was especially a cause for concern among the Presbyterians who had in 1840 carried out a union of the Synod of Ulster and the Secession Church, and in an ecclesiastical sense the authority of orthodoxy should have been increased. In terms of maintaining authority among the ordinary people, however, the 'intellectualist' Presbyterian system, and the rationalism in the church court system, had its limitations when it came to controlling the passions of the people in a time of sectarian anxiety. This was a difficult period for an orthodox enthusiast to consider imposing godly discipline upon both the elect and the non-elect.[133]

There is evidence of a growing spiritual intensity among some Presbyterian congregations, however, and from the pulpits came appeals to the personal conscience of the worshipper, the need for personal knowledge of the grace of Christ, and the acceptance of the guidance of the Holy Spirit. This new pietistic expression of the faith was sufficiently strong that when reports came in from America of a major revival movement among Protestant churches the General

Assembly of 1858, meeting in Londonderry sent two senior representatives to investigate the phenomenon and to report back what was happening.[134] What their visit revealed was a very emotional religious revival taking place, not unlike that of the Great Awakening a century earlier. It was a time of great anxiety in New York city following a major stock market crash, and of popular talk that this was a judgment of God upon a sinful society. The revival was unexpected, without direction from professional evangelists, with the leadership assumed by laymen. For the most part an urban phenomenon the revival spread rapidly to Philadelphia, Chicago and other cities, where multitudes attended daily prayer meetings. These were conducted on a non-denominational basis, and examples of religious 'enthusiasm' were soon to be found in small towns and in the countryside, as the movement produced a whole new generation of evangelists, such as one of the greatest conversionist preachers since the days of Wesley and Edwards, Dwight Lyman Moody.

Apart from the Presbyterians there was among Irish Protestants a popular evangelical movement which tended to break down denominational barriers, and to encourage meetings for discussion and bible study in private houses. This had begun in the 1827 period when independent churches began to appear, such as those associated with John Nelson Darby and his Brethren movement, with their 'built in corrective to the contagion of the evils of power' which were to be found in the churches as well as society. Without an organized ministry their pietism demanded an on-going spirit of revivalism, with devotees engaging in practices such as renouncing secular occupations judged not to be compatible with new testament standards.[135] Such churches, along with the Methodists, Moravians and others were well established in the latter half of the nineteenth century, and with their unstructured denominational organizations they too were readily influenced by the spirit of 'enthusiasm' which appeared in Ulster following, or at the same time as the great revival which took place in America.

The first sign of revivalism in Ulster was in the large Connor congregation of County Antrim where conversions were reported in prayer and cottage meetings. Most Presbyterian congregations still had cold, formal services, however, and when news spread of 'enthusiasm' appearing in various congregations, and then stories of 'physical prostration' in Ahoghill and elsewhere the excitement among the Protestants was immense. The new sense of joy and assurance of salvation obviously had more appeal to the masses than the 'fairly rigid Calvinism' they were used to and the reported number of conversions were disturbing to the Presbyterian authorities. Especially was this so when those who were conscious of a conversion experience chose to become Baptists or Plymouth Brethren.[136] Fortunately for the ecclesiastical authorities the revival subsided soon after peaking with a great mass meeting in Botanical Gardens, Belfast, and an assessment of the significance of the phenomenon began, although the *Banner of Ulster*, the official Presbyterian paper chose to pass over what had happened without making comment.

The Revival of 1859 could not be ignored by historians because in terms of involvement of large numbers of people in sustained activity it was the most important folk event between 1798 and 1913. It is true that there were no conversions in Fermanagh, few in Tyrone and in Belfast they were concentrated in some areas like Sandy Row. It has been noted that those converted were more apt to be female textile hands than shipyard workers in Belfast, and rather elaborate theories have been advanced to explain away the significance of the religious phenomena.[137] It has also been admitted that this 'rural popularization of enthusiastic Protestantism' had profound effect because its use of common speech, and a fundamentalist interpretation of the bible began the separation of the minister from his flock. Those who had had the experience of conversion had a diminishing respect for clerical rationalism and intellectualism. What they wanted now of the ministers was that they act as 'chaplains' of the fellowship of the converted, rather like clergy acted as chaplains of the Orange Order. If anything the converted now wanted the kind of 'enthusiastic' leadership they were to find in the future in Edward Carson, the Unionist politician.[138]

What seems undeniable is that the 1859 revival was widely accepted by a newly emergent popular Protestant community as: 'both a historical event and a supernatural encounter invested with almost mythical significance', and an event of 'cultural revitalization', long and nostalgically remembered.[139]

> It stimulated many in their religious enthusiasm and clearly remained an important if unacknowledged influence on the northern psyche. Its monuments are the innumerable mission halls and tents, evangelical crusades, and evangelical associations that make Northern Ireland an Irish extension of the Bible belt.[140]

An immediate consequence of the revival was the reinforcement it gave to the popular anti-Catholic preachers of the time like Hugh Hanna, Tommy Toye or Thomas Drew in Belfast. The Presbyterian Toye even brought converted people from Ahoghill for a meeting in Belfast in May, 1859. Whereas in America revivalism was important in revitalizing the life of the individual frontiersmen or immigrant who was moving forward to establish a new culture in a land that seemed to have no boundaries, in Ireland there was no frontier to be pushed back, but rather one to be defended, and the legacy of conversion was more apt to be important in a communal than in merely a personal sense. The intense evangelical spirit which grew in Ulster after the revival and became a form of popular Protestantism, was interpreted in terms of the on-going historical experience of the Ulster Protestants:

> Evangelical religion... imbued the Ulster Protestant community with a sense of divine approval in its continued resistance to assimilation into the wider Irish culture, in which the Roman Catholic religion was

regarded as the most central and most pernicious element.[141]

Following the Ulster Revival the transcending of denominations by Protestant evangelicals was a continuing process. They watched glumly the rise of Fenianism in the rest of Ireland, and few would have disagreed with Henry Cooke when, in his last public appearance, he exhorted the huge crowd assembled on 30 October, 1867 at Hillsborough, County Down, to resist the never-ending attack on Protestant institutions in Ireland: 'the vast bulk of the Protestants of Ireland believed that their rights and liberties were in danger'.[142] The Orange Order was once more becoming important, its populist militant atmosphere interpreted as the 'carrying out of the spirit of Bible Christianity', and whatever the church or political occasion the popular Protestant view of Irish history was promoted. Providence was on their side, as their long and successful defence of their 'open bible' faith revealed. The revival of 1859 confirmed for them that they were not alone in their struggle with priestcraft and superstition, and they saw themselves as a faithful remnant of righteousness in a land threatened by an authoritarian and heretical power.

Then came the shock of Disestablishment of the Church of Ireland, which even the General Assembly protested against, and the last reservations about an Ulster pan-Protestant movement led by the Presbyterians and the Episcopalians began to fade away. There still remained, of course, lingering resentment over members of the Church of Ireland remaining dominant in law and local government, and the retention by the episcopalians of their church's name, but the two communities were significantly united now in a common movement to defend Ulster's Protestant heritage, as the many demonstrations of the period made clear.[143] The Presbyterian-Episcopalian alliance was helped after Disestablishment was carried out, and the Church of Ireland in its reorganization recognized a new lay authority in church affairs, and chose to revise the Prayer Book in a modestly Protestant fashion.[144] No Presbyterian was going to doubt the Protestant loyalties of someone like the border rector who told Orangemen in County Monaghan that when it came to serving the crown, 'Protestant loyalty... is conditional'. The Queen should be reminded:

> One of her ancestors who swore to maintain the Protestant religion forgot his oath, and his crown was kicked into the Boyne. We must speak out boldly, and tell our gracious Queen that, if she breaks her oath, she has no longer any claim to the Crown.[145]

There was an increasing conviction on the part of many Ulster Protestants that they were very much on their own after Disestablishment, and that the concessions of the crown to a militantly ultramontane Roman Catholic church would never end:

Persuaded by the revival of 1859 that God was still on their side, forced to accept in 1869 that the State would no longer shore up Irish Protestantism, and faced with the defeat of their national and cultural aspirations... Ulster Protestants dug deep into their historical tradition and once again found strength in adversity.[146]

One 'adversity' that threatened the Ulster Protestants from 1879 was the popular power in Roman Catholic Ireland of the Land League, led by the 'apostate' Parnell, and the convert to Roman Catholicism M.P. for Belfast, Joseph Biggar. Protestants did not fail to notice how often priests appeared on Land League platforms, and archbishop T.W. Croke of Cashel became a passionate champion of the cause. They knew the popular power of the Land League was organized by ex-Fenians, and the use of intimidation and other means of agrarian terror was becoming commonplace. Members of the hierarchy joined archbishop Croke in defence of the League's 'principles of justice', and the official organ of the Vatican appeared to be willing to justify the campaign of what the Protestants viewed as criminal activity.[147]

The Land League tried to establish itself among the Ulster Protestant tenantry, Parnell made a visit to Belfast and Newry in October, 1879, and some historians have argued that between then and 1882 there was: 'a calculating approach to the most effective agrarian strategies, which unquestionably weakened the hegemony of pan-Protestantism'.[148]   As the political manoeuvering went on, however, pressures from Protestant leaders brought the Protestant countrymen into line when the political interests of the Land League became clearer. In the words of Lord Enniskillen, in the *Fermanagh Times*, 20 January, 1881:

> The Land League is essentially a disloyal organization, and although landlordism may be the immediate object of its attack, the ultimate separation of the two countries is its aim.

By late 1881 Protestant support for the Land League was waning rapidly, because of its close association with nationalist aims and the continuing agrarian violence in the south and the west of Ireland. By 1885 when Parnell's Home Rulers won 85 of Ireland's 103 parliamentary seats, the movement made no headway in the predominantly Protestant areas of Ulster. The energetic labours of the Roman Catholic nationalist leader, Joe Devlin, supported by the priests and the ancient Order of Hibernians, helped in the separation of the two communities, by encouraging the deepening of the traditional sense of siege. By the beginning of 1886 the Presbyterians, the Methodists and the other Protestant churches had closed ranks with the Church of Ireland in opposition to Home Rule.[149] They were eagerly supported by a revitalized Orange Order, with its appeal that transcended Protestant denominational or social differences.

When the new Liberal Prime Minister, W.E. Gladstone announced his intention to introduce a bill to give Ireland Home Rule in 1885 the Protestant churches united in support of the opponents of the bill, with even the Quakers joining in the resistance. Every Protestant publication had something to say about 'fullness of conviction' and 'solidarity of opinion',[150] and out of the crisis of the first Home Rule bill emerged a popular Protestant mind, a way of thinking that gave Ulster Protestantism an identity of its own.[151] The Protestant welcome of Lord Randolph Churchill, when he spoke to a monster meeting of Unionists in the Ulster Hall in 1886, was immense. Few disapproved when he proclaimed in an open letter: 'Ulster will fight, and Ulster will be right'. The news of the defeat of the bill on 8 June, 1886 brought out enthusiastic rejoicing in the streets of Protestant Belfast, as well as the most serious sectarian riots of the nineteenth century. The fighting caused more blood to be spilled than in the 1803 Emmet rebellion or the 1848 Young Ireland rising, or the 1867 Fenian rebellion, or the Land War of the 1870's and 1880's, The common Protestant people had no intention of allowing themselves to be coerced into what they feared would be a tyrannical impoverished Roman Catholic state. Hugh Hanna had eager listeners when he thundered about Ulster's 'godly right of resistance'. Even the usually restrained *Irish Ecclesiastical Gazette* of 27 March, 1886 warned of the danger of a foreign and ultramontane church led by the Jesuits attempting to overthrow Protestantism in Ireland:

> If we and Rome cannot live together on terms of peace, we must do so with the sword in our hands. No surrender.

The Methodist *Christian Advocate* urged a united Protestant front against the Roman political and religious threat:

> Home Rule for Ireland means not only war against the Crown Rights of England but war against the Crown rights of Christ... its inspiration is religious antipathy, its methods plunder, its object Protestant annihilation.[152]

This popular Protestant mind had been formed through historical experience; it was to develop and become increasingly intransigent during the long struggle over Home Rule, which was to come to a climax during the events of the World War I period and led to the partition of Ireland. To persuade Gladstone that his Irish policy was mistaken, and that there was a more substantial opposition to Home Rule than mere Orange bigotry, a great banquet was held in Belfast in 1888 attended by the leaders of the Irish Presbyterian, Methodist, Congregational and Baptist churches, who discoursed upon an address against any form of Home Rule which had been signed by 864 out of 990 nonconformist ministers. They were convinced that any form of Home Rule would inevitably weaken historical

Protestantism by denying it the freedom to preach Biblical Christianity, and to maintain its influence culturally and socially. Their commitment to the cause of religious liberty was unqualified, and their stand applauded:

> The religious heroes of Ulster Protestantism have not been theologians or pietists, but rather those who have most resolutely defended the rights of Ulster Protestants to adhere to the reformed faith against the unwelcome encroachments of the Roman church.[153]

Future citizenship in a state where representatives of the imperialist-minded, persecution-prone Roman Catholic church were in authority was simply (as they say in Ulster) 'not on'. A fully-formed Ulster popular Protestant ideology came into being during the Home Rule crisis, and it was to be little qualified in succeeding years. Rome was as militant and aggressive as ever. The Ulstermen believed the papacy would seek to be all-pervasive in its influence, and it would never tolerate a pluralist religious establishment. There was no way that Ulster Protestants would be allowed to find peaceful accommodation in a culture where the value-systems of the Vatican would be enforced on society by an oppressive Roman Catholic nationalist government. 'Home Rule' would inevitably mean 'Rome rule'.[154]

What the outside world saw in Ulster from this time forward was not the firmness of religious and ideological commitment which sustained popular Protestantism but the posturing of extremists like those in the Orange Order. Large scale demonstrations against Home Rule were whipped up throughout the countryside by the Orangemen, they began to drill with wooden guns, and their leader William Johnston was deliberately provocative whenever possible:

> We are prepared to take the Bible in one hand and the sword in the other... We will defend the Protestant religion and our liberties won at the Boyne with our rifles in our hands.[155]

With the defeat of Gladstone's Second Home Rule bill in 1892, which the Orangemen did not take seriously, the death of Parnell and the divisions in the nationalist movement, the Orangemen stopped drilling, and the Ulster Protestants began to return to their normal existence. In the autumn of 1892 when the American evangelist, D.L. Moody held his last mission in Belfast to call for a new 'wave of divine awakening', the huge crowds that attended the meetings used a temporary structure that had been built on vacant ground near the Presbyterian college in the summer to protest the Second Home Rule bill.[156]

The weakness of the Ulster Protestant position, in political terms was, then and now, that it felt it needed the support of the imperial government in London, if it was to withstand the imperial authority of Rome. This it felt was lacking on the mainland where the Methodists and others believed the authorities had 'gone soft on Rome'.[157] The result of this 'abandonment' was a deepening of Ulster's intransigent resolve to defend the Protestant faith, and the political settlement that had hitherto allowed it to flourish. By the time that the Liberal government under Asquith was about to introduce the Third Home Rule Bill, some nationalists doubted the ultimate resolve of the Ulstermen, but in quiet determination the Protestant leaders, including most of the clergy, prepared themselves with the rest of the faithful to defend their inheritance and their territory. From December, 1911, the Ulster Orangemen formed a Provincial Grand Lodge to work in closest harmony with the Ulster Unionist Council. By the following year, although the Home Rule bill of the time merely granted Ireland local self-government powers under the Crown, the popular passions in the north were almost uncontrollable by either the churches or the state. After an assault upon Sunday School children by armed Hibernians near Castledawson in County Londonderry, there was a widespread hysteria that led to vicious rioting in the Belfast shipyards, and at a Celtic/Linfield football game. Rudyard Kipling added to the tension when he wrote a poem for the *Morning Post*, 'Ulster 1912':

> We know the war prepared
> On every peaceful home,
> We know the hells declared
> For such as serve not Rome.[158]

On Easter Tuesday 1912 a huge gathering at Balmoral in south Belfast listened to prayers conducted by the Primate of All Ireland and the Moderator of the Presbyterian church. Then came a march past of more than 100,000 which was described by the correspondent of the Liverpool *Daily Courier*:

> Not since the marshalling of Cromwell's Puritan army have we had anything approaching a parallel; as a body of men they were magnificent. The hardy sons of toil from shipyards and factories marched shoulder to shoulder with clergy and doctors, professional men and clerks.[159]

The great event in the display of popular Protestantism in this crisis was the signing of the Covenant in Belfast City Hall and elsewhere by some 471,414 Protestant men and women who pledged themselves not only to preserve the Union but, if Home Rule was forced upon them, they would: 'solemnly and mutually pledge ourselves to refuse to recognize its authority'.[160] Religious services were held throughout Belfast, and elsewhere in the countryside, with the congregations 'in this our time of threatened calamity' singing 'O God, our help in ages past'. For the Covenant ceremonies a faded yellow silk banner had been found which, it was claimed, had been carried before William III at the Boyne.

There were still English sceptics who considered such theatricals mere posturing by Edward Carson and his religious and secular supporters, but they could not sense the atmosphere in the province, or the reaction to words like those of the Presbyterian minister who preached to Edward Carson and others on Covenant Day:

> The Irish question is at bottom a war against Protestantism. It is an attempt to establish a Roman Catholic ascendancy in Ireland to begin the disintegration of the Empire by securing a second Parliament in Dublin... We are plain blunt men. We will not have Home Rule.[161]

By the end of 1912 Protestants were drilling all over Ulster, and the following year the Ulster Volunteer Force, limited to 100,000 men who had signed the Covenant, came into being. When guns were landed at Larne for Protestant resistance use in 1914, the operation was clearly one that had widespread tacit support. One popular clergyman who recorded the intense excitement associated with the gun-running, with even police in support of what was happening, exclaimed: 'This is the Lord's doing, and it is marvellous in our eyes'.[162] The popular Protestant passion only subsided with the outbreak of World War I, and the attempt to sublimate sectarianism into the 'higher cause' of serving the British Empire. The fear of the Home Rule demon never disappeared, however, and many of the Ulster Volunteer forces were hesitant to enlist in the 36th Ulster Division, and leave Ulster undefended: 'they feared the south'. Nor was their anxiety unjustified for, while they prepared for the holocaust of the Somme, the *Belfast News Letter* of 5 April, 1915, reported the review of various nationalist forces, numbering some 25,000 who marched past Parnell's statue in Dublin.

V   Popular Religious Ideology in Protestant Ulster

To look at the speeches and writings of Protestant leaders in 1966, the fiftieth anniversary of the two blood-sacrifices of 1916, the battle of the Somme, and the Easter Rising, is to realize that, although few were expressed with the venom and militancy of Ian Paisley, today a great ideological block exists between the minds of Ulster's Protestants and Ireland's Roman Catholics. To the Protestants the Easter Rising was a 'stab in the back', redolent of 1641 and 1789; to nationalist Catholics the slaughter on the Somme, or indeed the whole tragedy of World War I, was a memory you tried to erase from folk-recall with as much grace as possible. There remains in Ulster a very deep sectarian divide, based on old hurts, old memories, which is not much different from that which existed on the eve of World War I. Superficial accord is, of course, easily maintained by the middle classes, and in an age of ecumenism it would be politically incorrect to use the pulpit for religious polemics. Yet both Protestants and

Catholics have their lives governed by myths, and this is why provocations connected with the Protestant marching season, or the pilgrimages to I.R.A. 'shrines' are still potentially dangerous in Ulster society. The Ulster Protestants certainly recognize the passion associated with the I.R.A. which regularly produces martyrs for causes whose origins lie in the mists of history:

> The strength of traditional militant Irish Republicanism does not lie in reasoned arguments for independence from Britain, or for a particular form of government, but in the strong emotions evoked by memories and legends surrounding past leaders.[163]

It is not only the Ulster Protestants who choose to look upon militant Republicanism in this way: 'the Irish are not preoccupied with history but obsessed with divisive and largely sectarian mythologies'.[164]

An anomaly of the Ulster 'troubles' is that the 'sectarian mythologies' of the Roman Catholics are mainly political in nature, those of the Protestants 'religious'. There are exceptions, of course, such as Bishop Charles McHugh of Derry protesting against partition in the early 1920's, because of the perilous position in which religion and Catholic education would be placed in Ulster.[165] The Roman Catholic religious establishment has prospered in Northern Ireland, however, and the Ulster Roman Catholics seldom acknowledge the religious element in what to them is a straight-forward political struggle: the fulfilling of the 'manifest destiny' of the Irish Republic, made clear in Articles 2 and 3 of the Constitution of 1937. When James Craig declared in 1934 that Ulster was a Protestant state, with a Protestant parliament in Belfast, De Valera countered by declaring Ireland a Catholic nation, but such reference to religious identity has been comparatively rare on the part of the nationalists, although they live in one of the most Roman and Catholic nations in the modern world. When they refer to sectarianism they think in a tribal sense, rather than religious:

> It was the attempt to establish and maintain a separate sectarian-defined state in the north of Ireland, in opposition to the wishes of the majority in the rest of the country, and of the very substantial minority in the north itself which was at the root of the problem.[166]

The Ulster Protestants, of course, have no difficulty in explaining why the nationalists eliminate mention of the religious element when they talk of their crusade to bring the six counties into a united Ireland. Spiritual affairs in a Roman Catholic culture are the concern of the hierarchy, and ultimately of the Vatican, and there is no encouragement given to the nominally Roman Catholic foot soldiers in the I.R.A., or other front-line formations, to bring religious issues into their campaign. It will be only when the armed conflict is completed and there is no Protestant-dominated Northern Ireland to contend with that the process of acculturalization will begin; then the Ulster Protestant population will suffer the fate of the once substantial Protestant population in the Republic, which has almost disappeared since 1922. This is why the popular Protestant shibboleth remains the same as it has been since the 1880's: 'Home Rule is Rome Rule':

> They see the south of Ireland as priest-ridden, controlled in some way by the Vatican, and ready at every opportunity to take away their civil and religious liberties.[167]

The Church of Rome represents to the majority of Ulster Protestants an 'intolerant ecclesiastical tyranny':

> Ulster trembled when the shadow of the Vatican fell across her as men once trembled at an eclipse of the sun: and the Union seemed the only guarantee that recurrent eclipses would not be the harbingers of a perpetual darkness... the encyclical 'Libertas Praestantissimum' of Leo XIII in 1888 made it clear that religious liberty as we understand it was an evil, only to be permitted when the attempt to enforce conformity would produce still greater evils.[168]

In the midst of the 'troubles' the Methodists revealed the popular Protestant fear of what to them appeared to be a Rome-directed form of ethnic-cultural-religious cleansing:

> To many people in Ireland Roman Catholic education seems to be divisive and calculated to lead to a Gaelic Catholic society. Is it the policy of the Irish Roman Catholic church to have a Gaelic Catholic Ireland with the Protestants either absorbed or driven out?[169]

The popular Protestant response to militant Roman Catholicism is also, of course, represented in the still powerful Orange Order, which is so influential that in 1975 the General Assembly of the Presbyterians felt compelled to deny its influence in the church:

> The part played by the Order in the life of the various Protestant churches is... often exaggerated. Thus, a substantial majority of the ministers, elders and members of the Presbyterian Church are not members of the Order; and there would be strong objections if attempts were made, for instance, to dictate policies to the General Assembly.[170]

The majority of Ulster Protestants do not support the extremism of Paisleyism, and on occasion go to some trouble in working class areas to indicate their rejection of Ian Paisley as another Edward Carson,[171] but even when the value of Paisley's stentorian voice of anti-Catholic defiance is criticized there are those among the working class Protestants especially who do not question the central message of 'No Surrender' he delivers, in the manner of William Johnston in 1886:

> Speak gently, they tell us. Speak gently indeed and believe Luther and Calvin. Speak gently of the Inquisition, of Jesuit assassinations, and the dark deeds of priestcraft. Speak gently of the massacre of the Huguenots. Speak gently of the system which God's word denounces as 'Mystery, Babylon the Great, the Mother of Harlots and abominations of the earth'. Rev. 17:5.[172]

Popular Protestantism in Ulster is filled with justified fear; there is a steady exodus of Protestants from some border areas and parts of Belfast, where they have found themselves in the front-line.[173] Those who remain on the border, as in the predominantly Protestant village of Aughnacloy, County Tyrone, live in a community where in the winter of 1988 there was a close communion between the three Protestant clergymen, but the new Roman Catholic priest had not been spoken to by any of them in the six months he had then been in the community. The priest confessed to the *Irish Times* journalist who interviewed him that he had never before experienced such polarization in a community, nor so much bitterness among a mere one hundred people.[174] The situation in Aughnacloy, of course, is far from unique, and it is social realities of this nature, together with a long history of religious and tribal struggle that immediately influence the popular mind of the Ulster Protestants.[175] In the general Protestant population the memory of massacres such as those in the Pentecostal Church of Darkley, or at the Cenotaph in Enniskillen will be a long time in passing.[176]

The influence of this kind of history is what makes the popular Protestant mind in Ulster reluctant to even consider seriously the value of ecumenism, which is so important to many churchmen in the last decades of the twentieth century. When a comment was made on the reception of the Anglican-Roman Catholic International Commission final report in the spring of 1982, the *Church of Ireland Gazette* opined there was 'No need for alarm'. The Church of Ireland and the other Protestant denominations in Ulster were still to be masters in their own houses, 'in spite of the talk of accepting Roman primacy'.[177] There would be a reserved incredulity among Ulster Protestants of any denomination if they ever heard about the new centre for 'Catholic and Evangelical Theology' in Northfield, Minnesota.[178] The popular Protestant mind in Ulster can understand, in the event of a world-wide evangelical revival, churches uniting in a religious culture that is judged by Scripture, but history has persuaded reformed churchmen to be deeply suspicious of ecclesiastical organizations that are the creation of men, not the Holy Spirit. On the popular level most Protestants question the spiritual credentials of the Roman Catholic church, so that ecumenical endeavours are simply not a priority with them.

At the same time the Ulster Protestants are sometimes spiritually uneasy over the response of their churches to the twenty-five years of mayhem their society has had to endure. The message of the Protestant clergy following some atrocity has usually been given in a funeral address, and it has been one of cautionary pietism. Direct challenging of the cause of the suffering of the people, a call for all denominations to transcend the evil of sectarianism has been rare in Ulster; and now the churches are finding themselves under secular if not divine judgment.[179] It may be argued, nevertheless, that the pietism preached, especially in working class areas has had a spiritually calming or cautionary effect upon the minds of would be Protestant militants or terrorists. It is remarkable how well a 'turning the other cheek' ethic has operated in Protestant Ulster during the years of relentless attack upon themselves and their community since 1969. It has only been from November and December 1992 that the Protestant paramilitarists have begun to talk about a campaign against 'the entire Republican community' with 'a ferocity never imagined'[180]—though few Ulstermen have forgotten the 1972 outrages of the 'Shankhill butchers'.

The Ulster Protestants have difficulty in understanding why their struggle to remain as part of the United Kingdom, where they can be sure of religious tolerance in a pluralist society, has received so little sympathy from so few people. Theirs has been a lonely struggle for independence from a society which wants to assimilate them into a culture which they abhor. They also reject totally a religious system based on clerical control of the laity which to them is anathema, but is still passively if not enthusiastically embraced by the Roman Catholic laity in the Republic of Ireland, who seem to affirm their submissiveness every time they attend mass:

> The priest does whatever it is up there; the worshipper lets it wash over. And feels alone with God, though protected by the sacred place and the rest of the congregation. I don't think that the idea of belonging to a Christian community, or the idea that the people themselves are the Church—that is no more than all its people—are as yet congenial to Irish Catholics. I think they still want the old ways.[181]

There is no way in the popular Protestant mind that Ulster will willingly become part of the confessional Roman Catholic Republic of Ireland. No *dragonnade* or other pressure can force them to accept what would be to them a return to spiritual bondage, a repudiation of the religious freedom their forefathers lived and died for. Perhaps it was to assure the constituency that shares this mind that the new moderator of the Presbyterian Church in 1994: 'insisted that during his year-long term of office he would not be involved in talks with Catholic Church leaders'.[182]

Chapter XIV

Epilogue, 1992

The Tyranny of the Dead

'Of all that was done in the past, you eat the fruit, either rotten or ripe'
T.S. Eliot, quoted by Paul Blanshard,
Irish and Catholic Power. London,
1954, p. 35.

The 'notable public servant' C.S. Andrews in his autobiographical musings expressed the misgivings felt by many Irish, whether Catholic or Protestant, when they have considered the almost overwhelming cultural influence brought to bear upon them by the society on the 'mainland', and their instinctive response to British pressure:

> Since my schooldays, I had a deep emotional conviction that the only way by which Ireland could survive as an entity distinct from the Anglo-Saxon world which surrounded it was by identifying itself with the continent of Europe culturally... I felt very strongly that unless we absorbed something of the traditions and manners of Europe and acquainted ourselves with its art, architecture, and literature we would inevitably degenerate to the level of a province of Britain, second rate suppliants for small privileges.[1]

Andrews' 'deep emotional conviction' has been shared by generations of Irishmen, especially those who identified themselves with the major religious movements within 'the traditions and manners of Europe'. As we have seen throughout this study the reactive response of the Irish who resented the oppressive power of British imperialism was to place themselves under the protection of the imperial power which resided in Rome. Until the Reformation crisis the two imperial powers had uneasily maintained their 'dual protectorate' over the Irish and their 'barbarous culture' which London and Rome both despised. In the early modern period the great struggle between the two authorities began, and since then the perennial and often bloody ideological dispute between Britain and Rome has brought strife, both ecclesiastical and political, upon the Catholic and the Protestant peoples of Ireland. That such strife should have occurred in the seventeenth century, during the great struggle between Reformation and Counter-Reformation powers, is historically understandable:

> The notorious Cromwellian massacres at Drogheda and Wexford in 1649 take their place, not as uniquely barbaric episodes, but as part of a pattern of violence which was central to the historical experience of the inhabitants of the island...[2]

That such violent contention should have continued into the late twentieth century seems almost inconceivable. It begs the question of what has, and still does, motivate the Irish people to continue their atavistic activities.

The answer, this study has attempted to suggest, lies in the tenacious conservatism in thought of the Irish people, Catholic or Protestant; as has been so often remarked 'the tyranny of the dead' is omnipresent in their communal relations. Within the psyche of the Irish is an acceptance that the folk struggle between the adherents of the differing faiths is inevitable, non-ending, and must be borne with the attitude of long-suffering endurance which the outside world finds almost incomprehensible. After noting that until the 1990's phase of the struggle Protestant retaliation had been tiny compared to what the Catholic paramilitarists had perpetrated, the Workers' Party leader, Proinsias de Rossa, has commented: 'whatever the semantics of Republican propaganda, the murders of the I.R.A. are now accepted widely as a piecemeal pogrom imposed without mercy by Catholics upon Protestants'.[3] This sounds uncomfortably like the thinking of the wars of religion of a bygone era not the twentieth century. Yet, when a struggle has been as prolonged and vicious as the Irish one, it is likely that lurking in the unconscious of the combatants are the convictions of other ages; the belief that the suffering imposed, or the martyrdom assumed has somehow the blessing if not of the deity at least of an intransigent religious system which asserts the Way for all Christians to follow. When John Charles McQuaid, archbishop of Dublin, could assure the faithful during a Christian unity week that the 'unity' which should characterize the one, true church was denied by 'the errors and sins' of the 'separated brothers',[4] his words would have considerable sectarian consequence. So too would the utterances of the Ulster Presbyterians who in their Assembly chose to discuss whether the pope in Rome was the biblical Antichrist.

Some liberal churchmen, of course, would like to avoid any historical analysis of Irish society which seems to perpetuate the concept of continuing sectarian division between the Catholic and Protestant peoples. Catholics especially would like to forget the tensions produced by the ideology of ultramontanism, that: 'vision of the church as a complete society, Vatican based, with all the answers for an unheeding world'.[5] They prefer to see ultramontane arrogance as a regrettable aberration which dominated Ireland from the coming of Paul Cullen in 1850 until the retirement of John Charles McQuaid in 1971.

Gone for all time, they trust, is the old Catholicism which the popes perpetuated for over a century: 'imperialist, authoritarian, and totalitarian in action and intent', 'serene, medieval and triumphalist', 'impervious to the scorn and antagonism of secular society'. The liberal Catholics affirm:

Pius XII was the last of the emperor popes, and with him the modern form of papal absolutism, inaugurated by Pio Nono reached its culmination and probably its end.[6]

They remain convinced of the unlikeliness of anyone still sharing the unswerving commitment of a Joseph de Maistre, or a Paul Cullen, to papal authority: 'no European religion without Christianity, no Christianity without Catholicism, no Catholicism without the Pope, no Pope without the supremacy that belongs to him'.[7]

Not all churchmen are so sanguine about the disappearance of the authoritarian model of the Roman Catholic church, however, and they would argue that in Ireland the church is still: 'a coercive organization, primarily interested in maintaining its moral power'.[8] As in the past, the indirect influence of the church in political affairs is still 'immense'.[9] Some critics of the Roman Catholic church in the Republic would even argue that its belief in the 'sanctified volk' persuasively influences the government in its irredentist policies, as it seeks a united Ireland, in which recalcitrant heretics would be encouraged to return to the one true fold: 'that form of colonization which aims at the assimilation of the conquered'.[10] Others would maintain that clearly in southern secular affairs the power of Rome is still to be reckoned with:

Every single Roman Catholic Republican leader in the South can readily be shown invariably to have given his first loyalty not to the Republic, or to a united Ireland, but to Rome.[11]

As we have seen, however, it does appear in the last decades of the twentieth century the power of Rome has a declining influence, especially among the young. Gone is the coercive power that the novelist John McGahern and others experienced in the time of John Charles McQuaid, the unholy oppression of the young through 'parental violence and priestly hypocrisy'.[12] The huge youth population of Ireland no longer grants authority to the secular and religious authorities which influenced earlier generations, and this is of crisis importance according to professor Liam Ryan of Maynooth. Commenting on the social orders established by past taoisigh, Eamon de Valera and Sean Lemass, he has compared them with that of modern Ireland:

In one, integration was achieved on the basis of ideology (Catholicism and nationalism) in the second, integration was founded on the promise of the good life in terms of education, jobs, houses, and the benefits of the consumer society. In the third, we have a rapidly-growing section of the population who will be integrated neither by ideology nor by employment, whose difficulties and frustrations cannot be resolved by the twin safety valves of the past—borrowing and emigration—and who will increasingly become a problem.[13]

The old 'integration' is of the past. When the media in Ireland now considers the future it focuses on unexpected new phenomena such as the revived interest in the Irish who died on the Somme, as well as the rebels of 1916, and the emerging dominant role for the laity in the Catholic church in both parts of Ireland.[14] Above all, people in Irish society are concerning themselves with the new Europe.

Interest in the role of the laity in the Roman Catholic church in Ireland is a reflection of an institutional malaise throughout the universal church—the great decrease in clerical vocations. This phenomenon has become of paramount importance since the 1960's because it has resulted in a loss of direct clerical control in the areas of education, health and social welfare. Cardinal O'Fiaich startled a Galway audience in 1989 by remarking on the possibility of priests and religious being brought in from Africa to make up for the decline in Irish vocations.[15] Not only are the numbers of those entering the seminaries reduced, but the educational qualities of the new entrants have deteriorated.[16] Such is the dispirited state of many of the serving clergy that in a way that would have been unthinkable only a generation ago there is a growing spirit of latitudinarian toleration, as the *Irish Times* noted on 11 May, 1990:

> The steady drip... drip of pluralism is ever so slowly beginning to work its way through Irish society, even in the rural areas, as can be observed in the spread of fundamentalist pentecostal churches through such staunchly Catholic counties as Mayo and Roscommon.

Although there are still indications that mass attendance is high compared to anywhere else in Europe, the young are no longer worshipping as a matter of course. Social investigators claim that while in the Republic about sixty percent of senior secondary students still attend mass, the figures are much lower in Northern Ireland, down to as low as twenty percent in some areas. The press has shown immense interest in the phenomenal weakening of the church's authority, particularly in Dublin and the other urban centres.[17]

The *Irish Times,* which of recent years has become increasingly nationalist in its viewpoint, and an 'establishment' paper on many issues, has nevertheless slowly joined the prevailing criticism of traditional control of Irish culture by the Roman Catholic hierarchy—although it has been praised by the bishop of Ferns, Brendan Comiskey, for the 'extent and space' it gives to religious matters unlike: 'the shabby treatment of the Catholic Church in the *Sunday Independent* which seems to lose no opportunity to malign our church'.[18] Even so the *Irish Times* has begun to admit the public resentment of hierarchical intimidation, and the social bullying which demands conformity and even hypocrisy on the part of: 'former Catholics who go along with the externals of their belief, so that their children won't feel like outsiders... Catholicism is so vast here, so saturates all aspects of life and death, that to leave it means leaving the protection of the pack, being alone'.[19] The paper is still mild and cautious in its criticism, but it cannot ignore the changing mores in Irish society:

> What happened in the 1970's and 1980's therefore, was not that Irish Catholics started to use forms of birth control, but simply that they started to discover forms of birth control that were more pleasant and less painful than the ones which the church had created for them in the nineteenth century: late marriage, non-marriage, a fear and ignorance about the sexual side of human nature.[20]

The *Irish Independent* is more outspoken in its criticism of the authoritarian control of the Roman Catholic church in society, however, and in its issue of 1 December, 1990 it expressed satisfaction that the Irish were becoming in terms of values and activities not much different from the rest of European culture: '"a la carte" Catholicism prevails, with most adherents of the faith selective in their response to clerical direction of their lives.'

The criticisms of Roman Catholicism which appear in the press reflect the convictions of thoughtful churchmen of both communities, in both the south and the north, who are beginning to argue that the days of triumphalism of the order of the Eucharistic Congress of 1932, or even the papal visit of 1979 are now of the past:

> Theological pluralism is necessary for the health of the church. Not only are regional needs different, but we need each other's insights and priorities in order to correct the deficiencies and imbalances in our own. Authority may indeed prefer an unadventurous or conformist theology, but if it has learned anything from history it will never again seek to impose such a theology on the whole church in the name of orthodoxy.[21]

The month of December, 1990 marked the coming to positions of authority of Mary Robinson, as the new president of the Republic, and Cahal Daly, as the new archbishop of Armagh. The former is a convinced pluralist who has had much to say about the 'patriarchal male-dominated presence of the Catholic church' as an 'oppressive force' in Irish society.[22] The latter understands well the Protestant mind from his many years as an academic at Queen's University,

Belfast, and from his utterances during and after the meetings of the New Ireland Forum it is clear that he appreciates what could be the value of pluralism in Ireland. As a conservative in theology, archbishop Daly may not prove to be as committed a pluralist as president Robinson, who resigned from the Labour Party in 1985 over the Anglo-Irish Agreement which ignored the aspirations of the Ulster Unionists, but liberal churchmen are hopeful of new influences appearing which will promote the concept of pluralism in both parts of Ireland.

Nothing demands the need for pluralism in Ireland more than the promised merger of Irish affairs with those of Europe. It is accepted that after 1992 the southern Protestant protest over an issue like the ethos of the Adelaide hospital will not be decided by authorities who think in insular 'ourselves alone' terms.[23] A laudable concern such as the British government's attempt to produce a common history course for Ulster schools, as a means to break down sectarian barriers among children, will now receive comment from continental as well as Irish and British authorities. Perhaps political matters like the irredentist claims of the Republic to govern the northern province will be brought under outside review, and even some concept of the old union between the islands of the archipelago will be reconsidered.

The Ulster Protestants, however, remain convinced that whatever new political arrangement appears, it will be as difficult as it has been in the past for them to develop religiously and culturally without experiencing assimilative pressures to bring them into the Roman Catholic church:

> The very heart of Protestant fears is the historic Catholic claim to be the one true universal church and the ultimate arbiter of religious truth... This feeling of Protestants and the sense of insecurity and vulnerability which goes with it... is strengthened by their widespread conviction that the Church would wish to impose an exclusive Catholic ethos throughout the state, and through the power of the state to impose its moral and social teaching on all members of society.[24]

When the Protestants read contemporary media accounts of the Republic's concerns about losing its 'Catholic ethos' in some form of united Europe in the future, they notice the continuing southern obsession with cultural Catholicism:

> The fact that we are a Catholic country is the single most important thing about us. More than that we're an agricultural country, or an island, or... an English-speaking country, or a former colony... when it comes to individual people trying to work out their lives and trying to touch depths in themselves, it is to their religion they look.[25]

They see, of course, the growing 'secularism' in society in the Republic, but they note that the hierarchy shows no sign of changing its *Ne Temere* attitude when mixed marriages occur. They also cannot escape the reality of the unrelenting attack upon themselves and their chosen way of life by the body which calls itself the I.R.A.: 'exclusive, millennialist, unworldly...self-obsessed...dedicated to an imagined past'.[26] The Ulster Protestants feel caught in a struggle between 'competing religious traditions'. They are convinced that if their resolve ever weakened they would find themselves sooner or later under the Roman yoke their forefathers fought so valiantly against:

> If ever the Catholics should come to power in Northern Ireland, a theocratic tyranny would be instituted... something like the Browne case was taken as proof positive of Rome rule in the Republic.[27]

Ulster Protestant intransigence is a unique phenomeonon and it is not only the ARCIC ecumenists of the present day who have shown fascinated interest in the 'mind' of the Ulster Protestants. William Connor Magee, who was to become archbishop of York in 1891, wrote of his long experience of Protestantism in Enniskillen where his family had lived for many generations. He had a very difficult time in understanding either the clergy or the laity of the district, particularly their spirited support of the Orange order:

> This town is split into sects, religious, political and social beyond any place I ever knew of... To do the people justice they are very well disposed to follow any man who can make good his claim to lead them, but they will not be driven an inch.[28]

Magee's insight pointed to the essence of Ulster, and indeed Irish Protestantism as a whole; few churchmen are so wedded to the idea of Paul Tillich's 'Protestant Principle', referred to in the introduction of this study. No people are more stubborn when it comes to matters of ecclesiastical or any other kind of authority being imposed upon them—as their history has made clear.

It is this 'Protestant mentality' which explains much of the support given to Ian Paisley since the present 'troubles' began in 1969. When he began his rise to political power his rallying cry which brought him support was a denunciation of those liberal Protestant leaders who would put the reformed religion of Ulster in jeopardy: those men who were 'showing weakness in the face of Republican pressure'.[29] In places like Armagh, 'notorious for ambush and outrage' since the eighteenth century, Crossmaglen where murder was found to be almost common by nineteenth century judges, or centres like Lurgan and Belfast with a long history of sectarian rioting, the appeal of Paisley in large part reflected his intransigent stance.[30] 'Not an inch' was to be granted either in concession to territorial demands by Dublin, or religious and ecclesiastical assertion by the Roman church. When Paisley in a radio interview in the Republic admitted that co-operation between north and south was possible, 'if the theocratic nature of the 1937 Free State Constitution was altered', there was such a howl of protest from his followers that he quickly 'withdrew to his usual position'.[31] So long as they feel themselves threatened by Dublin or Rome the Protestant extremists remain committed to their stance of 'combative sectarianism' defending their: 'distinct Ulster Protestant nation whose democratic right to self-determination was threatened by a nationalist movement'.[32] To withstand the Republican attack upon their chosen way of life which, they are convinced, is aided by 'the priest in politics', they will accept the support of the British government, but only so far as it bends its will to protect their Protestant religion and culture: 'it is no disloyalty to the Queen to refuse loyalty to ministers or governments that fail in their duty to give loyal subjects the blessing of the Queen's peace'.[33]

Not all Northern Ireland Protestants react to the 'Roman threat' in the same manner, of course, and many would feel uncomfortable with the description of the Roman Catholic church described by a committee of the Presbyterian General Assembly as:

> ... a world wide religious organization that seeks to gain control of the institutions of mankind and of public life generally... thus the Protestant often fears the dangers of the violation of his freedom and of ecclesiastical power in religious, political and social affairs.[34]

It has been argued that the 'two nations' division in Ulster society is one that has less and less appeal as secularism becomes increasingly common among the urban middle classes.[35] When an attempt is made to avoid or transcend the sectarian tensions, however, it is usually because some Protestants have abandoned those more traditional religious values which still, nevertheless, continue to influence the culture of Northern Ireland. Among these people, there is often the acceptance that 'at the end of the day' (as is often said by journalists and other commentators) 'the Protestants will lose'; at lease in the sense that 'tribalism' will be of less and less importance as both parts of Ireland identify more with the European community.[36]

It is probably easier for Protestants in the Republic to transcend traditional sectarian divisions in society, to view the Roman Catholic church as a comparatively benign institution, in spite of the continuing annoyance over matters like mixed marriages and the attempt by the hierarchy to control social legislation. Many of them, in the view of some northern Protestants, have been conditioned to eschew any form of anti-Catholic sentiment, to avoid the continuing reference to historical experience that means so much to their co-religionists in Northern Ireland such as the Free Presbyterians:

> An absence of evidence of evil Roman Catholic intent poses no problem for anti-Catholicism because one can always posit a secret conspiracy... The Roman Catholic church may seem to act like one

denomination among others but those people who know the truth about history and who have the correct interpretation of the Scriptures can penetrate this miasma and see the global conspiracy.[37]

This way of thinking has little appeal to an increasing number of Protestants, especially in the Republic. Among those who identify with the liberal and secular values of late twentieth-century European society, the idea of identifying the papacy with the Antichrist which is still reportedly to be found on the Shankhill road in Belfast, is dismissed as an historical absurdity.[38] It is probable that most Irish Protestants share the belief of the Church of Ireland primate, archbishop Eames, that everywhere 'cooperation between Roman Catholics and Protestants in community affairs' is increasing, and that more and more churchmen 'desire the path to peace'.[39]

In terms of historical precedent this Protestant attitude as it is found in the Republic, and among an unknown number of churchmen of all denominations in Northern Ireland, is not unlike that first tentatively advanced by William Bedell and the minority of ecumenists of his age. Among political leaders in the south many voices have joined with Garret Fitzgerald and others in the call for religious pluralism in Irish society, and a toleration by Catholics and Protestants of each other's traditions. Increasingly the churches are working together in areas of mutual concern, such as overcoming social scourges like unemployment, drug addiction and violence among the young. Even in areas of the north where sectarian tensions have caused much social suffering 'Inter-Church Community Groups' under local leadership from both the Catholic and Protestant communities are becoming more common.[40] It is now much more rare to encounter popular disparagement of the religious customs, rites and traditions of either the Catholics or the Protestants. Does this mean that the traditional fears of the Irish Protestants concerning the court of Rome, and its threat to their existence, may finally be laid to rest?

Some Protestants would say 'yes' for since the 1970's there has emerged within the Catholic world a form of 'protestant' critique of the papacy and the curia. Supporters of old ideas of papal absolutism are by the year 1992 very much a minority, increasingly defensive as they observe: 'the emergence of a universal Church from the transient clothing of ultramontanism':[41]

The problem of the limits of the primacy and of the teaching authority forces itself upon us. Its investigation is... one of the most urgent tasks to be undertaken by modern theology.[42]

Powerful voices are being raised in the Catholic theological world decrying the Counter-Reformation mentality which the Protestants of Ireland have so long feared, that system: 'still characterized by a spiritual absolutism, a formal and often inhuman juridicism, a terrifying spiritual absolutism and a traditionalism fatal to genuine renewal that are truly shocking to modern man'. The criticism is extended to include even the papal office itself:

> The Pope exists for the Church, and not the Church for the Pope. His primacy is not the primacy of sovereignty but the primacy of service. The holder of the Petrine office must not set himself up as overlord either of the Church or the gospel, which is what he does today when, after all the negative experiences of the past... he interprets theology and Church policy in the light of an uncritically adopted tradition.[43]

As for the relationship with 'separated brethren' many Catholic churchmen now wonder whether the way forward in ecumenism is to: 'accept pluralism... to accept that faith can legitimately express itself in different theologies'.[44]

An interesting result of the development of this Catholic critique of ultra-montane 'Romanism' is that Protestant leaders have become concerned Vatican-watchers, slowly abandoning some of that insularity that has for so long characterized Ulster protestantism in particular, and was a contributing factor to the decision of the Presbyterian church in Ireland to withdraw from the World Council of Churches in 1980.[45] They read about the division within the Catholic church which had accompanied the reassertion of worldly authority under the leadership of the politically-minded pontiff, John-Paul II, with the aid of conservative theologians such as cardinal Joseph Ratzinger.[46] They are concerned about the latter's reviving what looks so much like the spirit of the papal inquisition of the past, with its demand for a 'veil of silence' as a means to control theological questioning.[47] Protestant leaders are wary of the favour shown to the conservative secular institute, Opus Dei, by the pope, and its influence in new bodies like the private Catholic university in Dublin.[48]

The tensions within Irish Catholicism ensure that the question of ultra-montane authority in the Republic is not forgotten by the Protestants. They watch with unease the social and religious division over the prohibition of a young girl rape victim going to Britain for an abortion, underlined by the media making the charge that the southern Irish people live in: 'a moral police state'. While the Church of Ireland expressed its concern that constitutional prohibitions were being used to deal with complex moral and social problems, the influential historian-journalist Conor Cruise O'Brien bluntly said that the issue was not about the 'right to life of the unborn', but 'the power of the Catholic church'.[49] In the *Irish Independent* of 29 February, 1992, he wrote an open letter to the Irish Catholic hierarchy, 'I accuse you of abusing your power':

> You may preach your peculiar doctrines to those who are willing to listen to you, even restlessly, but please don't try any more to impose those doctrines on the rest of us by manipulating the laws of the State. Hierarchy and democracy go ill together, both in theory and practice.

During the crisis public feeling ran high when a High Court judge, who had doubts about the wisdom of Ireland joining in the movement towards a unified Europe, admitted that he was a member of *Opus Dei:* 'can anyone now remain in doubt as to the permeating scale and extent of Catholic fundamentalism in Irish society'.[50] When the scandal concerning the moral life of bishop Eamonn Casey became public knowledge it was clear that the authority of the Roman Catholic church was such that it might well: 'lead to a rapid secularization of Irish society'.[51] The Protestants generally choose to say little about these developments.

There are, of course, a minority of Protestants like the Free Presbyterians of Ulster whose reaction is to ignore what is taking place in the body which they believe is governed by the Antichrist.[52] The mainstream of Irish Protestants, however, have appreciated what they believe to be the taking up of their traditional cause by liberal Irish Catholics. With them they share anxiety about a papal resurgence, and the reimposition of centralized Vatican control in the Catholic church. They know, as the probability of European union becomes more likely, that the Vatican has control of one of the most powerful political infrastructures in Europe (as well as in many of the one-time colonial areas). They suspect that the collapse of the Soviet empire has reawakened among conservative Roman Catholics dreams of reviving a new 'Christendom'. The Protestants are uneasy when they hear of plans for a Roman Catholic synod which 'will be the first in the history of the Catholic church to bring together bishops from throughout Europe' for debate 'on the church's role after Eastern Europe's democratic revolution'.[53]

However much the Protestants of Ireland welcome ecclesiological debate with liberal Catholics, and 'good inter-community relations' with their Catholic neighbours, they remain, as in the past, steadfastly opposed to any reassertion of monarchical power on the part of the papacy. The response of the Church of Ireland General Synod to the report of ARCIC-1 made very clear what the Protestants believed was the essence of the papal authority which they rejected:

> The care of the whole flock of Christ has been entrusted to the Supreme Pontiff. It belongs to him, according to the changing needs of the Church during the passage of time, to determine the way in which it is fitting for this care to be exercised, whether personally or collegially. The Roman Pontiff proceeds according to his own discretion and in view of the welfare in the church in structuring, promoting and endorsing any exercise of collegiality.[54]

Like their fellow Anglicans, and their fellow Irish Protestants, the Church of Ireland leaders remain 'troubled by the Catholic claim that the Pope has universal and immediate jurisdiction' without any limits on his authority.[55] In ecumenical affairs the way forward in Ireland, and elsewhere, is for a new tolerance in religious affairs, they believe, an acknowledgment of the value of ecclesiastical pluralism. This they hope, and pray, is appearing, as an ecclesiological revolution seems to be a possibility within Roman Catholicism. Yet in the words of one liberal Catholic theologian:

> There can be no hope whatsoever for Christian union if Catholic bishops have not the courage to stand against the pope, even publicly not so much about the doctrine as the manner of papal government, the creeping advance of monarchy over collegiality, the intolerance of ultramontanism.[56]

To this the Protestants of Ireland would say 'Amen'.

As the twentieth century draws to a close the voice of the Protestants in the Republic of Ireland has been a muted one after so many years of struggle to avoid assimilation, while the inter-faith marriage regulations of Roman Catholicism have steadily reduced their numbers. In Northern Ireland, however, where the Protestants are still a majority people in their community, their demand for the toleration of religious pluralism in Ireland as a whole has become insistent. Yet there has been little evidence, in their reading of history, to persuade them that they are not under an abiding threat of domination and assimilation by militant Roman Catholicism. They live in a continuing sense of siege, giving to the world the phenomenon of a people who choose to remain ungovernable by any authority which is not of their choosing. History has prepared them to survive as a people, willing to exist even in the midst of their long-experienced state of 'anarchy':

> ... an anarchy in the mind and in the heart, an anarchy which forbade not just unity of territories, but also 'unity of being', an anarchy within a small and intimate island of seemingly irreconcilable cultures, unable to live together or to live apart, caught inextricably in the web of their tragic history.
>> Out of Ireland have we come;
>> Great hatred, little room,
>> Maimed us at the start.[57]

Endnotes

Foreword

[1] Lovejoy, Arthur, 'Nature as Norm in Tertullian', *Essays in the History of Ideas*, N.Y., 1948, p. 315.

Preface

[1] Beckett, J.C., *Short History of Ireland*, London, 1967, p. 176.

[2] Canning, B.J., *Bishops of Ireland, 1870–1987*, Ballyshannon, 1987, p. 54.

[3] Darby, J., *Conflict in Northern Ireland*, Dublin, 1976, p. 114.

[4] *Irish Times,* 22 July, 1985.

[5] *Belfast Telegraph*, 15 September, 1987.

[6] *Ibid.*, 28 May, 1988. I have had personal discussion with cardinal O'Fiaich about the problems of ecumenism in Ireland, and Protestant 'sensibilities'.

[7] Fitzgerald, Garret, *Towards a New Ireland*, London, 1972, p. 35.

[8] Fitzgerald Garrett, *Towards a New Ireland*, Dublin, 1981, pp. 8–9

[9] Brown, Terence, *Whole Protestant Community: Making of a Historical Myth,* Londonderry, 1985, pp. 5–20.

[10] *Linenhall Review*, 1985, II, p. 24.

[11] Harbison, E.C., *Christianity and History,* Princeton, 1964, p. 152; *cf.* Tillich, Paul, *Idea of Protestantism: C.J. Jung Memorial Lecture*, N.Y., 1962, pp. 28–32.

[12] McDonagh, Enda, *Doing the Truth*, Notre Dame, 1979, p. 159.

[13] Curran, Charles, *Towards an American Catholic Moral Theology*, Notre Dame, 1987, p. 149.

[14] *Belfast Telegraph*, 18 May, 1989.

[15] Canny, Nicholas, 'Why the Reformation Failed in Ireland: Une Question Mal Posée', *Journal of Ecclesiastical History*, 1979, XXX, p. 430.

[16] Connolly, S.J., *Priests and People in Pre-Famine Ireland*, N.Y., 1982, p. 278.

[17] Shaw, F., 'Canon of Irish History—a Challenge', *Studies*, 1972, LXI, pp. 113–153.

[18] Corish, P., *Irish Catholic Experience*, Dublin, 1985, pp. 108, 214, 246-247.

[19] *V.* Gillingham, John, 'Origins of English Imperialism', *History Today*, 1987, XXXVII, pp. 16–22.

[20] Buckland, Patrick, *Anglo-Irish and the New Ireland*, Dublin 1972, p. 285.

[21] Browne, Noel, *Against the Tide*, Dublin, 1987, p. 167.

[22] Hegarty, Kevin, 'Is Irish Catholicism Dying', *Furrow*, 1985, XXXVI, pp. 44–47.

[23] *Irish Independent*, 16 January, 1984.

[24] *Irish Times*, 14 January, 1984.

[25] Bradshaw, Brendan, 'Nationalism and historical scholarship in modern Ireland', *I.H.S.*, 1989, XXVI, p. 351.

[26] Bloch, Marc, *Historian's Craft*, Manchester, 1954, p. 48.

[27] Evennett, H.O., *Spirit of the Counter-Reformation*, Notre Dame, 1970, pp. 96–109; *cf.* Bossy, John, 'Counter-Reformation and the People of Catholic Ireland, 1569–1641', *Historical Studies*, Dublin, 1971, VIII, pp. 155–169.

[28] Stubbs, William, *Constitutional History*, London 1878, III, p. 639.

[29] Bowen, Desmond, *Protestant Crusade in Ireland*, Dublin, 1978, p. xiv.

[30] 'Viewpoint', *Belfast Telegraph*, 21 September, 1987.

[31] *Fortnight*, 1981, No. 183, pp. 10–11.

[32] The wisdom of archbishop Donald Caird of Dublin, 1987.

Chapter I

[1] Toynbee, A.J., *Study of History*, Oxford, 1963, VIIB, p. 697.

[2] Emerton, E., *Correspondence of Pope Gregory VII*, N.Y., 1932, p. 167.

[3] MacNiocaill, G., *Ireland Before the Vikings*, Dublin, 1972, pp. 127.

[4] Hughes, K., *Church in Early Irish Society*, London, 1966, p. 34.

[5] Richter, Michael, *Medieval Ireland: the Enduring Tradition*, N.Y., 1988, p. 62.

[6] *Ibid.*, p. 66.

[7] Hughes, *op. cit.*, p. 156.

[8] O'Fiaich, T., 'The Celts', *People of Ireland*, 1968, p. 33. *Cf.* Enright, M.J., 'Medieval Ireland and the Continent', *Irish Historical Studies*, 1990, XXVII, p. 75.

[9] Barlow, Frank, *English Church, 1000–1066*, London, 1963, p. 289.

[10] Barraclough, G., *Origins of Modern Germany*, N.Y., 1963, p. 103.

[11] Corish, P.J., 'Christian Mission', *History of Irish Catholicism*, Dublin, 1972, I, p. 44.

[12] Watt, John, *Church in Medieval Ireland*, Dublin, 1972, p. 1. For the authority of the kings in church affairs *cf.* Kelly, Fergus, *Guide to Early Irish Law*, Dublin, 1987, pp. 234–5.

[13] MacDonald, A.J., *Lanfranc*, Oxford, 1926, p. 194; *cf.* Gwynn, A., 'Lanfranc and the Irish Church', *I.E.R.*, 1941, LVII, pp. 481–500

[14] Watt, *Church in Medieval Ireland*, p. 2.

[15] Gwynn, A., 'Twelfth Century Reform', *History of Irish Catholicism*, Dublin, 1968, II, p. 5,

[16] *Ibid.*, p. 12.

[17] Smith, Charles, *Ancient and Present State of the County and City of*

Waterford, Dublin, 1746, p. 115.

18 Lawlor, H.J., *St. Bernard of Clairvaux's Life of St. Malachy of Armagh*, N.Y., 1920, P. 37; *cf.* Gwynn, A., 'St. Malachy of Armagh', *I.E.R.*, 1948, LXX, pp. 961–978; *ibid.*, 1949, LXXI, pp. 134–138, 317–331.

19 Gwynn, A., 'Centenary of the Synod of Kells', *I.E.R.*, 1952, LXVII, 161–176, 250–264.

20 Knowles, M.D., *Monastic Order in England*, London, 1940, pp. 208–226.

21 Brooke, Z.N., *English Church and the Papacy*, London, 1931, pp. 193 *ff.*

22 Curtis, E. and McDowell, R.B., *Irish Historical Documents, 1172–1922*, London, 1968, p. 17; *cf.* Sheehy, M., 'The bull *Laudabiliter*: a problem in medieval diplomatique and history', *Journal of the Galway Archaeological and Historical Society*, 1961, XXIX, pp. 45–70.

23 Ulmann, Walter, *Principles of Government and Politics in the Middle Ages*, London, 1966, p. 86; *cf.* Ulmann, Walter, *Growth of Papal Government in the Middle Ages*, London, 1965, pp. 342, 429.

24 Rymer, T., and Sanderson, R., *Foedera*, London 1816, I, p. 45; *cf.* Flanagan, M.T., *Irish Society, Anglo-Norman Settlers, Angevin Kingship*, Oxford, 1989, p. 277.

25 Watt, *Church in Medieval Ireland*, p. 40.

26 Watt, John, *Church and the Two Nations in Medieval Ireland*, Cambridge, 1970, p. 107.

27 Paris, Matthew, *Chronic Majora*, ed. Luard, H.R., London 1872–1883, III, pp. 389–390,

28 Mollat, G., *Popes at Avignon*, N.Y., 1963, pp. 330–331.

29 Grosseteste, *Epistolae*, ed., Luard, H., London, 1861, p. 436.

30 Lydon, James, *Ireland in the Later Middle Ages*, Dublin, 1973, prologue; *cf.* Frame, R., 'Bruces in Ireland, 1315–1318', *I.H.S.*, 1974, XIX, pp. 3–38.

31 Lydon, James, *Lordship of Ireland in the Middle Ages*, Toronto, 1972, p. 208.

32 Curtis and McDowell, *Historical Documents*, p. 44.

33 Watt, *Church in Medieval Ireland*, p. 142.

34 *Ibid.*, p. 148.

35 Mooney, Canice, 'Church in Gaelic and Gaelicized Ireland, Thirteenth to Fifteenth Centuries', *History of Irish Catholicism*, Dublin, 1969, II, pp. 59–60.

36 Gwynn, A., 'Anglo-Irish Church Life, Fourteenth and Fifteenth Centuries', *History of Irish Catholicism*, 1968, II, pp, 19–20; *cf.* Walsh, Katherine, *Fourteenth Century Scholar and Primate: Richard FitzRalph in Oxford, Avignon and Armagh*, Oxford, 1981, pp. 363–368.

37 Gwynn, A., 'Richard FitzRalph, Archbishop of Armagh', *Studies*, 1933, XXII, pp. 389–405; 'Archbishop FitzRalph and the Friars', *Studies*, 1936, XXV, pp. 81–96.

38 Curtis and McDowell, *Irish Historical Documents*, pp. 52–59.

39 *Cf.* Aubenas, R., 'Papacy and the Catholic Church'. *New Cambridge Modern History*, Cambridge, 1957, I, p. 76, how papal dedication to 'temporal glory and artistic splendour pushed spiritual matters into the background'.

40 Lydon, *Lordship of Ireland*, p. 261.

41 Gwynn, 'Anglo-Irish Church Life', *op. cit.*, p. 65.

42 O'Connell, J., 'Church in Ireland in the Fifteenth Century; Diocesan Organization, Kerry', *Proceedings of the Irish Catholic Historical Committee*, Dublin, 1956, p. 4. *Cf.* Mooney, Canice, 'Irish Church in the Sixteenth Century', *PICHC*, 1963, p. 6, 'there were certain "levitical families" in the Ireland of the fifteenth and sixteenth centuries'.

43 Corish, P., *Irish Catholic Experience*, Dublin, 1986, p. 57.

44 Mooney, 'Church in Gaelic Ireland', *op. cit.*, p. 55.

45 Nicholls, K., *Gaelic and Gaelicized Ireland in the Middle Ages*, Dublin, 1972, p. 105.

46 Watt, *Church in Medieval Ireland*, pp. 192, 199.

47 Creighton, M., *History of the Papacy from the Great Schism to the Sack of Rome*, London, 1907, I, p. 299.

48 Oberman, Heiko, *Forerunner of the Reformation: the Shape of Late Medieval Thought*, N.Y., 1966, pp. 238–239.

49 Corish, *Irish Catholic Experience*, p. 55. *Cf. Calendar of Papal Letters, Great Britain and Ireland, 1492–1498*, Dublin, 1986, p. 230 on ecclesiastical violence in Ireland in the pontificate of Alexander VI.

50 Edwards, R.D., 'Ecclesiastical Appointments in the Province of Tuam, 1399–1477', *Archivium Hibernicum*, 1975, xxxiii, pp, 91–100.

51 *Cf.*, Watt, *Church in Medieval Ireland*, 'Church in Decline', pp. 181–193,

52 Cosgrove, A., 'Writing of Irish medieval history', *IHS*, XXVII, 1990, p. 99. Rome was not always accomodating, *cf.* Haven, M. and Pontfarcy, Y.A., *Medieval Pilgrimage to St. Patrick's Purgatory and the European Tradition*, Enniskillen, 1988, p. 242 on the closing of the shrine by papal edict in 1497.

Chapter II

1 Phillips, W.A., *History of the Church of Ireland*, Oxford, 1934, I, p. 176.

2 Corish, *Irish Catholic Experience*, p. 49.

3 Watt, *Church in Medieval Ireland*, pp. 182–3.

4 Lawlor, *Bernard's Life of Malachy*, p. 37.

5 Hennessey, W.M., and MacCarthy, B., *Annals of Ulster (Annala Uladh) 431–1541*, Dublin, 1887–1901, III, p. 417.

6 Gwynn, 'Anglo-Irish Church Life in the Fourteenth and Fifteenth Centuries', *op. cit.*, p. 73; *cf.* Mooney, 'Church in Gaelic Ireland', *op. cit.*, pp. 60–62.

7 Maxwell, Constantia, *Irish History from Contemporary Sources 1509–1610*, London, 1923, p. 79.

8 *State Papers, Henry VIII, Ireland,* II, p. 15. *Cf.* Mooney, 'Irish Church in the Sixteenth Century', *op. cit.*, p. 5; 'many of the clergy were unworthy of their sacred calling'.

9 Curtis, E., *History of Ireland*, London, 1966, p. 161.

10 Scarisbrick, J.J., *Henry VIII*, Berkeley, 1968, p. 397.

11 Parker, T.M., *English Reformation to 1558*, London, 1960, p. 66.

12 Mant, Richard, *History of the Church of Ireland*, London, 1840, I, pp. 165-166.

13 Curtis, *History of Ireland*, p. 162.

14 Bradshaw, Brendan, 'Opposition to Ecclesiastical Legislation in the Irish Reformation Parliament', *I.H.S.*, 1969, XVI, p. 303.

15 Ellis, S.G., 'Kildare rebellion and the early Henrican Reformation', *Historical Journal*, 1976, XIX, pp. 809–812. *Cf.* Ellis, S.G., 'Tudor Policy in Ireland 1496–1534', *I.H.S.*, 1977, XX, p. 271.

16 Shirley, E.P., *Original Letters and Papers Illustrative of the History of the Church of Ireland*, London, 1851, p. 169; *cf. State Papers, Henry VIII*, Correspondence II, pt. 111, p. 481.

17 Phillips, *History of the Church of Ireland*, II, pp. 226–227.

18 Bradshaw, Brendan, 'George Browne, First Reformation Archbishop of Dublin', *Journal of Ecclesiastical History*, 1971, XXI, p. 305.

19 Corish, *Irish Catholic Experience*, p. 79.

20 Phillips, *History of the Church of Ireland*, II, p. 239.

21 *Ibid.*, II, p. 241.

22 *Ibid.*, II, p. 243.

23 MacCurtain, M., *Tudor and Stuart Ireland*, Dublin, 1972, p. 38.

24 Curtis, *History of Ireland*, p. 166.

25 Daniel-Rops, H., *Catholic Reformation*, N.Y., 1964, I, p. 127.

26 *Ibid.*, p. 221. For differing assessments of Pius v, a 'grim and narrow man' *cf.* O'Connell, M.R., *Counter-Reformation, 1560–1610*, N.Y., 1974, p. 117; Dickens, A.G., *Counter Reformation*, London, 1968, p. 135.

27 Elliott, J.H., *Imperial Spain, 1469–1716*, London, 1963, p. 282.

28 Gontard, Friederich, *The Popes*, London, 1964, p. 246.

29 Moorman, J.R.H., *History of the Church of England*, London, 19558, p. 183.

30 Nichols, J.G., *Diary of Henry Machyn*, London, 1847, p. 178.

31 Corish, *Irish Catholic Experience*, p. 82.

32 Canny, Nicholas, *From Reformation to Restoration: Ireland 1534–1660*, Dublin, 1987, p. 56.

33 Bradshaw, Brendan, 'Fr. Wolfe's Description of Limerick', *North Munster Antiquarian Journal*, 1975, XVII, p. 51.

34 Canny, Nicholas, 'Why the Reformation Failed in Ireland: Une Question Mal Posée', *Journal of Ecclesiastical History*, 1979, XXX, p. 430.

35 *Ibid.*, p. 444.

36 Wilson, Philip, *Beginning of Modern Ireland*, London, 1914, p. 373.

37 Prothero, G.W., *Statutes and other Constitutional Documents Illustrative of the Reigns of Elizabeth I and James I*, Oxford, 1913, pp. 195–196.

38 Meyer, A.O., *England and the Catholic Church under Elizabeth I*, London, 1916, p. 271.

39 Daniel-Rops, *Catholic Reformation*, I, p. 241.

40 Black, J.B., *Reign of Elizabeth*, Oxford, 1936, p. 151. On the fate of the Armada survivors in Ireland *cf.* Maxwell, *Stranger in Ireland*, pp. 38–53; Mattingly, Garrett, *Armada*, Boston, 1959, p. 369; De Yturriaga, J.A., 'Attitudes in Ireland towards the Survivors of the Spanish Armada', *Irish Sword*, 1990, XVII, pp. 244–254.

41 *New History of Ireland*, Oxford, 1976, III, p. 77.

42 Canny, N., 'Protestants, planters and apartheid in early modern Ireland', *I.H.S.*, 1986, XXV, pp. 111–113.

43 Strype, John, *Memorials of Thomas Cranmer*, Oxford, 1840, p. 54.

44 Phillips, *History of the Church of Ireland*, II, p. 313.

45 Jefferies, H.A., 'Irish parliament of 1560: the Anglican reforms authorized', *I.H.S.*, 1988, XXVI,. P. 137.

46 Canny, 'Protestants, planters and apartheid', *op. cit.*, p. 108.

47 Canny, 'Why the Reformation Failed in Ireland', *op. cit.*, p. 446.

48 Kearney, Hugh, 'Ecclesiastical Politics and the Counter-Reformation in Ireland, 1612–1648', *Journal of Ecclesiastical History*, 1960, II, pp. 202–212.

49 Bossy, John, 'Counter-Reformation and the People of Catholic Europe', *Past and Present*, May, 1970, p. 62.

50 *Cf.* Neill, Stephen, *History of Christian Missions*, London, 1965, p. 225 'Anglicans were not on the whole very good at spreading Christian civility'.

51 Ford, Alan, *Protestant Reformation in Ireland, 1590–1641*, Frankfurt, 1985, p. 228.

52 Bayne, C.G., *Anglo-Roman Relations, 1558–1565*, Oxford, 1913, p. 106.

53 Matthews, Thomas, *O'Neills of Ulster*, Dublin, 1907, III, p. 195.

54 Phillips, *History of the Church of Ireland*, II, p. 379.

55 Brady, W.M., *Irish Reformation*, London, 1867, pp. 174–177.

56 Caraman, Philip, *Other Face: Catholic Life under Elizabeth I*, London, 1960, p. 54.

57 Meyer, *England and the Catholic Church under Elizabeth*, p. 267.

58 *New History of Ireland*, III, p. 90.

59 *State Papers, Elizabeth*, lxvii, 41, 22 July, 1579.

60 *Carew Mss., 1575–1588*, p. 191, no. 230; 'the pope above... your imperial crown'.

61 Bagwell, Richard, *Ireland Under the Tudors*, London, 1962, I, p. 265.

62 Morgan, Hiram, 'End of Gaelic Ulster: a thematic interpretation of events between 1534 and 1610', *I.H.S.*, 1988, XXVI, p. 24.

63 Byrne, M.J., *Irish War of Defence, 1598–1600*, Cork, 1934, pp. 33–37.

64 Maxwell, *Irish History from Contemporary Sources*, p. 187.

65 Bagwell, *Ireland under the Tudors*, III, pp. 271–272.

66 Phillips, *History of the Church of Ireland*, II, p. 476.

67 Morgan, 'End of Gaelic Ulster', *op. cit.*, p. 32.

68 Canny, 'Why the Reformation Failed in Ireland', *op. cit.*, p. 446.

69 Spencer, Edmund, *View of the State of Ireland*, Dublin, 1633, p. 125 ff.

70 Webster, C.A., *Diocese of Cork*, Cork, 1920, p. 228.

71 Phillips, *History of the Church of Ireland*, II, p. 488.

72 Brady, *Episcopal Succession*, II, p. 88.

73 Corish, *Irish Catholic Experience*, p. 95.

74 Brady, W.M., *State Papers Concerning the Irish Church*, London, 1868, pp. 124–128; *cf.* Bottigheimer, Karl, 'The failure of the Reformation in Ireland: une question bien posée', *Journal of Ecclesiastical History*, 1985, XXXVI, pp. 196–207.

75 Canny, Nicholas, *Elizabethan Conquest of Ireland*, London, 1976, pp. 117-136.

76 Phillips, *History of the Church of Ireland*, II, p. 493; *cf.* Ellis, S.G.,

'Economic Problems of the church: Why the Reformation Failed in Ireland', *Journal of Ecclesiastical History*, 1990, XLI, pp. 239–266.

77 Bossy, J., 'Counter-Reformation and the people of Catholic Ireland, 1596–1641', *Historical Studies*, Dublin, 1971, VIII, pp. 155–171,

78 *State Papers, Ireland, Elizabeth (1601–1603)*, p. 556.

79 *Pacata Hibernia, Ireland Appeased and Reduced*, Dublin, 1810, III, pp. 695-706.

80 Maxwell, *Irish History from Contemporary Sources*, pp. 137–138.

81 Maxwell, Constantia, *History of Trinity College, Dublin, 1591–1892*, Dublin, 1946, p. 26.

82 Maxwell, *Irish History from Contemporary Sources*, p. 134; *cf.* Walshe, H.C., 'Enforcing the Elizabethan settlement: the vicissitudes of Hugh Brady, bishop of Meath, 1563–1584,' *I.H.S.*, 1989, XXVI, pp. 352–377.

83 *Ibid.*, pp. 79–86, the famous State Paper of 1515.

84 Corish, *Irish Catholic Experience*, p. 92.

85 Phillips, *History of the Church of Ireland*, II, p. 620.

86 *Pacata Hibernia, Ireland Appeased and Reduced*, III, pp. 695–706.

87 Ellis, S.G., 'Economic Problem of the Church: Why the Reformation Failed in Ireland', *JEH*, 1990, XLI, p. 264.

88 Bradshaw, B., 'Sword, Word and Strategy in the Reformation in Ireland', *Historical Journal*, 1978, XXI, p. 502; *cf.* Ford, *Protestant Reformation* , p. 228.

89 Corish, P., *Catholic Community in the Seventeenth and Eighteenth centuries*, Dublin, 1981, p. 23.

90 Daniel-Rops, *Catholic Reformation*, II, p. 116.

91 Phillips, *History of the Church of Ireland*, II, p. 410.

92 Evennett, H.O., *Spirit of the Counter-Reformation*, Notre Dame, 1970, p.

93.

53 O'Grady, Hugh, *Strafford and Ireland*, Dublin, 1923, I, pp. 465-466.

Chapter III

1 Corish, *Irish Catholic Experience*, p. 94

2 Canny, Nicholas, *From Reformation to Restoration: Ireland, 1534–1660*, Dublin, 1987, p. 135.

3 Phillips, *History of the Church of Ireland*, II, p. 498.

4 O'Grady, *Strafford*, I, p. 434.

5 Canny, 'Why the Reformation Failed in Ireland', *op. cit.*, p. 433. *Cf.* Bossy, John, 'Counter-Reformation and the people of Catholic Ireland, 1596–1641', *Historical Studies*, 1971, VIII, pp. 155–171; *Calendar State Papers*, (Papal) 1558–1571, no. 845, pp. 467–8, Edmund Tanner to Cardinal Moroni in 1571.

6 Egan, P.K., 'Royal Visitation of Clonfert and Kilmacduagh in 1615', *Journal of the Galway Archaeological and Historical Society*, 1976, XXXV, pp. 67–76.

7 Daniel-Rops, *Catholic Reformation*, I, p. 259.

8 Jordan, W.K., *Development of Religious Toleration in England*, London, 1932, II, p. 208.

9 Willson, D.H., *King James VI and I*, London, 1956, pp. 148–9.

10 Caraman, Philip, *Years of Siege*, London, 1966, p. 122.

11 McIlwain, C.H., *Political Works of James I*, Cambridge, 1918, p. 307.

12 Ranke, L., von, *History of the Popes*, N.Y., 1901, II, p. 223.

13 Jordan, *Development of Religious Toleration*, II, p. 72.

14 Pawley, B. and M., *Rome and Canterbury*, London, 1974, p. 26.

15 Canny, *From Reformation to Restoration*, p. 172.

16 Ranger, T.O., 'Richard Boyle and the Making of an Irish Fortune', *I.H.S.*, 1957, X, pp. 257–297.

17 Lennon, Colm, 'Richard Stanihurst (1547–1618) and Old English Identity', *I.H.S.*, 1978, XXI, p. 138. *Cf.* Lennon, Colm, *Lords of Dublin in the Age of Reformation*, Dublin, 1989, pp. 216–217.

18 Lennon, *op. cit.*, p. 124.

19 Jackson, R.W., *Archbishop Magrath: the Scoundrel of Cashel*, Dublin, 1974, p. 68.

20 *State Papers, Ireland, James I, (1603–1606)*, p. 143.

21 Davies, John, *Historical Tracts*, London, 1786–7, I, pp. 240–1.

22 O'Grady, *Strafford and Ireland*, I, p. 434.

23 Morgan, 'End of Gaelic Ulster', *op. cit.*, p. 31.

24 Canny, *From Reformation to Restoration*, pp. 172, 175. *Cf.* Curtis, *History of Ireland*, p. 229 on the warning of the king of a rebellion under 'the veil of religion and liberty'.

25 Ridley, J., *John Knox*, Oxford, 1968, p. 321; *cf.*, Reid, J.S.. *History of the Presbyterian Church in Ireland*, London, 1853, I, pp. 89–90.

26 Neil,, *Christian Missions*, p. 225; Moody, T.W., 'Treatment of the Native Population under the Scheme of the Plantation of Ulster', *I.H.S.*, 1939, I, p. 63.

27 Moody, T.W., *Londonderry Plantation*, Belfast, 1939, p. 329; *cf.* Perceval-Maxwell, M., *Scottish Migration in Ulster in the Reign of James I*, London, 1973, pp. 8–9.

28 Stewart, A.T.Q., *Narrow Ground*, London, 1977, p. 48.

29 Reid, J.S., *History of the Presbyterian Church in Ireland*, London, 1853, I, p. 93.

30 *Ibid.*, I, p. 114.

31 Blair, Robert, *Autobiography and Life*, ed. T. McCrie, Edinburgh, 1848, p. 99.

32 Bailie, W.D., *Six Mile Water Revival of 1625*, Newcastle, 1976, p. 18.

33 O'Grady, *Strafford*, I, p. 447.

34 Phillips, *Church of Ireland*, II, p. 564.

35 Canny, 'Protestants, planters and apartheid', *op. cit.*, p. 110.

36 Silke, John, 'Primate Lombard and James I', *Irish Theological Quarterly*, 1955, xxii, pp. 124–150.

37 Phillips, *History of the Church of Ireland*, II, p. 523. *Cf.* Hill, George, *Historical Account of the Plantation of Ulster, 1608–1620*, Belfast, 1877, pp. 348–350.

38 *State Papers*, Venetian, 1622, XVII, pp. 397, 450. *Cf.* Phillips, *Church of Ireland*, II, pp. 516–518; Hughes, P., *Rome and the Counter-Reformation in England*, London, 1944, pp. 271–430; Silke, J.J., 'Primate Peter Lombard and Hugh O'Neill', *I.T.O.* 1955, XXII, pp. 15–30.

39 Wedgwood, C., *Thirty Years War*, London, 1944, p. 526.

40 McElwee, William, *Wisest Fool in Christendom: the Reign of King James I and VI*, London, 1958, p. 129.

41 Maxwell, Constantia, *History of Trinity College, Dublin, 1598–1892*, Dublin, 1946, p. 29.

42 Lee, Maurice, *James I and Henry IV: an Essay in English Foreign Policy, 1603–1610*, Illinois, 1970, p. 174 *ff.*

43 Norwich, J.J., *History of Venice*, London, 1983, p. 516. For the Roman Catholic view of Sarpi *v.* Jedin, Hubert and Dolan, John, *History of the Church*, London, 1980, V, p. 510, 551, 617–618.

44 Jedin, H., *History of the council of Trent*, London, 1961, I, pp. 7,

439–440; *cf.* Polano Petro Soave (Sarpi, P.) *Historie of the Council of Trent*, transl. Brent, Nicholas, London, 1920; Atterbury, Lewis, *Some Letters Relating to the Council of Trent*, London, 1705, p. 2 *ff.*: V. Acton, London, 'Paolo Sarpi' *Essays on Church and State*, London, 1952, p. 258 on the papacy and the assassination attempt.

45 Bouwama, W.J., *Venice and the Defence of Republican Liberty*, Berkeley, 1968, pp. 545–6. *Cf.* Wootton, D., *Paolo Sarpi*, Cambridge, 1983, pp. 34–35; Livesay, J.L., *Venetian Phoenix: Paolo Sarpi and his English Friends*, Lawrence, 1973, pp. 19–25.

46 Ranke, *Popes*, II, p. 222.

47 Brown, H.R.F., 'Paolo Sarpi', *Studies in European Literature: the Taylorian Lectures, 1888–1889*, Oxford, 1900, pp. 209–251: Wright, A.D., 'Why the Venetian Interdict?' *E.H.R.*, 1974, LXXXIX, pp. 534–550.

48 Shuckburgh, E.S., *Two Biographies of William Bedell, Bishop of Kilmore*, Cambridge, 1902, p. 5.

49 Wooton, D., *Paolo Sarpi*, pp. 94–101.

50 Shuckburgh, *Bedell*, p. 82.

51 *Copies of Certain Letters Between Master James Wadesworth a Late Pensioner of the Holy Inquisition of Seville and William Bedell as Minister of the Gospel of Jesus Christ in Suffolk*, London, 1624, *cf.* Hudson, E., ed. *Some Original Letters of Bishop Bedell*, London, 1742, pp. 132–133.

52 Bedell, William, *Letter to James Waddesworth upon the Principal Points of Controversy between Papists and Protestants*, London, 1826, p. 133.

53 Powicke, Maurice, *Cambridge Platonists*, London, 1926, p. 56.

54 Rupp, Gordon, *William Bedell, 1571–1642*, Cambridge, 1971, p. 11.

55 Powicke, *op. cit.*, p. 7.

56 Nugent, Donald, *Ecumenism in the Age of the Reformation*, Harvard, 1974, pp. 226–228.

57 *State Papers, Ireland, James I, 1615–1625*, pp. 451–2.

58 Jordan, *Religious Toleration*, II, p. 115.

59 Albion, Gordon, *Charles I and the Court of Rome*, London, 1935, p. 240. *Cf.* Fitzpatrick, Brendan, *Seventeenth Century Ireland*, Dublin, 1988, p. 187 on the importance of Urban VIII's pro-French policies on the missions in England and Ireland: *State Papers, Venetian*, XXIV, p. 273, 25 September, 1637.

60 Bossy, John, 'Catholicism and Nationalism in the Northern Counter-Reformation', *Studies in Church History*, Oxford, 1982, XVIII, p. 294. *Cf.* Corish, P.J., 'Reorganization of the Irish Church, 1603–1641', *PICHC*, 1957, pp. 9–14; Bossy, John, 'Counter-Reformation and the People of Catholic Ireland', *Historical Studies*, 1971, VIII, pp. 153–170.

61 Corish, P., *Catholic Community in the XVII and XVIII Centuries*, Dublin, 1981, p. 29.

62 Brady, *Episcopal Succession*, II, pp. 71–72.

63 *Archbishop Ussher's Answer to a Jesuit with Other Tracts on Popery*, Cambridge, 1835, p. 1.

64 Knox, R.B., *James Ussher, Archbishop of Armagh*, Cardiff, 1977, p. 16; *cf*, Bolton, F.R., *Caroline Tradition of the Church of England*, London, 1958, pp. 4–8.

65 Knowler, W., *Earle of Strafford's Letters and Dispatches*, Dublin, 1740, I, pp. 212–214.

66 Bernard, Nicholas, *Life of Ussher*, London, 1656, pp. 59–60.

67 Knox, *James Ussher*, p. 16.

68 Reid, *Presbyterian Church*, I, p. 88.

69 Rupp, Gordon, *Just Men: Historical Pieces*, London, 1977, p. 109.

70 McIlwaine, W., *Life and Times of Bishop Bedell*, Belfast, 1854, p. 15.

71 Burnet, Gilbert, *Life of Bedell*, London, 1736, pp. 26–28.

72 Shuckburgh, *Bedell*, p. 25.

73 Rupp, *William Bedell*, Cambridge, 1972, p. 10 on his Irish labours.

74 Mahaffy, J.P., *Epoch in Irish History: Trinity College, Its Foundation and Early Fortunes, 1591–1600*, London, 1906, pp. 201–202.

75 Maxwell, *Trinity College*, p. 34. *Cf.* Stubbs, J.W., *University of Dublin from its Foundation to the end of the Eighteenth Century*, London, 1889, pp. 57–58 on Bedell and the need for Irish instruction, and his own study of Irish.

76 Shuckburgh, *Bedell*, p. 332.

77 *Ibid.*, p. 30.

78 Knox, Ussher, pp. 41–46. *Cf.* Carr, J.A., *Life of James Ussher*, London, 1895, p. 213.

79 Rupp, *Bedell*, p. 10.

80 Shuckburgh, *Bedell*, p. 348.

81 Gamble, W., *William Bedell, his Life and Times*, Dublin, n.d., p. 41.

82 Shuckburgh, *Bedell*, p. 118.

83 Shuckburgh, *Bedell*, p. 317.

84 Reid, *Presbyterian Church*, I, p. 165.

85 Ussher, James, *Works*, ed. Elrington, C., Dublin, 1864, XV, p. 459.

86 Bernard, *Ussher*, pp. 59–60; *cf.* Parr, Richard, *Life of James Ussher*, London, 1686, I, p. 28.

87 Knox, *Ussher*, p. 35.

88 Burnet, *Bedell*, p. 147.

89 Abbott, T.K., 'On the History of the Irish Bible', *Hermathena*, 1913, XVII, pp. 29–50; *cf.* Jones, T. Wharton, *True Relations of the Life and Death of*

William Bedell, Lord Bishop of Kilmore in Ireland, Camden Society, 1872, p. 171 *ff.*

90 Burnet, *Bedell*, p. 177.

91 Shuckburgh, *Bedell*, p. 75.

92 Gee, H. and Hardy, W.J., *Documents Illustrative of English Church History*, London, 1896, p. 527n.

93 Gardiner, S.R., *Constitutional Documents of the Puritan Revolution*, London, 1906, pp. 202–203.

94 Bramhall, John, *Works*, Oxford, 1842, I, pp. lxxix–lxxx.

95 *Ibid.*, I, pp. 83–279, 'Just Vindication of the Church of England'.

96 *Ibid.*, I, p. lxxxi.

97 Burghclere, *Strafford*, London, 1931, II, p. 144.

98 Knowler, *Strafford's Letters*, I, pp. 187–188,

99 Maxwell, *Trinity College*, p. 39.

100 Heron, D.C., *Constitutional History of the University of Dublin*, Dublin, 1848, p. 53.

101 Maxwell, *Trinity College*, p. 42.

102 Knowler, *Strafford's Letters*, I, pp. 187–9, 212–214.

103 Reid, *Presbyterian Church*, I, p. 118.

104 Kearney, H.F., *Strafford in Ireland, 1633–1634*. Manchester, 1959, pp. 115–116.

105 Shirley, E.P., *Papers Relating to the Church of Ireland, 1631–1639*, Dublin, 1874, p. 41.

106 Stevenson, D., 'Conventicles in the Kirk, 1619–1637', *Records of the Scottish Church History Society*, 1972, XVIII, p. 111 *ff.*

[107] Knowler, *Strafford's Letters*, II, p. 219.

[108] Mant, R., *History of the Church of Ireland*, London, 1840, I, p. 549.

[109] Knowler, *Strafford's Letters*, p. 103.

[110] Reid, *Presbyterian Church*, I, p. 271.

[111] Bagwell, Richard, *Ireland under the Stuarts*, London, 1909, I, p. 331.

[112] Bramhall, *Works*, I, p. xviii; *cf.* McAdoo, H.R., *John Bramhall and Anglicanism*, London, 1964, p. 28.

[113] Hill, Christopher, *Antichrist in Seventeenth Century England*, London, 1971, p. 21; Welsby, P.A., *George Abbott: the Unwanted Archbishop*, London, 1962, p. 22.

[114] Ussher, *Works*, xvi, p. 9; Parr, *Ussher*, II, p. 477.

[115] Leslie, J.B., *Ossory Clergy and Parishes*, Enniskillen, 1933, p. 17.

[116] Leslie, J.B., *Ferns Clergy and Parishes*, Dublin, 1936, p. 8; Phillips, *Church of Ireland*, II, p. 556.

[117] Shuckburgh, *Bedell*, p. viii. *Cf.* many popular accounts of Bedell's life in catalogue of British Library, and modern studies by Gordon Rupp.

Chapter IV

[1] Daniel-Rops, H., *Church in the Seventeenth Century*, London, 1963, pp. 127, 148.

[2] Bossey, John, 'Editor's Postscript' in Evenett, *Spirit of the Counter-Reformation*, p. 145.

[3] Bradshaw, B., *Irish Constitutional Revolution of the Sixteenth Century*, Cambridge, 1979, p. 138.

[4] Ogg, David, *Europe in the Seventeenth Century*, London, 1963, p. 132.

[5] Daniel-Rops, *Church in the Seventeenth Century*, pp. 127. 140–141.

6 Trevor-Roper, H., *Archbishop Laud*, London, 1965, pp. 109–110.

7 Kent, John, *Unacceptable Face, the Modern Church in the Eyes of the Historian*, London, 1987, p. 61.

8 Perceval-Maxwell, M., 'Ulster Rising of 1641 and the depositions'. *I.H.S.*, 1978, XXI, p. 166.

9 Perceval-Maxwell, M., 'Strafford, the Ulster Scots and the covenanters', *I.H.S.*, 1973, XVIII, p. 534.

10 Lecky, W.E.H., *History of Ireland in the Eighteenth Century*, London, 1892, I, p. 39.

11 MacCurtain, M., *Tudor and Stuart Ireland*, Dublin, 1972, p. 144.

12 Froude, J.A., *English in Ireland in the Eighteenth Century*, London, 1887, I, p. 39.

13 Perceval-Maxwell, 'Ulster Rising", p. 165.

14 *Remonstrance of Divers Remarkable Passages Concerning the Church and Kingdome of Ireland*, London, 1642, pp. 2, 7.

15 Lindley, K.J., 'Impact of the 1641 Rebellion upon England and Wales, 1641–1645', *I.H.S.*, 1972, XVIII, p. 146; *cf. State Papers, Venetian*, 1641, XXV, p. 240.

16 Lindley, *op. cit.*, p. 153.

17 Nelson, John, *Impartial Collection of the Great Affairs of State*, London, 1683, II, p. 536.

18 Moody, *Londonderry Plantation*, p. 330.

19 MacCurtain, *Tudor and Stuart Ireland*, p. 142.

20 Bagwell, *Stuart Ireland*, II, p. 119. *Cf.* Hollick, Clive, 'Owen Roe O'Neill's Ulster Army of the Confederacy', *Irish Sword*, 1991, XVIII, pp. 220–226 for O'Neill as a military commander.

21 Clarke, Aidan, *Old English in Ireland*, London, 1966, p. 216.

22 Hickson, Mary, *Ireland in the Seventeenth Century*, London, 1884, I, p. 298.

23 Reid, *Presbyterians in Ireland*, I, p. 310.

24 Bagwell, *Stuart Ireland*, I, p. 358; *cf.* Colles, R., *History of Ulster*, London, 1919, III, p. 40.

25 Brady, *Episcopal Succession*, I, p. 256.

26 Lecky, *Eighteenth Century Ireland*, I, p. 92.

27 Bagwell, *Stuart Ireland*, II, pp. 137, 148.

28 Lowe, J., 'Charles I and the Confederation of Kilkenny', *I.H.S.*, 1964, XIV, pp. 1–19.

29 Lecky, *Ireland in the Eighteenth Century*, I, p. 87.

30 Bagwell, *Stuart Ireland*, II, p. 16.

31 Canny, *From Reformation to Restoration*, p. 206.

32 Malcolm, J.L., 'All the king's men: the impact of the crown's Irish soldiers on the English civil war', *I.H.S.*, 1979, XXI, p. 252.

33 Wedgwood, C.V., *King's Peace, 1637–1641*, N.Y., 1969, pp. 480–1.

34 Carte, Thomas, *Life of Ormond*, Oxford, 1851, II. app. p. 10.

35 Bagwell, *Stuart Ireland*, II, pp. 97–98.

36 Gilbert, J.T., *Contemporary History of Affairs in Ireland 1641–1652*, Dublin, 1879, I, p. 66.

37 Fitzpatrick, Brendan, *Seventeenth Century Ireland: the Wars of Religion*, Dublin, 1988, p. 199; *cf.* Gilbert, J.T., *Contemporary History of Affairs in Ireland, 1641–1652*, Dublin, 1879, I, p. 66; Gilbert, J.T., *History of the Irish Confederacy, 1641–9*, Dublin, 1882–1891, IV, p. 270; Canny, *From Reformation to Restoration*, pp. 212–214; Kearney, H.F., 'Ecclesiastical Politics and the Counter-Reformation in Ireland, 1618–1648', *Journal of Ecclesiastical History*, 1960, XI, pp. 211 *ff*.

38 Foster, R.F., *Modern Ireland, 1600–1972*, London, 1988, pp. 98–99. Rinuccini was probably the most important leader in what contemporaries called the Catholic Confederation; he destroyed the unity between its Old English and Old Irish factions.

39 Corish, *Irish Catholic Experience*, p. 108.

40 Bagwell, *Stuart Ireland*, II, p. 177. *Cf*. Corish, *Catholic Community*, p. 45 on the opposition to Rinuccini, and his support coming from Gaelic leaders 'formed on the continent, in the world of Spain'.

41 Hutton, A., *Embassy in Ireland of Monsignor G.B. Rinuccini, 1645–1649*, Dublin, 1873, p. 475.

42 *Ibid.*, pp. 143, 204,

43 *Ibid.*, p. 283.

44 Stewart, A.T.Q., *Narrow Ground*, London, 1977, p. 52.

45 Adair, P., *True Narrative of the Rise and Progress of the Presbyterian Church in Ireland, 1623–1670*, ed. Killen, W.D., Belfast, 1886, pp. 93–99.

46 Hill, *Antichrist*, p. 31.

47 Henderson, G.D., *Religious Life in Seventeenth Century Scotland*, Cambridge, 1937, p. 169.

48 Holmes, Finlay, *Our Irish Presbyterian Heritage*, Belfast, 1985, pp. 35–36.

49 Shearman, Hugh, *Not an Inch*, London, 1942, p. 34.

50 *Loc. cit.*

51 Phillips, *Church of Ireland*, III, p. 75. *Cf*. Hickson, *Ireland in the Seventeenth Century*, I, p. 190 *passim* for similar tales.

52 Phillips, *op. cit.*, III, p. 86.

53 Shuckburgh, *Bedell*, pp. 205–206.

54 *New History of Ireland*, III, p. 330.

55 Esson, D.M.R., *Curse of Cromwell*, London, 1971, p. 90.

56 Canny, *From Reformation to Restoration*, p. 216.

57 Ellis, P.B., *Hell or Connaught*, London, 1975, pp. 18–19.

58 Esson, *Curse of Cromwell*, p. 102.

59 Lecky, *Ireland in the Eighteenth Century*, I, p. 101.

60 Lomas, S.C., ed. *Letters and Speeches of Oliver Cromwell*, London, 1904, I, p. 469, *Cf.* Burke, James, 'New Model Army and the Problems of Siege Warfare', *I.H.S.*, 1990, XXVII, pp. 12–13, and p. 26 for 'contemporary perspective' on Drogheda.

61 Lecky, *Ireland in the Eighteenth Century*, I, p. 103.

62 Daniel-Rops, *Church in the Seventeenth Century*, pp. 164, 209–12. *Cf. New History of Ireland*, III, p. 367.

63 Ellis, *Hell or Connaught*, p. 126.

64 Canny, *Reformation to Restoration*, p. 223.

65 Ellis, *Hell or Connaught*, p. 71.

66 Reid, *Presbyterian Church*, II, p. 195.

67 Bagwell, *Stuarts*, II, pp. 350–351, 360.

68 Godkin, James, *Religious History of Ireland*, London, 1873, p. 193.

69 Fraser, A., *Cromwell*, N.Y.A, 1975, p. 659. *Cf. ibid.*, p. 657 on Cromwell's personal reaction to Fox; Van Etten, H., *George Fox*, London, 1959, pp. 53–54.

70 Ashley, M., *Greatness of Oliver Cromwell*, N.Y., 1962, p. 319,

71 Ellis, *Hell or Connaught*, p. 88.

72 Bottigheimer, Karl, 'Restoration land settlement in Ireland', *I.H.S.*, 1972, XVIII, p. 6.

[73] Gardiner, S.R., *Constitutional Documents of the Puritan Revolution*, London, 1906, pp. 465–467.

[74] Lane, J., *Reign of King Covenant*, London, 1956, p. 275.

[75] *State Papers, Ireland*, 1660–1662, p. 195.

[76] Bramhall, *Works*, I, p. 257.

[77] *Ibid*, I, p. 113.

[78] *Ibid*, III, p. 520, his 'Vindication of Himself and the Episcopal Clergy from the Presbyterian Charge of Popery' 1658–1660. On the toleration of Bramhall as primate compared to his harrying of nonconformity earlier in Derry *v.* Phillips, *Church of Ireland*, III, pp. 122–124.

[79] Hill, *Antichrist*, p. 153.

[80] Baxter, R., *Reliquiae Baxterianae*, London, 1696, pp. 238–240.

[81] May, E.H., *Dissertation on the Life, Theology and Times of Dr. Jeremy Taylor*, London, 1892, pp. 259, 270, 281–283.

[82] King, William, *State of the Protestants*, London, 1691, I, pp. i, ii. *cf.* Petty, William, *Political Anatomy of Ireland*, Shannon, 1969, p. 9.

[83] Reid, *Presbyterian Church*, II, p. 273.

[84] *State Papers, Ireland*, 1669–1670, pp. 225–227.

[85] Holmes, *Presbyterian Heritage*, p. 43. *Cf.* Ramsbottom, John, 'Presbyterians and Partial Conformity in the Restoration Church of England', *JEH*, 1992, XLIII, pp. 249–271.

[86] Seymour, S.J., *Puritans in England, 1647–1661*, Oxford, 1921, p. 20 *ff.*

[87] Holmes, *Presbyterian Heritage*, p. 45.

[88] Craig, Maurice, *Dublin, 1660–1860*, Dublin, 1980, pp. 38–39.

[89] Phillips, *Church of Ireland*, III, p. 146.

[90] Trevelyan, G.M., *History of England*, London, 1947, p. 462. *Cf.* Kenyon,

J.P., *Popish Plot*, London, 1972, pp. 224–225, 234 for influence of the plot in Ireland. It was ignored in Scotland.

91 Voltaire, *Age of Louis XIV*, Everyman, n.d., p. 135,

92 Acton, J.E., *Lectures on Modern History*, London, 1950, p. 226.

93 Ranke, *Popes*, III, p. 122.

94 Daniel-Rops, *Church in the Seventeenth Century*, p. 205.

95 McGuire, J.I., 'Why Ormond was dismissed in 1669', *I.H.S.*, 1973, XVIII, p. 311.

96 Walsh, William, *History and Vindication of the Irish Remonstrance*, London, 1674, pp. 694, 698.

97 Carte, *Life of Ormond*, II, p. 172.

98 *Diary of Abraham de la Pryme*, London, Surtees Society, 1870, p. 13.

99 Boulenger, J., *Seventeenth Century in France*, N.Y., 1963, p. 264.

100 Smiles, Samuel, *Huguenots in England and Ireland*, London, 1876, p. 192.

101 Ashley, M., *Glorious Revolution of 1688*, London, 1968, pp. 31–32.

102 *New History of Ireland*, III, p. 487. *Cf.* Louis XIV, *Memoires*, Paris, 1860, I, p. 209 , and II, 303, 315 for the religious element in the continental struggle.

103 Baxter, S.B., *William III*, N.Y., 1966, p. 186,

104 Chadwick, Owen, *The Popes and European Revolution*, Oxford, 1981, pp. 302–305; *cf.* Judge, H.G., *Louis XIV*, London, 1965, pp. 62–64.

105 Clark, G.N., *Seventeenth Century*, Oxford, 1960, p. 128.

106 Bagwell, *Stuarts*, III, pp. 180–184.

107 Mant, *Church of Ireland*, I, p. 725.

108 Caldicott, E., Gough, H., Pittion, J.P., *Huguenots and Ireland*, Dublin,

1987, p. 266.

[109] *Humble Petition of the Protestants of France Presented to his Most Christian Majesty by Marshal Schomberg and Marquis de Ruvigny*, London, 1685, pp. 1–4.

[110] Anon. *History of the Persecutions of the Reformed Churches in France, Orange and Piedmont*, London, 1699, p. 7 *ff.*

[111] Simms, J.G., *Jacobite Ireland, 1685–1691*, London, 1969, p. 51.

[112] *New History of Ireland*, III, p. 506.

[113] *State Papers, Ireland*, 1666–1669, p. 261.

[114] *State Papers, Domestic*, 1691–1692. pp. 55–56.

[115] *Cf.* Anon. *Account of the Present Condition of the Protestants in the Palatinate*, London, 1699, pp. 3 *ff.*

[116] Jurieu, Pierre, *Policy of the Clergy of France*, London, 1681; Jurieu, P., *Last Efforts of Afflicted Innocence, an Account of the Persecution of the Protestants in France*, London, 1682; Gwynn, R.D., 'James II in the Light of his Treatment of Huguenot Refugees in England', *E.H.R.*, 1977, XCII, pp. 820–3.

[117] Phillips, *Church of Ireland*, III, p. 160.

[118] *New History of Ireland*, III, p. 625.

Chapter V

[1] Simms, J.G., 'Bishop's Banishment Act of 1697', *I.H.S.*, 1970, XVII, p. 190.

[2] Mant, *Church of Ireland*, III, p. 73. *Cf.* 'Bishop's Banishment Act', p. 186 on their 'disturbance of the peace'; Corish, P.J., *Catholic Community in the Seventeenth and Eighteenth Centuries*, Dublin, 1981, p. 90 on the 'Romans' in Galway; Simms, *Jacobite Ireland*, p. 261 on the 'seditious' Irish bishops at St. Germain.

[3] Roebuck, P., ed., *Plantation to Partition: Essays in Ulster History*, Belfast, 1981, pp. 57–58.

4 Landa, L.A., *Swift and the Church of Ireland*, Oxford, 1954, p. 20.

5 Trevelyan, G.M., *England under the Stuarts*, London, 1965, pp. 483–497.

6 Hayton, David, 'Crisis in Ireland and the disintegration of Queen Anne's last ministry', *I.H.S.*, 1981, XXII, pp. 193–216; Simms, J.G., 'Irish parliament of 1713', *Historical Studies*, 1963, IV, pp. 83–84.

7 *Cf.* Wettenhall, Edward (Bishop of Cork), *Case of the Irish Protestants in Relation to Swearing Allegiance to and Praying for King William and Queen Mary Stated and Resolved*, London, 1691.

8 King, W., *State of the Protestants of Ireland under the Late King James' Government in which their Carriage Towards him is Justified*, Cork, 1768, p. I.

9 Leslie, Charles, *Answer to a Book Entitled the State of the Protestants in Ireland*, London, 1692, pp. 2, 187.

10 King, William, *Discourse Concerning the Inventions of Men in the Worship of God and Two Admonitions to the Dissenting Inhabitants of the Diocese of Derry*, Northampton, 1840, p. 136 *ff.*

11 Mant, *Church of Ireland*, II, p. 331.

12 Stokes, G.T., *Some Worthies of the Irish Church*, London, 1900, p. 157; *cf.* Craig, *Dublin, 1660–1860*, p. 88.

13 King, William, *Vindication of the Answer to the Considerations that Obliged Peter Manby to Embrace the Catholic Religion*, Dublin, 1688, pp. 33–35. His viewpoint was typical for his age; *cf, Preservative against Popery Published by the Most Eminent Divines of the Church of England, chiefly in the Reigns of King James II*, London, 1848–9, XVIII vols.

14 King, Simeon, *Great Archbishop of Dublin: William King, 1650–1729*, London, 1906, p. 221.

15 *Ibid.*, p. 29.

16 Hayton, David, 'Crisis in Ireland, the disintegration of queen Anne's last ministry', *I.H.S.*, 1981, XXII, p. 202.

[17] Mant, *Church of Ireland*, II, p. 299.

[18] *Ibid.*, II, p. 332.

[19] Witherow, Thomas, *Historical and Literary Memorials of Presbyterianism in Ireland*, London, 1879, I, p. 159.

[20] Phillips, *Church of Ireland*, III, p. 164.

[21] Leslie, J.B., *Biographical Succession of the Clergy of the Diocese of Down*, Enniskillen, 1936, p. 9.

[22] *State Papers, Ireland*, 1694–1695, p. 70.

[23] Mant, *Church of Ireland*, II, p. 290.

[24] Swanzy, H.B., *Succession Lists of the Diocese of Dromore*, Belfast, 1933, p. 6.

[25] Mant, *Church of Ireland*, II, p. 366.

[26] Leslie, J.B., *Derry Clergy and Parishes*, Enniskillen, 1937, p. 15.

[27] Leslie, J.B., *Clogher Clergy and Parishes*, Enniskillen, 1929, pp. 15–16; *Cf.* Mant, *Church of Ireland*, II, p. 282.

[28] *Ibid.*, II, p. 349.

[29] Harris, Walter, *James Ware's Works Concerning Ireland*, Dublin, 1739, I, p. 543.

[30] *Ibid.*, I, p. 619.

[31] Phillips, *Church of Ireland*, III, p. 206.

[32] Winnet, A.R., *Peter Browne*, London, 1974, p. 71.

[33] Landa, *Swift*, p. 182.

[34] Synge, Edward, *Defence of the Established Church and Laws in Answer to a Book Entitled a Vindication of Marriage as Solemnized by Presbyterians in the North of Ireland*, Dublin, 1705, p. 301. *Cf.* Leslie, J.B., *Raphoe Clergy and Parishes*, Enniskillen, 1940, p. 8.

35 Mant, *Church of Ireland*, II, p. 293.

36 *Ibid.*, II, p. 165.

37 *Ibid.*, II, p. 217.

38 Maxwell, *Trinity College*, p. 74.

39 *Ibid.*, p. 89.

40 Leslie, *Clogher Clergy*, p. 67; *cf.* Anderson, Christopher, *Brief Sketch of the Various Attempts which Have been Made to Diffuse a Knowledge of the Holy Scriptures Through the Medium of the Irish Language*, Dublin, 1818, p. 28.

41 Richardson, J., *Proposal for the Conversion of the Popish Natives of Ireland to the Established Religion*, London, 1712, pp. 153–4; Richardson, J., *Short History of the Attempts that Have Been Made to Convert the Popish Natives of Ireland to the Established Religion*, London, 1713, p. 23.

42 Leslie, *Down Succession Lists*, p. 12. *Cf.* Mant, *Church of Ireland*, II, p. 370.

43 Mant, *Church of Ireland*, II, p. 230.

44 *Ibid.*, II, p. 212.

45 Blackerly, Samuel, *History of the Penal Laws*, London, 1689, p. 136; *cf.* Burke, William, *Irish Priest in Penal Times, 1660–1760*, Shannon, 1969, pp. 200–201; Brennan, W.J., *Ecclesiastical History of Ireland*, Dublin, 1840, II, p. 348.

46 Burns, R.E., 'Irish Penal Code and Some of its Historians', *Review of Politics*, 1959, XXI, p. 276; *cf.* Burns, R.E., 'Irish Popery Laws: a Study of Eighteenth Century Legislation and Behaviour', *Review of Politics*, 1962, XXIV, pp. 485–508.

47 Macgrath, Kevin, 'Dublin Clergy in 1695', *Irish Ecclesiastical Record*, 1950, LXXIV, p. 193.

48 Moran, P.F., *Spicilegium Ossoriense*, Dublin, 1884, II, p. 404.

[49] Magrath, K., 'John Garzia, Noted Priest-Catcher and his Activities, 1717–1723', *I.E.R.*, 1949, LXXII, pp. 496–514.

[50] Creighton, S., 'Penal Laws in Ireland and the Documents in the Archives of Propaganda (1632–1731)', *Proceedings of the Irish Catholic Historical Committee*, 1961, p. 9.

[51] Cullen, Louis, 'Catholics and the Penal Laws', *Eighteenth Century Ireland*, London, 1986, I, pp. 25–29; *cf.*, Wall, Maureen, *Penal Laws*, Dundalk, 1961, pp. 24–27.

[52] Beckett, J.C., *Protestant Dissent in Ireland, 1687–1780*, London, 1948, p 38.

[53] Holmes, *Presbyterian Heritage*, p. 60,

[54] Mant, *Church of Ireland*, II, p. 471.

[55] Synge, Edward, *Happiness of a Nation or People: Sermon Preached at Christ Church Dublin, before the Government and the House of Lords, 29 May, 1716*, Dublin, 1716, p. 30; *cf*. Leslie, *Raphoe Clergy*, p. 9.

[56] Ogg, *Europe in the Seventeenth Century*, p. 281.

[57] Parton, J., *Life of Voltaire*, Boston, 1882, II, p. 367; Desnoiresterres, G., *Voltaire et la société française*, Paris, 1971, VI, p. 493; Smith, P., *History of Modern Culture*, N.Y., 1930, II, p. 555.

[58] Goodwin, A., *European Nobility in the Eighteenth Century*, London, 1953, p. 31.

[59] Downes, Henry, *Sermon by the Lord Bishop of Killala in Christ Church, Dublin, 1719*, Dublin, 23 October, 1719, p. 21.

[60] Madden, John, *Thanksgiving Sermon on the Late Unnatural Rebellion*, Dublin, 1746, p. 12.

[61] Giblin, Cathaldus, 'Stuart Nomination of Irish Bishops', *Proceedings of the Irish Catholic Historical Committee, 1965–1967*, Dublin, 1968, pp. 35–40.

[62] Murray, R.H., *Revolutionary Ireland and Its Settlement*, London, 1911, pp. 73, 372, 275.

63 Corish, *Catholic Community*, p. 74.

64 Simms, J.G., 'Connaught in the Eighteenth Century', *I.H.S.*, 1958, XI, p. 119.

65 Brady, J., *Catholics and Catholicism in the Eighteenth Century Press*, Maynooth, 1965, pp. 226–227. *Cf. Vindication of Sir Robert King's Designs and Actions: an Answer to a Scandalous Libel*, London, 1699, pp. 46–69.

66 Corish, *Irish Catholic Experience*, p. 128.

67 *Ibid.*, p. 129.

68 Jenney, Henry, *Sermon Preached at St. Andrew's Dublin, before the Honourable the House of Commons, 5 November, 1731*, Dublin, 1731, p. 12; *cf.*, Leslie, J.B., *Armagh Clergy and Parishes*, Dundalk, 1911, p. 61,

69 Clayton, R., *Sermon Preached at Christchurch, Dublin, 30 January, 1731*, Dublin, 1731, p. 2.

70 Mant, *Church of Ireland*, II, p. 487.

71 Wall, Maureen, 'Penal Law 1691–1760', *Catholic Ireland in the Eighteenth Century: Collected Essays of Maureen Wall*, Dublin, 1989, p. 60.

72 Moran, P.F., *Catholics of Ireland under the Penal Laws in the Eighteenth Century*, London, 1899, p. 170.

73 Kelly, Patrick, 'Lord Galway and the Penal Laws', *Huguenots and Ireland*, pp. 239–250; *cf.* Nary, Cornelius, 'Case of the Roman Catholics of Ireland, 1724', *Impartial History of Ireland*, Dublin, 1742, p. 142. *Cf.* Savory, D.L., *Pope Innocent XI and the Revocation of the Edict of Nantes*, London, 1940, pp. 4–5.

74 Lee, Grace, *Huguenot Settlements in Ireland*, London, 1939, p. 3. *Cf.* Ireland, J. de Courcy, 'Maritime Aspects of the Huguenot Immigration into Ireland', *Huguenots and Ireland*, pp. 341–351.

75 Knox, S.J., *Ireland's Debt to the Huguenots*, London, 1959, p. 17.

76 *State Papers, Domestic, 1691–1692*, pp. 55–56. *Cf.* Hylton, R.P.,

'Huguenot Settlement at Portarlington, 1692–1771', *Huguenots and Ireland*, pp. 297–315; Savory, D.L., *Huguenots*, Belfast, 1938, pp. 12–14,

[77] Leslie, J.B., *Armagh Clergy and Parishes*, Dundalk, 1911, p. 19.

[78] Sercesi, James., *Popery Always the Same: an Authentic Account of the Persecutions Against the Protestants in the South of France*, London, 1746, p. 11 *ff.*

[79] *Historical Memoir of the Most Remarkable Proceedings Against the Protestants in France, 1744–1751*, Dublin, 1752, p. v.

[80] Leslie, J.B., *Ferns Clergy and Parishes*, Dublin, 1936, p. 136; *cf.* Combe, J.C., *Huguenots in the Ministry of the Churches in Ireland: their Place and Contribution*, Queen's University, Belfast, 1970, Ph.D. thesis.

[81] *Cf.* Le Fanu (Dean of Emly), 'French Church in the Lady Chapel of St. Patrick's, 1666–1816', Lawlor, H.J., *Fasti of St. Patrick's, Dublin*, Dundalk, 1930, Appendix.

[82] Bolton, T., *Sermon Preached at St. Andrew's, Dublin, on Monday, 23 October, 1721, being the Anniversary of the Irish Rebellion*, Dublin, 1721, pp. 43–44.

[83] Anon. *Humble Address of the French Refugees for Religion in Ireland to the Earl of Wharton, Lord Lieutenant*, Dublin, 1709, p. 1; *cf.* Taylor, C., *The Camisards*, London, 1973 on the repression of Protestant dissidents in 1702–1704, 1709 by Louis XIV.

[84] Crookshank, C.H., *History of Methodism in Ireland*, Belfast, 1885, I, p. 147.

[85] Neely, W.G., *Kilcooley: Land and People in Tipperary*, Belfast, 1983, p. 77: *cf.* Savory, D.L., *Huguenot and Palatine Settlement*, London, 1948, p. 230.

[86] *Huguenots in Ireland*, Conclusion, p. 424. *Cf.* Dodge, G., *Political Theory of the Huguenots in the Dispersion*, Columbia, 1947, p. 120.

[87] Jenkins, Brian, *Era of Emancipation*, Montreal, 1988, p. 118.

[88] Lee, *Huguenot Settlements in Ireland*, p. 202.

89 Combe, *Huguenots in the Ministry of the Churches in Ireland*, p. 96 *ff*. *Cf*. Browning, W.S., *History of the Huguenots, 1598–1838*, London, 1839, pp. 238–239; Smiles, Samuel, *The Huguenots: Their Settlements, Churches and Industries in England and Ireland*, London, 1876, pp. 155 *ff*.

90 Trench, Richard le Poer, *Memoir of the le Poer Trench Family*, Dublin, 1874, pp. 1–5.

91 Daniel-Rops, H., *Church in the Eighteenth Century*, N.Y., 1966, p. 193.

92 Armstrong, A., *Church of England., the Methodists and Society, 1700–1850*, London, 1973, p. 104.

93 Wesley, John, *Works*, Michigan, 1959, X, p. 160.

94 Campbell, Thomas, *Jesuits*, N.Y., 1921, pp. 482–487.

95 Burton, Edwin, *Life and Times of Bishop Challoner*, London, 1909, II, p. 208.

96 Anon. *Historical Account of the Life and Writings of Mr. John Toland by One of his most Intimate Friends*, London, 1722, p. 53; *cf*. Simms, J.G., 'John Toland (1670–1722) a Donegal Heretic', *I.H.S.*, 1969, XVI, p. 319. Toland considered himself a 'trew protestant and a loyal subject', a man of 'anti-authoritarian principle', *ibid*, pp. 305, 312.

97 Law, William, *Letters to a Lady Inclined to Enter the Church of Rome*, London, 1779, pp. 1 *ff*.

98 Maxwell, *Trinity College*, p. 161.

99 Lecky, *Ireland in the Eighteenth Century*, I, p. 304.

100 Synge, Edward, *Authority of the Church in Matters of Religion*, London, 1718, p. 36; *cf. Sermon Against Persecution on Account of Religion at Christ Church, Dublin, 23 October, 1721*, Dublin, 1721, pp. 27–28. For the eirenical opinions of the younger Edward Synge *v. Case of Toleration Considered: Sermon in St. Andrew's, Dublin, 23 October, 1725, Being the Anniversary of the Irish Rebellion*, Dublin, 1726, p. 2.

101 Synge, Edward, *Gentleman's Religion with the Ground and Reason of It*, London, 1752, seventh edition, pp. 82, 92.

[102] Leslie, J.B., *Ferns Clergy and Parishes*, Dublin, 1936, p. 13.

[103] Aveling, J.C.H., *Handle and the Axe: Catholic Recusants in England*, London, 1976, p. 254.

[104] Mathew, *Catholicism in England*, p. 143.

[105] Pawley, *Rome and Canterbury*, p. 68.

[106] Bossy, John, 'Challoner and the Marriage Act', *Challoner and his Church*, London, 1981, p. 128.

[107] Mathew, *Catholicism in England*, p. 148.

[108] Abercrombie, Nigel, 'First Relief Act', *Challoner*, p. 192.

[109] Sykes, Norman, *William Wake*, Cambridge, 1957, I, p. 309; *cf.* Sykes, N., *Old Priest and New Presbyter*, Cambridge, 1956, p. 200.

[110] Sykes, *William Wake*, p. 209.

[111] Pawley, *Rome and Canterbury*, p. 51.

[112] Andrieux, Maurice, *Daily Life in Papal Rome in the Eighteenth Century*, London, 1968, p. 189: *cf.* Chadwick, *Popes and European Revolution*, pp. 273–290.

[113] Andrieux, *Daily Life in Papal Rome*, p. 191.

[114] Campbell, *Jesuits*, pp. 517–518. Pastor, Ludwig von, *History of the Popes*, London 1938–1953, XXXVII, pp. 292–336.

[115] Cragg, G.R., *Church and the Age of Reason*, London, 1960, p. 211.

[116] Giblin, C., 'Material Relating to Ireland in the Albani Collection in the Vatican Archives', *Proceedings of the Irish Catholic Historical Commission*, Dublin, 1965, pp. 12–13.

[117] Acts of Chapter, *Meetings of the Friars Minor, Dublin, 1717*, Dublin, 1729, p. 19.

[118] Corish, *Catholic Community*, p. 106.

119 Freyne, Sean, 'Laity and the Church', *Doctrine and Life*, 1987, XXXVII, p. 234.

120 Burns, 'Irish Penal Code', *Review of Politics*, p. 306.

121 Corish, *Irish Catholic Experience*, p. 138.

122 Propaganda Fide Archives, *Scritture riferite nei congressi Irlanda*, 1781–1784, XV, 68: *cf.* O'Flaherty, Eamon, 'Ecclesiastical politics and the dismantling of the penal laws in Ireland, 1774–1782', *I.H.S.*, 1988, XXVI, pp. 33–51. Bishop P.J. Plunket of Meath was considered to be a strong Gallican.

123 Dickson, R.J., *Ulster Emigration to Colonial America*, Belfast, 1966, p. 41.

124 Barkley, J.M., *Westminster Formularies in Irish Presbyterianism*, Belfast, 1956, pp. 8–10.

125 Holmes, *Irish Presbyterian Heritage*, p. 67.

126 Corish, *Catholic Community*, p. 119.

127 Boulter, H., *Foundation of Submission to our Governors Considered: Sermon Preached at St. Olave's, Southwark, 26 November, 1725*, London, 1725, p. 20, on the 'popish bigotted Pretender'.

128 Boulter, H., *Primary Visitation Charge*, Drogheda, 1725, p. 15.

129 Sykes, *William Wake*, II, p. 238.

130 Boulter, Hugh, *Letters, 1724–1738*, Dublin, 1770, I, p. 210.

131 Boulter, H., *Report Made by the Lord Primate for the Lords Committee Appointed to Inquire into the Present State of Popery in this Kingdom*, Dublin, 1732, pp. 5, 10.

132 Boulter, *Letters*, I, p. 223.

133 *Ibid.*, I, p. 182.

134 Boulter, Hugh, *Charge Given to the Primate of All Ireland at the Triennial Visitation of the Clergy*, Dublin, 1736, p. 9.

135 Phillips, *Church of Ireland*, III, p. 18.

136 Anon. *Brief Review of the Rise and Progress of the Incorporated Society in Dublin from the...Royal charter of 6 February, 1733 to 2nd of November, 1748*, Dublin, 1748, p. 38 *ff*.

137 Boulter, H., *Charge Given at the Triennial Visitation at Trim 30 June, 1730*, Dublin, 1730, p. 18

138 Anon. *Boulter's Monument, a Panegyrical Poem*, Dublin, 1745, pp. 59–96.

139 Lecky, *Ireland in the Eighteenth Century*, I, pp 188, 237.

140 Harris, *James Ware's Works*, I, 'Bishops of the Kingdom', p. 133; *cf.* Maxwell, *Country and Town under the Georges*, p. 331.

141 Boulter, *Letters*, I, p. 181.

142 Falkiner, C. Litton, *Essays Relating to Ireland*, London, 1909, p. 88.

143 Stone, G., *Sermon Preached at Christ Church, Dublin, before the Lord Lieutenant and the Lords Spiritual and Temporal 23 October, 1751*, Dublin, 1751, pp. 25–26; *Cf.* his *Sermon at Christ Church Dublin*, 1741, p. 17.

144 Beckett, *Making of Modern Ireland*, p. 194.

145 Stone, G., *Thanksgiving Sermon for Victories at Sea and on the Land, 29 November, 1759*, London, 1760, p. 12.

146 Berkeley, G., *Passive Obedience or the Christian Doctrine of Not Resisting the Supreme Power Proven Vindicated Upon the Principles of the Law of Nature*, London, 1712, p. 5.

147 Johnston, Joseph, *Bishop Berkeley's Querist in Historical Perspective*, Dundalk, 1970, p. 6.

148 Berkeley, G., *The Querist...to which is Added a Word to the Wise or An Exhortation to the Roman Catholic Clergy*, London, 1750, p. 12.

149 Stock, Joseph, *Memoirs of George Berkeley*, London, 1784, p. 173.

150 Berkeley, G., *Impartial History of the Life and Death of James II and a*

Letter to the Roman Catholics of his Diocese, Dublin, 1746, p. 41.

[151] Anderson, James, *Bishop Berkeley on the Roman Catholic Controversy: a Letter to Sir John James written in 1741*, London, 1850, pp. 15–25,

[152] *Querist...Word to the Wise*, p. 65.

[153] King, William, *Divine Predestination and Foreknowledge Consistent with the Freedom of Man's Will, Sermon at Christ Church, Dublin, 15 May, 1709*, Dublin, 1709, p. 8.

[154] Clayton, John, *Sermon Preached at St. Michan's, 23 February 1700, Upon Receiving into the Church of Ireland Converts*, Dublin, 1700, pp. 2, 16; *cf.* Layton, W.T., *Discoverer of Gas Lighting*, London, 1926, pp. 20–34.

[155] Hort, Josiah, *Instructions Given by the Lord Bishop of Kilmore and Ardagh to his Clergy at his Visitations in 1729*, Dublin, 1731, pp. 17–19.

[156] Hort, J., *Instructions to his Clergy on his Primary Visitation 8 July, 1742*, London, 1790, pp. 11, 23.

[157] Hort, J., *Sixteen Sermons*, Dublin, 1738, p. 181.

[158] Bacon, B., *Sermon at St. Andrew's, Dublin, 23 October, 1743, the Anniversary of the Irish Rebellion*, Dublin, 1743, p. 18.

[159] Maxwell, Constantia, *Country and Town in Ireland under the Georges*, Dundalk, 1949, p. 350.

[160] Vicar of the Church of Ireland, *Bishop Clayton on the Nicene and Athanasian Creeds Republished with a Memoir*, Dublin, 1876, p. 9.

[161] Burdy, S., *Life of Philip Skelton*, Oxford, 1914, p. xxv.

[162] *Ibid.*, pp. 112, 122, 222, 243.

[163] Skelton, Philip, 'Marks of Dangerous Corruption Found in the Church of Rome', *Protestant's Manual*, ed. Cochrane, James, Edinburgh, 1839, pp. 35–63.

[164] Skelton, P., 'Case of the Protestant Refugees from France Considered', *Complete Works*, London, 1824, III, pp. 375–384.

165 *Protestant's Manual*, pp. 59, 71.

166 Corish, *Catholic Community*, p. 85.

167 *Ibid.*, pp. 119, 106.

168 Maxwell, *Country and Town in Ireland under the Georges*, p. 351.

169 Wall, *Penal Laws*, p. 115.

170 Brady, *Catholics and Catholicism in the Eighteenth Century Press*, pp. 226–7.

171 Kenny, Colum, 'Exclusion of catholics from the legal profession in Ireland, 1537–1829', *I.H.S.*, 1987, XXV, pp. 337–358; *cf*, Boulter, *Letters*, I, p. 226.

172 Froude, J.A., *English in Ireland*, London, 1887, p. 5; *cf.* McCartney, D., 'James Anthony Froude and Ireland: a historiographical controversy of the nineteenth century', *Historical Studies*, 1971, VIII, pp. 171–190.

173 Wall, Maureen, 'Catholic loyalty to King and Pope in Eighteenth Century Ireland', *Catholic Ireland in the Eighteenth Century: Collected Essays*, Dublin, 1989, pp. 107–114.

174 Morton, Desmond, *Military History of Canada*, Edmonton, 1985, pp. 41–42.

175 Brady, *Eighteenth Century Press*, pp. 186–187.

176 Wall, *Catholic Ireland in the Eighteenth Century*, p. 191, n. 67.

177 Foster, R.F., *Modern Ireland, 1600–1972*, London, 1988, p. 245.

178 Corish, *Irish Catholic Experience*, p. 138.

179 Bossy, *Irish Catholic Community*, p. 316.

180 Propaganda Fidei, *Scritture*, 1779–1781, XIV, p. 106; *cf.* XV, 66; XVII, 93–96 *passim*.

181 *Ibid.*, 1773–1776, XII, p. 539.

182 *Ibid.*, XVI, 60–63.

183 Berington, Joseph, *State and Behaviour of English Catholics from the Reformation to 1781*, London, 1781, pp. vi, 199.

184 Berington, Joseph, *Memoir of Gregorio Panzani*, London, 1793, pp. 24, 461–464.

185 Buckley, M.B., *Life and Writings of Rev. Arthur O'Leary*, Dublin, 1868, p. 97; *cf.* O'Leary, A., *Address to the Lords...of the Parliament of Great Britain*, London, 1800, p. 6.

186 Troy, J.T., *Pastoral Instruction of the Duties of Christian Citizens Addressed to the Roman Catholics of the Dublin Archdiocese*, Dublin, 1793, p. 41; *cf.* O'Flaherty, Eamon, 'Ecclesiastical politics and the dismantling of the penal laws in Ireland, 1774–1782', *I.H.S.*, 1988, XXVI, p. 45. *V.* Menczer, Bela, *Catholic Political Thought, 1789–1848*, London, 1953, pp. 12–13 on Bossuet and Gallican theories of authority.

187 Stuart, James, *Historical Memoirs of the City of Armagh*, Dublin, 1900, p. 400.

188 Childe-Pemberton, W.S., *Earl Bishop: Life of Frederick Hervey, Bishop of Derry*, London, 1924, I. p. 97.

189 Reynolds, E.E., *Edmund Burke: Christian Statesman*, London, 1948, p. 22 *passim*; Mahoney, T.D., *Edmund Burke and Ireland*, Harvard, 1960, p. 314.

190 Anon. *Alarm to the Unprejudiced and Well-Minded Protestants of Ireland...Upon the Rise and Danger and Tendency of the Whiteboys*, Cork, 1762, pp;. 17–24; *cf.* Donnelly, J.S., 'Whiteboy Movement, 1761–1765', *I.H.S.*, 1978, XXI, pp. 20–55.

191 O'Connell, Philip, ''Plot against Fr. Nicholas Sheehy: the historical background', *Proceedings of the Irish Catholic Historical Commission 1965*, Dublin, 1968, p. 53.

192 Corish, *Irish Catholic Experience*, p. 141,

193 Moran, P.F., *Spicilegium Ossoriense*, Dublin, 1874, III, pp. 372, 384; *cf*, Lecky, *Ireland in the Eighteenth Century*, II, p. 36 *ff.*

194 Propaganda Fidei, *Scritture*, XVI, 52–53, *cf.* fol. 32.

195 Woodward, Richard, *Present State of the Church of Ireland Containing a Description of its Precarious Situation and the Consequent Danger to the Public and a General Account of the Origin and Progress of the Insurrection in Munster*, Dublin, 1787, 9th edition, pp. 76, 85.

196 Butler, James, *Justification of the Tenets of the Roman Catholic Religion and a Refutation of the Charges Against Its Clergy*, Dublin, 1787, pp. 3–27, *Cf.* Connolly, S.J., *Religion, Law and Power: the Making of Protestant Ireland, 1660–1760*, Oxford, 1992 for an appreciation of the objective reality of Protestant fears.

197 Authenticus, *Defence of the Protestant Clergy in the South of Ireland*, Dublin, 1788, pp. 41–108; *cf.* Hales, William, *Observation on the Political Influence of the Doctrine of the Pope's Supremacy*, London, 1987, pp. 41. *ff.*

198 O'Leary, Arthur, *Address to the Common People of Ireland Particularly to Such of Them as are called Whiteboys*, Cork, 1786, p. 13.

199 O'Leary, Arthur, *Defence against the Ill-Grounded Insinuations of Dr. Woodward, Lord Bishop of Cloyne*, Dublin, 1787, pp. 30, 116,

200 O'Leary, Arthur, *Address to the Common People of Ireland, loc. cit.*

201 O'Leary, Arthur, *Defence against Insinuations*, pp. v. 15; *cf.* O'Leary, *Third Address to the Whiteboys, Particularly Those of the County of Cork*, Dublin, 1786, p. 4.

202 Clifford, Brendan, *Belfast in the French Revolution*, Belfast, 1989, pp. 1–148.

203 Gwynn, D., *John Keogh: Pioneer of Catholic Emancipation*, Dublin, 1930, p. 31.

204 Ireland, House of Lords, *Report from the Secret Committee*, Dublin, 1798, p. 14.

205 Foster, *Modern Ireland*, p. 273.

206 McAnally, Henry, *Irish Militia, 1793–1816*, Dublin, 1949, pp. 14–27.

207 Livingstone, Peadar, *Monaghan Story*, Enniskillen, 1980, p. 170.

208 Lecky, *Ireland in the Eighteenth Century*, IV, p. 370. *Cf.* Beckett, J.C., *Making of Modern Ireland, 1603–1923*, London, 1966, p. 263 on the Wexford rising being 'essentially religious' in character: Protestants were 'to be attacked...even slaughtered simply for being Protestant'.

209 Pakenham, Thomas, *Year of Liberty*, London, 1969, pp. 190, 199; Lecky, *op. cit.*, IV, p. 394; Taylor, George, *History of the Rebellion in the County Wexford in the Year 1798*, Dublin, 1800, pp. 60–61; Musgrave, R., *Memoirs of the Rebellions in Ireland*, London, 1802, pp. 525–6.

210 Dewar, M., Brown, J. and Long, S., *Orangeism*, Dublin, 1967, p. 110.

211 Pakenham, *Year of Liberty*, p. 228.

212 Lecky, *op. cit,*, IV, p. 415.

213 McDowell, R.B., *Ireland in the Age of Imperialism and Revolution, 1760–1801*, Oxford, 1979, p. 419.

214 *Times*, 1 January, 28 May, 1799.

215 Leadbeater, Mary, *Leadbeater Papers*, London, 1862, II, pp. 208 *ff.*

216 Pakenham, *Years of Liberty*, pp. 340–341.

217 *Ibid.*, p. 339.

218 Madden, R.R., *Life and Times of Robert Emmet*, Dublin, 1847, pp. 122–124.

219 Moran, *Spicilegium Ossoriense*, III, pp. 588–594.

220 Troy, J.T., *To the Reverend Pastors of the Dublin Archdiocese*, Dublin, 1798, p. 13.

221 Holmes, *Irish Presbyterian Heritage*, p. 83.

222 Chart, D.A., *Drennan Letters, 1776–1819*, Belfast, 1931, pp. 232, 311.

223 Falkiner, C.L., *Studies in Irish History*, London, 1902, p. 44.

224 Beckett, *Making of Modern Ireland*, p. 266.

225 Phillips, *Church of Ireland*, III, p. 270.

Chapter VI

1 Chamberlin, E.R., *Bad Popes*, N.Y., 1969, p. 281. for the 'mood of the day;' on the eve of the Revolution, 'suspicious, fearful Gallican, erastian anti-clerical' *cf.* McManners, John, *French Revolution and the Church*, London, 1969, p. 43.

2 Daniel-Rops, H., *Church in an Age of Revolution, 1789–1870*, N.Y., 1967, I, p. 125.

3 *Ibid.*, p. 221.

4 Rohrbacher, R-F., *Histoire universelle de l'Eglise catholique*, Paris, 1857–1859, XXVIII, p. 363.

5 Costigan, R.F., 'Ecclesiological Dialectic', *Thought*, 1974, 49, p. 141; *cf.* Costigan, R.F., *Rohrbacher and the Ecclesiology of Ultramontanism*, Rome, 1980, p. xiv.

6 Mathew, David, *Catholicism in England, 1535–1935* London, 1937, p. 146.

7 Burton. E.H., *Life and Times of Bishop Challoner, 1691–1781*, London, 1909, II. p. 190.

8 Bossy, *English Catholic Community*, p. 335.

9 Milner, John, *Divine Right of Episcopacy Addressed to the Catholic Laity of England*, London, 1791, p. 116.

10 Husenbeth, F.C., *Life of Rt. Rev. John Milner*, Dublin, 1862, p. 49.

11 *Cf.* Milner, John, *Democracy Detected: Being a Review of the Controversy between the Laymen and the Clergymen Concerning the Appointment of Bishops*, London, 1793.

12 Ward, Bernard, *Catholic England a Century Ago*, London, 1905, p. 7 *ff*. *Cf.* Ward, Bernard, *Dawn of the Catholic Revival in England*, London, 1909, I, p. 130.

13 Butler, Charles, *Address to the Protestants of Great Britain and Ireland*, Exeter, 1813, p. 25.

14 Butler, Charles, *Historical Memoirs of the English and Scottish Catholics Since the Reformation*, London, 1822, IV, p. 69.

15 *Ibid.*, III, p. 392.

16 Butler, Charles, *Book of the Roman Catholic Church*, London, 1825, pp. 216–222.

17 Butler, *Address to the Protestants*, p. 10.

18 Milner, J., *Inquiry into Certain Vulgar Opinions Concerning the Catholic Inhabitants of Ireland*, London, 1808, pp. 4, 203.

19 MacDonagh, Oliver, 'Politicization of the Irish Catholic Bishops, 1800-1850', *Historical Journal*, 1975, xviii, p. 38.

20 MacDonagh, O., *Hereditary Bondsman: Daniel O'Connell, 1775–1829*, London, 1988, p. 100.

21 *Freeman's Journal*, 9 March, 1810.

22 MacDonagh, Michael, *Daniel O'Connell and the Story of Catholic Emancipation*, Dublin, 1929, p. 91; *cf. Freeman's Journal*, 9 May 1814, on the rescript from Msgr. Quarantotti vice-prefect of Propaganda.

23 Fitzpatrick, W.J., *Life and Times of Rt. Rev. Dr. Doyle*, Dublin, 1880, I, p. 451.

24 de Tocqueville, Alexis, *Journeys to England and Ireland*, London, 1958, p. 172; *cf.* Murphy, J.A., 'Support of the Catholic Clergy in Ireland, 1750-1850', *Historical Studies*, 1965, V, p. 118.

25 O'Connell, J., ed., *Life and Speeches of Daniel O'Connell, M.P.*, Dublin, 1846, II, pp. 178, 207–216.

26 MacDonagh, *Hereditary Bondsman*, p. 130.

27 *Ireland and Irish Catholics: Consisting of the Leading Articles of the First Seven Numbers of the British Lion Newspaper*, London, 1825, p. 8.

28 Grattan, Henry, *Speech on the Catholic Question in the House of Commons, 18 May, 1810*, London, 1810, pp. 4–5.

29 O'Conor, C., *Columbanus's Third Letter on the Liberties of the Irish Church*, London, 1810, pp. 41, 112.

30 O'Conor, Charles, *Columbanus ad Hibernos: Fourth Letter on the Liberties of the Catholics of Ireland*, London, 1811, p. 8 *ff.*

31 O'Conor, Charles, *Columbanus Number VI: Unpublished Correspondence between Rt. Rev. Dr. Poynter and Dr. O'Connor*, London, 1812, p. 185. *Cf. Dublin Evening Post*, 1 Sept., 1812.

32 Ryan, Edward, *Strictures on Dr. Milner's Tour*, Dublin, 1809, p. 9.

33 Milner, J., *Letters to a Roman Catholic Prelate of Ireland*, Dublin, 1811, p. 13.

34 Milner, J., *Instructions to Catholics of the Midlands*, Wolverhampton, 1811, p. 9.

35 Propaganda Fide Archives, *Scritture riferite nei congressi Irlanda*, 1811-1815, XIX, 30, May 3, 1812.

36 Husenbeth, *Life of Milner*, p. 251.

37 Prop. Fidei, *Scritture*, XIX, 1812, 30.

38 Grier, Richard, *Reply to the End of Religious Controversy*, London, 1821, p. 463 on Milner and the papacy.

39 Phillpotts, Henry, *Letters to Charles Butler on his Book of the Roman Catholic Church*, London, 1825, p. 306.

40 Ellis, John Tracy, *Cardinal Consalvi and Anglo-Papal Relation*, Washington, 1942, pp. 75–97.

41 *Life and Speeches of Daniel O'Connell*, II, p. 209.

42 Butler, *Historical Memoirs*, IV, pp. 536–548.

43 Ward, Bernard, *Eve of Catholic Emancipation*, London, 1911, I, p. 24.

44 Bossy, *English Catholic Community*, p. 298.

45 Bowen, Desmond, *Paul Cardinal Cullen and the Shaping of Modern Irish Catholicism*, Dublin, 1983, pp. 34–35. *Cf.* Slater, Edward, *Letter to Sir John Hippisley on the Nature and Extent of Papal Authority*, Liverpool, 1813, p. 25.

46 O'Flaherty, E., 'Ecclesiastical politics and the dismantling of the penal laws in Ireland', *I.H.S.*, 1988,, XXVI, p. 44.

47 Broeker, G., *Rural Disorder and Police Reform in Ireland, 1812–1836*, London, 1970, pp. 5, 27, 42. Stuart, J., *Armagh*, Dublin, 1900, p. 270.

48 Longford, Elizabeth, *Wellington: Pillar of State*, N.Y., 1972, p. 118.

49 Troy, J.T., *Dialogue between a Protestant and a Papist*, London, 1776, p. 7.

50 Connolly, S.J., *Priests and People in Pre-Famine Ireland, 1780–1845*, Dublin, 1982, p. 127.

51 Troy, J.T., *Pastoral Instructions on the Duties of Christian Citizens*, Dublin, 1793, pp. 112, 97.

52 Kerr, D.A., *Peel, Priests and Politics*, Oxford, 1982, p. 226.

53 Troy, J.T., *To the Rev. Pastors and other Roman Catholic Clergy of the Dublin Archdiocese*, Dublin, 1798, p. 11.

54 Troy, J.T., *Pastoral Instructions to the Roman Catholics of the Archdiocese of Dublin*, Dublin, 1798, pp. 12–14.

55 Troy, J.T., *Pastoral Address to the Roman Catholics of the Archdiocese of Dublin on the Happy Event of General Peace*, Dublin, 1802, pp. 12–14.

56 Anon. *Catholic Emancipation*, London, 1805, pp. 16–42.

57 Melancthon, *Letter to Dr. Troy on the Coronation of Bonaparte*, London, 1805, p. 95.

58 Lewis, Robert, *Reply to Melancthon's Letter to Dr. Troy*, London, 1805, pp. 5, 66.

59 *Trial of Henry Delahay Symons for a Libel against John Thomas Troy in*

the Court of King's Bench, 11 July, 1805, London, 1806, pp. 29 and appendix, p. 107. *Cf.* MacDonagh, Oliver, *Hereditary Bondsman*, London, 1988, p. 162 on Troy ('the pliant Trojan') whose 'traffic at the Castle is long notorious'.

60 O'Tuahaigh, G., *Ireland before the Famine, 1798–1848*, Dublin, 1972, p. 57.

61 Broeker, *Rural Disorder*, p. 4, 7. *Cf.* Coppinger, William, *Remonstrance Addressed to the Lower Order of Roman Catholics in the Dioceses of Cloyne and Ross*, Cork, 1798, pp. 1–5.

62 Moylan, Francis, *Pastoral Instruction to the Roman Catholics of the Diocese of Cork*, Dublin, 1798, p. 13.

63 Connolly, S.J., *Priests and People in Pre-Famine Ireland, 1780–1845*, Dublin, 1982, pp. 219, 233, 235.

64 Finnegan, Francis, 'Irish Catholic Convert Rolls', *Studies*, March 1949, pp. 73–83; Burns, R.E., 'Parsons, Priests and the People: the Rise of Irish Anti-Clericalism, 1785–1789', *Church History*, 1962, XXXI, p. 160.

65 Malcolmson, A.P.W., *John Foster: Politics of the Anglo-Irish Ascendancy*, Oxford, 1978, pp. 438–439.

66 Anon. *Strictures and Remarks on Dr. Hussey's Late Pastoral to the Clergy of Lismore and Waterford*, Dublin, 1797, p. 11. *cf.* Hussey, Thomas, *Pastoral Address to the Catholic Clergy of Waterford and Lismore*, Dublin, 1797, pp. 4–5.

67 McKee, Robert, *Remarks on a Pastoral Letter Written by Dr. Hussey*, Waterford, 1797, p. 2.

68 Anon. *Short Account of the Public Prayers in the Spanish Chapel for his Holiness Pope Pius VI, 14 May, 1798*, London, 1798, p. 7. *Sermon Preached by Rt. Rev. Dr. Hussey in the Spanish Chapel on Sunday 2 March, 1800 and Taken in Shorthand by a Gentleman Present*, London, 1800, pp. 8–9.

69 Healy, John, *Maynooth College*, Dublin, 1895, p. 176.

70 *Ibid.*, p. 694; *cf.* O'Brien, William, *Edmund Burke as an Irishman*, Dublin, 1926, pp. 306, 318.

71 Cornwallis, Charles, *Correspondence*, London, 1859, III, pp. 58–63.

72 Broeker, *Rural Disorder and Police Reform in Ireland*, p. 26.

73 Lewis, Cornewall, *Local Disturbances in Ireland, London*, 1836, p. 99.

74 Neely, W.G., *Kilcooley: Land and People in Tipperary*, Belfast, 1983, p. 95.

75 White, James Grove, *Account of the Yeomanry of Ireland, 1796–1834*, Cork, 1893, p. 3.

76 Foster, *Modern Ireland*, p. 282.

77 Carr, John, *Stranger in Ireland on a Tour Through the South and West Parts of the Country in 1805*, London, 1806, pp. 407–415.

78 Connolly, *Priests and People*, pp. 64–65.

79 Murphy, John A., 'Support of the Catholic Clergy in Ireland, 1750–1850', *Historical Studies*, London, 1965, V, p. 104.

80 O'Leary, A., *Address to the Lords Spiritual and Temporal of the Parliament of Great Britain*, Dublin, 1800, p. 11.

81 Propaganda Fidei, *Scritture*, XVIII, 161, 28 Sept., 1802.

82 British Observer, *Letter to the Lords and Commons of Great Britain on the Catholic Claims*, London, 1805, p. 29. *Cf.* MacDonagh, *Hereditary Bondsman*, p. 94.

83 Hill, Jacqueline, 'National festivals, the State and protestant ascendancy in Ireland, 1790–1829', *I.H.S.*, 1984, XXIV, p. 34.

84 Nassau, John, *Cause of the Roman Catholics Pleaded in an Address to the Protestants of Ireland*, Dublin, 1792, p. 41.

85 Tone, T.W., *Argument on Behalf of the Catholics of Ireland*, Dublin, 1792, p. 12.

86 *Speech of Mr. Grattan in the House of Commons on the Catholic Question*, Dublin, 1808, p. 95.

87 Anon. *Thoughts on the Protestant Ascendancy in Ireland*, London, 1805, pp. 97–108.

88 Pawley, *Rome and Canterbury*, p. 83–84. He was 'provisionally pensioned'.

89 Brady, W.M., *Essays on the English State Church in Ireland*, London, 1869, p. 393.

90 Hanna, A.G., *Enniskillen Methodism*, Enniskillen, 1967, p. 6.

91 Crookshank, C.H., *History of Methodism in Ireland*, Belfast, 1885, I, p. 45; *cf.* Mant, *Church of Ireland*, II, p. 593.

92 Hempton, David, *Methodism and Politics in British Society, 1750–1850*, London, 1984, p. 36.

93 Wesley, John, *Journal: Abridged by Nehemiah Curnock*, N.Y., 1963, p. 372, entry for 4 March, 1778.

94 Crookshank, *Methodism*, I, p. 339.

95 O'Leary, Arthur, *Remarks on the Rev. Mr. Wesley's Letter in Defence of the Protestant Association in England*, Dublin, 1780, pp. 76–80.

96 O'Leary, *Address to the Lords, 1800*, pp. 6–38

97 *Freeman's Journal*, 1 and 5 Aug., 1839; *cf.* Campbell, Graham, *Apostle of Kerry: Life of Charles Graham*, Dublin 1868, pp. 37–46.

98 Elrington, Thomas, *Reflections on the Appointment of Dr. Milner as the Political Agent of the Roman Catholic Clergy*, Dublin, 1809, p. 3 *passim*.

99 Leslie, J.B., *Ferns Clergy and Parishes*, Dublin, 1936, p. 19.

100 Le Mesurier, Thomas, *Reply to Certain Observations of Rt. Rev. Dr. Milner*, London, 1807, p. 193,

101 Hippisley, John, *Substance of Additional Observation on the Petition of the Roman Catholics of Ireland*, London, 1806, p. 111.

102 Donnelly, J.S., 'Pastorini and Captain Rock: Millenarianism and

Sectarianism on the Rockite Movement of 1821–4', *Irish Peasants: Violence and Political Unrest, 1780–1914*, Dublin, 1983, p. 111.

[103] *Derriana: Collection of Papers Relative to the Siege of Derry and Illustrative of the Revolution of 1688*, Derry, 1794, p. 65.

[104] Jebb, John, *Charge to the Clergy of Limerick*, Dublin, 1823, pp. 20–25.

[105] Maxwell, C., *Dublin Under the Georges*, London, 1936, p. 144.

[106] Kirwan, Wilhelmina, *Sermons by the Late Rev. Walter Blake Kirwan, Dean of Killala, with a Sketch of his Life*, London, 1814, pp. v–xv.

[107] Jebb, John, *Sermons on Subjects Chiefly Practical*, London, 1915, p. 357.

[108] Jebb, John, *Tract for All Times: the Peculiar Character of the Church of England*, London, 1839, p. 11. For a Roman Catholic appreciation of Jebb *cf.* Begley, John Archdeacon, *Diocese of Limerick from 1691 to the Present Time*, Dublin, 1938, pp. 444–447.

[109] Jebb, John, *Primary Visitation Charge 19 June, 1823*, Dublin, 1823, pp. 42–44.

[110] Forster, Charles, ed., *Thirty Years Correspondence between John Jebb and Alexander Knox*, London, 1934, II, pp. 40, 412. *Cf.* Wolffe, John, *Protestant Crusade in Britain, 1829–1860*, Oxford, 1991, p. 38 on Jebb and evangelical missions.

[111] Knox, Alexander, *Remains*, London, 1834, III, pp. 188, 316, IV, 461–2.

[112] Jebb, John, *Religious Patriotism Nurtured in the House of God: Sermon at Limerick, 15 February, 1829*, pp. 14–15. For Jebb's 'Thoughts on the State of Ireland' *cf.* TCD *Mss.* 6395, f. 42 addressed to Sir Robert Inglis.

[113] Jebb, John, *Biographical Memoir of William Phelan*, London, 1832, p. 2; *cf.* Neely, W.G., *Kilkenny: an Urban History 1391–1843*, Belfast, 1989, p. 270 for another response.

[114] *Ibid.*, p. 13.

[115] Phelan, W., *The Bible not the Bible Society*, Dublin, 1817, p. 47. *Cf.* St. Canice Cathedral Library, Kilkenny *Mss*, Phelan to archbishop J.G. Beresford, 23 March, 1825 on rejection of papal authority by the Irish

hierarchy.

[116] *Ibid.*, p. 55.

[117] Phelan, W., *Brief Exposure of the Principles Advanced, the Intellect Displayed and the Spirit Manifested by the Rev. Robert J. M'Ghee in his Late Publication*, Dublin, 1817, p. 47.

[118] *Parliamentary Papers*, 1825, VIII, (129), p. 494.

[119] Phelan, W., *History of the Policy of the Church of Rome in Ireland*, London, 1854, 3rd edition, p. xiv.

[120] Godkin, James, *Religious History of Ireland*, London, 1873, pp. 231–238.

[121] McNamee, Brian, 'Second Reformation in Ireland', *I.T.Q.*, 1966, XXXIII, pp. 60–61.

[122] *Ibid.*, p. 59.

[123] Forster, C., *Life of Bishop Jebb*, pp. 187–188.

[124] Longford, *Wellington: Years of the Sword*, pp. 265–266.

[125] MacDonagh, *Hereditary Bondsman*, pp. 220–221. *Cf. Prop. Fidei, Scritture*, 1823–1827, 24, 807 for Rome's view of Irish affairs.

[126] Fitzpatrick, W.J., *Life and Times of the Rt. Rev. Dr. Doyle*, Dublin, 1880, I, pp. 199–200; *cf. ibid.*, I, p. 335 on his union proposal.

[127] *Ibid.*, I, p. 208.

[128] J.K.L., *Letter to Dr. Magee, Protestant Archbishop of Dublin*, Carlow, 1822, p. 9.

[129] *Dublin Evening Post*, 14 December, 1822.

[130] J.K.L., *Vindication of the Religious and Civil Principles of the Irish Catholics Addressed to the Marquis of Wellesley*, Dublin, 1823, p. 40.

[131] The letter is often said to have been sent to Frederick Robinson, Chancellor of the Exchequer *cf.* Fitzpatrick, *Doyle*, I, p. 330; Pawley, *Rome and*

Canterbury, pp. 112–113 for text and address.

132 Ward, *Eve of Catholic Emancipation*, III, pp. 150, 496.

133 Husenbeth, *Life of Milner*, p. 496.

134 Fitzpatrick, *Doyle*, I, p. 338.

135 *Letters on a Reunion of the Churches of England and Rome From and To Rt. Rev. Dr. Doyle, John O'Driscol, Alexander Knox and Thomas Newenham*, Dublin, 1824, p. 11; *cf. Morning Chronicle*, 18 May, 1824,

136 *Letters on Reunion*, p. 15.

137 *Ibid.*, p. 28.

138 *Ibid.*, p. 20.

139 *Ibid.*, p. 35.

140 Fitzpatrick, *Doyle*, II, pp. 15–25.

141 Elrington, C.R., (F.T.C.D.) *Remarks Upon the Reply of J.K.L. to the Charge of his Grace the Archbishop of Dublin*, Dublin, 1827, p. 93.

142 Fitzpatrick, *Doyle*, II, pp. 72–73; *cf.* Brady, *Essays on the English State Church in Ireland*, pp. 397–404. *Cf.* Chadwick, *Popes and European Revolution*, pp. 567 *ff.* on papal absolutism of the time.

143 Fitzpatrick, *Doyle*, I, p. 166.

144 de Tocqueville, *Journey to England and Ireland*, p. 142.

145 Jenkins, *Era of Emancipation*, pp. 182–183.

146 Fitzpatrick, *Doyle*, I, p, 204.

147 Donnelly, J.S., 'Pastorini and Captain Rock: Millenarianism and Sectarianism in the Rockite Movement of 1821–1824', *Irish Peasants: Violence and Political Unrest, 1780–1914*, Dublin, 1983, pp. 136–137.

148 MacDonagh, *Hereditary Bondsman*, p. 102.

149 *Ibid.*, pp. 162–163.

150 O'Faolain, Sean, *King of the Beggars*, London, 1938, p. 229.

151 Fitzpatrick, *Doyle*, I, 452, II, 340.

152 Gwynn, Denis, *Daniel O'Connell*, Cork, 1938, p. 145; *cf.* Wyse, T., *Sketch of the late Catholic Association of Ireland*, London, 1829, I, pp. 83, 329–340.

153 MacDonagh, O., 'Politicization of the Irish Catholic Bishops, 1800–1850', *Historical Journal*, 1975, XVIII, p. 43.

154 Wyse, *Catholic Association*, I, p. 408.

155 *Irish Times*, 6 August, 1975, Supplement, p. ii.

156 MacDonagh, *Hereditary Bondsman*, p. 267.

157 O'Ferrall, Fergus, *Catholic Emancipation: Daniel O'Connell and the Birth of Irish Democracy, 1820–1830*, Dublin, 1985, p. 280.

158 *Hansard*, 1829, XXI, 69–70.

159 Lecky, *Ireland in the Eighteenth Century*, III, p. 142.

160 Duigenan, Patrick, *Speech in the House of Commons of Ireland On the Union with Great Britain, 5 February, 1800*, Dublin, 1800, p. 27.

161 Duigenan, Patrick, *Speech of Dr. Duigenan Delivered in the House of Commons of the Imperial Parliament, 10 May, 1805*, London, 1805, p. 24.

162 Duigenan, Patrick, *Nature and Extent of the Demands of the Irish Roman Catholics Fully Explained*, Stockdale, 1810, p. 5.

163 Hales, William, *Observations on the Political Influence of the Doctrine of the Pope's Supremacy*, London, 1787, pp. 1–47; *cf.* Hales, W., *Letters on the Religious and Political Tenets of the Romish Hierarchy*, London, 1813, pp. 118–121.

164 Sirr, Henry, *Ipsissima Verba: Strictures on R.R. Madden's United Irishmen*, Dublin, 1911, p. 6.

165 Flood, Peter, *Letter to a Member of Parliament in London*, Dublin, 1800, p. 1.

166 Bellew, R., *Observation on the Opinions of Patrick Duigenan*, London, 1803, p. iii.

167 MacDonagh, M., *Viceroy's Post-Bag*, London, 1904, pp. 98–100.

168 *Annual Review, Appendix to Chronicle*, 1822, p. 138.

169 Brynn, E., 'Some Repercussions of the Act of Union on the Church of Ireland, 1801–1820', *Church History*, 1971, XL, pp. 284–296.

170 Brynn, E., 'Church of Ireland Diocese in the Age of Catholic Emancipation', *Historical Magazine of the Protestant Episcopal Church*, June, 1971, pp. 188–191.

171 Magee, William, *Charge to the Clergy of Raphoe in the Primary Visitation of 17 October, 1821*, London,1823, p. 70.

172 Elrington, Thomas, *Charge Delivered at the Visitation of the Dioceses of Leighlin and Ferns, June, 1824*, Dublin, 1824, p. 43; *cf.* Elrington, T., *Charge of August 1828 in Leighlin and Ferns*, Dublin, 1828, p. 2.

173 Romish Priest, *Renunciation of Popery Made by a Native of Ireland*, London, 1824, p. 23.

174 Roe, Peter, *Address in St. Mary's, Kilkenny 11 March, 1828 at the Internment of Major Kenney of the 73rd Regiment*, p. 2.

175 Phillips, *Church of Ireland*, III, p. 328.

176 Madden, Samuel, *Life of Peter Roe*, Dublin, 1842, p. 2 *passim*.

177 Leslie, J.B., *Ossory Clergy and Parishes*, Enniskillen, 1933, pp. 298–9; *cf.* Bible Society in Ireland, *Full Account of the Meeting of 9 November, 1824 at Carrick on Shannon between Protestants and Catholics on Distributing the Scriptures Among the Population of that Country*, London, 1824, p. 35.

178 Crookshank, *History of Methodism*, III, p. 3; *Conference Reviewed: Late Occurrences among the Methodists of Ireland*, Dublin, 1819, pp. 104–111.

179 *Newry Telegraph*, 28 August, 1821.

180 *Cf.* Otway, Caesar, *Sketches in Ireland: Description of Interesting Portions of the Counties of Donegal, Cork and Kerry*, Dublin, 1839, pp. 104–105.

181 Elrington, Thomas, *Remarks on Dr. Milner's Tour in Ireland*, Dublin, 1809, p. 37; Fitzpatrick, *Doyle*, II, p. 41.

182 O'Sullivan, Mortimer and Martin, J.C., *Remains of Rev. Samuel O'Sullivan*, Dublin, 1853, III, p. 170.

183 Pinnington, John, 'Church of Ireland's Apologetic Position in the Years before Disestablishment', *Irish Ecclesiastical Record*, 1967, CVIII, p. 305.

184 Curtis, Patrick, *Two Letters from the Most Reverend Dr. Curtis Respecting the Horrible Act of Placing a Calf's Head on the Altar of Ardie and Also his Answer to the Protestant Archbishop Magee's Charge against the Roman Catholic Religion*, Dublin, 1822, p. 8.

185 Hierophilos, *Brief Reply to the Charge of His Grace William Magee in Two Letters*, Dublin, 1822, pp. 1–33. *Cf. Letters of the Most Rev. John MacHale, D.D.*, Dublin, 1847, p. 580 on his belief in the government's 'deadly hate of Catholicism'. *V.* MacDonagh, Oliver, *The Emancipist*, London, 1989, p. 265 on MacHale: 'prone to identify Catholic and Irish values'.

186 British Museum, *Mss* . 40329, fol. 157, d. 27 Sept., 1823.

187 Magee, William, *Evidence of his Grace the Archbishop of Dublin before the Select Committee of the House of Lords on the State of Ireland*, Dublin, 1825, pp. 5–13.

188 Daunt, W.J.O., *Eighty-Five Years of Irish History, 1800–1885*, London, 1886, I, p. 93.

189 Bowen, Desmond, *Protestant Crusade in Ireland, 1800–1870*, Dublin, 1978, p. 106 *ff.*

190 *Authentic Report of the Discussion between the Rev. Richard T.P. Pope and the Rev. Thomas Maguire in Dublin*, London, 1827, pp. 10–11.

191 *Ibid.*, p. 382.

192 Bushe, William, *Lecture on the Doctrines of the Church of Rome, 5 November, 1823*, Dublin, 1824, p. 15.

193 Cahill, D.W. and Kinsella, W., *Letter on the Subject of the New Reformation Addressed to the Editor of the Carlow Morning Post*, Carlow, 1827, p. 4.

194 *Life, Letters and Lectures of the Late Dr. Cahill*, Dublin, n.d., p. 14.

195 *Ibid.*, p. 174.

196 O'Sullivan, Mortimer, *Captain Rock Detected, or the Origin and Character of the Recent Disturbances*, Dublin, 1824, p. 419.

197 Phelan, William, *Bible not the Bible Society*, Dublin, 1817, pp. 50–51. *Cf.* MacDonagh, *Hereditary Bondsman*, p. 218 for complaints of 'disloyalty to the British government' of Maynooth graduates. *V.* also Connolly, *Priests and People*, p. 54 on social identification of the minority of Maynooth priests prior to the famine: Connell, K.H., *Irish Peasant Society*, Oxford, 1968, p. 86.

198 O'Sullivan, *Captain Rock*, p. 394.

199 O'Sullivan, Mortimer, *Evidence of the Rev. Mortimer O'Sullivan Before the Select Committees of the Houses of Lords and Commons on the State of Ireland*, Dublin, 1825, p. 43. On the state of the countryside *cf.* Broeker, Galen, *Rural Disorder and Police Reform in Ireland, 1812–1836*, London, 1970, pp. 108–9, 153.

200 O'Sullivan, Mortimer, *Evidence*, p. 11. *Cf.* Hall, S.C. and Mrs., *Ireland: Its Scenery and Character*, London, 1841–3, II, pp. 279–280 on priests and popular agitation.

201 O'Sullivan, *Captain Rock*, p. 395.

202 O'Sullivan, *Evidence*, p. 43; *Cf.* Connolly, *Priests and People in Pre-Famine Ireland, 1780–1845*, pp. 91, 112, 169, 235 on Everard as a reformer.

203 O'Sullivan, *Evidence*, p. 2; *Cf.* Connolly, *Priests and People*, p. 13 on popular ballads and 'overthrow of heretics' theme as a 'peripheral role' in agrarian disturbances. *V.* Jenkins, Brian, *Era of Emancipation*, Montreal,

1988, p. 186 on 1822 clash of Orangeman and O'Connellites in Dublin.

204 O'Sullivan, *Captain Rock*, p. 380.

205 O'Sullivan, *Evidence*; *Cf.* O'Driscol, John, *Views of Ireland, Moral, Political and Religious*, London, 1823, I, p. 155.

206 *Evidence*, p. 2.

207 *Ibid.*, p. 29.

208 *Encyclical Letter of Pope Leo XII to Which are Annexed Pastoral Instructions by the Roman Catholic Archbishops and Bishops to the Clergy and Laity Throughout Ireland*, Dublin, 1824, p. 16.

209 *Ibid.*, p. 7, 15.

210 *Pastoral Address of the Roman Catholic Archbishops and Bishops to the Clergy and Laity of Ireland*, Dublin, 1826, pp. 1–20.

211 Castlereagh, Viscount, *Memoirs and Correspondence*, London, 1848–1853, IV, p. 224.

212 Holmes, Finlay, *Henry Cooke*, Belfast, 1981, pp. 63–66.

213 Parl. Papers, *State of Ireland*, 1825, VIII, pp. 48–85.

214 *Cf.* p. 287 *supra*. Wyse, *Catholic Association*, I, pp. 401–418; Rushe, D.C., *Historical Sketches of Monaghan*, Dublin, 1895, pp. 84–5.

215 O'Ferrall, *Catholic Emancipation*, p. 214.

216 Marshall, J.J., *Annals of Aughnacloy*, Dungannon, 1925, p. 51.

217 Colles, Ramsay, *History of Ulster*, IV, p. 179.

218 Livingstone, Peadar, *Monaghan Story*, Enniskillen, 1980, p. 189.

219 Bardon, J., *Belfast*, 1982, p. 83.

220 Macaulay, A., *Patrick Dorrian*, p. 27, n. 14.

Chapter VII

1 Daniel-Rops, H., *Church in an Age of Revolution*, N.Y., 1967, I, p. 243. On Roman illiberality at this time *v.* Chadwick, *Popes and European Revolution*, pp. 567–572, and Latourette, K.S, *Christianity in a Revolutionary Age: the Nineteenth Century*, N.Y., 1958, I, p. 258.

2 Hales, E.E.Y., *Catholic Church in the Modern World*, N.Y., 1960, p. 89.

3 MacDonagh, O., *The Emancipist: Daniel O'Connell, 1830–1870*, London, 1989, p. 62.

4 Costigan, 'Ecclesiological Dialectic', *op. cit.*, p. 141.

5 Rohrbacher, *Universal History*, vol. XXI, p. 172. For an ultramontane appreciation of Gregory XVI *v .* Wiseman, Nicholas, *Recollections of the Last Four Popes and of Rome in Their Times*, London, 1858, part IV, pp. 415–532. Gregory was a strong supporter of missions.

6 Daniel-Rops, *Church in an Age of Revolution*, II, p. 64. For a consideration of nineteenth century ultramontanism *v.* Acton, Lord, 'Ultramontanism', *Essays on Church and State*, London, 1952, pp. 373–86. *Cf.* Costigan, Richard, S.J., 'Ecclesiological Dialectic', *Thought*, 1974, XLIX, pp. 134–144 for an analysis of ultramontanism as a 'great movement of thought and sentiment'.

7 Ward, *Eve of Catholic Emancipation*, II, pp. 32–40, III, pp. 62–65; *cf.* Bossy, *Catholic Community*, p. 322 on the 'complicated whole' in the development of Catholicism in England at this time.

8 Gilley, S., 'Roman Catholic Mission to the Irish in London', *Recusant History*, 1969, X, p. 126.

9 Amhurst, W.J.S., *Catholic Emancipation and the Progress of the Catholic Church in the British Isles, 1771–1820*, London, 1886, II, p. 333.

10 Fitzpatrick, W.J., *Correspondence of Daniel O'Connell*, London, 1888, I, p. 186.

11 Stanley, Edward, *Few Words in Favour of our Roman Catholic Brethren, An Address to his Parishioners*, London, 1829, p. 8; *cf.* Stanley, E., *Few Observations on Religion and Education in Ireland*, London, 1835, p. 36.

12 Bickersteth, E., *Remarks on the Progress of Popery, and the Difficulties and Duties of Protestants in These Days*, London, 1836, p. 8.

13 *Times*, April 5, 20, May 18, 1838.

14 *British Critic*, 1835, XVIII, p. 148.

15 *Blackwood's Magazine*, 1838, XLIV, pp. 494–498.

16 Cahill, Gilbert, 'Irish Catholicism and English Toryism', *Review of Politics*, 1957, XIX, pp. 68–69.

17 Hexter, J.H., 'Protestant Revival and the Catholic Question in England, 1778–1829', *Journal of Modern History*, 1936, VIII, pp. 297 *ff*.

18 *Blackwood's Magazine*, 1838, XLIV, p. 730.

19 Cobban, Ingram, 'Essay on Popery', *Foxe's Book of Martyrs*, London, 1875, p. iv.

20 Neal, Frank, *Sectarian Violence: the Liverpool Experience, 1819–1914*, Manchester, 1988, p. 41.

21 Ward, W.R., *Religion and Society in England, 1790–1850*, London, 1972, p. 212.

22 *Freeman's Journal*, 29 January, 1831.

23 Webb, S. and B., *History of Trade Unionism*, London, 1920, p. 104.

24 O'Higgins, Rachel, 'Irish Influence in the Chartist Movement', *Past and Present*, 1961, XX, p. 92.

25 Read, D. and Glasgow, E., *Feargus O'Connor, Irishman and Chartist*, London, 1961, p. 7 *ff*.; *cf.* Ward, J.T., *Chartism*, London, 1973, p. 77.

26 Pawley, *Rome and Canterbury*, p. 115.

27 Froude, Hurrell, *Remains*, London, 1838, I, p. 336.

28 Gwynn, D., *Lord Shrewsbury, Pugin and the Catholic Revival*, London, 1946, pp. 59 *ff*.

29 Mozley, Anne, ed., *Letters and Correspondence of J.H. Newman*, London, 1898, II, p. 286.

30 Mathew, *Catholicism in England*, p. 194,

31 Bossy, *English Catholic Community*, p. 297.

32 Ward, Bernard, *Sequel to Catholic Emancipation*, London, 1915, I, p. 66.

33 Gwynn, D., *Fr. Luigi Gentile and his Mission, 1801–1848*, Dublin, 1951, p. 10; *cf.* Gwynn, D., *Fr. Dominic Barberi*, Dublin, 1947, pp. 243–244.

34 Bossy, *English Catholic Community*, p. 388.

35 Parker, Charles, *Sir Robert Peel*, London, 1899, III, pp. 334–356.

36 *Times*, 3 April, 1845; *Hansard*, LXXIX, pp. 18–38.

37 *Fraser's Magazine*, 1845, II, p. 104.

38 *Times*, April 7, 17, 26, May 1, 1845. *Cf.* Martineau, Harriet, *History of the Thirty Year's Peace*, London, 1878, pp. 245–247, 'the subject on which society seemed to be going mad'.

39 *Hansard*, LXXIX, p. 657.

40 Thelwall, A.S., ed., *Proceedings of the Anti-Maynooth Conference of 1845*, London, 1845, p. xviii.

41 Greville, Charles, *Past and Present Policy of England towards Ireland*, London, 1845, p. 312.

42 *Proceedings of Anti-Maynooth Conference*, p. xii.

43 Purcell, E.S., *Life of Cardinal Manning*, London, 1895, I, p. 301; *cf.* Norman, E.R., *Anti-Catholicism in Victorian England*, London, 1968, p. 38; Norman, E.R., 'Maynooth Question of 1845', *I.H.S.*, 1967, XV, pp. 407–438,

44 Knox, A., *Essays on the Political Crisis of Ireland*, London, 1798, p. 18.

45 Gentleman in Ireland, *Strictures on a Pamphlet Entitled Thoughts on the*

Protestant Ascendancy in Ireland, London, 1805, pp. 99, 53.

[46] *Proceedings, Resolutions and Addresses of the Protestants of County Roscommon Assembled on 25 November, 1812 to Take into Account the Claims of the Roman Catholics of Ireland*, Dublin, 1813, pp. 50–51.

[47] *Plain Truths on a Motion for Going into a Committee of the Whole House Upon the State of Ireland*, London, 1825, pp. 10–11.

[48] Urwick, William, *Life and Letters*, edited by his Son, Dublin, 1870, p. 70.

[49] *Full and Authentic Report of the First Annual Meeting of the Brunswick Constitutional Club in the Rotunda, 4 January, 1828*, Dublin, 1828, pp. 4–9.

[50] North of Ireland Man, *View of the Catholic Question as It Relates to Ireland*, London, 1829, p. 9.

[51] Erck, John, *Account of the Ecclesiastical Establishment Subsisting in Ireland*, Dublin, 1830, pp. lvi on tithes to impropriate landowners.

[52] Brynn, Edward, 'Irish Tithes in British Politics', *Historical Magazine of the Protestant Episcopal Church*, Sept., 1970, p. 298.

[53] Elrington, Thomas, *An Inquiry Whether the Disturbances in Ireland Have Originated in Tithes*, Dublin, 1822, p. 7.

[54] Bowen, Desmond, *Protestant Crusade in Ireland*, Dublin, 1978, pp. 157–177.

[55] Committee of the Parish of Blackrath, Killiney, *Short Statement Relative to the Bishop's Court in Ireland and the Conduct of Tithe Proctors in that Country*, London, 1824, p. 6.

[56] Clark, Samuel, 'Importance of Agrarian Classes in Nineteenth Century Ireland', *Journal of Sociology*, 1978, XXIX, p. 29. *Cf. Letter of an Irish Dignitary to an English Clergyman on the Subject of Tithes in Ireland*, Dublin, 1822, p. 18.

[57] Ensor, George, *Observations on the Present State of Ireland*, Dublin, 1814, pp. 38–39 on the extortions of tithe proctors.

[58] *Edinburgh Review*, 1825, XL, p. 381.

59 Fitzpatrick, *Life of Doyle,* I, p. 199.

60 Hammond, J.L. and B., *Village Labourer*, London, 1948, I, ch. X and XI; *cf.* Ward. W.R., 'Tithe Question in England in the Early Nineteenth Century', *Journal of Ecclesiastical History*, 1965, XVI, p. 78.

61 Townsend, T.S., *Facts and Circumstances Relating to the Condition of the Irish Clergy*, Dublin, 1832, p. 5,

62 Hicks, Edward, *What is to be Done with the Tithes in Ireland*, London, 1832, p. 19.

63 Cotton, Henry, *Cui Bono: Letter to the Rt. Hon. E.G. Stanley*, Dublin, 1833, p. 89.

64 *Dublin University Magazine*, May, 1833, p. 30; *ibid.*, March, 1833, p. 266.

65 Neely, *Kilcooley*, pp. 97–98.

66 *Hansard*, 1834, XXVI, 523; *Kilkenny Moderator*, 24 Dec., 1834,

67 Broadhurst, J., *Letter to Lord Melbourne on the Irish Church and Irish Tithes*, London, 1835, p. 69; *Corrected Report of the Proceedings in the Freemason's Hall, 3 December, 1835, the Archbishop of Canterbury in the Chair, for the Relief of the Irish Clergy*, London, 1835, pp. 12–14.

68 O'Sullivan, M., *Case of the Protestants in Ireland*, London, 1836, pp. 3–20.

69 Meagher, William, *Notices of the Life and Character of Most Rev. Daniel Murray*, Dublin, 1853, p. 183.

70 Editor of the Church of England Quarterly Review, *Political Aspect of Popery*, London, 1838, pp. 5, 10.

71 *Dublin Evening Post*, 16 Feb., 1830.

72 O'Donnell, P., *Faction Fighters of the Nineteenth Century*, Dublin, 1975, pp. 28, 146; *cf.* Croly, David, *Essay Religious and Political*, London, 1834, p. 61.

[73] Murphy, J.A., 'Priests and People in Modern Irish History', *Christus Rex*, 1969, XXIII, p. 245.

[74] Fitzpatrick, *Doyle*, I, pp. 202, 204.

[75] O'Beirne, E.F., Late Student of Maynooth College, *Maynooth in 1834*, Dublin, 1835, pp. 18. 82.

[76] de Tocqueville, *Journeys to England and Ireland*, p. 130.

[77] d'Alton, Ian, *Protestant Society and Politics in Cork, 1812–1844*, Cork, 1980, p. 205.

[78] Broderick, J.F., *Holy See and the Irish Movement for Repeal of the Union*, Rome, 1951, p. 58,

[79] MacIntyre, Angus, *The Liberator*, London, 1964, p. 113.

[80] Bowen, Desmond, *Souperism: Myth or Reality*, Cork, 1971, pp. 54–65.

[81] Broderick, *Holy See*, p. 65.

[82] *Ibid.*, pp. 97–107.

[83] *Cf., True Tendency of the Irish Church Bill Developed by Lord Melbourne, the Noble Apologist for Popery*, London, 1835.

[84] *Representation of the Present State of Religion with Regard to Infidelity, Heresy, Impiety and Popery*, Dublin, 1712, p. 18.

[85] *Humble Proposal for Obtaining a Royal Charter to Incorporate a Society for Promotion Christian Knowledge Among the Poor Natives of the Kingdom of Ireland*, Dublin,1740, p. 15.

[86] *Cf.* Dewar, Daniel, *Observation of the Character, Customs and Superstitions of the Irish*, London, 1812; and Anderson, Christopher, *Memorial on Behalf of the Native Irish*, London, 1814.

[87] Mason, H.J. Monck, *Catholic Religion of St. Patrick and St. Columbkill*, Dublin, 1823, p. 142; Mason, H.J. Monck, *History of the Origins and Progress of the Irish Society*, Dublin, 1846, p. 120.

[88] Foster, *Modern Ireland*, p. 341.

89 *Scriptural Education in Ireland: a Full Report of the Great Protestant Meeting Held in Exeter Hall, 8 February, 1832*, p. 13; *cf.* Gordon, J.E., *Six Letters on the Subject of Irish Education Addressed to the Right Hon. E.G. Stanley, Chief Secretary for Ireland*, London, 1831, p. 17.

90 Bowen, Desmond, 'Lord John George Beresford', *New Divinity*, 1972, III, p. 101.

91 Incumbent of the Church of England and Ireland, *Three Letters on the Speeches Made at the Last Public Meeting of the Church Educational Society at the Rotunda*, Dublin, 1853, pp. 22–23.

92 Holmes, *Cooke*, p. 137.

93 Boynton, Charles, *Speech at a Meeting of the Protestant Conservative Society, 10 July, 1832*, Dublin, 1832, p. 17.

94 Sirr, J.D., *Memoir of Power le Poer Trench*, Dublin, 1845, p. 384.

95 Condon, Mary D., 'Irish Church and the Reform Ministries', *Journal of British Studies*, 1964, I, pp. 120–121; *cf.* Lister, T.H., 'State of the Irish Church', *Edinburgh Review*, 1835, LXI, pp. 490–525.

96 de Beaumont, Gustave, *Ireland: Social, Political and Religious*, London, 1839, II, pp. 252–259. *Cf.* Akenson, D.H., *Church of Ireland, 1800–1835*, Yale, 1971, pp. 165, 210, tables 34, 36 for statistics of the period.

97 Phillips, *Church of Ireland*, III, p. 297.

98 Faber, G., *Oxford Apostles*, London, 1954, p. 320.

99 Cotton, *Cui Bono*, p. 49.

100 M'Ghee, R.J., *Last Stand for the Church: a Letter to the Deans, Archdeacons and Clergy of the Church of Ireland*, Dublin, 1833.

101 Stopford, Edward, *Letter Addressed to the Clergy of the Diocese of Raphoe Caused by Two Letters of the Rev. R.J. M'Ghee*, Dublin, 1833, pp. 9, 48.

102 *Edinburgh Review*, 'State of the Irish Church', 1835, LXI, p. 509.

103 M'Ghee, *Last Stand*, pp. 1–7, 11.

104 Prop. Fidei, *Scritture*, 1808, XVIII, f. 480.

105 Meagher, *Life of Murray*, pp. 171–173.

106 M'Ghee, R.J. and O'Sullivan, M., *Romanism as It Rules in Ireland, Being a Full and Authentic Report of the Meetings Held in Which the Theology Secretly Taught, the Commentary on the Bible Clandestinely Circulated, the Law of Papal States as Surreptitiously Set Up to Govern Ireland, and the Secret Diocesan Statutes of the Province of Leinster Have Been Successively Detected and Exposed*, London, 1835, II, p. 498.

107 *Irish Ecclesiastical Gazette*, 23 August, 1876.

108 Brooke, *Recollections*, p. 22.

109 Gregg, T.D., *Protestant Ascendancy Vindicated and National Regeneration Through the Instrumentality of National Religion Urged*, Dublin, 1840, preface and p. 82.

110 Gregg, T.D., *Free Thoughts on Protestant Matters*, Dublin, 1846, p. 371.

111 Daunt, *Eighty-Five Years of Irish History*, p. 147.

112 Hill, Jacqueline, 'Protestant Response to Repeal: the Dublin Working Class', *Ireland Under the Union: Varieties of Tension*, Oxford, 1980, pp. 35–69.

113 Gregg, *Protestant Ascendancy Vindicated*, p. 222. *Cf.* Hempton, David, and Hill, Myrtle, *Evangelical Protestantism in Ulster Society, 1740–1890*, London, 1992, p. 161 on the 'Protestant mind' being shaped by 'observation, experience, intuition, historical facts and facts of daily life'.

114 *Scriptural Unity of the Protestant Churches Exhibited in Their Published Confessions*, Dublin, 1835, pp. 1–28 on the 1615 Articles.

115 *Christian Herald*, Dublin, 1830–1835, V volumes.

116 Coad, R., *History of the Brethren Movement*, Exeter, 1976, pp. 21 *ff.*

117 Clarke, Richard, 'Dublin Connection: Two Archbishops and the Oxford Movement', *Search*, 1983, VI, pt. II, pp. 17–23.

118 *Irish Ecclesiastical Record*, 1842, II, p. 29.

119 McRedmond, L., 'Church in Ireland', *Church Now*, Dublin, 1980, p. 30.

120 Connolly, *Priests and People*, p. 113.

121 *Cf.* Miller, David, 'Irish Catholicism and the Great Famine', *Journal of Social History*, 1975, IX, I, pp. 86–88, and Corish, *Irish Catholic Experience*, pp. 166, 187.

122 O'Donoghue, David, *Life of William Carleton*, London, 1896, I, p. xxii; *cf.* Otway, Caesar, *Sketches in Ireland*, Dublin, 1839, p. 284.

123 D'Alton, *Protestant Society and Politics in Cork*, p. 231.

124 *Ibid.*, p. 55.

125 Foster, *Modern Ireland*, p. 303.

126 *Sympathy of the Irish Presbyterians with the Church of Scotland: Speeches in May St. Church, Belfast, 26 Feb., 1840*, Belfast, 1840, p. 40.

127 *Northern Whig*, 7 January, 1841.

128 Killen, W.D., *Memoir of John Edgar*, Belfast, 1867, p. 196.

129 Daunt, W.J. O'Neill, *Personal Recollections of Daniel O'Connell*, London, 1848, I, p. 156. *Cf.* MacIntyre, A., *The Liberator*, Oxford, 1964 on the O'Connell 'interest' in Kerry.

130 Broderick, *Holy See*, p. 23.

131 MacDonagh, *The Emancipist*, p. 25.

132 *Ibid.*, p. 26.

133 Porter, J.L., *Life and Times of Henry Cooke*, Belfast, 1875, p. 345.

134 Nowlan, Kevin, *Politics of Repeal*, London, 1965, p. 52.

135 O'Faoláin, Seán, *King of the Beggars*, London, 1938, p. 332.

136 *Ibid.*, p. 336.

137 MacDonagh, *The Emancipist*, p. 235.

138 MacSuibhne, Peadar, *Paul Cullen and his Contemporaries*, Naas, 1961, I, p. 246.

139 Nowlan, Kevin, B., *Politics of Repeal*, London, 1965, p. 66.

140 Parker, C.S., *Sir Robert Peel from his Private Papers*, London, 1891, III, p. 132. *Cf.* O'Connell in *The Nation*, 31 August, 1844; *Freeman's Journal*, 11 January, 1845.

141 Broderick, *Holy See*, pp. 186–187.

142 *Pilot*, 24 January, 1845.

143 MacSuibhne, *op. cit.*, I, pp. 255–258.

144 MacDonagh, *The Emancipist*, p. 265.

145 Bowen, *Paul Cardinal Cullen*, p. 94.

146 *Times*, 13 April, 1846.

147 Duffy, Charles Gavan, *Young Ireland*, London, 1980, pp. 645–646.

148 *Ibid.*, p. 630.

149 Foster, T.C., *Letters on the Condition of the People of Ireland*, London, 1846, p. 6.

150 MacSuibhne, *Paul Cullen, I*, p. 392. *Cf.* Anon. *History of Popery*, London, 1838, pp. 420-423 on popular intimidation.

151 *Nation*, 31 October, 1846.

152 *Freeman's Journal*, 20 August, 1846.

153 MacDonagh, *The Emancipist*, p. 272.

154 MacSuibhne, *Paul Cullen*, I, p. 301.

155 Nowlan, *Politics of Repeal*, p. 124.

[156] Macaulay, Ambrose, *Patrick Dorrian*, Dublin, 1987, p. 61.

[157] Tierney, M., *Murroe and Boher*, Dublin, 1966, p. 144.

[158] Neely, *Kilcooley*, pp. 106–107.

[159] McConville, M., *Ascendancy to Oblivion*, London, 1986, p. 230; O'Brien, W.P., *Great Famine in Ireland*, London, 1896, pp. 76–81.

[160] Maguire, W.A., *Downshire Estates in Ireland*, Oxford, 1972, p. 247.

[161] O'Brien, Barry, *Irish History, 1691–1870*, p. 410.

[162] O'Brien, Barry, *Fifty Years of Concessions to Ireland, 1831–1881,* London, n.d. II, p. 269.

[163] Fry, Edward, *James Hack Tuke: a Memoir*, London, 1899, pp. 55–70.

[164] Bowen, Desmond, *Souperism: Myth or Reality*, Cork, 1971, p. 191.

[165] *Tyrawly Herald*, 2 December, 1847.

[166] Bardin, Charles, *Duties of Repentance and Charity Enforced: Sermon for Relief of the Peasantry in Distressed Districts*, Dublin, 1822, p. 16.

[167] Seaver, George, *St. Ernan's, Donegal*, Donegal, n.d., p. 10.

[168] Trench, Francis, *Few Notes from Past Life*, Oxford, 1862, pp. 232–238.

[169] Noel, Baptist, *Notes of a Short Tour Through the Midland Counties of Ireland in the Summer of 1836*, London, 1837, p. 103 *ff.*

[170] Seddall, Henry, *Edward Nangle: the Apostle of Achill*, London, 1884, pp. 143–144.

[171] *Freeman's Journal*, 23 July, 1850, Sept. 11, 1851.

[172] Fitzpatrick, William, *Achill as It Is Compared with What It Was*, Dublin, 1886, pp. 22 *ff.*

[173] Bowen, *Paul Cardinal Cullen*, p. 94.

174 *Ibid.*, p. 95. *Cf.* MacSuibhne, *Cullen, I*, pp. 61–70 on Maher's politics.

175 Fisher, W.A., *Forty Years in the Church of Ireland*, London, 1882, p. 28.

176 Bowen, *Protestant Crusade*, p. 187.

177 Hickey, Patrick, *Study of Four Peninsular Parishes*, University College of Cork, 1980, M.A. thesis, p. 541. *Cf.* Richard Webb, a Quaker, reporting from Erris in May, 1847 on dereliction by Catholic clergy *PROI*, IA42–34.

178 Thompson, Mrs. D.P., *Brief Account of the Change in Religious Opinion Now Taking Place in Dingle*, London, 1846, p. 188.

179 Bowen, *Paul Cardinal Cullen*, pp. 70–71.

180 *Morning Chronicle*, 23 Feb., 1847 on Munster priests denying any overpopulation.

181 Cahill, *Life, Letters and Lectures*, p. 201.

182 O'Rourke, John, *Battle of the Faith in Ireland*, Dublin, 1887, p. 554; *cf.*, O'Rourke, John, *History of the Great Irish Famine of 1847*, Dublin, 1847.

183 MacDonagh, Oliver, 'Irish Catholic Clergy and Emigration During the Great Famine', *I.H.S.*, 1947, V, p. 292.

184 Whately, Richard, *Life and Correspondence*, London, 1866, II, p. 242; *cf.* Killen, W.D., *Ecclesiastical History of Ireland*, London, 1875, II, p. 495.

185 Miller, David, 'Irish Catholicism and the Great Famine', *Journal of Social History*, 1975, IX, pp. 92–93.

Chapter VIII

1 Daniel-Rops, *Church in an Age of Revolution*, II, p. 38. *Cf. ibid.*, II, 35–36 on the character of Antonelli. On the relationship between Pius IX and Antonelli *v.* Hales, E.E.Y., *Pio Nono*, London, 1952, pp. 151–2; Hales, E.E.Y., *Catholic Church in the Modern World*, New York, 1960, p. 105. *Cf.* Coppa, F.J., *Cardinal Giacomo Antonelli and Papal Politics in European Affairs*, N.Y., 1990, pp. 6–7, 71, 124.

2 Blakiston, Noel, *Roman Question: Extracts from the Despatches of Odo Russell from Rome, 1858–1870*, London, 1962, pp. 111-112.

3 Daniel-Rops, *Church in an Age of Revolution*, II, p. 81.

4 Butler, Cuthbert, *The Vatican Council*, London, 1930, II, p. 35.

5 Latourette, K.S., *The Nineteenth Century in Europe: Background and the Roman Catholic Phase*, N.Y., 1958, p. 467. On the increase of papal authority during this time of retreat *v.* Bury, J.B., *History of the Papacy in the Nineteenth Century*, London, 1930, pp. 163–164.

6 Mathew, *Catholicism in England*, pp. 182–183.

7 Wiseman, Nicholas, *Appeal to the Reason and Good Feeling of the English People on the Subject of the English Hierarchy*, London, 1850, p. 8.

8 Ward, *Sequel to Catholic Emancipation*, II, p. 287.

9 Chadwick, Owen, *Newman*, Oxford, 1983, p. 15; *cf.* Chadwick, *Victorian Church*, I, 271–309; Albion, Gordon, 'Restoration of the Hierarchy', *English Catholics, 1850–1950*, London, 1950, p. 99 *ff.*; Joyce, T.P., *Restoration of the Catholic Hierarchy in England and Wales, 1850: a Study of Certain Public Reactions*, Rome, 1966, pp. 17–28.

10 *Times*, 14 October, 1850. Wiseman's pastoral appeared in the 29 October issue.

11 On the almost frenetic debate in parliament *v. Hansard*, 4 Feb., 1851, cxiv, 97; Ward, Wilfrid, *Life and Times of Cardinal Wiseman*, London, 1897, I, pp. 540, 548–550.

12 Norman, E.R., *Anti-Catholicism in Victorian England*, London, 1968, p. 66.

13 MacSuibhne, *Paul Cullen*, II, p. 93; *cf.* Cullen, Paul, *Pastoral Letters and Other Writings*, ed. Moran, P.F., Dublin, 1882, I, p. 123.

14 Mathew, *Catholicism in England*, p. 205. *Cf.* Gilley, Sheridan, 'Newman, conservatism and orthodoxy', *Christianesimo nella storia*, 1991, XII, p. 620, 'even as a Cardinal Newman wore his Rome with a difference'.

15 Leslie, Shane, 'Manning and Newman', *Manning: Anglican and Catholic*, London, 1951, p. 80.

16 Ward, W., *W.G. Ward and the Catholic Revival*, London, 1893, p. 194.

17 *Ibid.*, p. 18.

18 Kenny, Terence, *Political Thought of John Henry Newman*, London, 1957, p. 158; Ker, Ian, *John Henry Newman: a Biography*, O.U.P., 1989, p. 657.

19 Costigan, 'Ecclesiological Dialectic', *op. cit.*, p. 141.

20 Hales, E.E.Y., *Pio Nono: Creator of the Modern Papacy*, N.Y., 1954, p. 329; *cf.* Ward, Wilfrid, *Aubrey de Vere: a Memoir*, London, 1904, p. 113.

21 Bowen, *Paul Cardinal Cullen*, p. 276; *cf.* Leslie, Shane, 'Irish Pages from the Postbags of Manning, Cullen and Gladstone', *Dublin Review*, October, 1919, p. 163.

22 Ker, Ian, *Achievement of John Henry Newman*, Notre Dame, 1990, pp. 127–128; *cf.*, Newman, *Apologia pro Vita Sua*, Oxford, 1967, pp. 237–238.

23 Newman, J.H., *Autobiographical Writings*, ed. Tristram, H., London, 1956, pp. 270–271.

24 *Hansard*, 22 April, 1873, ccxvi, 320; *cf.* MacCaffrey, James, *History of the Catholic Church in the Nineteenth Century*, Dublin, 1909, II, p. 76; Court of Queen's Bench (Ireland), *Report of the Action for Libel Brought by Rev. Robert O'Keeffe, PP Against Cardinal Cullen*, London, 1874.

25 Norman, *Anti-Catholicism in Victorian England*, p. 93.

26 Gladstone, W.E., *Vaticanism: an Answer to Replies and Reproofs*, London, 1875, p. 16. *Cf.* Birkenhead, Lord, *Rudyard Kipling*, London, 1980, p. 283 on the papacy as 'civilization's great enemy'.

27 Bowen, *Paul Cardinal Cullen*, pp. 207–208.

28 Gladstone, W.E. *Rome and the Newest Fashions in Religion*, London, 1875, preface, p. iv.

29 Chadwick, Owen, *Victorian Church*, London, 1966, I, p. 300.

30 Chadwick, *Newman*, p. 64. *Cf.* Holmes, Derek, *More Roman than Rome: English Catholicism in the Nineteenth Century*, London, 1978, pp. 201–251.

31 Coulson, J., Allchin, A.M., *Rediscovery of Newman*, London, 1967, p. xxix.

32 Doyle, James (J.K.L.), *Letters on the State of Ireland*, Dublin, 1825, p. 58.

33 Maxwell, Constantia, *Stranger in Ireland*, London, 1954, p. 294.

34 Connolly, *Priests and People*, p. 73; *cf.* Larkin, Emmet, 'Devotional Revolution in Ireland, 1850–1875', *American Historical Review*, 1972, LXXVII, pp. 633–634.

35 Larkin, Emmet, 'Church and State in Ireland in the Nineteenth Century', *Church History*, 1962, XXXI, pp. 304–5.

36 Whyte, J.H., 'Appointment of Catholic Bishops in Nineteenth Century Ireland', *Catholic Historical Review*, 1962, XLVIII, pp. 24–25.

37 Berington, Joseph, *Memoirs of Gregorio Panzani*, Birmingham, 1793, p. 464.

38 Larkin, 'Devotional Revolution', *op. cit.*, p. 627; *cf.* Anon, *Ireland: Observations on the People, the Land and the Laws in 1851 with Especial Reference to the Incumbered Estates Court*, Dublin, 1852, p. 3.

39 Nowlan, *Politics of Repeal*, pp. 224–226; Machin, G.I.T., 'Maynooth Grant, the Dissenters and Disestablishment', *English Historical Review*, 1957, XLIII, pp. 308–310; Cahill, Gilbert, 'Protestant Association and the Anti-Maynooth Agitation of 1845', *Catholic Historical Review*, 1967, LXXXII, p. 74.

40 MacSuibhne, *Cullen*, II, p. 29; on the debate *cf. Nation*, 14 June, 1845; *Morning Herald*, 19 August, 1845; *Hansard*, 1845, LXXX, pp. 377–800, LXXXI, pp. 1037–1043.

41 MacSuibhne, *Cullen*, I, pp. 309–310.

42 Larkin, Emmet, *Making of the Roman Catholic Church in Ireland*, Chapel Hill, 1980, p. 57. *Cf.* Carey, F.C., *Archbishop Murray of Dublin*, n.d., p. 16 *passim*; Connolly, *Priests and People*, p. 71.

43 Bowen, *Paul Cardinal Cullen*, p. 117.

44 *Freeman's Journal*, 23 August, 1850.

45 *Belfast News Letter*, 18 October, 1850; *ibid.*, 20 Dec., 1850.

46 O'Sullivan, Mortimer, *Plea for Inquiry into the Political Constitution of Romanism*, London, 1851, pp. 7–8.

47 Murphy, 'Priests and People in Modern Irish History', *op. cit.*, p. 250.

48 MacSuibhne, *Cullen*, II, p. 199.

49 *Ibid.*, III, p. 194; *cf.* Corish, P.J., 'Gallicanism at Maynooth: Archbishop Cullen and the Royal Visitation of 1853', *Studies in Irish History Presented to R.D. Edwards*, Dublin, 1979, pp. 176–189.

50 Bowen, *Paul Cardinal Cullen*, p. 257.

51 *Ibid.*, pp. 121, 125; *cf.* Perraud, A., *Ireland in 1862*, Dublin, 1963, p. 454.

52 Gwynn, Denis, *O'Connell, Davis and the College's Bill*, Cork, 1948, p. 21.

53 Norman, E.R., *Catholic Church and Ireland in the Age of Rebellion*, London, 1965, p. 10.

54 *Cullen Papers*, Dublin Archdiocesan Archives, 7 April, 1852; *Dublin Evening Mail*, 2 February, 1852.

55 Bowen, *Paul Cardinal Cullen*, p. 131.

56 MacSuibhne, *Cullen*, III, pp. 103–194. The hotel entry was in Hunter's Hotel, Rathnew, Co. Wicklow, 8 September, 1858.

57 Duffy, C.G., *My Life in Two Hemispheres*, London, 1898, II, p. 102, 83. *Cf. New York Times*, 25 October, 1855, 'a mere province or spiritual appendage of the Vatican'.

58 MacSuibhne, *Cullen*, I, p. 394. *Cf.* Whyte, John, 'Political Problems, 1850–1860', *History of Irish Catholicism*, 1967, V, p. 24; Lucas, E., *Life of Frederick Lucas*, London, 1886, II, pp. 122–123.

59 Corish, *Irish Catholic Experience*, p. 195.

60 Walpole, Spencer, *Life of Lord John Russell*, London, 1889, II, pp. 309–29.

61 MacSuibhne, *Cullen*, IV, p. 84.

62 Cullen, Paul, *Letter to the Clergy and Laity of the Diocese of Dublin on Some Recent Instances of Bigotry and Intolerance*, Dublin, 1859, p. 31.

63 Bowen, *Paul Cardinal Cullen*, p. 200.

64 *Ibid.*, p. 204.

65 *Belfast Newsletter*, 7 February, 1860.

66 Cullen, Paul, *Pastoral Letters and Other Writings of Cardinal Cullen*, Dublin, 1882, III, p. 98. *Cf.* Larkin, *Making of the Roman Catholic Church in Ireland*, pp. 485–486 for a discussion of Cullen as 'a species of ultramontane ogre'.

67 *Nation*, 28 January, 1854.

68 Lucas Papers, *National Library of Ireland Mss.*, 24 January, 1855.

69 Bowen, *Paul Cardinal Cullen*, pp. 151–152; Larkin, *Making of the Roman Catholic Church*, p. 124.

70 McRedmond, Louis, 'Warm Hearts and Cold Comfort: Newman in Ireland', *Doctrine and Life*, 1990, XL, p. 236 on Newman's view of Irish concerns. *Cf.* Gilley, S., *Newman and his Age*, London, 1990.

71 MacSuibhne, *Cullen*, IV, p. 45.

72 Bowen, *Paul Cardinal Cullen*, p. 267–268; *cf.* Comerford, R.V., 'Patriotism as pastime: the appeal of Fenianism in the 1860's', *IHS*, 1981, XXII, p. 249; Comerford, R.V., *Charles J. Kickham, a Study In Irish*

Nationalism and Literature, Dublin, 1979, pp. 68–9 on the parish priests' and Fenians' struggle to control parish life.

73 Bowen, *Paul Cardinal Cullen*, p. 270; Cullen, *Pastoral Letters*, II, pp. 388-404.

74 Corish, P.J., 'Cardinal Cullen and Archbishop MacHale', *Irish Ecclesiastical Record*, 1959, XCI, p. 405.

75 Parliamentary Papers, 'Primary Education (Ireland)', *Reports from Commissioners*, 1870, XXXVIII, Pt. 4, pp. 1222, 1247.

76 Armstrong, John, *Oath Taken by Roman Catholic Bishops to the Pope and the Oath Taken by Roman Catholic Members of the House of Commons*, London, 1865, p. 2.

77 Anon. *Letter to Cardinal Cullen: a Freemason's Answer to the Attack Made by His Eminence on the Masonic Order*, London, 1869, p. 6.

78 *Belfast Newsletter*, 6 August, 1866.

79 *Dublin Evening Post*, 26 June, 1866.

80 *Dublin Evening Mail*, 16 June, 1866.

81 Wiseman, N., 'State of Catholic Affairs', *Dublin Review*, 1857, XLII, p. 213.

82 *Cullen Papers*, Dublin Archdiocesan Archives, 29 November, 1865.

83 Bowen, *Paul Cardinal Cullen*, p. 197.

84 Walsh, Katherine, 'The First Vatican Council, the Papal State, and the Irish Hierarchy: Recent Research on the Pontificate of Pope Pius IX', *Studies*, Spring 1982, p. 58.

85 *Ibid.*, p. 70; *cf. Ireland and the Holy See, a Retrospect: the 1866 and 1883 Illegal and Seditious Movements in Ireland Contrasted with the Principles of the Catholic Church Shown in the Writings of Cardinal Cullen*, Rome, Propaganda Press, 1883, p. 4.

86 Neill, Stephen, *History of Christian Missions*, London, 1964, p. 209.

87 Magnus, Philip, *Gladstone*, London, 1963, pp. 41, 170, 198.

88 *Edinburgh Review*, 1835, LXI, p. 523.

89 Bell, P.M.H., *Disestablishment in Ireland and Wales*, London, 1969, p. 41.

90 Anon, *Ireland: Encumbered Estates Court, Should it be Continued*, Dublin, 1852, p. 59.

91 Urwick, William, *Life and Letters*, Dublin, 1870, p. 218.

92 Whately, Richard, *Thoughts on the Proposed Evangelical Alliance in a Letter to a Clergyman*, Dublin, 1846, p. 2.

93 Chadwick, Owen, *Victorian Church*, London, 1966, I, p. 440.

94 Urwick, *Life*, pp. 36–37. On the 'spiritual impoverishment' of the people argument *v.* Dallas, A.R.C., *Letter to the Roman Catholics of Kilkenny*, London, 1856 with reproduction of the controversial broadsides of the time.

95 *Edinburgh Review*, 1851, XCIII, p. 301.

96 *Irish Ecclesiastical Journal*, 1852, VIII, p. 144, 1 July, 1852.

97 Cullen, Paul, *Two Letters to Lord St. Leonards on the Management of the Patriotic Fund and on the Second Report of the Royal Commissioners*, Dublin, 1858, p. iv.

98 *Letter of His Grace the Most Rev. Dr. Cullen to the Lord Lieutenant Relative to the Appointment of Officials and Teachers in the Royal Hibernian Military School, Phoenix Park*, Dublin, 1866, pp. 2–4; *cf. Freeman's Journal*, 27 March, 1865.

99 Cullen, *Letters to Lord St. Leonards*, p. 5.

100 Lucas, Edward, *Life of Frederick Lucas*, London, 1882, II, p. 371.

101 Corish, *Irish Catholic Experience*, p. 201.

102 MacSuibhne, *Cullen*, II, pp. 152–153.

103 *Express*, Dublin, 10 September, 1869.

104 Bowen, Desmond, 'Alexander R.C. Dallas: the Warrior Saint', *View from the Pulpit: Victorian Ministers and Society*, Toronto, 1978, pp. 17–45.

105 Religious Tract Society, *Alexander R.C. Dallas: Soldier and Missionary*, London n.d., p. 21. For his ecclesiology *v*. Dallas, A.R.C., *Story of the Irish Church Missions*, London, 1875, p. x.

106 Bowen, *Protestant Crusade*, p. 223.

107 Bowen, *Paul Cardinal Cullen*, p. 170.

108 Irish Peer, *Letter to His Grace the Archbishop of Dublin on Proselytism*, Dublin, 1865, p. 10.

109 Colquhoun, J.C., *Reply to Charges Against the Irish Church Missions Made by the Rev. George Webster*, London, 1864, p. 6.

110 Plunket, Thomas, *Charge to the Clergy of Killala and Achonry at The Annual Visitation, 29 September, 1854*, Dublin, 1855, pp. 9–10.

111 Bowen, *Paul Cardinal Cullen*, p. 262.

112 Bowen, *Souperism*, pp. 163–173.

113 Plunket, W.C., *Short Visit to the Connemara Missions*, London, 1863, p. 66.

114 *Mission Church and Schools, Lower Jarvis Street, Dublin, Service at the Laying of the Foundation Stone, 12 October, 1864*, Dublin, 1864, pp. 17–19.

115 Whately, *Whately*, II, pp. 229–231; "cf. Whately, Richard, *Letter to a Clergyman of the Diocese of Dublin on Religious Controversy*, Dublin, 1850, p. 4.

116 O'Rourke, Canon, *Battle of the Faith in Ireland*, Dublin, 1887, p. 539.

117 MacSuibhne, *Cullen*, III, pp. 364–372.

118 Cahill, D.W., *Reply to the Challenge of the Protestant Clergy of Sligo to a Public Discussion*, Dublin, 1855, p. 13.

119 MacSuibhne, *Cullen*, II, p. 178.

120 Committee for the Guidance of Agents, *Principles and Arrangements of the Society for Irish Church Missions to the Roman Catholics*, London, Exeter Hall, 1951, p. 5.

121 *Christian Examiner*, November, 1868, IV, p. 117.

122 *Ibid.*, December, 1864, XII, p. 309.

123 *Ibid.*, February, 1865, XIV, p. 34.

124 *Ibid.*, November, 1867, LXIX, p. 276.

125 O'Faolain, Sean, *The Irish*, London, 1947, pp. 110–111.

126 Neely, *Kilcooley*, pp. 117–118.

127 Brooke, R.S., *Recollections of the Irish Church*, Dublin, 1878, Second Series, p. 5.

128 Gregg, R.S., *Faithful unto Death: Memorials of the Life of John Gregg, Bishop of Cork, Cloyne and Ross*, Dublin, 1879, p. 15; *cf.* Webster, C.A., *Diocese of Cork*, Cork, 1920, p. 354. Gregg spent the tithe war years serving in Portarlington and Kilsallaghan.

129 Mansergh, Nicholas, *Irish Question: 1840–1921*, Toronto, 1975, p. 21; *cf.* Seymour, M.H., *Experience of the Church of Ireland: Letter to Lord Derby*, London, 1868, p. 6 on the intimidation and murder of converts to Protestantism instigated by 'agitating priests'.

130 Norman, *Catholic Church and Ireland in the Age of Rebellion*, p. 105; *cf.* Johnston, William, *Ribbonism and its Remedy: a Letter to the Earl of Derby*, Dublin, 1858, p. 3.

131 Bowen, *Cullen*, p. 219; *Guardian*, 20 February, 1867, 12 February, 1868; *Freeman's Journal*, 18 February, 1867.

132 *Dublin Evening Mail*, 10 January, 1865.

133 Begley, John, *Diocese of Limerick from 1691 to the Present Time*, Dublin, 1938, pp. 543–548. On Cullen's relations with Butler *v.* Bowen, *Paul Cardinal Cullen*, pp. 222–223; MacSuibhne, *Cullen*, IV, pp. 141–146.

134 Maturin, William, *Unfaithfulness the True Source of the Church's Danger, Address to the Irish Church Society, 15 May, 1868*, Dublin, 1868, p. 19.

135 Godkin, *Religious History of Ireland*, p. 275.

136 Trench, R.C., *Charge at Triennial Visitation, September, 1868*, Dublin, 1868, pp. 35, 36, 51.

137 Lee, A.T., *Facts Respecting the Present State of the Church in Ireland*, London, 1868, pp. iii, 25,

138 *Ibid.*, p. iii.

139 Simms, G.O., 'James Henthorn Todd', *Hermathena*, 1969, CIX, p. 19.

140 Ewald, A.C., *Life of Sir Joseph Napier*, London, 1887, p. 359.

141 Lee, A.T., *Irish Church: Its Present Condition: Its Future Prospects*, London, 1866, p. 47; *cf.* Hardinge, W.H., *Narrative Proof of the Uninterrupted Consecrational Descent of the Bishops of the Church of Ireland*, Dublin, 1867, p. 6.

142 Brady, W.M., *Alleged Conversion of the Irish Bishops to the Reformed Religion at the Accession of Queen Elizabeth Disproved*, London, 1866, p. 4 *passim*.

143 *Census of Ireland for the Year 1861, Part IV, Report and Tables Relating to the Religious Professions*, Dublin, 1863, pp. 7, 34.

144 Clergymen of the Established Church in Ireland, *Essays on the Established Church*, London, 1866, p. 241.

145 Shearman, Hugh, *How the Church of Ireland was Disestablished*, Dublin, 1970, pp. 17–18.

146 Public Record Office, Northern Ireland, *Mss.* Dio 4/11/14/1, Marcus Beresford to C.K. Irwin, 19 March, 1868.

147 *Loc. cit.*, Dio 4/11/14/1.

148 Plunket, W.C., *Dangers of Silence at the Present Crisis*, Dublin, 1869, p. 13; *cf.* Plunket, W.C., *The Church and the Census in Ireland*, Dublin , 1965, p. 35.

149 Propaganda Fidei, *Scritture*, XVIII, 23 November, 1804, p. 262.

150 Livingstone, *Monaghan Story*, pp. 246–247; Bowen, *Paul Cardinal Cullen*, pp. 181–182.

151 *Authentic Report of Downpatrick Discussion 22–30 April, 1828*, Belfast, 1829, p. 281.

152 Macaulay, *Patrick Dorrian*, 1987, p. 90.

153 *Belfast Newsletter*, 10 November, 1865; *cf.* Hempton, David and Hill, Myrtle, *Evangelical Protestantism in Ulster Society, 1740–1890*, London, 1992, p. 126 on Dorrian as 'a stout-hearted churchman and a vigorous constitutional nationalist'.

154 *Correspondence between Rev. W. McIlwaine and Most Rev. Dr. Dorrian*, Belfast, 1865; *cf.* Macaulay, Ambrose, *Patrick Dorrian*, Dublin, 1987, p. 133.

155 Godkin, *Religious History of Ireland*, pp. 277, 281.

156 Cooke, Henry, *Lecture on Popery Delivered at Belfast, 3 December, 1850*, London, 1851, pp. 6, 26.

157 *Northern Whig*, 22 November, 1867.

158 Godkin, *Religious History*, p. 275.

159 *Report of the Fifth Annual Conference of the Dioceses of Down, Connor, and Dromore*, Belfast, 1863, p. 35.

160 Smith, C.F., *James Nicholson Richardson of Bessbrook*, London, 1925, p. 78.

161 Bardon, Jonathan, *Belfast*, 1982, p. 107.

162 Stewart, A.T.Q., *Narrow Ground*, London, 1977, p. 123. *Cf.* Dewar, M., Brown, J. and Long, S.F., *Orangeism: A New Historical Appreciation*, Belfast, 1967 on the Orange 'victory' at Dolly's Brae, Castlewellan, Co. Down in 1849 over Ribbonmen.

163 Coad, Roy, *History of the Brethren Movement*, Exeter, 1976, pp. 170–3.

164 Gibson, William, *Year of Grace*, Edinburgh, 1909, p. 215.

165 Stopford, E.A., *The Work and Counterwork of the Religious Revival in Belfast with an Explanation of the Physical Phenomenon*, Dublin, 1859, p. 6; *cf.* Carson, J.T., *God's River in Spate*, Belfast, 1959, pp. 4 *passim*.

166 Trench, W.S., *Realities of Irish Life*, London, 1870, p. 333.

167 Ford, Alan, 'Protestant Reformation in Ireland', Brady, C. and Gillespie, R., *Natives and Newcomers: the Making of Irish Colonial Society, 1534–1641*, Dublin, 1986, pp. 50–74.

168 Hempton and Hill, *Evangelical Protestantism in Ulster*, p. 160.

Chapter IX

1 Daniel-Rops, H., *Fight for God*, N.Y., 1965, I, p. 127. *Cf.* Wood, C.J., 'Ireland and Anglo-Papal Relations', 1880–1885', *IHS*, 1972, XVIII, pp. 29–61 on Rome's seeking of regular diplomatic relations with England, and the use of 'unofficial' envoys to end the isolation felt by the Holy See.

2 Paul, Herbert, *Letters of Lord Acton to Mary Gladstone*, London, letter of 15 March,1881.

3 Ward, W., *Life and Times of Cardinal Wiseman*, London, 1897, II, p. 49.

4 Bebbington, D.W., *Evangelical in Modern Britain*, London, 1989, p. 150.

5 *The Christian*, 11 March, 1886, p. 18. *Cf.* Cadoux, C.J., *Catholicism and Christianity*, London, 1928, p. 55.

6 Gwynn, D.R., *Hundred Years of Catholic Emancipation*, London, 1929, p. xviii.

7 Leslie, Shane, *Henry Edward Manning*, London, 1921, p. 469.

8 Sullivan, W.R., 'Key to the Social Problem', *Westminster Review*, Feb., 1894, p. 128.

9 Snead-Cox, J.G., *Life of Cardinal Vaughan*, London, 1910, I, pp. 407–418.

10 Leslie, S., ed., *Letters of Herbert Cardinal Vaughan to Lady Herbert of Lea*, London, 1942, p. 405.

11 *Times*, 17 August, 1892. *Cf*. Mathew, David, *Catholicism in England.*, London, 1937, p. 220 on Vaughan's 'ardent chivalrous devotion to the Holy See'.

12 Pawley, *Rome and Canterbury*, p. 241; Hastings, Adrian, *History of English Christianity, 1920–1985*, London, 1987, pp. 145, 147.

13 Holmes, Derek, *More Roman than Rome*, London, 1978, p. 218; Vaughan, *Letters to Lady Herbert of Lea*, p. 89.

14 Hemmer, H., *Fernand Portal: Apostle of Unity*, London, 1961, p. 40.

15 Pawley, *op. cit.*, p. 245.

16 Hastings, *History of English Christianity*, p. 147; *cf*. Williams, M., *The Venerable English College, Rome: a History, 1579–1979*, London, 1979, p. 161 *ff*.

17 Hastings, *op. cit.*, p. 273; *cf*., Oldmeadow, E., *Francis, Cardinal Bourne*, London, 1944.

18 Bebbington, *Evangelicalism in Modern Britain*, p. 150.

19 Harrison, J.F.C., *The Early Victorians, 1832–1851*, London, 1971, p. 133.

20 Brown, K.D., *Social History of the Nonconformist Ministry in England and Wales, 1800–1930*, Oxford, 1988, p. 5.

21 Sell, A.P.F., *Defending and Declaring the Faith: Scottish Examples, 1860–1900*, London, 1987, p. 14.

22 Masterman, C.F.G., *Condition of England*, London, 1960, p. 205.

23 Hilton, Boyd, *Age of Atonement*, Oxford, 1988, p. 377.

24 Gray, Robert, *Cardinal Manning*, London, 1985, p. 199, 223; *cf* McLelland, V.A., *Cardinal Manning, his Public Life and Influence*, London, 1962, p. 164.

25 *Daily Express*, 20 Jan., 6 Feb., 1868.

26 *Banner of Ulster*, 8 Aug., 1868.

27 *Irish Ecclesiastical Record*, June, 1868, p. 460.

28 O'Farrell, Patrick, *England and Ireland Since 1800*, Oxford, 1975, p. 151; *cf.* MacSuibhne, *Cullen*, III, pp. 186–188.

29 Bell, P.M.H., *Disestablishment in Ireland and Wales*, London, 1969, p. 83.

30 *Gazette*, 6 January, 1868.

31 *Saturday Review*, 14 March, 1868.

32 *Times*, 3 October, 1868.

33 *Freeman's Journal*, 2 November, 1868.

34 Comerford, R.V., *Fenians in Context: Irish Politics and Society, 1832–1882*, Dublin, 1985, pp. 183–184.

35 Barnes, Jane, *Irish Industrial Schools, 1868–1908*, Dublin, 1989, pp. 33–41; *cf.* Kelleher, D.V., *James Dominic Burke: Pioneer of Irish Education*, Dublin, 1988, pp. 164–187.

36 Bence-Jones, W., *Irish Church from the Point of View of One of Its Laymen*, London, 1868, pp. 4, 46.

37 Godkin, James, *Ireland and her Churches*, Dublin, 1867, p. 509.

38 Byrne, James, 'Influences Exerted in Ireland by the Irish Church Establishment', *Essays on the Irish Church,* London, 1868, p. 329. For the personal strengths of the church leaders *v.* Phillips, *Church of Ireland*, III, pp. 367 *ff.*; Alexander, E., *Primate Alexander: a Memoir*, London, 1913, pp.

164–194; Trench, M., *Richard Chenevix Trench: Letters and Memorials*, London, 1888, I, p. 54 *ff.*

[39] Patton, H.E., *Fifty Years of Disestablishment*, Dublin, 1922, p. 10.

[40] Lee, A.T., *Journal of the General Convention of the Church of Ireland*, Dublin, 1871, p. 14. *Cf.* Roberts, G.B., *History of the English Church Union, 1859–1894*, London, 1895, p. 404 *ff.* on the hysteria of some of the agitators.

[41] *Church Times*, 5 Feb., 1988, Anniversary Supplement p. iii.

[42] Clarke, R.L., *Disestablishment Revision of the Irish Book of Common Prayer*, Ph.D. Thesis, Trinity College, Dublin, 1989, p. 141.

[43] Griffin, J.N., *Call for the Revision of the Book of Common Prayer*, Dublin, 1871, p. 101.

[44] Salmon, George, *Thoughts on the Present Crisis of the Church of Ireland*, Dublin,1870, p. 11.

[45] Maberly, L.F.S., *Introduction and Spread of Ritualism in the Church of Ireland under Archbishop Trench from 1870–1879*, Dublin, 1879, pp. 15, 40' *cf. Dublin Evening Mail*, 19 April, 1870.

[46] *Daily Express*, 18, 19 May, 4, 22, 24 June, 1870.

[47] Trench, Maria, *Richard Chenevix Trench, Archbishop: Letters and Memorials*, London, 1888, II, p. 52.

[48] Clarke, *Disestablishment*, p. 284.

[49] Patton, *Fifty Years of Disestablishment*, p. 146.

[50] Milne, Kenneth, *St. Bartholomew's: History of a Dublin Parish*, Dublin, 1963, pp. 6–46.

[51] MacDonnell, J.S., *Life and Correspondence of William Connor Magee, Archbishop of York*, London, 1896, II, pp. 55–6.

[52] Sherlock, William, *Story of the Revision of the Irish Prayer Book*, Dublin, 1910, pp. 22–23.

53 *Irish Church Advocate*, December, 1870.

54 *Irish Ecclesiastical Gazette*, 31 October, 1890.

55 McDowell, R.B., *Church of Ireland. 1869–1969*, London, 1975, p. 80.

56 *Dublin Evening Mail*, 3 May, 1878.

57 *Irish Ecclesiastical Gazette*, 1 April, 1866.

58 *Daily Express*, 26 December, 1867,

59 *Freeman's Journal*, 24 January, 1900; *cf.* Milne, *St. Bartholomew's*, pp. 18 *ff.*

60 Lloyd, Roger, *Church of England, 1900–1965*, London, 1966, p. 133.

61 McDowell, *Church of Ireland*, p. 17.

62 How, F.D., *William Conyngham Plunket*, London, 1900, p. 230 *ff.*

63 *Freeman's Journal*, 27 September, 1894; *Church Times* , 12 October, 1894; Snead-Cox, *Cardinal Vaughan*, II, pp. 164–174.

64 McDowell, *Church of Ireland*, p. 95.

65 How, *Plunket*, p. 115.

66 Stanford, W.B. and McDowell, R.B., *Mahaffy: Biography of an Anglo-Irishman*, London, 1971, p. 235.

67 *Ibid.*, pp. 117–118.

68 Clark, S. and Donnelly, J.S., *Irish Peasants: Violence and Political Unrest, 1780–1914*, Dublin, 1983, p. 306: *cf.* Corfe, T.H., 'Troubles of Captain Boycott', *History Today*, 1964, XIV, pp. 758–764, 854–862.

69 Foster, *Modern Ireland*, p. 419.

70 O'Shea, James, *Priest, Politics and Society in Post-Famine Ireland*, Dublin, 1983, p. 247; *cf.* Clark and Donnelly, *Irish Peasants*, p. 329.

71 O'Shea, *Priest, Politics and Society*, p. 232.

72 O'Farrell, Patrick, *Ireland's English Question*, London, 1971, p. 164.

73 Hamilton, Ernest, *Forty Years On*, London, 1922, p. 213.

74 Massy, Dawson, *Secret History of Romanism*, London, 1876, pp. 547–548.

75 Rhodes, Anthony, 'Persico Papers', *Encounter*, February, 1980, p. 10 based on 'secret' documents of the pontificate of Leo XIII made available in 1980 (1887–1888, Rubrica 278, fascicoli 1–3).

76 *Ibid.*, p. 11. *Cf.* Larkin, Emmet, *The Roman Catholic Church and the Plan of Campaign, 1886–1888*, Cork, 1978, pp. 147–193, 'Roman Interlude' on the papal decision 'to take a new line with regard to Ireland'. On the influence of the Christian Brothers *v.* Coldrey, Barry, *Faith and Fatherland: the Christian Brothers and the Development of Irish Nationalism, 1838–1921*, Dublin, 1988.

77 Rhodes, 'Persico Papers', *op. cit.*, p. 12; *v.* Larkin, *Roman Catholic Church and the Plan of Campaign*, p. 194 on Walsh 'and the availability to him and his designates of the columns of the *Freeman's Journal'*. *Cf. Freeman's Journal*, 29 August, 1887.

78 Rhodes, *op. cit.*, pp. 16–17.

79 Curtis, L.P., *Coercion and Conciliation in Ireland, 1880–1892*, Princeton, 1963, p. 272.

80 Larkin, *Roman Catholic Church and the Plan of Campaign in Ireland*, p. 242.

81 Rhodes, *op. cit.*, p. 18.

82 Larkin, Emmet, *Roman Catholic Church and the Creation of the Modern Irish State, 1878–1886*, Philadelphia, 1975, p. 298.

83 Tierney, Mark, *Croke of Cashel: Life of Archbishop Thomas W. Croke*, Dublin, 1976, p. 222. *Cf.* Lyons, F.S.L., *Charles Stewart Parnell*, London, 1977, p. 256 on Walsh 'a firm nationalist, not in the flamboyant

manner of the archbishop of Cashel'. *V.* also *Tablet*, 5 and 12 December, 1886.

84 Tierney, *Croke of Cashel*, p. 142.

85 *Ibid.*, p. 145.

86 O'Shea, Patrick, *Politics and Society*, p. 95; *cf.* Tierney, *Croke of Cashel*, pp. 214–215; *United Ireland*, 2 April, 1887. Another politically active Matthew Ryan was curate of Tipperary 1861–1865,

87 *Tipperary Nationalist*, 1 Jan., 1887; Tierney, *Croke of Cashel*, p. 206.

88 Propaganda Fidei, *Scritture, Irlanda*, XLII, ff. 735–744.

89 Tierney, *Croke of Cashel*, p. 224.

90 Propaganda Fidei, *Scritture, Irlanda*, XLIII, ff. 551–2.

91 Begley, J., *Diocese of Limerick from 1691 to the Present Time*, Dublin, 1938, p. 572; *United Ireland*, 26 October, 1889.

92 *Freeman's Journal*, 8 May, 1888.

93 Bowen, *Cardinal Cullen*, p. 7, 3 January, 1871.

94 O'Shea, *Priest, Politics and Society*, p. 188.

95 Gregory, William, *Autobiography*, London, 1894, p. 60; *cf.* Young, A.B.R., *Reminiscences of an Irish Priest, 1845–1920*, Dublin, n.d., p. 101.

96 Leslie, Shane, *Henry Edward Manning: his Life and Labours*, London, 1921, p. 206.

97 Thornley, David, *Isaac Butt and Home Rule*, London, 1964, p. 145; *cf.* Larkin, E., *Roman Catholic Church and the Home Rule Movement in Ireland, 1870–1874*, Chapel Hill, 1990, pp. xxviii–xix on Cullen's dislike of Butt and his politics.

98 *Freeman's Journal*, 5, 6 February, 1874.

99 Norman, *Catholic Church and Ireland in the Age of Rebellion, 1859–1873*, p. 458.

100 *Report on the Action for Libel brought by the Rev. Robert O'Keeffe, P.P. against His Eminence Cardinal Cullen*, London, 1874, pp. 302–315.

101 Foster, R.F., *Charles Stewart Parnell: the Man and his Family*, Sussex, 1979, p. 20; *cf.* O'Connor, T.P., *Life of C.S. Parnell*, London, 1891, pp. 170–171 on Parnell's 1886 confession: 'I believe in the religion I was born in'.

102 *Ibid.*, p. 256.

103 Healey, T.M., *Letters and Leaders of My Day*, London, 1929, I, p. 87.

104 O'Farrell, *Ireland's English Question*, p. 189.

105 Lyons, F.S.L., *Charles Stewart Parnell*, London, 1977, p. 349.

106 O'Farrell, *op. cit.*, p. 176. *Cf.* Lyons, *Parnell*, p. 350 on his failure to appreciate 'the fears of Irish Protestantism in general, and of Ulster Protestantism in particular'. *V. Times*, 28 June, 1886 on Orangemen as a 'miserable gang who trade upon the name of religion'.

107 Foster, *Modern Ireland*, p. 415.

108 *Ibid.*, p. 418.

109 Larkin, *Roman Catholic Church and the Creation of the Modern Irish State, 1878–1886*, p. 391.

110 *Freeman's Journal*, 8 May, 1888.

111 Larkin, Emmet, *Roman Catholic Church in Ireland and the Fall of Parnell, 1888–1891*, Chapel Hill, 1979, pp. 81–85.

112 Lyons, F.S.L., *John Dillon*, London, 1968, p. 97.

113 Buckland, Patrick, *Irish Unionism*, Dublin, 1972, I, p. 6.

114 *Times*, 9 June, 1886. *Cf.* Lyons, *Dillon*, p. 189 on Lecky, with Edward Carson, the other unionist M.P. for Dublin University supporting Dillon

regarding the proposed Catholic university in 1898. *V.* also Stewart, A.T.O., *Narrow Ground*, London, 1977, p. 166 on the 'closed ranks' tactics of the Protestants. For the small minority of Protestant Home Rulers *v.* Loughlin, J., 'Irish Protestant Home Rule Association and Nationalist Politics', *I.H.S.*, 1985, XXIV, pp. 341–360.

115 Livingstone, Peadar, *Monaghan Story*, Enniskillen, 1980, pp. 345–352.

116 *Nation*, 14 March, 14 November, 1885; Buckland, Patrick, *Ulster Unionism*, Dublin, 1973, p. xxxii; *cf.* Lyons, *Parnell*, p. 354.

117 Bew, Paul, *C.S. Parnell*, Dublin, 1980, pp. 142–143.

118 Lyons, *Dillon*, p. 113. *Cf.* Larkin, Emmet, 'Roman Catholic Hierarchy and the Fall of Parnell'. *Victorian Studies*, 1961, IV, p. 332.

119 Larkin, E., *Roman Catholic Church and the Creation of the Modern Irish State*, p. 71.

120 O'Brien, William, *Recollections*, London, 1905, pp. 222–223.

121 Glaser, J.F., 'Parnell's Fall and the Nonconformist Conscience', *I.H.S.*, 1960, XII, p. 121. *Cf. Methodist Times*, 20 November, 1890.

122 Lyons, F.S.L., *Fall of Parnell, 1890–1891*, London, 1962, p. 311.

123 Larkin, Emmet, 'The Roman Catholic Hierarchy and the Fall of Parnell', *Victorian Studies*, 1961, IV, p. 334.

124 Bence-Jones, W., *Life's Work in Ireland of a Landlord who Tried to Do his Duty*, London, 1880, p. 64. *Cf.* O'Farrell, *Ireland's English Question*, p. 200 on the view of some bishops that Parnell's scandal was 'providential', a deliverance from 'a bold unscrupulous despot'.

125 Tierney, *Croke of Cashel*, p. 220.

126 Larkin, E., *The Roman Catholic Church and the Plan of Campaign*, p. 165.

127 Irish College, Rome, *Kirby Papers*, Croke to Kirby, 15 July, 1885. *Cf.* Larkin, *Roman Catholic Church and the Plan of Campaign*, pp. 214–217 on where Walsh and Croke were 'not fully in accord' over the 'clerical-nationalist' alliance and Roman authority.

128 Leslie, *Henry Edward Manning*, p. 441.

129 *Ibid.*, p. 436; *cf.* Walsh, P.J., *William J. Walsh, archbishop of Dublin*, Dublin, 1928, p. 409.

130 Larkin, Emmet, 'Mounting the Counter-Attack: The Roman Catholic Hierarchy and the Destruction of Parnellism'. *Review of Politics*, 1963, XXV, p. 182.

131 Lyons, *Charles Stewart Parnell*, p. 471.

132 Larkin, *Roman Catholic Church in Ireland and the Fall of Parnell*, p. 201.

133 Larkin, 'Mounting the Counter-Attack', *op. cit.*, p. 157.

134 *Times*, 9 December, 1890.

135 Lyons, *Fall of Parnell*, p. 173; *cf.* Woods, C.J., 'General Election of 1892: the Catholic Clergy and the Defeat of the Parnellites', *Ireland Under the Union: Varieties of Tension*, Oxford, 1980, pp. 300–301.

136 Leslie, *Manning*, p. 435.

137 Tierney, *Croke*, p. 243.

138 O'Shea, *Priest, Politics and Society*, p. 220.

139 Tierney, M., *Murroe and Boher*, Dublin, 1966, p. 172; *cf.*, *Limerick Reporter*, 17 Nov., 1891.

140 *Irish Catholic*, 9 July, 1892.

141 *Minutes of the General Assembly*, 1886, p. 104.

142 Buckland, *Ulster Unionism*, p. xxxii. For Protestant treatment of the Ulster Catholics who 'threatened' them *v.* Boyle, John, *Irish Labour Movement in the Nineteenth Century*, Washington, 1988, p. 293 *ff.*

143 Macaulay, *Patrick Dorrian*, p. 33.

144 *Cf.* Mansergh, Nicholas, *Irish Question, 1840–1921*, Toronto, 1975, p. 207–208; Maxwell, *Stranger in Ireland*, pp. 288–289 on the anti-Catholic, anti-nationalist Protestant ethos of Ulster in 1842 recorded by the German, J.G. Kohl. *Cf.* Hempton, David and Hill, Myrtle, *Evangelical Protestantism in Ulster Society, 1740–1890*, London, 1992, ch. 9, 'Home Rule and the Protestant Mind, 1860–90', pp. 160–187 for Ulster's anti-Catholic heritage.

145 *Northern Whig*, 29 April, 1825; *Belfast Newsletter*, 29 April, 1825,

146 *Northern Whig*, 3 November, 1834,

147 Porter, J.L., *Henry Cooke*, Belfast, 1875, pp. 286–287; *cf. Northern Whig*, 22 August, 1837. *Cf.* Hempton and Hill, *Evangelical Protestantism*, p. 186: 'Irish Ultramontanist Catholicism provided them with a... comprehensible enemy'.

148 Wright, Frank, 'Protestant Ideology and Politics in Ulster', *European Journal of Sociology*, 1973, XIV, p. 324.

149 Buckland, *Ulster Unionism*, p. xxxv.

150 Bew. *Parnell*, p. 139.

151 Livingstone, Peadar, *Monaghan Story*, Enniskillen, 1980, p. 342.

152 Macknight, Thomas, *Ulster As It Is: Twenty Eight Years Experience as an Irish Editor*, London, 1896, II, p. 44.

153 Buckland, *Ulster Unionism*, p. xxxiii. *Cf. Irish Ecclesiastical Gazette*, 27 March, 1886 on resistance to Ultramontane church 'worked by the Jesuits' calling for Protestant defence 'with swords in our hands': *Christian Advocate*. 8 January, 1886, on threat of 'Protestant annihilation'.

154 *Cf.* Conaty, N., *Catholic Church Proved to be the Church of Christ with an Anatomy of Protestantism*, Dublin, 1852.

155 Walker, *Ulster Politics*, p. 185.

156 Lucas, Reginald, *Colonel Saunderson, M.P.*, London, 1908, p. 199.

157 Lyons, F.S.L., *Ireland Since the Famine*, London, 1971, p. 291.

158 Macknight, *Ulster As It Is*, II, p. 331.

159 Walker, *Ulster Politics*, p. 60. Johnston was Church of Ireland.

160 *Belfast Newsletter*, 5 February, 1874.

161 Savage, D.C., 'Origins of the Ulster Unionist Party', *I.H.S.*, 1961, XII, p. 203. For Johnston's theological position *v.* his novel, *Nightshade*, denouncing both Jesuits and liberal Protestants.

162 O'Farrell, *Ireland's English Question*, pp. 241–2, from *Irish Catholic*, January, 1889.

163 Buckland, Patrick, *History of Northern Ireland*, Dublin 1981, p. 9.

164 Baker, S.E., 'Orange and Green: Belfast 1832–1912', *Victorian Cities Images and Realities*, London, 1973, I, p. 803.

165 *Cf.* Nowlan, K.B., *Politics of Repeal*, Dublin, 1965, p. 228 on the Orange 'victory' at Dolly's Brae, county Down in 1849 referred to earlier. *V. Freeman's Journal*, 16 July, 1849.

166 *Belfast Newsletter*, 5 July, 1865.

167 Bardon, Jonathan, *Belfast*, Belfast, 1982, pp. 144–145. *Cf. Belfast Newsletter*, 21 August, 1872.

168 Macknight, *Ulster As It Is*, pp. 149–151.

169 Buckland, *Ulster Unionism*, pp. 39–41. *Cf.* Bardon, *op. cit.*, p. 150 on the 1886 riots as 'the worst episode of violence in Ireland in the nineteenth century'.

170 Connell, K.H., *Irish Peasant Society*, Oxford, 1968, pp. 145–146.

171 Gwynn, Stephen, *Holiday in Connemara*, Dublin, 1909, p. 285.

172 Plunkett, Horace, *Ireland in the New Century*, Dublin, 1905, p. 330.

173 *The Witness*, 24 June, 1892.

174 Armour, W.S., *Armour of Ballymoney*, London, 1934, pp. 96–117; *cf.* McMinn, R.B., *Against the Tide: J.B. Armour*, Belfast, 1989, *v. Freeman's Journal*, 6, 24, 26 April, 1893.

175 Holmes, *Irish Presbyterian Heritage*, p. 134.

176 *Authorized Report of the Church of Ireland Conference held at Dublin on October 3, 4, 5, 1899*, Dublin, 1899, p., 49.

177 Walker, *Ulster Politics*, p. 27.

178 *Weekly Examiner*, 6 March, 1886; *cf. Presbyterian Churchman*, 1886, p. 95.

179 *Catholic Bulletin*, March, 1912, quoted O'Farrell, *Ireland's English Question*, p. 245. *Cf. ibid.* p. 250 on the government's belief that Ulster loyalty was a fraud: 'masking their bigoted determination not to be ruled by a Catholic parliament, cloaking that old hatred, suspicion and contempt of the Church of Rome'.

Chapter X

1 O'Farrell, *Ireland's English Question*, p. 241.

2 Daniel-Rops, H., *Fight for God, 1870–1939*, N.Y., 1967, I, p. 211.

3 Falconi, Carlo, *Popes in the Twentieth Century*, London, 1967, p. 65.

4 Gaselee, Stephen, 'British Diplomatic Relations with the Holy See', *Dublin Review*, 1939, CCIV, pp. 1–9.

5 Pawley, *Rome and Canterbury*, p. 276. *Cf.* Daniel-Rops, *Fight for God*, I, pp. 87–95.

6 Snead-Cox, *Life of Cardinal Vaughan*, I, p. 470.

7 Holmes, *More Roman than Rome*, p. 212.

8 Hastings, A., *History of English Christianity, 1920–1985*, London, 1987, p. 144.

9 *Ibid.*, pp. 148–149.

[10] de Mendieta, E.A., *Rome and Canterbury*, London, 1962, p. 242.

[11] Sykes, Norman, *Man as Churchman*, Cambridge, 1960, p. 67.

[12] Leonard, Ellen, *George Tyrell and the Catholic Tradition*, London, 1982, p. 138.

[13] Hastings, *English Christianity*, p. 152. *Cf. Times*, 2 November, 1907.

[14] Reynolds, E.E., *Roman Catholic Church in England and Wales*, Wheathampstead, 1973, p. 349.

[15] O'Farrell, Patrick, *England and Ireland Since 1800*, Oxford, 1975, pp. 137-138.

[16] Supple, Jennifer, 'Ultramontanism in Yorkshire, 1850–1900', *Religion in Victorian Britain*, Open University, 1988, IV, p. 139.

[17] *Leeds Mercury*, 11 May, 1895.

[18] Hastings, *English Christianity*, p. 131.

[19] Neal, Frank, *Sectarian Violence: the Liverpool Experience, 1819–1914*, Manchester, 1988, p. 244.

[20] Anon. *Popery in Power: an Address to the People*, London, 1874, p. 15.

[21] Walsh, James, *Political Aspects of Popery*, London, 1905, p. 66.

[22] Robertson, Alexander, *Roman Catholic Church in Italy*, 7th edition, London, 1915, p. vii.; *cf.* Robertson, Alexander, *Papal Conquest, Italy's Warning: Wake up John Bull*, London, 1918.

[23] An Irishman, *Intolerance in Ireland: Fact not Fiction*, London, 1913, p. 154.

[24] *Hansard*, 7 Feb., 1911, XXI, col. 169.

[25] Henson, Hensley, *Letters*, ed. E.F. Braley, London, 1950, p. 26.

[26] O'Farrell, *Ireland's English Question*, p. 200.

27 *Ibid.*, p. 201.

28 Canning, B.J., *Bishops of Ireland, 1870–1987*, Ballyshannon, 1987, p. 39.

29 Curtis, *Coercion and Conciliation in Ireland, 1880–1892*, p. 276.

30 Walsh, P.J., *William J. Walsh, Archbishop of Dublin*, Dublin, 1928, p. 365.

31 *Irish Catholic Directory*, 1902, p. 428.

32 Birrell, A., *Things Past Redress*, London, 1937, p. 203.

33 Moody, T.W., 'Irish University Question of the Nineteenth Century', *History*, 1958, xliii, pp. 90–109; *cf.* Maxwell, *Trinity College*, p. 189.

34 Miller, David, *Church, State and Nation in Ireland, 1898–1921*, Dublin, 1973, p. 41; *cf. The Leader*, I, 15 Sept., 1900.

35 *The Leader*, 27 July, 1901. *Cf.* Brown, Terence, *Ireland: a Social and Cultural History, 1922–1979*, London, 1981, p. 56 on Moran's 1905 *Philosophy of Irish Ireland*; Foster, *Modern Ireland*, p. 454 on Moran's 'the Irish nation is *de facto* a Catholic nation'.

36 Miller, *op. cit.*, p. 43.

37 O'Sullivan, T.F., *Story of the G.A.A.*, Dublin, 1916, pp. 9–10.

38 Hyde, Douglas, 'The Necessity for De-Anglicizing Ireland', *The Revival of Irish Literature*, London, 1894, p. 119.

39 Bredin, A.E.C., *History of the Irish Soldier*, Belfast, 1987, p. 371.

40 *Cf.* the many regimental histories, Jourdain, H.F.N., *Connaught Rangers*, London, 1926, II, pp. 368–373; Gretton, G.le M., *Campaigns and History of the Royal Irish Regiment*, London, 1911, pp. 309–319 etc.

41 Verney, Peter, *The Micks: Story of the Irish Guards*, London, 1970, p. 12.

42 Macardle, Dorothy, *Irish Republic*, London, 1968, pp. 65, 95.

43 *Irish Catholic*, 22 May, 1909.

44 Miller, *op. cit.*, p. 284.

45 McCarthy, M.J.F., *Priests and People in Ireland*, Dublin, 1903, p. vi.

46 *Ibid.*, p. 266. *Cf. ibid.*, p. xv for the 'encomium' of this work.

47 McCarthy, M.J.F., *Rome in Ireland*, London, 1904, pp. 64–92.

48 *Cf.* Larkin, Emmet, 'Mounting the Counter-Attack: the Roman Catholic Hierarchy and the Destruction of Parnellism', *Review of Politics*, 1963, XXV, pp. 157–182; 'Launching the Counter-Attack: Part II of the Roman Catholic Hierarchy and the Destruction of Parnellism', *Review of Politics*, 1966, XXVIII, pp. 359–383.

49 O'Farrell, *Ireland's English Question*, p. 256; *cf.* Lyons, *Fall of Parnell*, p. 287.

50 Lyons, *John Dillon*, p. 152.

51 *Annual Conference of the Church of Ireland held in Belfast, 18, 19, 20 October, 1893*, Belfast, 1893, pp. 15–17.

52 Killen, W.D., *Reminiscences of a Long Life*, London, 1902, pp. 110, 235; *cf.* Godkin, James, *Religious History of Ireland*, London, 1873, ch. XIX, 'Progress of Romanism', pp. 270–282 on those who shared Killen's anxieties about Roman Catholic authority.

53 Irwin, C.H., *History of Presbyterianism in Dublin and the South and West of Ireland*, London, 1890, p. 159.

54 *Journal of the General Synod, 1893*, Dublin, 1893, pp. xiv–lii.

55 *Mss.* 'Conference of Friends upon the Home Rule Question', 21 April, 1893, Friends Library, London, Box 382 (23) 66.

56 Neely, *Kilcooley*, p. 128.

57 Lysaght, Edward, *Sir Horace Plunkett*, Dublin, 1916, p. 12.

58 Plunkett, Horace, *Ireland in the New Century*, London, 1904, pp. 80–82.

59 Lyons, *Ireland Since the Famine*, p. 211.

60 Birmingham, George, *Irishmen All,* London, 1913, pp. 193–207.

61 McDowell, *Church of Ireland, 1869–1969,* p. 101.

62 *Church of Ireland Gazette,* 4 March, 1904.

63 Hyman, Louis, *Jews of Ireland,* Shannon, 1972, pp. 212–217.

64 Fletcher, Dudley, *Rome and Marriage: the Recent Papal Decree Ne Temere,* Dublin, 1911, p. 9.

65 Patton, *Fifty Years of Disestablishment,* p. 264.

66 Cole, L.R., *History of Methodism in Ireland,* Belfast, 1960, IV, p. 82.

67 McDowell, *Church of Ireland,* p. 103.

68 Stanford and McDowell, *Mahaffy,* p. 219. *Cf.* Miller, *Church, State and Nation,* p. 290 on the hierarchy's expectation that Home Rule would 'make it possible to move toward greater denominationalism', an extension of ecclesiastical authority in education.

69 *Fermanagh Times,* 29 February, 1912; *Belfast Newsletter,* 6 January, 1911.

70 *The Witness,* 26 January, 1912.

71 *Belfast Newsletter,* 8 July, 1912.

72 *Ibid.,* 20 January, 1912; *cf. ibid.,* 13 July, 1912.

73 Blake, R., *Unknown Prime Minister: Life of Andrew Bonar Law,* London, 1955, p. 22. *Cf.* D'Arcy, C.F., *Adventures of a Bishop,* London, 1934, p. 188: 'a truly religious conviction animated the opposition to Home Rule' hence the solemn religious service before signing the Covenant.

74 D'Arcy, *Adventures of a Bishop,* pp. 191–192.

75 *The Witness,* 4 October, 1912.

76 *Times,* 6 May, 1913.

77 Armour, W.S., *Armour of Ballymoney,* London, 1934, pp. 280–283.

78 McDowell, R.B., *Alice Stopford Green*, Dublin, 1967, pp. 75–96.

79 Holmes, *Irish Presbyterian Heritage*, p. 137; *cf.* Orr, Philip, *Road to the Somme*, Belfast, 1987, pp. 4–5.

80 *Irish Catholic*, 2 August, 1913.

81 Hyde, Montgomery, *Carson*, London, 1953, p. 343.

82 Lyons, F.S.L., *Culture and Anarchy in Ireland, 1890–1923*, Oxford, 1979, p. 86; Pearse, P.H., *Political Writings and Speeches*, Dublin, 1922, pp. 215–218; *cf.* Gilley, Sheridan, 'The Catholic Church and Revolution' in Boyce, D.G., ed., *Revolution in Ireland, 1879–1923*, Dublin, 1988, pp. 157–173.

83 O'Farrell, *Ireland's English Question*, pp. 267–268. *Cf* . Foster, *Modern Ireland*, p. 483 on Pearse's 'theology of insurrection'.

84 Stanford and McDowell, *Mahaffy*, p. 223.

85 Inge, W.R., *Diary of a Dean*, London, 1949, p. 29: Temple, William, *Challenge to the Church*, London, 1917, pp. 4–6.

86 *Irish Independent*, 29 September, 1914. *Cf. Irish Catholic* , 3 October, 1914 for Logue's account of what his comments had been. The 10th and 16th divisions were considered to be 'Irish Catholic' in composition.

87 Gwynn, D., *Life of John Redmond*, London, 1932, p. 449.

88 Miller, *Church, State and Nation*, p. 312.

89 Lee, J.J., *Ireland, 1912–1985*, Cambridge, 1990, p. 23. *Cf.* Callan, Patrick, 'Recruiting for the British Army in Ireland during the First World War', *Irish Sword*, 1987, XVII, p. 53, on: 'the national quota of fifty-five catholic recruits during the war to every forty-five protestants'.

90 O'Kennedy, Richard, 'Most Rev. E.T. O'Dwyer', *Irish Monthly*, 1918, XLVI, pp. 29–30.

91 Macardle, *Irish Republic*, p. 138.

92 Miller, *op. cit.*, p. 313.

93 Code, Pauline, 'Recruiting and Responses to the War in Wexford', *Ireland and the First World War*, ed. Fitzpatrick, D., Dublin, 1986, p. 25.

94 Tierney, M., Bowen, P. and Fitzpatrick, D., 'Recruiting Posters', *ibid.*, p. 55.

95 Leonard, Jane, 'Lest We Forget', *ibid.*, pp. 60–67.

96 Foster, *Modern Ireland*, p. 472.

97 Smyth, John, *In This Sign Conquer*, London, 1968, p. 158.

98 Purcell, William, *Woodbine Willie*, London, 1962, p. 29.

99 O'Rahilly, Alfred, *Father William Doyle, S.J.*, London, 1930, p. 556; *cf. Glasgow Weekly News*, 1 Sept., 1917; Gibbs, Philip, *From Bapaume to Passchendaele*, London, 1917, p. 254.

100 Leonard, Jane, 'Catholic Chaplaincy', *Ireland and the First World War*, p. 5.

101 Lee, *op. cit.*, p. 26; *cf.* Orr, *Road to the Somme*, p. 45 on some unionists and the Kaiser as 'a latter-day William of Orange'.

102 McDowell, *Church of Ireland*, p. 108; *cf.* Murray, R.H., *Archbishop Bernard*, London, 1911, p. 276.

103 D'Arcy, *Adventures of a Bishop*, p. 200. D'Arcy almost lost a son through wounds at the first battle of Ypres.

104 Holmes, *Presbyterian Heritage*, p. 143.

105 Ryan, Desmond, *The Rising*, Dublin, 1957, p. 68.

106 Walsh, *Walsh*, pp. 592–593.

107 *Irish Weekly Independent*, 29 April–13 May; *cf.* Miller, *Church, State and Nation*, p. 323.

108 Falls, Cyril, 'Maxwell, 1916 and Britain at War', *Leaders and Men of the Easter Rising: Dublin, 1916*, London, 1967, pp. 203–213.

109 Coogan, T.P., *Ireland Since the Rising*, London, 1966, p. 20.

110 Miller, *Church, State and Nation*, pp. 341–342, on their catholicism.

111 *Daily Mail*, 22 May, 1917. *Cf. Daily Telegraph*, 17 May, 1917.

112 Foster, *Modern Ireland*, p. 479.

113 Harris, Henry, *Irish Regiments in the First World War*, Cork, 1968, p. 83.

114 MacDonagh, Michael, *Irish on the Somme*, London, 1917, p. 27.

115 Foster, *Modern Ireland*, p. 486.

116 *Hansard*, 5 Jan., 1916, LXXVII, 1043.

117 *Irish Independent*, 5 October, 1918.

118 *Ibid.*, 31 October, 1918.

119 Middlebrook, Martin, *Kaiser's Battle: 21 March, 1918*, pp. 325–327.

120 Boyce, David G., 'British Opinion, Ireland and the War, 1916–1918', *Historical Journal*, 1974, XVII, p. 507.

121 Earl of Longford and O'Neill, T.P., *Eamon de Valera*, Boston, 1971, p. 72.

122 Marlowe, N., 'Irish Bishops, the War and Home Rule', *Contemporary Review*, 1918, CXIV, p. 404. *Cf.* Callan, Patrick, 'Recruitment for the British Army in Ireland during the First World War', *Irish Sword*, 1987, XVII, pp. 42–56 for enlistment figures.

123 Longford and O'Neill, *Eamon de Valera*, p. 73.

124 Buckland, *Irish Unionism, I*, p. 166.

125 Travers, Pauric, 'The Priest in Politics: the Case of Conscription', *Irish Culture and Nationalism: 1750–1950*, Canberra, 1985, pp. 167–168; *cf. Irish Independent*, 25 April, 1918.

126 O'Fiaich, Tomas, 'Irish Bishops and Conscription', *Capuchin Annual*, Dublin, 1968, p. 363.

127 Augusteijn, Joost, 'Ideas and the Volunteers in Mayo and Tipperary', *Revolution?: Ireland 1917–1923*, ed. Fitzpatrick, D., Dublin, 1990, p. 41;

Travers, *op. cit.*, pp. 173–7.

128 Murray, *Archbishop Bernard*, pp. 323–324.

129 Buckland, *Irish Unionism, I*, p. 168.

130 Miller, *Church, State and Nation*, p. 419.

131 Walsh, J.R., 'Bishops of Derry', *Derry Journal*, 22 March, 1974.

132 Colvin, Ian, *Life of Lord Carson*, London, 1936, III, p. 313. *Cf.* Marjoribanks, Edward, *Life of Lord Carson*, London, 1932, I, pp. 6, 9, 69 on Carson's Protestantism. An Orangeman from the age of 19 he encountered priestly intimidation in law courts during the Plan of Campaign. His early intention had been to become a clergyman.

133 Hyde, *Carson*, p. 444. *Cf.* Marjoribanks, *op. cit.*, p. 131 for Carson's experience as a crown prosecutor; 'Coercion Carson' in a murder trial involving a priest, the famous 'Gweedore case'.

Chapter XI

1 Daniel-Rops, *Fight for God*, II, p. 26.

2 *Ibid.*, II, p. 38. *Cf.* Sullivan, Francis A., *Magisterium: Teaching Authority in the Catholic Church*, N.Y., 1983, p. 157 on the teaching of Pius XI in *Mortalium Animos* of 1928 'binding on the Catholic rulers of Catholic nations to suppress Protestant evangelism'. V. Bell, G.K.A., *Documents on Christian Unity, 2nd Series, 1924–1929*, Oxford, 1930, pp. 51–64, for the 'missionary' ethos of Rome during the inter-war years.

3 Daniel–Rops, *op. cit.*, II, p. 244. *Cf.* Granfield, Patrick, *Limits of the Papacy*, N.Y., 1987, p. 46 on papal authority and the canon law: 'no human authority can legitimately impede papal action; any attempt to do so would be a crime… religious submission of intellect and will is due the teaching on faith and morals'. *V.* also Vischer, L., 'Holy See, the Vatican State and the Church's Common Witness: a Neglected Ecumenical Problem', *Journal of Ecumenical Studies*, 1974, II, 617–636

4 Thomas, Hugh, *The Spanish Civil War*, London, 1977, p. 695.

5 Pawley, *Rome and Canterbury*, p. 301.

6 Smyth, *G.F. Garbett: Archbishop of York*, London, 1959, p. 375.

7 Neal, Frank, *Sectarian Violence: the Liverpool Experience, 1819–1914*, Manchester, 1988, p. 245.

8 *Ibid.*, p. 246.

9 Bowman, John, *De Valera and the Ulster Question, 1917–1973*, Oxford, 1989, 'The Play of English Interest, 1932–1937', pp. 89–109. *V.* p. 112 on British reluctance to reconsider issues, and p. 121 on the Irish Situation Committee not meeting at all in 1935,

10 *Freeman's Journal*, 5 May, 1916.

11 Phillips, W.A., *Revolution in Ireland, 1906–1923*, London, 1923, p. 105.

12 White, Jack, *Minority Report: Protestant Community in the Republic of Ireland*, Dublin, 1975, p. 78.

13 *Irish Times*, 8 May, 1917; Miller, *Church, State and Nation*, p. 363.

14 *Irish Catholic*, 13 October, 10 November, 1917.

15 MacDonagh, Oliver, *States of Mind: a Study of Anglo-Irish Conflict 1780–1983*, London, 1983, p. 102.

16 Miller, *Church, State and Nation*, p. 470.

17 O'Farrell, *Ireland's English Question*, p. 290.

18 Younger, Carlton, *Ireland's Civil War*, London, 1968, p. 117.

19 Keogh, *Vatican, Bishops and Irish Politics*, pp. 25, 29, 37.

20 *Freeman's Journal*, 29 November, 1920.

21 Savory, D., *History of Home Rule, 1886–1949*, London, 1956, p. 81.

22 Bence-Jones, Mark, *Twilight of the Ascendancy*, London, 1987, p. 214.

23 Kee, *Green Flag*, p. 744.

24 Bowen, Kurt, *Protestants in a Catholic State*, Dublin, 1983, p. 22; *cf. Irish Times*, 30 October, 1922, 'easy marks for lawlessness and greed'. Fanning, Ronan, *Independent Ireland*, Dublin, 1983, p. 41 on the I.R.A.'s justification of attack on 'imperialist residences'. *V.* also Bence-Jones, *op. cit.*, pp. 195–196, and Buckland, *Irish Unionism*, I, pp. 210–215. On the emigration of Irish Protestant clergy *v. Church of Ireland Gazette*, 19 March, 1920.

25 Pakenham, Frank, *Peace by Ordeal*, London, 1972, p. 225.

26 Younger, *Ireland's Civil War*, p. 502.

27 Curtis, L.P., 'Anglo-Irish Predicament', *Twentieth Century Studies*, 1970, IV, p. 57.

28 *Irish Times*, 13 June, 1922.

29 Buckland, *Irish Unionism, I*, pp. 286–287.

30 *Irish Times*, 1 May, 1922; *cf.* White, *Minority Report*, p. 85.

31 *Irish Times*, 13 May, 1922; *cf. Church of Ireland Gazette*, 28 January 1921, 'every day the Irish press reeks of blood'.

32 Fitzpatrick, D., *Politics and Irish Life, 1913–1921: Provincial Experience of War and Revolution*, Dublin, 1977, p. 78.

33 Garvin, Tom, 'Great Hatred, Little Room: Social Background and Revolutionary Activists in Ireland, 1890–1922', Boyce, *Revolution in Ireland*, p. 109.

34 Moloney, J.C., *Ireland*, London, 1936, p., 196; *cf.* Moloney, J.C., *Riddle of the Irish*, London, 1927, pp. 158–179.

35 O'Farrell, *England and Ireland Since 1800*, p. 151. *Cf. Church of Ireland Gazette*, 23 January, 1920 on the 'open warfare' and *ibid.* 30 January, 1920 on a labour delegation on tour meeting with Sinn Fein.

36 Seaver, George, *John Allen Fitzgerald Gregg: Archbishop*, Dublin, 1963, pp. 113–114.

37 *Ibid.*, p. 121.

[38] O'Casey, S., *I Knock at the Door*, London, 1939, p. 27; White, *Minority Report*, p. 63.

[39] Lee, *Ireland, 1912–1985*, p. 157; *cf.* W.B. Yeats on the measure as 'grossly oppressive', Fanning, Ronan, *Independent Ireland*, Dublin, 1983, p. 56.

[40] *Belfast Telegraph*, 12 February, 1925.

[41] McDowell, *Church of Ireland*, p. 110.

[42] *Ibid.*, p. 115.

[43] D'Arcy, C.F., *Adventures of a Bishop*, London, 1934, pp. 11, 62.

[44] Bowen, *Protestants in a Catholic State*, pp. 20–21; White, *Minority Report*, pp. 10–11.

[45] *Nation*, 13 December, 1930.

[46] *Irish Independent*, 31 December, 1930; *cf. Irish Times*, 20, 29 and 31 December, 1930, 7 January, 1931; *v.* also *Daily Debates*, 17 June, 1931, XXXIX, 418–452.

[47] *Connaught Telegraph*, 3 January, 1931.

[48] Lee, *Ireland, 1912–1985*, p. 166.

[49] *Round Table*, 1932, LXXXVI, p. 369; *Catholic Bulletin*, 1931, XXI, p. 3.

[50] *Catholic Mind*, February 1931, p. 28; *Cf.* Lee, *op. cit.*, p. 167.

[51] *Standard*, 13 December, 1930; *cf. Irish Independent*, 7 January, 1931.

[52] Canning, B.J., *Bishops of Ireland, 1870–1987*, Ballyshannon, 1987, p. 319,

[53] Longford and O'Neill, *De Valera*, p. 203.

[54] *Ibid.*, p. 220.

[55] *Ibid.*, p. 10.

[56] Miller, *Church, State and Nation*, pp. 404, 393.

57 Longford and O'Neill, *De Valera*, p. xviii.

58 Whyte, J.H., *Church and State in Modern Ireland, 1923–1979*, Dublin, 1980, p. 27.

59 *Irish Catholic Directory, 1925*, p. 568, 8 April, 1924; *cf. Irish Independent*, 9 April, 1924.

60 O'Faolain, Sean, *Vive Moi! An Autobiography*, London, 1975, p. 264.

61 Bromage, Mary, *De Valera and the March of a Nation*, London, 1956, pp. 228–229.

62 Miller, *Church, State and Nation*, p. 493.

63 Whyte, *Church and State*, p. 42.

64 *Irish Independent*, 15 March, 1932.

65 Keogh, *Vatican, the Bishops and Irish Politics*, p. 192.

66 *Irish Independent*, 22 June, 1932.

67 Murphy, John A., *Ireland in the Twentieth Century*, Dublin, 1975, p. 159; Murphy, J.J., *Peoples' Primate*, Dublin, 1945, p. 45.

68 Seaver, *Gregg*, p. 192.

69 O'Duffy, Eoin, *Crusade in Spain*, Dublin, n.d., pp. 38–39. *Cf. Irish Catholic Directory*, 1929, p. 602 for his speech on leaving Down and Connor.

70 Manning, Maurice, *The Blueshirts*, Dublin, 1987, pp. 198–208.

71 Daniel-Rops, *Fight for God*, II, p. 128.

72 Manning, *op. cit.*, pp. 222, 228.

73 Whyte, *Church and State*, pp. 72–73; *Standard*, 16 December, 1938; 20 February, 1942.

74 Dignan suffered under the Black and Tans; was congratulated by Sinn Fein on his appointment and served on a Fianna Fail committee on national

health insurance (Dignan Report) *v. Irish Press*, 13 April, 1953.

75 *United Irishman*, 19 May, 1934.

76 *Irish Times*, 23 September, 1969; Whyte, *Church and State*, p. 56; *cf.* Faughnan, Sean, 'Jesuits and the drafting of the Irish constitution of 1937', *I.H.S.*, 1988, XXVI, pp. 99–101; *Irish Times*, 31 July, 1987; *Belfast Telegraph*, 2 July, 1987 on cardinal Pacelli and the constitution.

77 Blanshard, Paul, *Irish and Catholic Power*, London, 1954, p. 199.

78 Whyte, *Church and State*, p. 164.

79 *Irish Times,* 16 April, 1949.

80 Whyte, *op. cit.*, p. 169.

81 Longford and O'Neill, *Eamon de Valera*, p. 300; *cf.* McDonagh, Enda, 'Church and State in the Constitution of Ireland', *Irish Theological Quarterly*, 1961, XXVIII, pp. 131–144.

82 Lee, *Ireland, 1912–1985*, p. 205.

83 *Ibid.*, p. 159.

84 Edwards, O.D., *Eamon de Valera*, Cardiff, 1987, p. 122.

85 *Cork Examiner*, 28 October, 1931.

86 Murphy, J.A., 'Achievement of de Valera', *De Valera and his Times*, ed. O'Carroll, J.P. and Murphy, J.A., Cork, 1983, p. 7.

87 Seaver, *Gregg*, p. 126.

88 Sheehy, Michael, *Is Ireland Dying?*, London, 1968, pp. 150–151.

89 Whyte, *Church and State*, p. 92.

90 *Irish Statesman*, 17 November, 1928, p. 208.

91 O'Connor, Frank, 'Future of Irish Literature', *Horizon*, 1942 *v.* pp. 56–7.

92 O'Faolain, Sean, 'A Broken World', *Finest Stories of Sean O'Faolain*,

London, 1959, p. 81.

93 Brown, Terence, *Ireland: a Social and Cultural History, 1922–1979*, Glasgow, 1981, pp. 159, 154–155.

94 Wright, Frank, 'Protestant Ideology and Politics in Ulster', *European Journal of Sociology*, 1973, XIV, p. 224.

95 Buckland, *History of Northern Ireland*, p. 45.

96 Buckland, P., *Factory of Grievances: Devolved Government in Northern Ireland, 1921–1939*, Dublin, 1979, p. 195.

97 Ervine, St. John, *Craigavon: Ulsterman*, London, 1949, p. 4.

98 Buckland, Patrick, *James Craig: Lord Craigavon*, Dublin, 1980, p. 109. For Roman Catholic resentment of the Protestant ascendancy of the Craig era *v.* Macardle, D., *Irish Republic*, London, 1937, p. 620; de Paor, Liam, *Divided Ulster*, London, 1973, p. 109.

99 Ervine, *Craigavon*, pp. 108–109.

100 *Loc. cit.*

101 *Witness*, 2 February, 1912.

102 *Daily Herald*, 31 August, 1920: Buckland, *Craig*, p. 47.

103 King, C., *Orange and the Green*, London, 1965, p. 100.

104 Boyce, D.G., 'British Conservative Opinion, the Ulster Question, and the Partition of Ireland, 1912–1921', *I.H.S.*, 1970, XVII, p. 106.

105 Taylor, Peter, 'Britain's Irish Problem', *Crane Bag*, 1980–1981, IV, p. 48. *Cf.* Canning, *Bishops of Ireland, 1870–1987*, p. 120 on MacRory's part in 'trying days of a pogrom'. *V.* also Brewer, J.D., *Royal Irish Constabulary: an Oral History*, Belfast, 1990, p. 95 on priests in the north aiding the R.I.C.

106 *Irish News*, 14, 25, 27 February, 1922; Buckland, *History of Northern Ireland*, pp. 56–57.

107 Farrell, Michael, *Arming the Protestants*, London, 1983, pp. 188–195.

[108] Buckland, *History of Northern Ireland*, pp. 64–65, p. 63.

[109] Buckland, *Craig*, p. 112.

[110] *Ibid.*, p. 115.

[111] *Freeman's Journal*, 3, 5, 12 November, 1917.

[112] *Gaelic American*, 3 April, 1920.

[113] Bowman, John, *De Valera and the Ulster Question, 1917–1973*, Oxford, p.; 109. *Cf.* Longford and O'Neill, *De Valera*, p. 366 for his abiding suspicion of British intentions.

[114] Longford and O'Neill, *op. cit.*, p. 71.

[115] Coogan, Tim Pat, *The I.R.A.*, London, 1981, pp. 211–212.

[116] Brown, T., and Reid, A., *Time Was Away*, Dublin, 1974, p. 23.

[117] Inglis, Brian, *Roger Casement*, London, 1973, p. 387.

[118] Barton, Brian, *Brookeborough: Making of a Prime Minister*, Belfast, 1988, p. 25.

[119] Lee, *Ireland, 1912–1985*, p. 138.

[120] Hezlet, Arthur, *The 'B' Specials*, London, 1972, pp. 70–71.

[121] *Irish News*, 27 February, 1922; *cf.* Longford, *Peace by Ordeal*, p. 235.

[122] Keogh, *Vatican, the Bishops and Irish Politics*, p. 263, n. 57.

[123] Bowman, *De Valera and the Ulster Question*, p. 128n.

[124] Lyons, *Ireland Since the Famine*, p. 716.

[125] *Glasgow Observer*, 26 February, 1938.

[126] *Ibid.*, 28 May, 1938.

[127] Beckett, J.C., *Anglo-Irish Tradition*, London, 1976, p. 152.

128 *Irish Press*, 24 June, 1937; *cf.* Lee, *Ireland, 1912–1985*, pp. 206, 239.

129 Longford and O'Neill, *De Valera*, pp. 356–357.

130 Bell, J.B., *Secret Army: History of the I.R.A.*, Cambridge, Mass., 1970, p. 180.

131 Farrell, *Arming the Protestants*, p. 288.

132 Bowman, *De Valera and the Ulster Question*, p. 276; *cf.* Tierney, M., 'Ireland and the Anglo-Saxon Heresy', *Studies*, 1940, XXIX, pp. 3 *ff.* *United Irishman*, 24, 31 March, 1934.

133 Harkness, David, *Northern Ireland Since 1920*, Dublin, 1983, p. 80.

134 Gibbon, Peter, *Origins of Ulster Unionism*, Manchester, 1975, p. 85.

135 O'Farrell, *Ireland's English Question*, p. 305.

136 *Ibid.*, p. 306.

137 Lyons, F.S.L., *Culture and Anarchy in Ireland, 1890–1939*, Oxford, 1979, pp. 173–174.

138 Rose, Richard, *Governing without Consensus: an Irish Perspective*, London, 1971, especially chapter V.

139 *Belfast Telegraph*, 28, 29 August, 1973, the words of bishop Arthur Butler of the Protestant diocese of Connor in a memorial address; *cf.* Barton, *Brookeborough*, p. 233.

Chapter XII

1 Chadwick, Owen, *Britain and the Vatican During the Second World War*, Cambridge, 1986, pp. 316–317.

2 Falconi, Carlo, *Silence of Pius XII*, London, 1970, p. 350.

3 Camus, Albert, *Resistance, Rebellion and Death*, N.Y., 1961, p. 71; *cf.* Bowen, Desmond, 'History and the Shaping of Irish Protestantism', *Journal of the Irish Christian Study Centre*, Belfast, 1984, pp. 63–4.

4 Pawley, *Rome and Canterbury*, p. 313–314. The Marian dogma was based on the *ipse dixit* of Pius himself.

5 Williams, Michael, *Venerable English College, Rome: a History 1579-1979*, London, 1979, pp. 165–166.

6 Hastings, *History of English Christianity*, p. 480.

7 Heenan, J., *Not the Whole Truth*, London, 1971, pp. 289–304. *Cf.* Hastings, *op. cit.*, p. 564 on Heenan's 'conservative' ultramontanism, any questioning Roman theology as 'speculation' would be 'unworthy of a priest'.

8 Hastings, *History of English Christianity*, p. 579; *cf.* Martin, Malachi, *The Jesuits*, N.Y., 1987, pp. 336–341 on the 'mind-set for change' among Jesuits. *V.* Butler, Christopher, 'Bishop of Rome', *Tablet*, 6 March, 1982, p. 222; Butler, C., *Theology of Vatican II*, London, 1967, p. 105, 'the Church lives by conscientious charity rather than by law'.

9 *Times*, 30 September, 1978. *Cf.* Hebblethwaite, Peter, 'John Paul I', *Modern Catholicism: Vatican II and After*, ed. Hastings, A., London, 1991, pp. 444–446.

10 Granfield, Patrick, *Limits of the Papacy*, London, 1987, p. 8.

11 *Sunday Times*, 2 December, 1984.

12 Swidler, Leonard, 'Hans Küng: a Theologian for Our Time', *Doctrine and Life*, April, 1984, pp. 179–184.

13 Jeanrond, Werner, 'Authentic Christian Leadership?' *Furrow*, 1987, XXXVIII, pp. 265–266. *Cf. Sunday Tribune*, 22 February, 1987, 'His Master's Choice'.

14 *Cf. Universe*, 10 September, 1989.

15 *Guardian Weekly*, 21 October, 1990.

16 ARCIC, *Final Report*, London, 1982, pp. 99–100.

17 Hastings, *History of English Christianity*, pp. 643–644.

18 *Times*, 20 September, 1989.

19 *Manchester Guardian Weekly*, 8 October, 1989.

20 *Irish Independent*, 2 October, 1990; *Daily Telegraph*, 4 October, 1990.

21 *Times*, 3 October, 1989.

22 Churchill, W., *World Crisis: the Aftermath*, London, 1929, p. 319.

23 Harkness, *Northern Ireland*, p. 102.

24 Mitchel, A. and Snodaigh, P., *Irish Political Documents, 1916–1949*, Dublin, 1985, pp. 233–239; Barton, *Brookeborough*, pp. 234–235.

25 Blake, J.W., *Northern Ireland in the Second World War*, Belfast, 1956, pp. 233–234.

26 Bardon, Jonathan, *Belfast: an Illustrated History*, Belfast, 1983, p. 240.

27 Bew, P. and Gibbon, P., and Patterson, H., *State in Northern Ireland, Political Forces and Social Classes*, Manchester, 1979, p. 112.

28 Lee, *Ireland, 1912–1985*, p. 265.

29 Lyons, *Ireland Since the Famine*, p. 721.

30 Foster, *Modern Ireland*, p. 563n; *cf.* Lee, *Ireland, 1912–1985*, pp. 183–4.

31 Brown, *Ireland: a Social and Cultural History*, pp. 196–197.

32 O'Faolain, Sean, 'Ireland and the Modern World', *The Bell*, March, 1943, V, p. 423.

33 O'Donnell, Peadar, 'Cry Jew', *The Bell*, February, 1943, V, p. 344.

34 Fanning, Ronan, *Four Leaved Shamrock*, Dublin, 1983, pp. 16–17.

35 *Irish Catholic Directory*, 1949, p. 705.

36 Coogan, *I.R.A.*, p. 100; Bell, *Secret Army*, pp. 130–137.

37 Whyte, *Church and State*, p. 158.

38 Blanshard, *Irish and Catholic Power*, p. 197 *ff. Cf.* also Stanford, W.B., *Recognized Church: the Church of Ireland in Eire*, Dublin, 1944, p. 43.

39 Whyte, *Church and State*, p. 191 on the Catholic Protection and Rescue Society in existence since 1913.

40 *Irish Times*, 31 July-12 September, 1950.

41 Bowen, *Protestants in Catholic State*, p. 43. *V.* O'Briain, Felim, 'Silken Tyranny', *Irish Independent* articles of November 1952 on the state having 'no primary goal of its own'.

42 *Irish Catholic Directory*, 1945, p. 674.

43 *Irish Times*,13 April, 1955.

44 Clarkson, J.D., 'Big Jim Larkin: a footnote to nationalism', *Nationalism and Internationalism*, N.Y., 1950, p. 55.

45 Fennell, D., *Changing Face of Catholic Ireland*, London, 1968, p. 65.

46 Adams, Michael, *Censorship: the Irish Experience*, Dublin, 1968, p. 65.

47 Whyte, *Church and State*, p. 193.

48 *Loc. cit.*

49 McInerney, M., 'Noel Browne: a Political Portrait', *Irish Times*, 11 October, 1967.

50 Browne, Noel, *Against the Tide*, Dublin, 1987, p. 164.

51 *Ibid.*, p. 171.

52 *Irish Times*, 12 April, 1951.

53 Whyte, *Church and State*, p. 246; for crisis details *cf.* pp. 196–272.

54 *Bell*, XVII, pp. 6–7, 3 June, 1951.

55 *Irish Catholic Directory*, 1952, pp. 687–688, 2 July, 1951.

56 Browne, M., 'Why Catholic priests should concern themselves with social and economic questions', *Christus Rex*, 1947, I, pp. 3–4.

57 Browne, *Against the Tide*, p. 218.

58 Blanchard, Jean, *Church in Contemporary Ireland*, Dublin, 1963, p. 17.

59 Bowman, *De Valera and the Ulster Question*, p. 277.

60 Fanning, Ronan, 'Fianna Fail and the Bishops II,' *Irish Times*, 14 February, 1985: *cf. Irish Times*, 13 February, 1985.

61 Cromlyn (John Barry), 'The Shocking Truth', *Church of Ireland Gazette*, 16 January, 1987, p. 12: *cf. Irish Independent*, 8 November, 1986 on 'the submission to Rome'.

62 *Irish Times*, 4 March, 1957; *cf.* McCaffrey, L.J., 'Irish Nationalism and Irish Catholicism: a Study in Cultural Identity', *Church History*, 1973, XLII, p. 532.

63 Coogan, T.P., *Ireland Since the Rising*, London, 1966, p. 224.

64 Feeney, John, *John Charles McQuaid: the Man and his Mask*, Dublin, 1974, p. 3.

65 *Ibid.*, pp. 34, 16.

66 Inglis, Brian, *West Briton*, London, 1962, pp. 162–3.

67 Feeney, *op. cit.*, p. 35.

68 *Irish Times*, 26 June, 1970.

69 *Irish Times*, 8 July, 1957, 12 August, 1957; *cf.* Bowen, *Protestants in a Catholic State*, p. 72; *Dail Debates*, CLXIII, 731.

70 Coogan, T.P., *Disillusioned Decades: Ireland, 1966–1987*, Dublin, 1987, p. 85.

71 Feeney, *McQuaid*, pp. 41–44.

72 *Irish Times*, 17 October, 18 October, 20 October, 1955. *Cf.* Feeney, *op. cit.*, p. 40.

73 Feeney, *McQuaid*, p. 55.

74 *Ibid.*, p. 65. *Cf.* Lennon, Peter, 'Grey Eminence', *Guardian*, 11 January, 1964. Neither of the Protestant archbishops of Dublin, A.W. Barton nor G.O. Simms were likely to contend with McQuaid.

75 Feeney, *op. cit.*, pp. 70–71.

76 *Catholic Bulletin*, 1935, XXV, p. 273.

77 *Irish Times*, 2, 3, 4, 5 January, 1957. *Cf.* Feeney, *op. cit.*, p. 77 on the 'whirlpool of charge and counter-charge' following McQuaid's unexplained visit to Sean MacStiofain.

78 *Tablet*, 14, 21, 28 April, 1973; *Times*, 9 April, 1973.

79 Fanning, *Independent Ireland*, p. 202.

80 Coogan, *Disillusioned Decades*, p. 74.

81 *Ibid.*, p. 76–77.

82 Lee, *Ireland, 1912–1985*, p. 477.

83 *Sunday Press*, 7 March, 1976; *Church of Ireland Gazette*, 14 May, 1976.

84 Lee, *op. cit.*, p. 498; *cf.* Coogan, *Disillusioned Decades*, pp 76, 94..

85 *Church of Ireland Gazette*, 10 April, 1981.

86 Brennan, Pat, 'Backlash and Blackmail', *Magill*, July, 1982, pp. 14–24.

87 *Belfast Telegraph*, 20 February, 1982.

88 *Irish Times*, 26 August, 1983.

89 *Irish Times*, 12 August, 1983, letter of Joe Foyle on 'Catholic Coercion'.

90 *Ibid.*, 2 September, 1983.

91 Coogan, *Disillusioned Decades*, p. 77.

92 *Tablet*, 1 December, 1984.

93 *Sunday Tribune*, 10 February, 1985.

94 *Belfast Telegraph*, 16 February, 1985; 'The Kerry Babies and the Contraception Debate'.

95 Lee, *Ireland, 1912–1985*, p. 656,

96 Kirby, Peadar, *Is Irish Catholicism Dying*, Cork, 1984, pp. 1–93; *cf.* Hegarty, Kevin, 'Is Irish Catholicism Dying', *Furrow*, 1985, XXXVI, p. 46.

97 *Belfast Telegraph*, 11 February, 1985.

98 *Irish Times*, 13 February, 1985.

99 *Ibid.*, 16 February, 1985.

100 *Belfast Telegraph*, 29 July, 1985.

101 *Irish Times*, 13 June, 1986; *cf.* Coogan, *Disillusioned Decades*, pp. 105-106; *Irish Independent*, 10 January, 1991.

102 *Ibid.*, 4 November, 1986.

103 *Irish Times*, 10 April, 1986.

104 *Sunday Times*, 1 September, 1985; *Belfast Telegraph*, 19 September, 1985.

105 Coogan, *Disillusioned Decades*, p. 79.

106 *Sunday Tribune*, 22 February, 1987.

107 *Irish Times*, 30 April, 1987.

108 *Irish Independent*, 25 September, 1987.

109 *Ibid.*, 14 October, 1987.

110 *Irish Times*, 7 March, 1987, review of Inglis, T., *Moral Monopoly: The Catholic Church in Modern Irish Society*, Dublin, 1987.

111 *Irish Independent*, 9 July, 1987.

112 *Belfast Telegraph*, 12 March, 1983.

113 *Irish Times*, 23 May, 1990, letters to the editor.

114 *Church of Ireland Gazette*, 21 November, 1980.

115 Lee, *Ireland, 1912–1985*, p. 479.

116 *Irish Times*, 1 December, 1983. *Cf.* McGuckian, Michael, S.J., 'Can the Church of Christ be said to subsist in other churches', *Doctrine and Life*, 1988, XXXVIII, pp. 421–428 for the difficulties in Irish ecumenism.

117 Beckett, J.C., in Eccleston, G. and Elliott, E., *The Irish Problem and Ourselves*, London, 1977, p. 9.

118 Fitzgerald, Garret, *Towards a New Ireland*, London, 1972, p. 35. *Cf.* Inglis, Brian, *Story of Ireland*, London, 1970, p. 237 on the 1950's in the Republic: 'unconscious pressure of an overwhelming majority is sometimes oppressive'.

119 White, *Minority Report*, p. 130; *cf.* Inglis, *Moral Monopoly*, pp. 187–8.

120 *Church of Ireland Gazette*, 1 September, 1972.

121 *Irish Times*, 24 August, 1982.

122 *Ibid.*, 18 November, 1983; *cf. ibid.*, 14 June, 1984. *V.* Hastings, Adrian, 'Church and State in a Pluralist Society', *Theology*, 1992, XCV, p. 176 on Garret Fitzgerald, the papacy and pluralism in Ireland.

123 *Belfast Telegraph*, 19 November, 1983.

124 *Cf.* O'Connor, K.D., 'Ireland—a nation caught in the middle of an identity crisis', *Irish Independent*, 20 July, 1985 for the argument that it is not only

the Protestants who need liberation from 'the three-leaved shamrock of race, language and Catholicism which were an imposition by nineteenth century nationalists'.

125 *Church of Ireland Gazette*, 4 April, 1974.

126 Presbyterian Church in Ireland, *Pluralism in Ireland*, Belfast, 1977, p. 7.

127 Fitzgerald, G., *Towards a New Ireland*, Dublin, 1981, p. 7 (R.T.E. interview of 27 September, 1981).

128 Lee, *Ireland, 1912–1985*, p. 645.

129 *Church of Ireland Gazette*, 19 September, 1969.

130 *Ibid.*, 31 January, 1975.

131 *Presbyterian Herald*, October, 1979, p. 3.

132 Heskin, K., *Northern Ireland: a Psychological Analysis*, Dublin, 1980, pp. 105–106; Harris, Rosemary, *Prejudice and Tolerance in Ulster*, Manchester, 1972, pp. 176–177.

133 *Belfast Telegraph*, 8 May, 1985.

134 *Ibid.*, 7 June, 1986.

135 *Ibid.*, 3 November, 1987.

136 O'Malley, Padraig, *Uncivil Wars: Ireland Today*, Belfast, 1983, p. 5.

137 *Belfast Telegraph*, 17 November, 1990; figures from John Hume of the S.D.L.P. nationalist party. By 1992 Protestant terrorism was almost as prevalent as that of the Republicans.

138 Mawhinney, B. and Wells, R., *Conflict and Christianity in Northern Ireland*, London, 1975, p. 122.

139 *Irish Times*, 22 November, 1983, 11, 12 May, 1987.

140 *Belfast Telegraph*, 13 November, 1987.

141 *Irish Times*, 21 March, 1988.

142 *Belfast Telegraph*, 27 October, 1990.

143 *The Times*, 10 May, 1990.

144 *Sunday Times*, 13 May, 1990; *cf.* Flackes, W.D., *Northern Ireland: a Political Directory, 1968–1979*, Dublin, 1980, pp. 60–61.

145 Coogan, *Disillusioned Decades*, p.78.

146 Kearney, Richard, 'I.R.A.'s Strategy of Failure', *Crane Bag*, 1981, IV, p. 67; *cf.* Coogan, T.P., *On the Blanket*, Dublin, 1981, p. 15 *ff*; O'Malley, *Uncivil Wars*, p. 272.

147 Bishop, Patrick and Mallie, Eamonn, *Provisional I.R.A.*, London, 1980, p. 360.

148 *Times*, 27 May, 1981.

149 *Irish Times*, 22 July, 1985; *Irish News*, 20 July, 1985.

150 *Irish Independent*, 18 July, 1984.

151 *Irish Times*, 22 July, 1985.

152 *Fortnight*, February, 1983, p. 14.

153 *Irish Times*, 23 July, 1985. *Cf.* Murphy, Seamus, 'Political Prejudice of Irish Catholics', *Doctrine and Life*, XLII, 1992, pp. 381–382.

154 *Ibid.*, 22 July, 1985; *cf. Church of Ireland Gazette*, 16 August, 1985.

155 *Observer*, 28 February, 1988.

156 *Belfast Telegraph*, 16 August, 1985; *cf. ibid.*, 12 August, 1985.

157 *Daily Telegraph*, 21 March, 1988: *cf.* Faul, Denis and Murray, Raymond, 'Alienation of Northern Ireland Catholics', *Doctrine and Life*, 1984, XXXIV, pp. 63–72.

158 *Belfast Telegraph*, 17 January, 1984.

159 *Ibid.*, 5 October, 1987.

160 *Ibid.*, 29 November, 1989.

161 *Daily Telegraph*, 9 May, 1990. *Cf.* Canning, *Bishops of Ireland*, pp. 56–64 for his pastoral attributes and personality traits.

162 Marrinan, Patrick, *Paisley: Man of Wrath*, Tralee, 1973, p. 10; *cf.* O'Malley, *Uncivil Wars*, p. 175.

163 *Protestant Telegraph*, 24 November, 1981, p. 11.

164 Moloney, Ed. and Pollak, Andy, *Paisley*, Dublin, 1986, p. 89. *Cf.* Paisley, I.R.K., *Massacre of St. Bartholomew*, Belfast, 1972; *The Jesuits, their start, sign, system, secrecy and strategy*, Belfast, n.d.; *The EEC and the Vatican*, Belfast, 1984, for his view of historical Roman Catholicism. *V.* also, Gallagher, Tom, 'Religion, Reaction and Revolt in North Ireland: the Impact of Paisleyism in Ulster', *Journal of Church and State*, 1981, XXIII, pp. 425–428 on Free Presbyterian mentality.

165 Moloney, Ed., 'Northern Issue', *Crane Bag*, 1890–1981, IV, p. 24.

166 *Belfast Telegraph*, 12 October, 1988: *cf. Sunday Telegraph*, 25 August, 1991 on John Paul's vision of a 'Holy European Empire'.

167 O'Neill, Terence, *Autobiography of Terence O'Neill: Prime Minster of Northern Ireland, 1963–1969*, London, 1972, p. 50 *ff.*

168 *The Revivalist*, July, 1963.

169 Nelson, Sarah, *Ulster's Uncertain Defenders*, Syracuse, 1984, p. 56.

170 Bruce, Steve, *God Save Ulster*, Oxford, 1989, p. 264, pp. 73–74.

171 O'Malley, *Uncivil Wars*, p. 178.

172 Paisley, Ian, 'Call to the Protestants of Ulster', *Protestant Telegraph*, 9 January, 1982, pp. 6–9.

173 *Belfast Telegraph*, 30 November, 1981.

174 *Irish Times*, 14 October, 1989.

175 White, Barry, 'Rev. Ian Paisley', *Belfast Telegraph*, 19 February, 1981.

176 *Irish Times*, 14 January, 1984: *Irish Independent*, 16 January, 1984. *Cf.* Bew, Paul, and Patterson, H., *British State and the Ulster Crisis*, London, 1985, pp. 128 *ff.*

177 White, Barry, *John Hume*, Belfast, 1984, pp. 257–258.

178 *Ibid.*, p. 259; *cf. Irish Times*, 14 January, 1984.

179 *Belfast Telegraph*, 10 February, 1984.

180 O'Malley, Padraig, 'Hollow Assumptions of the Unitary Staters', *Fortnight*, July/August, 1984, p. 13; *cf.* McRedmond, Louis, 'Storm in Ireland', *Tablet*, 21 January, 1984.

181 Lee, *Ireland, 1912–1985*, p. 656: *cf.* Falconer, A., McDonagh, E., and MacReamoinn, S., *Freedom to Hope? The Catholic Church in Ireland Twenty Years After Vatican Council II*, Dublin, 1985, p. 6 *ff.*

182 *Irish Times*, 10 February, 1984: *Belfast Telegraph*, 10 February, 1984.

183 *Times*, 9 January, 1984: *Irish Times*, 31 December, 1983. Letters to the editor.

184 *Belfast Telegraph*, 16 September, 1985.

185 *Ibid.*, 3 April, 1986.

186 *Belfast Telegraph*, 9 July, 1987.

187 *Irish News*, 21 January, 1988. *Cf.* Flackes, *Northern Ireland: a Political Directory*, p. 129 on the ideas of the S.D.L.P. for 'condominium' by the British and Irish governments outlined in *Towards a New Ireland*, 1972.

188 *Irish Times*, 20 May, 1987; *cf. Sunday Tribune*, 26 April, 1987.

189 *Belfast Telegraph*, 11 October, 1990.

190 *Belfast Telegraph*, 6 May, 1989.

191 *Irish Independent*, 31 March, 1989.

192 V. Cumming, J. and Burns, F., eds., *Church Now: an Inquiry into the Present State of the Catholic Church in Britain and Ireland*, London, 1980; Falconer, McDonagh and MacReamoinn, *Freedom to Hope, op. cit.*

193 *Times*, 23 May, 1989; *cf.* McElroy, Gerald, *Catholic Church and the Northern Ireland Crisis, 1968–1986*, Dublin, 1991.

194 *Irish Times*, 18, 19 May, 1990; *Belfast Telegraph*, 7 July, 1989.

195 *Belfast Telegraph*, 9 August, 1990.

196 *Irish Times*, 9 September, 1989.

197 *Belfast Telegraph*, 14 November, 1990.

198 *Irish Independent*, 6 August, 1990.

199 *Irish Times*, 29 September, 1989; May 26, 1990.

200 O'Leary, Joseph S., 'Religion, Ireland in Mutation', in *Across the Frontiers: Ireland in the 1990's*, ed. Kearney, R., Dublin, 1990, p. 239.

201 *Irish Times*, 8 February, 1988, 26 March, 1988, 20 September, 1989.

202 *Irish Times*, 13 September, 1989.

203 *Irish Independent*, 19 October, 1990; *cf.* Lyng, R.A., 'Catholic Church and the New Ireland', *Furrow*, 1991, XLII, p. 17; Flannery, Tony, 'Religion in Decline', *Furrow*, 1992, XLIII, pp. 31–36 on the loss of traditional Catholic authority; NicGhiolla, Maire, 'Trends in Religious Practice in Ireland', *Doctrine and Life*, 1992, XLII, pp. 3–12.

204 *Irish Times*, 18 September, 1989.

205 *Irish Independent*, 27 March, 1989; *Irish Times*, 28 May, 1990.

206 *Irish Times*, 27 September, 1989.

207 *Ibid.*, 9 February, 1983.

208 *Ibid.*, 4 October, 1989.

209 *Ibid.*, 19 May, 1988; 3 June, 1989; 13 October, 1989; *Belfast Telegraph*, 4 October, 1989.

210 *Belfast Telegraph*, 6 October, 1990.

211 *Ibid.*, 13 October, 1990.

212 *Ibid.*, 9 June, 28 June, 1989.

213 *Ibid.*, 18 October, 1982. Archbishop Daly became a cardinal in June, 1991.

214 MacNee, Columbanus, 'Open Letter to Bishop Cahal Daly', *Fortnight*, March, 1984, p. 2.

215 *Belfast Telegraph*, 21 September, 1987.

216 *Irish Times*, 23 March, 1988.

217 *Belfast Telegraph*, 18 January, 1990. *Cf.* Canning, *Bishops of Ireland*, pp. 104–111. For Daly's engagement in nationalist controversy *v. Times*, 13 December, 1982; *Derry Journal*, 4 February, 1983; *Irish Press*, 28 January, 1985.

218 *Ibid.*, 3 September, 1985.

219 *Ibid.*, 6 November, 1990.

220 *Irish Times*, 11 June, 1990.

221 *Fortnight*, October, 1981, p. 11.

Chapter XIII

1 McCartney, R.L., *Liberty and Authority in Ireland*, Belfast, 1985, p. 25.

2 *Ibid.*, p. 27.

3 Gillespie, Raymond, 'Historical Revisit: T.W. Moody, *the Londonderry Plantation, 1609–1641*', *I.H.S.*, 1994, XXIX, p. 112.

4 Registrar General, Northern Ireland, *Northern Ireland Census, 1991*, Belfast, 1993, Appendix, p. xvi.

5 Ozment, Steven, *Protestants: The Birth of a Revolution*, N.Y., 1992, p. 49 *passim*..

6 Greely, A.M. *Denominational Society*, N.Y., 1972, p. 186: *cf.* Littell, F.H., *From State Church to Pluralism: a Protestant Interpretation of Religion in American History*, N.Y., 1962, pp. 19–20.

7 *Republicanism, Loyalism and Pluralism in Ireland: Studies Presented to the General Assembly of the Presbyterian Church in Ireland*, Belfast, 1977, p. 17.

8 Harbison, E.H., *Christianity and History*, Princeton, 1964, p. 285.

9 Calvin, John, *Theological Treatises*, Philadelphia, 1954, XXII, pp. 77, 78, 79–92, 'Ordinances for the Supervision of Churches'.

10 Bouwsma, W.J., *John Calvin*, Oxford, 1988, p. 219.

11 *Ibid.*, p. 223.

12 Skinner, Quentin, *Foundations of Modern Political Thought*, Cambridge, 1978, II, pp. 189–358.

13 Laski, Harold, *Defence of Liberty Against Tyrants*, London, 1924, pp. 96–7, 109–111.

14 Burns, J.H., 'Knox and Bullinger', *S.H.R* ., 1955, XXXIV, pp. 90–1.

15 Goodman, Christopher, *How Superior Powers Ought to be Obeyed, 1558*, 1931, Columbia University Press, pp. 148–150, 183–185.

16 Woodhouse, A.S.P., *Puritanism and Liberty*, Chicago, 1951, pp. 317–318, from Lilburne's *Freeman's Freedom Vindicated*, 1656.

17 McNeill, J.T., *History and Character of Calvinism*, Oxford, 1967, p. 412. Samuel Rutherford was the celebrated author of *Lex Rex, a Dispute for the Just Prerogative of King and People*, 1644.

18 *Ibid.*, p. 327.

19 Bonnar, A.A., *Letters of Samuel Rutherford*, London, 1894, pp. 192, 333.

20 Withero, Thomas, *Historical and Literary Memorials of Presbyterianism in Ireland, 1623–1731*, Belfast, 1879, I, p. 42.

21 Reid, J.S., *History of the Presbyterian Church in Ireland*, London, 1853, I, pp. 102–103; Bailie, W.D., *The Six Mile Water Revival of 1625*, Newcastle, 1976, pp. 4–11.

22 Withero, *op. cit.*, I, p. 33. From the *Short Account*, III, of Andrew Stewart of Donaghadee.

23 Maguire, W.A., *Kings in Conflict: the Revolutionary War in Ireland and Its Aftermath, 1689–1750*, p. 168, the words of William King, 1719.

24 Stewart, *Narrow Ground*, p. 49.

25 Browne, Robert, *A Treatise of Reformation without Tarrying for Anie*, Middelburg, 1582. Browne had migrated from Norwich to Holland with his Independent flock and was an influence in the development of English Congregationalism.

26 Baxter, Richard, *Reliquiae Baxterianae*, London, 1696, I, p. 50, a contemporary appreciation of these 'hot-headed' sectaries by a moderate of the period. *Cf.* Walzer, Michael, 'Puritanism as a revolutionary ideology', *History and Theory*, 1963, III, pp. 59–70.

27 Baker, Frank, *John Wesley and the Church of England*, London, 1970, p. 55.

28 Fawcett, A., *The Cambuslang Revival*, London, 1971.

29 Hempton and Hill, *Evangelical Protestantism in Ulster Society*, p. 11 have detailed information about the growth of Methodism and its divisions.

30 Woodward, Josiah, *Account of the Rise and Progress of the Religious Societies in London and their Endeavours for Reformation of Manners*, London, 1701.

31 Crookshank, C.H., *History of Methodism in Ireland*, Belfast, 1885, I, p. 11.

32 Wesley, John, *Journal* (Abridged), N.Y. 1963, p. 372. For Wesley's anti-

Roman Catholic animus *v.* his *Letters*, London, 1931, IV, pp. 136–138; and his *Works*, London, 1872, X, pp. 86–128, 133–140. *Cf.* also his 1753 work, *Advantage of the Members of the Church of England over those of the Church of Rome*, and *Popery Calmly Considered* of 1779.

33 Miller, Kerby, *Emigrants and Exiles*, Oxford, 1985, p. 152; *cf.* Dickson, R.J., *Ulster Emigration to Colonial America, 1718–1775*, Belfast, 1976, pp. 60–69; Glasgow, Maude, *Scotch-Irish in Northern Ireland and the American Colonies*, N.Y., 1926, pp. 157 *ff.*

34 Withero, *Presbyterian Memorials*, II, p. 68.

35 Armstrong, M.W., Loetscher, L.A., and Anderson, C.A., *The Presbyterian Enterprise*, Westminster, 1956, pp. 21–22.

36 Leckey, A.G., *In the Days of the Laggan Presbytery*, Belfast, 1908, pp. 36–37; Schlenther, B.S., *Life and Writings of Francis Makemie*, Philadelphia, 1971, p. 13 *ff.*

37 Salisbury, W.S., *Religion in American Culture*, Homewood, 1964, p. 29.

38 Chambers, George, *Tribute to the Principles, Virtues, Habits and Public Usefulness of the Irish and Scotch Early Settlers of Pennsylvania*, Chambersburg, 1856, p., 10.

39 Leyburn, J.G., *Scotch-Irish*, Chapel Hill, 1962, p. 230.

40 Chambers, *Tribute to the Irish and Scotch Early Settlers*, p. 73.

41 Barton, Thomas, *Conduct of the Paxton Men, Impartially Represented*, Philadelphia, 1764, p. 1 *ff.* It was widely justified by the Scotch-Irish.

42 Armstrong, Loetscher and Anderson, *Presbyterian Enterprise*, pp. 21-22.

43 Tebbel, John, *History of the Indian Wars*, N.Y., 1966, p. 38.

44 Armstrong, Loetscher and Anderson, *op. cit.*, p. 42.

45 Olmstead, C.E., *History of Religion in the United States*, Englewood Cliffs, 1960, p. 158.

46 Mode, P.G., *Sourcebook and Bibliographical Guide for American Church History*, N.Y., 1921, p. 525. *Cf.* Miller, Perry, *Jonathan Edwards* , N.Y.,

1959, p. 137 *ff.*

[47] Olmstead, *Religion in the United States*, p. 166.

[48] Winslow, O.E. *Jonathan Edwards, 1703-1758*, N.Y., 1961, pp. 272-283.

[49] Olmstead, C.E., *Religion in America: Past and Present*, Englewood Cliffs, 1961, pp. 47–49.

[50] Bushman, Richard, *From Puritan to Yankee: Character and the Social Order in Connecticut, 1690–1765*, N.Y., 1967, p. 194; Tennent, Gilbert, *Danger of an Unconverted Ministry*, Boston, 1742, p. 4.

[51] Sweet, W.W., *Methodism in American History*, Abingdon, 1954, p. 76; Jones, Rufus, *Quakers in the American Colonies*, N.Y., 1966, pp. 128, 410, on Methodist missions.

[52] *Freeman's Journal*, 30 March, 1775.

[53] Olmstead, *History of Religion in the United States*, p. 199.

[54] Froude, J.A., *English in Ireland in the Eighteenth Century*, London, 1887, II, p. 154. *Cf.* Hibbert, Christopher, *Redcoats and Rebels*, London, 1990, pp. 239–240 on Irish loyalist units, many of their members deserters from Washington's army.

[55] Carman, H.J., Syrett, H.C., Wishy, B.W., *History of the American People*, N.Y., 1967, I, p. 43.

[56] Bagenal, P.H., *American Irish and their Influence on Irish Politics*, London, 1882, pp. 12–13; cf. Doyle, D.N., *Ireland, Irishmen and Revolutionary America, 1760–1820*, Dublin, 1981, V. Irwin, Clark, *History of Presbyterianism in Dublin and the South West of Ireland*, London, 1890, pp. 40–41, on the Philadelphia Presbytery being 'essentially a missionary Presbytery'.

[57] Lecky, *Ireland in the Eighteenth Century*, II, p. 226.

[58] Hamilton, Thomas, *History of the Irish Presbyterian Church*, Edinburgh, 1887, pp. 133–134.

[59] Miller, *Emigrants and Exiles*, p. 163.

[60] Leyburn, *Scotch-Irish*, p. 319.

61 Bacon, L.W., *History of American Christianity*, N.Y., 1900, pp. 234–7.

62 Roosevelt, T., *Winning of the West*, N.Y., 1904, I, 168n.

63 Olmstead, *History of Religion in the United States*, p. 327.

64 Westerkamp, M.J., *Triumph of the Laity: Scots-Irish Piety and the Great Awakening, 1625–1760*, Oxford, 1988; O'Brien, S., 'A transatlantic community of saints: the Great Awakening and the first evangelical network, 1735–1755', *A.H.R.*, 91, pp. 811–832.

65 *Records of the General Synod of Ulster*, II, p, 254.

66 *Ibid.*, p. 445.

67 *Ibid.*, p. 467.

68 Withero, *Presbyterian Memorials*, I, pp. 218–219.

69 Anderson, A.C., *Story of the Presbyterian Church in Ireland*, Belfast, 1985, p. 72; *cf.* Barkley, J.M., *The Westminster Formularies in Irish Presbyterianism*, Belfast, 1956, p. 9 *ff.* For modern controversy over the Westminster Confession *v.* Haire, J.L.M., *Challenge and Conflict: Essays in Irish Presbyterian History and Doctrine*, Belfast, 1981, pp. 170–182.

70 Reid, *Presbyterian Church in Ireland*, III, p. 441.

71 Beckett, J.C., *Protestant Dissent in Ireland, 1687–1780*, London, 1948, p. 135.

72 Wight, T., and Rutty, J., *History of the Rise and Progress of the People Called Quakers in Ireland*, London, 1811, p. 328; *cf.* Grubb, I., *Quakers in Ireland, 1654–1900*, London, 1927.

73 Hempton, D., *Methodism and Politics in British Society, 1750–1850*, London, 1984, pp. 34–43; *cf.* Haire, R., *Wesley's One and Twenty Visits to Ireland*, London, 1947.

74 Hempton, D. and Hill, M., *Evangelical Protestantism in Ulster Society*, London, 1992, p. 17.

75 Elliott, Marianne, *Watchmen in Zion: the Protestant Idea of Liberty*,

Belfast, 1985, p. 1.

76 *Ibid.*, p. 9.

77 *Cf. Irish Times*, 12 July, 1994, p. 11 for the nationalist argument that the memory of William III and the Boyne was largely forgotten.

78 Withero, *Presbyterian Memorials*, II, pp. 45–6, sermon of 9 Oct. 1746 'Delivery of... Ireland from Popery, Slavery and the Pretender'.

79 Grob, G.N. and Beck, R.N., *Ideas in America*, N.Y., 1970, p. 92.

80 McDowell, R.B., *Irish Public Opinion, 1750–1800*, London, 1944, p. 44; *cf.* O'Connell, M.R., *Irish Politics and Social Conflict in the Age of the American Revolution*, Philadelphia, 1965, pp. 22 *ff.*

81 Brooke, Peter, *Ulster Presbyterianism*, Dublin, 1987, p. 125.

82 *Ibid.*, p. 123.

83 Bailie, W.D., 'William Steel Dickson, D.D.', *Bulletin of the Presbyterian Historical Society of Ireland*, 1976, VI, p. 15.

84 Miller, D.W., 'Presbyterianism and Modernization', *Past and Present*, LXXX, pp. 77–84.

85 Miller, D.W., 'The Armagh Troubles, 1784–1795', *Irish Peasants Violence and Political Unrest*, Dublin, 1983, p. 187.

86 Wesley, John, *Journal*, London, 1827, IV, pp. 115–116.

87 Rogers, P., *Irish Volunteers and Catholic Emancipation, 1778–1793*, London, 1934, p. 154.

88 Colles, Ramsey,*History of Ulster*, London, 1920, IV, p. 97.

89 O'Callaghan, J.C., *History of the Irish Brigades in the Service of France*, Glasgow, 1886, p. 584.

90 Stewart, *Narrow Ground*, pp. 116–117.

91 Miller, 'Armagh Troubles'. *op. cit.*, p. 166.

92 Foster, *Modern Ireland, 1600–1972*, p. 272.

93 Byrne, J., *An Impartial Account of the Late Disturbances in the County of Armagh, 1784–1791*, Dublin, 1792.

94 Bartlett, T., 'Defenders and Defenderism in 1793', *I.H.S.*, 1985, XXIV, p. 376.

95 County of Meath Freeholder, *Candid and Impartial Account of the Disturbances in the County of Meath in the Years, 1792, 1793, and 1794*, Dublin, 1794, pp. 6–7; *cf.* Lecky, *Ireland in the Eighteenth Century*, III, p. 213.

96 Curtin, Nancy, 'Transformation of the Society of United Irishmen into a mass-based revolutionary organization, 1794–1796', *I.H.S.*, 1985, pp. 463–493.

97 *Ibid.*, p. 479.

98 Bartlett, *op. cit.*, p. 389.

99 Senior, H., *Orangeism in Ireland and Britain, 1795–1836*, London, 1966, p. 18 *ff.*

100 Reid, *Presbyterian Church*, III, p. 508.

101 Latimer, W.T., *History of the Irish Presbyterians*, Belfast, 1893, p. 182,

102 Hamilton, *Irish Presbyterians*, p. 140.

103 Pakenham, Thomas, *Year of Liberty*, London, 1969, p. 198, and pp. 164–170 on the suffering of the Quakers at Ballitore.

104 *Ibid.*, p. 199.

105 Lecky, *Ireland in the Eighteenth Century*, IV, p. 403.

106 Beckett, *Protestant Dissent*, p. 137; Barkley, J.M., 'Presbyterian Minister in Eighteenth Century Ireland', *Challenge and Conflict: Essays in Irish Presbyterian History and Doctrine*, pp. 46–71.

107 *Records of the General Synod of Ulster*, III, p. 208.

108 *Ibid.*, p. 209.

109 Tone, Wolfe, *Life*, Washington, 1826, I, p. 51.

110 Stewart, *Narrow Ground*, pp. 108–109, 164.

111 Latimer, *Irish Presbyterianism*, p. 182.

112 Beckett, J.C., 'Ulster Protestantism', *Ulster Since 1800*, Belfast, 1957, pp. 160–161.

113 Holmes, *Presbyterian Heritage*, p. 105; Holmes, F., *Henry Cooke*, Belfast, 1981, pp. 63–66 on his opposition to Catholic Emancipation.

114 *The Repealer Repulsed: a Corrective Narrative of the Rise and Progress of the Repeal Invasion of Ulster*, Belfast, 1841, p. 47.

115 MacDonagh, *Hereditary Bondsman*, p. 258.

116 Milner, Joseph, *Works*, London, 1810, VIII, p. 199.

117 Bebbington, D.W., *Evangelicalism in Modern Britain: a History from the 1730's to the 1980's*, London, 1989, pp. 1–5; Hilton, Boyd, *Age of Atonement: the Influence of Evangelicalism on Social and Economic Thought, 1785–1865*, Oxford, 1988, p. 8; Anstey, Roger, *Atlantic Slave Trade and British Abolition, 1760–1810*, London, 1975, pp. 157–199.

118 Helmstadter, R.J., 'Nonconformist Conscience', *Religion in Victorian Britain*, Manchester, 1988, IV, p. 69.

119 Murray, S.W., *City Mission Story*, Belfast, n.d., p. 5.

120 Magee, H., *Fifty Years in the Irish Mission*, Belfast, n.d., pp. 188–90.

121 Hempton and Hill, *Evangelical Protestantism*, p. 37.

122 Woodward, R., *Present State of the Church of Ireland: Containing a Description of its Precarious Situation and Consequent Dangers to the Public*, Dublin, 1787, 6th edition.

123 Hempton, D.N., 'Methodist Crusade in Ireland, 1795–1845', *I.H.S.*, 1980, XXII, p. 36.

124 *Dublin Evening Mail*, 10 April, 1825.

125 Campbell, W.G., *Apostle of Kerry: Life of Charles Graham*, Dublin, 1826, pp. 124–126.

126 *Report of a Deputation from the London Hibernian Society Respecting the Religious State of Ireland*, Dublin, 1808, pp. 26–8.

127 Porter, J.L., *Life of Henry Cooke*, Belfast, 1875, pp. 410, 451–2.

128 McClelland, Aiken, 'Later Orange Order', *Secret Societies in Ireland*, Dublin, 1973, p. 128. Crommelin Irwin, an Orange leader, argued this case at Sixmilecross.

129 Boyd, Andrew, *Holy War in Belfast*, Tralee, 1972, pp. 36, 41.

130 *The Watchman*. 15 September, 1841; 8 January, 1845.

131 Macaulay, Ambrose, *Patrick Dorrian*, Dublin, 1987, pp. 83–84.

132 *Cf.* Hempton, David, *Methodism and Politics in British Society, 1750–1850*, London, 1984, pp. 92–96; Hempton, D. and Hill, M., 'Godliness and good citizenship: evangelical Protestantism and social control in Ulster, 1790–1850', *Saothar*, 1988, XIII, pp. 65–80.

133 Miller, David, *Queen's Rebels*, Dublin, 1978, p. 83.

134 Holmes, *Presbyterian Heritage*, p. 121.

135 Coad, Roy, *History of the Brethren Movement*, Exeter, 1968, p. 181 on Brethren influences in the secular career of T.J. Barnardo.

136 Holmes, *Presbyterian Heritage*, p. 123; *cf.* Gibson, William, *Year of Grace*, Edinburgh, 1909, especially ch. xviii on the revival's 'pathological affections'; Carson, Herbert, *God's River in Spate*, Belfast, 1958.

137 Miller, David, 'Presbyterianism and Modernization', *Past and Present*, 1978, LXXX, pp, 69–90.

138 Gibbon, Peter, *Origins of Ulster Unionism*, Manchester, 1975, pp. 44, 64.

139 Hempton and Hill, *Evangelical Protestantism*, p. 146.

140 Brown, Terence, *The Whole Protestant Community: the Making of a Historical Myth*, Belfast, 1985, pp. 17–18.

141 Hempton and Hill, *op. cit.*, p. 44.

142 Porter, *Henry Cooke*, pp. 451–452.

143 *Irish Church Bill: the Great Protestant Demonstration in Belfast*, Belfast, 1869.

144 Protestant Defence Association of the Church of Ireland, *Revision of the Prayer Book*, Dublin, 1875, pp. 3–4.

145 McClelland, Aiken, 'Later Orange Order', *op. cit.*, p. 129.

146 Hempton, David, 'For God and Ulster: Evangelical Protestantism and the Home Rule Crisis of 1886', *Protestant Evangelicalism: Britain, Ireland, Germany and America, 1750–1950*, Oxford, 1990, p. 253.

147 Palmer, N.D., *The Irish Land League Crisis*, N.Y., 1940, p. 120.

148 Bew, Paul and Wright, Frank, 'The Agrarian Opposition in Ulster Politics, 1848–1887, *Irish Peasants, Violence and Political Unrest*, p. 219.

149 *Irish Ecclesiastical Gazette*, 27 February, 1886.

150 *Christian Advocate*, 15 January, 1886. There were, of course, a minority of Protestant Home Rulers, such as J.B. Armour.

151 'General Assembly, 1886', *Presbyterian Churchman*, 1886, pp. 193–7.

152 *Christian Advocate*, 8 January, 1886.

153 Hempton and Hill, *Evangelical Protestantism*, pp. 178, 182.

154 MacKnight, Thomas, *Ulster as it is, or twenty eight years experienced as an Irish editor*, London, 1896, II, p. 205; *cf. Londonderry Standard*, 31 October, 1887

155 McClelland, Aiken, 'Later Orange Order', *op. cit.*, p. 132.

156 Murray, S.W., *City Mission Story*, Belfast, 1977, p. 29.

157 *Christian Advocate*, 7 May, 1886.

158 Stewart, A.T.Q., *Ulster Crisis*, London, 1967, p. 56.

159 McNeill, Ronald, *Ulster's Stand for Union*, London, 1922, p. 163.

160 Ervine, St. John, *Craigavon*, London, 1949, p. 237, the account of the 28 September proceedings is given by Martin Ross writing for the *Spectator*.

161 Bardon, Jonathan, *Belfast*, 1983, p. 180.

162 Moeran, Francis M., *Memoirs: the Good Fight*, Dublin, 1951, p. 52, son of a T.C.D. professor, Moeran served in many Ulster parishes; *cf.* An Irishman, *Intolerance in Ireland: Fact not Fiction*, London, 1913, pp. 154–156 on popular opposition to *Ne Temere* etc.

163 *Republicanism, Loyalism and Pluralism in Ireland*, p. 17. Nationalists suppress 'memories' such as that of the many Irish Catholics who served in the British Army; *cf.* Denman, Terence, *Ireland's Unknown Soldiers: the 16th (Irish) Division in the Great War*, Dublin, 1992, and Johnstone, Tom, *Orange, Green and Khaki: the Irish Regiments in the Great War*, Dublin, 1992.

164 *Northern Ireland and the Two Traditions in Ireland*, Belfast, 1984, p. 15, wisdom of John Magee, late head of history department, St. Joseph's College of Education, Belfast.

165 Canning, B.J., *Bishops of Ireland 1870–1987*, Ballyshanon, 1987, p. 96.

166 Farrell, Michael, *Arming the Protestants*, Dingle, 1983, p. 291.

167 Crawford, R.G., *Loyal to King Billy: Portrait of the Ulster Protestants*, Dublin, 1987, p. 53.

168 Report of the Committee on National and International Problems to the General Assembly, *Republicanism—the Aims, Ideals and Methods of Irish Republicanism*, Belfast, 1974, p. 6.

169 *Methodist Church in Ireland: Report of Special Committee to Examine the Current Situation in Ireland*, Belfast, 1979, p. 11.

170 *Republicanism, Loyalism and Pluralism in Ireland*, p. 48.

171 *Shankill Bulletin*, 18 April, 1981, 'Shankill Opinion Poll Rejects Paisley'.

172 *Protestant Telegraph*, 20 June, 1981, p. 6, article on William Johnston of Ballykilbeg and the anti-Home Rule Orange movement.

173 *Independent*, 28 July, 1992, report of Presbyterian Moderator, John Dunlop on 'siege mentality' of his people.

174 *Irish Times*, 27 February, 1988, a few days earlier a Catholic, Aidan McAnespie, had been killed by an accidental ricochet from a British border post; *cf.* Bew, Paul and Gillespie, Gordon, *Northern Ireland: Chronology of the Troubles, 1968–1993*, Dublin, 1993, p. 211.

175 Harris, Rosemary, *Prejudice and Tolerance in Ulster*, Manchester, 1972, pp. 162–163 on Orangeism transcending denominationalism.

176 Bew and Gillespie, *op. cit.*, pp. 173, 208.

177 *Church of Ireland Gazette*, 2 April, 1982; *cf.* 'Cromlyn', *ibid.*, 11 June, 1982 on the need to read again George Salmon and J.F.A. Gregg regarding Roman authority.

178 'Evangelicals and Catholics Together: a Declaration', *First Things*, May, 1994, p. 22.

179 University of Ulster's Centre for the Study of Conflict, *The Churches and Inter-Community Relationships, a study of Roman Catholic, Church of Ireland, Presbyterian and Methodist relations. Cf. Belfast Telegraph*, 8 May, 1991.

180 Bew and Gillespie, *op. cit.*, pp. 276, 283. Until the end of 1992 the overwhelming number of victims have been Protestant: *cf.* Evangelical Contribution on Northern Ireland (ECONI), *For God and His Glory Alone*, Belfast, February, 1994, p. 7 for popular pietism: 'the root cause of the Ulster problem is that we are all sinners... pride, bitterness and bigotry have the same root cause as racketeering, kidnapping and murder'.

181 O'Faolain, Nuala, 'Our religion will colour our vote in more ways than one', *Irish Times*, 15 June, 1992.

182 *Irish Independent*, 7 June, 1994.

Chapter XIV

1 Andrews, C.S., *Man of no Property*, Dublin, 1982, p. 197; quoted in Lee, *Ireland, 1912–1985*, p. 464.

2 Bradshaw, Brendan, 'Nationalism and Historical Scholarship in Modern Ireland', *I.H.S.*, 1989, XXVI, p. 339.

3 *Belfast Telegraph*, 1 September, 1990, church page editorial.

4 Feeney, *John Charles McQuaid*, p. 70.

5 *Tablet*, 19 May, 1990, comment on cardinal Hinsley.

6 McSweeney, Bill, *Roman Catholicism: the Search for Relevance*, Oxford, 1980, pp. 86–87.

7 Granfield, Patrick, *Limits of the Papacy*, London, 1987, p. 42.

8 Inglis, *Moral Monopoly*, p. 63.

9 Chubb, Basil, *Government and Politics of Ireland*, London, 1982, p. 18.

10 O'Brien, C.C., 'Nationalism and the Reconquest of Ireland', *Crane Bag*, 1977, I, pp. 8–13.

11 Browne, Noel, 'Pope rules South', *Irish Times*, 23 August, 1985.

12 *Sunday Times*, 29 April, 1990; *cf.* Kirby, Peadar, *Is Irish Catholicism Dying*, Cork, 1984, p. 70.

13 *Belfast Telegraph*, 8 September, 1984, survey for Conference of Major Religious Superiors.

14 *Irish Independent*, Supplement '1991: Year of Challenge', 28 December, 1990. *Ibid.*, 8 June, 1992 on the bishop of Derry and the new 'dialogue' with the I.R.A.

15 *Daily Mirror*, 22 August, 1989.

16 Inglis, T., 'Decline in Numbers of Priests and Religious in Ireland', *Doctrine and Life*, 1979, XXX, pp. 87–98; *cf. Irish Times*, 30 April, 1990.

17 Gilley, Sheridan, 'Religion in Modern Ireland', *Journal of Ecclesiastical History*, 1992, XLIII, p. 114 on the media's 'vulgarly Voltairian anti-religious work'; *cf. Belfast Telegraph*, 3 November, 1990 on the Irish Inter-Church, 'Challenge of the City' movement; *Ibid.*, 29 December, 1990 on Curtice, J., Gallagher, T., 'British Social Attitudes: the Seventh Report'; *Irish Times*, 4 May, 1990.

18 *Irish Times*, 28 June, 1990.

19 *Ibid.*, 1 February, 1988.

20 *Ibid.*, 24 May, 1990. *Cf.* O'Brien, C.C., 'Testing Time for Catholicism', *Irish Independent*, 5 September, 1992.

21 Daly, Gabriel, 'Catholic Theology During the Last Two Decades', *Doctrine and Life*, 1984, XXXIV, p. 61.

22 *Belfast Telegraph*, 2 November, 1990, her interview with 'Hot Press'.

23 *Irish Times*, 11 June, 1990. *Cf. Belfast Telegraph*, 20 May, 1992 on the Church of Ireland synod 'demanding' maintenance of the Adelaide hospital's 'Protestant ethos'.

24 *Study Conference to Explore Models of Political Co-operation: Background Papers, Corrymeela Community*, Belfast, 1981, p. 19.

25 *Irish Times*, 15 June, 1992.

26 de Paor, Liam, 'Rebel Mind' in Kearney, R., *Irish Mind.*, Dublin, 1985, pp. 186–7.

27 de Paor, Liam, *Divided Ulster*, London, 1973, pp. 143–4.

28 Dundas, W.H., *Enniskillen, Parish and Town*, Dundalk, 1913, p. 76; *cf.*, Leslie, J.B., *Clogher Clergy and Parishes*, Enniskillen, 1929, p. 57.

29 Boyd, Andrew, *Holy War in Belfast*, London, 1972, p. 182.

30 Stewart, *Narrow Ground*, p. 182.

31 Crawford, R.G., *Loyal to King Billy: a Portrait of the Ulster Protestants*, Dublin, 1987, p. 90; *cf.* Heskin, K., *Northern Ireland: a Psychological*

Analysis, Dublin, 1980, p. 123.

32 Patterson, Henry, *Class Conflict and Sectarianism: the Protestant Working Class and the British Labour Movement, 1868–1920*, Belfast, 1980, p. 145.

33 Miller, David, *Queen's Rebels*, Dublin, 1978, p. 155.

34 *Records of the General Assembly*, 1950, pp. 87–91.

35 Whyte, J.H., 'Interpretations of the Northern Ireland Problem: an Appraisal', *Economic and Social Review*, 1978, IX, pp. 257–282.

36 Bruce, *God Save Ulster*, p. 268; *cf.* Presbyterian General Assembly committee report in *Loyalism in Ireland*, 1975, p. 35 regarding 'tribalism'.

37 Bruce, *God Save Ulster*, pp. 222–3.

38 *Ibid.*, pp. 228–9.

39 Lee, Simon, ed., *Freedom from Fear: Churches Together in Northern Ireland*, Belfast, 1990, p. 113.

40 *Ibid.*, pp. 21–51.

41 Norman, Edward, 'Outsider's Evaluation' in *Modern Catholicism: Vatican Council II and After*, London, 1991, p. 458.

42 de Vries, Wilhelm, 'Limits of Papal Primacy', *Cardinal Bea Studies II: Dublin Papers on Ecumenism*, Manila, 1972, p. 162.

43 Kung, Hans, *Infallible?*, London, 1980, p. 22.

44 Sullivan, F.A., *Magisterium: Teaching Authority in the Catholic Church*, Ramsey, New Jersey, 1983, p. 210.

45 *Minutes, General Assembly*, 1980, pp. 54–55.

46 Cornwell, John, 'Dues of the Fisherman', *Independent on Sunday*, 15 April, 1990.

47 *Irish Times*, 27 June, 1990; *cf. Tablet*, 24, 31 December, 1988, 14 January, 4 February, 1989.

48 Bull, George, *Inside the Vatican*, London, 1982, p. 201; Martin, M., *Jesuits*, N.Y., 1987, p. 507 on this 'pliant' organization; *Irish Times*, 28 May, 1990.

49 *Irish Independent*, 19 February, 1992, 11 April, 1992.

50 *Irish Times*, 6 April, 1992.

51 *Guardian Weekly*, 24 May, 1992.

52 *Belfast Telegraph*, 20 May, 1992, Church of Ireland General Synod address by archbishop Caird of Dublin on churches in Northern Ireland who 'make no significant contribution to inter-community relations'.

53 *Irish Times*, 28 April, 1990; *Times*, 23 April, 1990.

54 *Response of the General Synod of the Church of Ireland to the Final Report of ARCIC-I*, Oxford, 1987, pp. 38–39.

55 Granfield, *Limits of the Papacy*, p. 184.

56 Hastings, *History of English Christianity*, p. 647; *cf.* Misner, P., 'Papal Primacy in a Pluriform Polity', *Journal of Ecumenical Studies*, 1974, XI, pp. 239–261; Ernst, C., 'Primacy of Peter: Theology and Ideology', *New Blackfriars*, 1969, L, pp. 347–355, 399–404; 'Faith and Theology: the Ultramontane Influence', *Tablet*, April 18–25, 1981, pp. 380–381.

57 Lyons, *Culture and Anarchy*, p. 177.

APPENDIX

Chronological List of Pontiffs Referred to in the Text

Celestine I,	422-432	Gregory XIII,	1572-1585
Leo I,	440-461	Sixtus V ,	1585-1590
Gelasius I,	492-496	Clement VIII,	1592-1605
Gregory I,	590-604	Paul V,	1605-1621
Nicholas I,	858-867	Gregory XV,	1621-1623
Sergius III,	904-911	Urban VIII,	1623-1644
John XI,	931-935	Innocent X,	1644-1655
John XII,	955-964	Alexander VII,	1655-1667
Leo IX,	1049-1054	Clement IX,	1667-1669
Alexander II,	1061-1073	Clement X,	1670-1676
Gregory VII,	1073-1085	Innocent XI,	1676-1689
Urban II,	1088-1099	Alexander VIII,	1689-1691
Eugenius III,	1145-1153	Innocent XII,	1691-1700
Anastasius IV,	1153-1154	Clement XI,	1700-1721
Hadrian IV,	1154-1159	Innocent XIII,	1721-1724
Alexander III,	1159-1181	Benedict XIII,	1724-1730
Lucius III,	1181-1185	Clement XII,	1730-1740
Innocent III,	1198-1216	Benedict XIV,	1740-1758
Gregory IX,	1227-1241	Clement XIII,	1758-1769
Boniface VIII,	1294-1303	Clement XIV,	1769-1774
John XXII,	1316-1334	Pius VI,	1775-1799
Martin V,	1417-1431	Pius VII,	1800-1823
Callistus III,	1455-1458	Leo XII,	1823-1829
Pius II,	1458-1464	Pius VIII,	1829-1830
Innocent VIII,	1484-1492	Gregory XVI,	1831-1846
Alexander VI,	1492-1503	Pius IX,	1846-1878
Julius II,	1503-1513	Leo XIII,	1878-1903
Leo X,	1513-1521	Pius X,	1903-1914
Hadrian VI,	1522-1523	Benedict XV,	1914-1922
Clement VII,	1523-1534	Pius XI,	1922-1939
Paul III,	1534-1549	Pius XII,	1939-1958
Paul IV,	1555-1559	John XXIII,	1958-1963
Pius IV,	1559-1565	Paul VI,	1963-1978
Pius V,	1566-1572	John Paul I,	1978
		John Paul II,	1978...

Selected Bibliography

The issue of Roman Catholic influence in Ireland, and the Protestant response to it, has been of perennial interest to commentators and scholars, and it would be impossible to provide in a single interpretative volume such as this a comprehensive bibliography of such a dialectical process. What is presented here are those studies, many of them referred to in the text, which provide insight enabling us to begin to understand the many facets of Ireland's unremitting religious, ecclesiastical and cultural struggle between its warring peoples. All books cited in the bibliography may be assumed to have been published in London, unless otherwise noted. Manuscript and newspaper sources are referred to fully in the text of the study.

Abbreviations

ACHR	American Catholic Historical Review
AH	Archivium Hibernicum
AHR	American Historical Review
CHR	Catholic Historical Review
CJH	Canadian Journal of History
CQR	Church Quarterly Review
EHR	English Historical Review
HIC	History of Irish Catholicism
HS	Historical Studies
IER	Irish Ecclesiastical Record
IHS	Irish Historical Studies
IS	Irish Sword
ITQ	Irish Theological Quarterly
JEH	Journal of Ecclesiastical History
JSH	Journal of Social History
PP	Past and Present
PICHC	Proceedings of the Irish Catholic Historical Committee
SH	Studia Hibernica
SHR	Scottish Historical Review

Surveys, Collections and Interpretative Studies

Aveling, J.C.H., *Handle and the Axe: Catholic Recusants in England from the Reformation to Emancipation*, 1976.

Bailey, K.C., *History of Trinity College, Dublin, 1892–1945*, Dublin, 1947.

Beck, G.A., (ed.) *English Catholics, 1850–1950*, 1950.

Beckett, J.C., *Making of Modern Ireland, 1603–1923*, 1966.

_____ *Anglo-Irish Tradition*, 1976.

Bossy, John, *English Catholic Community, 1570–1850*, 1975.

_____ 'Mass of a Social Institution, 1200–1700', *PP*, 100, 1983.

Bowen, Desmond, 'History and Shaping of Irish Protestantism', *Journal of Irish Christian Study Centre*, II, Belfast, 1984.

Boyd, A., *Holy War in Belfast*, Tralee, 1972.

Brady, W. Maziere, *Episcopal Succession in England, Scotland and Ireland, 1400–1875*, 1971, III vols.

Briggs, James, *Historical Survey of the Relations that have Subsisted between the Church and State of England and Ireland and the See and Court of Rome from the Norman Conquest*, 1868.

Browne, L., *Their Name is Pius: Portraits of Five Great Modern Popes*, Milwaukee, 1941.

Canning, B.J., *Bishops of Ireland, 1870–1987*, Ballyshannon, 1987.

Canny, N., 'Formation of the Irish Mind: Religion, Politics and Gaelic Irish Literature, 1580–1750', *PP*, 95, 1982.

_____ *Kingdom and Colony: Ireland in the Atlantic World, 1560–1800*, Baltimore, 1988.

Crookshank, C.H., *History of Irish Methodism in Ireland*, Belfast, 1888, III vols.

Curtis, E. and McDowell, R.B., *Irish Historical Documents, 1172–1922*, 1968.

Daniel-Rops, Henri, *Protestant Reformation*, N.Y., 1962, II vols.

_____ *Catholic Reformation*, N.Y., 1964, II vols.

_____ *Church in the Seventeenth Century*, N.Y., 1963.

_____ *Church in the Eighteenth Century*, N.Y., 1966.

_____ *Church in an Age of Revolution*, N.Y., 1967, II vols.

_____ *A Fight for God*, N.Y., 1967, II vols,

Dewer, M.W., Brown, John and Long, S.F., *Orangeism: a New Historical Appreciation, 1688–1979*, Belfast, 1967.

Foster, R.F., *Modern Ireland, 1600–1972*, 1988.

Hastings, Adrian, (ed.) *Bishops and Writers: Aspects of the Evolution of Modern English Catholicism*, 1977.

Healy, John, *Maynooth College, Its Centenary History, 1795–1895*, Dublin, 1895.

Heyer, F., *Catholic Church from 1649–1870*, 1969.

Holmes, Finlay, *Our Irish Presbyterian Heritage*, Belfast, 1985.

Holmes, J.D., *More Roman than Rome: English Catholicism in the Nineteenth Century*, 1978.

Hughes, P., *History of the Church, 1934–1937*, III vols.

_____ *Popes' New Order: Systematic Summary of the Social Encyclicals and Addresses from Leo XIII to Pius XII*, 1943.

Hurley, Michael, (ed.) *Irish Anglicanism, 1869–1969*, Dublin, 1970.

Jordan, W.K., *Development of Religious Toleration in England*, 1932–1940, IV vols.

Killen, W.D., *Ecclesiastical History of Ireland*, 1975, II vols.

Latourette, K.S., *Nineteenth Century in Europe: Background and the Roman Catholic Phase*, N.Y., 1958.

MacDonagh, Oliver, *States of Mind: a Study of Anglo-Irish Conflict, 1780–1980*, 1983.

Mason, W. Monck, *History of the Cathedral Church of St. Patrick near Dublin from 1190–1818*, Dublin, 1820.

Mathew, David, *Catholicism in England, 1535–1935*, 1936.

Maxwell, Constantia, *History of Trinity College, Dublin, 1591–1892*, Dublin, 1946.

McDowell, R.B., *Church of Ireland, 1869–1969*, 1975.

McDowell, R.B. and Webb, D.A., *Trinity College, Dublin, 1592–1952: an Academic History*, Cambridge, 1982.

Miller, David, *Queen's Rebels: Ulster Loyalism in Historical Perspective*, Dublin, 1980.

Moody, T.W. and Beckett, J.C., *Queen's Belfast: History of a University*, 1959, II vols.

Moran, P.F., *Spicilegium Ossoriense: Collection of Original Letters and Papers Illustrative of the History of the Irish Church from the Reformation to 1800*, Dublin, 1874, III vols.

New History of Ireland, Moody, T.W. et al. (eds.), II, 1169–1534, Oxford, 1987
III, 1534–1691, Oxford, 1976
IV, 1691–1800, Oxford, 1986
V, 1801–1870, Oxford, 1989

Nielsen, Fredrik, *History of the Papacy in the Nineteenth Century*, 1906, II vols.

Nippold, Friedrich, *Papacy in the Nineteenth Century*, N.Y., 1900.

Norman, E.R., *English Catholic Church in the Nineteenth Century*, 1984.

_____ *Roman Catholicism in England from the Elizabethan Settlement to the Second Vatican Council*, Oxford, 1985.

O'Farrell, Patrick, *Ireland's English Question, Anglo-Irish Relations 1534–1970*, N.Y., 1971.

_____ *England and Ireland since 1800*, Oxford, 1975.

Pastor, Ludwig, *History of the Popes*, 1891–1953, XL vols.

Pawley, B. and M., *Rome and Canterbury through the Centuries*, 1974.

Phillips, W.A., (ed.) *History of the Church of Ireland from the Earliest Times to the Present Day*, 1933, III vols.

Ranke, L. von, *History of the Popes During the Last Four Centuries*, 1908, III vols.

Reid, James, *History of the Presbyterian Church in Ireland,* Killen, W.D., (ed.) Belfast, 1867, III vols.

Renehan, L.F., *Collections on Irish Church History*, McCarthy, D., (ed.) Dublin, 1861, II vols.

Stewart, A.T.Q., *Narrow Ground, Aspects of Ulster, 1609–1969*, 1977.

Stubbs, J.W., *History of the University of Dublin from its Foundation to the End of the Eighteenth Century*, 1889.

I   Ireland's Dual Protectorate: prior to the Reformation

Barraclough, G., *Medieval Papacy*, 1968.

Binchy, D.A., 'Patrick and his Biographers: Ancient and Modern', *SH*, II, 1962.

Brooke, Z.N., *English Church and the Papacy*, Cambridge, 1931.

Byrne, F.J., 'Ireland of St. Columba'. *HS*, V, 1970.

Calendar of Papal Letters Relating to Great Britain and Ireland, 1198–1492, vols. 1–xiv, 1893–1960.

Calendar of Entries in the Papal Registers Relating to Great Britain and Ireland: Papal Letters, XV: Innocent VIII: Lateran Registers, 1484–1492, Dublin, 1978.

Calendar of Papal Letters Relating to Great Britain and Ireland: XVI: Alexander VI, Dublin, 1986.

Corish, P.J., 'Christian Mission', *HIC*, I, 1972.

Cosgrove, A., 'Writing of Irish medieval history', *IHS*, XXVII, 1990.

Curtis, E., *History of Medieval Ireland*, 1968.

Dunning, P.J., 'Pope Innocent III and the Irish Kings', *JEH*, VIII, 1957.

_____ 'Irish Representatives and Irish Ecclesiastical Affairs at the Fourth Lateran Council', *Medieval Studies Presented to Aubrey Gwynn*, Dublin, 1961.

Edwards, R.D., 'Kings of England and Papal Provisions in Fifteenth Century Ireland', *Medieval Studies Presented to Aubrey Gwynn*, Dublin, 1961.

_____ 'Ecclesiastical Appointments to the Province of Tuam, 1399–1477', *AH*, XXXIII, 1975.

Ellis, S.G., 'Nationalist historiography and the English and Gaelic worlds in the late middle ages', *IHS*, XXV, 1986.

Enright. M.J., 'Medieval Ireland and the Continent', *IHS*, XXVI, 1990.

Flanagan, U.G., 'Papal Letters of the Fifteenth Century as a Source for Irish History', *PICHC*, 1958

_____ 'Papal Provisions in Ireland, 1305–1378', *HS*, III, 1961.

Frame, Robin, 'English Officials and Irish Chiefs in the Fourteenth Century', *EHR*, XC, 1975.

_____ *English Lordship in Ireland, 1318–1361*, Oxford, 1982.

Gwynn, Aubrey, 'Lanfranc and the Irish Church', *IER*, LVII, 1941.

_____ *Medieval Province of Armagh, 1470–1545*, Dundalk, 1946.

_____ 'St. Malachy of Armagh', *IER*, LXX, 1948, LXXI, 1949

_____ 'Centenary of the Synod of Kells', *IER*, LXVII, 1952.

_____ 'Twelfth Century Reform', *HIC*, II, 1, Dublin, 1968.

_____ 'Anglo-Irish Church Life, Fourteenth and Fifteenth Centuries', *HIC*, II, 4, Dublin, 1968.

Hand, Geoffrey, *English Law in Ireland, 1290–1324*, Cambridge, 1967.

_____ 'Church in the English Lordship', *HIC*, II, 3, Dublin, 1968.

Hanson, R.P.C., *Saint Patrick, His Origins and Career*, Oxford, 1968.

Hughes, Kathleen, 'Church and the World in Early Christian Ireland', *IHS*, XIII, 1962.

_____ *Church in Early Irish Society*, 1966.

Hull, R., *Medieval Theories of the Papacy*, 1934.

Jalland, T.B., *Church and the Papacy*, 1964.

Kelly, Fergus, *Guide to Early Irish Law*, Dublin, 1987.

Lawrence, C.H., (ed. *English Church and the Papacy in the Middle Ages* , 1965.

Lydon, J.F., *Lordship of Ireland in the Middle Ages*, Dublin, 1972.

_____ *Ireland in the Later Middle Ages*, Dublin, 1973.

Mooney, Canice, 'Church in Gaelic Ireland, Thirteenth to Fifteenth Centuries', *HIC*, II, 5, Dublin, 1969.

Norgate, Kate, 'The Bull *Laudabiliter*', *EHR*, VIII, 1893.

O'Connell, J., 'Church in Ireland in the Fifteenth Century: Diocesan Organization, Kerry', *PICHC*, 1956.

O'Doherty, J.F., 'Rome and the Anglo-Norman Invasion of Ireland', *IER*, XLII, 1933.

Otway-Ruthven, A.J., *History of Medieval Ireland*, 1968.

Phillips, J.R.S., 'Irish remonstrance of 1317: an international perspective', *IHS*, XXVII, 1990.

Richter, M. and Ni Cathain, P. (eds.) *Ireland and Europe: the Early Church,* Stuttgart, 1984.

Richter, M., 'Interpretations of medieval Irish history', *IHS,* XXIV, 1985.

_____ *Medieval Ireland: the Enduring Tradition,* N.Y., 1988.

Sheehy, M.J., 'The bull *Laudabiliter:* a problem in medieval *diplomatique* and history', *Galway Archaeological and Historical Journal,* XXIX, 1961.

Sheehy, M.P., (ed.) *Pontifica Hibernica: Medieval Papal Chancery Documents Concerning Ireland, 600–1261,* Dublin, 1962–5, II vols.

Ullmann, Walter, *Short History of the Papacy in the Middle Ages,* 1972.

Walsh, Katherine, *Fourteenth Century Scholar and Primate: Richard Fitzralph in Oxford, Avignon and Armagh,* Oxford, 1981.

Watt, J.A., Negotiations between Edward II and John XXII concerning Ireland', *IHS,* X, 1956.

_____ 'Laudabiliter in medieval diplomacy and propaganda', *IER,* LXXXVII, 1967.

_____ 'Papacy and episcopal appointments in thirteenth century Ireland', *PICHC,* 1959.

_____ *Church and the Two Nations in Medieval Ireland,* Cambridge, 1970.

_____ *Church in Medieval Ireland,* Dublin, 1972.

II   Ireland and the English Reformation: the Tudor Period

Antony, C.M., *Life of St. Pius V,* 1911.

Bagwell, R., *Ireland under the Tudors,* 1962, III vols.

Bayne, C.G., *Anglo-Roman Relations, 1558–1565,* Oxford, 1913.

Bossy, John, 'Rome and the Elizabethan Catholics: a question of geography', *Historical Journal,* VII, 1964.

_____ 'Character of Elizabethan Catholicism' in *Crisis in Europe, 1560–1660*, ed. T. Aston, 1965.

_____ 'Social History of the Confessional in the Age of the Reformation', *Transactions of the Royal Historical Society*, XXV, 1975.

Bottigheimer, Karl, 'Failure of the Reformation in Ireland: une question bien posée', *JEH*, XXXVI, 1985.

Bradshaw, Brendan, 'Opposition to ecclesiastical legislation in the Irish Reformation parliament', *IHS*, XVI, 1969.

_____ *Dissolution of the Religious Orders in Ireland under Henry VIII*, Cambridge, 1974.

_____ 'Edwardian reformation in Ireland', *AH*, XXVI, 1977.

_____ 'Sword, word and strategy in the reformation in Ireland', *Historical Journal*, XXI, 1978.

Brady, Ciaran, 'Conservative subversives; community of the Pale and the Dublin administration, 1556–1584', in *Radicals, Rebels and Establishments* (Historical Studies XV), Belfast, 1985.

Brady, Ciaran and Gillespie, R., (eds.) *Natives and Newcomers: Essays on the making of Irish Colonial Society, 1534–1641*, Dublin, 1986.

Brady, W. Maziere, *Alleged Conversion of the Irish Bishops to the Reformed Religion at the Accession of Queen Elizabeth,*, 1866.

_____ *Irish Reformation*, 1867.

Canny, Nicholas, *Formation of the Old English élite in Ireland*, Dublin, 1975.

_____ *Elizabethan Conquest of Ireland: a Pattern Established, 1565–1576*, Hassocks, Sussex, 1976.

_____ 'Why the Reformation failed in Ireland: une question mal posée', *JEH*, XXX, 1979

_____ 'Formation of the Irish Mind: Religion, Politics and Gaelic Irish Literature', *PP*, XCV, 1982.

_____ *From Reformation to Restoration: Ireland, 1534–1660*. Dublin, 1988.

_____ 'Protestants, planters and apartheid in early modern Ireland', *IHS*, xxv, 1986.

Caraman, P., *Other Face: Catholic Life under Elizabeth I*, 1960.

Corish, P.J., 'An Irish Counter-Reformation bishop, John Roche', *ITQ*, XXV, XXVI, 1958, 1959.

Cregan, D., 'Social and cultural background to a Counter-Reformation episcopate' in *Studies in Irish History Presented to R. Dudley Edwards*, Dublin, 1979.

Dickens, A.G., *Counter-Reformation*, 1968.

Edwards, R. Dudley, *Church and State in Tudor Ireland: a History of Penal Laws against Irish Catholics, 1534–1603*, Dublin, 1935.

Ellis, S.G., 'Tudor policy and the Kildare ascendancy in the lordship of Ireland, 1496–1534', *IHS*, XX, 1977

_____ *Tudor Ireland: Crown, Community and the Conflict of Cultures, 1470–1603*, 1985.

_____ 'Economic problems of the church: why the Reformation failed in Ireland', *JEH*, XLI, 1990.

Evennett, G.O., H.O., *Spirit of the Counter-Reformation*, Notre Dame, 1970.

Ford, Alan, *Protestant Reformation in Ireland, 1590–1641*, Frankfurt-am-Main, 1985.

Froude, J.A., *Lectures on the Council of Trent*, N.Y., 1896.

Hammerstein, Helga, 'Aspects of the continental education of Irish students in the reign of Elizabeth I', *HS*, VIII, 1971.

Hübner, J.A., *Life and Times of Sixtus V*, 1872.

Janelle, P., *Counter-Reformation*, Milwaukee, 1949.

Jedin, H., *Papal Legate at the Council of Trent: Cardinal Seripando*, 1947.

_____ *History of the Council of Trent,* 1957, II vols.

_____ *Crisis and Closure of the Council of Trent,* 1967.

Jefferies, H.A., 'Irish parliament of 1560: the anglican reforms authorized', *IHS,* XXVI, 1988.

Kidd, B.J., *Counter-Reformation,* 1933.

Lennon, Colm, *Richard Stanihurst: the Dubliner, 1547–1618,* Dublin, 1981.

_____ 'Counter-Reformation in Ireland, 1542–1641', in *Natives and Newcomers: Making of Irish Colonial Society, 1534–1641,* Dublin, 1986.

_____ *Lords of Dublin in the Age of the Reformation,* Dublin, 1989.

McGrath, P., *Papists and Puritans under Elizabeth I,* 1937.

McNally, R., 'Council of Trent, the *Spiritual Exercises* and the Catholic Reform', *Church History,* XXXV, 1965.

Meyer, A.O., *England and the Catholic Church under Queen Elizabeth,* London, 1916.

Pollen, J.H., 'Fomenting the Irish rebellion of 1579 b y Gregory XIII', *Month,* July, 1902.

Ronan, M.V., *Reformation in Ireland under Elizabeth,* 1930.

Scarisbrick, J., *Reformation and the English People,* Oxford, 1984.

Schroeder, H.J., *Canons and Decrees of the Council of Trent,* 1941.

Shirley, E.P. (ed.) *Original Letters and Papers Illustrative of the History of the Church of Ireland during the Reigns of Edward VI, Mary and Elizabeth,* 1851.

Silke, John, 'Primate Peter Lombard and Hugh O'Neill', *ITQ,* XXII, 1955.

Walsh, T.J., *Irish Continental College Movement,* Dublin, 1973.

Walshe, H.C., 'Enforcing the Elizabethan settlement: the vicissitudes of Hugh Brady, bishop of Meath, 1563–1584', *IHS,* XXVI, 1989.

III   William Bedell's Ireland, 1600–1641

Abbot, T.K., 'History of the Irish Bible', *Hermathena, XVII, 1913.

Acton, Lord, 'Fra Paolo Sarpi' in Acton, *Essays on Church and State, 1952.

Albion, G., *Charles I and the Court of Rome, 1935.

Bagwell, Richard, *Ireland under the Stuarts and during the Interregnum, 1963, III vols.

Bedell, William, *Letter to James Waddesworth upon the Principal Points of Controversy between Papists and Protestants, 1827.

Berington, Joseph, *Memoirs of Gregorio Panzani, Birmingham, 1793.

Bossy, John, 'Counter-Reformation and the People of Catholic Europe', *PP, No. 47, 1970.

_____ 'Counter-Reformation and the People of Catholic Ireland', *HS, VIII, Dublin, 1971.

Bouwsma, W.J., *Venice and the Defence of Republican Liberty: Renaissance Values in the Age of Counter-Reformation, Berkeley, 1968.

_____ 'Venice and the Political Education of Europe' in *Renaissance Venice, ed. Hale, J.R., 1973.

Brady, J., 'Irish Colleges in Europe and the Counter-Reformation;', *PICHC, 1975.

Burke, P., 'Great Unmasker: Paolo Sarpi, 1552–1623', *History Today, XV, 1965.

Burnet, Gilbert, *Life of William Bedell, Bishop of Kilmore, 1736.

Canny, Nicholas, *Upstart Earl: a Study of the Social and Mental World of Richard Boyle, First Earl of Cork, 1566–1643, Cambridge, 1982.

Carr, J.A., *Life and Times of James Ussher, 1896.

Clancy, Thomas, 'English Catholics and the Dispensing Power, 1570–1640', *Recusant History, VI, 1961.

Clarke, Aidan, 'Pacification, plantation and the Catholic question, 1603–1623', *New History of Ireland,* III, Oxford, 1976.

_____ 'Colonial Identity in early seventeenth century Ireland', *HS,* XI, Belfast, 1978.

_____ *Old English in Ireland, 1625–1642,* 1966.

Corish, P.J., 'Reorganization of the Irish Church, 1603–1641', *PICHC,* 1957.

_____ *Catholic Community in the Seventeenth and Eighteenth Centuries,* Dublin, 1981.

Frere, Walter, *English Church in the Reigns of Elizabeth I and James I, 1558–1625,* 1904.

Gamble, W., *William Bedell, his Life and Times,* 1951.

Gilbert, F., 'Venice in the Crisis of the League of Cambrai', in *Renaissance Venice,* ed. Hale, J.R., 1973.

Gillespie, Raymond, *Colonial Ulster: the Settlement of East Ulster, 1600–1641,* Cork, 1985.

Hill, Christopher, *Antichrist in Seventeenth Century England,* Oxford, 1971.

Hughes, P., *Rome and the Counter-Reformation in England,* 1944.

Kearney, Hugh, 'Ecclesiastical Politics and the Counter-Reformation in Ireland, *JEH,* II, 1960.

_____ *Strafford in Ireland, 1633–1641: a Study in Absolutism,* Manchester, 1961.

Kilroy, P., 'Sermon and pamphlet literature in the Irish reformed church, 1613–1634', *AH,* XXXIII, 1975.

Knox, R. Buick, 'Ussher and the Church of Ireland', *CQR,* April, 1960.

_____ *James Ussher, Archbishop of Armagh,* Cardiff, 1967.

Lennon, Colm, 'Civic Life and Religion in Early Seventeenth Century Dublin', *AH,* XXXVIII 1983.

Mackie, J.D., 'Secret Diplomacy of James VI in Italy Prior to his Accession to the English Throne', *SHR,* XXI, 1923–4.

Mason, H.J. Monck, *Life of William Bedell,* 1843.

MacCarthy-Morrogh, M., *Munster Plantation: English Migration to Southern Ireland, 1583–1641,* Oxford, 1986.

McIlwaine, W., *Life and Times of Bishop Bedell,* Belfast, 1854,

Meyer, A.O., 'Charles I and Rome', *AHR,* XIX, 1913.

Moody, T.W., 'Treatment of the Native Population under Scheme of the Plantation of Ulster', *IHS,* I, 1939.

_____ *Londonderry Plantation,* Belfast, 1939.

Morley, H., (ed.) *Ireland under Elizabeth and James I,* 1890.

Parr, Richard, *Life of James Ussher,* 1686.

Perceval-Maxwell, M., 'Strafford, the Ulster Scots and the Covenanters', IHS, XVIII, 1973.

_____ *Scottish Migration to Ulster in the Reign of James I,* 1973.

_____ 'Ulster Rising of 1641 and the Depositions;, *IHS,* XXI, 1978–9.

_____ 'Protestant faction: the impeachment of Strafford, and the origins of the Irish civil war', *CJH,* XVI, 1982.

Rupp, Gordon, *William Bedell, 1571–1642,* Cambridge, 1971.

Sheehan, A.J., 'Recusancy Revolt of 1603: a Reinterpretation', *AH,* XXXVIII, 1983.

Shuckburgh, E.S., *Two Biographies of William Bedell, Bishop of Kilmore,* 1902.

Silke, J.J., 'Primate Lombard and James I' *,ITQ,* XXII, 1955.

_____ *Ireland and Europe, 1559–1707,* Dundalk, 1966.

_____ *Kinsale: the Spanish Intervention in Ireland at the End of the Elizabethan Wars,* N.Y., 1976.

Simpson, W.J. Sparrow, *Archbishop Bramhall,* 1927.

Smith, L.P., *Life and Letters of Sir Henry Wotton,* Oxford, 1907, II vols.

Stone, J.M. 'Corporate Reunion in the Reign of Charles I', *SHR* April, 1889.

Sykes, Norman, 'James Ussher as churchman' *Theology,* March, 1957.

Ward, A.W., 'James VI and the Papacy', *SHR,* II, 1905.

Wootton, David, *Paolo Sarpi: between Renaissance and Enlightenment,* Cambridge, 1983.

Yates, F.A., 'Paolo Sarpi's History of the Council of Trent', *Journal of the Warburg and Courtauld Institute,* VII, 1944.

IV   Ireland's Wars of Religion: 1641–1691

Adair, Patrick, *True Narrative of the Rise and Progress of the Presbyterian Church in Ireland, 1623–1670,* Belfast, 1866.

Barnard, T.C., 'Planters and policies of Cromwellian Ireland', *PP,* 1973.

_____ *Cromwellian Ireland: English Government and Reform in Ireland, 1649–1660,* Oxford, 1975.

Beckett, J.C., 'Confederation of Kilkenny Reviewed', *HS,* II, 1959.

Borlase, Edmund, *History of the Execrable Irish Rebellion* , Dublin, 1743.

Brady, John, 'Oliver Plunkett and the Popish Plot', *IER,* XXXIX, 1958, XC, 1958.

Burke, J., 'New Model Army and the problem of siege warfare, 1649–51' *IHS,* XXVII, 1990.

Carpenter, Andrew, 'William King and the threats to the Church of Ireland during the reign of James II', *IHS,* XVIII, 1972.

Casway, J.L., *Owen Roe O'Neill and the Struggle for Catholic Ireland,* Philadelphia, 1984.

Clarke, Aidan, 'Genesis of the Ulster Rising of 1641' in *Plantation to Partition: Essays in Honour of J.L. McCracken,* Belfast, 1981.

Coonan, T.L., *Irish Catholic Confederacy and the Puritan Revolution,* Dublin, 1954.

Corish, P.J., 'Rinuccini's Censure of 27 May, 1648', *ITQ,* XVIII, 1951.

_____ 'Crisis in Ireland in 1648: the Nuncio and the Supreme Council: Conclusions', *ITQ,* XXII, 1955.

_____ 'Origins of Irish Nationalism', *HIC,* III, 8, 1968.

_____ 'Cromwellian Regime, 1650–1660', *New History of Ireland,* III, Oxford, 1976.

Ellis, P.B., *Hell or Connaught: Cromwellian Colonization of Ireland, 1652–1660,* 1975.

Esson, D.M.R., *Curse of Cromwell,* 1971.

Fitzpatrick, T., *Bloody Bridge and other papers relating to the Insurrection of 1641,* Dublin, 1903.

Grubb, Isabel, *Quakers in Ireland, 1654–1700,* 1927.

Hamilton, E., *Irish Rebellion of 16421,* 1920.

Hickson, Mary (ed.) *Ireland in the Seventeenth Century; or the Irish Massacres of 1641–2,* 1884, II vols.

Hutton, A., *Embassy in Ireland of Monsignor G.B. Rinuccini,* Dublin, 1873.

Kenyon, J.P., *Popish Plot,* 1974.

Malcolm, J.L., 'All the king's men: impact of the crown's Irish soldiers on the English civil war', *IHS,* XXI, 1979.

McGuire, J., 'Why Ormond was dismissed in 1669', *IHS,* XVIII, 1973.

Meehan, C.P., *Confederation of Kilkenny*, Dublin, 1905.

Murphy, J.A., 'Politics of the Munster Protestants, 1641–9', *Cork Historical Society Journal*, LXXVI, 1971.

O'Fiaich, Tomas, 'Appointment of Blessed Oliver Plunkett to Armagh', *ITQ*, XXV, 1958.

Petty, William, *Political Anatomy of Ireland*, Shannon, 1979.

Prendergast, J.P., *Cromwellian Settlement of Ireland*, Dublin, 1922.

Seymour, S.D., *Puritans in Ireland, 1647–1661*, 1921.

Simms, J.G., *Jacobite Ireland, 1685–1691*, 1969.

Stevenson, David, *Scottish Covenanters and Irish Confederates: Scottish-Irish Relations in the Mid-Seventeenth Century*, Belfast, 1981.

Troost, W., *William III and the Treaty of Limerick, 1691–1697: a Study of his Irish Policy*, Leiden, 1983.

Walsh, P., *History and Vindication of the Irish Remonstrance*, 1674.

Wight, Thomas and Rutty, John, *History of the Rise and Progress of the People Called Quakers in Ireland from the year 1653 to 1700*, Dublin, 1751.

Witherow, Thomas, *Historical and Literary Memorials of Presbyterianism in Ireland, 1623–1731*, Belfast, 1979, II vols.

V   The Age of Protestant Domination: the Eighteenth Century

Anderson, James, *Bishop Berkeley on the Roman Catholic Controversy*, 1860.

Andrieux, Maurice, *Daily Life in Papal Rome in the Eighteenth Century*, 1968

Aulard, A., *Christianity and the French Revolution*, 1927.

Barkley, J.M., *Westminster Formularies in Irish Presbyterianism*, Belfast, 1956.

Bartlett, Thomas, *Fall and Rise of the Irish Nation: the Catholic Question,*

1690–1830, Dublin, 1992.

Bartlett, T., and Hayton, D., (eds.) *Penal Era and golden Age: Essays in Irish History, 1682–1800,* Belfast, 1979.

Beckett, J.C., *Protestant Dissent in Ireland, 1687–1780,* 1948.

Berington, Joseph, *State and Behaviour of English Catholics from the Revolution to 1781,* 1781.

Blackerly, Samuel, *History of the Penal Laws,* 1689.

Boulter, Hugh, *Report by the Lord Primate for the Lords Committee on the Present State of Popery in this Kingdom,* Dublin, 1732.

Brady, John, *Catholics and Catholicism in the Eighteenth Century Press,* Maynooth, 1965.

Brady, John and Corish, P.J., 'Church under the Penal Code', *HIC,* IV, 2, Dublin, 1971.

Brady, W. Maziere, *Memoirs of Cardinal Erskine, Papal Envoy to the Court of George III,* 1890.

Brennan, W.J., *Ecclesiastical History of Ireland,* Dublin, 1840, II vols.

Buckley, M.B., *Life and Writings of Arthur O'Leary,* Dublin, 1868.

Burdy, S., *Life of Philip Skelton,* Oxford, 1914.

Burke, N., 'A Hidden Church?: the Structure of Catholic Dublin in the mid-Eighteenth Century', *AH,* XXXII, 1974.

Burke, W.P., *Irish Priests in the Penal Times, 1660–1760,* Shannon, 1969.

Burns, R.E., 'Irish Penal Code and Some of its Historians', *Review of Politics,* XXI, 1959.

_____ 'Irish Popery Laws: a Study in Eighteenth Century Legislation and Behaviour', *Review of Politics,* XXIV, 1962.

_____ 'Parsons, Priests and the People: The Rise of Irish Anti-clericalism, 1785–9', *Church History,* XXXI, 1962.

_____ 'Catholic Relief Act in Ireland, 1778', *Church History,* XXXII, 1963.

Burton, E.H., *Life and Times of Bishop Challoner,* 1909.

Butler, James, *Justification of the Tenets of the Roman Catholic Religion,* Dublin, 1787.

Caldicott, E., Gough, H. and Pittion, J.P., *Huguenots of Ireland,* Dublin, 1987.

Childe-Pemberton, W.S., *Earl-Bishop: Life of Frederick Hervey, Bishop of Derry,* 1924.

Connolly, S.J., *Religion and Power: the Making of Protestant Ireland, 1660–1760,* Oxford, 1992.

Creighton, S., 'Penal Laws in Ireland and the Documents in Propaganda, 1631–1731', *PICHC,* 1961.

Daniel-Rops, H., *Church in the Eighteenth Century,* N.Y., 1966.

Donnelly, J.S., 'Rightboy Movement', *SH,* XVII-XVIII, 1977–8.

_____ 'Whiteboy movement, 1761–5', *IHS,* XXI, 1978.

_____ 'Hearts of Oak, Hearts of Steel', *SH,* XXI, 1981.

Duffy, Eamon, *Challoner and his Church: a Catholic Bishop in Georgian England,* 1981.

Froude, J.A., *English in Ireland in the Eighteenth Century,* 1882, III vols.

Giblin, Cathaldus, 'Stuart Nomination of Irish Bishops', *PICHC,* 1968.

Goodwin, M.C., *Papal Conflict with Josephism,* N.Y., 1938.

Gwynn, D., *John Keogh: Pioneer of Catholic Emancipation,* Dublin, 1930.

Gwynn, Robin, D., *Huguenot Heritage: the History and Contribution of the Huguenots in Britain,* 1985.

Hemphill, Basil, *Early Vicars-Apostolic of England, 1685–1750,* 1954.

Jervis, W.H., *Gallican Church and the Revolution,* 1882.

King, C.S., (ed.) *Great Archbishop of Dublin, William King: his Autobiography and Correspondence,* 1906.

King, William, *Vindication of the Answer to the Considerations that Obliged Peter Manby to Embrace the Catholic Religion,* Dublin, 1688.

King, William, *State of the Protestants of Ireland under the late King James Government,* 1691.

Landa, L.A., *Swift and the Church of Ireland,* Oxford, 1965.

Lecky, W.E.H., *History of Ireland in the Eighteenth Century,* 1892, V vols.

Lee, Grace, *Huguenot Settlements in Ireland,* 1936.

Leslie, Charles, *Answer to a Book Entitled the State of the Protestants in Ireland,* 1692.

Mackenzie, J., *Narrative of the Siege of Londonderry,* 1690.

Mahoney, T.D., *Edmund Burke and Ireland,* Harvard, 1960.

Mant, Richard, *History of the Church of Ireland,* 1840, II vols.

McLean, G.R.D., 'Archbishop Wake and Reunion with the Gallican Church', *CQR,* CXXXI, 1941.

Moran, P.F., *Catholics of Ireland under the Penal Laws in the Eighteenth Century,* 1899.

Murphy, J.A., 'Support of the Catholic Clergy in Ireland, 1750–1800', *HS,* V, 1965.

O'Boyle, James, *Irish Colleges on the Continent,* Dublin, 1935.

O'Connell, P., 'Plot against Fr. Nicholas Sheehy: the Historical Background', *PICHC,* 1968.

O'Flaherty, Eamon, 'Ecclesiastical politics and the dismantling of the penal laws in Ireland 1774 –1782', *IHS,* XXV, 1988.

Richardson, J., *Proposal for the Conversion of the Popish Natives of Ireland to the Established Religion,* 1712.

Savory, D.L., *Huguenots*, Belfast, 1938.

_____ *Huguenots and Palatine Settlements*, Belfast, 1948.

Sercesi, James, *Popery Always the Same: an Authentic Account of the Persecutions Against the Protestants in the South of France*, 1746.

Simms, J.G., *Williamite Confiscation in Ireland, 1690–1703*, 1956

_____ 'Connaught in the eighteenth century', *IHS*, XI, 1958.

_____ 'Making of a penal law, 1703–4', *IHS*, XII, 1960.

_____ 'Bishops banishment act of 1697', *IHS*, XVII, 1970.

Smiles, S., *Huguenots in England and Ireland*, 1876.

Sykes, Norman, *William Wake, Archbishop of Canterbury, 1657–1737*, Cambridge, 1957, II vols.

Synge, Edward, *Sermon Against Persecution on Account of Religion*, Dublin, 1721.

_____ *Gentleman's Religion with the Ground and Reason of It*, Dublin, 1752, 7th edition.

Wall, Maureen, 'Catholic loyalty to king and pope in eighteenth century Ireland', *PICHC*, 1961.

_____ *Penal Laws, 1691–1760*, Dundalk, 1961.

_____ 'Whiteboys' in *Secret Societies in Ireland*, Dublin, 1973.

_____ *Catholic Ireland in the Eighteenth Century: Collected Essays of Maureen Wall*, Dublin, 1989.

VI   Catholic Resurgence After the Union (1800–1829)

Allies, Mary H., *Life of Pope Pius VII*, 1875.

Anon. 'New Reformation', *British Critic*, III, 1828.

_____ 'Reasons for Excluding Catholics from Power', *Anti-Catholic Magazine*, I, 1829.

Armstrong, J., *History of the Presbyterian Church in the City of Dublin*, Dublin, 1829.

Authentic Report of the Discussion between Rev. T.P. Pope and the Rev. Thomas Maguire, Dublin, 1827.

Authentic Report on the Controversial Discussion upon the Supremacy of St. Peter which Took Place between Rev. Bernard M'Auley, P.P., and Rev. Robert Stewart, 24, 25 and 26 July, 1827 at Ballymena, Belfast, 1827.

Authenticated Report of the Discussion between Rev. T.D. Gregg and the Rev. Thomas Maguire from 29 May to 2 June, 1838, Dublin, 1939.

Bickersteth, Edward, 'Progress of Popery', *Blackwood's Magazine*, XLIV, 1838.

Brady, W. Maziere, *Essays on the English State Church in Ireland*, 1869.

Brennan, M., *Reasons for Renouncing the Errors of the Church of Rome*, Dublin, 1825.

Broderick, J.F., *Holy See and the Irish Movement for the Repeal of the Union with England, 1829–1847*, Rome, 1951.

Brynn, E., 'Some Repercussions of the Act of Union on the Church of Ireland, 1801–1820', *Church History*, XL, 1971.

_____ 'Church of Ireland Diocese in the Age of Catholic Emancipation', *Historical Magazine of the Protestant Episcopal Church*, June, 1971.

Bushe, William, *Lecture on the Doctrines of the Church of Rome*, Dublin, 1824.

Butler, Charles, *Address to the Protestants of Great Britain and Ireland*, Exeter, 1813.

_____ *Philological and Biographical Works*, 1817, V vols.

_____ *Historical Memoirs of the English Catholics*, 1822, IV vols.

_____ *Book of the Roman Catholic Church in a series of Letters addressed to*

R. Southey, 1825.

Campbell, Graham, *Apostle of Kerry: Life of Charles Graham*, Dublin, 1868.

Carr, John, *Stranger in Ireland*, 1806.

Connell, K.H., *Irish Peasant Society*, Oxford, 1968.

Connolly, S.J., 'Catholicism in Ulster, 1800–1850', *Plantation to Partition*, Belfast, 1981.

_____ *Priests and People in Pre-Famine Ireland, 1780–1845*, Dublin, 1982.

Costigan, Richard, 'Ecclesiological Dialectic', *Thought*, XLIX, 1974.

_____ *Rohrbacher and the Ecclesiology of Ultramontanism*, Rome, 1980.

Daunt, W.J.O., *Eighty-Five Years of Irish History, 1800–1885*, 1886.

Donnelly, J.S., 'Pastorini and Captain Rock: Millenialism and Sectarianism in the Rockite Movement of 1821–4' in *Irish Peasants: Violence and Political Unrest, 1780–1914*, Dublin, 1985.

Doyle, James, *Letters on the State of Education in Ireland and Other Works, Together with a Reply to a Charge by Dr. Magee, Archbishop of Dublin*, Dublin, 1824.

_____ *Vindication of the Religious and Civil Principles of the Irish Catholics Addressed to the Marquis of Wellesley*, Dublin, 1823.

Duigenan, Patrick, *Nature and Extent of the Demands of the Irish Roman Catholics Fully Explained*, Stockdale, 1810.

Ellis, J.T., *Cardinal Consalvi and Anglo-Papal Relations, 1814–1824*, Washington, 1942.

Elrington, Thomas, *Reflections on the Appointment of Dr. Milner as Political Agent of the Roman Catholic Clergy*, Dublin, 1809.

_____ *Remarks on Dr. Milner's Tour of Ireland* Dublin, 1809.

Encyclical Letter of Pope Leo XII to which are Annexed Pastoral Instructions by the Roman Catholic Archbishops and Bishops to the Clergy and Laity

Throughout Ireland, Dublin, 1824.

Fitzpatrick, W.J., *Life and Times and Correspondence of the Right Reverend Dr. Doyle,* Dublin, 1880, II vols.

Forster, Charles, *Life of John Jebb,* 1936, II vols.

Gasquet, Aidan, *Great Britain and the Holy See, 1792–1806,* Rome, 1919.

Graduate of Trinity College, *Prophecies of Pastorini Analyzed and Refuted,* Dublin, 1823.

Grattan, Henry, *Speech on the Catholic Question, 18 May 1810,* 1810.

Gwynn, Denis, *Struggle for Catholic Emancipation,* 1928.

_____ *Daniel O'Connell,* Cork, 1938.

Hales, William, *Letters on the Religious and Political Tenets of the Romish Hierarchy,* 1813.

Hanna, A.G., *Enniskillen Methodism,* Enniskillen, 1967.

Hempton, David, *Methodism and Politics in British Society, 1750–1850,* 1984.

Hempton, David and Hill M. *Evangelical Protestantism in Ulster Society, 1740–1890,* 1992.

Henriques, Ursula, *Religious Toleration in England, 1787–1833,* 1961.

Hill, Jacqueline, 'National Festivals, the State and Protestant Ascendancy in Ireland, 1790–1829, *IHS,* XXIV, 1984.

Holmes, Finlay, *Henry Cooke,* Belfast, 1981.

Hoppen, K.T., *Ireland since 1800: Conflict and Conformity,* 1989.

Horne, T.H., *Romanism Contradictory to the Bible: the Peculiar Tenets of the Church of Rome Contrasted with Holy Scripture,* 1827.

Husenbeth, F.C., *Life of John Milner,* Dublin, 1862.

Hussey, Thomas, *Pastoral Address to the Catholic Clergy of Waterford and*

Lismore, Dublin, 1797.

Jebb, John, *Biographical Memoir of William Phelan, 1832.*

Keenan, Desmond, *Catholic Church in Nineteenth Century Ireland*, Dublin, 1983.

Kiernan, V., 'Evangelicalism and the French Revolution', *PP*, I, 1952.

Letters on the Reunion of the Churches of England and Rome from and to Dr. Doyle, Roman Catholic Bishop of Kildare, John O'Driscol, Alexander Knox and Thomas Newenham, Dublin, 1824.

MacDermott, Brian, *Catholic Question in Ireland and England, 1798–1822: the Papers of Denys Scully*, Dublin, 1988.

MacDonagh, M., *Daniel O'Connell and the Story of Catholic Emancipation*, Dublin

MacDonagh, Oliver, 'Politicization of the Irish Catholic Bishops, 1800–1850', *Historical Journal*, XVIII, 1975.

_____ *Hereditary Bondsman: Daniel O'Connell, 1775–1829*, 1988.

_____ *The Emancipist: Daniel O'Connell, 1830–1847*, 1989.

Machin, G.I.T., *Catholic Question in English Politics, 1820–30*, 1964.

MacNamee, Brian, 'Second Reformation in Ireland', *ITQ*, XXXIII, 1966.

Madden, Samuel, *Life of Peter Roe*, Dublin, 1842.

M'Ghee, Robert J., *Case Plainly Stated and Proved on the Papal Laws Established over Ireland: Speech to the Electors of the University of Dublin, 8 January, 1840*, Dublin, 1840.

_____ *Pope and Popery Exposed in their Present Power and Plots Against the Religious Laws and Liberties of the Empire*, 1843.

M'Ghee, R.J., and O'Sullivan, Mortimer, *Romanism as it Rules in Ireland... Successively Detected and Exposed*, 1840, II vols.

Meagher, William, *Notices of the Life and Character of Most Reverend Daniel*

Murray, Dublin, 1853.

Milner, John, *Divine Right of Episcopacy Addressed to the Catholic Laity of England,* 1791.

_____ *Inquiry into Certain Vulgar Opinions Concerning the Catholic Inhabitants of Ireland,* 1808.

_____ *Letters to a Roman Catholic Prelate of Ireland,* Dublin, 1911.

Neely, W.G., *Kilcooley: Land and People in Tipperary,* Belfast, 1983.

O'Brien, W., *Edmund Burke as an Irishman,* Dublin, 1926.

O'Connell, J., *Life and Speeches of Daniel O'Connell,* Dublin, 1846, II vols.

O'Leary, Arthur, *Address to the Lords Spiritual and Temporal of the Parliament of Great Britain,* Dublin, 1800.

O'Reilly, B., *John MacHale, Archbishop of Tuam,* N.Y., 1890, II vols.

O'Sullivan, Mortimer, *Captain Rock Detected, or the Origin and Character of the Recent Disturbances,* Dublin, 1824.

_____ *Remains of Rev. Samuel O'Sullivan,* Dublin, 1853, III vols.

Otway, Caesar, *Letter to the Roman Catholic Priests of Ireland on the Nature and Value of Quarantotti's Rescript,* 1814.

Parliamentary Papers, *State of Ireland,* Minutes of Evidence, VIII (129), 1829.

State of Ireland, Minutes of Evidence, Lords Select Committee, IX, (181), (521), 1825.

Phelan, William, *History of the Policy of the Church of Rome in Ireland,* 1854.

Reynolds, James, *Catholic Emancipation Crisis in Ireland, 1823–1829,* New Haven, 1954.

Rushe, Desmond, *Edmund Rice: the Man and his Times,* Dublin, 1981.

Senior, Hereward, *Orangeism in Ireland and Britain, 1795–1836,* 1966.

Slater, Edward, *Letter to Sir John Hippisley on the Nature and Extent of Papal Authority*, Liverpool, 1813.

Vidler, A.R., *Prophecy and Papacy*, 1954.

Ward, Bernard, *Dawn of Catholic Revival in England, 1780–1803*, 1909, II vols.

_____ *Eve of Catholic Emancipation*, 1911–12, III vols.

Wyse, T., *Sketch of the Late Catholic Association of Ireland*, 1829, II vols.

VII   The Struggle for Catholic Ascendancy (1829–1850)

Ahern, John, 'Plenary Synod of Thurles', *IER*, LXXV, 1951.

Akenson, D.H., *Irish Education Experiment*, 1970.

Barry, P.C., 'National Synod of Thurles (1850)', *IER*, LXXXV, 1956.

_____ 'Holy See and the Irish National Schools', *IER*, XCII, 1959.

Beaumont, Gustave de, *Ireland, Social, Political, Religious*, 1939, II vols.

Beckett, J.C., 'Ulster Protestantism' in *Ulster Since 1800*, Moody, T.W. and Beckett, J.C. (eds.), 1957.

Blackburn, John, *Maynooth Grant: Facts and Observations Relating to the Popish College of St. Patrick*, 1845.

Bowen, Desmond, *Souperism: Myth or Reality*, Cork, 1971.

_____ 'Alexander R.C. Dallas: Warrior-Saint of Wonston' in *View from the Pulpit: Victorian Ministers And Society*, Toronto, 1976.

_____ *Protestant Crusade in Ireland*, Dublin, 1978.

_____ *Paul Cardinal Cullen and the Shaping of Modern Irish Catholicism*, Dublin, 1983.

Brady, John, 'Oath of Allegiance at Maynooth', *IER*, XCIV, 1960.

Brose, Olive, 'Irish Precedent for English Church Reform: the Church

Temporalities Act of 1833', *JEH*, VII, 1956.

Colquhon, J.C., *Ireland: Popery and Priestcraft, the Cause of her Misery and Crime*, Glasgow, 1836.

Croly, David, *Address to the Lower Orders of the Roman Catholics of Ireland with Dr. Doyle's Letter on the Union of the Churches*, Cork, 1835.

Crotty, Michael and Crotty, William, *Catholic not the Roman Catholic Church*, Dublin, 1836.

Dallas, A.R.C., *Real Romanism as Stated in the Creed of Pope Pius IV*, 1845.

_____ *Popery in Ireland: a Warning to Protestants in England*, 1847.

d'Alton, Ian, *Protestant Society and Politics in Cork, 1812–1844*, Cork, 1980.

Daly, M.E., *Famine in Ireland*, Dundalk, 1986.

Edgar, John, *Cry from Connaught: an Appeal for a Land that Fainteth by Reasons of a Famine of Bread and of Hearing the Word of the Lord*, Belfast, 1846.

Fisher, William, *Forty Years in the Church of Ireland*, 1882.

Gilley, S., 'Roman Catholic Mission to the Irish in London', *Recusant History*, X, 1969.

_____ 'Papists, Protestants and the Irish in London, 1835–1870', *Studies in Church History*, VIII, 1971.

Gregg, T.D., *Protestant Ascendancy Vindicated*, Dublin, 1840.

_____ *Free Thoughts on Protestant Matters*, Dublin, 1846.

Gwynn, Denis, *Hundred Years of Catholic Emancipation*, 1929.

_____ *Second Spring, 1818–1852: Catholic Revival in England*, 1942.

_____ *Father Dominic Barberi*, Dublin, 1947.

_____ *Father Luigi Gentili and his Mission: 1801–1848*, Dublin, 1951.

_____ 'Rome and the British Veto, 1829–1847', *IER*, LXXV I, 1951.

Hales, E.E.Y., *Catholic Church in the Modern World*, N.Y., 1960.

_____ *Revolution and the Papacy, 1796–1846*, 1965.

Hempton, D., 'Methodist Crusade in Ireland, 1795–1845', *IHS*, XXII, 1980.

Hexter, J.H., 'Protestant Revival and the Catholic Question in England, 1778–1829', *Journal of Modern History*, VIII, 1936,

Hill, Jacqueline, 'Protestant Response to Repeal, the Dublin Working Class', in *Ireland under the Union: Varieties of Tension*, ed. Lyons, F.S.L. and Hawkins, R., Oxford, 1980.

Holmes, J.D., *More Roman than Rome: English Catholicism in the Nineteenth Century*, 1978.

Kerr, D.A., *Peel, Priests and Politics: Sir Robert Peel's Administration and the Roman Catholic Church in Ireland, 1841–1846*, Oxford, 1982.

Killen, W.D., *Memoir of John Edgar*, Belfast, 1869.

Macaulay, Ambrose, *Patrick Dorrian*, Dublin, 1987.

Mant, Richard, *Church of Rome and England Compared in their Declared Doctrines and Practices*, 1836.

Mason, H. Monck, *Catholic Religion of St. Patrick and St. Columcille*, Dublin, 1823.

_____ *History of the Origins and Progress of the Irish Society*, Dublin, 1846.

M'Ghee, R.J., *Last Stand for the Church: Letter to Deans Archdeacons and the Clergy of the Church of Ireland*, Dublin, 1833.

Miller, David, 'Irish Catholicism and the Great Famine', *JSH*, IX, 1975.

Murphy, J.A., 'Priests and People in Modern Irish History, *Christus Rex*, XXIII, 1969.

Neal, Frank, *Sectarian Violence: the Liverpool Experience, 1819–1914*, Manchester, 1988.

Norman, Edward, *Supremacy of the Pope: Lecture at Kingscourt, Co. Cavan, 7 April, 1841,* Dublin, 1841.

Norman, E.R., 'Maynooth Question of 1845', *IHS,* XV, 1967.

_____ *Anti-Clericalism in Victorian England,* 1968.

O'Beirne, Eugene, *Maynooth in 1834,* Dublin, 1835.

_____ *Succinct and Accurate Account of the System of Discipline, Education and Theology in the Popish College of Maynooth,* Dublin, 1840.

O'Grada, Cormac, *Ireland Before and After the Famine,* Dublin, 1988.

O'Sullivan, Mortimer, *Case of the Protestants in Ireland,* 1836.

Parliamentary Papers, Collection and Payment of Tithes, Lords Select Committee, XXII, 1831–1832, (271), (663)

_____ *Orange Lodges, Ireland,* Report of Select Committee, XV, 1835, (377).

_____ *Education in Ireland,* Lords Select Committee Report, Minutes of Evidence, VIII, 1837, Pts. I and II, (543-I) and (543-II).

_____ *Maynooth College,* Select Committee Report, Minutes of Evidence, XXII, 1854–1855, (1896) (1896–I),

Pinnington, John, 'Church of Ireland's Apologetic Position in the Years before Disestablishment', *IER* CVIII, 1867.

Porter, J.L, *Life and Times of Henry Cooke,* 1877.

Ralls, Walter, 'Papal Aggression of 1850: a Study in Victorian Anti-Catholicism', *Church History,* XLIII, 1974.

Seddall, Henry, *Edward Nangle: Apostle of Achill,* 1884.

Sirr, J.D., *Memoir of Power le Poer Trench,* Dublin, 1845.

Thelwall, A.S., (ed.) *Proceedings of the Anti-Maynooth Conference of 1845,* 1845.

Thompson, Mrs. D.P., *Brief Account of the Change in Religious Opinion now*

Taking Place In Dingle, 1846.

Ward, W., *W.G. Ward and the Catholic Revival,* 1912.

——— *Sequel to Catholic Emancipation,* 1915, II vols.

Williams, H.E., *Venerable English College, Rome,* 1979.

Wiseman, Nicholas, *Recollections of the Last Four Popes and of Rome in their Times,* 1875.

VIII   The Ultramontane Advance (1850–1878)

Anon. *The Confessional Unmasked, Showing the Depravity of the Priesthood: Being extracts from the Theological Works of Liguori, Peter Dens, Bailly, Delahogue and Cabassutius,* 1851.

Anon. *Dr. Cullen's Pastoral Answered: or the Celebration of the Birthday of Pope Pius's Creed on the 9th of December, 1851,* Dublin, 1852.

Armstrong, J., *Oath Taken by the Roman Catholic Bishops to the Pope and the Oath Taken by Roman Catholic Members of the House of Commons,* 1865.

Arnstein, W.L., *Protestant Versus Catholic in Mid-Victorian England,* 1982.

Aubert, R., *Le Pontificat de Pie IX, 1846–1878,* Paris, 1952.

Barry, P.C., 'Holy See and the Irish National Schools', *IER,* XCII, 1959.

Beck, G.A., (ed.) *English Catholics, 1850–1950.* 1950.

Beckett, J.C., 'Gladstone, Queen Victoria and the Disestablishment of the Irish Church, 1868–1869', *IHS,* XIII, 1962.

——— 'Disestablishment in the Nick of Time', *Theology,* LXIII, 1970.

Bell, P.M.H., *Disestablishment in Ireland and Wales,* 1969.

Berkeley, G.H.F., *Irish Battalion in the Papal Army of 1860,* Dublin, 1929.

Blakiston, N.A., (ed.) *Roman Question: Extracts from the Despatches of Odo*

Russell from Rome, 1858–1870, 1962.

Brooke, R.S., *Recollections of the Irish Church,* Dublin, 1878, II vols.

Brooke, W.G., *Irish Church Act of 1869,* Dublin, 1871.

Bury, J.B., *History of the Catholic Church in the Nineteenth Century, 1864–1878,* 1930.

Butler, Cuthbert, *Vatican Council, 1869–1879,* 1930, II vols.

Byrne, James, et. al. *Essays on the Irish Church,* Oxford, 1866.

Cahill, D.W., *On the Sacriligeous Conduct of the Coombe Soupers,* Dublin, 1861.

Cahill, Gilbert, 'Protestant Association and the Anti-Maynooth Agitation of 1845', *CHR,* XLIII, 1957.

Carson, J.T., *God's River in Spate,* Belfast, 1959.

Cesare, R. de., *Last Days of Papal Rome, 1850–1870,* 1909.

Cooke, Henry, *Lecture on Popery Delivered in Belfast, 3 December, 1850,* 1851.

Corish, P.J., 'Cardinal Cullen and Archbishop MacHale', *IER,* XCI, 1959.

_____ 'Cardinal Cullen and the National Association of Ireland', *Reportium Novum,* III, 1962

_____ 'Political Problems, 1860–1878', *HIC,* V, 3, Dublin, 1967.

_____ 'Gallicanism at Maynooth: Archbishop Cullen and the Royal Visitation of 1853', in *Studies in Irish History Presented to R. Dudley Edwards,* Dublin, 1979.

Cullen, Paul, *Pastoral Letters and Other Writings,* Dublin, 1882–3, III vols.

Dallas, A.R.C., *Roman Teaching: What it is and What it is not,* 1857.

_____ *Story of the Irish Church Missions Continued to the Year, 1869,* 1875.

de Vere, Aubrey, *Church Settlement of Ireland, or Hibernia Pacanda,* 1866.

Dobbin, O.T., *Plea for Tolerance towards our Fellow-Subjects in Ireland who Profess the Roman Catholic Religion*, 1866.

Dollinger, Ignaz von. *Lectures on the Reunion of the Churches*, 1872.

Faber, G.S., *Fate of Papal Rome and the Premillenial and Postmillenial Theories Considered*, Dublin, 1850.

Forbes, F.A., *Life of Pius IX*, 1918.

Fothergill, B., *Nicholas Wiseman*, 1897, II vols.

Gibson, W., *Year of Grace*, Edinburgh, 1909.

Gladstone, W.E., *Vatican Decrees in their Bearing on Civil Allegiance*, 1874

‗‗‗‗‗ *Vaticanism: an Answer to Replies and Reproofs*, 1875

Godkin, James, *Ireland and her Churches*, 1867.

Gwynn, Denis, *Cardinal Wiseman*, Dublin, 1929.

‗‗‗‗‗ *O'Connell, Davis and the Colleges Bill*, Cork, 1948.

Hales, E.E.Y., *Pio Nono: Creator of the Modern Papacy*, N.Y., 1959.

‗‗‗‗‗ 'First Vatican Council', *Studies in Church History*, Cambridge, 1971.

Hammond, J.L., *Gladstone and the Irish Nation*, 1938.

Harper, S.B.A., *Conspiracy against the Religion and Liberties of the States of the Church* 1860.

Hoppen, T.K., 'W.G. Ward and Liberal Catholicism', *JEH*, XXII, 1972.

How, F.D., *William Conyngham Plunket, Archbishop of Dublin*, 1900.

Hume, A., *Results of the Irish Census of 1866 and the Condition of the Church of Ireland*, 1964.

Hurley, M., (ed.) *Irish Anglicanism: 1869–1969*, Dublin, 1970.

Ker, Ian, *John Henry Newman: a Biography*, Oxford, 1989.

King, Robert, *History of the Holy Catholic Church in Ireland from the Introduction of Christianity to the Formation of the Modern Irish Branch of the Church of Rome,* Dublin, 1845–51, III vols. 3rd edition.

Larkin, Emmet, 'Church and State in Ireland in the Nineteenth Century', *Church History,* XXXI, 1962.

_____ 'Devotional Revolution in Ireland, 1850–1875', *AHR,* LXXVII, 1972.

_____ *Making of the Roman Catholic Church in Ireland, 1850–1860,* Chapel Hill, 1980.

_____ *Consolidation of the Roman Catholic Church in Ireland, 1860–1870,* Chapel Hill, 1987.

_____ *Roman Catholic Church and the Home Rule Movement in Ireland, 1870–1874,* Chapel Hill, 1990.

Latimer, W.T., *History of Irish Presbyterians,* Belfast, 1902.

Lee, A.T., *Facts Respecting the Present State of the Church of Ireland,* 1868.

Leslie, Shane, *Henry Edward Manning: his Life and Labours,* 1921.

Lucas, Edward, *Life of Frederick Lucas,* 1882, II vols.

MacGregor, Geddes, *Vatican Revolution,* 1958.

Machin, G.I.T., 'Maynooth Grant, the Dissenters and Disestablishment', *EHR,* LXXXII, 1967.

MacSuibhne, Peadar, 'Ireland at the Vatican Council', *IER,* XCIII, 1960.

_____ *Paul Cullen and his Contemporaries,* Naas, 1961–1977, V vols.

Maguire, J.F., *Rome, Its Ruler and Its Institutions,* 1859.

_____ *Pius IX,* 1878.

Manning, H.E., *Vatican Decrees in their Bearing on Civil Allegiance,* 1875.

_____ *True Story of the Vatican Council,* 1877.

Marrable, William, *Sketch of the Origin and Operations of the Society of Irish Church Missions to the Roman Catholics,* 1852.

Massy, Dawson, *Secret History of Romanism,* 1876, 4th edition.

McClelland, V.A., *Cardinal Manning, his Public Life and Influence, 1865–1892,* Oxford, 1962.

McWalter, J.G., *Irish Reformation Movement,* Dublin, 1852.

Monsell, William, *Lecture on the Roman Question,* 1860.

Moriarty, David, *Letter on the Disendowment of the Established Church,* Dublin, 1867.

Murphy, James, 'Role of Vincentian parish missions in the Irish Counter-Reformation of the mid-nineteenth century', *IHS,* XXIV, 1984.

Murphy, Patrick, *Popery in Ireland,* 1865.

Norman, E.R., *Catholic Church and Ireland in the Eighteen Sixties,* Dundalk, 1965.

_____ *Catholic Church and Ireland in the Age of Rebellion, 1859–1873,* 1965.

_____ *English Catholic Church in the Nineteenth Century,* 1984.

O'Keeffe, Robert, *Cardinal Cullen and the Parish Priest of Callan,* Dublin, 1872.

O'Reilly, Bernard, *John MacHale, His Life, Times and Correspondence,* N.Y., 1890, II vols.

O'Rourke, John, *Battle of the Faith in Ireland,* Dublin, 1887.

O'Sullivan, Mortimer, *Plea for Inquiry into the Political Constitution of Romanism,* Dublin, 1851.

Parliamentary Papers, Report of Commissioners, Riots in Belfast, July, September, 1857, XXVI, 1857–1858, (2309).

_____ *Powis Commission on Primary Education in Ireland,* Minutes of Evidence, 1870, XXVIII, (C6-II). (C6-III) vols. III and IV.

Patton, H.E., *Fifty Years of Disestablishment,* Dublin, 1922.

Phillips, Ambrose de Lis*le, Letter to the Earl of Shrewsbury on the Reestablishment of the Hierarchy of the English Catholic Church,* 1950.

Pope, Thomas, *Council of the Vatican and the Events of the Time,* Dublin, 1871.

Purcell, E.S., *Life of Cardinal Manning,* 1895, II vols.

Randall, A., 'British Agent at the Vatican: Mission of Odo Russell', *Dublin Review,* 479, 1959.

Roe, Thomas, *Church of Ireland before the Reformation or the Present Established Church in Ireland Proved to be the Same Church as Founded by St. Patrick,* Belfast, 1866.

Salmon, George, *Infallibility of the Church,* 1888.

Shearman, H., *How the Church of Ireland was Disestablished,* Dublin, 1970.

Simpson, W.J. Sparrow, *Roman Catholic Opposition to Papal Infallibility,* 1909.

Stanford, C.S., *Handbook to the Romish Controversy: a Refutation of the Creed of Pope Pius IV on the Grounds of Scripture and Reason,* Dublin, 1852.

Trollope, T.A., *Story of the Life of Pius IX,* 1877, II Vols.

Urwick, William, *Life and Letters,* Dublin, 1870.

Wallace, L.P., *Papacy and European Diplomacy, 1869–1878,* Chapel Hill, 1948.

Waller, J.T., *Fenianism and Romanism,* Dublin, 1866.

Walsh, Katherine, 'First Vatican Council, the Papal State and the Irish Hierarchy: Recent Research on the Pontificate of Pope Pius IX', *Studies,* Spring, 1982.

Ward, W., *Life and Times of Cardinal Wiseman,* 1897, II vols.

Whately, Richard, *Letter to a Clergyman of the Diocese of Dublin on Religious*

Controversy, Dublin, 1850.

_____ *On the Errors of Romanism: Essays*, 1856.

Whyte, J.H., 'Influence of the Catholic Clergy on Elections in Nineteenth-Century Ireland', *EHR*, LXXV, 1960.

_____ 'Appointment of Catholic Bishops in Nineteenth Century Ireland', *CHR*, XLVIII, 1962.

_____ 'Political Problems, 1850–1860', *HIC*, V, 2, 1967.

Wiseman, Nicholas, *Pastoral, Out of the Flaminian Gate, 7 October, 1850*, 1950.

IX   The Protestant Resistance, 1878–1900

Armour, W.S., *Armour of Ballymoney*, 1934.

Ball, J.T., *Reformed Church of Ireland*, Dublin, 1886.

Bernard, J.H., *Present Position of the Irish Church*, 1904.

Brownlow, W.R., *Reunion of England and Rome*, 1896.

Buckland, P.J., 'Southern Irish Unionists and British Politics', *IHS*, XII, 1961.

_____ *Irish Unionism*, Dublin, 1972–3, II vols.

Curran, Michael, 'Late Archbishop of Dublin: 1841–1921', *Dublin Review*, CLXIX, 1921.

D'Arcy, C.F., 'Religious Difficulty under Home Rule: the Church View', in *Against Home Rule*, Rosenbaum, S., (ed.) 1970.

Fulop-Miller, Rene, *Leo XIII and his Times*, N.Y.,1937.

Glaser, J.F., 'Parnell's Fall and the Nonconformist Conscience', *IHS*, XII, 1960.

Gray, Robert, *Cardinal Manning*, 1985.

Halifax, Viscount, *Leo XIII and Anglican Orders*, 1912.

Hughes, J.J., *Absolutely Null and Void*, 1968.

Jones, Spencer, *England and the Holy See: an Essay Towards Reunion*, 1902.

Larkin, Emmet, 'Roman Catholic Hierarchy and the Fall of Parnell', *Victorian Studies*, IV, 1961.

_____ 'Mounting the Counter-Attack: the Roman Catholic Hierarchy and the Destruction of Parnellism', *Review of Politics*, XXV, 1963.

_____ 'Socialism and Catholicism in Ireland', *Church History*, XXXIII, 1964.

_____ 'Launching the Counter-Attack: the Roman Catholic Hierarchy and the Destruction of Parnellism', *Review of Politics*, XXVIII, 1964.

_____ *Roman Catholic Church and the Creation of the Modern Irish State, 1878–1886*, Philadelphia, 1975.

_____ *Roman Catholic Church and the Plan of Campaign, 1886–88*, Cork, 1978.

_____ *Roman Catholic Church and the Fall of Parnell, 1888–1891*, Chapel Hill, 1979.

Lucas, R.J., *Colonel Saunderson, M.P.: a Memoir*, 1908.

Lyons, F.S.L., *Fall of Parnell, 1890–1891*, 1960.

_____ *John Dillon*, 1968.

MacDevitt, John, *University Education in Ireland and Ultramontanism*, Dublin, 1886.

MacKnight, Thomas, *Ulster as it is, or Twenty-Five Years Experience of an Irish Editor*, 1896, II vols.

McCarthy, *Five Years in Ireland*, 1901.

_____ *Priests and People in Ireland*, Dublin, 1902.

_____ *Rome in Ireland*, 1904.

McCormack, Arthur, *Cardinal Vaughan*, 1966.

McMinn, R.B., *Against the Tide: J.B. Armour*, Belfast, 1989.

Nicholas, William, *Why are the Methodists of Ireland Opposed to Home Rule*, Dublin, 1893.

O'Riordan, M., *Catholicity and Progress in Ireland*, 1905.

O'Shea, James, *Priest, Politics and Society in Post-Famine Ireland: a Study of County Tipperary, 1850–1891*, Dublin, 1983.

Rhodes, Anthony, 'Persico Papers', *Encounter*, February, 1980.

Savage, D.C., 'Origins of the Ulster Unionist Party, 1885–6', *IHS*, XII, 1961.

Sherlock, W., *Story of the Revision of the Irish Prayer Book*, Dublin, 1910.

Snead-Cox, J.G., *Life of Cardinal Vaughan*, 1910.

Stanford, W.B., and McDowell, R.B., *Mahaffy: Biography of an Anglo-Irishman*, 1971.

Walsh, Patrick, *William J. Walsh, Archbishop of Dublin*, Dublin, 1928.

Woods, C.J., 'Ireland and Anglo-Papal Relations, 1880–1885', *IHS*, XVIII, 1972.

_____ 'General Election of 1892: the Catholic Clergy and the Defeat of the Parnellites' in *Ireland under the Union: Varieties of Tension*, Lyons, F.S.L. and Hawkins, R. (eds.) Oxford, 1980.

Wright, Frank, 'Protestant Ideology and Politics in Ulster', *European Journal of Sociology*, XIV, 1973.

X   The Road to Partition, 1900–1918

Altholz, J., *Liberal Catholic Movement in England*, 1962.

Atkinson, James, *Rome and Reformation*, 1966.

Barmann, L.F., *Friederich von Hugel and the Modernist Crisis in England*,

1972.

Baum, Gregory, *That They May be One: a Study of Papal Doctrines, Leo XIII-Pius XII*, 1958.

Bernard, J.H., *Present Position of the Irish Church*, 1904.

Birmingham, George, *Irishmen All*, 1913.

Boyce, D.G., 'British Opinion, Ireland and the War, 1916–18', *Historical Journal*, XVII, 1979.

Bredin, A.E.C., *History of the Irish Soldier*, Belfast, 1987.

Cole, L.R., *History of Methodism in Ireland, 1860–1960*, Belfast, 1960.

Falconi, Carlo, *Popes in the Twentieth Century*, 1967.

Fitzpatrick, D., *Ireland and the First World War*, Dublin, 1986.

Fletcher, Dudley, *Rome and Marriage: the recent Papal Decree, Ne Temere*, Dublin, 1911.

Garvin, Tom, 'Priests and patriots: Irish separatism and fear of the modern, 1890–1914', *IHS*, XXV, 1986.

Gaselee, Stephen, 'British Diplomats and Relations with the Holy See', *Dublin Review*, CCIV, 1939.

Hammer, H., *Fernand Portal: Apostle of Unity*, 1961.

Harris, H.E.D., *Irish Regiments in the First World War*, Cork, 1968.

Heenan, J., *Cardinal Hinsley*, 1944.

Irishman, An, *Intolerance in Ireland: Fact not Fiction*, 1913.

Killen, W.D., *Reminiscences of a Long Life*, 1902.

Lee, J.J., *Ireland, 1912–1985*, Cambridge, 1990.

Leonard, Ellen, *George Tyrell and the Catholic Tradition*, 1982.

Longford, earl of, and O'Neill, T.P., *Eamon de Valera*, Boston, 1971.

Lyons, F.S.L., *Culture and Anarchy in Ireland, 1880–1939*, Oxford, 1980.

MacDonagh, Michael, *Irish on the Somme*, 1917.

Marlowe, N., 'Irish Bishops, the War and Home Rule', *Contemporary Review*, CXIV, 1918.

Merry del Val, R., *Memories of Pope Pius X*, 1939.

McHugh, R., 'Catholic Church and the Rising' in *1916: the Dublin Rising*, Edwards, D.R., and Pyle, F., (eds.) 1968

Miller, David, *Church, State and Nation in Ireland, 1898–1921*, Dublin, 1973..

Moynihan, Michael, *God on our Side: the British Padre in the First World War*, 1983.

Newsinger, John, 'I Bring not Peace but a Sword: the Religious Motif in the Irish War of Independence', *Journal of Contemporary History*, XIII, 1978.

O'Fiaich, T., 'Irish Bishops and Conscription', *Capuchin Annual*, Dublin, 1968.

O'Kennedy, R., 'Most Reverend E.T. O'Dwyer', *Irish Monthly*, XLVI, 1918.

Oldmeadow, Ernest, *Francis Cardinal Bourne*, 1944.

O'Rahilly, Alfred, *Fr. William Doyle, S.J.*, 1930.

Orr, Philip, *Road to the Somme*, Belfast, 1987.

Reynolds, E.E., *Roman Catholic Church in England and Wales*, Wheathamsted, 1973.

Robertson, Alexander, *Roman Catholic Church in Italy*, 1915, 7th edition.

_____ *Papal Conquest, Italy's Warning: Wake up John Bull*, 1918.

Ryan, W.P., *Pope's Green Island*, 1912.

Schultenover, G., *George Tyrell: in Search of Catholicism*, 1981.

Stewart, A.T.Q. *Ulster Crisis: Resistance to Home Rule, 1912–1914*, 1967.

Supple, Jennifer, 'Ultramontanism in Yorkshire, 1850–1900' in *Religion in Victorian Britain, IV*, Open University, Manchester, 1988.

Travers, Pauric, 'Priest in Politics: the Case of Conscription', *Irish Culture and Nationalism: 1750–1950*, Canberra, 1985.

Walsh, James, *Political Aspects of Popery*, 1905.

Whyte, J.H., '1916—Revolution and Religion' in *Leaders and Men of the Easter Rising: Dublin, 1916*, 1967.

Wilkinson, A., *Church of England in the First World War*, 1978.

XI   The Confessional Republic, 1918–1945

Akenson, D.H., *Mirror to Kathleen's Face: Education in Independent Ireland, 1922–1960*, 1975.

Barton, Brian, *Bookeborough: Making of a Prime Minister*, Belfast, 1988.

Bence-Jones, M., *Twilight of the Ascendancy*, 1987.

Blanchard, P., *American Freedom and Catholic Power*, Boston, 1951.

_____ *Irish and Catholic Power*, 1954.

Bolster, Evelyn, *Knights of Columbanus*, Dublin, 1979.

Bowen, Kurt, *Protestants in a Catholic State*, Dublin, 1983.

Bowman, John, *De Valera and the Ulster Question, 1917–1973*, Oxford, 1989.

Boyne, Don, *I Remember Maynooth*, 1937.

Browne, Noel, *Against the Tide*, Dublin, 1987.

Butler, Hubert, 'The Bell: an Anglo-Irish View', *Irish University Review*, VI, 1976.

Chadwick, Owen, 'The Papacy and World War II', *JEH*, XXVII, 1967.

_____ *Britain and the Vatican During the Second World War,* Cambridge, 1988.

Cianfarra, C.M. *War and the Vatican,* 1945.

Conway, John, 'Silence of Pope Pius XII', *Review of Politics,* XXVII, 1965

D'Arcy, C.F., *Adventures of a Bishop,* 1934.

Delzell, C., 'Pius XII, Italy and the Outbreak of the War', *Journal of Contemporary History,* II, 1967.

_____ *Papacy and Totalitarianism between the Two World Wars* (ed.), N.Y., 1974.

Ervine, St. John, *Craigavon: Ulsterman,* 1949.

Falconi, Carlo, *Silence of Pius XII,* 1970.

Faughnan, Sean, 'Jesuits and the drafting of the Irish Constitution of 1937', *IHS,* XXVI, 1988

Feeney, J., *John Charles McQuaid: the Man and the Mask,* Dublin, 1974.

Friedlander, S., *Pius XII and the Third Reich: a Documentation,* 1966.

Gregg, J.A.F., *Primitive Faith and Roman Catholic Developments,* Dublin, 1909.

_____ *The 'Ne Temere' Decree,* Dublin, 1935.

Gwynn, D., *Hundred Years of Catholic Emancipation,* 1929.

Hachey, T.E., (ed.) *Anglo-Vatican Relations, 1914–1939,* Boston, 1972.

Holmes, J.D., 'English Catholicism from Wiseman to Bourne', *Clergy Review,* LXI, 1976.

_____ 'English Catholicism from Hinsley to Heenan', *Clergy Review,* LXII, 1977.

Jackson, J.A., *The Irish in Britain,* 1963.

Keogh, D.F., *Vatican, the Bishops and Irish Politics, 1919–1939*, Cambridge, 1986.

Lee, R.M., 'Intermarriage, Conflict and Social Control in Ireland: the Decree *Ne Temere*', *Economic and Social Review*, XVII, 1985.

Manning, Maurice, *The Blueshirts*, Dublin, 1971.

McDonagh, Enda, 'Church and State in the Constitution of Ireland', *ITQ*, XXVIII, 1961.

Meehan, Denis, *Window on Maynooth*, Dublin, 1949.

Meenan, James, *Italian Corporative System*, Cork, 1944.

Moloney, T., *Westminster, Whitehall and the Vatican: the Role of Cardinal Hinsley, 1935–1943*, 1985.

Murphy, J.A., *Ireland in the Twentieth Century*, Dublin, 1975.

Murphy, J.J., *Peoples' Primate*, Dublin, 1945.

O'Doherty, J.F., 'Catholic Church in 1937', *IER*, LI, 1938.

O'Duffy, Eoin, *Crusade in Spain*, Dublin, 1938.

Phillips, W.A., *Revolution in Ireland, 1906–1923*, 1923.

Savory, D. *History of Home Rule, 1889–1949*, 1950.

Seaver, G., *John Allen Fitzgerald Gregg, Archbishop*, Dublin, 1963.

Stanford, W.B., *Recognized Church: the Church of Ireland in Eire*, Dublin, 1944.

Tierney, Michael, 'Ireland and the Anglo-Saxon Heresy', *Studies*, XXIX, 19

Waller, B.C., *Pope's Claims and Why We Reject Them*, Dublin, 1932.

Walsh, B.M., 'Trends in the Religious Composition of the Population in the Republic of Ireland', *Economic and Social Review*, VI, 1975.

White, J., *Minority Report: the Protestant Community in the Irish Republic*,

Dublin, 1975.

Whyte, J.H., *Church and State in Modern Ireland, 1923–1979*, Dublin, 1980.

XII Struggle for Pluralism

Adams, Michael, *Censorship: the Irish Experience*, Dublin, 1968.

Akenson, D.H., *Education and Enmity*, Newton Abbot, 1973.

Bell, G., *Protestants of Ulster*, 1976.

Blanshard, J., *Church in Contemporary Ireland*, Dublin, 1963.

Boyle, J., 'Belfast Protestant Association and the Independent Orange Order', *IHS*, XIII, 1962–3.

Browne, Michael, 'Why Catholic Priests Should Concern Themselves with Social and Economic Questions', *Christus Rex*, I, 1947.

Bruce, Steve, *God Save Ulster: the Religion and Politics of Paisleyism*, Oxford, 1989.

Butler, H., 'Portrait of a Minority', *Bell*, XIX, 1954.

Connolly, P.R., 'Church in Ireland since Vatican Council II', *Furrow*, XXX, 1979.

Coogan, T.P., *Disillusioned Decades: Ireland, 1966–1987*, Dublin, 1987.

Daly, Cahal, 'Future of Christianity in Ireland', *Doctrine and Life*, XXVII, 1977.

Daly, Gabriel, 'Catholic Theology During the Last Two Decades', *Doctrine and Life*, XXXIV, 1984.

Doyle, D.N., 'Contemporary Irish Identity: a Roman Catholic's Reflections', *Crane Bag*, IX, 1985.

Easthope, Gary, 'Religious War in Northern Ireland, *Sociology*, X, 1976.

Falconer, A., McDonagh, E., MacReamoinn, S., (eds.) *Freedom to Hope? the*

Catholic Church in Ireland Twenty Years After Vatican II, Dublin, 1985.

Fennell, D., *Changing Face of Catholic Ireland*, 1968.

Fitzgerald, G., *Towards a New Ireland*, Dublin, 1972.

Gallagher, E. and Worrall, S., *Christians in Ulster, 1969–1980*, Oxford, 1982.

Gallagher, J.F., and DeGregory, G.C., *Violence in Northern Ireland: Understanding Protestant Perspectives*, Dublin, 1985.

Graham, Aelred, 'Pathos of Vatican II', *Encounter*, December, 1965.

Grey-Stacks, C.M., 'Mystery of the Empty Chair', *Focus*, IX, 1966.

Hastings, Adrian, *History of English Christianity, 1920–1985*, 1987.

Hegarty, Kevin, 'Is Irish Catholicism Dying', *Furrow*, XXXVI, 1985.

Inglis, Tom, 'Decline in Numbers of Priests and Religious in Ireland, *Doctrine and Life*, XXX, 1979.

_____ *Moral Monopoly: Catholic Church in Modern Irish Society*, Dublin, 1987.

Kirby, Peadar, 'Irish Church: Shifting Sands', *Doctrine and Life*, October, 1977.

_____ *Is Irish Catholicism Dying*, Cork, 1984.

Larkin, E., 'Church, State and Nation in Modern Ireland', *AHR*, LXXX, 1975.

Lyng, R.A., 'Catholic Church and the New Ireland'. *Furrow*, XLII, 1991.

Lyons, F.S.L., 'Dilemma of the Irish Contemporary Historian', *Hermathena*, CXV, 1973.

Marrinan, Patrick, *Paisley: Man of Wrath*, Tralee, 1973.

McCaffrey, L.J., 'Irish Nationalism and Irish Catholicism in Cultural Identity', *Church History*, XLII, 1973.

McDonagh, Enda, 'Ireland's Divided Disciples', *Furrow*, XXXIII, 1982.

McKee, Eamonn, 'Church-state relations and the development of Irish health policy: the mother-and child scheme, 1944–1953', *IHS*, XXV, 1986.

McKevitt, P., 'Epilogue: Modern Ireland', *HIC*, V, 10, Dublin, 1970.

McSweeney, Bill, *Roman Catholicism: Search for Relevance*, Oxford, 1980.

Moloney, E., 'Paisley', *Crane Bag*, iv, 1980.

Moloney, E. and Pollak, A., *Paisley*, Swords, 1986.

Murray, S.W., *W.P. Nicholson: Flame for God and Ulster*, Belfast, 1979.

Nelson, S., 'Protestant Ideology Considered', *British Political Sociology Yearbook*, II, 1975.

_____ *Ulster's Uncertain Defenders*, Belfast, 1984.

Noel, G.E., *Montini Story: Portrait of Paul VI*, 1963.

O'Leary, James, 'Religion: Ireland in Mutation', *Across the Frontiers: Ireland in the 1990's*, Kearney, R., (ed.) Dublin, 1990.

Padellaro, N., *Portrait of Pius XII*, 1956.

Paisley, Ian, *No Hope Here*, Belfast, 1982.

Pawley, Bernard, *Looking at the Vatican Council*, 1962.

Presbyterian Church in Ireland, *Pluralism in Ireland*, Belfast, 1977.

Ramsey, Michael, *Rome and Canterbury: Public Lecture in Dublin, 23 June, 1967*, 1967.

Rhodes, A., *Vatican in the Age of the Dictators*, 1973.

Roberts, D.A., 'Orange Order in Ireland: a Religious Institution', *British Journal of Sociology*, XXII, 1971.

Ryan, Liam, 'Church and Politics: the Last Twenty-Five Years', *Furrow*, XXX, 1979.

_____ 'The Church Now', *Furrow*, XXXII, 1981.

Shaw, Francis, 'Canon of Irish History—a Challenge', *Studies*, LXI, 1972.

Sheeny, M., *Is Ireland Dying?* 1968.

Stewart, A.T.Q., *Ulster Crisis*, 1967.

Viney, Michael, *The Five Percent*, Dublin, 1965.

Wallis, Roy, Bruce, Steve and Taylor, David, *'No Surrender': Paisleyism and the Politics of Ethnic Identity in Northern Ireland*, Belfast, 1986.

White, T. de Vere, *Anglo-Irish*, 1972.

Whyte, J.H., 'Church, State and Society, 1950–1970' in *Ireland, 1945–1970*, Lee, J.J. (ed.) Dublin, 1979.

_____ 'How Much Discrimination was there under the Unionist Regime, 1921–1968', *Contemporary Irish Studies*, Gallagher, T., and O'Connell, J., (eds.) Manchester, 1983.

XIII   Ulster's Popular Protestantism

Anderson, A.C., *Story of the Presbyterian Church in Ireland*, Belfast, 1985.

Armstrong, M.W., Loetscher, L.A., and Anderson, C.A., *The Presbyterian Enterprise*, Westminster, 1956.

Bacon, L.W., *History of American Christianity*, N.Y., 1900.

Bagenal, P.H., *American Irish and their Influence on Irish Politics*, London, 1882.

Bailie, W.D., *The Six Mile Water Revival of 1625*, Newcastle, 1976.

Baker, Frank, *John Wesley and the Church of England*, London, 1870.

Barkley, J.M., *Westminster Formularies in Irish Presbyterianism*, Belfast, 1956.

Bartlett, T., 'Defenders and Defenderism in 1793', *IHS*, 1985, XXIV, pp. 373–395.

Barton, Thomas, *Conduct of the Paxton Men, Impartially Represented,*

Philadelphia, 1764.

Bebbington, D.W., *Evangelicalism in Modern Britain: a History from the 1730's to the 1980's*, London, 1989.

Beckett, J.C., *Protestant Dissent in Ireland, 1687–1780*, London, 1948.

_____ 'Ulster Protestantism', *Ulster Since 1800*, Belfast, 1957.

Bouwsma, W.J., *John Calvin*, Oxford, 1988.

Boyd, Andrew, *Holy War in Belfast*, Tralee, 1972.

Brown, Terence, *The Whole Protestant Community: the Making of a Historical Myth*, Belfast, 1985.

Brooke, Peter, *Ulster Presbyterianism*, Dublin, 1987.

Burns, J.H., 'Knox and Bullinger', *SHR*, 1955, XXXIV, pp. 90–91.

Byrne, J., *An Impartial Account of the Late Disturbances in the County of Armagh, 1784–1791*, Dublin, 1792.

Campbell, W.G., *Apostle of Kerry: Life of Charles Graham*, Dublin, 1826.

Carson, Herbert, *God's River in Spate*, Belfast, 1958.

Chambers, George, *Tribute to the Principles, Virtues, Habits and Public Usefulness of the Irish and Scotch Early Settlers of Pennsylvania*, Chambersburg, 1856.

Coad, Roy, *History of the Brethren Movement*, Exeter, 1968.

Cole, R.L., *History of Methodism in Ireland, 1860–1960*, Belfast, 1960.

Connolly, S.J., 'Catholicism in Ulster, 1800–1850', *Plantation to Partition: Essays in Ulster History in Honour of J.L. McCracken*, Belfast, 1981, pp. 157–172.

County of Meath Freeholder, *Candid and Impartial Account of the Disturbances in the County of Meath in the Years 1792, 1793, 1794*, Dublin, 1794.

Crawford, R.G., *Loyal to King Billy: Portrait of the Ulster Protestants*, Dublin,

1987.

Crookshank, C.H., *History of Methodism in Ireland*, Belfast, 1885, III vols.

Curtin, Nancy, 'Transformation of the Society of United Irishmen into a mass-based revolutionary organization, 1794–1796', *IHS*, 1985, pp. 463–493.

Dickson, R.J., *Ulster Emigration to Colonial America, 1718–1775*, Belfast, 1976.

Doyle, D.N., *Ireland, Irishmen and Revolutionary America, 1760–1820*, Dublin, 1981.

Elliott, Marianne, *Watchmen in Zion: the Protestant Idea of Liberty*, Belfast, 1985.

Froude, J.A., *English in Ireland in the Eighteenth Century*, London, 1887, II, p. 154.

Gibbon, Peter, *Origins of Ulster Unionism*, Manchester, 1975.

Gibson, William, *Year of Grace*, Edinburgh, 1909.

Gillespie, Raymond, 'Historical Revisit: T.W. Moody, the Londonderry Plantation, 1609–1641, *I.H.S., 1994*, XXIX, pp. 109–114.

Glasgow, Maude, *Scotch-Irish in Northern Ireland and the American Colonies*, N.Y., 1926.

Greely, A.M. *Denominational Society*, N.Y., 1972.

Grob, G.N. and Beck, R.N., *Ideas in America*, N.Y., 1970.

Grubb, I., *Quakers in Ireland, 1654–1900*, London, 1927.

Haire, J.L.M., ed. *Challenge and Conflict: Essays in Irish Presbyterian History and Doctrine*, Antrim, 1981.

Haire, R., *Wesley's One and Twenty Visits to Ireland*, London, 1947.

Hamilton, Thomas, *History of the Irish Presbyterian Church*, Edinburgh, 1887.

Harris, Rosemary, *Prejudice and Tolerance in Ulster*, Manchester, 1972.

Helmstadter, R.J., 'Nonconformist Conscience', *Religion in Victorian Britain*, Manchester, 1988, IV, pp. 61–96.

Hempton, D.N., 'Methodist Crusade in Ireland, 1795–1845', *I.H.S.*, 1980, XXII, pp. 33–48.

Hempton, David, *Methodism and Politics in British Society, 1750–1850*, London, 1984.

_____ 'For God and Ulster: Evangelical Protestantism and the Home Rule Crisis of 1886', *Protestant Evangelicalism: Britain, Ireland, Germany and America, 1750–1950*, Oxford, 1990, pp. 225–255.

Hempton, David and Hill, Myrtle, *Evangelical Protestantism in Ulster, 1740–1890*, London, 1992.

Hibbert, Christopher, *Redcoats and Rebels,* London, 1990.

Hilton, Boyd, *Age of Atonement: the Influence of Evangelicalism on Social and Economic Thought, 1785–1865*, Oxford, 1988.

Holmes, Finlay, *Our Presbyterian Heritage*, Belfast, 1985.

Irish Church Bill: the Great Protestant Demonstration in Belfast, Belfast, 1869.

Irishman, *Intolerance in Ireland: Fact not Fiction*, London, 1913.

Irwin, Clark, *History of Presbyterianism in Dublin and the South West of Ireland*, London, 1890.

Jones, Rufus, *Quakers in the American Colonies*, N.Y., 1966.

Laski, Harold, *Defence of Liberty Against Tyrants*, London, 1924.

Latimer, W.T., *History of the Irish Presbyterians*, Belfast, 1893.

Lecky, A.G., *In the Days of the Laggan Presbytery*, Belfast, 1908.

Lecky, W.E.H., *Ireland in the Eighteenth Century*, London, 1892, V vols.

Leyburn, J.G., *Scotch-Irish*, Chapel Hill, 1962.

Littell, F.H., *From State Church to Pluralism: a Protestant Interpretation of*

Religion in American History, N.Y., 1962.

Macaulay, Ambrose, *Patrick Dorrian*, Dublin, 1987.

MacKnight, Thomas, *Ulster as it is, or twenty eight years experienced as an Irish editor*, London, 1896, II vols.

Magee, H., *Fifty Years in the Irish Mission*, Belfast, n.d.

Maguire, W.A., ed., *Kings in Conflict: the Revolutionary War in Ireland and Its Aftermath, 1689–1750*, Belfast, 1990.

McCartney, R.L., *Liberty and Authority in Ireland*, Belfast, 1985.

McClelland, Aiken, 'Later Orange Order', *Secret Societies in Ireland*, Dublin, 1973, pp. 126–138.

McDowell, R.B., *Irish Public Opinion, 1750–1800*, London, 1944.

McNeill, J.T., *History and Character of Calvinism*, Oxford, 1967.

McNeill, Ronald, *Ulster's Stand for Union*, London, 1922, p. 163.

Methodist Church in Ireland: Report on Special Committee to Examine the Current Situation in Ireland, Belfast, 1975.

Miller, D.W., *Queen's Rebels*, Dublin, 1978.

_____ 'Armagh Troubles, 1784–1795', *Irish Peasants, Violence and Political Unrest*, Dublin, 1983, pp. 155–192.

Miller, Kerby, *Emigrants and Exiles*, Oxford, 1985.

Miller, Perry, *Jonathan Edwards*, N.Y., 1959.

Mode, P.G., *Sourcebook and Bibliographical Guide for American Church History*, N.Y., 1921.

Moeran, Francis M., *Memoirs: the Good Fight*, Dublin, 1951.

Murray, S.W., *City Mission Story*, Belfast, n.d.

O'Brien, S., 'A transatlantic community of saints: the Great Awakening and the first evangelical network, 1735–1755', *A.H.R.*, 91, pp. 811–832.

O'Connell, M.R., *Irish Politics and Social Conflict in the Age of the American Revolution*, Philadelphia, 1965.

Olmstead, C.E., *History of Religion in the United States*, Englewood Cliffs, 1960 .

____ *Religion in America: Past and Present*, Englewood Cliffs, 1961.

Ozment, Steven, *Protestants: The Birth of a Revolution*, N.Y., 1992.

Pakenham, Thomas, *Year of Liberty*, London, 1969.

Porter, J.L., *Life of Henry Cooke*, Belfast, 1875.

Records of the General Synod of Ulster, 1691–1820, Belfast, 1890, III vols.

Registrar General, Northern Ireland, *Northern Ireland Census, 1991*, Belfast, 1993.

Reid, J.S., *History of the Presbyterian Church in Ireland*, London, 1853, III vols.

Repealer Repulsed: a Corrective Narrative of the Rise and Progress of the Repeal Invasion of Ulster, Belfast, 1841.

Report of a Deputation from the London Hibernian Society Respecting the Religious State of Ireland, Dublin, 1808.

Republicanism, Loyalism and Pluralism in Ireland: Studies Presented to the General Assembly of the Presbyterian Church in Ireland, Belfast, 1977.

Roosevelt, T., *Winning of the West*, N.Y., 1904.

Salisbury, W.S., *Religion in American Culture*, Homewood, 1964.

Schlenther, B.S., *Life and Writings of Francis Makemie*, Philadelphia, 1971.

Senior, H., *Orangeism in Ireland and Britain, 1795–1836*, London, 1966.

Stewart, A.T.Q., *Ulster Crisis*, London, 1967.

Sweet, W.E., *Methodism in American History*, Abingdon, 1954.

Tebbel, John, *History of the Indian Wars*, N.Y., 1966.

Tennent, Gilbert, *Danger of an Unconverted Ministry*, Boston, 1742.

Tone, Wolfe, *Life*, Washington, 1826, II vols.

Walzer, Michael, 'Puritanism as a revolutionary ideology', *History and Theory*, 1963, III, pp. 59–70.

Wesley, John, *Advantage of the Members of the Church of England over those of the Church of Rome*, London, 1753.

_____ *Popery Calmly Considered*, London, 1779.

Westerkamp, M.J., *Triumph of the Laity: Scots-Irish Piety and the Great Awakening, 1625–1760*, Oxford, 1988.

Wight, T., and Rutty, J., *History of the Rise and Progress of the People Called Quakers in Ireland*, London, 1811.

Winslow, O.E. *Jonathan Edwards, 1703-1758*, N.Y., 1961.

Withero, Thomas, *Historical and Literary Memorials of Presbyterianism in Ireland, 1623–1731*, Belfast, 1879, II vols.

Woodhouse, A.S.P., *Puritanism and Liberty*, Chicago, 1951.

Woodward, Josiah, *Account of the Rise and Progress of the Religious Societies in London and their Endeavours for Reformation of Manners*, London, 1701.

XIV   Epilogue, 1992: The Tyranny of the Dead

Bradshaw, Brendan, 'Nationalism and Historical Scholarship in Modern Ireland', *IHS,* 1989, XXVI, pp. 329–352.

Bull, George, *Inside the Vatican*, London, 1982.

de Paor, Liam, *Divided Ulster*, London, 1973.

de Vries, Wilhelm, 'Limits of Papal Primacy', *Cardinal Bea Studies, II: Dublin*

Papers on Ecumenism, Manila, 1972.

Ernst, C., 'Primacy of Peter: Theology and Ideology', *New Blackfriars*, 1969, L, pp. 347–355, 399–404.

Gilley, Sheridan, 'Religion in Modern Ireland', *JEH*, 1992, XLIII, pp. 111–119.

Granfield, Patrick, *Limits of the Papacy*, London, 1987.

Harris, M., *Catholic Church and the Foundation of the Northern Irish State, 1912–1930*, Cork, 1993.

Kearney, R., *Irish Mind*, Dublin, 1985.

Kung, Hans, *Infallible?* London, 1980.

Lee, Simon, ed. *Freedom from Fear: Churches Together in Northern Ireland*, Belfast, 1990.

Martin, M., *Jesuits*, N.Y., 1987.

Misner, P., 'Papal Primacy in Pluriform Polity', *Journal of Ecumenical Studies*, 1974, XI, pp. 239–261.

Patterson, Henry, *Class Conflict and Sectarianism: the Protestant Working Class and the British Labour Movement, 1868–1920*, Belfast, 1980.

Rafferty, O.P., *Catholicism in Ulster, 1603–1983: an Interpretative History*, London, 1993.

Response of the General Synod of the Church of Ireland to the Final Report of ARCIC-I, Oxford, 1987.

Study Conference to Explore Models of Political Co-operation: Background Papers, Corrymeela Community, Belfast, 1981.

Sullivan, F.A., *Magisterium: Teaching Authority in the Catholic Church*, Ramsey, New Jersey, 1983.

Whyte, J.H., 'Interpretations of the Northern Ireland Problem: an Appraisal', *Economic and Social Review*, 1978, IX, pp. 257–282.

INDEX

DATE DUE			
FEB 26 '97			
			Printed in USA